AIR AND SPACE HISTORY

GARLAND REFERENCE LIBRARY
OF THE HUMANITIES
(Vol. 834)

Milestones of Flight Gallery, The National Air and Space Museum.

AIR AND SPACE HISTORY
An Annotated Bibliography

Edited by
Dominick A. Pisano *and* Cathleen S. Lewis

National Air and Space Museum
Smithsonian Institution

GARLAND PUBLISHING, INC. • NEW YORK & LONDON
1988

Library of Congress Cataloging-in-Publication Data

Air and space history: an annotated bibliography / editors, Dominick
A. Pisano and Cathleen S. Lewis.

p. cm.—(Garland reference library of the humanities ; v. 834)
Includes index.
ISBN 0–8240–8543–4
1. Aeronautics—History—Bibliography. 2. Astronautics—History—
Bibliography. 3. Space sciences—History—Bibliography.
I. Pisano, Dominick, 1943– . II. Lewis, Cathleen S., 1958– . III. Series.

Z5060.A44 1988 [TL515] 016.6291′09—dc 19
88–342 CIP

Printed on acid-free, 250-year-life paper
Manufactured in the United States of America

CONTENTS

ILLUSTRATIONS

The V–2 guided missile, which was assembled from
components of several rockets, on display in Space Hall in
the National Air and Space Museum. Developed during World
War II by German engineers at Peenemunde under the
leadership of Wernher von Braun, the V–2 was the world's
first long–range ballistic missile. In the last year of the war,
more than three thousand of these rockets were launched
against Allied targets. After the war, both American and
Soviet engineers utilized captured V–2 components,
engineers, and technicians to augment their own rocket
programs. The first launch vehicles to send the artificial
satellites into earth orbit were based on this technology. The
paint design of the craft on display is the same at that of the
first successfully launched V–2 from 3 October 1942.   330

A Proof Test Capsule of the Viking Lander on display on
simulated Martian terrain in the Milestones of Flight Gallery
at the National Air and Space Museum. This capsule was
assembled from flight type hardware and was refurbished by
Martin Marietta Corporation before donation to the National
Air and Space Museum. Two identical spacecraft, Viking 1
and Viking 2 were launched from the Kennedy Space Center
on 20 August and 9 September 1975 and landed on Mars on 20
July and 3 September 1976. The Viking 1 lander is NASM's
only space artifact on another planet.   380

The Air and Space Museum's recreation of the Apollo–Soiuz
Test Project, the first international piloted space mission
during which an Apollo spacecraft docked with Soiuz 19 in
space on 18 July 1975. This mock–up consists of an Apollo
Command Service Module which had formerly been used for
ground tests; an engineering model of the docking module,
which was designed specifically for this mission, and a
mock–up of a Soiuz spacecraft, which is on loan from the Soviet
Academy of Sciences. A similar display is exhibited in
Moscow in the Kosmos Pavilion of the Exhibition of
Economic Achievements.   468

PREFACE

Aviation and spaceflight are very young in the history of civilization. Younger still are the communities of scholars who study aspects of the history of flight. There are no common scholarly journals, few consistently useful professional organizations for the communication of interests, and still fewer institutions willing to support serious scholarly research in the area. More important, there is little or no way in which a researcher can gain ready access to bibliographic information about the history of air and space.

Although both general and specialist bibliographies exist in the realms of air and space, none reflect the overall state of the literature on the subject. In fact, that literature appears to be very spotty and, in some cases, virtually nonexistent. Unquestionably, there is a compelling need for an entry-level bibliography of the history of aviation and spaceflight. Such a bibliography should not only introduce the subject to nonspecialists, but also mirror the status of the body of scholarly literature available and show, in its lacunae, areas of research that require attention. It should also answer questions efficiently and assist researchers in locating specific information about the subject.

There is simply no way that one person could perform such a bibliographic task alone. Air and space, although they are allied subject areas, are distinct and rather diverse. Therefore, when this bibliography was conceived, it seemed natural that the curatorial staff of the Smithsonian Institution's National Air and Space Museum should work together to compile it.

At the outset, a number of curators in both the Department of Aeronautics and the Department of Space Science and Exploration met to establish general guidelines and to develop a broad outline of the diverse subject matter that might be covered. We included all possible topics and fields, whether or not there were specialists competent to handle them. With a broad outline established, the two persons chosen as departmental editors turned to available staff to research and compile each identified area. Assignments were made, and systematic literature searches were carried out. The next steps in the process—writing and editing annotations and editorial review—were undertaken by the two departments with wide latitude as to methodology.

Curators within the Department of Aeronautics and the Department of Space Science and Exploration developed their own search strategies, subject matter boundaries, and annotation styles. Curators in the Department of Aeronautics concentrated on the history of flight, both civil and military, the technology that made it possible, and the social, cultural, and political context of that technology. Curators in the Department of Space Science and Exploration focused on the history of space science, with a natural emphasis on post–World War II issues in science, science policy, and technology and society, as well as the manned exploration of space.

Each compiler then submitted annotated selections to the editors, who worked together to make the body of information collected as consistent and useful as possible. The result is an important first step in documenting the largely uncharted domain of the history of air and space. The compilers and editors believe that the selections will assist the reader in establishing his or her own knowledge of the literature and that the bibliography will serve as a foundation upon which others will build in the years to come.

David H. DeVorkin
National Air and Space Museum
October 1987

INTRODUCTION

The history of air and space is so relatively new that few efforts have been made to create either a comprehensive or a selective bibliography. Paul Brockett's extensive and pioneering *Bibliography of Aeronautics* (see item 5), which covers the years from 1909 to 1937, is the first systematic attempt to gather bibliographic information in aeronautics and issue it annually. Since Brockett's work, however, few comprehensive bibliographies on the subject have appeared. Coverage became uneven and then dropped off in the years after World War II.

The reasons for this lapse in bibliographic work in aerospace studies are complex. The growth in aviation, and, later, space exploration in the postwar years produced voluminous amounts of technical materials as well as reams of popular books and articles. Subsequently, the widespread use of computer-generated, on-line databases also contributed to the neglect of the art of published bibliography. The sheer quantity of materials, both published and unpublished, appeared to have outstripped any single person's or organization's ability to keep up with it.

Although few bibliographies cover the full scope of air and space history, a number of excellent short selective bibliographies are available. In the history of aviation, the work of Richard P. Hallion, Jr., Roger Bilstein, and Bernard Mergen deserves special mention. Hallion's bibliographic essay, "A Source Guide to the History of Aeronautics and Astronautics," *American Studies International* 20, no. 3 (Spring 1982), pp. 3–50, reprinted as part of the U.S. Air Force's Project Warrior Monograph series (see item 8), surveys the literature chronologically from antiquity to the space age. Bilstein's "Notes," in *Flight in America, 1900–1983: From the Wrights to the Astronauts* (Baltimore: Johns Hopkins University Press, 1984, pp. 331–350; see item 4), provide a bibliographic survey of the significant literature. And, although aimed at recreational flying, Mergen's bibliographic essay "Flying," in *Recreational Vehicles and Travel: A Resource Guide* (Westport, Conn.: Greenwood Press, 1985, 143–174, see item 12), contains a great deal of information about the literature of flight in general.

Although not as recent, some attempts have been made to provide selective access to the space literature. Mildred C. Benton's *Liter–*

ature of Space Science and Exploration (Washington, D.C.: U.S. Naval Research Laboratory, 1958; see item 1004), an annotated bibliography, lists more than 2,000 monographs, articles, and research reports from 1903 to 1958. Katherine M. Dickson's *History of Aeronautics and Astronautics: A Preliminary Bibliography* (Washington, D.C.: U.S. National Aeronautics and Space Administration, 1968; see item 1008) is an introduction to the historical literature and sources published mainly from 1945 to 1967. The more recent work of John J. Looney, *Bibliography of Space Books and Articles from Non–Aerospace Journals, 1957–1977* (Washington, D.C.: U.S. National Aeronautics and Space Administration, 1979; see item 1019), deals primarily with the journal literature of space science and exploration.

This volume, *Air and Space History: An Annotated Bibliography*, follows and expands on the work done by all these researchers. As such, it fits well the aspiration of the National Air and Space Museum to be not only the focal point of the scholarly pursuit of the history of flight, but also to serve as a clearinghouse for information on the subject. Consequently, it was our goal to produce a selective, annotated bibliography of international dimensions to give the beginning (or advanced) researcher access to the best literature in the field. In fact, we have tried to be not so much exhaustive as selective. And although the bibliography tends to reflect the research interests of the staff of the National Air and Space Museum, it is not restricted to or by those interests, and is broad in scope.

The youthfulness of the history of aviation and the coexistence of a wide variety of popular or so–called buff literature and very highly technical material, along with a handful of scholarly works, has forced us to make some hard decisions about what to include so as to remain faithful to the title of the bibliography, *Air and Space History*. In some areas of aeronautics—engineering, communication, and navigation, for example—there is very little analytical, historical work extant; in these cases, we opted for whatever technical material seemed to define the area. In general aviation, especially in the newly emerging areas of hang gliding, human–powered and ultralight flight, we have had to rely primarily on popular works.

In the field of space science and exploration, the span of titles is similarly mixed, ranging from the well–established history of astronomy to the newly emerging cultural history of space exploration. Thus, the differing approaches to the subject have forced us to accommodate a plethora of popular, technical, and historical titles.

We are optimistic that the relative size of the body of synthetic historical analysis will be increased as time goes on and as the study of the history of air and space becomes legitimized by historians of technology and of social, political, and cultural subjects. Indeed, in the past few years, the history of air and space has attracted the attention of numerous scholars and academic historians. Increasing interest in the field on the part of young scholars and the growing number of academic programs accommodating this interest are encouraging signs.

The organization of the bibliography reflects the diversity of the materials included and the peculiarities of aviation and space research. In some cases, it seemed appropriate to simply arrange titles alphabetically within a section. In other cases, subdivisions had to be introduced. Despite these variations, points of form and style are consistent throughout and conform with the University of Chicago Press *Manual of Style*, 12th edition. In the text, we have followed the Library of Congress system of transliteration.

Each section of the bibliography opens with a brief essay explaining the organization therein and the method of selection. These essays not only present the compilers' rationale in making selections but also indicate directions for future research and writing.

A few final words. The editors have tried laboriously to eliminate duplicate entries from section to section and from air to space. Nevertheless, some purposeful duplication exists where the subject matter of a title has relevance in more than one context. In such cases, it was considered necessary to repeat the entry with a different annotation so that its application in another subject area would be illuminated. And, despite the best efforts of a good many persons, a bibliography of such scope and magnitude as this is bound to have some inaccuracies. The editors and compilers take full responsibility for them.

Dominick A. Pisano
Cathleen S. Lewis
National Air and Space Museum
October 1987

ACKNOWLEDGMENTS

The editors would like to thank the staff of the Departments of Aeronautics and Space Science and Exploration for their cooperation. Certain persons made substantial contributions. They should not remain anonymous: in the Department of Aeronautics, Debbie Douglas, for her preliminary work, administration, coordination, verification, and editorial assistance and advice; Tom Noon, who, when Debbie was called away, stepped in and took over these tasks and performed excellently; and Barbara Irwin, who not only contributed to a number of sections, but verified entries and provided editorial help. Thanks also to Dorothy Cochrane and Peter Jakab for editorial assistance during crucial periods, and Anita Mason for her administrative expertise. Outside the department, special thanks go to Tom Crouch, National Museum of American History; Dick Hallion, Department of the Air Force; and John Greenwood, Department of the Army, for reviewing various parts of the manuscript.

In the Department of Space Science and Exploration, special thanks go to Frank Winter for nurturing the project during its earliest days, Edith Smith for the patience with which she read the roughest of drafts, and Addison Wells for methodically checking bibliographic data.

Finally, the editors are grateful to Roger Bilstein, University of Houston at Clear Lake City, Joe Guilmartin, U.S. Naval War College, and Pam Mack, Clemson University, for their invaluable work in reading the manuscript and recommending last-minute alterations. Also, our thanks go to Von Hardesty, chairman, Department of Aeronautics, Joe Tatarewicz, chairman, Department of Space Science and Exploration, and Trish Graboske, chief, Office of Publications, for their unstinting support and encouragement. Last but not least, our thanks to Vicky Macintyre for her meticulous copy editing and for compiling the index.

AIR AND SPACE HISTORY

AN ANNOTATED BIBLIOGRAPHY

AIR

Dominick A. Pisano, Editor

with the special assistance of Deborah G. Douglas,

Thomas J. Noon and Barbara J. Irwin

BIBLIOGRAPHIES

The lack of continuous, systematic bibliographic coverage of the history and technology of aviation has long been a consistent problem for scholars. Brockett's *Bibliography of Aeronautics* (see item 5), the first and most extensive work in the field, covers the years from 1909 to 1937 quite uniformly. After Brockett, however, the coverage, although yearly, becomes uneven and, ironically, in light of the enormous development of aviation in the postwar era, virtually ends in 1947.

Picking up where Brockett's work leaves off, the Library of Congress's aeronautical indexes cover the years 1938 and 1939. These compilations overlap somewhat with the Works Progress Administration's *Bibliography of Aeronautics* (see item 23), which deals with the period 1936 to 1940. The years from 1943 to 1947 are covered in Willard Kelso Dennis's *Recent Periodical Articles: A Selective Subject Index* (see item 6), but it lists only periodicals. Since 1947, there have been no serious attempts to survey the literature systematically, with the exception of the Smithsonian Institution, National Air and Space Museum's *The Aerospace Periodical Index, 1973–1982* (see item 1), which is limited to magazine articles and is rather difficult to use.

In view of the overall spottiness of bibliographic work in the field, this section serves as an introduction to the most important and most readily available general sources of bibliographic information. Only those sources deemed most representative are included. Sources of bibliographic information on more specific topics are in the introductory essays that appear in other sections of the bibliography.

Dominick A. Pisano

1. *The Aerospace Periodical Index, 1973–1982.* Smithsonian Insti-
    tution Libraries, Research Guide no. 3. Boston: G.K. Hall,
    1983. Pp. vii + 660.

    Begun as an internal information tool for the National Air and
    Space Museum in 1973, this index continues the work of Hanni-
    ball's *Aircraft, Engines and Airmen* (cited herein as item 9).
    The *Index* covers a variety of topics (history of air and space,
    flight technology, ballooning and lighter–than–air technology,
    rocketry, satellites, astronomy, and earth and planetary sci-
    ences) that have appeared in both popular and technical aero-
    space magazines and journals. Because the subject headings are
    somewhat esoteric (authors, for example, are listed as headings)
    the *Index* may be difficult to use. Nonetheless, it is the only
    source of information on periodical articles that relate to aero-
    space topics in the relatively recent past.

2. *The Air University Library Index.* Maxwell Air Force Base, Ala.:
    Department of the Air Force Library, 1949–.

    Begun in 1949 as a quarterly index to 23 periodicals (formerly
    titled *Air University Periodical Index*), the *AU Index* has
    been greatly enlarged over the years and now indexes some 75
    aeronautically related periodicals, including *Aerospace His-
    torian, Air University Review, Interavia, Soviet Military
    Review*, and *U.S. Naval Institute Proceedings*. Heavy on air
    doctrine and policy, but nonetheless indispensable.

3. *Applied Science and Technology Index.* New York: H.W. Wilson,
    1958–.

    Primarily a general sci–tech periodical index, but useful for
    aeronautics. Continues *Industrial Arts Index* (cited herein as
    item 10) with approximately the same coverage.

4. Bilstein, Roger E. "Notes." In *Flight in America, 1900–1983:
    From the Wrights to the Astronauts*, 331–350. Baltimore, Md.:
    Johns Hopkins University Press, 1984.

    Bilstein's "notes" to his survey of aviation in the United States
    are in reality an excellent, readable, and thoughtful extended
    bibliographic essay that surveys the significant literature in the
    field. A fine bibliographic introduction to the subject. Highly
    recommended both for beginning students and for seasoned
    veterans.

5. Brockett, Paul, comp. *Bibliography of Aeronautics.* Washington,
    D.C.: U.S. National Advisory Committee for Aeronautics
    [1909–1937].

    Begun as vol. 55 of the Smithsonian *Miscellaneous Collec-
    tions,* "Brockett's," as it is more familiarly known, was insti-
    tuted as a reflection of the Smithsonian Institution's early
    interest in flight as overseen by the National Advisory Commit-
    tee for Aeronautics. Undoubtedly the best source of biblio-
    graphic information on early flight and the only continuous
    source for aeronautical literature through the 1930s.

6. Dennis, Willard Kelso, comp. *Recent Periodical Articles: A
    Selective Subject Index [Recent Aeronautical Literature: A
    Selective Subject Index].* East St. Louis, Ill.: Parks Air
    College [Wichita, Kansas: Beech Aircraft Corporation]
    [1943–1947].

    A periodical index to aeronautical literature initially issued by
    the Parks Air College Library (1943–1944), then by Beech
    Aircraft Corp. (1945–1947).

7. Gamble, William B., comp. *History of Aeronautics: A Selected
    Bibliography of References to Material in the New York Public
    Library.* Reprint. New York, 1971.

    Excellent introductory bibliography. Originally published in
    1936 and 1937 as a series of articles in the *Bulletin of the New
    York Public Library,* then in 1938 as a monograph. Reprinted in
    1971.

8. Hallion, Richard P. *A Source Guide to the History of Aeronau-
    tics and Astronautics.* Project Warrior Monograph. Edwards
    Air Force Base, Calif.: Air Force Flight Test Center, History
    Office, 1982. Pp. i + 71.

    An excellent, thorough bibliographic essay that surveys the
    literature of aviation and spaceflight in chronological fashion
    from antiquity to the space age. Includes a useful section on
    general reference sources that covers the history of technology,
    research perspectives, periodical sources, chronologies, air-
    craft, biographical guides, and bibliographic sources. Indispen-
    sable for the beginning student.

9. Hanniball, August. *Aircraft, Engines and Airmen: A Selective Review of the Periodical Literature, 1930–1969.* Metuchen, N.J.: Scarecrow, 1972. Pp. xxiv + 825.

   Fine, unannotated survey of periodical literature on aviation in three parts. Strong on individual aircraft, but less useful for engines and biography.

10. *Industrial Arts Index.* (Subject Index to a Selected List of Engineering, Trade and Business Periodicals, Books, and Pamphlets). New York: H.W. Wilson, 1913–1957.

    Contains a great deal of bibliographic material on aeronautical subjects. Indexes (especially for the 1930s) such journals as *Aero Digest, Air Commerce Bulletin, Aviation, Royal Aeronautical Society Journal, S.A.E* [Society of Automotive Engineers] *Journal, Scientific American.* Complements coverage in *Readers' Guide to Periodical Literature.* Title changes to *Applied Science and Technology Index* in 1958.

11. *International Aerospace Abstracts.* New York: American Institute of Aeronautics and Astronautics, Technical Information Service, 1961–.

    Difficult to use but indispensable index to technical abstracts in both aeronautics and astronautics. Alternates publication with NASA's *Scientific and Technical Aerospace Reports* (Washington, D.C.: Scientific and Technical Information Branch, 1963–). Divided into two major sections: abstracts and index. Abstracts section contains bibliographic citations with abstracts arranged by subject. Index section contains five indexes: subject, personal author, contract number, meetings paper, and report index and accession number. Each index is prefaced by explanatory notes.

12. Mergen, Bernard. "Flying." In *Recreational Vehicles and Travel: A Resource Guide*, 143–174. Westport, Conn.: Greenwood, 1985.

    An excellent and entertaining bibliographic essay that is aimed at recreational flying but manages to impart a great deal of information about the literature of flight in general. Covers ballooning, powered flight, gliding, and sky diving and includes a checklist of both books and articles. Recommended reading for all serious students of aviation.

13. Miller, Samuel Duncan, comp. *An Aerospace Bibliography.* Washington, D.C.: Office of Air Force History, 1978. Pp. vii + 341.

    Good introductory aviation bibliography with special emphasis on the U.S. Air Force. See also Mary Ann Cresswell and Carl Berger, *United States Air Force History, An Annotated Bibliography* (Washington, D.C.: Office of Air Force History, 1971), an earlier edition of Miller.

14. *The New York Times Index.* New York: New York Times, 1913–.

    A virtual record of this newspaper's comprehensive coverage of aviation from the origins to the present. Although entries are scattered over a number of subject headings, the *Index* is especially good for the developmental period of the interwar years, World War II, and the postwar era of jet propulsion.

15. *Readers' Guide to Periodical Literature.* New York: H.W. Wilson, 1901–.

    One of the best sources for surveying the periodical literature in the field from the beginnings of aviation to the present day. Provides surprisingly good coverage of the subject in the nonaviation, general periodicals, especially for the interwar and postwar years.

16. Royal Aeronautical Society. *A List of the Books, Periodicals, and Pamphlets in the Library of the Royal Aeronautical Society, with Which Is Incorporated the Institution of Aeronautical Engineers.* London: Royal Aeronautical Society, 1941; reprint, New York: Arno, 1980.

    Contains a complete and extensive list of the library collections of the Royal Aeronautical Society in 1941, listed by author and subject. Also includes listings of many foreign-language works. Useful for locating historical and technical-scientific material.

17. U.S. Civil Aeronautics Administration. *A Selected and Annotated Bibliography on the Social, Political, Economic, and International Aspects of Aviation.* Washington, D.C.: U.S. Department of Commerce, Civil Aeronautics Administration, Office of Aviation Training, 1946.

A sampling of books and pamphlets, this bibliography is geared toward use by teachers to help them examine the social implications of aviation. The entries are representative of the most current literature available at the time of publication. A subject index indicates the grade level appropriate to each entry.

18. U.S. Civil Aeronautics Administration. *A Selected and Annotated Bibliography of Recent Air Age Education Textbooks.* Washington, D.C.: U.S. Department of Commerce, Civil Aeronautics Administration, Office of Aviation Training, 1947.

One of the "bibles" of the so–called air age education movement that gained some legitimacy in the early 1940s and lasted throughout the war years. See also, Stanford University, School of Education, *Aviation Education Source Book* (New York: Hastings House, 1946) and the Aviation Education Research Group, Columbia University, Teachers College, *Bibliography of Aviation Education Materials* (New York: Macmillan, 1942).

19. U.S. Library of Congress. Division of Aeronautics. *Subject Index to Aeronautical Periodical Literature and Reports for the Year 1938.* New York, 1939.

Subject–oriented index of American and foreign periodicals and serials received in the Library of Congress. Prepared primarily from the card index maintained by the library's Division of Aeronautics, but includes articles from other sources. Issued in cooperation with the Institute of the Aeronautical Sciences and prepared for publication by workers under the supervision of the Federal Works Agency, Works Projects Administration, for the city of New York. Covers only the year 1938.

20. U.S. Library of Congress. Division of Aeronautics. *The Aeronautical Index for 1939: A Subject and Author Index to Aeronautical Periodicals and Technical Reports.* New York: Sherman Fairchild Publication Fund, Institute of the Aeronautical Sciences, 1943.

The second in a brief series, the project was terminated on June 30, 1941. Subject–author index follows the same general guidelines as used the previous year. Also contains entries for numerous bulletins, reports, government documents, and pamphlets in aeronautics. See also, *Subject Index to Aeronautical Periodical Literature and Reports for the Year 1938.*

21. U.S. Library of Congress. Science and Technology Division. *Aeronautical and Space Serial Publications: A World List.* Washington, D.C., 1962.

Not a bibliography per se, but an international index of aero-space serial publications (periodicals, documents, annuals, numbered monographs, etc.). Although out of date, a very useful compilation. Supersedes *A Checklist of Aeronautical Periodicals and Serials in the Library of Congress*, published in 1948.

22. U.S. National Advisory Committee for Aeronautics. *Index of NACA Technical Publications.* 9 vols. Washington, D.C.: 1915–1949.

Historic compilation of technical publications issued by NACA from the time it was established (1915) to 1949. A classified bibliography that includes 12 general subject headings, among which are aerodynamics, propulsion, meteorology, instruments and research equipment, and techniques.

U.S. National Aeronautics and Space Administration. Scientific and Technical Information Branch. *Scientific and Technical Aerospace Reports.* Washington, D.C., 1963–.

Alternates publication with *International Aerospace Abstracts* (cited herein as item 11).

23. U.S. Works Progress Administration [Work Projects Administration]. *Bibliography of Aeronautics.* New York, 1936–1940.

Compiled from the index of aeronautics of the Institute of the Aeronautical Sciences. Consists of 50 parts arranged by subject. Focuses on flight technology, but surprisingly good on aviation medicine, laws and regulations, aerial photography, and women in aeronautics. Along with Brockett's (q.v.), one of the most ambitious aviation bibliography projects in scope and comprehensiveness ever undertaken. Produced in the late 1930s by the Work Projects Administration (later, Works Progress Administration) under the sponsorship of the Institute of the Aeronautical Sciences. A supplement to each part was issued in 1940–1941.

GENERAL SOURCES

Researchers in the history of aviation are faced with a confusing plethora of published and unpublished references and documents, in addition to factual and statistical information. Up to now there has been little hope of being guided to it in a systematic way. Aside from a brief section of Eugene P. Sheehy's *Guide to Reference Books* (Chicago: American Library Assn., 1976) titled "Aeronautical and Space Engineering," little effort has been made to classify these materials.

Particularly frustrating is the lack of comprehensive information on manuscript and documentary collections that relate to the history of aviation. Lawrence J. Paszek's *United States Air Force History: A Guide to Documentary Sources* (see item 54), and Catherine D. Scott's *Aeronautics and Space Flight Collections* (see item 55) are important first steps. The forthcoming *Directory of Aerospace Information Resources*, which will be published in the near future by Smithsonian Institution Press, should also be an important contribution.

This section of the bibliography is an attempt to remedy these deficiencies somewhat, particularly in the area of published sources on the history and technology of aviation. The works listed here are a representative sampling of the most frequently used general references on the subject. The section is subdivided into chronologies, dictionaries, encyclopedias, biographical dictionaries, handbooks, yearbooks, and documentary sources.

Barbara J. Irwin
William T. Judkins

Chronologies

24. Emme, Eugene M. *Aeronautics and Astronautics: An American Chronology of Science and Technology in the Exploration of Space, 1915–1960*. Washington, D.C.: National Aeronautics and Space Administration, 1961. Pp. xi + 240. Index, Bibliog.

A detailed, in–depth chronology that contains a large pool of historical information concerning events leading up to the formation of the National Aeronautics and Space Administration. Appendixes include chronicles of earth satellites and space probes, world airplane records, select balloon flights, and awards and honors given in aeronautics and astronautics. Also includes a membership roster of the National Advisory Committee for Aeronautics (1915–1958). Good bibliography and exhaustive name and subject index.
Continued for 1962 by U.S. Congress, House, Committee on Science and Astronautics, *Astronautical and Aeronautical Events of 1962*: Report of the National Aeronautics and Space Administration, 88th Cong., 1st sess., June 12, 1963, and in yearly cumulations published by NASA titled *Astronautics and Aeronautics*, 1963–.

25. Payne, L.G.S. *Air Dates*. London: Heinemann, 1957. Pp. vii + 565. Index.

A chronological presentation of aeronautical events that covers the period from 1783 to 1956. Serves as an accurate historical timetable, especially during World War II, in which events are recorded almost daily.

26. Shrader, Welman. *Fifty Years of Flight: A Chronicle of the Aviation Industry in America, 1903–1953*. Cleveland, Ohio: Eaton, 1953. Pp. 178. Illustr.

Presents a chronological history of aviation and the aviation industry in a brief outline format. Includes a summary of annual statistical information.

27. Taylor, Michael J.H., and David Mondey, eds. *Milestones of Flight*. London: Jane's, 1983. Pp. 288. Index, Illustr.

A profusely illustrated, chronologically formatted record of all the important events in aviation and aerospace history from

863 B.C. to 1982. A detailed index helps the reader without chronological knowledge locate topics and events.

Dictionaries

28.   Frenot, G.H., and A.H. Holloway, eds. *AGARD Aeronautical Multilingual Dictionary*. New York: Pergamon, 1960. Index.

NATO's Advisory Group for Aerospace Research and Development produced this technical dictionary for use within the aerospace industry worldwide. Presents terms and indexes in English, Spanish, French, German, Italian, Dutch, Turkish, and Russian. Holloway edited a supplement to the dictionary (Pergamon, 1963), adding additional terms as well as Greek-language definitions.

29.   Gentle, Ernest J., and Lawrence J. Reithmaier, eds. *Aviation and Space Dictionary*. Fallbrook, Calif.: Aero, 1980. Pp. 272. Illustr.

Attempts to assign standardized meanings to the many terms that have evolved with the recent rapid growth of aerospace technology. Thus, it also includes terminology of aerospace-related fields such as geophysics, astronomy, and electronics. Although the dictionary is geared toward the intelligent layman, it is extremely technical and complete.

30.   Wragg, David W. *A Dictionary of Aviation*. New York: Frederick Fell, 1973. Pp. 286.

Written for the layman, the material includes terms related to lighter–than–air flight and spaceflight as well as aviation. Terminology from five specific areas is covered: military and civil; historical and contemporary; individuals and companies; events; equipment; organizations, agreements and alliances, and aerospace jargon. Word definitions are concise without being overly technical.

Encyclopedias

31.   Sencier, Paul, et al. *Annuaire de l'Aéronautique Diction-naire Encyclopédique des Locomotions Aériennes* (Annual

encyclopedic directory of air travel). Paris: C. Goblet and H. Marchal, 1910. Pp. 289.

A French–language dictionary that describes narratively balloon and dirigible evolution, airplane and helicopter construction, and use in early days. Part 2 contains an alphabetical listing of the names and addresses of aeronautical personalities. Part 3 lists alphabetically aeronautical terms, functions, balloons, dirigibles, airplanes, and aero engines of the period. Illustrated throughout with photographs, drawings, and graphs.

32. Hitzmann, Ivan. *Annuaire International De l'Aéronautique Encyclopédie Générale des Locomotions Aériennes* (Annual general encyclopedic directory of air travel). Paris: 1913–1914. Pagination varies. Illustr.

French–language narrative history of balloons, dirigibles, and airplanes. Lists aeronautical events chronologically and by national location. Includes considerable discussion of early military and naval aviation. Part 2 contains alphabetical listings of aeronautical terms and brief descriptions of aeronautical vehicles, engines, instruments, and clothing of the period. Part 3 lists names and addresses of aeronautical personalities and aero clubs or organizations. Part 4 lists names and addresses of scientific, industrial, and commercial establishments concerned with aeronautics. Representative photographs and drawings illustrate the text.

33. Burge, C.G. *Encyclopaedia of Aviation*. London: Sir Isaac Pitman and Sons, 1935. Pp. 642. Index, Illustr.

Illustrated alphabetical listing of aeronautical terms, aircraft maneuvers, aircraft types, and historical facts. Contains brief technical details devoted primarily to British usage and some foreign and international listings. Also includes sketchy biographies of 116 people who contributed to the development of aviation.

34. Garriga–Jové, Xavier, José Sanchez–Rocha, and Juan–Antonio Miquel Casado. *Enciclopedia de Aviación y Astronauticá* (Encyclopedia of aviation and astronautics). 8 vols. Barcelona: Ediciónes Garriga, 1972. Illustr.

Eight–volume, Spanish language, alphabetical listing of aeronautical terms, aircraft and missile types, instruments, engines, and miscellaneous service equipment. Historical and brief technical descriptions. Judicious use of charts, graphs, and photographs throughout the text. Lists abbreviated biographies of world–renowned airmen alphabetically within the text.

35.   Mancini, Luigi. *Grande Enciclopedia Aeronautica* (Great Encyclopedia of Aeronautics). Milan: Edizioni, "Aeronautica" L. Mancini, 1936. Pp. 660.

Italian–language alphabetical listings of international aero-nautical personalities, organizations, airports and air routes, manufacturers, and aircraft and aero–engine descriptions. Illustrated by numerous drawings, charts, and photographs.

36.   Mondey, David, et al. *The International Encyclopedia of Aviation.* New York: Crown, 1977. Pp. 480. Index, Illustr.

Narrative descriptions of aeronautical creative ideas, de-velopment of airframes, engines, flying boats, airships, rotor-craft, V/STOL, rocketry, and space exploration. Chapters devoted to facts, feats and records, air disasters, and aviation law. Lists famous names and includes an aeronautical chronol-ogy, a glossary of aviation terms, air museums, and index. Profusely illustrated throughout with drawings, charts, and photographs.

37.   Taylor, Michael J.H., et al. *Jane's Encyclopedia of Aviation.* 5 vols. London: Jane's and Grolier, 1980. Pp. 1078. Index, Illustr.

An illustrated alphabetical listing of the most significant types of aircraft and space vehicles. Historical descriptions in directory form include photographs and brief technical details. In addition, Volume 1 contains an abbreviated aeronautical glossary, a brief chronology of aviation milestones, a world directory of air forces, and aerospace world records. A preface contains a listing of photo credits. Volume 5 also includes indexes to chronology and to aircraft and space vehicles.

Biographical Dictionaries

38.   Gardner, Lester D. *Who's Who in American Aeronautics.* 3 vols. New York: Aviation Publishing. Pagination varies. Illustr.

Published in only three editions, (1922, 1925, and 1928), *Who's Who* lists personnel from nearly every organization, military or otherwise, that had anything to do with aircraft, aviation, and aeronautics of that era. Its major drawback lies in the brevity of the biographical sketches, especially in comparison with *The Blue Book of Aviation*. A large advertising section is included in each edition.

39. Hoagland, Ronald W., ed. *The Blue Book of Aviation.* Los Angeles, Calif.: Hoagland Co., 1932. Pp. 292. Index, Illustr.

    Basically a who's who in aviation up to and including the year 1932, this volume lists prominent men and women flyers as well as those connected with the aviation industry. Also contains a section titled "American Aviation during the World War," with a complete list of U.S. air victories. Includes a list of air aces from other countries and a chronological index.

40. *Who's Who in Aviation and Aerospace.* Boston: National Aero- nautical Institute, 1983. Pp. xi + 1415.

    Focuses on important figures in the industry, such as aero- space engineers, educators, and researchers, as well as pilots, flight instructors, managerial personnel, and fixed-base operators. Limited in scope, with extremely short biographies that contain only cursory information. Includes indexes for locating names by geographical area and firm affiliation.

Handbooks

41. Burge, C.G., ed. *Handbook of Aeronautics.* London: Gale and Polden, 1931. Pp. xvi + 703. Index, Illustr.

    Compendium of the modern practice of aeronautical engi- neering with appropriate mathematical tables and formulas. Illustrated with graphs and charts.

42. Burge, C.G., ed. *Handbook of Aeronautics.* 2d ed. London: Sir Isaac Pitman and Sons, 1934. Pp. xxii + 721. Index, Illustr.

    Compilation of modern aeronautical engineering practice covering aerodynamics, performance, construction, materials, meteorology, instruments, wireless, air survey, and photography. Design data and formulas illustrated by tables, graphs, and charts. One volume is devoted to aircraft engine design and practice. Volume 3 covers aircraft and airscrew design details.

43.   Hildreth, C.H., and Bernard C. Nalty. *1001 Questions Answered about Aviation History.* New York: Dodd, Mead, 1969. Pp. xii + 419. Index, Bibliog., Illustr.

A basic text for the layman, this book answers general questions relating to aviation history. Although the material is easy to understand, it refrains from being superficial and simplistic.

44.   Judge, Arthur W. *Handbook of Modern Aeronautics.* London: Library Press, 1919. Pp. xxiii + 1005. Index, Illustr.

A technical reference book for manufacturers, designers, draftsmen, students, and others interested in aeronautical practice and theory. Generally useful information and mathematical tables. Covers screw threads, wire gauges, limits and tolerances, weights, and weight estimates for aero design. Also contains information on strengths and properties of materials, aerodynamics, fittings, instruments, and performance data. Discusses aero–engine, airscrew, flying boat, and seaplane design criteria, meteorology, and air navigation.

45.   Mason, Francis K., and Martin C. Windrow. *Know Aviation: Seventy Years of Man's Endeavor.* Garden City, N.Y.: Doubleday, 1973. Pp. 244. Index, Illustr.

A detailed account of aviation history that focuses not so much on chronology (although a chronology is included), as on aspects of individual people, machines, and events. Sections include the world's air forces, airlines, aircraft (both modern and classic), and aviation's great personalities. Includes an appendix titled "The Highest Awards for Gallantry Made to Military Airmen."

46.   Schulz, Richard, G.W. Feuchter, and Werner von Langsdorff. *Handbuch der Luftfahrt (Handbook of air travel).* Munich: J.F. Lehmanns Verlag, 1936, 1937–1938, 1939. Pp. 473. Index.

German–language listing, by nation, of worldwide military air organizations and air base locations, civil airlines, and airports. Part 2A lists, in alphabetical order, international aircraft design and manufacturing firms. Part 2B lists, with photographs where available, currently produced military aircraft. Part 2C lists civil aircraft, and Part 2D lists aeronautical engines. The 1939 issue was expanded to 596 pages of text and includes sections on naval aircraft carriers and aero engines.

47. Taylor, John W.R., Michael J.H. Taylor, and David Mondey, eds. *Air Facts and Feats*. New York: Two Continents, 1974. Pp. 228. Index, Bibliog., Illustr.

Examines significant events in the international development of flight. It differs from Michael J.H. Taylor's *Milestones of Flight* (cited herein as item 27) in its emphasis on "famous firsts" in aviation as opposed to aerospace (although a chapter on rocketry and spaceflight is included). Chapters cover lighter–than–air and rotorcraft as well as military, maritime, and commercial aviation. Includes an extensive index. Previously published in 1970 and compiled by Francis K. Mason and Martin C. Windrow.

Yearbooks

48. *The Aircraft Year Book*. New York: Manufacturers Aircraft Association; Aeronautical Chamber of Commerce of America, 1919–1962(?). Index, Illustr.

Although the first of these annual volumes was published in 1919, *The Aircraft Year Book* is most helpful to the researcher for its coverage of the critical period of aviation history—the late 1920s to the end of the 1940s. The yearbooks contain excellent statistical information and reference material, and are also useful records of legislative and governmental activities concerning aviation, outstanding achievements in aviation, new aircraft and accessories, and scientific developments. (These sections are especially detailed during the World War II years.) Although published into the 1960s (the title was changed to *The Aerospace Year Book* in 1957), it is less valuable as a reference source after 1950.

49. Cleveland, Reginald M., and Frederick P. Graham. *The Aviation Annual*. Garden City, N.Y.: Aviation Research Associates, 1944–1946. Pp. vii + 224; xiv + 205; x + 245. Index, Bibliog., Illustr.

A narrative description of World War II aviation. Devotes chapters to the Army Air Forces, naval aviation, training aircraft manufacturing, aeronautical research, the civil air patrol, and U.S. air transport. Includes an annual directory of aviation organizations and associations and an annual bibliography of aviation books. A valuable reference for students of World War II aviation.

50. Cleveland, Reginald M., et al. *The Aviation Annual.* New York: Harper and Brothers, 1947. Pp. xiv + 250. Index, Illustr.

Post–World War II narrative description of civil aviation, international flying, aeronautical research for peace, new prime movers for aircraft, military aviation, manufacturing, and education. Covers the transition from war to peace.

51. *Jane's All the World's Aircraft.* London: Jane's, 1909–. Index, Illustr.

An annual narrative and alphabetical listing, by nation, of airships, dirigibles, airplanes, specialized aircraft, satellites and spacecraft, and aero engines. Contains photographs (where available), drawings, and historical and brief technical details for each entry. Also includes timely topical articles and tabulations. Presents annual sections that deal with first flights in each calendar year along with official aeronautical records. The classified advertising and the aerial trades directory of "Who's Who" are useful reference material.

52. Manoury, Paul. *L'Annuaire de L'Air* (Aerial directory). Paris: Atmos, 1910. Pp. 225. Index.

Published in both English and French, contains alphabetical listings divided into a chronology of aeronautics, early builders of aircraft, other classes of associated aerial industry and trade such as aerodromes, aviators, clubs and societies, flying schools, personally owned aircraft and aerodromes, records of aviation feats and aerostation, bibliography, and recommended firms (mostly French).

53. Mingos, Howard, ed. *The Junior Aircraft Yearbook (Flying).* New York: Aeronautical Chamber of Commerce of America, 1934–1938. Index, Illustr.

Contains nontechnical narrative descriptions of current events in air transportation, governmental activities, annual noteworthy flights, aerial service, airways and airports, military aviation, manufacturing, elementary aircraft, and engine design. A topical handbook for aviation enthusiasts.

Documentary Sources

54. Paszek, Lawrence J. *United States Air Force: A Guide to Documentary Sources*. Washington, D.C.: Office of Air Force History, 1973. Pp. v + 245. Index, Illustr.

   Lists nearly 150 repositories of significant collections. Although emphasis is on official air force materials, also includes information on larger research facilities such as the National Archives, the Library of Congress, and major university libraries. An essential guide for the researcher interested in U.S. Air Force–related topics.

55. Scott, Catherine D., ed. *Aeronautics and Space Flight Collections*. New York: Haworth, 1985. Pp. xi + 229. Illustr.

   Consists of a series of articles written by specialists that contain a great deal of information on aerospace documentary and book collections such as those in the Smithsonian Institution's National Air and Space Museum, Library of Congress, New York Public Library, University of Texas at Dallas, and U.S. Air Force Academy. Although by no means comprehensive, a useful and necessary compilation for historians of aerospace.

PERIODICALS

Aeronautical journalism traces its roots to the period before the invention of the airplane. In France, the birthplace of ballooning, for example, journals devoted to aerostation, or the science of ballooning, began to appear as early as the turn of the century. Yet it was not until well after the invention of the airplane in 1903 that a branch of concerted journalistic endeavor devoted solely to heavier–than–air flight began to make its appearance around the world, especially in Europe, Great Britain, and the United States. Many of the periodicals that developed in the years following the advent of powered flight have long ceased publication, but historians and researchers who would find them useful can take solace in the fact that they still exist (albeit in varying stages of deterioration, depending on their age) on library shelves throughout the world. In the United States, many will be found in the collections of the Library of Congress, the New York Public Library, and other major libraries.

Since there are virtually hundreds of aviation periodicals covering almost every aspect of lighter–than–air and heavier–than–air flight, the scope of this essay is limited to those considered most representative or useful to a beginning researcher in aviation. Moreover, the discussion focuses more heavily on English–language sources than on foreign–langage journals. Those who wish to pursue the subject in more depth should consult *Aeronautical and Space Serial Publications: A World List* (Washington, D.C., 1962), published by the Library of Congress. Although sadly out of date, this listing is still the best overall source of information relating to aerospace periodicals. It contains brief descriptions of many periodicals and magazines published throughout the world and is the most comprehensive source of information on periodicals that specialize in aviation and space. Information concerning aviation–space periodicals currently published in the United States will be found in recent editions of *The Standard Periodical Directory* (New York: Oxbridge Communications) under the heading "Aeronautics and Astronautics."

United States and Canada

The oldest known American periodical devoted to the science and technology of flight, the *Aerial Reporter*, began publication as a semimonthly in Washington, D.C., in May 1852, focusing its attention on lighter–than–air flight in the United States. Edited by the pioneer American technical journalist Rufus Porter, *Aerial Reporter* was issued as a means of keeping investors in Porter's dirigible airship project up to date on the progress of the venture. Although *Aerial Reporter* was short–lived and ended publication in August 1852, it did contain useful material on other flying machine projects and a series of fascinating editorials. Porter, the founding editor of *Scientific American*, began the tradition of covering aeronautics in that journal as well.

Other attempts at dispensing information on the current state of aeronautics were made by *Aeronautics*, which was published by the *American Engineer and Railroad Journal* from October 1893 to September 1894 and included the proceedings of the International Conference on Aerial Navigation held in Chicago in 1893. *The Aeronautical Annual*, published by Clarke Co. in Boston from 1895 to 1897 and edited by James Means, was another early source of information on developments in aeronautics.

The *Aeronautical World*, published in Glenville, Ohio, from 1902 to 1903, was another early American periodical devoted solely to heavier–than–air flight. The journal was a priceless mix of crank proposals, captivating editorials, and solid news of the early aeronautical community.

One of the earliest aeronautical journals in the United States to enjoy more than an ephemeral existence was also called *Aeronautics*, like its 1893 predecessor. This periodical originated in New York in July 1907 as *American Magazine of Aeronautics*, but in February 1908 its title was changed to *Aeronautics*, the name it held until its demise in 1915. At various times during its existence, *Aeronautics* was the official organ of the Aero Club of Pennsylvania and the Aeronautical Society of America.

Edited by Ernest L. Jones, *Aeronautics* provided sound coverage of the latest aircraft and aviation developments, American and European, during the early days of heavier–than–air flight. *Aeronautics* contained many interesting and useful advertisements, and focused on the technical development of aviation, with features such as "Our Recent Experiments in North Carolina" (June 1908), by Wilbur and Orville Wright. Although the magazine continued into the World War I years, it gave surprisingly little coverage to the air war in Europe.

Next in chronological order of appearance is *Fly; The National Aeronautic Monthly*, published in Philadelphia from November 1908 to October 1912. *Fly* was started by Alfred Lawson, the developer of the first multi–engined passenger aircraft in the United States and eccentric founder of "Lawsonomy," a quasi–religious political-economic theory. Lawson was also *Fly's* first editor and publisher.

The first issue of *Fly* set the tone for the magazine with Lawson at the helm: "New and original ideas wanted. . . . Art, science, fiction, wit, epigram, poetry, prose, drawing; anything from a single sentence to a 5000 word article, or a ludicrous cartoon will be accepted, provided that it relates to the subject of mechanized flight." In its first year, *Fly* often showed the mark of Lawson's energetic approach and his eccentricity. By November 1909, however, Lawson had sold his shares in the company that published *Fly* to John F. Kelley, his partner. After that, *Fly* settled down to become a rather ordinary aviation journal not unlike *Aero* or *Aerial Age Weekly*, and in January 1914, it was absorbed by *Aeronautics*.

Another early aviation periodical was *Aero*, published in St. Louis, which first appeared on October 8, 1910, and ran until November 14, 1914. Billing itself as "the first weekly aeronautic publication in America," *Aero*, beginning with the July 6, 1912 issue, became *Aero and Hydro*, and shifted location to Chicago.

Aero and Hydro was a mixture of up–to–date reportage of early aviation events and features such as a serialized translation, by David Douglas of Edinburgh of Heinrich Gatke's "Fifty Years of Bird Flight" (June 15, 1912). The magazine also contains the standard aviation advertising for flying schools, equipment, a directory of licensed aviators, aircraft drawings for the homebuilder, coverage of activi- ties at various flying fields, and, probably most important, up–to–date information on "hydroaeroplanes," as the amphibious aircraft of those days were called. During the earliest days of the war, *Aero and Hydro* reported regularly on aerial activity at the front, but publication ended shortly after World War I began. All in all, *Aero and Hydro* offers the best detailed day–by–day coverage of U.S. aeronautical activity available for this period.

Another impressive early aeronautical journal is *Aero Club of America Bulletin*. This journal, the official organ of the Aero Club of America, was founded in 1911 by Robert J. Collier, Henry A. Wise Wood, and Henry Woodhouse, and by 1920 had on its editorial con- tributing board Robert E. Peary, Augustus Post, A.F. Zahm, and Alberto Santos–Dumont. In October 1912, the title of the magazine was changed to *Flying*, and on August 1, 1921, it was consolidated with *Aerial Age Weekly*. Throughout its lifetime, the journal main- tained its affiliation with the Aero Club of America.

Edited primarily by Henry A. Wise Wood, Henry Woodhouse, and G.D. Wardrop, *Aero Club of America Bulletin—Flying* put forth its editorial policy in the January 1912 issue: "The purpose of this peri- odical is to gather and present, for the information of the member- ship of the Aero Club of America and its affiliated clubs, an accurate monthly summary of the progress of aeronautics throughout the world. Its policy will aim to encourage scientific research, develop the various branches of aerial sport, assist the growth of contributory industries and arouse an active public interest in aerial travel. Bound only to serve the broad interests of the aeronautical movement in America, its pages will be found wholly free of personal, sectional, or commercial bias." To a large extent, the journal lived up to its original promise. Later issues also announced that the journal was dispensing with normal copyright restrictions and inviting other publications to reproduce "articles and cuts" without payment and only a credit to the *Bulletin*.

Aero Club of America Bulletin—Flying offered comprehensive and objective coverage of all the early U.S. aeronautical activity until World War I. Although it was one of the only aeronautical periodicals to report extensively on military aviation before the war, wartime coverage became overtly militaristic. For example, numerous articles dealt with the aerial defense of the United States (not a real concern in 1918, given the primitive state of aviation technology).

Aerial Age Weekly (later, *Aerial Age*, a monthly), which absorbed *Aero Club of America Bulletin—Flying*, is another important aeronautical journal of the pre–World War I period. Published in New York from March 1915 until July 1923, *Aerial Age* was one of the few of the early aviation magazines to survive into the 1920s. Important because it allows the researcher to follow the development of the aviation industry during its formative years, *Aerial Age* is also a good source of information on developments in lighter–than–air flight, and on women in aviation, with frequent articles by Ruth Law and Katherine and Marjorie Stinson. The magazine also featured in–depth analyses of the major aircraft of the period. During the World War I years, *Aerial Age* devoted extensive space not only to American aeronautical efforts but also to those of France, Great Britain, and Germany.

The most long–lived of the second–generation aero magazines is undoubtedly *Aviation*, a New York publication that began on August 1, 1916, as *Aviation and Aeronautical Engineering*. In the 1920s, *Aviation* was a weekly, edited and published by Lester Gardner (Gardner Publishing). Considered by many to be the foremost aviation publicist in the United States—he was founder of the Institute of the Aeronautical Sciences, promoter of aviation causes from the 1920s through the 1940s, and air traveler extraordinaire—Gardner made *Aviation* the showcase of aviation journalism in the United States during the 1920s.

An editorial in the first issue of *Aviation* proclaimed: "Aeronautics has passed through the period of rule of thumb designing and empirical experimentation. It is now a recognized science subdivided into many branches, and those who are working in aeronautical engineering can rightly claim that it has reached the dignity of a profession." If anything, Gardner and *Aviation* helped the burgeoning technology attain legitimacy.

In March 1929, *Aviation* was purchased by McGraw–Hill, and in the July 6, 1929, issue, the eminent Edward P. Warner took on the editorial duties for the magazine. With Warner at the helm, *Aviation* became the voice of the aeronautical industry in the 1930s and reflected the changing image of aviation during the decade. Later,

when Warner became a member of the Civil Aeronautics Administration, S. Paul Johnston took over as editor. *Aviation* provided
excellent coverage of World War II, both in terms of news and technology. Continuing into the space age, *Aviation* became known as
Aviation Week and Space Technology on January 11, 1960. As *Aviation Week*, it has become the most familiar and comprehensive
aerospace magazine of the present day, providing continuity into the
space age and weekly coverage of current developments.

After its first four numbers were issued as the official bulletin of
the World's Board of Aeronautical Commissioners (1921–1922), *Aero
Digest*, published in Washington, made its appearance in August 1922
as *Aeronautical Digest*, a monthly. In April 1924, the title was
changed to *Aero Digest* (Charles J. Glidden, editor) and the magazine
enjoyed a long run until December 1956.

For much of its lifetime, *Aero Digest* was edited and published by
Frank Tichenor and J.E. Horsfall, who had a long reign as the magazine's first and second in command. Like its contemporary, *Aviation,
Aero Digest* presented a well-rounded view of aviation with articles
of general interest on commercial, military, and general aviation and
current news of the industry, along with eccentric and provocative
reviews and comments by Tichenor and Cy Caldwell. At the same
time, *Aero Digest* was, in its heyday, more of a "nuts and bolts"
aviation magazine with a heavy concentration on products and various aspects of aeronautical engineering. This tradition began in July
1933, when *Aero Digest* absorbed *Aviation Engineering*. Beginning in
November 1940 and lasting throughout the war years, *Aero Digest*
published *Aviation Engineering* as a special section.

Other significant sources of aviation information concerning
technological developments for the interwar and post–World War II
years are *Western Flying* (later *Western Aviation, Missiles and Space*,
and *Western Aerospace*, January 1926 to ?) and *Southern Aviation*
(September 1929 to May 1933) for good regional coverage; *U.S. Air
Services* (February 1919 to December 1956) for broad coverage;
AOPA Newsletter (1939 to the present); *Air Line Pilot* (1931 to the
present); *Journal of the Aeronautical Sciences*, later called *Journal of
the Aerospace Sciences* (1934–1958); *Ninety-Nine News*, official
publication of International Women Pilots (1933 to the present), and
Soaring (1937 to the present).

Researchers who wish to survey the milieu of aviation in the
nation's capital, especially during the 1920s and 1930s, will want to
look at *National Aeronautics*, an interest-group organ designed to
promote aviation, published by the National Aeronautic Association.
This journal, which originated as the *National Aeronautic Association
Review* in December 1923, went through a number of title changes
until it emerged in March 1956 as *National Aeronautics*.

The heyday of *National Aeronautics* was the 1930s, with U.S.
Senator Hiram Bingham (later censured by his congressional peers for
an apparent conflict of interest) as president and a veritable who's

who of aviation as board members: Joseph S. Ames, Richard Byrd, Amelia Earhart, Harry Guggenheim, David S. Ingalls, Charles A. Lindbergh, and Clarence Young.

On the political side of aviation, mention must be made of *American Aviation* and its sister publication *American Aviation Daily*, both published in Washington, D.C. More comprehensive than *National Aeronautics* in its political coverage, *American Aviation*, first published in June 1937, is, according to Civil Aeronautics Administration historian John R.M. Wilson, "the best source of continuing analysis of aviation issues." Although its editor, Wayne W. Parrish, was often candid (and sometimes thoroughly in error) in his assessment of those issues, *American Aviation* cannot be faulted because its coverage of events from the late 1930s through the late 1960s was in every way comprehensive. Also important is *American Aviation's* companion, *American Aviation Daily*, which began in January 1939 as a news digest of day–by–day aviation developments. Its forte has been coverage of aviation legislation and developments on Capitol Hill. Still published today by the Ziff–Davis group as *Aviation Daily*, this news digest continues to be the best overall source of daily information on aerospace developments in the United States.

Those interested in more specialized publications that deal with the legal issues in aviation should see the *Air Law Review* (1930–1941), *Journal of Air Law* (1930–1938) and its successor, *Journal of Air Law and Commerce* (1938–1942), and *Aviation Law Reports* (1931 to the present).

On the civil air side, the general workings of the Bureau of Air Commerce, aviation's regulatory agency during the 1920s (later, the Civil Aeronautics Authority and Civil Aeronautics Administration in the 1930s and 1940s), were covered in depth in its house organ, *Air Commerce Bulletin* (1929–1939), later known as *Civil Aeronautics Journal* (1940–1944), and *C.A.A. Journal* (1945–1952). This publication presents a handy digest of developments within the agency that relate to investigations, safety, airports, air transportation, and general aviation.

On the military side, one of the most comprehensive and useful sources of information on flying in the U.S. Air Service and its successors during the interwar years and World War II is the unpretentious, mimeographed *D.M.A. Weekly News Letter*. This publication, which began on September 21, 1918, changed its title to *Air Service News Letter* in April 1919. In December 1926, it became known as *Air Corps Newsletter*, the title it held until September 1941, when it became *Air Force; Official Service Journal of the U.S. Army Air Forces*. The *Journal* continues into the present day as *Air Force Magazine*.

Although less sophisticated than *Air Force Magazine*, the U.S. Navy's counterpart *Naval Aviation News* (formerly *BuAer News*, 1943 to the present) covers naval aviation developments in a systematic way. Also, much valuable information concerning naval aviation can be found in the *Naval Institute Proceedings*, which began publication in 1874 and continues into the present.

Another useful and informative source of information on aviation is the company organ. Of particular interest are such publications as *The Curtiss Flyleaf* (1917–1918), later called *Curtiss Fly Leaf* (1936–1945), published by the Curtiss Aeroplane and Motor Corp. and Curtiss–Wright, respectively; *Sperryscope* (1919–?), published by Sperry Rand; *The Beehive* (1926–), published by United Aircraft Corp., and *Esso Air World*, later called *Exxon Air World* (1947–).

One should not assume, however, that all of aviation journalism was focused on technology, the industry, or political developments. A number of publications were designed to appeal to the general public. The most famous of these was undoubtedly *Popular Aviation*, published in New York as a monthly from August 1927 to the present, and currently known as *Flying*. Known especially for its wonderfully illustrated and colorful covers, *Popular Aviation* hit the newsstands shortly after Lindbergh's transatlantic flight in May 1927 proved that there was, indeed, a popular interest in flying. The formula turned out to be successful.

Air Trails, another aviation magazine of general interest, first came out in New York in February 1934. Published by Street and Smith, *Air Trails* began as *Bill Barnes, Air Adventurer*. Throughout the 1930s, aerial hero Barnes ("Bill slammed his stick all the way forward and went into an outside loop at a speed that left him giddy"), written by George L. Eaton, continued his aerial adventures on a monthly basis. *Air Trails* continued publication into the 1950s, with a mix of general interest articles on current aviation developments and features of interest to model aviation enthusiasts. The magazine was noted for its excellent model aircraft plans and striking cover illustrations.

Other popular aviation magazines were *Model Airplane News* (1929 to the present) and *Flying Aces* (1928–1945). Finally, the action-packed aviation pulps—*Aces, Dare-Devil Aces, Battle Aces, Sky Fighters, George Bruce's Contact, War Birds*—were fictionalized treatments of war in the air generally set in the World War I period. These were especially popular during the 1930s and into the 1940s. Along with aviation films, the pulps helped to popularize aviation in the United States during the interwar years and should be of special interest to students of popular culture.

Finally, *The Sportsman Pilot* (1929–1943) stands in a category by itself because of its appeal to aviation's elite class, the well–heeled "sportsman" pilot. Representative of the type of audience cultivated, especially during the 1920s, are members of the Aviation Country Club movement and people who considered themselves part of the "smart set." Later, the magazine shifted its emphasis and became more democratic in its articles and advertisements.

Among current periodicals that concern themselves with historical aviation are *Aerospace Historian* (1954–); *Astronautics and Aeronau-*

tics (1932–); *Aviation Quarterly* (1974–); *C.A.H.S.* (Canadian Aviation Historical Society) *Journal* (1963–); *Canadian Aviation* (1928–); *Cross and Cockade Journal* (1959–); *Flight International* (1909–); *Historical Aviation Album* (1965–); *Journal of the American Aviation Historical Society* (1956–); *Technology and Culture* (1959–), and *World War I Aero* (1961–), among others.

Great Britain, Europe, and the Rest of the World

Although this discussion focuses mainly on periodicals of the United States, mention must be made of at least a few of the more important foreign publications. In Great Britain, some important titles are *Aeronautics* (1907–1957), *The Aeroplane* (1911–1967), *Air International* and its companion *Air Enthusiast* (1971–), *Air Pictorial* (1941 to the present), *Flight* (Royal Aero Club, 1909–1962) and *Flight International* (1962 to the present), and *Journal of the Royal Aeronautical Society* (January 1897 to the present). France is represented mainly by *L'Aerophile* (1893–1947), *Les Ailes* (1921–), and *Icare* (1957 to the present). Some representative German titles are *Deutsche Luftfahrt* (1897–1931), *Der Flieger* (1922–), and *Flugsport* (1908–1944). In the USSR, *Aviatsiya i kosmonavtika* (1918 to the present), a monthly journal of the Soviet air force enjoys a broad appeal, and *Kryl' ya rodiny* (Wings of the Motherland) touches on both civil and military aviation history.

The best overall source of information worldwide on aerospace periodicals is the Library of Congress's *Aeronautical and Space Serial Publications: A World List* (Washington, D.C., 1962), which covers 76 countries in North America, South and Central America, the Caribbean, Europe, Africa, Asia, and Australia. *Aeronautical and Space Serial Publications* lists over 250 periodicals each for France and Great Britain and over 300 for Germany. These consist of popular, technical, irregular or ephemeral, and philatelic publications, along with some of limited duration, and some of questionable value.

Dominick A. Pisano

GENERAL HISTORIES

The scholarly study of the history of aviation is still so new that a comprehensive, synthesized overview has yet to be written. Nevertheless, the handful of works listed here at least provide a place to begin.

These works are of two basic types: broad overviews of world aviation history that include analytical texts, popular surveys, and pictorial essays; and national histories of aeronautical activity in countries that have played the most significant roles in aviation.

Admittedly, the list is brief, and many nations for which literature exists have been omitted. The intent is to introduce the reader to the classic works that provide an overview of the field as well as to illustrate the various approaches and styles that characterize general histories of aviation. These are the standard references for the principal names, dates, and events in aviation history. For more specific and analytical studies, the reader should refer to the specialized sections of the bibliography.

Peter L. Jakab

28

56. Abate, Rosario. *Storia della Aeronautica Italiana* (History of Italian aeronautics). Milan: Bietti, 1974. Pp. 396. Index, Bibliog. Illustr.

   Covers the history of Italian aviation thoroughly. Especially useful is the first section, which includes chapters on early figures, such as Leonardo da Vinci. The chapters that cover the relationship between Mussolini's Fascist government and aviation are very valuable. Extensive bibliography.

57. Amnleyev, N.I., et al. *Aviatsiya i Kosmonavtika SSSR* (Aviation and cosmonautics in the USSR). Moscow: Voyenizdat, 1968. Pp. 599. Illustr.

   Provides coverage of important historical trends, personalities, and events from a Soviet perspective, with particular emphasis on military developments. Excellent overview of aviation and cosmonautics in the Soviet Union.

58. Bilstein, Roger E. *Flight Patterns: Trends of Aeronautical Development in the United States, 1918–1929*. Athens: University of Georgia Press, 1983. Pp. xi + 236. Index, Bibliog., Illustr.

   Analytical survey of U.S. aeronautical development from 1918 to 1929. Focuses on long–term trends established during the 1920s. Discussion includes the airmail, burgeoning airlines, research and development, the beginnings of an aircraft industry, an emerging infrastructure for the airplane, and the establishment of the airplane as an integral part of military thinking. Well researched and documented. Extensive bibliography.

59. Bilstein, Roger E. *Flight in America, 1900–1983: From the Wrights to the Astronauts*. Baltimore, Md.: Johns Hopkins University Press, 1984. Pp. xii + 356. Index, Bibliog., Illustr.

   An excellent survey of American aviation from the Wright brothers to the present. Although the sheer quantity of the information precludes a thorough treatment in a single volume, Bilstein does a fine job of writing a substantive, thematic text on U.S. aviation history. A strong work, *Flight in America* is recommended reading for beginners and old hands alike.

60. Dollfus, Charles, and Henri Bouché. *Histoire de L'Aéronautique*

(History of aeronautics). Paris: Saint–Georges, 1942. Pp. xxv + 613. Index, Illustr.

Accurate, comprehensive, large–format, narrative overview of the history of aviation. Lavishly illustrated with several full-color plates. One of the best works of its kind. Its only drawback is that, because it was published in 1942, it stops before the conclusion of World War II.

Ellis, Frank. *Canada's Flying Heritage.* 2d ed. Toronto: University of Toronto Press, 1954. Pp. xv + 388. Index, Illustr.

Cited herein as item 533.

61. Emme, Eugene M., ed. *Two Hundred Years of Flight in America: A Bicentennial Survey.* San Diego, Calif.: American Astro-nautical Society, 1977. Pp. xvi + 310. Index, Bibliog., Illustr.

Published proceedings of "Two Hundred Years of Flight in America," a symposium sponsored by the American Institute of Aeronautics and Astronautics and held at the National Air and Space Museum, Smithsonian Institution, Washington, D.C., in honor of the American bicentennial. A series of papers by prom-inent scholars in the field covering lighter–than–air flight, gen-eral aviation, military aviation, commercial aviation, and spaceflight. Excellent collection of essays by some of the best people in the field, with extensive notes.

62. *The Epic of Flight.* 23 vols. Alexandria, Va.: Time–Life, 1980–84. Index, Bibliog., Illustr.

Accurate, well–illustrated overview of the history of aviation. Arranged by subject, with each volume standing alone. The one–stop reference for the field.

63. Gibbs–Smith, Charles H. *Aviation: An Historical Survey from Its Origins to the End of World War II.* London: Her Majesty's Stationery Office, 1970. Pp. xvi + 316. Index, Bibliog., Illustr.

An expansion of the author's *The Aeroplane: An Historical Survey* (London: Science Museum, 1960) that surveys analytically the history of aviation from antiquity to the end of World War II. Emphasizes the early history of powered flight through World War I. The treatment of the period following World War I is admittedly brief, making it something less than a true overview. Nevertheless, it is the most analytical of any general history of aviation and remains the standard work.

64. Gordon, Arthur. *The American Heritage History of Flight.* Edited by Alvin M. Josephy, Jr. New York: American Heritage, 1962. Pp. 416. Index, Illustr.

Narrative overview of the history of aviation from antiquity to the beginnings of the space age, with an emphasis on the United States. A nicely illustrated introduction to the subject.

65. Kohri, Katsu, Ikuo Komori, and Ichiro Naito, comps. *The Fifty Years of Japanese Aviation, 1910–1960.* 2 vols. Translated by Kazuo Oyauchi. Tokyo: Kantosha, 1961. Pp. 324 + 169. Illustr.

Summarizes briefly the history of Japanese aviation from 1785 to 1960. (The dates given in the title are misleading.) Fairly well-balanced between civil and military aspects. Excellent chronology that compares Japanese civil and military aviation with aeronautical happenings in the rest of the world. Profusely illustrated.

66. Miller, Francis Trevelyan. *The World in the Air: The Story of Flying in Pictures.* 2 vols. New York: G.P. Putnam's Sons, 1930. Pp. 320 + 336.

Two-volume annotated pictoral history of aviation to 1930. Contains many excellent photographs as well as artists' impressions of flight. A unique and valuable visual reference that contains much information. Volume 1, which deals with the pre-Wright brothers era, is particularly strong. Over 1,200 illustrations.

67. Morris, Lloyd R., and Kendall Smith. *Ceiling Unlimited: The Story of American Aviation from Kitty Hawk to Supersonics.* New York: Macmillan, 1953. Pp. 417. Index, Illustr.

Surveys aviation from the Wrights through World War II, with the principal focus on the United States. Approximately half the book is devoted to the invention of the airplane and its first decade of development. Good source of the essential names, dates, and events.

68. Penrose, Harald. *British Aviation.* 5 vols. London: Putnam; Her
    Majesty's Stationery Office, various dates. Pp. 607 + 620 + 727
    + 339 + 317. Illustr.

    Covers aircraft, designers, and the development of the
    industry in Great Britain from the pioneer era to World War II in
    a comprehensive and authoritative way. Very thorough overview.

69. Percheron, Maurice. *L'Aviation Française* (French aviation).
    Paris: Fernand Nathan, 1938. Pp. 159. Illustr.

    Overview of some of the principal aircraft, aviators, and
    builders in French aviation from the beginnings to the
    mid–1930s. Major focus is on the pioneer era of heavier–than–air
    flight and the World War I period.

70. Supf, Peter. *Das Buch der deutschen Fluggeschichte* (History of
    German flight). 2 vols. Berlin–Grunewald: Hermann Klemm,
    1935. Pp. 515 + 637. Index, Illustr.

    Best pre–World War II survey of German aviation. Covers the
    period from the Middle Ages to 1935. Heaviest concentration is
    on the pioneer era from Lilienthal through the first decade of
    the 20th century and World War I. Excellent illustrations.

71. Taylor, John W.R., and Kenneth Munson. *History of Aviation.*
    New York: Crown, 1972. Pp. 511. Index, Illustr.

    Well–illustrated with a large format, this volume provides a
    general overview of the history of aviation from antiquity to the
    space age. Good introduction to the major names, dates, and
    events. Also provides some sense of major technological trends
    in aviation.

EARLY FLIGHT

The works in this section provide an introductory overview of the history of aviation, from antiquity to World War I. They should help familiarize the researcher with basic names, dates, events, and themes related to the invention and early development of heavier–than–air flight. Because this list is introductory and highly selective, an effort has been made to include works that are broad in scope. Specific case studies have been omitted. The only biographies cited are about the most influential figures in the field or works that provide useful insights into the overall subject or period. Two contemporary works of the period are listed, but only because they were widely consulted. Many books about early flight were written at the time or shortly thereafter by participants or on–the–scene observers. For an entry into this literature, see Paul Brockett, *Bibliography of Aeronautics*, Smithsonian Miscellaneous Collections, vol. 55 (Washington, D.C.: Smithsonian Institution, 1910).

Peter L. Jakab

72. Chandler, Charles deForest, and Frank P. Lahm. *How Our Army Grew Wings: Airmen and Aircraft before 1914.* New York: Ronald, 1943. Pp. xiii + 333. Index, Illustr.

General overview of early American military aviation. Begins with the use of balloons during the American Civil War and at the end of the 19th century, and carries the story through the Signal Corps' first airplane purchase from the Wright brothers in 1909 and the training and experiments conducted at College Park, Maryland, until 1912. Also details the emergence of other U.S. Army airfields before World War I.

73. Chanute, Octave. *Progress in Flying Machines.* Long Beach, Calif.: Lorenz and Herweg, 1976; original work published in 1894. Pp. iv + 308. Index, Illustr.

One of the most widely circulated and often referred to works available to late 19th–century aeronautical experimenters. Because it was a primary book consulted by many early experimenters, it provides the historian with an entree into turn–of–the–century aeronautical thinking.

74. Combs, Harry, and Martin Caidin. *Kill Devil Hill: Discovering the Secret of the Wright Brothers.* Boston: Houghton Mifflin, 1979. Pp. xx + 389. Index, Bibliog., Illustr.

In–depth study of the Wright brothers' inventive process. Combs mistakenly characterizes the Wrights as scientists rather than engineers, but the book is still a detailed and, for the most part, accurate account of the invention of the airplane. One of the best books on the Wright brothers to date.

75. Crouch, Tom D. *A Dream of Wings: Americans and the Airplane, 1875–1905.* New York: W.W. Norton, 1981. Pp. 349. Index, Bibliog., Illustr.

An authoritative, analytical treatment of the community of late 19th– and early 20th–century aeronautical experimenters principally involved with the invention of the airplane. Places particular emphasis on the role of Lilienthal, Chanute, Langley, and the Wright brothers. Among the best books on the subject of early aviation and the invention of the airplane. Well re-searched and documented. Strong bibliography.

December 17, 1903, Kitty Hawk, North Carolina: With Orville Wright at the controls, the Wright Flyer, the world's first successful airplane, rises into the air as Wilbur Wright looks on.

76.   Crouch, Tom D. *Bleriot XI: The Story of a Classic Aircraft.*
      Famous Aircraft of the National Air and Space Museum, vol.
      5. Washington, D.C.: Smithsonian Institution Press, 1982. Pp.
      vii + 143. Bibliog., Illustr.

      A brief history of the most influential aircraft built by Louis
      Bleriot, the Type XI. Discusses the evolution of the design and
      its central role in the development of pioneer aviation. Also
      includes a particularly useful chapter that analyzes early
      structural problems characteristic of pioneer monoplanes.
      Concludes with a discussion of the restoration of the National
      Air and Space Museum's Bleriot XI, along with detailed draw-
      ings and photographs.

77.   Davy, M.J.B. *Henson and Stringfellow: Their Work in Aero-
      nautics.* London: His Majesty's Stationery Office, 1931. Pp.
      114. Index, Bibliog., Illustr.

      The standard work on Henson and Stringfellow's aeronautical
      activities. Although there is some brief biographical informa-
      tion, the book is not a genuine biography. It is primarily an
      account of Henson and Stringfellow's aeronautical work and
      provides the essential facts of their contributions to flight.

78.   Davy, M.J.B. *Interpretive History of Flight: A Survey of the
      History and Development of Aeronautics with Particular
      Reference to Contemporary Influences and Conditions.*
      London: His Majesty's Stationery Office, 1948. Pp. viii + 191.
      Index, Bibliog., Illustr.

      A general treatment of aviation, beginning with a discussion
      of flight in nature and early human desires and attempts to fly.
      It takes the story up through the invention and development of
      lighter–than–air flight. The book concludes with a section on
      the then–modern phase (1919–1929). The book is old, but
      provides an adequate overview of the major events and
      personalities associated with the early development of flight.

79.   Gibbs–Smith, Charles H. *Sir George Cayley's Aeronautics,
      1796–1855.* London: Her Majesty's Stationery Office, 1962.
      Pp. xxiii + 269. Index, Bibliog., Illustr.

      Detailed, annotated chronology of Cayley's aeronautical
      work. Provides technical information and descriptions on all of
      Cayley's designs as well as critical insights into his aeronautical
      thinking. The reference work on Cayley.

80. Gibbs–Smith, Charles H. *The Invention of the Aeroplane (1799–1909)*. New York: Taplinger, 1965. Pp. xxiii + 360. Index, Bibliog., Illustr.

General overview of the development of heavier–than–air flying machines from the time of Cayley to the pivotal year 1909. Includes not only a discussion of the Wrights, but also the other principal aeronautical experiments of the first decade of powered flight. Also contains several appendixes that provide technical information and statistics on these early aircraft.

Gibbs–Smith, Charles H. *Aviation: An Historical Survey from Its Origins to the End of World War II*. London: Her Majesty's Stationery Office, 1970. Pp. xvi + 316. Index, Bibliog., Illustr.

Cited herein as item 63.

81. Gibbs–Smith, Charles H. *The Rebirth of European Aviation, 1902–1908: A Study of the Wright Brothers' Influence*. London: Her Majesty's Stationery Office, 1974. Pp. xx + 387. Index, Bibliog., Illustr.

An authoritative discussion of how the Wright brothers' experiments with powered flight influenced the reemergence and development of European aviation after 1902. Provides a critical examination of the European understanding of and response to the Wrights' technology. One of the most important books on the subject of early aviation.

82. Gollin, Alfred M. *No Longer an Island: Britain and the Wright Brothers, 1902–09*. London: William Heinemann, 1984. Pp. x + 478. Index, Bibliog.

A lengthy analytical account of the Wright brothers' efforts to sell their invention, the airplane, to the British government. Gollin counters the traditional argument that it was the Wrights' secrecy and paranoia that led to problems with negotiation by suggesting it was more a problem of British bureaucracy and bumbling, an equally unsatisfying thesis. Yet, the book does present a great deal of information related to the Wright–British interaction. Should be read with Walker, *Early Aviation at Farnborough: The History of the Royal Aircraft Establishment* (cited herein as item 102).

83.   Hallion, Richard P., ed. *The Wright Brothers: Heirs of Prometheus*. Washington, D.C.: Smithsonian Institution Press, 1978. Pp. xiii + 146. Bibliog., Illustr.

An anthology of short articles about the Wright brothers and their aircraft. In addition to articles by prominent Wright historians, there are pieces by some of the participants in the Wright story, a guide to research, a photographic essay, and a chronology. A handy reference.

84.   Harris, Sherwood. *The First to Fly: Aviation's Pioneer Days*. New York: Simon and Shuster, 1970. Pp. 316. Index, Bibliog., Illustr.

Generally good overview of major aeronautical events and personalities from 1900 to 1915. The focus is principally on the United States. Bibliography is very brief.

85.   Hart, Clive. *The Dream of Flight: Aeronautics from Classical Times to the Renaissance*. New York: Winchester, 1972. Pp. 200. Index, Bibliog., Illustr.

Provides an overview of aeronautical devices from antiquity to Leonardo. The book discusses everything from simple wind socks and banners to kites, parachutes, tower jumps, and the complex ornithopter designs of Leonardo da Vinci. Hart has a better grasp of these early manuscripts than just about anyone. Well illustrated, and has the best published bibliography of medieval primary material anywhere.

86.   Hart, Clive. *The Prehistory of Flight*. Berkeley: University of California Press, 1985. Pp. xvii + 279. Index, Bibliog., Illustr.

A follow-up to Hart's previous work, *The Dream of Flight*, this book carries the story to the 18th century. The book also supplements Hart's earlier work with a more in-depth discussion of medieval conceptions of the air and bird flight, as well as the medieval understanding of aerodynamics. As with *Dream of Flight*, this book is well illustrated and has an excellent bibliography. Together, these works are the definitive source on pre-Cayley aeronautics.

87.   Jarrett, Philip. *Another Icarus: Percy Pilcher and the Quest for*

Flight. Washington, D.C.: Smithsonian Institution Press, 1987. Pp. xi + 226. Index, Illustr.

Well-researched and documented account of the aeronautical work of the British pioneer Percy Pilcher, one of the most significant of the pre-Wright era experimenters. Includes a treatment of Pilcher's relationships with other major aeronautical pioneers like Otto Lilienthal, Octave Chanute, Lawrence Hargrave, and Hiram Maxim. Contains useful appendixes.

88. Kelly, Fred C. *The Wright Brothers: A Biography Authorized by Orville Wright*. New York: Harcourt, Brace, 1943. Pp. 340. Index, Illustr.

   The standard biography of the Wrights. Since Kelly was the authorized biographer, the book is, understandably, very sympathetic. Nevertheless, it remains one of the most useful works on the subject.

89. Kelly, Fred C., ed. *Miracle at Kitty Hawk: The Letters of Wilbur and Orville Wright*. New York: Farrar, Straus, and Young, 1951. Pp. ix + 482. Index, Illustr.

   A very selective collection of Wright correspondence dating from 1881 to 1946, with running commentary by Kelly. The book serves best as a companion to the larger collection of published papers of the Wrights, edited by Marvin McFarland.

90. Lieberg, Owen S. *The First Air Race: The International Competition at Reims, 1909*. Garden City, N.Y.: Doubleday, 1974. Pp. viii + 229. Index, Bibliog., Illustr.

   Ostensibly a book about the first major flying meeting for powered airplanes, it also provides a general picture of the events and personalities of the first decade of powered flight. As he describes each day's events, Lieberg digresses to provide background information on the activities and accomplishments of the participants. Some minor factual errors, but, on the whole, a useful book.

91. Lilienthal, Otto. *Birdflight as the Basis of Aviation*. London: Longmans, Green, 1911. Pp. 142. Index, Illustr.

   One of the most important and influential aeronautical works available to late 19th– and early 20th–century experimenters. This is an English translation, published 22 years after the original German edition of Lilienthal's seminal work on the effects of air pressure on a plane surface and airfoil shapes. The Wright brothers, among others, were particularly influenced by Lilienthal's efforts. Many tables, equations, and diagrams.

92.   McFarland, Marvin W., ed. *The Papers of Wilbur and Orville Wright: Vol. 1 (1899–1905), Vol. 2 (1906–1948)*. New York: McGraw–Hill, 1953. Pp. lv + xxvii + 1278. Index, Bibliog., Illustr.

Selected from the Wright brothers' manuscript collection in the Library of Congress, these published papers cover the period 1899–1948. The emphasis is on the experimental period 1899–1908. Carefully organized and well annotated, *The Papers* is the primary reference work on the Wrights' aeronautical work. Also includes several appendixes on the Wrights' wind tunnel, motor, and propeller research, and related documents of Octave Chanute.

93.   Means, James, ed. *Epitome of the Aeronautical Annual*. Boston: W.B. Clarke, 1910. Pp. 214. Index, Illustr.

A collection of articles and papers produced by the pathfinders of aviation between 1809 and 1910. The early observations by Otto Lilienthal, Karl Mullenhoff, Octave Chanute, William H. Pickering, Hiram S. Maxim, Percy S. Pilcher, Samuel P. Langley, Alexander G. Bell, Abbot L. Rotch, George Cayley, and F.H. Wenham pertaining to flying and gliding, aerial navigation, and meteorology. An excellent reference work for students of aeronautical science.

94.   Moolman, Valerie. *The Road to Kitty Hawk*. Alexandria, Va.: Time–Life, 1980. Pp. 176. Index, Bibliog., Illustr.

Brief, popular account, in the Time–Life Epic of Flight series, of the path to the invention of heavier–than–air flight, culminating with the Wright brothers and their powered 1903 Flyer. A profusely illustrated, well–written general overview of the subject.

95.   Morrow, John Howard. *Building German Airpower, 1909–1914.*

Knoxville: Univ. of Tennessee Press, 1976. Pp. ix + 150. Index, Bibliog., Illustr.

Analytical discussion of the emergence of the German and Austro–Hungarian aircraft industries before World War I. Places the industrial–technical development of aviation in these countries in the context of military organizational institutions and demands. Well researched and documented.

96. Parkin, John H. *Bell and Baldwin: Their Development of Aerodromes and Hydrodromes at Baddeck, Nova Scotia.* Toronto: University of Toronto Press, 1964. Pp. xvi + 555. Index, Bibliog., Illustr.

Detailed and authoritative discussion of Alexander Graham Bell and Frederick Walker (Casey) Baldwin's work with aircraft and hydrofoil craft. Strong treatment is given to the Aerial Experiment Association and its other principal members: Glenn Curtiss, Thomas E. Selfridge, and J.A.D. McCurdy. Also provides a good deal of technical data. Only glaring omission is that it has neither footnotes nor bibliography.

97. Penrose, Harald. *British Aviation: The Pioneer Years, 1903–14.* Fallbrook, Calif.: Aero, 1967. Pp. 607. Index, Illustr.

Part of Penrose's five–volume study of British aviation, this book covers the topic from the experimental years up to World War I. Essentially a discussion of early British aircraft, designers, and the beginnings of the British aircraft industry. A comprehensive and authoritative work.

98. Prendergast, Curtis. *The First Aviators.* Alexandria, Va.: Time–Life, 1980. Pp. 176. Index, Bibliog., Illustr.

Brief, popular account of the first decade of powered flight. Details the principal events and personalities in aviation from 1903 to World War I. Profusely illustrated, well–written general overview of the subject. Part of the Time–Life Epic of Flight series.

99. Pritchard, J. Laurence. *Sir George Cayley: The Inventor of the Aeroplane.* London: Max Parrish, 1961. Pp. xxii + 277. Index, Bibliog., Illustr.

The standard biography of Cayley. Complements Gibbs–Smith's *Sir George Cayley's Aeronautics*, a chronology of Cayley's designs.

100. Roseberry, Cecil R. *Glenn Curtiss: Pioneer of Flight.* Garden City, N.Y.: Doubleday, 1972. Pp. x + 514. Index, Bibliog., Illustr.

The standard biography of Glenn Curtiss. Detailed and complete treatment of Curtiss's aeronautical career. Generally accurate, except for the section on Curtiss's work with the Langley Aerodrome in 1914.

101. Villard, Henry S. *Contact! The Story of the Early Birds.* New York: Crowell, 1968. Pp. 263. Index, Bibliog., Illustr.

Basically a chronicle of the major events and personalities of the first decade of powered flight. Provides most of the essential names and dates, but not terribly analytical. Good place to start for an introduction to the subject.

102. Walker, Percy B. *Early Aviation at Farnborough: The History of the Royal Aircraft Establishment.* 2 vols. London: Macdonald, 1971. Pp. 283 + 375. Index, Illustr.

Two–volume history of the Royal Aircraft Establishment at Farnborough, England. Volume 1 covers the history of British lighter–than–air craft, and Volume 2, early British airplanes. The work not only discusses the aircraft and their builders, but also provides insights into the British government's aviation policy and thinking, including its negotiations with the Wright brothers regarding the sale of their inventions. Should be read with Gollin, *No Longer an Island: Britain and the Wright Brothers, 1902–09* (cited herein as item 82).

103. Walsh, John Evangelist. *One Day at Kitty Hawk: The Untold Story of the Wright Brothers and the Airplane.* New York: Thomas Y. Crowell, 1975. Pp. x + 305. Index, Bibliog., Illustr.

Ostensibly an account of the Wrights' invention of the airplane. Walsh's main goal is to demonstrate that Wilbur was the critical figure and that, at best, Orville played the role of a technical assistant. Moreover, Walsh claims that Orville deliberately attempted to distort the truth about the brothers' aeronautical contributions. A valiant, yet unsuccessful, attempt to prove a contrived thesis. A book of limited usefulness.

104. Whitehouse, Arthur George J. [Arch]. *The Early Birds: The Wonders and Heroics of the First Decades of Flight.* Garden City, N.Y.: Doubleday, 1965. Pp. xxii + 288. Index, Bibliog., Illustr.

General overview of the accomplishments of early aeronautical pioneers. The book begins with a very brief discussion of aviation from medieval times to the 19th century and closes with early military uses of the airplane in 1914. Most of the book covers the period 1890–1910 and highlights the activities of the principal inventors and developers of the airplane. Lots of names and dates, but not terribly analytical.

Wolko, Howard S., ed. *The Wright Flyer: An Engineering Perspective.* Proceedings of a Symposium Held at the National Air and Space Museum, December 16, 1983. Washington D.C.: Smithsonian Institution Press, 1986. Pp. ix + 106. Illustr.

Cited herein as item 418.

105. Wykeham, Peter. *Santos–Dumont: A Study in Obsession.* London: Putnam, 1962. Pp. 278. Index, Bibliog., Illustr.

The standard biography of Alberto Santos–Dumont. Fairly good treatment of this critical figure in early aviation. Unfortunately, there are no footnotes and only a limited bibliography.

LIGHTER–THAN–AIR FLIGHT

The story of lighter–than–air flight is the oldest and, perhaps, most romantic in the history of aviation. It ranges from the ascension of the Montgolfier brothers' balloon in 1783 to the crash of the airship *Hindenburg* in 1937, to the revival of ballooning and the attempted resurrection of the airship in the mid–1970s. In this era of jumbo jets and supersonic transports, lighter–than–air flight continues to enchant students of aviation. The study of its development, decline, and revival holds a particular fascination. Historical, technical, and popular works on the subject exist in abundance.

The works cited should give the researcher a selection of the most representative titles on the history and technology of lighter–than–air flight. Because of the international nature of the subject, titles of foreign works have been included whenever possible. In general, however, the works were chosen for their excellence, usefulness, and availability.

Those interested in other studies on ballooning will find additional titles in "A Select Bibliography of Materials on the History of the Balloon in the United States," pp. 721–731, of Tom D. Crouch's *The Eagle Aloft: Two Centuries of the Balloon in America* (see item 109). Those who wish to find more references to airship literature should consult the bibliographies of the books listed in the subsection titled "Airships."

Richard K. Smith

Balloons

106. Chaintrier, Louis A. *Balloon Post of the Siege of Paris, 1870–71*. Washington, D.C.: American Air Mail Society, 1976. Pp. vi + 163.

    Although compiled primarily for philatelists, contains a wealth of quantitative data relating to the Parisian "airlift" of the Franco–Prussian War.

107. Chandler, Charles deForest, and Walter S. Diehl. *Balloon and Airship Gases. Part I—Hydrogen and Helium Production Processes, the Compression and Storage of Gases*. New York: Ronald, 1926. Pp. x + 226. Illustr.

    A classic textbook treatment of its subject. Chandler was one of the founders of U.S. Army aviation; Diehl, a Navy officer and aeronautical engineer who became a salient figure in American aviation's research and development. Although long since out of print, a softcover photocopy reproduction may be obtained from University Microfilms, Ann Arbor, Michigan.

108. Cohn, Ernst M. *The Flight of the Ville d'Orléans*. Chicago: Collectors' Club of Chicago, 1978. Pp. 175. Illustr.

    Although the focus is on the *Ville d'Orléans*, a balloon that accidentally flew from Paris to northern Norway, there is a wealth of other information relating to French balloon operations during the siege of Paris, 1870–1871.

109. Crouch, Tom D. *The Eagle Aloft; Two Centuries of the Balloon in America*. Washington, D.C.: Smithsonian Institution Press, 1983. Pp. 770. Index, Bibliog., Illustr.

    Its title should be self–explanatory; this is a truly magnificent production, almost encyclopedic in its scope.

110. Duhem, Jules B. *Histoire des idées aéronautique avant Montgolfier* (A history of aeronautical ideas before Montgolfier). Paris: Fernand Sorlot, 1943. Pp. 458. Bibliog.

    An extraordinarily detailed history of aeronautic thought and endeavors up to the end of the 18th century. Published in occupied France during World War II, it and its companion volume, *Musée aéronautique avant Montgolfier*, had a very limited press run and are difficult to find today.

111. Duhem, Jules B. *Musée aéronautique avant Montgolfier; recueil de figures et de documents pour servir a l'histoire des idées aeronautiques avant l'invention de aerostats* (Aeronautical representations before Montgolfier; collection of illustrations and documents to serve as a history of aeronautical ideas before the invention of balloons). Paris: Fernand Sorlot, 1944. Pp. 253. Bibliog., Illustr.

Whereas Duhem's *Histoire des idées* is devoted to text, *Musée aéronautique* consists almost entirely of illustrations. Practically a volume two to *Histoire des idées*.

112. Fisher, John. *Airlift 1870: The Balloon and Pigeon Post in the Siege of Paris*. London: Max Parrish, 1965. Pp. viii + 166. Illustr.

An adequate journalistic treatment of the French effort to use balloons to maintain communications between Paris and the rest of France while the city was being besieged by Prussian armies in 1870–1871.

113. Gillespie, Charles C. *The Montgolfier Brothers and the Invention of Aviation*. Princeton, N.J.: Princeton University Press, 1983. Pp. xi + 210. Index, Bibliog., Illustr.

This handsome book is filled with rich biographical information not previously available in the English language. Also contains some rare information on descendants of the Montgolfiers, namely, the Seguin brothers who developed the Gnome rotary engine used in airplanes of World War I. A classic treatment of the evolution of ideas in science and technology in a social context. The primary English–language source on the Montgolfiers.

114. Haydon, F. Stansbury. *Aeronautics in the Union and Confederate Armies with a Survey of Military Aeronautics prior to 1861*. Baltimore, Md.: Johns Hopkins University Press, 1941. Pp. 421. Illustr.

A classic history of its subject, with a heavily documented

text that provides a guide to primary sources. This book carries
the story to the Peninsular Campaign of 1862 and was to be the
first of a projected two–volume work, but the second volume
was never completed.

115. Hodgson, John E. *The History of Aeronautics in Great Britain
from the Earliest Times to the Latter Half of the Nineteenth
Century.* London: Oxford University Press, 1924. Pp. xxii +
436. Index, Bibliog., Illustr.

A chronological narrative of the period when aeronautics was
just beginning to develop as a science. Though dated, this
remains the finest survey of ballooning in Great Britain.
Includes an annotated bibliography.

116. McCary, Charles. *Double Eagle.* Boston: Little, Brown, 1979.
Pp. viii + 278. Illustr.

A chronicle of the first successful transatlantic balloon
flight. It lacks a technical description of the balloon and its
equipment; and although there is a track chart in the end
papers, there is no flight profile.

117. Mason, Monck. *Aeronautica; or, Sketches Illustrative of the
Theory and Practice of Aerostation.* London: Westley, 1838.
Pp. vii + 355. Illustr.

Generally believed to be the first comprehensive history of
aeronautics (i.e., ballooning) written in English. Rare and
difficult to find, it is overdue for reprinting.

118. Mikesh, Robert C. *Japan's World War II Balloon Bomb Attacks
on North America.* Washington, D.C.: Smithsonian Institution
Press, 1973. Pp. v + 85. Illustr.

During World War II, the Japanese launched bomb–carrying
unmanned balloons that the prevailing wind carried across the
Pacific to North America's Pacific Northwest. This monograph
surveys these unusual operations.

119. Milbank, Jeremiah. *The First Century of Flight in America.*
Princeton, N.J.: Princeton University Press, 1943. Pp. x +
248. Bibliog., Illustr.

A classic first effort to cover the subject. Although it has been superseded by Crouch's *The Eagle Aloft*, the volume remains a useful short survey. The notes and bibliography are especially good.

120. Morris, Allan. *The Balloonatics*. London: Jarrolds, 1970. Pp. xi + 212. Bibliog., Illustr.

Deals with the use of observation balloons in World War I, a subject that otherwise has practically no literature outside of a few professional military periodicals.

121. Piccard, Auguste. *Between Earth and Sky*. Translated by Claude Apcher. London: Falcon, 1950. Pp. 157. Illustr.

The author's experiences in high-altitude ballooning in the 1930s, in which a spherical sealed gondola (a technological "first" in ballooning) was used to carry the crew.

122. Piccard, Auguste. *In Balloon and Bathyscaphe*. Translated by Christina Stead. London: Cassell, 1956. Pp. 192. Illustr.

The author's experiences in high-altitude ballooning in the 1930s and in exploring the ocean depths in the 1950s with his "bathyscaphe," a deep submergence vehicle that employed the aerostatic principles of an airship to achieve depth control in the ever more dense medium of the sea.

123. Reynaud, Marie-Helene. *Les frères Montgolfier: et leurs étonnantes machines* (The Montgolfier brothers and their astonishing machines). Vals-les-Bains: De Plein Vent, 1982. Pp. 231. Bibliog., Illustr.

Dr. Reynaud is probably the world's most knowledgeable student of Montgolfier history, and there is a great deal of information in these pages that is not available elsewhere.

124. Rolt, L.T.C. *The Aeronauts: A History of Ballooning, 1783-1903*. New York: Walker, 1966. Pp. 267. Bibliog., Illustr.

An excellent historical survey of international ballooning. Particularly strong on European events.

125. Schoendorf, Robert. *Catalog of Classic American Airposts and Aeronautica, 1784–1900*. Southfield, Mich.: Postilion, 1982. Pp. v + 99. Illustr.

 Although prepared primarily for philatelists, the book contains a wealth of useful information for historians.

126. Tissandier, Gaston. *Histoire des ballons et des aéronautes célèbres*. (History of balloons and famous aeronauts). 2 vols. Paris: H. Launette, 1887–90. Bibliog., Illustr.

 A classic history of ballooning from 1783 to 1890 written by one of the 19th century's great balloonists. A rare set, shelved only by major libraries, it is overdue for reprinting in an English translation.

127. Tissandier, Gaston, comp. *Bibliographie aéronautique* (Aeronautical bibliography). Amsterdam: B.M. Israel, 1971. Pp. 63.

 A reprint of Tissandier's original compilation of 1887; a priceless collection of early 19th-century references. Contains more than 800 entries.

128. Turner, Christopher Hatton. *Astra Castra: Experiments and Adventures in the Atmosphere*. London: Chapman and Hall, 1865. Pp. xxiii + 530. Bibliog., Illustr.

 A magnificently produced history of early ballooning; rare, held only by large libraries. Overdue for reprinting.

129. Upson, Ralph H., and Charles DeForest Chandler. *Free and Captive Balloons*. New York: Ronald, 1926. Pp. xiii + 331. Illustr.

 Upson was a famous pre-1914 balloonist and later an airship designer; Chandler was one of the founders of U.S. Army aviation. Together, they provide a classic textbook treatment of the subject. Although long since out of print, the book is available in a softcover photocopy from University Microfilms, Ann Arbor, Michigan.

130. Van Orman, Ward T., and Robert C. Hull. *Wizard of the Winds*. Saint Cloud, Minn.: North Star, 1978. Pp. xvi + 278. Illustr.

A very fine autobiography by the most successful balloon racer in the United States. Van Orman was also involved in engineering Goodyear balloons and airships.

131. Warner, Edward P. *Aerostatics.* New York: Ronald, 1926. Pp. ix + 112. Illustr.

One of the many volumes of the Ronald Aeronautical Library of the 1920s, a textbook of its subject. Although long since out of print, it is available in a softcover photocopy reproduction from University Microfilms, Ann Arbor, Michgan.

132. Wise, John. *Through the Air; A Narrative of Forty Years Experience as an Aeronaut. Comprising a History of the Various Attempts in the Art of Flying by Artificial Means from the Earliest Period down to the Present Time.* Reprint. New York: Arno, 1972. Pp. 650. Illustr.

A reprint of the original autobiographical narrative published in 1873 by John Wise (1808–1879), the greatest American balloonist of the 19th century.

133. Wise, John. *A System of Aeronautics.* Reprint. Fairfield, Wash.: Ye Galleon, 1979. Pp. 310. Index, Illustr.

A reprint of the original published in Philadelphia in 1850. Contains many useful insights to balloon design, materials, fabrication, and flight techniques of the mid–19th century.

Airships

134. Abbott, Patrick. *Airship: The Story of the R.34 and the First East–West Crossing of the Atlantic by Air.* New York: Charles Scribner's Sons, 1973. Pp. 163. Bibliog., Illustr.

A very good description of this first transatlantic flight by an airship, and the first transatlantic round trip made by any form of aircraft.

135. Amundsen, Roald, and Lincoln Ellsworth. *The First Flight across the Polar Sea.* New York: Doran, 1927. Pp. x + 324. Illustr.

A firsthand account of the flight of the Italian airship *Norge*, commanded by Umberto Nobile, from Europe across the North Pole to Alaska in 1926. Amundsen was the flight's organizer, Ellsworth its financial backer.

136. Blakemore, Thomas L., and W. Watters Pagon. *Pressure Airships*. New York: Ronald, 1927. Pp. xiii + 311. Illustr.

A textbook treatment of the design and construction of nonrigid and semirigid airships; the information is as valid today as it was at the time of the book's publication. Although long out of print, a softcover photocopy can be obtained from University Microfilms, Ann Arbor, Michigan.

137. Brooks, Peter W. *Historic Airships*. Greenwich, Conn.: New York Graphic Society, 1973. Pp. 69. Bibliog., Illustr.

Although the narrative amounts to only 38 pages, it studiously avoids adjectives and adverbs to provide a terse, telegraphic study that wants for nothing by way of significant information. Its industrial and economic analyses are especially good. The succinct text is well served by drawings, maps, graphs, and tabulated data.

138. Burgess, Charles P. *Airship Design*. New York: Ronald, 1927. Pp. xi + 300. Illustr.

A textbook on the subject; the only one of its kind written and published in America. The author was an engineer in the Navy's Bureau of Aeronautics and well known and respected internationally as an authority on this subject. Although long out of print, a softcover photocopy can be obtained from University Microfilms, Ann Arbor, Michigan.

139. Countryman, Barry. *R.100 in Canada*. Erin, Ontario: Boston Mills, 1982. Pp. 128. Bibliog., Illustr.

A charming and highly informative treatment of the R.100's flight from Britain to North America in 1930. In a rare *beau geste*, the book as originally published included a sleeve in its rear cover that held a 45-rpm phonograph record of the song "R.100," written in Canada for the airship's flight.

140. Dick, Harold G., and Douglas H. Robinson. *The Golden Age of the Great Passenger Airships: Graf Zeppelin and Hindenburg.* Washington, D.C.: Smithsonian Institution Press, 1985. Pp. 226. Index, Illustr.

   The quasi memoir of an American engineer (Dick), who was closely associated with Luftschiffbau Zeppelin. Unusual for its structural drawings of the two airships, that of the *Graf Zeppelin* being the only one in print.

141. Eckener, Hugo. *Count Zeppelin; The Man and His Work.* London: Massie, 1938. Pp. 275. Illustr.

   An uncritical biography of Ferdinand von Zeppelin (1838–1917), written by a man who knew him well, became part of the Zeppelin company, and later commanded the airship *Graf Zeppelin.*

142. Eckener, Hugo. *Im Zeppelin über Länder und Meere; Erlebnisse und Erinnerungen* (Over lands and seas in a Zeppelin; reminiscenses and adventures). Flensberg: Christian Wolff, 1949. Pp. 565. Illustr.

   The memoirs of the greatest of all airship commanders. A severely abridged English translation is available with the title *My Zeppelins* (translated by Douglas Robinson, London: Putnam, 1958).

143. Hansen, Zenon C.R. *The Goodyear Airships.* Bloomington, Ill.: Airship International, 1977. Pp. 110. Bibliog., Illustr.

   A well–illustrated history of the Goodyear blimps, other little–known airship projects, and Goodyear's ventures that were collateral to aeronautical designs—that is, lightweight railroad trains in the 1930s.

144. Italiaander, Rolf. *Hugo Eckener, ein moderner Columbus* (Hugo Eckener, a modern Columbus). Konstanz: Stadler, 1979. Pp. 191. Index, Illustr.

   An illustrated biography of Dr. Hugo Eckener (1868–1954) and history of Luftschiffbau Zeppelin and its airships.

145. Italiaander, Rolf. *Ein Deutscher namens Eckener* (A German named Eckener). Konstanz: Stadler, 1981. Pp. 562. Illustr.

    A biography of Dr. Hugo Eckener (1868–1954), associate of Count von Zeppelin, director of the Luftschiffbau Zeppelin and internationally known as the commander of the airship *Graf Zeppelin*.

146. Knaüsel, Hans G. *Zeppelin und die Vereinigten Staaten von Amerika* (Zeppelin and the United States of America: An important episode in German–American relations). Friedrichshafen: Luftschiffbau Zeppelin, 1981. Pp. 256. Illustr.

    An unusual examination of the Zeppelin airship as an extraordinarily effective instrument of political, commercial, and cultural international goodwill during the 1920s, especially between the United States and Germany.

147. Knaüsel, Hans G. *LZ-1, der erste Zeppelin: Geschichte einer Idee, 1874–1908* (LZ-1, the first Zeppelin: the history of an idea, 1874–1908). Bonn: Kirschbaum Verlag, 1985. Pp. 308. Index, Bibliog., Illustr.

    A far more detailed and analytical account than the author's book of a similar title (1975).

148. Leasor, James. *The Millionth Chance: The Story of the R.101*. New York: Reynal, 1957. Pp. 244. Bibliog., Illustr.

    A journalistic account of the British commercial airship program of the 1920s and its termination by the R.101 disaster.

149. Lewitt, Ernest H. *The Rigid Airship: A Treatise on the Design and Performance*. London: Sir Isaac Pitman and Sons, 1925. Pp. x + 283. Illustr.

    A textbook examination of its subject, but not as thorough as that prepared by Charles P. Burgess.

150. McPhee, John A. *The Deltoid Pumpkin Seed*. New York: Farrar, Straus and Giroux, 1973. Pp. 184. Illustr.

    An intelligently written narrative that deals with a novel,

aerodynamically formed hull for airships built and flown in small–scale prototype in the early 1970s.

151. Maitland, Edward M. *The Log of H.M.A. R.34 Journey to America and Back*. London: Hodder and Stoughton, 1921. Pp. xii + 168. Illustr.

The author was the Air Ministry's observer on board the airship during its return flight to America in 1919, the first transatlantic round–trip flight made by any form of aircraft. Its technical information is excellent.

152. Masefield, Peter G. *To Ride the Storm: The Story of the Airship R.101*. London: William Kimber, 1982. Pp. 560. Illustr.

An excellent account of the British commercial airship effort of the 1920s that culminated in the R.101 disaster of 1930 and was terminated shortly thereafter. Also provides a biography of Lord Thomson, the air minister killed in the R.101.

153. Meager, George. *My Airship Flights, 1915–1930*. London: William Kimber, 1970. Pp. 239. Illustr.

A veteran British airshipman, the author was aboard the R.101 during its flight to Canada in 1930.

154. Nobile, Umberto. *With the "Italia" to the North Pole*. New York: Dodd, Mead, 1931. Pp. 358. Illustr.

An aeronautical engineer, airship designer and operator, Umberto Nobile (1885–1978) was Italy's greatest airshipman and for almost a quarter of a century before World War II was world renowned as an exponent of the semirigid airship. The *Italia* was a semirigid of Nobile's design; the book provides a firsthand account of its polar flight of 1928 and its disaster on the ice pack.

155. Nobile, Umberto. *My Polar Flights: An Account of the Voyages of the Airships Italia and Norge*. Translated by Frances Fleetwood. New York: Putnam, 1961. Pp. 288. Illustr.

Deals with the intercontinental transpolar flight of the *Norge* in 1926 and the polar operations of the ill–fated *Italia* in 1928.

Both airships were designed by the author and commanded by him during operations.

156. Nobile–Stolp, Gertrude. *Bibliografia di Umberto Nobile* (A bibliography of Umberto Nobile). Florence: Leo S. Olschki, 1984. Pp. 113. Index, Bibliog., Illustr.

An awesome multilingual bibliography of Nobile's writings and items written about him, compiled and edited by the Italian airshipman's widow.

157. Rimell, Raymond L. *Zeppelin! A Battle for Air Supremacy in World War I.* London: Conway, 1984. Pp. 256. Index, Bibliog., Illustr.

Examines the German Zeppelin raids on England, 1915–1917, with emphasis on British defensive countermeasures.

158. Robinson, Douglas H. *Giants in the Sky: A History of the Rigid Airship.* Seattle: University of Washington Press, 1973. Pp. xxix + 376. Bibliog., Illustr.

The best English–language survey of its subject. An excellent narrative, it also serves as a wealth of ready–reference, tabulated quantitative data.

159. Robinson, Douglas H. *The Zeppelin in Combat: A History of the German Naval Airship Division, 1912–1918.* Seattle: University of Washington Press, 1980. Pp. xiv + 417. Bibliog., Illustr.

Originally published in 1962, this is the classic treatment of its subject, its data drawn almost entirely from the German navy archives. Deals not only with the Zeppelin raids on England but also the airship's place in German naval operations, industrial logistics, engine development, aeromedical effects on aircrews, and the concurrent development of airship technology in general.

160. Robinson, Douglas H. *Up Ship! A History of the U.S. Navy's Rigid Airships, 1919–1935.* Annapolis, Md.: U.S. Naval Institute, 1982. Pp. xiii + 236. Index, Bibliog., Illustr.

A historical survey of the Navy's five rigid airships, the ZR-1

Shenandoah, the faulty ZR–2 (British R.38 that never had a name), the German–built ZR–3 (Luftschiffbau Zeppelin LZ–126) *Los Angeles*, and the ZRS–4 *Akron* and ZRS–5 *Macon*, both built in the United States by Goodyear–Zeppelin, a subsidiary of the Goodyear Tire & Rubber Co., formed in partnership with Luftschiffbau Zeppelin of Germany.

161. Rosendahl, Charles E. *Up Ship!* New York: Dodd, Mead, 1931. Pp. xiv + 311. Illustr.

     Deals with the author's experiences with the USS *Shenandoah*, as commanding officer of the *Los Angeles*, and observer aboard the *Graf Zeppelin*, and the imminent availability of the *Akron*, of which he was the first commanding officer.

162. Rosendahl, Charles E. *What About the Airship? The Challenge to the United States*. New York: Charles Scribner's Sons, 1938. Pp. x + 437. Illustr.

     An early argument for reviving the rigid airship in America. Contains a wealth of contemporary information and quantitative data.

163. Rotem, Zevi. *David Schwarz, Tragödie des Erfinders; zur Geschichte des Luftschiffes* (David Schwarz, the tragedy of the inventor; contribution to the history of the airship). Bloomington, Ind.: Indiana University Printing Services, 1983. Pp. 187.

     Provides more information on Schwarz (1845–1897), inventor of the first all–metal airship and first aluminum aircraft of any form, than any other source.

164. Santos Dumont, Alberto. *My Airships*. New York: Dover, 1973. Pp. xviii + 122. Illustr.

     A reprint of the book originally published in 1904.Santos Dumont's (1873–1932) own memoirs of his "airship period," before he redirected his interests to airplanes.

165. Schiller, Hans von. *Kapitän Hans von Schiller's Zeppelinbuch* (Captain Hans von Schiller's Zeppelin book). Leipzig: Bibliographisches Institut, 1938. Pp. 235. Illustr.

The author was an officer aboard wartime Zeppelins and later one of the captains of the *Graf Zeppelin*. Although the book went to press after the *Hindenberg* disaster of 1937, it nevertheless shows the great hopes that the Germans continued to have for the airship as a vehicle of global air transportation.

166. Schiller, Hans von. *Zeppelin: Wegbereiter des Weltluftverkehrs* (Zeppelin: Pioneer of world air commerce). Bad Godesberg: Kirschbaum Verlag, 1967. Pp. 200. Illustr.

A quarter of a century after the Zeppelin airship came to its end in Germany, this former captain of the *Graf Zeppelin* looks back on that era, providing an excellent package of useful information.

167. Schütte, Johann, ed. *Der Luftschiffbau Schütte–Lanz, 1909–1925* (The airship construction company Schütte–Lanz, 1909–1925). Munich: R. Oldenbourg, 1926. Pp. 152. Illustr.

Until the mid–1920s, Schütte–Lanz was the Zeppelin Company's primary competitor, and this book illuminates the company's prewar activities, wartime design, and production from 1914 to 1918, and its abortive postwar commercial efforts.

168. Sinclair, James A. *Airships in Peace and War*. London: Rich and Cowan, 1934. Pp. 308. Illustr.

The author was a former British airshipman. Provides a good historical survey of the subject, albeit from a British point of view, up to the date of publication.

169. Sinclair, James A. *Famous Airships of the World*. London: Frederick Muller, 1959. Pp. 144. Illustr.

Given the limitations of its small size, it nevertheless provides good summaries of its subjects.

170. Smith, Richard K. *The Airships Akron & Macon: Flying Aircraft Carriers of the U.S. Navy*. Annapolis, Md.: Naval Institute, 1965. Pp. xxii + 228. Bibliog., Illustr.

A fine and detailed history of the efforts to develop these two airships into carriers of airplanes, namely, their design, construction, operations and politics. Also contains information on previous efforts to combine airship and airplane, details of the "skyhook" airplanes that operated with *Akron–Macon*, and the Navy's abortive airship efforts of 1935–1940.

171. *Symposium on the Future of the Airship, November 20, 1975.* London: Royal Aeronautical Society, 1975. Pp. 155. Bibliog., Illustr.

    Published only in mimeograph form and difficult to find in most libraries. The dozen or so papers of this symposium provide many useful insights to efforts to revive large airships in terms of recently illuminated utility.

172. U.S. Department of the Navy. Bureau of Aeronautics. *Rigid Airship Manual*. Washington, D.C.: U.S. Government Printing Office, 1927. Illustr.

    Although not credited, most of this operating manual was written by Dr. Hugo Eckener and his associates on contract to the Navy after they had delivered the airship LZ–126 to the United States in October 1924.

173. Vaeth, J. Gordon. *Graf Zeppelin: The Adventures of an Aerial Globetrotter*. London: F. Muller, 1959. Pp. xiii + 250. Index, Illustr.

    A nicely done, once–over–lightly biography of Dr. Hugo Eckener (1868–1953) and a history of the airship *Graf Zeppelin*. Basically, a sentimental journey with *Graf*.

174. Ventry, Arthur Frederick Daubeney Eveleigh–de Moleyns, and Eugene M. Kolesnik. *Jane's Pocket Book of Airship Development*. New York: Collier, 1977. Pp. 244. Index, Bibliog., Illustr.

    Although riddled with minor errors of fact that lead to a flawed interpretation, this little book can be a helpful reference if used with care.

175. Wellman, Walter. *The Aerial Age: A Thousand Miles by Airship over the Atlantic Ocean; Airship Voyages over the Polar*

*Sea; the Past, the Present, and the Future of Aerial
Navigation.* New York: A.R. Keller, 1911. Pp. 448. Illustr.

In 1907 and 1909, the author made abortive attempts in the
French–built airship *America* to fly from Spitzbergen to the
North Pole; and in 1910 he made an almost disastrously abortive
attempt to use the same airship to fly the Atlantic from the
United States to Europe. A good story told with admirable
sobriety.

AIRCRAFT

Among the broad range of titles encompassed by this section are many of the better-known aircraft compendiums. In these works, it should be possible to locate a good description, as well as photographs and drawings, of virtually every aircraft built throughout the world. They also contain specifications on military, civilian, and commercial aircraft. Where books of similar format are listed, one general description is given for the entire series.

These entries were selected for the thoroughness of the research and the utility of the work. Where several similar books exist, the most comprehensive work has been chosen in order to provide the greatest range of material for the reader. Where little material exists in a particular category of aircraft, the best available book has been selected.

Since the purpose of this section is to provide a broad introduction to the myriad aircraft designs that have been produced, a conscious effort has been made to exclude books about specific aircraft. Several of the more significant and popular types have been the subject of a wide variety of historical treatments. To include these books would make the list unnecessarily long. The items selected here should provide the reader with a satisfactory general background to the study of aircraft, past and present.

Additional information on aircraft specifications is available in the excellent *Jane's All the World's Aircraft* (see item 51), which has been published continuously since 1909. Further, *Air War Bibliography, 1939–1945: English Language Sources, Volume 4, Part VI—The Aircraft*, by Myron J. Smith, Jr. (Manhattan, Kans.: Aerospace Historian, 1977), provides an excellent selection of titles and articles on World War II–era military aircraft.

F. Robert van der Linden

176. Alexander, Jean. *Russian Aircraft since 1940*. Putnam Aero-
     nautical Books. London: Putnam, 1975. Pp. 555. Index, Illustr.

     Though now somewhat dated in the light of the latest devel-
     opments, this book provides excellent production and service
     histories of all the major Soviet aircraft produced since the
     beginning of World War II. Contains good tables and three–view
     line drawings, plus excellent appendixes of obscure types and
     U.S. and NATO code names.

177. Andrews, C.F. *Vickers Aircraft since 1908*. Putnam Aeronau-
     tical Books. New York: Funk and Wagnalls, 1969. Pp. x + 566.
     Illustr.

     Comprehensive guide to Vickers' wide range of aircraft from
     the Vimy bomber of World War I to the pioneering Viscount
     turbojet airliner. Arranged chronologically by type. Includes
     excellent three–view line drawings and appendixes. Production
     lists are especially complete.

178. Andrews, C.F., and E.B. Morgan. *Supermarine Aircraft since
     1914*. Putnam Aeronautical Books. London: Putnam, 1981. Pp.
     ix + 399. Index, Illustr.

     Well–documented work that traces the development of all the
     aircraft from this British firm that produced classic racing
     planes and the famous Spitfire fighter of World
     War II. Contains detailed appendix and index.

179. Barnes, C.H. *Shorts Aircraft since 1900*. Fallbrook, Calif.:
     Aero, 1967. Pp. x + 532.

     Barnes has written a thorough guide to this venerable British
     aircraft firm that became noted for its wide range of successful
     flying boats. Well illustrated. Arranged chronologically.

180. Barnes, C.H. *Bristol Aircraft since 1910*. 2d ed. Putnam
     Aeronautical Books. London: Putnam, 1970. Pp. 415. Index,
     Bibliog., Illustr.

     Famous for its F.2B Brisfit fighter of World War I and the
     four–engined turboprop Britannia airliner, the British firm of
     Bristol was an innovative company that built many landmark
     designs. Barnes provides an authoritative, concise, historical

guide to these aircraft with an index, excellent appendixes, including production lists and contractors' numbers, and a bibliography.

181. Barnes, C.H. *Handley Page Aircraft since 1907.* Putnam Aeronautical Books. London: Putnam, 1976. Pp. 663. Index, Illustr.

Well–documented book on Handley Page aircraft, particularly its string of renowned British bombers. Contains a good index with excellent appendixes that give all the type designations, production lists, registration numbers, and dispositions.

182. Bowers, Peter M. *Boeing Aircraft since 1916.* 2d ed. London: Putnam, 1968. Pp. 465. Index, Illustr.

Comprehensive work on this major American manufacturer of transports and bombers, although dated. Covers every Boeing aircraft except the post–1960s generation of jet transports. Indexed with thorough appendixes providing civil and military registrations. Originally published as part of the Putnam Aeronautical series.

183. Bowers, Peter M. *Curtiss Aircraft, 1907–1947.* Putnam Aeronautical Books. London: Putnam, 1979. Pp. 636. Index, Illustr.

The only authoritative work on Curtiss aircraft that highlights particularly the JN "Jenny" and the P–40, as well as virtually every other Curtiss machine. Thoroughly indexed with a good set of appendixes. Includes section on Curtiss's work with the Aerial Experiment Association.

184. Brown, Don L. *Miles Aircraft since 1925.* Putnam Aeronautical Books. London: Putnam, 1970. Pp. ix + 420. Index, Bibliog., Illustr.

The only major guide to Miles aircraft. Details the products of this small but important British manufacturer of utilitarian and experimental aircraft. Includes information on prototypes and projected designs.

185. Bruce, John M. *British Aeroplanes, 1914–1918.* London: Putnam, 1957. Pp. viii + 742. Index, Illustr.

Massive book that describes the British aircraft of World War I in depth. Concise production and service histories are arranged alphabetically.

186. Bruce, John M. *The Aeroplanes of the Royal Flying Corps (Military Wing)*. London: Putnam, 1982. Pp. xxv + 642. Index, Illustr.

Complete production and operational account of Royal Flying Corps aircraft written by one of aviation's most respected World War I historians. Thoroughly researched, well written and well illustrated.

187. Coble, Howard, and A.R. Payne. *Famous Aircraft*. London: W&R Chambers, 1937. Pp. 159. Illustr.

This excellent book examines the history of 61 of the most significant aircraft and related events in aviation history. Each two- to four-page story includes significant events and vignettes about these aircraft. A very useful introduction to aviation history before World War II.

188. Cross, Roy. *Great Aircraft and Their Pilots*. Greenwich, Conn.: New York Graphic Society, 1972. Pp. 154. Illustr.

Documents 21 important combat and record-setting aircraft in detail and relates their importance to aviation history. Among those included are the Bleriot XI, Fokker D.VII, Supermarine S.6B, and Bell X-1. Excellent two-page black and white drawings accompany the text.

189. Cynk, Jerzy B. *Polish Aircraft, 1893-1939*. Putnam Aeronautical Books. London: Putnam, 1971. Pp. xxii + 760. Index, Bibliog., Illustr.

The most authoritative book on the development of the varied and technologically advanced Polish aircraft industry up to the outbreak of World War II. Cynk describes the history of each aircraft in remarkable detail and provides an interesting overview of early Polish attempts at heavier-than-air flight. Thoroughly researched, with bibliography.

190. Duval, G.R. *British Flying-Boats and Amphibians, 1909-1952.* Fallbrook, Calif.: Aero, 1966. Pp. 268. Index, Illustr.

   Comprehensive work on British flying boats, arranged chronologically. Very thorough historical treatment is given to each aircraft, describing production and service. Complete with good appendixes and index. Originally published as part of the Putnam Aeronautical series.

191. Francillon, René J. *Japanese Aircraft of the Pacific War.* 2d ed. Putnam Aeronautical Books. London: Putnam, 1979. Pp. xiii + 570. Illustr.

   Very thorough volume that documents the development and operations of World War II Japanese aircraft. Excellent coverage of all major and minor types, but hampered by the lack of an index.

192. Francillon, René J. *McDonnell Douglas Aircraft since 1920.* Putnam Aeronautical Books. London: Putnam, 1979. Pp. xii + 721. Illustr.

   Definitive guide to McDonnell and Douglas aircraft, although hampered by the lack of an index. Francillon explains each significant aircraft from these two American manufacturers in detail, outlining the development and subsequent use of each of the major aircraft types.

193. Francillon, René J. *Lockheed Aircraft since 1913.* Putnam Aeronautical Books. London: Putnam, 1982. Pp. x + 526. Illustr.

   Well-researched guide to the numerous military, commercial, and experimental aircraft from Lockheed. Production and service histories are well documented. Lacks an index.

194. Gibbs-Smith, Charles H. *A Directory and Nomenclature of the First Aeroplanes, 1809 to 1909.* London: Her Majesty's Stationery Office, 1966. Pp. xi + 120. Index.

   Written by the foremost historian on the subject, this book provides a concise description and listing of the first airplanes. Also includes a list of first flights and engines, as well as the first aerodromes, schools, meets, and fatalities. A very useful reference for early aircraft.

195. Gray, Peter, and Owen Thetford. *German Aircraft of the First World War*. Rev. ed. Garden City, N.Y.: Doubleday, 1971. Pp. xxxviii + 600. Index, Illustr.

Revised edition of earlier 1962 work published for Putnam. This book provides an authoritative and exhaustive account of virtually every German World War I aircraft. Well illustrated with drawings for each of the major aircraft types.

196. Green, William. *Famous Fighters of the Second World War*. Rev. ed. Garden City, N.Y.: Doubleday, 1975. Pp. 276. Illustr.

Excellent operational and production coverage of 29 of the most significant fighters of all of the combatants. Includes good drawings and photographs.

197. Green, William. *The Warplanes of the Third Reich*. Garden City, N.Y.: Doubleday, 1970. Pp. 672. Index, Illustr.

Massive, comprehensive single volume provides a detailed developmental and service history of virtually every aircraft built by Germany between 1933 and 1945. Includes experimental and projected designs.

198. Green, William. *Warplanes of the Second World War*. 2d ed. 10 vols. Garden City, N.Y.: Doubleday, 1971. Index, Illustr.

Excellent 10-volume set examines all the major fighters, bombers, flying boats, float planes, and reconnaissance aircraft used by the combatants during World War II. Small format provides excellent reference. Each aircraft is given a detailed two- to six-page description.

199. Green, William. *Famous Bombers of the Second World War*. Rev. ed. Garden City, N.Y.: Doubleday, 1976. Pp. 282. Illustr.

Excellent detailed production and operational histories of 25 of the most significant bombers of all of the combatants. Includes good drawings and photographs.

200. Green, William, and Gordon Swanborough. *The Observer's Basic Military Aircraft Directory*. London: Frederick Warne, 1974. Pp. 224. Index, Illustr.

Good general reference to virtually every military aircraft in service. Provides performance data and brief histories with three-view drawings and photographs. Contains a good index.

201. Green, William, and Gordon Swanborough. *The Observer's Soviet Aircraft Directory*. London: Frederick Warne, 1975. Pp. 256. Index, Illustr.

Excellent reference tool despite confusing organization by NATO code names. One of the few good guides to Soviet aircraft available.

202. Griffin, John A. *Canadian Military Aircraft; Serials and Photographs, 1920–1968*. Ottawa: Queen's Printer, 1969. Pp. xv + 691. Illustr.

Large, well-illustrated book that consists of very detailed compilations of serial numbers and statistics on every Canadian military aircraft through 1968. Contains no written text.

203. Isaacs, Keith. *Military Aircraft of Australia, 1909–1918*. Canberra: Australian War Memorial, 1971. Pp. 190. Bibliog., Illustr.

Thorough work documenting the early years and the early aircraft of the Royal Australian Air Force. Well-detailed text, illustrated with drawings and paintings. Excellent appendixes provide statistical information on the aircraft, and serial numbers as well as a useful chronology.

204. Jackson, A.J. *Avro Aircraft since 1908*. Putnam Aeronautical Books. Fallbrook, Calif.: Aero, 1965. Pp. 470 Index, Illustr.

This well-researched guide to Avro aircraft documents all of this British firm's major and minor aircraft. Detailed production and service histories are accompanied by useful specification tables and three-view line drawings. Aircraft descriptions are arranged chronologically.

205. Jackson, A.J. *Blackburn Aircraft since 1909*. New York: Funk and Wagnalls, 1969. Pp. xi + 555. Index, Illustr.

Jackson describes well the aircraft built by the British firm

Blackburn and pays particular attention to those built for the Royal Air Force and Fleet Air Arm during the interwar period. Well–illustrated chronological histories of each major and minor type. Published in the United States as part of the Putnam Aeronautical series.

206. Jackson, A.J. *British Civil Aircraft since 1919*. Rev. ed. 3 vols. Putnam Aeronautical Books. London: Putnam, 1974. Pp. 567 + 560 + 636. Index, Illustr.

Massive three–volume work that details the production and service of virtually every civil and commercial aircraft built or registered in Great Britain. Includes three–view line drawings, specifications tables, and index.

207. Jackson, A.J. *de Havilland Aircraft since 1909*. 2d ed. Putnam Aeronautical Books. London: Putnam, 1978. Pp. 542. Index, Illustr.

One of the few detailed books on de Havilland aircraft. The author not only describes the development of the aircraft of this British company, but also the development of the firm's operations in Canada and Australia. Contains good index with appendixes that cover minor types.

208. James, Derek N. *Gloster Aircraft since 1917*. Putnam Aeronautical Books. London: Putnam, 1971. Pp. ix + 446. Index, Illustr.

Definitive book on Gloster, a pioneer in jet aviation and fighter aircraft design. Excellent index and appendixes including three–view drawings of projected types. Also includes complete production data, a list of test pilots, and factories.

Juptner, Joseph P. *U.S. Civil Aircraft*. 9 vols. Los Angeles, Calif.: Aero, 1962–. Index, Bibliog., Illustr.

Cited herein as item 674.

209. King, H.F. *Aeromarine Origins: The Beginnings of Marine Aircraft, Winged Hulls, Air–Cushion and Air–Lubricated Craft, Planing Boats and Hydrofoils*. Putnam Aeronautical Books. Fallbrook, Calif.: Aero, 1966. Pp. 93. Index, Illustr.

A unique book that covers the technological background of the development of the first successful seaplanes as well as the relationship between aeronautics and watercraft.

210. King, H.F. *Sopwith Aircraft, 1912–1920.* Putnam Aeronautical Books. London: Putnam, 1981. Pp. 322. Index., Illustr.

Only comprehensive single volume on Sopwith aircraft. Pays much attention to the famous Camel fighter of World War I fame. Presents in great detail the production and service listings of all Sopwith designs.

211. King, H.F., and John W.R. Taylor. *Milestones of the Air: Jane's 100 Significant Aircraft, 1909–1969.* New York: McGraw–Hill, 1969. Pp. viii + 157. Illustr.

Provides concise details on 100 aircraft that affected the course of the history of aviation. Includes photographs and drawings. Excellent reference.

212. Knott, Richard C. *The American Flying Boat: An Illustrated History.* Annapolis, Md.: Naval Institute, 1979. Pp. xiv + 262. Index, Bibliog., Illustr.

The most authoritative work on the American flying boat. Covers all of the major boats from Glenn Curtiss to the Martin P6M Seamaster. Excellent and well–researched text accompanied by a good selection of photographs. Recommended as one of the few works on the subject.

213. Lewis, Peter M.H. *British Aircraft, 1809–1914.* Putnam Aeronautical Books. London: Putnam, 1962. Pp. 576. Index, Illustr.

Details the history of virtually every British aircraft built before World War I. Contains good photographs and three–view drawings.

214. Mason, Francis K. *Hawker Aircraft since 1920.* Putnam Aeronautical Books. London: Putnam, 1961. Pp. 475. Index, Illustr.

Thorough guide to Hawker aircraft. Book is divided into an 80–page historical overview and a 280–page technical description section that covers individual aircraft types.

215. Molson, K.M., and H.A. Taylor. *Canadian Aircraft since 1909.*
Putnam Aeronautical Books. London: Putnam, 1982. Pp. 530.
Illustr.

Describes every major Canadian–designed and built aircraft
with special attention to Canadair and de Havilland. Includes
very detailed appendixes with a chronology and production
records.

216. Munson, Kenneth. *Civil Aircraft of Yesteryear.* London: Ian
Allan, 1967. Pp. vi + 122. Index, Illustr.

Primarily a photographic essay with detailed captions on
most of the older, historic civil aircraft. Provides a representative cross section of 50 years of aircraft development.

217. Munson, Kenneth. *Aircraft of World War II.* 2d ed. Garden
City, N.Y.: Doubleday, 1972. Pp. 272. Illustr.

Good, small–format, ready–reference guide. Provides a brief
description of every major aircraft type with one photograph
and specifications table. Contains a good section on minor types
with a photograph and very brief description.

The following nine books are part of the Blandford–Macmillan Pocket
Encyclopaedia of World Aircraft in Color series and are designed to
have a unified format. The first half of each book is devoted to
attractive single–page color three–view drawings with specifications
and performance figures. The second half provides a concise history
of the development and service of each type of aircraft. Provides a
well–chosen sampling of the most significant aircraft in each category. Serves as a convenient ready–reference guide.

218. Munson, Kenneth. *Bombers: Patrol and Reconnaissance Aircraft, 1914–19.* The Pocket Encyclopaedia of World Aircraft
in Color. New York: Macmillan, 1968. Pp. 180. Index, Illustr.

219. Munson, Kenneth. *Fighters: Attack and Training Aircraft,
1914–19.* The Pocket Encyclopaedia of World Aircraft in
Color. New York: Macmillan, 1968. Pp. 183. Index, Illustr.

220. Munson, Kenneth. *Pioneer Aircraft, 1903–1914.* The Pocket Encyclopaedia of World Aircraft in Colour. London: Blandford, 1969. Pp. 178. Index, Illustr.

221. Munson, Kenneth. *Bombers between the Wars, 1919–39: Including Patrol and Transport.* The Pocket Encyclopaedia of World Aircraft in Color. New York: Macmillan, 1970. Pp. 165. Index, Illustr.

222. Munson, Kenneth. *Fighters: Attack and Training Aircraft.* The Pocket Encyclopaedia of World Aircraft in Color. New York: Macmillan, 1970. Pp. 147. Index, Illustr.

223. Munson, Kenneth. *Fighters between the Wars, 1919–39.* The Pocket Encyclopaedia of World Aircraft in Color. New York: Macmillan, 1970. Pp. 164. Index, Illustr.

224. Munson, Kenneth. *Bombers in Service: Patrol & Transport Aircraft since 1960.* The Pocket Encyclopaedia of World Aircraft in Color. New York: Macmillan, 1972. Pp. 155. Index, Illustr.

225. Munson, Kenneth. *Bombers, 1939–45: Patrol and Transport Aircraft.* The Pocket Encyclopaedia of World Aircraft in Color. New York: Macmillan, 1975. Pp. 163. Index, Illustr.

226. Munson, Kenneth. *Fighters, 1939–1945: Attack and Training Aircraft.* The Pocket Encyclopaedia of World Aircraft in Color. New York: Macmillan, 1975. Pp. 163. Index, Illustr.

227. Nowarra, Heinz, and G.R. Duval. *Russian Civil and Military Aircraft, 1884–1969.* London: Fountain, 1971. Pp. 288. Index, Illustr.

A good narrative guide, particularly for the earliest aircraft. Well illustrated with photographs and 70 pages of black-and-white plates. Contains a good index and appendixes.

228. Smith, J.R., and Antony Kay. *German Aircraft of the Second World War.* Putnam Aeronautical Books. London: Putnam, 1978. Pp. xiii + 745. Index, Illustr.

Contains very detailed developmental and operational descriptive information on every major, minor, and projected aircraft. Comprehensive work on World War II German aircraft. Very well indexed, with good tables and explanatory notes.

229. Stroud, John. *European Transport Aircraft since 1910*. Fall-brook, Calif.: Aero, 1967. Pp. xiv + 680. Index, Illustr.

Authoritative survey of the more important transport aircraft built in continental Europe. Examines over 300 types, including airships. Provides specifics on production and operation. Excellent appendix of civil registrations. Published in the United States as part of the Putnam Aeronautical series.

230. Stroud, John. *Soviet Transport Aircraft since 1945*. New York: Funk and Wagnalls, 1968. Pp. ix + 318. Index, Illustr.

Well-researched although dated on the subject. Describes in detail all the postwar Soviet transports. Includes photographs and drawings.

231. Swanborough, Gordon, and Peter M. Bowers. *United States Military Aircraft since 1908*. Rev. ed. Putnam Aeronautical Books. London: Putnam, 1971. Pp. xi + 675. Index, Illustr.

Excellent one-volume guide. Detailed descriptions of each major aircraft type with three-view drawings and photographs. Well indexed with good appendixes and explanation of designation and marking schemes. Separate section deals with history and minor aircraft types.

232. Swanborough, Gordon, and Peter M. Bowers. *United States Navy Aircraft since 1911*. 2d ed. Annapolis, Md.: Naval Institute, 1976. Pp. ix + 545. Index, Illustr.

One of the most thorough single-volume works on the subject. Describes the development and subsequent service history of each major aircraft type and includes three-view drawings and photographs. Separate sections deal with history and minor aircraft types. Well indexed with good appendixes and good explanations of designation and marking systems. Originally published by Putnam.

233. Taylor, H.A. *Airspeed Aircraft since 1931*. Putnam Aeronautical Books. London: Putnam, 1970. Pp. x + 206. Index, Illustr.

Brief history of Airspeed aircraft with complete type summaries and individual aircraft histories and registrations.

234. Taylor, H.A. *Fairey Aircraft since 1915*. Putnam Aeronautical Books. London: Putnam, 1974. Pp. viii + 450. Index, Illustr.

A major builder of aircraft for the British armed forces,
Fairey was also known for experimental types such as the
Rotodyne transport. Details the history of the aircraft with
special emphasis on development. Includes a good index and
appendix.

235. Taylor, John F. *British Aircraft of World War 2*. New York:
Stein and Day, 1976. Pp. 143. Index, Illustr.

Good introductory work to World War II British aircraft. The
first part examines the aircraft with concise text with photographs and charts; the second provides rare color photographs
of the aircraft. Part three gives a brief history of Royal Air
Force and Fleet Air Arm combat during the war.

236. Taylor, John W.R., and Gordon Swanborough. *Civil Aircraft of
the World*. New York: Scribner's, 1972. Pp. 169. Index, Illustr.

Small book with brief one–page descriptions of all the major
commercial and civilian types with one photograph, specifications table, and three–view drawing. Second section details
the minor types.

237. Taylor, Michael J.H. *Warplanes of the World, 1918–1939*. New
York: Scribner's, 1981. Pp. 192. Index, Illustr.

Very convenient reference guide to the many important
though lesser known military planes developed during the
interwar period. Lists major types alphabetically and gives a
one–page description with photograph and specification table.
Though less comprehensive, similar coverage of minor types
appears in a separate section. Very thorough coverage on an
often neglected, though extremely important, time.

The following eight books are part of the Jane's pocket book series and are similar in format. Each is a convenient softcover book that provides a handy thumbnail sketch of the important aircraft in the various categories. Each aircraft profile is accompanied by a three-view line drawing, photograph, and specifications table. All serve as excellent aircraft recognition guides.

238. Munson, Kenneth, and John W.R. Taylor, eds. *Jane's Pocket Book of Record-Breaking Aircraft.* New York: Collier, 1981. Pp. 264. Index, Illustr.

239. Taylor, Michael J.H., and Kenneth Munson. *Jane's Pocket Book of Commercial Transport Aircraft.* New York: Collier, 1974. Pp. 263. Index, Illustr.

240. Taylor, Michael J.H., and Kenneth Munson. *Jane's Pocket Book of Major Combat Aircraft.* New York: Collier, 1974. Pp. 263. Index, Illustr.

241. Taylor, Michael J.H., and Kenneth Munson. *Jane's Pocket Book of Military Transport and Training Aircraft.* New York: Macmillan, 1974. Pp. 262. Index, Illustr.

242. Taylor, Michael J.H., and Kenneth Munson. *Jane's Pocket Book of Light Aircraft.* New York: Collier, 1976. Pp. 260. Index, Illustr.

243. Taylor, John W.R., and Kenneth Munson. *Jane's Pocket Book of Remotely Piloted Vehicles: Robot Aircraft Today.* New York: Collier, 1977. Pp. 239. Illustr.

244. Taylor, Michael J.H., and John W.R. Taylor, eds. *Jane's Pocket Book of Home-Built Aircraft.* New York: Collier, 1977. Pp. 261. Index, Illustr.

245. Taylor, Michael J.H., and John W.R. Taylor. *Jane's Pocket Book of Research and Experimental Aircraft.* New York: Collier, 1977. Pp. 259. Index, Illustr.

246. Tapper, Oliver. *Armstrong Whitworth Aircraft since 1913.*
     Putnam Aeronautical Books. London: Putnam, 1973. Pp. vii +
     390. Index, Illustr.

     Thoroughly describes the production and operational history
     of Armstrong Whitworth, a British aircraft company noted for a
     long line of civil and military transports. Includes a good index
     and appendixes.

247. Thetford, Owen. *Aircraft of the Royal Air Force since 1918.*
     London: Putnam, 1962. Pp. 581. Index, Illustr.

     An excellent single–volume guide. Concise production and
     operational histories of each major aircraft type with three-
     view drawing and photographs. Separate sections deal with
     history and minor aircraft types.

248. Thetford, Owen. *British Naval Aircraft since 1912.* Rev. ed.
     London: Putnam, 1978. Pp. 488. Index, Illustr.

     Excellent one–volume guide. Detailed descriptions of the
     development and service careers of each major aircraft type
     with three–view drawings and photographs. Separate sections
     deal with history and minor aircraft types.

249. Thompson, Jonathan. *Italian Civil and Military Aircraft, 1930–
     1945.* Los Angeles, Calif.: Aero, 1963. Pp. 304. Index,
     Bibliog., Illustr.

     The only single–volume English reference available on Italian
     aircraft of this period. Information on all aircraft very sparse.
     Good photographs and drawings. No index.

250. Urech, Jakob. *The Aircraft of the Swiss Air Force since 1914.*
     Stäfa, Switzerland: Verlag Th. Gut, 1975. Pp. 366. Index,
     Illustr.

     Good reference tool. Two–page description with full–page
     three–view drawing, large photograph, and detailed specifica-
     tions of each aircraft type. Descriptions are very brief.

251. Wagner, Ray. *American Combat Planes.* 3d ed. Garden City,
     N.Y.: Doubleday, 1982. Pp. viii + 565. Index, Bibliog., Illustr.

A large–format book that provides information concerning every major and minor aircraft that served with the Air Force or Navy. Though dated, it provides a very useful guide, especially to the more obscure designs. Good, though brief text. Well illustrated.

252. Wagner, Ray, and Heinz Nowarra. *German Combat Planes*. Garden City, N.Y.: Doubleday, 1971. Pp. 400. Index, Bibliog., Illustr.

This well–illustrated large–format book is a handy reference to virtually every major and minor type to serve with the German armed forces through World War II. Good, though brief, text.

253. Windrow, Martin C., ed. *Aircraft in Profile*. Garden City, N.Y.: Doubleday, 1967–. Illustr.

Excellent 14–volume set with a total of over 250 concise, well–illustrated and documented accounts of a wide variety of aircraft types. Each profile is written by a noted historian and specialist on the particular aircraft. Includes high–quality reproductions. Serves as a reliable source of information on many significant aircraft.

HELICOPTERS AND AUTOGIROS

The selections in this part of the bibliography represent the available, nonscientific literature on rotary-wing aviation (also known as vertical flight—specifically, helicopters and autogiros). These titles fall into three main categories: (1) the personalities who pioneered and developed the technology; (2) the history of the technology itself, and (3) descriptions and analyses of the machines and how they are flown.

The amount of literature about rotary-wing aviation is quite small in comparison with what has been written about fixed-wing flying. Vertical flight is not a popular topic because it is still a specialized and exclusive area of aviation. In fact, statistics extrapolated from information in a recent issue of the British periodical *Flight International* (October 8, 1983, p. 941) indicate that in 1981 only 4 percent of the free world's aircraft were helicopters. Also, it took much longer to develop the practical helicopter than the airplane, and helicopters have been mass-produced only since World War II.

In general, most of the work to date has centered on hardware, and provides lists of helicopter types and manuals on how they fly. Few books analyze the broad history of the helicopter and explain how designers exchanged ideas and the social impact of vertical flight. However, *Vertical Flight: The Age of the Helicopter*, by Walter J. Boyne and Donald S. Lopez (see item 255), is one of the best of the broad surveys.

The U.S. Works Progress Administration's *Bibliography of Aeronautics* (see item 23) is recommended for further reading. First published in 1938, this expansive bibliographic coverage of aviation technology includes a section on autogiros, helicopters, and other types of vertical flight craft. It lists over 1,000 articles and includes an author's index.

Another useful source is the *Bibliography of Rotary Wing Aircraft*, prepared by the Air Service Command of the U.S. Army Air Forces, Wright Field, Dayton, Ohio. Like the WPA *Bibliography*, this publication lists articles that were compiled from some 200 periodicals. Although the date of publication is not known precisely, the *Bibliography of Rotary Wing Aircraft* is thought to have appeared around September 1943, and the addendum in 1944.

Additional bibliographic information on rotary wing vehicles will be found in Willard Kelso Dennis, *Recent Periodical Articles: A Selective Subject Index* [*Recent Aeronautical Literature: A Selective Subject Index*] (see item 6). This periodical index to aeronautical literature was published by the Parks Air College Library in 1943–1944, then by Beech Aircraft Corp. from 1945 to 1947.

Russell E. Lee
Peter W. Brooks

254. Apostolo, Giorgio. *The Illustrated Encyclopedia of Helicopters.* New York: Bonanza, 1984. Pp. 140. Index, Illustr.

Over 500 excellent drawings and illustrations accompanied by an excellent text with few errors make this an excellent reference book and primer on helicopters.

255. Boyne, Walter J., and Donald S. Lopez. *Vertical Flight: The Age of the Helicopter.* Washington, D.C.: Smithsonian Institution Press, 1984. Pp. xiii + 257. Bibliog., Illustr.

A collection of articles written by important pioneers in helicopter development. Fills a number of long–standing historical gaps and addresses a variety of specific topics, including the evolution of helicopters in Europe. A chapter on famous firsts in helicopter history and an excellent bibliography complete the work.

256. Brie, R.A.C., comp. *A History of British Rotorcraft, 1866–1965.* Yeovil, England: Westland Helicopters, 1968. Pp. vi + 141. Bibliog., Illustr.

One of the best works to date on the history of British rotorcraft. The autogiro, in particular, is examined in detail in this well–illustrated publication.

257. Brown, Eric M. *The Helicopter in Civil Operations.* New York: Van Nostrand Reinhold, 1981. Pp. 180. Index, Illustr.

Deals mainly with helicopter operations in Europe, with emphasis on present–day capabilities and performance requirements. Occasionally, the author strays to events in the United States, usually for a comparison with European operations. An illustrated list of the major types of European helicopters with performance data blocks for each round out the book.

258. de la Cierva, Juan. "The Development of the Autogiro." *Journal of the Royal Aeronautical Society*, January 1926, 8–29. Illustr.

First of three classic papers read to the Royal Aeronautical Society in London by Juan de la Cierva, inventor of the autogiro. The autogiro was an intermediate form of rotary–wing

aircraft that first flew in 1923, 21 years before the first practical helicopters entered service in 1944. Autogiros differ from
helicopters in having unpowered rotors, which turn only under
the influence of air forces resulting from their motion. This
paper, which was read in 1925, records Cierva's pioneering
development of the first autogiros to fly.

259. de la Cierva, Juan. "The Autogiro." *Journal of the Royal Aero-*
     nautical Society, November 1930, 902–921. Illustr.

     Second of de la Cierva's classic papers read to the Royal
     Aeronautical Society in London in 1930. Gives full account of
     the development of the first fixed–spindle autogiros to go into
     production. Undue attention, however, is given to the de-
     flected–slipstream method of rotor spin–up before takeoff,
     which was about to be overtaken by the first practical engine
     spin–up drive developed in the United States.

260. de la Cierva, Juan. *Wings of Tomorrow: The Story of the Auto-*
     giro. New York: Brewer, Warren and Putnam, 1931. Pp. 300.
     Illustr.

     A popular account of the development of the Cierva autogiro
     which covers most of the period from the first experiments in
     Spain in the early 1920s up to the appearance of direct control
     in 1932. A final chapter by test pilot James G. Ray describes
     the flying characteristics of fixed–spindle autogiros.

261. de la Cierva, Juan. "New Developments of the Autogiro." *Jour-*
     nal of the Royal Aeronautical Society, December 1935, 1125–
     1143. Illustr.

     Third of de la Cierva's classic papers read to the Royal
     Aeronautical Society in London in 1935. Records the remarka-
     ble progress in autogiro technology during the 1930s for which
     Cierva was mainly responsible. Cierva's death in an airline
     accident the following year prevented him from completing his
     contribution to the development of the helicopter.

262. Dorland, Peter, and James Nanney. *Dust Off: Army Aeromed-*
     ical Evacuation in Vietnam. Washington, D.C.: U.S. Army
     Center of Military History, 1982. Pp. vi + 134. Index, Bibliog.,
     Illustr.

Although not heavily illustrated, this book is well documented and easy to read. Includes very good material on the use of helicopters for medical evacuation during the Vietnam War.

263. Fay, John. *The Helicopter: History, Piloting, and How It Flies.* New York: Hippocrene, 1987. Pp. xiv + 223. Index, Bibliog., Illustr.

Fine book of basics on the technical aspects of the helicopter and autogiro. Emphasizes aerodynamics and control functions. Includes a good listing of the important dates in helicopter history.

264. Gablehouse, Charles. *Helicopters and Autogiros: A Chronicle of Rotating–Wing Aircraft.* Philadelphia: J.B. Lippincott, 1967. Pp. xi + 254. Index, Bibliog. Illustr.

Traces the helicopter's development in easy–to–read text. Although not heavily illustrated, the photographs are nevertheless unique and informative. The chapter on aerodynamics contains a full amount of detail with simple line drawings to illustrate some concepts. Appendix contains a history of the word "helicopter." Also includes a brief glossary with more detailed definitions of helicopter terminology.

265. Gregory, H. Franklin. *Anything a Horse Can Do: The Story of the Helicopter.* Introduction by Igor Sikorsky. New York: Reynal and Hitchcock, 1944. Pp. vii + 243. Illustr.

An anecdotal narrative that traces the history of rotary–wing vertical flight until just before the end of World War II. The author touches on the early pioneers while concentrating on the U.S. Army Air Corps' work to perfect the helicopter. Contains good photographs.

266. Gunston, Bill. *An Illustrated Guide to Military Helicopters.* New York: Arco, 1981. Pp. 159. Illustr.

A pocket–sized book that provides quick reference to most modern post–World War II helicopters. In addition to a brief history of the aircraft and table of specifications, each entry has a three–view drawing. Photographs, many in color, illustrate each type. Although there is no index, a table of contents lists each helicopter type alphabetically.

267. Gunston, Bill. *Helicopters of the World.* Combat Aircraft Library. New York: Crescent, 1983. Pp. 80. Illustr.

An accurate and well-written book that features almost 200 excellent color and profile drawings of helicopters. Oversize format gives added visual impact, has perhaps more appeal to young readers. Emphasis is on modern military aircraft.

268. Harrison, P.G., et al. *Military Helicopters.* Brassey's Battlefield Weapons Systems and Technology Series. London: Brassey's Defence, 1985. Pp. xvi + 155. Index, Illustr.

A textbook of modern military helicopters now operating around the world. Excellent section on the principles of helicopter flight; thorough question–and–answer section after each chapter for advanced students of modern vertical flight.

269. Lambermont, Paul, and Anthony Pirie. *Helicopters and Autogyros of the World.* Rev. ed. Foreword by Igor I. Sikorsky. New York: A.S. Barnes, 1970. Pp. 255. Index, Illustr.

With hundreds of black–and–white photographs, Lambermont and Pirie's work is among the most thorough and well researched for the time period. Includes difficult–to–find information on a number of obscure types. Table of contents and index are well organized and easy to use.

270. McDonald, John J. *Flying the Helicopter.* Blue Ridge Summit, Pa.: TAB, 1981. Pp. 255. Index, Illustr.

Concentrates on helicopter aerodynamics and flight controls. The appendix contains the complete pilot's flight manual for the Hughes 500 helicopter, an excellent complement to the sections on aerodynamics and flight controls. Includes section on the history of helicopters.

271. Montross, Lynn. *Cavalry of the Sky: The Story of U.S. Marine Combat Helicopters.* New York: Harper and Brothers, 1954. Pp. xv + 270. Index, Bibliog., Illustr.

Gives accurate, detailed coverage of U.S. Marine helicopter operations during the Korean War. This detailed work includes maps, photographs, and a thorough bibliography.

272. Morris, Charles L. *Pioneering the Helicopter*. Alexandria, Va.:
      Helicopter Association International, 1985. Pp. 161. Bibliog.,
      Illustr.

      Concentrates on Igor Sikorsky's efforts to perfect his VS–300
      series helicopters from test pilot Morris's viewpoint. Includes
      historical summary of helicopter history. Also contains very
      good black–and–white photographs.

273. Munson, Kenneth. *Helicopters and Other Rotorcraft since 1907*.
      Rev. ed. London: Blandford, 1973. Pp. 199. Index, Illustr.

      A handy pocket reference with 94 color plates of the world's
      rotorcraft. Specifications accompany the illustrations, grouped
      at the front of the book. Short, concise, and informative his-
      tories appear at the back.

274. *The Piasecki Story of Vertical Lift, Pioneers in Progress for
      over Forty Years*. Lakehurst, N.J.: Piasecki Aircraft Corpor-
      ation, 1967. N.p. Illustr.

      A company–published chronicle that describes all test and
      production vehicles built by the Piasecki Aircraft Corporation.
      Inroductory reference for all Piasecki aircraft.

275. Pitcairn, Harold F. "The Autogiro: Its Characteristics and
      Accomplishments." *Annual Report of the Board of Regents of
      the Smithsonian Institution*, 1930. Pp. 265–271. Illustr.

      Harold Pitcairn, who introduced the autogiro into North
      America in 1928, read this paper to a meeting of the Franklin
      Institute on November 20, 1929. It was then published in the
      Journal of the Franklin Institute (vol. 209, no. 5, May 1930) and
      subsequently reproduced in the 1930 Smithsonian report. De-
      scribes Cierva's early evolution of the autogiro and Pitcairn's
      development of the first American autogiro in 1929.

276. Polmar, Norman, and Floyd D. Kennedy, Jr. *Military Helicop-
      ters of the World: Military Rotary-Wing Aircraft since 1917*.
      Annapolis, Md.: Naval Institute, 1981. Pp. x + 370. Index,
      Illustr.

      Contains several minor contradictions but is nonetheless an
      excellent reference on military helicopters. Aircraft are

grouped by nationality with adequate history of each type. Includes good black–and–white photographs.

277. Prouty, Raymond W. *Practical Helicopter Aerodynamics*. Peo–ria, Ill.: PJS, 1982. Pp. 86. Illustr.

     Depth of coverage, clarity of explanation, and attention to detail make this one of the definitive textbooks on helicopter aerodynamics for the educated layman.

278. Schafer, Joseph. *Basic Helicopter Maintenance*. Riverton, Wyo.: International Aviation, 1980. Pp. vii + 343. Illustr.

     The definitive work on the mechanics of modern rotorcraft. Describes the most popular domestic and foreign production helicopters with text and drawings. Should be considered an advanced maintenance textbook.

279. Smith, Frank Kingston. *Legacy of Wings: The Story of Harold F. Pitcairn*. New York: Jason Aronson, 1985. Pp. x + 371. Index, Illustr.

     Well–researched story of Harold Pitcairn's airline operation and aircraft manufacturing activities between the world wars and through World War II. Approximately half of the book is devoted to Pitcairn's development, production, and marketing of autogiros in the United States. Provides good account of the Autogiro Company of America's successful lawsuit against the U.S. government to protect its rotary–wing patents.

280. Taylor, John W.R. *Helicopters and VTOL Aircraft*. Garden City, N.Y.: Doubleday, 1968. Pp. 96. Index, Illustr.

     A pocket–sized reference book that contains one–page de–scriptions of helicopters of the period. Each entry includes specifications, a brief history, and a black–and–white photograph.

281. Taylor, Michael J.H. *Jane's Pocket Book 20 Helicopters*. Lon–don: Macdonald and Jane's, 1978. Pp. 260. Index, Illustr.

     Good source of historical and statistical reference informa–tion about helicopters. Although limited to two pages for each type, all entries include a photograph, accurate three-view drawing, and descriptive text. Covers only modern types.

282. Taylor, Michael J.H., and John W.R. Taylor. *Helicopters of the World*. New York: Charles Scribner's Sons, 1978. Pp. 112. Index, Illustr.

   Accurate, well-researched reference book that includes more than 100 entries and is illustrated with quality black-and-white photographs. A comprehensive index makes the book easy to use.

283. Thomas, Kas, and Jack Lambie. *The Complete Guide to Home-built Rotorcraft: The Essentials of Building and Flying Your Own Helicopter*. Blue Ridge Summit, Pa.: TAB, 1982. Pp. viii + 120. Index, Illustr.

   Clearly explains construction techniques for small, personal helicopters built from plans or kits. Easy-to-read text and adequate illustrations. Includes a source list for plans and kits.

284. Tolson, John J. *Airmobility, 1961–1971*. Vietnam Studies. Washington, D.C.: U.S. Department of the Army, 1973. Pp. xiv + 304. Index, Illustr.

   Superb work that traces the helicopter's evolution during the Vietnam War into a mass-airlift tool. Detailed narrative is supplemented by adequate photos.

285. Townson, George. *Autogiro: The Story of "The Windmill Plane."* Fallbrook, Calif.: Aero, 1985. Pp. 160. Index, Illustr.

   A technically detailed record of the development of autogiros in the United States. Gives much attention to the Kellett company's products under license from Pitcairn as to those of the Pitcairn company itself. In 1934, Kellett was the first to produce and sell direct-control autogiros in the United States. Includes a glossary of autogiro terms, an excellent elementary explanation of the theory of the autogiro, and a useful specification table for American autogiros.

286. Wragg, David W. *Helicopter at War: A Pictorial History.* New York: St. Martin's, 1983. Pp. 283. Index, Illustr.

A well-written history of military helicopters. Includes all known military conflicts in which helicopters were involved.

PROPULSION

The engine is the one element common to all forms of powered aircraft. It is truly the heart of an airplane, because it is the component whose proper functioning is vital to flight safety. The function and the development of this critical component are treated in a variety of technical and historical works. We have tried to provide a comprehensive cross section of these works, by including not only general histories of propulsion, but also mechanics' textbooks, books on the theory of design and performance, government specification standards, historical monographs on selected types of engines, books written by or about engine manufacturers, reports from major engine conferences, congressional reports, and biographies of famous engine designers. The principal criterion for selecting a particular book for this section was its usefulness as a research tool.

Most research in the history of propulsion is organized around rather fixed chronological intervals. Several major library collections as well as bibliographies in the field are arranged in this manner. Hence, the section has been divided into 10-year intervals. In general, books are placed in one of these sections according to their date of publication. A few works that cover more than one period are placed in the most pertinent decade. The last category, "Recurring Government Reports," covers recurring documents on a wide range of topics.

Finally, the annotations are intended to be informative descriptions of the aspects of a given book that would benefit researchers most. They occasionally include references to complementary texts that provide additional information.

Among the key reference works are *Aerosphere: Including World's Aircraft Engines with Aircraft Directory* by Glenn D. Angle (see item 301), *Aircraft Engines of the World* by Paul H. Wilkinson (see item 317), and *Development of Aircraft Engines; Development of Aviation Fuels—Two Studies of Relations between Government and Business* by Robert Schlaifer and S.D. Heron (see item 321). *Jane's All the World's Aircraft* (see item 51) is one of the definitive aircraft engine reference books. First published in 1909, this yearbook contains a section on aircraft engines that is subdivided by country of origin and by manufacturer. It provides the developmental history, description, and specifications for each engine model.

The researcher may also wish to consult several bibliographic works. August Hanniball's *Aircraft, Engines and Airmen: A Selection of the Periodical Literature, 1930–1969* (see item 9) classifies articles on engines by manufacturer for easy reference. Ernest F. Fiock's *Bibliography of Books and Published Reports on Gas Turbines, Jet Propulsion and Rocket Power Plants* (National Bureau of Standards Circular 482, Washington: U.S. Department of Commerce, National Bureau of Standards, 1949) classifies information on engines and accessories by type, nationality, and year of publication. The Works Progress Administration's *Bibliography of Aeronautics* (see item 23) is divided into 50 parts and includes an extensive list of books, pamphlets, and articles on selected propulsion topics. Those of particular interest are part 17, Diesel Aircraft Engines and Supplement; part 27, Aircraft Propellers; part 28, Fuels; part 29, Lubricants; part 32, Engines, Vol. I; part 33, Engines, Vol. II; part 34, Engines by Manufacturer; part 35, Engine Parts and Accessories; and part 36, Engine Instruments.

Rick Leyes
Deborah G. Douglas
William A. Fleming

Through 1919

287. André, H. *Moteurs d'aviation et de dirigeables* (Aviation and dirigible engines). Paris: L. Geisler, 1910. Pp. 190. Illustr.

Primarily a descriptive comparison of dirigible engines of the 1910 era. Also contains an engine theory analysis.

288. Burls, G.A. *Aero Engines: With a General Introductory Account of the Theory of the Internal-Combustion Engine.* London: Charles Griffin, 1917. Pp. x + 196. Illustr.

Outstanding collection of illustrations and foldout plates. Surveys engines by cylinder configuration. Includes a discussion on the theory of performance.

289. Haenig, Alfred. *Ballon und Flugmoteren: Ihre technische Entwicklung und gegenwärtige Gestaltung* (Balloon and aircraft engines: Their technical development and current state). Rostock: C.J.E. Volckmann Nachfolger, 1910. Pp. 196. Illustr.

Discusses history, theory, and technical data of balloon and airplane motors. Contains excellent photographs and illustrations of German, French, American, Belgian, Danish, English, and Italian engines.

290. Hayward, Charles. *Aviation Motors.* Chicago: American School of Correspondence, 1918. Pp. 88. Illustr.

Comparative technical analysis of aircraft engines of the 1910s. Contains specifications for many early aircraft engines. Well illustrated with photographs and schematics.

291. U.S. Department of Commerce. Bureau of Standards. *Technologic Papers of the Bureau of Standards, Department of Commerce.* Washington, D.C.: U.S. Government Printing Office, 1917, 1919.

An important series of papers that individually provide detailed technical analyses of engines or other propulsion components. Each focuses on performance and provides a wealth of information on specifications and design.

1920–1929

292. Angle, Glenn D. *Airplane Engine Encyclopedia.* Dayton, Ohio: Otterbein, 1921. Pp. 547. Index, Illustr.

Compiles and alphabetically arranges an enormous body of data on engine design construction. Most of the text is based on the manufacturers' data or other original sources. Contains summary tables of classification of engine types. Extremely valuable reference tool and useful survey of engines.

293. Dyke, Andrew L. *Dyke's Aircraft Engine Instructor.* 3d ed. Chicago: Goodheart–Willcox, 1929. Pp. x + 425. Index, Illustr.

One of the most important textbooks employed by mechanics during the 1920s and 1930s. Excellent schematics, maintenance diagrams, and photographs of engines of the 1920s. Exceptionally useful for aircraft restorers.

294. Hourwich, Iskander, and W.J. Foster. *Air Service Engine Handbook.* Dayton, Ohio: Chief of Air Service, Engineering Division, McCook Field, September 1925. Pp. xxv + 738. Index, Illustr.

The principal engineering reference text on aircraft engine materials for use in their design in the 1920s. The data in this book were derived from published aero propulsion research statistics from such sources as the U.S. Army Air Service, the Engineering Division (McCook Field), the U.S. Bureau of Standards, and the National Advisory Committee for Aeronautics.

295. Jones, Edward T., Robert Insley, Frank W. Caldwell, and Robert F. Kohr. *Aircraft Power Plants.* New York: Ronald, 1926. Pp. xiv + 208. Index, Illustr.

Comparative analysis of engines and propulsion theory of the 1920s. Significant collection of early writings by a group of engineers who later achieved substantial prominence in their respective fields of design, theory, and engineering.

296. Lucke, Charles E. *Thermodynamic Efficiency of Present Types of Internal Combustion Engines for Aircraft.* New York: Columbia University Press, 1922. Pp. 116.

Important (and perhaps only) survey of the evolution, design, and physical characteristics of aircraft engines of the 1920s. Provides data useful for assessing the historical value of specific engines. However, the appendix, which includes much bibliographic data and many engine test results, was not published along with the text.

297. Pagé, Victor W. *Modern Aviation Engines—Design, Construction, Operation and Repair.* 2 vols. New York: Norman W. Henley, 1929. Pp. 976 + 931 (continuous pagination to 1908). Illustr.

Pagé's tour de force of information about aircraft engines. Much of it was taken from factory publications and specifications. In essence, it has preserved these data for historians and anyone interested in aircraft engines of the time. Includes a brief historical summary of early aircraft engines. Similar important texts by Pagé are *Aviation Engines* (New York: Norman W. Henley, 1917) and *Aviation Engine Examiner* (New York: Norman W. Henley, 1930).

298. Park, Whyrill E. *A Treatise on Airscrews.* London: Chapman and Hall, 1920. Pp. xii + 308. Index, Illustr.

A work that is midway between the theoretical and the practical. Utilizes design theory rather than elaborate mathematical solutions of theories. The first part of the book discusses propeller design, while the second illustrates propeller construction techniques of the period.

299. Sherbondy, E.H., and G.D. Wardrop. *Textbook of Aero Engines.* New York: Frederick A. Stokes, 1920. Pp. 363. Illustr.

A major text of the early 1920s that describes the engines in detail. Includes schematics and photographs.

300. U.S. Army Air Corps. Propeller Section, Engineering Division, McCook Field, Dayton, Ohio. *The Airplane Propeller.* Washington, D.C.: U.S. Government Printing Office, 1921. Pp. 337.

The standard for propeller design specifications of the time. This work set the standard for aircraft propeller design, manufacturing, inspecting, and testing. A summary of the existing research data.

1930–1939

301. Angle, Glenn D. *Aerosphere: Including World's Aircraft Engines with Aircraft Directory*. 1939, 1941, 1942, 1943 eds. New York: Aircraft Publications, 1940, 1942, 1943, 1944. Pp. 1420 + n.p. + n.p. + n.p. Bibliog., Illustr.

   Aerosphere is the standard reference textbook for aircraft engine history and specifications for all engines developed prior to its publication. Each edition also includes descriptions of aircraft, aircraft statistics, and a product directory.

302. Brimm, Daniel J., Jr., and H. Edward Bogges. *Aircraft Engine Maintenance*. New York, Chicago: Pitman, 1939. Pp. ix + 470. Illustr.

   Best of the aircraft engine maintenance texts used in the 1940s. Covers all topics related to repair in voluminous detail. Provides tables, specifications, and illustrations for a significant number of aircraft engines. Excellent restoration reference book.

303. Caunter, C.F. *Light Aero Engines*. London: Pitman and Sons, 1930. Pp. xiii + 288. Index, Bibliog., Illustr.

   Surveys aircraft engines and components of the time. Schematics, tables, and photographs are very useful. Provides a list of engine manufacturers. Additional works by Caunter are *Small Four–Stroke Aero Engines* (London: Sir Isaac Pitman and Sons, 1936) and *Small Two–Stroke Aero Engines* (London: Sir Isaac Pitman and Sons, 1936).

304. Davy, M.J.B., and G. Tilghman Richards. *Handbook of the Collections Illustrating Aeronautics—III: The Propulsion of Aircraft*. 2d ed. London: His Majesty's Stationery Office, 1936. Pp. 104. Index, Bibliog., Illustr.

   A brief outline of the history and development of the aero–engine and propeller with reference to the collection of the Science Museum of London. Also contains a contemporary catalog of and labels for the museum's propulsion exhibits. A very functional reference work for early aircraft engine history. Well illustrated.

305. International Nickel Company. *A Directory of American Air-craft Engines*. New York, 1931. Pp. 69. Bibliog., Illustr.

Contains technical descriptions and photographs of a large number of American aircraft engines including several rare models. This volume is one of an annual series that International Nickel produced on engines using nickel parts. Known editions include the years 1930, 1931, and 1935.

306. Weick, Fred E. *Aircraft Propeller Design*. New York: McGraw-Hill, 1930. Pp. xiii + 294. Index, Illustr.

A comprehensive summary of propeller technology in the mid-1930s. Presents airfoil and propeller design theory and propeller performance data. Also describes propeller testing and propeller–airframe interaction. Lack of a bibliography is more than compensated for by the presence of extensive reference footnotes.

1940–1949

307. Aircraft Gas Turbine Engineering Conference [1945: Swamp-scott, Massachusetts]. *Aircraft Gas Turbine Engineering Conference, 1945*. West Lynn, Mass.: General Electric, 1945. Pp. xi + 286. Illustr.

This historic document is a compilation of scientific papers presented at the first engineering conference on aircraft and gas turbine engines. It is a particularly important work because it focuses on early aircraft gas turbine engine developments and technical problems.

308. American Society of Mechanical Engineers. *Development of the British Gas Turbine Jet Unit*. Reprint. London: Institution of Mechanical Engineers, 1947. Pp. 104. Illustr.

Reprints of a collection of lectures on British gas turbine units. Of particular value are two introductory essays by Hayne Constant that include a history of the axial type of gas turbine engines.

309. Fahey, James C. *U.S. Army Aircraft (Heavier-than-Air) 1908–1946*. New York: Ships and Aircraft, 1946. Pp. 64. Illustr.

This book, along with a subsequent companion volume called *USAF Aircraft, 1947–1956* (Falls Church, Va.: Ships and Aircraft, 1956), is extremely useful for propulsion research because it specifies the manufacturer, model, and horsepower or thrust of engines used in U.S. Army or U.S. Air Force aircraft.

310. Fedden, Roy. *Aircraft Power Plant—Past and Future*. Aeronautical Reprints. London: Royal Aeronautical Society, 1944. Pp. 120. Illustr.

Text of 1944 Wilbur Wright Memorial Lecture presented to the Royal Aeronautical Society. Historical survey of aircraft engines from very early reciprocating engines to turbine engines of the 1940s as seen from a British perspective. Provides a comparative analysis of aircraft engines and related accessories.

311. Judge, Arthur W. *Aircraft Engines*. 2 vols. London: Chapman and Hall, 1940. Pp. 371 + 434. Illustr.

Two–volume text for engineering students on aircraft engines. It is a superb reference tool with a large number of technical charts and illustrations. Volume 1 is principally concerned with the theoretical and experimental aspects of the aircraft engines; Volume 2 with the descriptive aspects as well as certain design considerations. A complementary text for students that describes and illustrates the steps in designing a reciprocating engine is *Aircraft Engine Design* (New York: McGraw–Hill, 1942) by Joseph Liston.

312. Linsley, H.L. *The Birth of Flight*. Patterson, N.J.: Wright Aeronautical Corp., July 6, 1944. Pp. 44. Index.

This unpublished manuscript is the only known history of the Wright Aeronautical Corporation. Begins with the Wright brothers and explains the corporate mergers that took place. Also describes the engine programs that the company pursued. A valuable engine index is included that lists the basic specifications of all of the major engines developed by the company through 1944.

313. Markey, Richard. *The Aircraft Propeller; Principles, Maintenance, and Servicing, with Sketches by the Author*. New York: Pitman, 1940. Pp. xi + 155. Illustr.

Popular explanation of the operation of the propeller that uses little technical terminology. A section of the text is devoted to defining aerodynamic terms. An excellent introduction to propellers that uses four examples of actual propellers to discuss methods of construction and maintenance techniques.

314. Moss, Sanford A. *Superchargers for Aviation.* New York: National Aeronautics Council, 1942. Pp. viii + 103. Illustr.

Excellent history of supercharging written by the principal figure in the development of this technology. Integrates technical and historical material, providing a comprehensive overview of this aspect of the modern internal combustion engine.

315. Neville, Leslie E., and Nathaniel F. Silsbee. *Jet Propulsion Progress: the Development of Aircraft Gas Turbines.* New York: McGraw–Hill, 1948. Pp. xii + 232. Bibliog., Illustr.

Excellent outline of the international, historical, and technical development of jet propulsion beginning in the mid–1930s. Uses fundamental mathematics to explain topics, but avoids extensive or highly technical discussions.

316. Sawyer, R. Tom. *The Modern Gas Turbine.* 2d ed. New York: Prentice–Hall, 1947. Pp. xx + 224. Index, Illustr.

Surveys the development, uses, and operating characteristics of the gas turbine in locomotives, ships, industry, and aircraft. Contains an especially useful history of early gas turbine engines. A companion book by Sawyer, *Gas Turbine Construction* (New York: Prentice–Hall, 1947), describes the construction and physical characteristics of gas turbines, including turbosuperchargers and early U.S. and British engines.

317. Wilkinson, Paul H. *Aircraft Engines of the World.* New York: Paul H. Wilkinson, n.d. Index, Illustr.

Complete, authoritative reference book devoted exclusively to modern aircraft engines. Over 23 editions (roughly annually) from the 1940s to the 1970s have been published, each of which contains data on engine characteristics, clear photographs, and a summary of trends in engine development.

318. Wilkinson, Paul H. *Aircraft Diesels*. New York, Chicago: Pitman, 1940. Pp. ix + 275. Illustr.

Historical overview of the development of diesel aircraft engines. Excellent technical summary of diesel powerplants. Includes diesel specifications, component and fuel analysis, and research on diesel development. Other useful aircraft diesel engine books written by Wilkinson are *Diesel Aircraft Engines* (Brooklyn, N.Y.: Paul H. Wilkinson, 1936) and *Diesel Aviation Engines* (New York: National Aeronautics Council, 1942).

1950–1959

319. Casamassa, Jack V., and Ralph D. Bent. *Jet Aircraft Power Systems*. 2d ed. New York: McGraw–Hill, 1957. Pp. ix + 329. Illustr.

Important text on jet–propulsion systems. Presents jet propulsion theory and technical data. Also illustrates U.S. and British engines and their aircraft applications in the mid–1950s just prior to Sputnik. (Updated in 1965.)
A related publication presenting jet engine and rocket theory and British design and operating experience is *Jets and Rockets* (London: Chapman and Hall, 1959) by A. Barker, T.R.F. Nonweiler, and R. Smelt.

320. Finch, Volney Cecil. *Jet Propulsion Turboprops*. Millbrae, Calif.: National, 1950. Pp. xvi + 256. Index, Illustr.

Comprehensive description of design theory, operation, and performance characteristics of turboprop engines and their components.

321. Schlaifer, Robert, and S.D. Heron. *Development of Aircraft Engines; Development of Aviation Fuels—Two Studies of Relations between Government and Business*. Boston: Harvard Graduate School of Business Administration, 1950. Pp. xviii + 754. Index.

Considered the definitive book on the history of aircraft engines and fuels. Explores the relationship between the federal government and technology and analyzes aspects of technical history that are not discussed in any other work.

322. Smith, G. Geoffrey. *Gas Turbines and Jet Propulsion for Air-
     craft*. 5th ed. New York: Aircraft, 1951. Pp. 394. Index,
     Illustr.

     Multifaceted work written by one of the principal proponents
     of gas turbine technology in Great Britain. Includes a broad
     survey of the historical approaches to the subject, an explana-
     tion of the basic principles and theories, and a summary of
     design characteristics of complete units and components.

323. United Aircraft Corporation. *The Pratt & Whitney Aircraft
     Story*. East Hartford, Conn.: Pratt & Whitney Aircraft
     Division. 1952. Pp. 172. Illustr.

     A history of Pratt & Whitney presenting a relatively detailed
     account of the people involved, the engines developed, and the
     aircraft in which the engines were used from 1925 to 1950. This
     book, when read with *An Account of Pratt & Whitney Aircraft
     Company, 1925–1950* (East Hartford, Conn.: Pratt & Whitney
     Aircraft, 1950) by Frederick B. Rentschler (cited herein as item
     998) and *Wings Over the World: The Life of George Jackson
     Mead* (Wauwatosa, Wisc.: Swannet, 1971) by Cary Hoge Mead
     (cited herein as item 990), provide an excellent historical
     background of Pratt & Whitney.

324. U.S. Congress. *Hearing before the Subcommittee on Research
     and Development of the Joint Committee on Atomic Energy:
     First Session on the Aircraft Nuclear Propulsion Program,
     July 23, 1959*. Washington, D.C.: U.S. Government Printing
     Office, 1959. Pp. 418. Bibliog., Illustr.

     Extensive history of the American research program in
     nuclear propulsion for aircraft. Contains a good bibliography
     plus a chronology, press releases, speeches, technical articles,
     and letters provided as appendixes. The U.S. government report:
     *Review of Manned Aircraft Nuclear Propulsion Program,
     Atomic Energy Commission and the Department of Defense*
     (Washington, D.C.: U.S. Government Printing Office, 1963), is
     considered a complementary document and describes the pro-
     cedures for planning and managing this program.

325. U.S. Department of the Air Force. Air Materiel Command.
     Model Designations of USAF Aircraft Engines. 9th ed. Wash-
     ington, D.C.: U.S. Government Printing Office, 1950. Various
     pagination.

Lists principal specifications and applications of air-breathing and non air-breathing military engines. Includes engines in use between 1945 and 1950.

326. U.S. Department of the Air Force, Air Research & Development Command; U.S. Department of the Navy, Bureau of Aeronautics; U.S. Department of Commerce, Civil Aeronautics Administration. *ANC-9 Bulletin Aircraft Propeller Handbook.* Washington, D.C.: U.S. Government Printing Office, 1956. Pp. 391. Index, Bibliog.

The standard reference textbook for propeller design. Represents the state of the art of propeller design in the 1950s.

Whittle, Sir Frank. *Jet: The Story of a Pioneer.* New York: Philosophical Library, 1954. Pp. 320. Index, Illustr.

Cited herein as item 388.

1960–1969

327. Dickey, Philip S. III. *The Liberty Engine, 1918–1942.* Smithsonian Annals of Flight, vol. 1, no. 3. Washington, D.C.: Smithsonian Institution Press, 1968. Pp. x + 110. Bibliog., Illustr.

Contains a detailed analysis of the design, production, and application of the Liberty engine, which was a significant contribution to the Allied cause in World War I and to American aviation in the postwar period.

328. Heiman, Grover. *Jet Pioneers.* New York: Duell, Sloan and Pearce, 1963. Pp. xiv + 235. Illustr.

Highlights many significant turbine engine developments. Each chapter tells the story of an individual who made a significant contribution to jet aviation history, such as Hans von Ohain, the inventor of the first jet engine.

329. Heron, S.D. *History of the Aircraft Piston Engines: A Brief Outline.* Detroit: Ethyl Corporation, 1961. Pp. 130. Bibliog., Illustr.

A classic text of aircraft piston engine history. One of the best reference books in the field. The author was one of the world's foremost aviation fuel experts.

330. Loh, W.H.T. *Jet, Rocket, Nuclear, Ion, and Electric Propulsion: Theory and Design.* New York: Springer–Verlag, 1968. Pp. xvii + 765. Illustr.

Surveys the developments during the 1960s in each of five fields of propulsion. Presents the fundamentals of jet engine aerodynamics and thermodynamics and reciprocating engine thermodynamics. Structured around a senior– or graduate–level engineering seminar in the propulsion field.

331. Meyer, Robert B., Jr. *First Airplane Diesel Engine: Packard Model DR–980 of 1928.* Smithsonian Annals of Flight, vol. 1, no. 2. Washington, D.C.: Smithsonian Institution Press, 1964. Pp. 48. Illustr.

Describes the development of the first diesel engine to power an airplane, which won the 1931 Collier Trophy for the Packard Motor Car Company. Outlines the history of the engine, describes how it functioned, and critically analyzes its performance characteristics.

1970–1979

332. Banks, Francis R. *I Kept No Diary: 60 Years with Marine Diesels, Automobile and Aero Engines.* Shrewsbury, England: Airlife, 1978. Pp. 247. Index, Bibliog., Illustr.

The autobiography of Francis R. Banks, who was active in the development of tetraethyl lead for aviation fuel and of British aircraft engines and accessories. Contains an interesting section on the history of Schneider Trophy race engines.

333. Boyne, Walter J., and Donald S. Lopez, eds. *The Jet Age: Forty Years of Jet Aviation.* Washington, D.C.: Smithsonian Institution Press, 1979. Pp. vii + 190. Bibliog., Illustr.

Collection of writings by several of the principal participants in the field of jet aviation. Articles written by von Ohain, Whittle, and Franz cover their pioneering roles in the development of aircraft gas turbine engines.

334. Byttebier, Hugo T. *The Curtiss D–12 Aero Engine*. Smithsonian Annals of Flight, no. 7. Washington, D.C.: Smithsonian Institution Press, 1972. Pp. vii + 109. Illustr.

Excellent history of the Curtiss D–12 engine and its impact on the evolution of high–performance engines.

335. General Electric Company. *Seven Decades of Progress: A Heritage of Aircraft Turbine Technology*. Fallbrook, Calif.: Aero, 1979. Pp. 232. Index, Bibliog., Illustr.

Comprehensive history of the development of General Electric turbine engines. A condensed version of William R. Travers's unpublished manuscript, *The General Electric Aircraft Engine Story* (a limited number of copies were printed by General Electric in 1978), which analyzed General Electric's turbine engine programs in great detail.

336. Gunston, Bill. *By Jupiter: The Life of Sir Roy Fedden*. London: Royal Aeronautical Society, 1978. Pp. ix + 157. Index, Illustr.

Biography of Sir Roy Fedden that traces the history of the development of Bristol aircraft engines. Bristol engines were among the most~widely produced aircraft engines in Great Britain. A section of the book is devoted to the Jupiter engine, a noted early British design.

337. Hobbs, Leonard S. *The Wright Brothers' Engines and Their Design*. Smithsonian Annals of Flight, no. 5. Washington, D.C.: Smithsonian Institution Press, 1971. Pp. 71. Index, Bibliog., Illustr.

The most comprehensive survey yet written on engines designed by the Wright Brothers. Well illustrated.

338. Lloyd, Ian. *Rolls–Royce: The Merlin at War*. London: Macmillan, 1978. Pp. xvii + 188. Index, Bibliog., Illustr.

A history of the production and development of the Rolls–Royce Merlin. Contains a very detailed recounting of the decisions of the firm, its production problems, and its engine applications. This book, along with Lloyd's *Rolls–Royce, the Years of Endeavor* (London: Macmillan, 1978) and *Rolls–Royce, the Growth of a Firm* (London: Macmillan, 1978), constitute a chronological history of Rolls–Royce, Ltd. through World War II. All three books contain aircraft engine production figures and are well illustrated.

339. McCready, Lauren S. "The Invention and Development of the Gnome Rotary Aero Engine: The World of Louis and Laurent Seguin." Master's Thesis, Polytechnic Institute of Brooklyn, 1973. Pp. ix + 80. Bibliog., Illustr.

The story of the design and development of the Gnome rotary engine. The Gnome engine and other rotary engines based on its fundamental ideas were very influential aircraft engines between 1910 and 1918. In addition to recounting its historical development, the book describes the engineering details of the engine, discusses its applications, and analyzes its performance.

340. Meyer, Robert B., Jr., ed. *Langley's Aero Engine of 1903*. Smithsonian Annals of Flight, no. 6. Washington, D.C.: Smithsonian Institution Press, 1971. Pp. xi + 193. Bibliog., Illustr.

A comprehensive history of the Langley–Manly–Balzer engine, one of the most significant early aircraft engines. Richly endowed with original source material, the book includes a comparative evaluation of its performance against other early aviation engines. Meyer's companion book, *Langley's Model Aero Engine of 1903* (Washington, D.C.: Aeroplanes and Engines, 1976), discusses the development of Langley's model aircraft engine that was used to calculate the power requirements for Langley's full–size aerodrome.

341. North Atlantic Treaty Organization, Advisory Group for Aerospace Research and Development. *Advanced Technology for Production of Aerospace Engines*. London: Technical Editing and Reproduction, 1970. Various pagination. Illustr.

A collection of papers from NATO's Advisory Group for Aerospace Research and Development conference, each of which is carefully documented and well researched, and provides valuable data. The conference focused on the most advanced research in manufacturing techniques, materials, and test methods as they applied to aerospace engines in the early 1970s. Appendix includes questions and comments on the papers by attendees, with responses by the authors.

342. *Proceedings: 3d International Symposium on Air Breathing Engines.* Munich: Deutsche Gesellschaft Fur Luft–und Raum-fahrt e.V., 1976. Pp. 955.

An international forum for top management, engineers, and scientists from the producers and users of air–breathing (non-rocket) flight–propulsion systems. Excellent source of information on the state of the art with respect to turbine engines and their components.

343. Setright, L.J.K. *The Power to Fly: The Development of the Piston Engine in Aviation.* London: George Allen and Unwin, 1971. Pp. 224. Illustr.

Presents the history of the development of aircraft piston engines with photos and schematics. Appendix includes important specifications of principal aircraft engines. Considered one of the best surveys of the evolution of aircraft piston engines.

344. Sloop, John L. *Liquid Hydrogen as a Propulsion Fuel, 1945–1959.* NASA SP–4404. Washington, D.C.: National Aeronautics and Space Administration, 1978. Pp. xiv + 325. Index, Bibliog., Illustr.

An important work on the application of hydrogen as a jet engine and rocket fuel and its experimental use on aircraft. The title is misleading because the book deals with the applications of hydrogen fuel, rather than hydrogen fuel as such.

345. Smith, Maxwell. *Aviation Fuels.* Henley–on–Thames: G.T. Foulis, 1970. Pp. xii + 495. Bibliog., Illustr.

Comprehensive study of aviation fuels. Provides information on fuel properties and the measurement of such data. The wealth of data and details of research are of enormous value to historical as well as scientific studies.

346. Taylor, C. Fayette. *Aircraft Propulsion: A Review of the Evolution of Aircraft Piston Engines.* Smithsonian Annals of Flight, vol. 1, no. 4. Washington, D.C.: Smithsonian Institution Press, 1971. Pp. viii + 134. Bibliog., Illustr.

Brief history of the development of the aircraft piston engine, internal engine components, and propulsion accessories.

Unconventional aircraft engines are reviewed. Extensive bibliography.

347. Treager, Irwin E. *Aircraft Gas Turbine Engine Technology.* New
     York: McGraw–Hill, 1970. Pp. ix + 463. Illustr.

     Widely used textbook for contemporary aircraft gas turbine
     engines. Covers history, theory, and mechanics. Includes
     reviews of engines by type.

348. U.S. Department of the Air Force. History Office. Aeronautical
     Systems Division. Air Force Systems Command. *An Encoun-
     ter between the Jet Engine Inventors, Sir Frank Whittle and
     Dr. Hans von Ohain, 3–4 May 1978.* Wright–Patterson Air
     Force Base, Ohio, 1978. Pp. xxvi + 136. Index, Illustr.

     A transcript of a conference held at Wright–Patterson Air
     Force Base in which Sir Frank Whittle and Dr. Hans von Ohain
     were interviewed by jet propulsion scientists and engineers.
     Both inventors discuss the development of their jet engines and
     compare their problems and performance. Includes biographies
     and photographs of the men and their engines.

1980 to the Present

349. Bingelis, Antoni. *Firewall Forward: Engine Installation Methods.*
     Edited by David A. Rivers. Austin, Tex. Tony Bingelis, 1983.
     Pp. 303. Illustr.

     Principally devoted to the actual installation of aircraft
     engines and accessories in homebuilt and antique aircraft. A
     practical guide that is widely used by experimental aircraft
     builders.

350. Brinks, Glenn. *Ultralight Propulsion: The Basic Handbook of
     Ultralight Engines, Drives and Propellers.* Ultralight Aviation
     Series, no. 4. Hummelstown, Pa.: Ultralight, 1982. Pp. 192.
     Illustr.

     Detailed description of ultralight powerplants and acces-
     sories. The final chapter provides engine specifications by man-
     ufacturer and is well illustrated. A similar book, *Engines for
     Homebuilt Aircraft and Ultralights* (Blue Ridge Summit, Pa.:

TAB, 1983), by Joe Christy, analyzes auto–engine conversions, type–certificated engines, and ultralight engines.

351. Constant, Edward W. II. *The Origins of the Turbojet Revolution.* Baltimore, Md.: Johns Hopkins University Press, 1980. Pp. xiv + 311. Index, Bibliog., Illustr.

    Historiographical case study examining history of the evolution of the turbojet. Useful discussion of various historical approaches to the study of technology. More concerned with method than actual history.

352. Donne, Michael. *Leader of the Skies: Rolls–Royce: The First Seventy–Five Years.* London: Frederick Muller, 1981. Pp. 157. Index, Bibliog., Illustr.

    A condensed history of Rolls–Royce aircraft engines replete with photographs of engines and the aircraft they were used in. Although this book traces the history of the company since 1906, the emphasis is on the development of later Rolls–Royce turbine engines, especially the RB211. Also includes industrial, marine, and future applications of turbine engines.

353. Finch, Richard. *Converting Auto Engines for Experimental Aircraft.* Titusville, Fla.: Finch, 1985. Pp. 186. Illustr.

    An in–depth review of automobile engines that are suitable for aircraft conversion. Discusses the advantages and disadvantages of the modifications necessary to convert specific engines and engine accessories for use in aircraft. Also includes a brief history of auto engines that have been used in aircraft as well as aircraft engines that have been used in automobiles.

354. Gas Turbine Division of the American Society of Mechanical Engineers. *1985 International Gas Turbine Technology Report.* Atlanta, Ga.: International Gas Turbine Center, annual. Pp. 84.

    Compiled and published by the International Gas Turbine Center, this is an annual publication that summarizes the activities of U.S. and foreign companies, universities, organizations, and committees involved in turbine engine and related component research and production.

355. von Gersdorff, Kyrill, and Kurt Grasmann. *Flugmotoren und Strahltriebwerke: Entwicklungsgeschichte der deutschen Luftfahrtantriebe von den Anfangen bis zu den europaischen Gemeinschaftsentwicklungen.* (Aircraft engines and jet engines: Developmental history of German aeronautical propulsion from the origins to the evolution of the European partnership). Munich: Bernard and Graefe Verlag, 1981. Pp. 303. Index, Bibliog., Illustr.

A comprehensive history of the development of German aircraft engines. Profusely illustrated and contains production statistics and an excellent engine bibliography.

356. Harvey–Bailey, Alec. *Rolls–Royce—The Formative Years, 1906–1939.* Derby, England: Rolls–Royce Heritage Trust, 1983. Pp. 95. Illustr.

A brief history of the aircraft engines developed and manufactured by Rolls–Royce. Each significant engine discussed in this book is illustrated with good photographs. Harvey–Bailey's book *The Merlin in Perspective—The Combat Years* (Derby, England: Rolls–Royce Heritage Trust, 1983) adds to this historic survey of the company by focusing on the Merlin, one of Rolls–Royce's most important engines.

357. Hooker, Sir Stanley, and Bill Gunston. *Not Much of an Engineer: An Autobiography.* Shrewsbury, England: Airlife, 1984. Pp. iv + 255. Index, Illustr.

Sir Stanley Hooker worked with Rolls–Royce and the Bristol Engine Division. Early in his career he was responsible for greatly increasing the power of the Rolls–Royce Merlin engine and was instrumental in furthering the development of many of Great Britain's most significant engines up through the RB211, the high–thrust fanjet engine used on wide–body jet aircraft.

358. National Air and Space Museum. Smithsonian Institution. *Aircraft Engines in Museums around the World.* 2 sections. Washington, D.C., 1982. N.p.

A reference book intended to assist in locating aircraft engines in museum collections. Section 1 lists engines by design firm and cross–references them to museums in which they are located. Section 2 lists the engine collection of each participating museum.

359. Neumann, Gerhard. *Herman the German: Enemy Alien U.S. Army Master Sergeant #10500000.* New York: William Morrow, 1984. Pp. 269. Illustr.

The author, head of General Electric's aircraft engine group, provides an inside look at key managerial decisions that went into the engineering of important General Electric engines. Among the more important engine projects discussed is the G.E. GOL–1590 engine, the prototype of the G.E. Collier Trophy-winning J79 engine.

360. Ogston, Alexander R., Robert V. Kerley, Robert Friedman, Ray Knipple, and John Thich. *Trends in Aviation Fuels and Lubricants.* "SP–492." Warrendale, Pa.: Society of Automotive Engineers, 1981. Pp. 63. Bibliog., Illustr.

Well-referenced set of articles that outline the history of aviation fuels and lubricants. Probably the only material of its type available for this topic, although the Coordinating Research Council's *Handbook for Aviation Fuel Properties* (Atlanta, Ga.: Coordinating Research Council, 1983) does contain comprehensive data on contemporary fuels and their properties.

361. Rosen, George, and Charles A. Anezis. *Thrusting Forward: A History of the Propeller.* N.p. Hamilton Standard Division of United Technologies and British Aerospace Dynamics Group, Hatfield–Lostock Division, 1984. Pp. 95. Illustr.

Profusely illustrated history of the aircraft propeller. Traces the development of the aircraft propeller from concepts proposed by Leonardo Da Vinci to contemporary prop-fan designs. Significant advances in propeller design, such as metal blade, composite blade and variable pitch, constant speed propellers are highlighted. A very readable history that is recommended for understanding the fundamentals of propeller design and application.

362. Smith, Herschel. *Aircraft Piston Engines: From the Manly Baltzer [sic] to the Continental Tiara.* New York: McGraw-Hill, 1981. Pp. xi + 255. Index, Bibliog., Illustr.

Although the quality of research is uneven, this is one of the most recent examinations of the development of aircraft piston engines.

363. U.S. National Aeronautics and Space Administration. Scientific and Technical Information Branch. *General Aviation Propulsion*. NASA CP–2126. Washington, D.C., 1980. Pp. vi + 432. Bibliog., Illustr.

A series of papers presented at a conference held at the NASA Lewis Research Center that discuss programs designed to improve general aviation powerplant technology. Supplementary information on rotary combustion engine technology was presented at a 1978 NASA conference on the subject, *The Rotary Combustion Engine—A Candidate for General Aviation* (Washington, D.C.: NASA Scientific and Technical Information Branch, 1978).

364. U.S. National Aeronautics and Space Administration. Scientific and Technical Information Branch. *Aircraft Engine Diagnostics*. NASA CP–2190. Washington, D.C., 1981. Pp. vi + 380. Illustr.

A collection of papers presented at a conference held at the NASA Lewis Research Center on the subject of how turbine engine peformance declines with operating time. A supplementary set of survey papers describing recent turbine engine technology advances is contained in NASA's conference publication *Aeropropulsion 1979*, NASA CP–2092 (Washington, D.C.: NASA Scientific and Technical Information Branch, 1979).

365. Wagner, William. *Continental! Its Motors and Its People*. Fallbrook, Calif.: Aero, 1983. Pp. ix + 240. Index, Illustr.

A corporate history of the Continental Motors Corporation, a major manufacturer of aircraft engines. A useful survey of the development and production of these engines.

Wolko, Howard S. *In the Cause of Flight: Technologists of Aeronautics and Astronautics*. Smithsonian Studies in Air and Space, no. 4. Washington, D.C.: Smithsonian Institution Press, 1981. Pp. iii + 121. Index, Bibliog., Illustr.

Cited herein as item 389.

Recurring Government Reports

366. British Aeronautical Research Committee. *Technical Reports.* London: Her Majesty's Stationery Office.

Technical reports on all aspects of aeronautics, including propulsion, that are prepared by the Royal Aeronautical Establishment or other British organizations and are compiled and published annually by the British Aeronautical Research Committee. Requests for assistance in locating reports can be directed to the Scientific and Technical Library, NASA Headquarters, Washington, D.C. Copies of some reports can be purchased from either the Defense Technical Information Center in Cameron Station, Virginia, or from the National Technical Information Service in Springfield, Virginia.

367. U.S. Department of Transportation. Federal Aviation Administration. *Airframe and Powerplant Mechanics Powerplant Handbook.* Advisory Circular 65–12A. Washington, D.C.: U.S. Government Printing Office, 1976. Pp. ix + 500. Illustr.

Continuously updated, this book is written for the airframe and powerplant mechanic and contains recommended procedures for inspecting, servicing, and overhauling aircraft engines.

368. U.S. Department of Transportation. Federal Aviation Administration. *Airworthiness Standards: Aircraft Engines.* Federal Aviation Regulations, part 33. Washington, D.C.: U.S. Government Printing Office, 1986. Various pagination.

These regulations carry the force of law and are binding on all aviation activities within the purview of the Federal Aviation Administration. These regulations set the standards that are to be met for type certificated engines. This document is continuously updated.

369. U.S. Department of Transportation. Federal Aviation Administration. *Summary of Airworthiness Directives for Small Aircraft, Vol. I; Summary of Airworthiness Directives for Large Aircraft, Vol. II.* Washington, D.C.: U.S. Government Printing Office.

In the case of aircraft, engines, propellers, or parts that the Federal Aviation Administration has certified, but later found

to be unsafe, the FAA issues airworthiness directives, which
require that the deficiency be corrected. Deficiencies and
appropriate corrective action are listed in these volumes.

370. U.S. Department of Transportation. Federal Aviation Adminis-
tration. *Type Certificate Data Sheets and Specifications: Vol.
V, Aircraft Engines and Propellers.* Washington, D.C.: U.S.
Government Printing Office.

The Federal Aviation Administration issues type certificates
for new aircraft models, engine models, and propeller models
when it determines that they meet prescribed safety standards.
Contains specifications for engines and propellers of all types
and models. *Type Certificate Data Sheets and Specifications:
Volume VI, Aircraft Listing and Aircraft and Propeller Listing*
(Washington, D.C.: U.S. Government Printing Office) is a companion volume that contains specifications of older aircraft
models of which 50 or less are in the FAA aircraft registry.

371. U.S. National Advisory Committee for Aeronautics. *Technical
Reports.* Washington, D.C.: U.S. Government Printing Office,
n.d.

The National Advisory Committee for Aeronautics produced
a prodigious number of technical reports from 1915 to 1958 on
aspects of aircraft propulsion. In addition to the formal technical reports, these reports consisted of technical memoranda,
research memoranda, technical notes, and wartime reports.
Collectively, such publications represent an important body of
data that can assist researchers. In addition, most have bibliographies and are well illustrated.
The only complete library of NACA reports that exists is at
NASA Headquarters in Washington, D.C. Requests for assistance in locating NACA reports should be directed to the
Scientific and Technical Library, NASA Headquarters, Washington, D.C. Reproduced copies of some NACA reports can be
purchased from the National Technical Information Service in
Springfield, Virginia.

372. U.S. National Aeronautics and Space Administration. Scientific
and Technical Information Branch. *Technical Reports* and
Technical Notes. Washington, D.C.

Since its establishment in 1958, NASA and its contractors
have produced a number of reports on the technical aspects of

aircraft propulsion. These reports extend the similar body of data on aircraft propulsion developed prior to that time by the National Advisory Committee for Aeronautics.

AERONAUTICAL ENGINEERING

This section of the bibliography differs somewhat from most of the other sections on specific subjects in that it contains both historical works and a large number of technical studies and scientific texts. The goal is to provide the researcher with a rather complete bibliography of materials that treat aerospace engineering from a historical perspective and to combine those studies with a wide enough selection of nonhistorical works to form a solid technical frame of reference. Since this section deals with the history of a technical discipline, it is important to have a good grasp of the technology itself when attempting to put it into historical context.

The historical works in this section consist of biographies of important engineeers and aerodynamicists and studies concerned with aeronautical research, flight testing, and wind tunnels. The balance of the entries are nonhistorical in nature and cover the following topics: aerodynamics, aircraft structures, aircraft design, wing design, and aircraft stability and control. Some of these are recent works, others are quite old. In addition to providing technical and scientific information, these works have historical value as primary sources if taken collectively, since they will allow the researcher to trace the changing state of knowledge in the field over the years.

In addition, information on aeronautical engineering can be found in the vast amount of technical periodical literature in such areas as aerodynamics; aircraft design, testing, and performance; aircraft stability and control; and research and support facilities. For entree into this literature, see *Scientific and Technical Aerospace Reports* (STAR), published by NASA, and *International Aerospace Abstracts* (IAA), published by the American Institute of Aeronautics and Astronautics. STAR and IAA alternate publication twice–monthly and for convenience are indexed with identical subject categories.

Thomas J. Noon
Howard S. Wolko

The Engineers

373. de Havilland, Sir Geoffrey. *Sky Fever; The Autobiography of Sir Geoffrey de Havilland.* Shrewsbury, England: Airlife, 1979. Pp. 239. Index, Bibliog. Illustr.

Sir Geoffrey de Havilland's autobiography portrays the history of one of the most significant British aircraft companies through the people de Havilland met and the events with which he was associated. Presents an inside view of the design and production phases of an airplane. Among the many aircraft covered in this work, de Havilland gives considerable attention to the versatile Mosquito and the Comet.

374. Delear, Frank J. *Igor Sikorsky, His Three Careers in Aviation.* Foreword by James H. Doolittle. New York: Dodd, Mead, 1969. Pp. xi + 272. Illustr.

This entertaining biography portrays Sikorsky as a great humanitarian as well as an aviation pioneer. The "three careers" mentioned in the title refer to the development of the practical helicopter, the multi-engined airplane, and the flying boat. The text is supported with the liberal use of photographs and information supplied by Sikorsky's family and friends. The book's only flaw lies in its tendency to be overly simplistic, especially for those familiar with the aviation industry.

375. Hanle, Paul A. *Bringing Aerodynamics to America.* Cambridge, Mass.: MIT Press, 1982. Pp. xiv + 184. Index, Bibliog., Illustr.

Discusses how Theodore von Kármán's expertise in theoretical aerodynamics contributed to the success and strength of the American aviation industry. Details the transfer of German aeronautical technology to the United States that took place when von Kármán organized a program of aerodynamics at Caltech.

376. Heinemann, Edward H., and Rosario Rausa. *Ed Heinemann, Combat Aircraft Designer.* Annapolis, Md.: Naval Institute, 1980. Pp. xv + 277. Index, Bibliog., Illustr.

A very enjoyable account of Ed Heinemann's contribution to military fighting aircraft during his productive career, which spanned the golden age of aviation. The text is narrated by Heinemann, giving it a personalized style, and his true appreciation for aviation comes through. Describes the events from the design–conception stage of an aircraft to production of the first test prototype.

377. Heinkel, Ernst. *Stormy Life: Memoirs of a Pioneer of the Air Age.* New York: E.P. Dutton, 1956. Pp. 256. Index, Illustr.

Written by one of Germany's leading aircraft designers, this autobiography discusses German aviation in World War I and II and pays particular attention to the reconstruction of the Luftwaffe between the wars. Although Heinkel was politically naive, he offers many insightful comments about the German aircraft industry and its relationship with the technical department of the Luftwaffe.

378. Hooker, Sir Stanley, and Bill Gunston. *Not Much of an Engineer: An Autobiography.* Shrewsbury, England: Airlife, 1984. Pp. iv + 255. Index, Illustr.

A personal book written by a mathematician turned engineer. Sir Stanley Hooker discusses his remarkable career in engine development, which spanned the period from his wartime work with the Merlin engine and his making the Whittle jet engine a production item, to his work with vectored thrust gas turbines that led to feasible VTOL jet flight. The appendixes contain technical information about specific engines and their performance characteristics. An enjoyable read in which technical matters become very clear.

379. Horikoshi, Jiro. *Eagles of Mitsubishi: The Story of the Zero Fighter.* Translated by Shojiro Shindo and Harold N. Wantiez. Seattle: University of Washington Press, 1981. Pp. xi + 160. Index, Bibliog., Illustr.

An autobiography of the aircraft designer responsible for the Type Zero Carrier Based Fighter, which serves as an excellent case study for all phases of the aircraft design process. This nontechnical work utilizes simple aeronautical terminology to discuss technical problems encountered in designing an aircraft and the evolution of solutions to solve them. Although a bit awkward owing to the translation, the work clearly explains the operation of this most effective World War II fighter.

380. Hughes, Thomas P. *Elmer Sperry; Inventor and Engineer.* Baltimore, Md.: Johns Hopkins University Press, 1971. Pp. xvii + 348. Index, Bibliog., Illustr.

A work supported by in–depth research and clarified through the liberal use of photographs and illustrations. An attempt to explain the motives behind Sperry's work, which is highlighted by his invention of the gyroscopic feedback control system. A detailed discussion of how Sperry founded his company, which gave him, at the age of 23, free rein to invent and manufacture his creations. The book is complete with technical discussions of his many inventions, and the appendixes contain Sperry patents, as well as the engineering and scientific papers of Elmer Sperry.

381. Johnson, Clarence L., and Maggie Smith. *Kelly: More than My Share of It All.* Washington D.C.: Smithsonian Institution Press, 1985. Pp. xii + 209. Illustr.

A personal narrative of Clarence L. "Kelly" Johnson's life during which he designed almost every outstanding Lockheed aircraft from the P–38 to the SR–71. Johnson emerged from a childhood of poverty and obscurity to become a leader in aircraft design. Unfortunately, the book does not reveal the internal operations of the "skunk works," but it does explain technical details of the development of his aircraft.

382. Kármán, Theodore von, and Lee Edson. *The Wind and Beyond; Theodore von Kármán, Pioneer in Aviation and Pathfinder in Space.* Boston: Little, Brown, 1967. Pp. iii + 376. Index, Bibliog., Illustr.

Recounts the life of the aerodynamicist whose theories and concepts in aerodynamics and space science have contributed greatly to our knowledge of aeronautics. Also discusses his more industrial involvements, such as his work with Aerojet-General Corporation and AGARD, the aeronautical research arm of NATO.

383. Langley, Samuel Pierpont, and Charles M. Manly. *Langley Memoir on Mechanical Flight.* Smithsonian Contributions to Knowledge, vol. 27, no. 3. Washington D.C.: Smithsonian Institution, 1911. N.p. Illustr.

A report of experimental glider and powered–model testing

performed by Dr. Langley at the turn of the century that led to the design and construction of his full-size, man-carrying "Aerodrome," which was unsuccessfully tested in 1903. Presents a review of available power sources that were best adapted to the requirements of mechanical flight, as well as previously employed aircraft configurations and launching apparatus. Gliders are used as examples in a discussion of aircraft stability.

384.   Morpurgo, J.E. *Barnes Wallis: A Biography*. London: Ian Allen, 1981. Pp. xvi + 400. Index, Bibliog., Illustr.

The English aircraft designer who was responsible for applying geodetics to aircraft construction. His many technological innovations helped to advance developments in aeronautics. He successfully designed the R.80, the R.100, the Wellesley, and the Wellington. His designs also included the very useful bouncing and tallboy bombs. This biography also spans his postwar career, during which his work with tailless aircraft led him to experiment with variable wing span aircraft designs.

385.   Pendray, G. Edward. *The Guggenheim Medalists: Architects of the Age of Flight*. New York: Daniel Guggenheim Medal Board of Award, 1964. Pp. 125. Illustr.

A discussion of Daniel Guggenheim and his great concern for the advancement to aeronautics and flight. Brief biographical essays of Guggenheim Medal recipients are presented. An excellent source of information on the individuals who have made significant contributions to flight.

386.   Rashke, Richard L. *Stormy Genius: The Life of Aviation's Maverick, Bill Lear*. Boston: Houghton Mifflin, 1985. Pp. 401. Index, Bibliog. Illustr.

A financially successful inventor-entrepreneur who held 150 patents, including the direction-finder, the first jet autopilot, and the familiar 8-track tape. Although he did more to make the skies safe for pilots than any other individual, he is best remembered for his corporate jet.

Roseberry, Cecil R. *Glenn Curtiss: Pioneer of Flight*. Garden City, N.Y.: Doubleday, 1972. Pp. x + 514. Index, Bibliog., Illustr.

Cited herein as item 100.

387. Weyl, Alfred R. *Fokker: The Creative Years*. New York: Funk and Wagnalls, 1968. Pp. 420. Index, Illustr.

An excellent explanation of pre–World War I European aircraft design and construction techniques that also includes many of Fokker's wartime efforts. Extensively researched, but unfortunately no bibliographical sources are cited.

388. Whittle, Sir Frank. *Jet, the Story of a Pioneer*. New York: Philosophical Library, 1954. Pp. 320. Index, Illustr.

A nontechnical autobiography that is predominantly concerned with the period in Sir Frank Whittle's professional career when he was most involved in the development of the turbojet engine. Provides an inside view of the operation of Power Jets Limited, and Whittle's bureaucratic fight to gain support for his work.

389. Wolko, Howard S. *In the Cause of Flight: Technologists of Aeronautics and Astronautics*. Smithsonian Studies in Air and Space, no. 4. Washington, D.C.: Smithsonian Institution Press, 1981. Pp. iii + 121. Index, Bibliog., Illustr.

Provides biographic material, arranged in chronological order, on 129 engineers and scientists who made prominent contributions to the technology of flight. These biographic sketches are accompanied by clear and concise surveys of the various fields within aviation technology. An excellent reference.

390. Yakovlev, Alexander S. *Notes of an Aircraft Designer*. New York: Arno, 1972. Pp. 273. Illustr.

Although propagandistic in nature, this work is informative on the emergence of the Soviet aircraft industry and one of its leading aircraft designers, Alexander Yakovlev. Soviet aircraft design techniques during World War II are also discussed.

391.   Zahm, Albert F. *Aeronautical Papers, 1885–1945.* 2 vols. Notre
        Dame, Ind.: University of Notre Dame, 1950. Pp. xi + 1001.
        Bibliog., Illustr.

        This chronological presentation of Dr. Zahm's published
        work includes his technical papers as well as narratives of
        early aeronautical events. Although this collection of reports
        provides historical insight into the technological achievements
        of early aeronautics, the reader must recognize that Zahm did
        not always express an objective point of view. The reports
        contain a wealth of technical information concerning a full
        range of topics.

Aerodynamics

392.   Allen, John E. *Aerodynamics, the Science of Air in Motion.*
        New York: McGraw–Hill, 1982. Pp. viii + 205. Index, Bib-
        liog., Illustr.

        Provides a clear analysis of the common patterns of air
        motion (boundary layers, vortices, wakes, and shock waves)
        and of the physical characteristics of airflows, such as
        viscosity, compressibility, and thermal conductivity. Presents
        applications of aerodynamics by nature and man in their
        historical context. Although mathematical formulas are used,
        this work should be considered nontechnical.

393.   Anderson, John D. *Introduction to Flight.* New York: McGraw–
        Hill, 1985. Pp. xvi + 560. Index, Bibliog., Illustr.

        An elementary text on aerodynamics suitable for a first
        course for engineers. Contains many interesting historical
        notes. Sample problems illustrate application of equation to
        propeller–driven and jet aircraft. Recommended reading.

394.   Durand, William F. *Aerodynamic Theory, a General Review of
        Progress.* 6 vols. New York: Dover, 1963. Bibliog., Illustr.

        An excellent treatment of the history of aerodynamics.
        Provides an insight and chronology of events for the nontech-
        nical reader.

395. Kármán, Theodore von. *Aerodynamics*. New York: McGraw–Hill, 1963. Pp. ix + 203. Illustr.

A nontechnical discussion of aerodynamics by one of the world's outstanding aerodynamicists. von Kármán's easy writing style is indicative of his greatness as a researcher and teacher.

396. Millikan, Clark B. *Aerodynamics of the Airplane*. New York: John Wiley and Sons, 1941. Pp. xi + 171. Illustr.

A very understandable treatment of elementary aerodynamics. Intended as a reference volume to be used by nonengineers familiar only with the elements of mechanics and having limited mathematical experience.

397. *NACA Annual Reports, 1915–1958*. Washington, D.C.: U.S. Government Printing Office. Annual. Illustr.

An authoritative treatment of aeronautical progress in the United States from 1915 to 1958. Technical reports are for the practicing engineer, but introductory section of each annual report summarizes progress on a year–by–year basis. Individual articles contain bibliographic references.

398. Perkins, Courtland D., and Robert E. Hage. *Airplane Performance, Stability and Control*. New York: John Wiley and Sons, 1949. Pp. vii + 493. Bibliog., Illustr.

Intended to meet the needs of the practicing engineer in the late 1940s. It is divided into two parts; the first deals with the problems of airplane design for performance, and the second, with airplane design for flying qualities.

399. Shevell, Richard S. *Fundamentals of Flight*. Englewood Cliffs, N.J.: Prentice–Hall, 1983. Pp. xxiv + 405. Index, Bibliog., Illustr.

An introduction to the essential elements of aeronautics that serves to illustrate the relationship between pure theory and the practical use of aerodynamic principles. To fully derive the intended benefits from the text, one needs to be technically inclined. The work presents a brief history of aeronautics that relates to the more functional information, which includes aerodynamic forces, compressible flow, aircraft structures and propulsion systems, performance estimation, and aircraft stability.

400. Von Mises, Richard. *Theory of Flight.* New York: Dover, 1959. Pp. 629. Illustr.

An excellent treatment of aerodynamics for the advanced student. Requires a facility with mathematics.

Structures

401. Langley, Marcus. *Metal Aircraft Construction.* Rev. ed. London: Sir Isaac Pitman and Sons, 1941. Pp. viii + 443. Illustr.

Provides a chronology of progress in metal construction up to the early 1940s. Contains many illustrations of structural details. The treatment is distinctly international as a result of the cooperative arrangements made with industry.

402. Niles, Alfred S., and Joseph S. Newell. *Airplane Structures.* New York: John Wiley and Sons, 1929. Pp. xi + 413. Bibliog., Illustr.

An excellent engineering text that describes the fundamentals of structures and their application to practical aircraft design. Written in 1929 and therefore somewhat limited in application. An excellent example of a late–1920s structures text.

403. Pippard, Alfred J.S., and J. Laurence Pritchard. *Aeroplane Structure.* London: Longmans, Green, 1919. Pp. xii + 359. Index, Illustr.

Intended primarily for use by British airplane designers. Reflects the authors' experience during World War I supervising experimental designs, from the standpoint of structural design and stress analysis.

404. Sechler, Ernest E., and Louis G. Dunn. *Airplane Structural Analysis and Design.* New York: John Wiley and Sons, 1942. Pp. xi + 412. Index, Illustr.

Written in 1942, this work is an advanced text on aircraft structures with emphasis on design. Text requires a competence in mathematics. In its day, an excellent textbook for engineering students.

405.   Titterton, George F. *Aircraft Materials and Processes*. New York: Pitman, 1941. Pp. xv + 340. Index, Illustr.

A practical text on aircraft materials of interest to technically inclined or trained readers.

Aircraft Design

406.   Blyth, John D. *Practical Performance Prediction of Aircraft*. London: Sir Isaac Pitman and Sons, 1935. Pp. xii + 80. Bibliog., Illustr.

Using mild technical treatment, this work presents aerodynamic calculations and methods for predicting the overall performance of the airplane. Also discusses performance characteristics of the propeller and engine. Provides insight into the engineering methods commonly used in the 1930s.

407.   Brimm, Daniel J. *Airplanes and Elementary Engineering*. Scranton, Pa.: International Textbook, 1939. Pp. v + 70. Illustr.

An excellent introductory source for a study of aeronautics and the basic physical principles of aerodynamics that is old but not dated. The strongest feature of the text is its very clear identification of the aircraft and its parts with definitions of commonly used nomenclature. Discusses aircraft configurations and constructions techniques of the period. This work, along with Anderson's *Introduction to Flight* (cited herein as item 393), is recommended for an introductory study of aeronautics.

408.   Burke, James D. *The Gossamer Condor and Albatross: A Case Study in Aircraft Design*. Pasadena, Calif.: AeroVironment, 1980. Various pagination. Bibliog., Illustr.

This account of the design and flight testing of two human-powered aircraft is predominantly concerned with the final

stages of the aircraft design process. Reviews the performance of· these aircraft from the initial flight tests to the
historic human–powered English Channel crossing. Presents
structural materials and instrumentation used in the final
configurations. The appendix contains an excellent set of
detailed drawings.

Combs, Harry, and Martin Caidin. *Kill Devil Hill: Discovering
the Secret of the Wright Brothers.* Boston: Houghton Mifflin,
1979. Pp. xx + 389. Index, Bibliog., Illustr.

Cited herein as item 74.

409.   Heinemann, Edward H., Rosario Rausa, and Kermit E. Van
Every. *Aircraft Design.* Annapolis, Md.: Nautical and
Aviation Publishing, 1985. Pp. xvi + 130. Index, Illustr.

An introduction to aircraft design that provides a sound
explanation of basic aerodynamic concepts. Elucidates the
design process from the initial conceptual phase to flight
controls and aircraft stability. Utilizes the design of an attack
trainer in a brief case study. The author has given the reader a
sound work that can be used as a basis for a more in–depth
study of the subject.

410.   Judge, Arthur W. *The Design of Aeroplanes.* London:
Whittaker, 1916. Pp. viii + 212. Bibliog., Illustr.

Written in 1916, this book presents a treatment of aircraft
structures as practiced in England. The book was written for
designers, draftsman, and students entering the field of
aeronautics.

411.   Lanchester, Frederick W. *The Flying Machine from an Engineering Standpoint.* London: Constable, 1916. Pp. viii + 135.
Illustr.

A reprint of the notable "James Forrest Lecture," presented
to the Institution of Civil Engineers in 1914, which epitomized
the state of scientific and technical aeronautical knowledge at
the time. Since this lecture was given three months before the
beginning of World War I, it represents the state of the art in
aeronautics and aircraft design before the technical revolution
in the aviation industry that took place during the war.

412. Nicolai, Leland M. *Fundamentals of Aircraft Design.* Dayton, Ohio: University of Dayton, School of Engineering, 1975. Pp. xvii + 523. Bibliog., Illustr.

A comprehensive technical treatment ranging from the conceptual design phase of an aircraft to the iterative process that serves to finalize a design. This text realistically represents the compromise of all the engineering disciplines involved in the aircraft design process.

413. Owens, Albert A., and Ben F. Slingluff. *How to Read Aircraft Blueprints.* Philadelphia, Pa.: John C. Winston, 1940. Pp. 257. Illustr.

An extensive study of blueprints common to the field of aviation. The work utilizes actual blueprints of aircraft that range from very simple drawings to highly technical diagrams. An excellent opportunity for aerospace engineering students to coordinate an academic and a practical knowledge of aircraft construction techniques.

414. Parkinson, Harold. *Examples and Charts for Aircraft Draughtsmen.* London: Sir Isaac Pitman and Sons, 1939. Pp. viii + 56. Bibliog., Illustr.

Excellent for an engineer who cannot draft, as it presents the essentials of detail design. Illustrates pre–World War II techniques in the design of aircraft structures. Many realistic examples support the analytical discussion persuading the reader to realize that practical considerations preclude theoretical requirements.

415. Steiner, J.E., American Institute of Aeronautics and Astronautics, and the Boeing Company. *Case Study in Aircraft Design, the Boeing 727.* New York: AIAA, 1978. Pp. 72. Illustr.

A sound engineering case study, especially with regard to functional aerodynamics, the aircraft design process, and flight testing. The work is directed toward those beginning to study aircraft design.

416. Stinton, Darrol. *The Anatomy of the Aeroplane.* New York: Granada, 1980. Pp. xxiii + 321. Index, Bibliog., Illustr.

A comprehensive aircraft design text that clarifies how aeronautical principles are applied to the construction of airplanes and reinforces the notion that the final aerodynamic and structural configuration of an aircraft is a function of the requirements that it is designed to satisfy. This nontechnical work covers a full range of flight envelopes, from low subsonic to supersonic, using the most elementary of mathematical formulas.

417.   Stinton, Darrol. *The Design of the Airplane*. New York: Van Nostrand Reinhold, 1983. Pp. xxix + 642. Index, Bibliog., Illustr.

A step–by–step approach to the design of single–pilot aircraft. The functional aspect of aircraft design is balanced with the theoretical. Well supported by examples of successfully designed aircraft that thoroughly cover aerodynamics, performance, and aircraft stability.

418.   Wolko, Howard S., ed. *The Wright Flyer: An Engineering Perspective*. Proceedings of a Symposium Held at the National Air and Space Museum, December 16, 1983. Washington D.C.: Smithsonian Institution Press, 1986. Pp. ix + 106. Illustr.

A successful attempt to understand the fundamental technological achievements embodied in the design and construction of the 1903 Wright Flyer. Five distinguished engineers contributed to the proceedings of a symposium held at the National Air and Space Museum to explore the specific elements of the aerodynamic, structural, and powerplant technology utilized by Wilbur and Orville Wright. The first detailed analytical account of the Wrights' achievement to take full advantage of current engineering knowledge.

Research in Aeronautics/Flight Testing/Wind Tunnels

419.   Anderton, David A. *Sixty Years of Aeronautical Research, 1917–1977*. Washington D.C.: National Aeronautics and Space Administration, 1978. Pp. 89. Illustr.

Although this work tends to glorify the National Advisory Committee for Aeronautics, it is a terse chronological history of the founding, development, and growth of the NACA Langley Research Center and its transition into the space age as one of the many research centers under the control of NASA.

420.   Baals, Donald D., and William R. Corliss. *Wind Tunnels of NASA*. Washington D.C.: National Aeronautics and Space Administration, Scientific and Technical Information Branch, 1981. Pp. 154. Index, Illustr.

Presents, in layman's terms, an early history of wind tunnels and their development and explains many of the latest technological achievements gained through wind tunnel testing. Describes the contributions of the many NASA research facilities to the science of flight. Through the liberal use of photographs provides much insight into wind tunnel operation. A comprehensive source that also discusses tunnel instrumentation.

421.   Burnet, Charles. *Three Centuries to Concorde*. London: Mechanical Engineering Publications, 1979. Pp. xii + 276. Index, Illustr.

An excellent if biased account of the events leading up to and beyond the advent of supersonic flight, told from a strongly British perspective. While Burnet is perceptive on the British story, he gives short shrift to the development of the Bell X-1, the first aircraft to fly faster than the speed of sound and to Aerospatiale and Société Nationale d'Etude et de Construction de Moteurs d'Aviation, the French participants in the Concorde project. Should be read in conjunction with Richard P. Hallion's *Supersonic Flight; The Story of the Bell X-1 and Douglas D-558* (cited herein as item 424).

422.   Gorlin, Samuil M., Isaak I. Slezinger, and NASA. *Wind Tunnels and Their Instrumentation*. Jerusalem: Israel Program for Scientific Translations, 1966. Pp. v + 592. Bibliog., Illustr.

A technical discussion, translated from Russian, complete with clear illustrations and diagrams. Reviews commonly used modern measuring techniques for wind tunnel instrumentation. The most important aspect of this work is that it explains how aerodynamic theory has developed from available experimental wind tunnel data. Intended for those familiar with the design and research results of wind tunnels.

423.   Gray, George W. *Frontiers of Flight: The Story of NACA Research*. New York: Alfred A. Knopf, 1948. Pp. ix + 362. Index, Illustr.

A review of the activities and significant results of the entire NACA scientific research program that supported developmental and technical advancements in aeronautics. Uses elementary terminology to clarify technical matters while adding historical perspective to NACA's work.

424.   Hallion, Richard P. *Supersonic Flight; The Story of the Bell X-1 and Douglas D-558*. New York: Macmillan, 1972. Pp. xxii + 248. Index, Bibliog., Illustr.

Covers two supersonic flight testing programs from the earliest studies of compressibility to the retirement of the X-1 in 1958. Repeatedly offers effective technical explanations of aerodynamic phenomena, while discussing contributions of individuals within the aeronautical engineering community and aircraft industry.

425.   Hallion, Richard P. *Test Pilots: The Frontiersmen of Flight*. Garden City, N.Y.: Doubleday, 1981. Pp. xii + 347. Index, Bibliog., Illustr.

An extensively researched and comprehensive history of flight research and flight testing from the earliest beginnings of powered flight to modern aviation. Through the many participants in various flight testing activities, the author illustrates the qualifications, attributes, and distinctive qualities that make up a successful flight researcher. The treatment of pre-NACA flight research programs is not as extensive as that in the rest of the text. A notable quality of this work is that it appropriately credits the achievements of the aircraft designers and engineers.

426.   Hallion, Richard P. *On the Frontier: Flight Research at Dryden, 1946-1981*. Washington D.C.: National Aeronautics and Space Administration, Scientific and Technical Information Branch, 1984. Pp. xix + 385. Index, Bibliog., Illustr.

A history of Dryden Flight Research Center that serves as a chronicle of supersonic flight research efforts. The book uses aeronautical terminology and is suitable for a reader without a technical background. After a comprehensive narrative on the

The X-15 #1, a rocket-powered research aircraft built by North American Aviation, is launched from a Boeing B-52 Stratofortress. The X-15, which could fly six times faster than the speed of sound, bridged the gap between manned flight in the atmosphere and beyond.

"X–series" of experimental aircraft and their achievements, the work proceeds with a discussion of research at Dryden that benefited NASA's space program. The appendixes (over one-quarter of the book) contain an excellent chronology of experimental flights at Dryden.

427. Hartman, Edwin P. *Adventures in Research; A History of Ames Research Center, 1940–1965.* Washington D.C.: National Aeronautics and Space Administration, Scientific and Technical Information Division, 1970. Pp. xviii + 555. Bibliog., Illustr.

An account of the establishment, evolutionary development, and activities of Ames Research Center that covers a period characterized by unprecedented scientific and technological revolution. Does not concentrate on peripheral subjects such as Ames Research Center's involvement with NASA or other research centers, but focuses on discussions of specific tests Ames carried out.

428. Hunsaker, Jerome C., et al. *Reports on Wind Tunnel Experiments in Aerodynamics.* Smithsonian Institution Miscellaneous Collections, vol. 62, no. 4. Washington D.C.: Smithsonian Institution, 1916. Pp. iii + 92. Illustr.

A report of wind tunnel construction, operation, and instrumentation that represents the advanced state of technical knowledge of the period. Included is an excellent presentation of experimentation with swept wings and an investigation into the effect of dihedral on a wing structure.

429. Hunsaker, Jerome C. *Aeronautics at the Mid–Century.* New Haven, Conn.: Yale University Press, 1952. Pp. ix + 116. Illustr.

Based on a lecture given in 1951 by the author, this work discusses the state of technology from which the Wright brothers' invention arose and outlines the subsequent development of aircraft. Describes the state of the art of aeronautics, principally as it applies to air transportation, with some speculation about apparent limitations and where evident trends may lead. Finally, examines the impact of both civil and military aeronautics on our society.

430. Langley Research Center. *Research in Aeronautics and Space.*
Rev. ed. Hampton, Va.: National Aeronautics and Space Administration, 1971. Pp. xv + 350. Illustr.

A nontechnical and general description of the aerospace
research programs and flight projects of the NASA Langley
Research Center. The program descriptions range from subsonic and supersonic flight to space systems. A commentary on
the corresponding electronics support is provided.

431. Miller, Ronald E., and David Sawers. *The Technical Development of Modern Aviation.* London: Routledge and Kegan
Paul, 1968. Pp. xvi + 351. Bibliog., Illustr.

Predominantly concerned with civilian aviation, the work
explains how inventions and innovations have entered into the
evolutionary process of technical change. Although the work
tends to digress in places, it effectively details the improvement of the airplane from its earliest days through to the jet
age of the 1960s.

432. Muenger, Elizabeth A. *Searching the Horizon: A History of the
Ames Research Center, 1940–1976.* Washington, D.C.:
National Aeronautics and Space Administration, Scientific
and Technical Information Branch, 1985. Pp. xiii + 299.
Index, Bibliog., Illustr.

A comprehensive overview of an important aerospace
research center. The author takes a broad approach that does
not get bogged down in technical detail and provides a strong
analysis of how personalities, management philosophies,
economics, politics, and military needs affected the research
goals and accomplishments of Ames during the period under
consideration. Well-researched and documented appendixes
and chronologies.

433. Pope, Alan. *Wind-Tunnel Testing.* New York: Wiley, 1947. Pp.
xi + 319. Illustr.

A thorough technical treatment that embraces wind tunnel
design, operations and testing procedures, and data correc-
tions. An excellent accompaniment to laboratory work. For a
more comprehensive treatment, the author later divided this
work into two textbooks: *Low-Speed Wind Tunnel Testing* and
High-Speed Wind Tunnel Testing.

434.   Randers–Pehrson, Nils H. *Pioneer Wind Tunnels*. Smithsonian Miscellaneous Collections, vol. 93, no. 4. Washington D.C.: Smithsonian Institution, 1935. Pp. 20. Bibliog., Illustr.

A short discussion of wind tunnels built between 1871 and 1909. Contains diagrams and photographs that illustrate their configuration and their accompanying instruments. Unfortunately, the author does not present a sufficiently detailed report of these early wind tunnels, perhaps because of the lack of documentation.

435.   Shortal, Joseph A. *A New Dimension: Wallops Island Flight Test Range, The First Fifteen Years*. Washington, D.C.: National Aeronautics and Space Administration, Scientific and Technical Information Office, 1978. Pp. xv + 774. Index, Bibliog., Illustr.

Describes the wide array of activities, tasks, projects, and experiments that have to do with the evolution and testing of aerospace technology from 1945 to 1960. A sound reference source for many of the obscure programs at Wallops Island. Using little technical jargon, Shortal gives the reader a clear view of the organization and operation of the facilities at this research and test center.

436.   Walker, Lois E., and Shelby E. Wickam. *From Huffman Prairie to the Moon: The History of Wright–Patterson Air Force Base*. Wright–Patterson Air Force Base, Ohio: Air Force Logistics Command, 1987. Pp. 496. Index, Bibliog., Illustr.

Detailed overview of the development of Wright–Patterson Air Force Base from the earliest activities of the Wright brothers to the present day. Although not very analytical, the book is an excellent reference to names, dates, organizational changes, events, and institutional developments. Profusely illustrated.

437.   Willmore, A.P., and S.R. Willmore. *Aerospace Research Index: A Guide to World Research in Aeronautics, Meteorology, Astronomy, and Space Science*. Harlow, England: F. Hodgson, 1981. Pp. 597. Index.

Provides details of establishments that conduct or promote research. Includes universities, government laboratories, public corporations, industrial firms, and research associations. Indexes facilities in over 70 countries.

Wing Design

438. Abbott, Ira H., and Albert E. von Doenhoff. *Theory of Wing Sections, including a Summary of Airfoil Data.* New York: Dover, 1959. Pp. x + 693. Illustr.

   An excellent reference for engineers that requires knowledge of calculus and mechanics. Presents theoretical and experimental results of research on the aerodynamics of wing sections. The appendixes, which comprise over half the book, contain NACA data pertaining to the aerodynamic characteristics of modern NACA wind sections.

439. American Institute of Aeronautics and Astronautics, Air Force Museum, and the University of Dayton. *The Evolution of Aircraft Wing Design.* Dayton, Ohio, 1980. Pp. vi + 154. Bibliog., Illustr.

   Does not discuss the process of designing a wing, but is strictly a chronological history of permutations in wing configurations. The informative text ranges from descriptions of the gliders of the 19th century to the supersonic configurations of the 20th. Swept, delta–arrow, and variable geometry wings are included in a discussion of state–of–the–art wing technology.

440. Lennon, Andy. *Canard: A Revolution in Flight.* Hummelstown, Pa.: Aviation, 1984. Pp. 200. Bibliog., Illustr.

   This work serves as a record of aircraft that have utilized the canard wing concept. The author stresses that Burt Rutan and success with the canard design (initiated by his search for inherent stall avoidance) provided the major breakthrough for the acceptance of the canard. Discusses design concerns, but without in–depth coverage of technicalities. The aviation enthusiast will find many of the accounts in the volume very interesting.

441. Lippisch, Alexander. *The Delta Wing: History and Development.* Translated by Gertrude L. Lippisch. Ames: Iowa State University Press, 1981. Pp. x + 126. Index, Bibliog., Illustr.

   This account of the author's more than 60 years of work with aircraft presents a concise technological history of delta wing development. The author's research dates back to 1903, when the concept of tailless aircraft originated. Detailed technical information pertaining to airfoils is contained in the appendix. The text outlines many aircraft designs that have utilized the delta wing.

442.   Wooldridge, E.T. *Winged Wonders: The Story of the Flying Wings*. Washington D.C.: Smithsonian Institution Press, 1983. Pp. xiv + 230. Index, Bibliog., Illustr.

A well-researched and extensively illustrated work that traces the development of tailless aircraft. Concentrates on John K. Northrop's ambitious attempts to achieve success with his flying wing design. The appendixes document the restoration of the Northrop N-1M by the National Air and Space Museum.

Aircraft Stability and Control

443.   Etkin, Bernard. *Dynamics of Atmospheric Flight*. New York: Wiley, 1972. Pp. xii + 579. Index, Bibliog., Illustr.

A very technical treatment of the subject that requires a prior knowledge of differential equations and aerodynamic theory. Discusses unsteady motion and stability characteristics in the longitudinal and lateral modes. The work offers an in-depth presentation of aircraft handling qualities, human factors in piloting an aircraft, and flight in turbulent atmosphere.

444.   McRuer, Duane T., Irving L. Ashkenas, and Dunstan Graham. *Aircraft Dynamics and Automatic Control*. Princeton, N.J. : Princeton University Press, 1973. Pp. xxv + 784. Index, Bibliog., Illustr.

A thorough, technical treatment of aircraft dynamics and flight control systems written by and for engineers. Presents the early history of aircraft dynamics and flight control along with a genealogy of automatic flight control systems. Covers equations of dynamic motion and feedback control systems. The appendixes contain stability derivatives for representative aircraft.

445.   Pallett, E.H.J. *Automatic Flight Control.* New York: Granada, 1983. Pp. ix + 286. Index, Illustr.

A clear, nontechnical text for a reader at the introductory level that instills a basic understanding of flight principles and aircraft stability. An evolution of automatic flight control systems is presented and a very convincing discussion is developed through the use of actual equipment.

MILITARY AVIATION

The theme of air power, or more broadly, military aviation, occupies an important place in aeronautical history. Representative titles contained in this section cover this historical area from an international perspective and deal with a variety of topics—key events, personalities, air force traditions, air power theories, and military campaigns.

The historiography of military aviation has been uneven, and, until recently, very few scholarly works have been published. Although military aviation has made a profound impact on the course of 20th-century history, in particular on the history of World War II, the number of specialists who conduct research and write in the field has been slow to expand. Before World War II, a body of literature arose, polemical in character, which dealt with the perceived threat of air power. Also, many popular books were written about famous aviators, the Army Air Service and Air Corps, and pivotal events. Few substantial histories have been written by independent scholars.

After World War II, the study of military aviation became more systematic, with careful attention to institutions and doctrinal factors, as well as traditional themes. This same scholarly interest, however, was limited for many years by security clearance barriers. The Department of Defense's decision in the 1970s to declassify many official records and documents has stimulated a considerable amount of historical research and writing. Coincidentally, the retirement of military aviators of various nations provided the occasion for the production of a rich body of memoirs and unit histories. Finally, institutional histories, prepared by various air forces, have been a welcome addition to the historical literature in the field.

Certain major references are available to guide the researcher working in the area of American military aviation. *A Guide to the Sources of U.S. Military History* (Hamden, Conn.: Archon, 1975), edited by Robin Higham, contains an excellent section on military aviation titled "The U.S. Army Air Corps and the United States Air Force, 1909–1973," by Robert F. Futrell. Myron J. Smith's comprehensive six–volume *Air War Bibliography, 1939–1945*, English Language Sources (Manhattan, Kans.: Aerospace Historian, 1977), provides an extensive list of titles on such topics as air power in the

European, Mediterranean, and Pacific theaters of operation; strategy and tactics; the air forces; and the aircraft of World War II.

Von D. Hardesty
Dorothy S. Cochrane
Peter L. Jakab
F. Robert van der Linden
Robert F. Dreesen
Barbara J. Irwin
Dominick A. Pisano

This Supermarine Spitfire Mk. VII, now in the collection of the National Air and Space Museum, is shown en route to its delivery to the U.S. Army Air Forces in May 1943. The agile Spitfire, flown by the Royal Air Force, was one of the most celebrated fighter aircraft of World War II. (SI Photo 866483)

446. Allen, H.R. *The Legacy of Lord Trenchard.* London: Cassell, 1972. Pp. xi + 228. Index, Bibliog.

Allen, a fighter pilot during World War II, retired from the Royal Air Force in order to write this controversial book. He attempts to present a cost–effective evaluation of the RAF's strategic air defense and prove that Trenchard's military philosophy of bombing large cities instead of smaller, specific installations was not only misguided, but also extremely detrimental to the RAF Bomber Command. Allen also states that the continuation of the Trenchard legacy will be harmful to future RAF policy and presents his own alternate philosophy.

447. Arnold, Henry H. *Global Mission.* New York: Harper and Brothers, 1949. Pp. xii + 626. Index, Illustr.

Provides an overview of military aviation from its genesis to 1949. Dealing with the turbulent events of this epoch from his own perspective, H.H. "Hap" Arnold, commander of the U.S. Army Air Forces in World War II, recounts his impressions of events and personalities with candor. Arnold ends the book with warnings about the Soviet Union and the danger of the Cold War, then taking shape.

448. Boyle, Andrew. *Trenchard: Man of Vision.* London: Collins, 1962. Pp. 768. Index, Bibliog., Illustr.

A detailed, thorough biography of Lord Hugh Montague Trenchard, the main instigator of the Royal Air Force. The book follows Trenchard's early years as a soldier in the Boer War, his relatively late metamorphosis to a pilot of the Royal Flying Corps in 1912 at the age of 40, through to his role in the development of the RAF. Good photos.

449. Broughton, Jack. *Thud Ridge.* Philadelphia: Lipincott, 1969. Pp. 254. Illustr.

A firsthand account of the Air Force's air war over North Vietnam by a senior F–105 pilot. The author's opinions are plainly stated, and the view he gives of the Rolling Thunder bombing offensive is valuable, whether one agrees with it or not.

450. Brown, David. *Carrier Operations in World War II.* Vol. 1. *The*

Royal Navy. Annapolis, Md.: Naval Institute, 1974. Pp. 160. Index, Illustr.

Recounts in a matter–of–fact way the operations of the British aircraft carriers during the period September 1939 to May 1945 and the events that necessitated the expansion of the Fleet Air Arm from a small striking force to a powerful strategic weapon. Specific aircraft and their weapons systems are discussed in relation to the missions they served in and how well they met the mission requirements. The appendixes present a brief examination of the evolution of British carriers from World War I to the present, as well as an index of British carriers from World War II.

451.   Brown, David. *Carrier Operations in World War II*. Vol. 2. *The Pacific Navies, December 1941–February 1943*. Annapolis, Md.: Naval Institute, 1974. Pp. 152. Index, Illustr.

Utilizing the same effective literary style as Volume 1, this work presents a description of the events that occurred between the attack on Pearl Harbor and the battle of Guadalcanal. Since the heavy aircrew losses incurred by the Japanese made Guadalcanal the last major attempt by the Imperial Japanese Naval Carrier Force to contest American amphibious operations for almost 20 months, the scope of this presentation ends in February 1943.

452.   Bueschel, Richard M. *Communist Chinese Air Power*. New York: Frederick A. Praeger, 1968. Pp. 238. Index, Bibliog., Illustr.

Virtually the only book on the subject, Bueschel's study is an admirable presentation of the short history of Communist Chinese military aviation and its reliance on foreign aircraft from the revolution to the war in Vietnam. Part 1 covers the history, beginning with 1923, and continues to the mid–1960s. Part 2 contains an alphabetical listing of aircraft utilized over the years. Includes 16 pages of photographs.

453.   Chennault, Claire L. *Way of a Fighter: The Memoirs of Claire Lee Chennault*. Edited by Robert Hotz. New York: G.P. Putnam's Sons, 1949. Pp. xxii + 375. Index, Illustr.

A personal account of the turmoil in China from 1937 to 1945 as witnessed by Chennault, pioneer air fighter tactician.

Chennault first advised the Chinese air force and later commanded the celebrated American Volunteer Group ("Flying Tigers"), and, finally, the American air forces in China. Despite his bombastic style, Chennault offers valuable insights into the China–Burma–India theater in World War II.

454. Clostermann, Pierre. *The Big Show: Some Experiences of a French Fighter Pilot in the R.A.F.* Translated by Oliver Berthoud. Foreword by Sir John Slessor. London: Chatto and Windus, 1958. Pp. 256. Illustr.

Personal account of the air war in Europe by a French officer who fought for the RAF and became a top-scoring Allied fighter pilot. The author had extensive combat experience from Dieppe onward. One of the best such accounts in terms of its literary merit.

455. Clostermann, Pierre. *Flames in the Sky*. Translated by Oliver Berthoud. London: Chatto and Windus, 1969. Pp. 199.

A further memoir from Clostermann on his experiences as a combat-seasoned World War II fighter pilot. Contains a series of narrative descriptions of various exemplary or critical air engagements of World War II (e.g., the attacks on the Meuse bridges in May of 1940, Pearl Harbor, the last large-scale Kamikaze attacks). Though not footnoted, this is extremely well written and offers operational insights not available elsewhere.

456. Collier, Basil. *A History of Air Power*. New York: Macmillan, 1974. Pp. 358. Index, Bibliog., Illustr.

Good general survey. The direction of the book is weighted toward the British experience, although the author does address most of the key questions concerning the story of airpower. Most of the material is drawn from secondary sources.

457. Cooper, Matthew. *The German Air Force, 1933–1945: An Anatomy of Failure*. London: Jane's, 1981. Pp. v + 406. Index, Bibliog., Illustr.

Well-written history that concentrates on the strategic development of the German Air Force. The author makes the bold assertion that the Luftwaffe was doomed to fail from the outset of World War II because of poor decisions made during its inception and expansion. Deliberately ignores the accomplishments of individual pilots and units, as these stories have been well documented elsewhere.

458. Copp, DeWitt S. *A Few Great Captains: The Men and Events that Shaped the Development of U.S. Air Power.* Garden City, N.Y.: Doubleday, 1980. Pp. xix + 531. Index, Bibliog., Illustr.

An insightful book that follows the development of U.S. air power between World War I and World War II by focusing on the careers of four major players in that development: Henry H. "Hap" Arnold, Frank M. Andrews, Carl Spaatz, and Ira C. Eaker. A key book for understanding the interwar years of the Air Force.

459. Copp, DeWitt S. *Forged in Fire: Strategy and Decisions in the Air War over Europe, 1940–1945.* Garden City, N.Y.: Doubleday, 1982. Pp. xvi + 531. Index, Bibliog., Illustr.

Excellent sequel to Copp's early work, *A Few Great Captains*, this book traces the story of those important American figures through their trials and triumphs in World War II. Unlike the previous volume, this work contains footnotes.

460. Craven, Wesley F., and James L. Cate, eds. *The Army Air Forces in World War II.* 7 vols. Chicago: University of Chicago Press, 1948–1958. Index, Illustr.

Prepared as an official seven-volume history of the U.S. Army Air Forces. Reflects perspective of wartime commanders on the role of air power, including the efficacy of strategic bombing. Subsequent historiography has either elaborated or revised aspects of this comprehensive multi-volume history. The approach of Craven and Cate is both chronological (European and Pacific theaters) and topical (e.g., doctrinal and logistical themes). The series remains an authoritative reference work.

Devlin, Gerard M. *Silent Wings: The Saga of U.S. Army and Marine Combat Glider Pilots during World War II.* New York: St. Martin's, 1985. Pp. xxii + 410. Index, Bibliog., Illustr.

Cited herein as item 635.

461. Emme, Eugene M. *The Impact of Air Power: National Security and World Politics.* Princeton, N.J.: Van Nostrand, 1959. Pp. xiv + 914. Index, Bibliog.

Provides coverage of the impact of air power in the 20th century through the 1950s. The large anthology contains a wealth of entries, including the writings of such diverse figures as Douhet, Goering, Churchill, Lindbergh, Zhukov, Doolittle, and Kissinger. Covers the broad development of air power, along with the early years of aerospace activities. Many entries, especially the post–1945 materials, touch on strategies and national security themes.

462. Flammer, Philip M. *The Vivid Air: The Lafayette Escadrille.* Athens: University of Georgia Press, 1981. Pp. xiv + 249. Index, Bibliog., Illustr.

Deals with the legendary Lafayette Escadrille, but from a detached historical perspective. The author endeavors to tell the story of the squadron without repeating the many myths that have arisen, and occasionally with gripping descriptions of the horror, fear, and fatigue of World War I aviation. Final chapter in the book covers the historical legacy of the squadron in France and the United States.

463. Foulois, Benjamin D., with C.V. Glines. *From the Wright Brothers to the Astronauts: The Memoirs of Major General Benjamin D. Foulois.* New York: McGraw–Hill, 1968. Pp. xi + 306. Index.

The history of the Air Force from its inception until the middle 1930s, as well as the biography of the Army's first aviator. Benny Foulois flew with Orville Wright for the Army's first aircraft acceptance flight in 1909 and retired as chief of the Air Corps in 1935. His personal story documents the problems and triumphs, the heroes and the villains, and the growth of the U.S. Air Force. An outspoken record of the formative period, this book is a necessity for studying U.S. military aviation.

464. Fredette, Raymond H. *The Sky on Fire: The First Battle of Britain, 1917–1918, and the Birth of the Royal Air Force.* New York: Holt, Rinehart and Winston, 1966. Pp. xxiii + 289. Index, Bibliog., Illustr.

Good treatment of the pioneering long–range bombing raids conducted by Germany against England during World War I. In addition to discussing their operational history, Fredette analyzes the psychological effects of the raids, which he suggests far outweighed the military gains and contributed significantly to the development of future military air doctrine.

465. Friedman, Norman. *U.S. Aircraft Carriers: An Illustrated Design History*. Annapolis, Md.; Naval Institute, 1983. Pp. vii + 427. Index, Bibliog., Illustr.

Since its inception, the aircraft carrier has been a focal point of analysis, rhetoric, and emotionalism. Most histories of the aircraft carrier are essentially a recounting of their action in battle. Friedman, however, provides a complete evolutionary design history, discussing both the technical and political issues behind each development. The author also provides a lucid explanation of the changing functions of carriers, from their origins as auxiliaries to their role as the main component of the force at sea. Detailed scale profiles, plan views, photographs, and data tables are included.

466. Futrell, Robert F. *The United States Air Force in Korea, 1950–1953*. Rev. ed. Washington D.C.: Office of Air Force History, 1983. Pp. 823. Index, Bibliog., Illustr.

This is the illustrated history of the USAF Far East Air Forces during the Korean conflict. The book's primary value is that it highlights actions in all the major command offices, while providing the accompanying detail of the Air Force's unit battle and battle–support response. This is equally the book's major deficiency, for it tends to indicate that any and all effective action by forces other than those of the USAF occurred because the commanders of those forces finally followed air staff recommendations. In all, however, this is recommended reading for background on the air contingent in Korea. Originally published in 1961 by Duell, Sloan and Pearce.

467. Futrell, Robert F. *Ideas, Concepts, Doctrine: A History of Basic Thinking in the United States Air Force, 1907–1964*. Maxwell Air Force Base, Ala.: Air University, 1974. Pp. viii + 520. Index, Bibliog.

Covers the development of the U.S. Air Force to 1964 with

detailed analysis of organizational, administrative, and doctrinal themes. The participation of the Air Force in various wars is covered along with attention to the various personalities that led and shaped this branch of the armed services. Futrell's history provides an invaluable reference tool and is authoritative on the history of the U.S. Air Force.

468. Galland, Adolf. *The First and the Last: The German Fighter Force in World War II.* London: Methuen, 1955. Pp. 360. Index, Illustr.

As commander of all Luftwaffe fighter forces, Galland provides a unique insight into the functioning of the German Air Force from its early victories in France to its defeat in 1945. The author tells the story through his own recollection of experiences during this time. An excellent book from one of the Luftwaffe's greatest pilots.

469. Goddard, George M., and DeWitt S. Copp. *Overview: A Life-Long Adventure in Aerial Photography.* Garden City, N.Y.: Doubleday, 1969. Pp. xiii + 415. Illustr.

The autobiography of the man responsible for the development of aerial photography and aerial reconnaissance in the Army Air Corps and U.S Air Force. Spanning over 40 years, this personal account includes technical developments, many pioneered by Goddard himself, and the fluctuating attitudes toward aerial photography in various branches of the military.

470. Hall, James Norman, and Charles Bernard Nordhoff, eds. *The Lafayette Flying Corps.* 2 vols. Boston and New York: Houghton Mifflin, 1920. Pp. xviii + 514; xiii + 361. Index, Illustr.

The classic history of the Lafayette Flying Corps. This twovolume work begins with three brief essays on the formation and general history of the group. The balance of the work is made up of biographical sketches and letters of the pilots who served in the unit. Comprehensive and informative.

471. Hallion, Richard P. *Rise of the Fighter Aircraft, 1914–1918.* Annapolis, Md.: Nautical and Aviation, 1984. Pp. vi + 200. Index, Bibliog., Illustr.

Demonstrates in a well–written and authoritative manner how the emergence of fighter aircraft represented a new benchmark in weaponry. Hallion's thesis is that the air war in World War I was not a peripheral episode in military history; points to important milestones established in military aircraft development and operations that have currency today. He sees in this critical period the genesis of certain tactical and strategic concepts that shaped the subsequent evolution of air power. The book has an interesting photographic essay showing the evolution of fighter aircraft.

472.   Hallion, Richard P. *The Naval Air War in Korea*. Baltimore, Md.: Nautical and Aviation, 1986. Pp. xii + 243. Index, Bibliog., Illustr.

Hallion focuses on the naval aviation war in Korea, while providing sufficient material to provide a broad background of the full scope of air and naval involvement in this near–forgotten "police action." The Korean period was the critical point in the evolution of naval aviation between the era of the propeller and that of the jet and of the modification of naval strategy and tactics to add continuous projection of power ashore to the classic wars at sea, including amphibious assault. In addition to providing a full history of this naval air engagement in Korea, the author highlights the advantages and limitations of air power in general, particularly during a politically limited war.

473.   Hardesty, Von. *Red Phoenix: The Rise of Soviet Air Power, 1941–1945*. Washington, D.C.: Smithsonian Institution Press, 1982. Pp. 288. Index, Bibliog., Illustr.

Provides a survey of Soviet air power in World War II. Coverage includes Operation Barbarossa, which nearly destroyed the Soviet Air Force, and its subsequent recovery in the battles for Stalingrad, the Caucasus, Kursk, Belorussia, and Berlin. One chapter provides commentary on the prewar antecedents. An extensive appendix includes data on Soviet aircraft types, organization, air armies, aircraft production, and specialized topics. Along with a glossary, the book contains a definitive Russian– and English–language bibliography with over 700 entries.

474.   Harris, Arthur T. *Bomber Offensive*. New York: Macmillan, 1947. Pp. 288. Index, Illustr.

Reveals the perspective of Sir Arthur Harris, Marshal of the Royal Air Force, who led Britain's World War II bombing campaign against Germany. Harris picks up the story in 1939, at the time he returned to England from Palestine, and then covers the wartime years. Harris was the foremost British proponent of the theories and effectiveness of strategic bombardment. His book attempts to confirm and justify these tenets on the basis of the experiences of RAF Bomber Command. Provides a useful, though subjective, insight into Harris's theories and practices. As expected, Harris asserts the tremendous effectiveness of strategic bombardment. A controversial figure, Harris provides his own forceful views on bombing, World War II, and the advent of the atomic age.

475.   Higham, Robin D.S. *Air Power: A Concise History*. New York: St. Martin's, 1972. Pp. xii + 282. Index, Bibliog., Illustr.

Good overview of the development of air power from the perspective of doctrine and theory. Emphasis is placed on those events and periods that most changed or influenced thinking on the use of air power. The work is heavily weighted toward the British and American air forces.

476.   Higham, Robin D.S., and Jacob W. Kipp, eds. *Soviet Aviation and Air Power: A Historical View*. Boulder, Colo.: Westview, 1978. Pp. xii + 328. Index, Bibliog., Illustr.

Surveys the historical development of Soviet aviation in 11 essays. An introductory essay by Higham defines major themes and background. Both chronological and topical approaches are adopted by the 12 contributors to this comprehensive anthology. Along with military themes and issues related to the strategic uses of air power, the collection includes an essay on Soviet civil aviation. The research notes that follow each essay provide an important reference to Russian- and English-language sources.

477.   Holley, I.B., Jr. *Buying Aircraft: Materiel Procurement for the Army Air Forces*. Washington, D.C.: Office of the Chief of Military History, Department of the Army, 1964. Pp. xviii + 643. Index, Bibliog., Illustr.

The definitive study of American aeronautical procurement during World War II. Holley goes far beyond the basic mechan–

ics of purchasing and contracting. He addresses the compu-
tation of requirements to the evolution of an internal organization to deal with procurement, conflicts between executive
and legislative agencies over procurement issues, and the
character and capabilities of the aircraft industry. An extremely thorough and thoughtful analysis.

478.　Holley, I.B., Jr. *Ideas and Weapons: Exploitation of the Aerial
Weapon by the United States during World War I; A Study in
the Relationship of Technological Advance, Military
Doctrine and the Development of Weapons*. Washington,
D.C.: Office of Air Force History. 1983. Pp. xii + 222. Index,
Bibliog.

Pivotal study of the relationship between weapons procurement, doctrine, and success in war. Using the airplane in World
War I as a focal point, Holley demonstrates how the development of weapons from a technical point of view is slowed if an
effective system for determining their future operational
function (i.e., doctrine) is not in place beforehand.

479.　Homze, Edward L. *Arming the Luftwaffe: The Reich Air
Ministry and the German Aircraft Industry, 1919–1939*.
Lincoln: University of Nebraska Press, 1976. Pp. xv + 296.
Index, Bibliog., Illustr.

This extremely well-researched book examines the growth
and development of the Luftwaffe during the interwar years.
Homze explores the intricate questions of politics, economics,
and technology upon the formation of the Luftwaffe and of the
rebirth of the German aircraft industry. Extensive notes
follow each chapter.

480.　Hudson, James J. *Hostile Skies*. Syracuse, N.Y.: Syracuse
University Press, 1968. Pp. xiv + 338. Index, Bibliog., Illustr.

Deals with the U.S. Air Service in World War I through a
uniquely human dimension that has previously been overlooked.
Through the use of the letters, diaries, logbooks, and personal
testimony, Hudson reconstructs the actual combat experiences
of the flyers, as well as the training, organization, and problems of the infant air service. Makes use of much unpublished,
obscure source material.

481. Hurley, Alfred F. *Billy Mitchell, Crusader for Air Power.* Bloomington: Indiana University Press, 1975. Pp. ix + 190. Index, Bibliog., Illustr.

The definitive work on Billy Mitchell. One of the only objective accounts of this controversial individual, it is extremely well researched and documented with footnotes and a bibliography of primary and secondary sources.

482. Infield, Glenn B. *Unarmed and Unafraid: The First Complete History of the Men, Missions, Training and Techniques of Aerial Reconnaissance.* New York: Macmillan, 1970. Pp. 308. Index, Bibliog., Illustr.

A complete history of aerial reconnaissance from the earliest attempts by the French in the 1790s and the United States in the 1840s to the extensive and complicated methods used in the late 1960s. Covers the events and people involved in both World Wars, Korea, the Cuban missile crisis, and Vietnam. Although dated, a section devoted to future trends describes the Lockheed SR-71 and the General Dynamics F-111, as well as the use of satellites for aerial reconnaissance.

483. Inoguchi, Rikihei, Tadashi Nakajima, with Roger Pineau. *The Divine Wind: Japan's Kamikaze Force in World War II.* Annapolis, Md.: Naval Institute, 1958. Pp. xxii + 240. Index, Illustr.

The incredible story of the suicidal Kamikaze or Special Attack Corps of World War II from the Japanese perspective, including a review of operations and the controversy surrounding the desperate tactic. More important, however, are the pilots themselves, whose dedication is revealed through final letters to their families. Three appendixes sum up the military results of the attacks.

484. Irving, David J.C. *The Rise and Fall of the Luftwaffe; The Life of Field Marshall Erhard Milch.* Boston: Little, Brown, 1974. Pp. xx + 443. Index, Bibliog., Illustr.

This extensive biography reveals the important role Milch, a former chief executive of Lufthansa, played in the rapid rejuvenation of the Luftwaffe. Recounts the German Air Force's early successes and eventual defeats during the war, as well as Milch's subsequent trial and conviction at Nuremburg. Provides a useful approach to the study of the Luftwaffe by examining one of its most important characters. Thorough endnotes.

485.   Johnson, James E. *Wing Leader*. Foreword by Douglas Bader. New York: Ballantine, 1957. Pp. 202.

The autobiographical account of the top–scoring British ace of World War II. Not only a fascinating personal narrative of the war in the air over Europe, it contains penetrating analytical observations on operational factors and tactics.

486.   Johnson, Robert S., and Martin Caidin. *Thunderbolt*. New York: Rinehart, 1958. Pp. 305. Illustr.

Though not so polished in a literary sense as J.E. Johnson's *Wing Leader*, or Pierre Clostermann's *The Big Show*, for example, this autobiography gives an accurate and gripping picture of World War II in the air over Europe through the eyes of a high–scoring American fighter pilot.

487.   Kelsey, Benjamin S. *The Dragon's Teeth? The Creation of United States Air Power for World War II*. Washington, D.C.: Smithsonian Institution Press, 1982. Pp. 148. Index, Illustr.

A brief account of the factors that led to the large–scale expansion of U.S. military aviation just prior to U.S. involvement in World War II. Provides insights into military aircraft procurement and its relationship to political factors. Although largely the memoir of a principal participant, it remains one of the few useful treatments of the subject.

488.   Kennett, Lee B. *A History of Strategic Bombing*. New York: Scribner, 1982. Pp. x + 222. Index, Bibliog., Illustr.

One of the best surveys written about strategic bombardment, this book is well documented and objective in its interpretations of sensitive issues. Intended for a general audience, it is nevertheless a very useful tool for the historian. The book covers the story from the first use of balloons in warfare to the end of World War II.

489.   LeMay, Curtis, E., and MacKinlay Kantor. *Mission with LeMay; My Story*. Garden City, N.Y.: Doubleday, 1965. Pp. xiv + 581. Illustr.

A frank and uncompromising autobiography by an acknowledged Air Force pioneer and leader. LeMay takes us from his early Air Corps days to his command and organization of the USAAF's bombing campaign in Germany and Japan. Later, LeMay became the legendary head of the postwar Strategic Air Command and Air Force chief of staff.

490.   Lewis, Cecil. *Sagittarius Rising*. New York: Harcourt, Brace, 1936. Pp. 301.

The classic account of a young aviator's experiences in World War I and his subsequent flying stint in China. A marvelously written book that details military action as well as the reaction of youth to the dangerous but exciting business of war. Strictly a personal account, however, with no notes or bibliography.

491.   MacIsaac, David. *Strategic Bombing in World War Two: The Story of the United States Strategic Bombing Survey*. New York: Garland, 1976. Pp. xi + 231. Index, Bibliog.

Provides a detailed and useful introduction to the Strategic Bombing Survey. Touches on prewar air themes and how the survey was organized and functioned. In the final chapter the author puts the survey into historical perspective. Should be read in conjunction with U.S. Strategic Bombing Survey, *The United States Strategic Bombing Survey* (cited herein as item 511).

492.   Mason, R.A., and John W.R. Taylor. *Aircraft, Strategy and Operations of the Soviet Air Force*. London: Jane's, 1986. Pp. 278. Index, Bibliog., Illustr.

Provides an overview of today's Soviet Air Force with reference to technology, air doctrine, and operational practice. Helpful, if brief, historical segments introduce successively the themes of air supremacy, tactical doctrine, naval aviation, long-range bombing capabilities, and air transport.

493. Mauer, Mauer, ed. *The U.S. Air Service in World War I.* 4 vols.
      Washington, D.C.: The Office of Air Force History, 1978.
      Pp. xiv + 448; xv + 460; ix + 794; xiv + 617. Index, Illustr.

      Virtually unknown until recently, these primary source doc-
      uments, many of them from Edgar S. Gorrell's, "History of the
      Air Service, AEF," provide valuable insight into American
      military thought during World War I. Volume 1 consists of *The
      Final Report*, which summarizes U.S. air actions in the war,
      and *A Tactical History*, which shows the rapid development of
      the Corps Air Service through chronological events.
      Volume 2, *Early Concepts of Military Aviation*, uses official
      documents written by various Air Service officers, as well as
      official orders and specifications, to illustrate differences of
      opinion concerning the use of aviation within the military.
      Volume 3, *The Battle of St. Mihiel* is a collection of
      documents on U.S. air operations at the Battle of St. Mihiel,
      including operations orders, reconnaissance and operations
      reports, and historical summaries of the various units involved.
      Volume 4, *Postwar Review*, contains two sections, "Lessons
      Learned," a valuable collection of firsthand accounts of the
      war operations from all levels of military aviation, and the
      "U.S. Bombing Survey," which examines the effects of U.S.
      aerial bombardment on the enemy.

494. Mersky, Peter B. *U.S. Marine Corps Aviation, 1912 to the
      Present*. Annapolis, Md.: Nautical and Aviation, 1983. Pp. x
      + 310. Index, Illustr.

      Traces Marine Corps aviation from the first flight by a
      USMC officer to the end of the Vietnam War. Essentially a
      combat history with extensive coverage of the deployment of
      squadrons and their aircraft in World War II, Korea, and Viet-
      nam. Concludes with a chapter on current Marine Corps
      aircraft. Well illustrated with over 200 photographs. Also
      contains two appendixes on Marine Corps pilots and a recom-
      mended reading list.

495. Mersky, Peter B., and Norman Polmar. *The Naval Air War in
      Vietnam*. Annapolis, Md.: Nautical and Aviation, 1981. Pp.
      xiii + 224. Index, Illustr.

      The first chronicle of the naval air war in Vietnam. Provides
      a limited examination of the factors that led up to this polit-
      ically and strategically complex and divisive war and con-

centrates on providing an air engagement account of the 10–year naval air war from the Gulf of Tonkin incident to the evacuation of Saigon. Should serve as the basis for more complete accounts of the naval air encounter in Vietnam.

496. Morrow, John Howard. *German Air Power in World War I.* Lincoln: University of Nebraska Press, 1982. Pp. xii + 267. Index, Bibliog.

A follow–up to Morrow's *Building German Airpower, 1909–1914* (cited herein as item 95), this work discusses the military–industrial relations of German aircraft acquisition and production during World War I. A thorough, well-researched study of all aspects of German aircraft production during the war, from logistics to technical data on the aircraft themselves. The definitive work on the subject.

Mrazek, James E. *Fighting Gliders of World War II.* New York: St. Martin's, 1977. Pp. 207. Index, Illustr.

Cited herein as item 640.

497. Murray, Williamson. *Luftwaffe.* Baltimore, Md.: Nautical and Aviation, 1985. Pp. xiv + 337. Index, Bibliog., Illustr.

Analyzes the evolution of the German Air Force during World War II. Breaks new ground on the history of the Luftwaffe by examining how certain strategic errors by the German leadership combined with the immense attrition in aircraft and crews during the war brought disaster to German air power. Excellent annotated bibliography supplements the text. The definitive history of the Luftwaffe.

498. Norman, Aaron. *The Great Air War.* New York: Macmillan, 1968. Pp. xi + 558. Index, Bibliog., Illustr.

A complete, classic work of World War I aviation with special emphasis on the experiences of the pilots involved, but marred by some errors of fact and interpretation. Includes an excellent section of drawings and specifications of World War I aircraft. Also contains impressive photos.

499. Overy, R.J. *The Air War, 1939–1945.* New York: Stein and Day, 1980. Pp. xii + 263. Index, Bibliog., Illustr.

Superb survey reviews the entire sweep of the air war in
Europe and the Pacific during World War II, giving attention to
"grand strategy" rather than military campaigns. Overy's aims
were twofold: to show why the Allies won and to demonstrate
the importance of strategic bombing to the overall victory.
Overy's analysis is keyed to crucial themes of evolving air
doctrines, research and development, industrial production in
wartime context, and mobilization. Excellent bibliography.

500.   Polmar, Norman, et al. *Aircraft Carriers: A Graphic History
         of Carrier Aviation and Its Influence on World Events.*
         Garden City, N.Y.: Doubleday, 1969. Pp. viii + 788. Index,
         Bibliog., Illustr.

This well–illustrated book is a thorough and comprehensive
account of the aircraft carrier's role in and contribution to
aerial and sea warfare, with especially excellent coverage of
the Pacific theater in World War II. The appendixes contain
many statistics and the bibliography is first–rate.

501.   Quester, George H. *Deterrence before Hiroshima: The Air-
         power Background of Modern Strategy.* New Brunswick,
         N.J.: Transaction, 1986. Pp. xxix + 193. Index.

Presents a convincing argument that ideas of deterrence and
limited war are neither peculiarly "American" nor totally new
concepts. The author discusses the possibility that such ideas
as "deterrence by punishment," in which a society receives a
painful enemy countervalue attack, had already been perceived well before nuclear weapons came to be. Finally, in a
discussion of strategic air power, the author argues that there
were many forerunners of our "modern" nuclear threat. The
chronological scope of the work is from 1899 to 1945.

502.   Raleigh, Walter A., and Henry A. Jones. *The War in the Air;
         Being the Story of the Part Played in the Great War by the
         Royal Air Force.* 6 vols. Oxford: Clarendon, 1922–1937.
         Index, Illustr.

Monumental history of the air war in World War I compiled
from British Air Ministry primary source documents. From the
first volume, which includes a historical background and
description of the Royal Flying Corps, predecessor of the
Royal Air Force, and the Royal Naval Air Service, to the
sixth, which deals with the events leading up to creation of the

RAF and the 1918 campaigns in the Middle East, Raleigh and Jones cover in roughly chronological fashion and comprehensive detail, Britain's role in the Great War in the air. Subsequent volumes cover naval operations; air operations on the Western and other fronts; the German airship attacks on Great Britain; the problems of supply administration, recruitment, and training; anti–aircraft defense; air raid shelters; and training pilots for night flying. Contains detailed charts and maps.

503.   Reynolds, Clark G. *The Fast Carriers: The Forging of an Air Navy.* Huntington, N.Y.: Robert E. Krieger, 1978. Pp. xvi + 502. Index, Bibliog., Illustr.

Thorough, analytical study of the development of the American Fast Carrier Task Force during World War II. Reynolds focuses on how this task force contributed to the transformation of the U.S. Navy from a battleship orientation to one that depended on air power. Includes statistical appendixes on Allied and Japanese carrier forces.

504.   Saundby, Robert H.M.S. *Air Bombardment: The Story of Its Development.* New York: Harper, 1961. Pp. 259. Illustr.

Vast in scope, this ambitious work successfully attempts to tell the story of air power in general and aerial bombardment in particular, from the earliest experiment to the nuclear age. Much of the book deals with the story and lessons of World War II. Provides a good general overview.

505.   Saunders, Hilary S. *Per Ardua; The Rise of British Air Power, 1911–1939.* London: Oxford University, 1945. Pp. 355. Index, Bibliog., Illustr.

Though dated, this work provides a solid fundamental history of the growth and development of British air power up to the beginning of World War II. Most of the book is devoted to the experiences of World War I. Well researched and written.

506.   Schaffer, Ronald. *Wings of Judgment: American Bombing in World War II.* New York: Oxford University Press, 1985. Pp. xiv + 272. Index, Bibliog.

Focuses on bombing tactics, conventional and nuclear, and

the moral decisions behind them. The author presents military and political leaders in a different light as they struggle with decisions affecting civilians in Europe and Asia as well U.S. military personnel. The epilogue is a fine chapter on postwar conflicts and the dilemmas facing a nuclear world.

507.   Sherrod, Robert L. *History of Marine Corps Aviation in World War II*. Washington, D.C.: Combat Forces, 1952. Pp. xiv + 496. Illustr.

Overview history of U.S. Marine Corps aviation during World War II. A very detailed narrative account with some analysis of high–level decisions regarding deployment of marine corps squadrons. Includes several statistical appendixes as well as one that provides thumbnail unit histories of the various squadrons.

508.   Sherry, Michael S. *The Rise of American Air Power: The Creation of Armegeddon*. New Haven, Conn.: Yale University Press, 1987. Pp. xiii + 435. Index, Bibliog., Illustr.

A provocative, controversial, and enlightened account of the history of air power. Sherry sees today's threat of nuclear annihilation as a continuum that originated with the strategic bombing in Europe and, especially, the fire–bombing of Japan in World War II. Unlike most histories of air power theory, which focus on technology and military strategy, Sherry's work takes a stand on the morality of strategic bombing and its effects on modern society. Should be read in conjunction with Ronald Schaffer's *Wings of Judgment: American Bombing in World War II* (cited herein as item 506).

509.   Shiner, John. *Foulois and the U.S. Army Air Corps.* Washington, D.C.: Office of Air Force History, 1983. Pp. xv + 346. Index, Bibliog., Illustr.

An official study of General Benjamin Foulois's tenure as chief of the Army Air Corps. The book includes a detailed but sympathetic look at Foulois's role in the so–called airmail scandal, in which the Army Air Corps was called upon to carry mail when FDR canceled the existing civilian airmail contracts. More important, it studies this period of transition in policy, organization, and all matters related to setting the stage for building a viable air arm of the United States.

510. Turnbull, Archibald D., and Clifford L. Lord. *History of United States Naval Aviation.* New Haven, Conn.: Yale University Press, 1949. Pp. xii + 345. Index, Bibliog., Illustr.

Covers the history of naval aviation from its inception through World War II. The author, a navy reserve captain and historian, gives considerable attention to the period before World War II. As a consequence, the historical coverage is weighted heavily toward events prior to Pearl Harbor and the Pacific War. The last chapter gives only passing attention to the critical period between 1941 and 1945. The major strength of the books is its treatment of the 1920s.

511. U.S. Strategic Bombing Survey. *The United States Strategic Bombing Survey.* 10 vols. Introduction by David MacIsaac. New York: Garland, 1976. Illustr.

Reprints 31 selected reports from the 321 issued by the U.S. Strategic Bombing Survey, a presidential commission established to evaluate the effects of strategic bombing on Germany and Japan. Each volume contains a brief introduction to the reports that provides a rationale for their selection and emphasizes points of controversy. Should be read in conjunction with David MacIsaac, *Strategic Bombing in World War Two: The Story of the United States Strategic Bombing Survey* (cited herein as item 491).

512. Wagner, Ray, and Leland Fetzer, eds. *The Soviet Air Force in World War II.* Garden City, N.Y.: Doubleday, 1973. Pp. vi + 440. Index, Illustr.

Published as an English translation of the official history by the Ministry of Defense of the USSR. The book focuses largely on major campaigns and the role of Soviet air power. Also concentrates on the Soviet Air Force, ignoring other aviation branches, such as the naval air arm. The perspective is a Soviet one, seeing in the "Great Patriotic War" a triumph of Soviet arms and political ideology. The editor has supplemented the text, translated in its entirety, with illustrations and a valuable index.

513. Watts, Barry D. *The Foundations of U.S. Air Doctrine: The Problem of Friction in War.* Maxwell Air Force Base, Ala.: Air University, 1984. Pp. xvii + 166. Index, Bibliog., Illustr.

A heterodox but tightly reasoned study of U.S. Air Force doctrine and its development. The historical analysis of pre–World War II developments is particularly well done and makes this the definitive work on the subject. The author's application of his conclusions to the Vietnam War, while controversial, is logically presented and well supported by historical evidence.

514. Webster, Charles K., and Noble Frankland. *The Strategic Air Offensive against Germany, 1939–1945*. 4 vols. London: Her Majesty's Stationery Office, 1961. Index, Bibliog., Illustr.

An important work that uses primary source documents to analyze the strategy, operations, and results of the strategic bombardment campaign against Germany in World War II from a British perspective. Volume 1 deals with the preparations for and opening of the offense; volume 2 with the role of Bomber Command and the Combined Bomber Offensive; volume 3 with the culmination of the offensive, and a concluding survey that evaluates critically the effects of strategic bombing on the war. Volume 4 contains useful annexes and appendixes.

515. Winter, Denis. *The First of the Few: Fighter Pilots of the First World War*. Athens: University of Georgia Press, 1983. Pp. 223. Index, Bibliog., Illustr.

An intelligently written and thorough account of British fighter pilots in World War I, from enlistment to postwar readjustment to civilian life. Avoiding the usual cliche–ridden, idolatrous narration, Winter deals squarely with the reality of air fighting in all its dimensions. Chapters 13 and 14, "The Dark Side—Physical Strain" and "The Dark Side—Dying" are particularly illuminating.

516. Wood, Derek, and Derek D. Dempster. *The Narrow Margin: The Battle of Britain and the Rise of Air Power, 1930–1940*. New York: McGraw-Hill, 1961. Pp. 536. Index, Bibliog., Illustr.

Provides an overview of the Battle of Britain with careful attention to the historical antecedents of German and British air power in the interim years. The author covers each phase of the 1940 clash between the Luftwaffe and the RAF in detail, showing the various factors—some fortuitous, others linked to the character of the combatants—that shaped the air battles. The authors also attempt to determine actual losses by both sides.

AIR TRANSPORTATION

Compared with some other branches of aviation, air transportion has been the subject of relatively few books. During the formative years of this worldwide industry, the airlines were gaining experience by trial and error and were unable to draw upon textbooks or technical reports, simply because there were none. Thus, the early literature on the airline business tends to be somewhat speculative, and by today's standards, a little naive. As to books on early air transportation history, such efforts were premature in that they were published just when the history itself was being made. Nevertheless, the works that did appear are valuable because they reflect the knowledge, the public attitudes, and the operational problems of an age that is centuries away in terms of technology and traveling habits, though it occurred only about 50 years ago.

This section attempts to cover the whole history of air transportation from the early 1920s up to the present day. It is arranged, for the most part, in geographical order according to the following categories: the World, North America, Europe, Asia, Australia and the South Pacific, Latin America, Africa, and the Middle East. Two additional categories are Airmail and Airports. Some books deal with the industry as a whole and explore its problems. Some are about groups of airlines, such as the U.S. industry; and many are histories of individual airlines. Some are about the great trunk airlines, others about bush operators. Some are meticulously researched scholarly works, others depend more on illustrations to make their impact on the reader. Some are aimed at those who are either in the airline business or possess a full knowledge of it, others are aimed at the beginner. In other words, the list attempts to cater to all tastes and requirements.

Moreover, almost half of the books deal with the United States. This is entirely appropriate as the United States has traditionally accounted for about one-half of the world's total air transportation activity. Some books, particularly in the sections on Europe, Asia, or Latin America, are in a foreign language. Nevertheless, they are invariably well presented, feature maps and charts, and are well worth the trouble of seeking help in the translation.

To supplement this bibliography, there is a two-volume work by Myron J. Smith, Jr., titled *The Airline Bibliography: The Salem*

College Guide to Sources on Commercial Aviation (West Cornwall, Conn.: Locust Hill Press, 1986). In addition to containing book lists, Smith's work offers a comprehensive catalog of all magazine articles written about the airlines and a variety of subjects associated with airline operation. It is strongly recommended to all serious students of air transportation.

R.E.G. Davies

World

517. Brooks, Peter W. *The Modern Airliner*. London: Putnam, 1961. Pp. 176. Index, Bibliog., Illustr.

   One of the vital ingredients that goes into making a good airline is the possession of a good fleet of airliners. It was not until the 1930s that these vehicles achieved sufficient economic efficiency to enable air transport to compete with surface modes without subsidy. Only since World War II have they been developed specifically for carrying passengers, mail, or freight. Brooks outlines the technical developments and their economic consequences in this succinct book. Revised edition published in 1982 by Sunflower University Press.

518. Davies, R.E.G. *A History of the World's Airlines*. London: Oxford University Press, 1967. Reprint. New York: AMS, 1983. Pp. xxx + 591. Index, Bibliog., Illustr.

   First published after World War II, this comprehensive work traces the complex development of air transport from 1914 until the introduction of commercial jets. It surveys the great transoceanic flag carriers, the regional and feeder airlines, and even the tiny bush outfits that often contributed to the economic development of their countries by opening up otherwise isolated regions to commerce, trade, and tourism.

519. Hudson, Kenneth, and Julian Pettifer. *Diamonds in the Sky: A Social History of Air Travel*. London: Bodley Head, 1979. Pp. 240. Index, Bibliog., Illustr.

   An excellent, one–of–a–kind study, based on a British Broadcasting Corporation television documentary of the same name, that focuses on "the ways in which flying has ministered to human needs, whims, and follies." Among other things, the book takes an unbiased and often disturbing look a jet–age mass tourism, especially in the developing nations. A follow–on, of sorts, to Hudson's *Air Travel: A Social History* (Totowa, N.J.: Rowman and Littlefield, 1972), which covers much of the same ground.

520. Lissitzyn, Oliver James. *International Air Transport and National Policy Studies in American Foreign Relations*. No. 3.

Percy W. Bidwell, ed. New York: Council on Foreign Relations, 1942. Pp. xviii + 478. Index, Bibliog., Illustr.

International air transport was built against a background of political rivalries, international jealousies, and considerations of national security. Lissitzyn analyzes comprehensively the importance of government subsidy in sponsoring the world's great flag carriers and also examines the problems that would confront postwar diplomacy from a pre–World War II viewpoint. Reprinted in 1983 by Garland Publishing.

521. Miller, Ronald E., and David Sawers. *The Technical Development of Modern Aviation.* London: Routledge and Kegan Paul, 1968. Pp. xvi + 351. Index, Bibliog., Illustr.

Systematically reviews the technical progress that led to the development of the so–called modern airliner, especially the later refinements of airframe design and the advent of jet propulsion, which revolutionized the airline industry. Miller and Sawers keep their sense of perspective with the somewhat controversial observation that "invention within the aircraft industry is most notable for its absence."

522. Newhouse, John. *The Sporty Game: The High–Risk Competitive Business of Making and Selling Commercial Airliners.* New York: Knopf, 1983. Pp. 242. Index, Bibliog.

A hard–hitting analysis of the manufacture, marketing, and sale of commercial airliners in the present day. Newhouse focuses on the corporate and international competition (the "sporty" in the title refers to the risks involved in playing the rough–and–tumble game required in this side of the aircraft industry) among aircraft manufacturers in capturing the commercial market. Full of insights by a skilled writer on international economics.

523. O'Connor, William E. *Economic Regulation of the World's Airlines: A Political Analysis.* New York: Praeger, 1971. Pp. 189. Index, Bibliog.

Detailed analytical study of airline regulation that focuses on the influence of political factors. Discusses the necessity, yet often hampering effect, of international cooperation in airline regulation.

524. Pahl, Walther. *Die Luftwege der Erde: Politische Geographie des Weltluft Verkhers* (The air routes of the earth: the political geography of world air commerce). Hamburg: Hanseatische Verlag, 1936. Pp. 128. Illustr.

Pahl first published his political geography of the world's airlines in 1936, and for almost 30 years it was the only textbook on the subject. It was translated into French and was farsighted enough to predict the use of Great Circle routes across the North Pole to link Europe with America.

525. Romeyer, Jean. *Les grands reseaux de l'air* (The great air networks). Paris: J. de Grigord, [1938]. Pp. 202. Illustr.

One of the few books devoted to air transport produced before World War II. Contains chapters on each country that had a substantial civil airline network, including all the major lines of Europe, the United States, South America, and Japan. Well illustrated with finely reproduced photographs. Also contains a well-chosen selection of maps and charts.

North America

526. Allen, Oliver. *The Airline Builders*. Alexandria, Va.: Time-Life, 1981. Pp. 176. Index, Bibliog., Illustr.

One of the better volumes of Time-Life's Epic of Flight series. Chronicles the growth and development of commerical aviation in the United States. Includes a chapter on European efforts before World War II.

527. Black, Archibald. *Transport Aviation*. New York, Chicago: Simmons-Boardman, 1926. Pp. 245. Index, Illustr.

Archibald Black, writing in 1926, gave an optimistic analysis of the potential of air transport business on the eve of the Great Depression. Black endeavored to show how the industry might grow by giving practical, and at times elementary, data on aircraft, aircraft design, and commercial aspects of air transport. His coverage makes reference to the international scene in the 1920s.

528. Bender, Marilyn, and Selig Altschul. *The Chosen Instrument.*

New York: Simon and Schuster, 1982. Pp. 605. Index, Bibliog.,
Illustr.

A parallel to Robert Daley's *An American Saga*, but with a
different slant. With skill and insight, Bender and Altschul
clinically analyze Pan American Airways' rise to greatness and
dissect the policies of Juan Trippe, whose single-minded drive
for dominance made Pan American the world's top international
carrier.

529. Cameron, Frank. *Hungry Tiger: The Story of the Flying Tiger
Line.* New York: McGraw-Hill, 1964. Pp. 277. Index, Illustr.

Chronicles the story of Robert Prescott, who founded the
all-cargo Flying Tiger Line after World War II, having been
introduced to the possibilities of air transport while serving in
the Chinese theater of World War II with the American Volunteer Group. Prescott struggled against enormous opposition,
including that of an entrenched U.S. airline industry supported
by the Civil Aeronautics Board.

530. Daley, Robert. *An American Saga: Juan Trippe and His Pan Am
Empire.* New York: Random House, 1980. Pp. 529. Index, Bibliog., Illustr.

One of the best of the many books written about Pan American Airways. Chronicles the story of Juan Trippe's influence
and control over this vast organization, giving full credit to his
accomplishments, but at the same time revealing flaws in
Trippe's character and ethics.

531. Davies, R.E.G. *Airlines of the United States since 1914.* London: Putnam, 1972. Reprint, rev. Washington, D.C.: Smithsonian Institution Press, 1982. Pp. xiv + 746. Index, Bibliog.,
Illustr.

A detailed narrative history of a selected group of airlines in
the United States, which accounts for almost half of the world's
air transport activity. Reviews in detail trunk, regional, commuter, freight, scheduled, and nonscheduled airlines from the
pioneering period to the present. Also chronicles the development of commercial aircraft, the influence of government
regulation, and the contributions made by gifted individuals.
The author considers this book to be the natural starting point
for a planned series of definitive airline histories.

532. Day, Beth. *Glacier Pilot: The Story of Bob Reeve and the Flyers Who Pushed Back Alaska's Air Frontiers.* New York: Henry Holt, 1957. Pp. 348. Illustr.

The fascinating account of Robert Reeve, who founded an airline in Alaska simply by volunteering to fly regularly to places where even hardened bush pilots were reluctant to go. Reeve's daredevil adventures in the northernmost ranges of the Rocky Mountains read more like fiction, but such men, using unorthodox methods, created a special kind of airline service quite alien to the established industry of the lower 48 states.

533. Ellis, Frank H. *Canada's Flying Heritage.* 2d ed. Toronto: University of Toronto Press, 1954. Pp. xv + 388. Index, Illustr.

This is such a comprehensive and authoritative book about Canada's aviation history during its pioneer years that it has been reprinted, including a second edition, four times. A flyer himself, Ellis combines the authority, born of experience, with the meticulous reporting and systematic chronological notations of a true researcher and a shrewd observer of events. This large-format volume is essential for anyone researching aviation in Canada.

Freudenthal, Elsbeth E. *The Aviation Business; From Kitty Hawk to Wall Street.* New York: Vanguard, 1940. Pp. xi + 342. Bibliog.

Cited herein as item 981.

534. Hopkins, George E. *The Airline Pilots: A Study in Elite Unionization.* Cambridge, Mass.: Harvard University, 1971. Pp. viii + 244. Bibliog., Illustr.

Takes the Airline Pilots Association from its founding in the late 1920s through the New Deal. Essential to an understanding of the origins of airline unions.

535. Hopkins, George E. *Flying the Line: The First Half Century of the Air Line Pilots Association.* Washington, D.C.: Air Line Pilots Association, 1982. Pp. x + 310. Index, Illustr.

Enlarges on his previous study and carries the story into the early 1980s.

536. Keith, Ronald A. *Bush Pilot with a Brief-Case: The Happy-Go-Lucky Story of Grant McConachie.* Toronto: Doubleday Canada, 1972. Pp. 322. Illustr.

Captures the spirit of Grant McConachie, adventurer of the air, who combined a strong element of luck with some remarkable intuition to lay the foundations of Canada's leading independent airline, Canadian Pacific Airways. Whereas Ellis's *Canada's Flying Heritage* (cited herein as item 533) covers the early pioneer years, Keith's biography admirably encompasses the period when Canadian air transport finally found its destiny.

537. Kennedy, Thomas H. *An Introduction to the Economics of Air Transportation.* New York: Macmillan, 1924. Pp. ix + 154. Index, Bibliog., Illustr.

One of the earliest books to address air transportation (the bibliography covers a single page and all of the books cited are about aviation or aeronautics in general). Considering that permanent airlines did not get under way until 1919, this book is a remarkably good review of the progress made in the first five years of the fledgling industry, which was before the passage of the Air Commerce Act of 1926. The book's special contribution is its review of the activities of air transportation operators such as the U.S. Air Mail Service, U.S. Army Model Airway, and Aeromarine Airways, Inc., all of which operated for only a few years. Much attention is given to the progress made in Europe, and the author includes a list of the world's air transportation services in 1923.

538. Komons, Nick A. *Bonfires to Beacons: Federal Civil Aviation Policy under the Air Commerce Act, 1926-1938.* Washington, D.C.: U.S. Department of Transportation, Federal Aviation Administration, 1978. Pp. viii + 454. Index, Bibliog., Illustr.

The first in a series of books on the history of the Federal Aviation Administration and its predecessors that studies the fledgling efforts by the U.S. government to organize and regulate the burgeoning American aircraft manufacturing and transport industry in the 1920s and 1930s and analyzes the foundations of air safety in the United States. An excellent and thoroughly researched work.

539. Kuter, Laurence S. *The Great Gamble: The Boeing 747; The Boeing Pan-Am Project to Develop, Produce and Introduce*

the 747. University, Ala.: University of Alabama Press, 1973.
Pp. ix + 134.

Detailed account of the history of the joint Boeing–Pan
American Airways venture to produce the Boeing 747 airliner.
Focuses on the tremendous financial outlays involved for both
sponsoring companies.

540. Lewis, W. David, and Wesley Philips Newton. *Delta—The
History of an Airline.* Athens: University of Georgia Press,
1979. Pp. xiii + 503. Index, Bibliog., Illustr.

A scholarly work written by professional historians who had
access to all of Delta's official records. Ranks as a classic
example of thorough research into the corporate and operational history of one of the largest and most successful airlines
in the United States, from C.E. Woolman's crop–duster days of
the 1920s to the time when Delta forced a reappraisal of the
traditional dominance of the "Big Four" companies.

541. Mills, Stephen E. *A Pictorial History of Northwest Airlines.*
New York: Bonanza, 1980. Pp. 192. Index, Bibliog., Illustr.

Well–illustrated account of one of the leading trunk airlines
of the United States. Full coverage of corporate history, aircraft, and route development, as well as the people involved in
this process. A good airline "case study." Originally published as
*More Than Meets the Sky; A Pictorial History of the Founding
and Growth of Northwest Airlines* (Seattle, Wash.: Superior,
1972).

542. Mudge, Robert W. *The Adventures of a Yellowbird.* Boston:
Branden, 1969. Pp. 374. Index, Illustr.

Northeast Airlines was a relatively small trunk airline,
always identified with New England. The author, a veteran
Northeast pilot, relates the postwar developments, but by far
the most interesting part deals with the little–known accomplishments of Northeast during World War II, when it pioneered
the establishment of strategic routes in northern Canada and
Greenland, serving points as distant as Winnipeg and Prestwick,
Scotland.

543. O'Neill, Ralph A., with Joseph F. Hood. *A Dream of Eagles.*

Boston: Houghton Mifflin, 1973. Pp. x + 324. Index, Illustr.

O'Neill promoted the New York, Rio, and Buenos Aires Airline (NYRBA), an enterprising attempt to launch a flying boat route from the United States to all the main cities of the east coast of South America, via the islands of the Caribbean. He found himself in competition with Juan Trippe and the might of Pan American, virtually sponsored by the U.S. Post Office, and was engulfed by that airline. O'Neill's story is one of pioneering endeavor, but also reveals the shortcomings of an idealistic approach, lacking other necessities such as an appreciation of sound economics and political reality.

544. Reeves, Earl. *Aviation's Place in Tomorrow's Business.* New York: B.C. Forbes, 1930. Pp. xv + 323. Illustr.

Provides a valuable insight into why American banks and corporations risked large fortunes in airline speculation almost simultaneously with the Wall Street crash. Yet the year 1930 marks the dawn of the commercial airline industry in the United States, and Reeves provides a glimpse of the public mood and the business background at a time when men of vision recognized the wide horizons of airline development.

545. Rochester, Stuart I. *Takeoff at Mid-Century: Federal Civil Aviation Policy in the Eisenhower Years, 1953-1961.* Washington, D.C.: U.S. Department of Transportation, Federal Aviation Administration, 1976. Pp. 352. Index, Bibliog.

Strong study of federal aviation policy that begins with the Federal Aviation Act of 1958 that created the FAA and proceeds through the rest of the Eisenhower administration. Focuses on the Eisenhower administration's attempt to make federal aviation policy more responsive to the problems brought on by the jet age.

546. Rowe, Basil L. *Under My Wings.* Indianapolis: Bobbs-Merrill, 1956. Pp. 256.

Pilots in the jet age fly under vastly different circumstances compared with those of a former generation. In the early days, many airlines were operated almost single-handedly by pilots. Such a pilot was Basil Rowe, who started off in the 1920s as a barnstormer, ran a small airline in the West Indies, and then flew about 6 million miles with Pan American. Epitomizes the

history of the airlines as seen through the eyes of a veteran
airline pilot.

547. Serling, Robert J. *Maverick: The Story of Robert Six and Con-
     tinental Airlines.* Garden City, N.Y.: Doubleday, 1974. Pp.
     viii + 351. Index, Illustr.

     The biography of Robert Six, who took over a shaky Varney
     Air Transport in the early 1930s, renamed it Continental Air-
     lines, and built it into one of the most respected U.S. trunk
     carriers. Handicapped by restrictive legislation, Six's forte was
     to extract every last ounce of advantage from those things that
     his airline could do well, achieving an enviable reputation for
     fine service. He showed commendable intuition in moving into
     the Pacific with military charters and was among the pace-
     setters of the jet age.

548. Serling, Robert J. *The Only Way to Fly: The Story of Western
     Airlines, America's Senior Air Carrier.* Garden City, N.Y.:
     Doubleday, 1976. Pp. viii + 494. Index, Illustr.

     Bob Serling takes the reader through the checkered history of
     the senior U.S. airline, from its contract mail years as Western
     Air Express in the 1920s, through the stormy years of battling
     for the big mail contracts of the Hoover administration, the
     "shotgun marriage" with TAT that produced TWA, and the
     subsequent development of the reconstituted Western Air Lines.

549. Serling, Robert J. *From the Captain to the Colonel: An Infor-
     mal History of Eastern Airlines.* New York: Dial, 1980. Pp.
     535. Index, Illustr.

     Very readable account of the history of Eastern Airlines,
     from its foundation as Pitcairn Aviation, through the flamboy-
     ant Rickenbacker years, to the reign of Frank Borman. Strong
     on anecdotes and character descriptions.

550. Serling, Robert J. *Howard Hughes' Airline: An Informal History
     of TWA.* New York: St. Martin's, 1983. Pp. xiii + 338. Index,
     Bibliog., Illustr.

     Another of Serling's fine books about individual airlines, this
     one tells the story of TWA from its foundation as a merger of
     Transcontinental Air Transport and Western Air Express until

the time when Hughes, who took over the airline in 1937, was forced to abdicate. Serling's approach reveals all sides of a complex personality and his bizarre ways of running the airline, but correctly narrates all the intuitive episodes that support the view that Howard Hughes was an eccentric genius.

551. Smith, Henry Ladd. *Airways; The History of Commercial Aviation in the United States*. New York: Alfred Knopf, 1942. Pp. xiv + 430. Index, Bibliog., Illustr.

This was a landmark in the literature of the airlines. There is no finer book that so intimately captures the drama of the Air Mail Scandal of 1934, vividly portraying the strong-minded individuals who were the founders of the airline industry in the United States. Smith shows how the foundation of air transport was the airmail, supported mainly by government subsidy, which provided the necessary finance to launch the airlines on their way to success.

552. Smith, Henry Ladd. *Airways Abroad, the Study of American World Air Routes*. Madison: University of Wisconsin Press, 1950. Pp. x + 355. Index, Bibliog., Illustr.

Immediately after the end of World War II, U.S. domestic airlines, formerly content to allow Pan American Airways to be the chosen instrument, suddenly realized the tremendous opportunities for expansion that the new long-range transport airplanes could provide and that the postwar world could stimulate. The bitter internal rivalries between the American giants and the conflicts with the foreign governments that led finally to the establishment of a world system are related in fine style by an accomplished wordsmith.

553. Solberg, Carl. *Conquest of the Skies: A History of Commercial Aviation in America*. Boston: Little, Brown, 1979. Pp. 441. Index, Bibliog., Illustr.

A general overview of some of the better-known historical episodes in commercial aviation from the 1920s to the 1960s, but stops very much short of important developments such as the jumbo jet. Focuses on such historical aspects of air transportation as airmail, transoceanic flights, and the development of the airlines. Conventional in approach but immensely readable as an introduction to the subject.

554. Taylor, Frank L. *High Horizons; Daredevil Flying Postmen to Modern Magic Carpet: The United Airlines Story.* Rev. ed. New York: McGraw–Hill, 1955. Pp. 284. Index, Illustr.

United Airlines has come to symbolize dependability, steadiness of purpose, and solid achievement, eschewing adventure and drama as pathways to success. In this tale of a great organization, Frank Taylor brings to life the boardroom dramas, from the early days when Bill Boeing fashioned a coast–to–coast organization, to the merger with Capital Airlines in 1961, at the time the biggest amalgamation in airline history. Includes excellent chronology.

555. Thruelson, Richard. *Transocean: The Story of an Unusual Airline.* New York: Henry Holt, 1953. Pp. 241.

The story of Orvis Nelson, a true entrepreneur of the airlines, who created a worldwide charter airline organization. Transocean was one of the first intercontinental nonscheduled airlines and the first to use the term "supplemental," later adopted by the Civil Aeronautics Board. This book also recounts Nelson's many speculative ventures in promoting, supporting, and guiding foreign airlines, some of which have become national flag carriers today.

556. [United Air Lines] *Corporate and Legal History of United Air Lines and Its Predecessors and Subsidiaries, 1925–1945 [1946–1955].* 2 vols. Pp. xiv + 847; xxiv + 1331. Index.

A comprehensive, meticulously researched history of the corporate growth and business activities of one of the largest air transportation systems in the United States, from its origins as a group of independent airmail routes to 1955. Discusses United's companies and their individual and intercorporate development. Compiled by the law firm of Mayer, Meyer, Austrian & Pratt.

557. Whitnah, Donald R. *Safer Skyways: Federal Control of Aviation, 1926–1966.* Ames: Iowa State University Press, 1966. Pp. xii + 417. Index, Bibliog., Illustr.

Books on safety, and the regulations that set the highest standards of conduct to attain a good safety record, do not normally provide exciting reading. But Whitnah's study of the airline's painful progress treats airline accidents and crashes as part of the hard–won experience toward the airlines' present level of excellence, and mercifully avoids the melodrama normally associated with such tragic events. The role of the Civil Aeronautics Administration and the Federal Aviation Administration in making the airways of the United States one of the safest paths to travel, compared with any transport mode, is well documented.

558. Williams, Brad. *The Anatomy of an Airline*. Garden City, N.Y.: Doubleday, 1970. Pp. 233. Index.

George "Ted" Baker was a cavalier torchbearer of independence in the world of the CAB–regulated U.S. airline industry. He founded National Airlines in 1934 with a handful of planes and a single route in Florida. A veritable David of his tribe, he challenged the might of Eastern Airlines to reach New York, and lived to see his airline become a transcontinental trunk. The title of this book belies its eventful story of a remarkable man.

559. Wilson, John R.M. *Turbulence Aloft: The Civil Aeronautics Administration amid War and Rumors of War, 1938–1953*. Washington, D.C.: U.S. Department of Transportation, Federal Aviation Administration, 1979. Pp. 346. Index, Bibliog., Illustr.

Strong study of the Civil Aeronautics Administration from 1938 to 1953. Discusses the internal workings of the CAA from the optimistic hopes following the passage of the Civil Aeronautics Act of 1938 through the troubled times when the agency struggled under the pressures of war and global conflict during the 1940s and early 1950s.

560. Woolley, James G., and Earl W. Hill. *Airplane Transportation*. Hollywood, Calif.: Hartwell, 1929. Pp. xii + 353. Illustr.

Woolley was an executive of Western Air Express, one of the earliest airlines of the United States. He collaborated with Earl Hill, trade and transportation lecturer at the University of Southern California, to write one of the earliest textbooks on how to run an airline. The work covers the history of air transportation (less than a decade old at the time), commercial application, types of aircraft and engines, theory of flight, training, operations, airports, meteorology, regulations, and investment prospects. A good case study of the knowledge, attitudes, and the aspirations of airlines in the embryo stage.

Europe

561. Alitalia. *Vent anni Alitalia* (Twenty years of Alitalia). Rome: Alitalia, 1967. Pp. 188. Illustr.

    Generally reviews all aspects of Alitalia's operations. A promotional book, but interesting because it treats, by separate chapters, every department in the airline, while providing broad coverage of the history. As such, it serves as a good introduction to airline business practices.

562. Allen, Roy. *A Pictorial History of KLM, Royal Dutch Airlines*. Amsterdam: KLM, 1969. Reprint. London: Ian Allan, 1978. Pp. 192. Illustr.

    Attractive compendium of published materials, including newspaper reports, magazine articles, and posters, supported by text, that provide a kaleidoscopic view of KLM's first 50 years. Superb illustrations, including scale drawings, in color, of all KLM's aircraft.

563. Banks, Howard. *The Rise and Fall of Freddie Laker*. London: Faber and Faber, 1982. Pp. 155.

    The best of many books written about the most charismatic airline promoter in British air transport history. Laker's rise, from postwar entrepreneur on the fringes of aviation to world-famous standard-bearer for the cause of freedom on the world's airways, is well chronicled.

564. Braunburg, Rudolf. *Kranich in der Sonne* (Crane in the sun). Munich: Kindler [1978]. Pp. 347. Illustr.

    A definitive account of the history of Lufthansa, Germany's national airline, and one of the most respected and influential in the world during the entire course of its history, including those of its antecedents going back to 1919.

565. CSA. *Ceskoslovenske Aerolinie, 1923–1973* (The Czechoslovak airlines, 1923–1973). Prague: CSA, 1973. Pp. 120. Illustr.

Succinct, well–illustrated history of the Czechoslovak airline, one of Europe's oldest. Starting service in 1923, its "OK" symbol became well–known at all the major European airports. Particularly interesting are the references to many unusual airliners from all countries, monopolized in recent years, of course, by Soviet types.

566. Daurat, Didier. *Dans le vent des helices* (In the propwash). Paris: Editions du Seuil, 1956. Pp. 251. Illustr.

A personal account of Aéropostale by the dynamic individual who helped to launch its predecessor, Lignes Latécoère, but who fell from grace when Bouilloux–Lafont took over in 1927. Daurat is the notorious despatcher mentioned in Saint-Exupéry's romanticized books, and his narrative provides a good idea of early air transport conditions at the dawn of the airline industry in Europe. Note that the history of Air France and its predecessors is being comprehensively covered by the lavish productions of the French publication *Icare*.

567. Endres, Günter G. *British Civil Aviation*. London: Ian Allen, 1985. Pp. 160. Illustr.

This book is aimed at the popular market, but also manages to be an excellent condensation of the history of British aviation: its airlines, aircraft, airports, and administration. Endres's reputation as an indefatigable compiler of facts and figures is evident; but these do not obtrude upon a readable summary of an enormous subject. The illustrations are well selected, attractive, and relevant, and the text is attractively laid out.

568. *50th Anniversary Edition of SABENA Review*. Brussels: SABENA, 1973. Pp. 100 , Illustr.

This artistically produced issue of a now–defunct series of high–quality literature by Belgium's national airline, SABENA, is mainly promotional, but is also a fine commentary on the history of a notable European airline. The colored illustrations and early photographs are particularly valuable as they capture perfectly the mood of European air transport in its embryo period.

569. Fleury, Jean–Gérard. *La Ligne Mermoz, Guillaumet, Saint Exupéry et de Leurs compagnons d'épopée* (The line of

Mermoz, Saint Exupéry and their contemporaries). Paris: Gallimard, 1949. Pp. 286. Illustr.

Definitive account of Aéropostale, the airline that became a legend for its pioneering of the South Atlantic air route. Gives full credit not only to famous pilots such as Mermoz, Guillamet, and Saint–Exupéry, but also to the visionary promoter, Marcel Bouilloux–Lafont.

570. Frentz, Robert. *Swissair in Kampf und Aufstieg* (Swissair's struggle and success). Zürich: Schweizer Verlagshaus, 1973. Pp. 319. Illustr.

Popular autobiographic history of Switzerland's national airline, which, like KLM in the Netherlands, has achieved prominence by efficiency and superb service and reliability, without even the stimulus (and hidden subsidy) of a distant overseas empire to serve.

571. Harper, Harry. *The Romance of a Modern Airway*. London: Sampson Low, Marston, 1930. Pp. xiii + 241. Illustr.

A nostalgic glimpse of the British airline scene during the romantic era when Imperial Airways was pioneering the route to India. Air travel was still a source of wonderment and the mood is enthusiastically reflected in Harper's writing. The generous illustrations portray the age before all–metal, aero–dynamically designed airliners.

572. Higham, Robin D.S. *Britain's Imperial Air Routes 1918–39; The Story of Britain's Overseas Airlines*. London: G.T. Foulis, 1960. Pp. 407. Index, Bibliog., Illustr.

Excellent account of the history of Imperial Airways and its development of the British Empire's air route system, until the formation of BOAC in 1939.

573. Instone, Alfred. *Early Birds: Air Transport Memories*. 2d ed. Cardiff: Western Mail and Echo, 1938. Pp. 196. Illustr.

An account of one of the predecessor airlines that merged to form Imperial Airways. It vividly portrays the conditions under which commerical aviation got under way in Great Britian in the early 1920s.

574. Kampen, A.C. *Plesman, Grondlegger van de Gouden* (Plesman, prospector for gold). Bussom: c. deBoer, 1969. Pp. 262.

Unlike the U.S. airlines during their formative years, the European companies did not customarily produce such dominating personalities as Juan Trippe, Eddie Rickenbacker, or C.R. Smith. A notable exception was Albert Plesman, who led the Dutch airline, KLM, to greatness, achieving an international stature far beyond the expectations of one of Europe's smallest nations.

575. Lindorm, Bo., ed. *Pa Sakra Vingar: 20 Ars Lufttrafik, 1924/ 1944* (On secure wings: Twenty years of air commerce, 1924–1944). Stockhölm: A.B. Wahlstrom and Widstrand, 1944. Pp. 169. Illustr.

History of the Swedish airline ABA's first 20 years, published by the airline that still operated during World War II—Sweden being a neutral country—although surrounded by the operations of Germany's Lufthansa. Like DDL, ABA was another component of SAS.

576. Lybye, Knud. *Det Danske Luftfartselskab gennen 25 Aar* (Twenty-five years of the Danish airline). N.p.: Det Danske Luftfautselskab, 1943. Pp. 210. Illustr.

The history of one of the predecessor companies that formed SAS, the Scandinavian airline consortium. DDL was founder-member of IATA (the International Air Traffic Association) in 1919, and one of Europe's first airlines. The author wrote the book while DDL was grounded during World War II.

577. MacDonald, Hugh. *Aeroflot: Soviet Air Transport since 1923.* Putnam Aeronautical Books. London: Putnam, 1975. Pp. 323. Index, Illustr.

This is one of the famous Putnam series of aviation books and does justice to its subject. The early development of Soviet air transport is covered, and of particular interest are the chapters on the secondary and feeder services of individual regional directorates. Sections on aircraft types and extensive appendixes containing operational data are included.

578. McIntosh, R.H. *All-Weather Mac: The Autobiography of Wing*

Commander R.H. McIntosh, DFC, AFC. London: Macdonald, 1963. Pp. 288. Illustr.

McIntosh was the chief pilot of Handley Page Air Transport, one of the pioneer British companies that merged in 1924 to form Imperial Airways. Contains much entertaining and personal observation of the progress of British air transport during the development of Imperial Airways.

579. *MALEV 1945–1975.* Budapest: Pannonia, 1961. Reprint. Budapest: MALEV, 1975. Pp. 126. Illustr.

Promotional booklet, and largely an illustrated history with loosely written text. An uncommon example of the story of the early years of a post–World War II airline entirely dominated by the technical and political influences of the USSR.

580. May, Garry. *The Challenge of BEA.* London: Wolfe, 1971. Pp. 176. Illustr.

A somewhat superficial account of British European Airways, Great Britain's flag carrier for domestic, European, and Mediterranean routes throughout the first quarter century of the post–World War II era. It was a fine airline before being forcibly merged with BOAC, as a political decision, to create British Airways.

581. Merton–Jones, A.C. *British Independent Airlines since 1946.* 4 vols. Uxbridge: LAAS International; Liverpool: Meyerside Aviation Society, 1976. Pp. 504. Bibliog., Illustr.

Magnificently encyclopedic in its scope, this is a production for the enthusiast. It lists, in alphabetical order, hundreds of independent British companies, down to the tiniest charter operator, in meticulous detail. It is not a scholarly work, in the sense that it analyzes environmental, operational, or political aspects, but it is invaluable as a standard reference on a complex airline subject.

582. Penrose, Harald. *Wings across the World: An Illustrated History of British Airways.* London: Cassell, 1980. Pp. 304. Index, Illustr.

A complete history of the British national airline, British

Airways, by a fine aviation historian. It covers the pioneer post–World War I companies, Imperial Airways and the independent companies of the interwar years, and the postwar BOAC, BEA, and BSAA state airlines that eventually formed British Airways.

583. Pudney, John. *The Seven Skies: A Study of BOAC and Its Fore-runners since 1919.* London: Putnam, 1959. Pp. 320. Index, Bibliog., Illustr.

The complete story of BOAC (component of the present–day British Airways) from its predecessor pre–World War II companies until the dawn of the jet age and the Comet. A comprehensive and literary work.

584. Stroud, John. *Annals of British Commonwealth Air Transport, 1919–1960.* London: Putnam, 1962. Pp. 675. Index, Illustr.

A meticulously researched diary of every significant event in the history of British air transport since its beginning, including a list of dates and events that could be termed the prelude to airline history. The book covers the United Kingdom, the British Dominions, and overseas possessions and also includes valuable fleet lists of all the pioneer companies as well as Imperial, BOAC, and BEA.

585. Stroud, John. *European Transport Aircraft since 1910.* London: Putnam, 1966. Pp. xiv + 680. Index, Illustr.

Although this is a comprehensive listing, by country, of all the transport aircraft that served European airlines for half a century, it also provides much valuable material on the airlines themselves, as Stroud fully recognizes that the airlines were a means to an end, rather than an end in themselves.

586. Thomas, G. Holt. *Aerial Transport.* London: Hodder and Stoughton, 1920. Pp. xviii + 259. Index, Illustr.

Written by the founder of Aircraft Transport and Travel, the first British airline, this is a remarkable book, outlining the basic problems and advantages of air transport at a time when the airlines as an industry were in their infancy.

587. *Twentieth Anniversary of the Yugoslav Airlines.* Zagreb: Infro–
      mator [1967]. Pp. 62. Bibliog., Illustr.

      Also commemorating the 40th anniversary of Aeroput, the
      first airline in the infant Yugoslav state in 1927, this is another
      promotional booklet. However, it is well produced and illus–
      trated, and is an interesting account of the determined survival
      of a beleagured airline against the vicissitudes of war and
      nationalistic rivalries.

588. Wachtel, Joachim. *The Lufthansa Story.* Cologne: Lufthansa
      German Airlines, 1980. Pp. 138. Illustr.

      Although produced as a promotional document by the German
      national airline, this is an excellent, well–organized history of
      German airline development since 1926. Accurate and devoid
      of the excessive self–serving exaggeration common in such
      productions.

589. Wegg, John. *Finnair, the Art of Flying since 1923.* Helsinki:
      Finnair, 1983. Pp. 283. Index, Illustr.

      A magnificent production, lavishly produced (and printed) by
      Finnair with copious illustrations—many in color—of aircraft,
      operations, and old promotional material. The appendixes
      include pictures of every single Finnair aircraft and a tabula–
      tion of the first airlines, showing Finnair to be the world's sixth
      oldest. Also includes chronology and statistics.

590. Wheatcroft, Stephen. *The Economics of European Air Trans–
      port.* Manchester: Manchester University Press, 1956. Pp. xxii
      + 358. Index, Bibliog.

      A sound analysis of the complex factors that surround the
      economic progress of the airlines of Europe: basic economics of
      operation, national interests, competition, and international
      agreements.

Asia

591. All Nippon Airways. *All Nippon Airways Corporate History.*
      Tokyo: Zen Nihon Kuyu Kabushiki Kaisha, 1983. 2 vols. Pp.
      545 + 243. Illustr.

This official history of the largest domestic airline in the world, outside the United States or the Soviet Union, is a monumental work. Its editors and promoters seem to have deliberately tried to produce a bigger and better corporate history than that of their rival, Japan Air Lines. It is in a larger format, in two volumes. The first is devoted to an extremely detailed history, the second to appendixes, which also include a detailed chronology and survey of aircraft types. Both volumes have large sections of colored photographs. As a result of All–Nippon's lavish challenge to its competition, this is possibly the most complete historical record ever compiled by a single airline.

592. *Japan Air Lines, 1951–1971*. Tokyo: Nihon Kōkū Kabushiki Kaisha, 1974. Pp. 674. Illustr.

This official airline history was compiled by a team of historians specially appointed by JAL. It is obviously the definitive work on one of the world's largest airlines, and records the astounding growth from the Japanese airline's rebirth in 1951. There is a chapter on prewar history and many appendixes, including detailed chronologies. Superbly printed, it contains sections of color pictures and tastefully toned graphics. Originally, there was to have been an English–language version, but the cost became prohibitive; hence the text is in Japanese.

593. Kohri, Katsu, Ikuo Komori, and Ichiro Naito, comps. *The Fifty Years of Japanese Aviation, 1910–1960*. 2 vols. Translated by Kazuo Oyauchi. Tokyo: Kantosha, 1961. Pp. 324 + 169. Illustr.

Succinct history of aviation in Japan from "prehistoric days" until 1960. Although the text is condensed and free of embellishment, there are good tables, excellent charts showing wartime progress and decline, and a well–researched chronological appendix, listing all important events—civil, military, and overseas. An excellent reference book.

594. Leary, William M. *The Dragon's Wings: The China National Aviation Corporation and the Development of Commercial Aviation in China*. Athens: University of Georgia Press, 1976. Pp. xiii + 279. Index, Bibliog., Illustr.

This is the first book of a trilogy on Chinese commercial aviation, by one of the finest air transport historians writing today. Leary manages to combine accurate recording of facts with pungent selective commentary, to produce a thoroughly readable narrative.

595. Leary, William M. *Perilous Missions: Civil Air Transport and CIA Covert Operations in Asia.* University, Ala.: University of Alabama Press, 1984. Pp. x + 281. Index, Bibliog., Illustr.

The second of Leary's trilogy on Chinese airline history, this one concentrates on a remarkable airline, Civil Air Transport (CAT), the brainchild of war hero Claire L. Chennault, which started as an airline in Taiwan, and later became the CIA's secret "air force," conducting extensive covert operations in East Asia, especially in Vietnam. This is a book of tremendous historical importance.

596. Rubin, Paul J. *Japan Air Transport Handbook.* Tokyo: JAL/Paul J. Rubin, 1981. Pp. 152. Illustr.

Comprehensive coverage of Japan's aviation industry, with particular reference to the scheduled airlines. Succinct historical summary of statistics, details of aircraft fleets, and operating data, including airfield information.

597. Santos, Enrique B. *Philippine Wings.* Manila: Philippine Airlines, 1969. Pp. 75. Illustr.

This is mainly the history of Philippine Air Lines, by its public relations director. Therefore, it is substantially the history of commercial aviation in the Philippines, whose many islands made it an ideal country for the development of an airline system necessary for essential communications.

598. Santos, Enrique B. *Trails in Philippine Skies.* Manila: Philippine Airlines, 1981. Pp. 328. Index, Illustr.

This is an even more ambitious book by Santos, faithfully chronicling the entire history of aviation in the Philippines, from 1909 to 1941. It covers the experiments and notable flying achievements of the early years and deals comprehensively with all subsequent developments, military and civil.

599. Tata, J.R.D. *The Story of Indian Air Transport.* Bombay: Air India [1953]. Pp. 40. Illustr.

This is the printed form of a lecture delivered by Mr. Tata to the Royal Aeronautical Society. It is a comprehensive account of the political, operational, and technical development of commercial air transport in India by the man most responsible for it. It is authoritative and personal, and a minor classic.

600. Wiethoff, Bods. *Luftverkehr in China, 1928–1949* (Air transportation in China, 1928–1949). Wiesbaden: Ottalttarrassowitz, 1975. Pp. 380. Index, Bibliog., Illustr.

A truly scholarly work about the complex political developments that led to the formation of the first airlines in China. The histories of the prewar CNAC and Eurasia are meticulously documented, as are their development in the postwar years during the Communist revolution.

Australia and the South Pacific

601. Bennett–Bremner, E. *Front–line Airline: Air Transport during the South–West Pacific War, 1934–44.* London: Paul Elek, 1945. Pp. 80. Illustr.

A modest little book, which, however, provides a penetrating, personal account of air transport in the Southwest Pacific theater of war from 1939 to 1944. Primarily, it records the role of QANTAS, the Australian national airline, in providing logistical support to the allied military forces in New Guinea, Indonesia, and the Solomon Islands. It is a vivid story of an airline doing its job under fire.

602. Driscoll, Ian H. *Flightpath South Pacific: The Flyers, the Airlines and the Aircraft.* Christchurch, New Zealand: Whitcombe and Tombs, 1972. Pp. 303. Index, Bibliog., Illustr.

Driscoll was a purser who worked for Imperial Airways and later joined New Zealand National Airways. The admirable historical narrative covers the history of the airlines of New Zealand in some detail and also reviews the airlines of the region. The author's personal reminiscences cover the formative years of the British Commonwealth air routes. The appendixes covering the chronology, airlines, routes, and equipment are splendidly complete and accurately researched.

603. Hocking, D.M., and C.P. Haddon–Cave. *Air Transport in Australia.* Sydney: Angus and Robertson, 1951. Pp. xvi + 188. Index.

Published under the auspices of the Australian Institute of International Affairs and the Institute of Pacific Relations, this is a methodically compiled factual history of Australian airlines from 1919 to 1950. An excellent factual reference book for the period, with important sections dealing with political developments, especially in the immediate post–World War II period.

604. Wigley, Harry. *Ski–Plane Adventure: Flying in the New Zealand Alps.* 2d ed. Wellington: A.H. and A.W. Reed, 1977. Pp. 222. Illustr.

An entertaining account of the adventurous life of a true pioneer who operated a remarkable airline in southern New Zealand. Mount Cook Airlines, founded by Wigley's father, a bus operator, is probably the only airline in the world that operates regularly on a glacier. Flying in the New Zealand Alps with ski–planes represents the far end of the air transport spectrum, of which a Pan American Boeing 747 represents the other.

Latin America

605. *La Aeronáutica Nacional al Servicio del Pais* (National aviation in the service of the state). Argentina: Secretariá de Aeronáutica de la Naciãn, 1948. Pp. 345. Illustr.

This handsome folio–size production is a comprehensive record of Argentine commercial aviation from the early 1920s until the immediate postwar period. It is especially important because the book was published immediately before the nationalization of all the Argentine airlines by the Perãn government in 1949. The production is lavish, with many colored charts and good illustrations; but the text is accurate and well researched, coming as it does from an official source.

606. Anderson, Dole A. *Aviação Comercial Brasileira* (Brazilian commercial aviation). João Pessoa: Editoria Universitária, 1979. Pp. 168.

This is a scholarly work that reviews concisely the place of Brazilian commercial aviation in the world today, its evolution, and recent regulatory control; and analyzes, with much statistical evidence, the problems of market development, equipment selection, and financial matters such as subsidy. A thought–provoking thesis.

607. Boy, Herbert. *Una História con Alas* (Winged history). Bogotá: Editorial Iqueima, 1963. Pp. 286. Illustr.

A personal account of one of the pilots of the Colombian airline, SCADTA, which later became the national flag carrier, AVIANCA. It tells the story from a pilot's viewpoint, of the difficulties in creating an air service in a country where roads were nonexistent and railroads very few. An interesting interlude occurred when, in 1932, war broke out between Colombia and Peru, and Boy took part of the airline fleet into the Amazon jungles to support the armed forces. A rare personal glimpse of pioneering in completely undeveloped territory.

608. Burden, William A.M. *The Struggle for Airways in Latin America*. New York: Council on Foreign Relations, 1943. Pp. xxiv + 245. Index, Bibliog., Illustr.

For many years, this was the only authoritative book about the development of air transport in Latin America. Although written with a political objective, it is comprehensive and accurate. The lavish production includes a well–selected collection of photographs and many maps, including several in full color, each of which was the result of much painstaking research. The book is a textbook of Latin American geography and economic conditions and a complete account of the commercial airplane's role in a hostile operating environment. Reprinted in 1977 by Arno Press.

609. Davies, R.E.G. *Airlines of Latin America since 1919*. Washington D.C.: Smithsonian Institution Press, 1983. Pp. xiv + 698. Index, Bibliog., Illustr.

One of the well–known Putnam aviation books, copublished with the Smithsonian, this is a companion volume to Davies's U.S. airline book. It charts the course of all Latin American airlines, country by country (there are eight chapters alone on Brazil) and is illustrated by more than 400 pictures, about 100 maps and charts, and a mass of tabulated information. This is a complete history of the development of air transport, and its effect on the national economies of a whole continent, over a period of 65 years.

610. Forero F., José Ignacio. *História de la Aviación en Colombia* (History of aviation in Colombia). Bogotá: Aedita, Editores, Ltda., 1964. Pp. 394. Index, Illustr.

Systematic account of the development of aviation in Colombia, both military and commercial, but containing a subsequent element of the epoch–making airlines of the 1920s. Colombia's airline industry is the oldest in all the Americas and thus this account, containing as it does many personal reminiscences, is especially important as source material for research.

611. Lavanère–Wanderley, Nelson Freire. *Historia de Forca Aérea Brasileira* (History of the Brazilian Air Force). Rio de Janeiro: Ministerio da Aeronáutica, 1966. Reprinted, 1975. Pp. 390. Index, Illustr.

Comprehensive account of the development of the Brazilian Air Force, both Army and Navy, since 1916, including a short summary of early aviation in Brazil, and ending with the Air Force's participation in the Congo conflict in the 1960s. The book is important for commercial air transport studies because the Brazilian Air Force deployed a substantial force toward the establishment of a mail and courier service into the undeveloped heartland of Brazil. This was in the early 1930s and predated many of the commercial airline routes that were subsequently flown by Brazilian airlines.

612. *Libro de Oro—Faucett, 1928–1978* (Book of Gold—Faucett, 1928–1978). Callao, Peru: Faucett Public Relations Office, 1978. Pp. 52. Illustr.

An attractive commemorative booklet, in color throughout, recording the history of one of the older airlines of Latin America. Founded by a U.S. citizen who developed his own special version of a basic design to cope with the stringent performance standards required in the formidable Peruvian terrain. Although bearing the stamp of a public relations exercise, this book is nevertheless valuable as it provides a good account of the growth of an airline in a developing country.

613. Medeiros, J.D., ed. *A História da Panair do Brasil* (History of Panair do Brasil). Rio de Janeiro: ETA–Editora Tecnica de Aviaçao, 1980. Pp. 104. Illustr.

A small commemorative booklet produced by the former employees of one of the pioneer airlines of Brazil that was absorbed by another company, under arbitrary circumstances, in 1965. The short historical text is also supplemented by many exhibits that bear witness to the importance of the airline during its existence, and is important because the history of airlines that became casualties is rare, especially in South America.

614. Newton, Wesley Phillips. *The Perilous Sky: Evolution of United States Aviation Diplomacy toward Latin America, 1919–1931.* Coral Gables, Fla.: University of Miami Press, 1978. Pp. 457. Index, Bibliog., Illustr.

Meticulously researched analysis of the early development of United States airlines in Latin America, the text concentrates particularly on the events leading up to Pan American's clandestine takeover of SCADTA, the Colombian–German airline founded in Bogota in 1919. Also outlines clearly the political influences that supported Juan Trippe and Pan Am on his almost ruthless quest for airline domination throughout Latin America.

615. Schleit, Philip. *Shelton's Barefoot Airlines.* Annapolis, Md.: Fishergate, 1982. Pp. x + 142. Index, Illustr.

This is a fine account of the accomplishments of an adventurous airline privateer. C.N. Shelton founded airlines in Latin America that were aimed to serve the local inhabitants, rather than U.S. businessmen and tourists. He used old planes, led the Civil Aeronautics Board a fine dance, always made profits, and never killed a passenger. The book also describes, with a sensitive feel for atmosphere, the problems of airlines in a turbulent political environment, as well as in arduous operating conditions.

616. Villela Gómez, José. *Breve História de la Aviación en México* (Brief history of aviation in Mexico). Mexico: José Villela Gómez, 1971. Pp. 48. Illustr.

This is a monumental work, especially commendable because it is the production of one man. He traces the entire history of aviation, from Aztec legend to the modern jets. His chapters on the airlines, well illustrated with rare photographs, comprise the only systematic record, from direct source materials, of this important airline country.

617. Yerex, David. *Yerex of TACA—A Kiwi Conquistador.* Canterton, New Zealand: Ampersand, 1985. Pp. 204. Illustr.

Written by his nephew, this is the story of an inspired New Zealander who was one of the great pioneers of air transport in Latin America. He founded TACA, an airline that became an institution in the small countries of Central America during the 1930s and that provided for many years the sole means of communications to countless small communities in the region. The painstaking and adventurous development of his airline, followed by his ruthless elimination from the field by Pan American Airways and the U.S. and British governments, make a fascinating story of one man's unique achievement.

Africa and the Middle East

618. *Dünden Bugüne Türk Hava Yollari* (Turkish airlines from yesterday to today). Istanbul: Turkish Airlines, 1983. Pp. 240. Illustr.

Lavishly produced book to commemorate 50 years of commercial aviation in Turkey, 1933 to 1983. Progress of the airline is meticulously annotated, year by year, with statistics and photographs, and supported by commentary and exhibits. A comprehensive reference book from an area where aviation literature is rare.

619. *From Mules to Jets: A Short History of Aviation in Ethiopia.* Switzerland: Ethiopian Airlines, 1981. Pp. 48. Illustr.

This is an attractive booklet, providing not only a well-illustrated history of the Ethiopian airline itself, but also a well-researched and equally well-illustrated history of aviation in Ethiopia since 1929. It is thus a rare commentary of aeronautical development in one of the few countries of black Africa which, except for the period of Italian occupation from 1935 to 1941, was never colonized by European powers, as was most of the continent.

Airmail

620. David, Paul T. *The Economics of Air Mail Transportation.* Washington, D.C.: Brookings Institution, 1934. Pp. xii + 235. Bibliog., Illustr.

A keen, objective analysis of the development of airmail service in the United States from the embryo period of experiment through the years of the U.S. Air Mail Service and into the first few years of contracted airmail by private carrier airlines. The author makes some penetrating observations on the interpretation (or misinterpretation) of the law, according to the Kelly and Watres airmail acts, and draws a sharp distinction between the subsidies granted for mail and those that indirectly subsidized passenger service.

621. Holmes, Donald B. *Air Mail, an Illustrated History, 1793–1981.* New York: Clarkson N. Potter, 1981. Pp. xiii + 226. Index, Bibliog., Illustr.

An extensively illustrated history of airmail that provides lengthy narratives of most of the major events in its evolution. Although it attempts to be international in scope, the emphasis of the work is on airmail in the United States.

622. Jackson, Donald D. *Flying the Mail.* Alexandria, Va.: Time–Life, 1982. Pp. 176. Index, Bibliog., Illustr.

A detailed and informative chronicle of the airmail in its evolutionary stages in the 1920s and 1930s. Extensively researched with a chapter on international developments. Effectively illustrated.

623. Leary, William M. *Aerial Pioneers, the U.S. Air Mail Service, 1918–1927.* Washington, D.C.: Smithsonian Institution Press, 1985. Pp. 309. Index, Bibliog., Illustr.

The aviation reading public, researchers, scholars, and historians alike have long awaited a definitive book on the history of the U.S. airmail service during the 1920s. Operated by the U.S. Post Office, the airmail was the greatest contribution made to the development of air transport by the United States during the formative years of the industry. Combines accurate historical reporting with sensitive observations that emphasize the hazardous nature of the pioneer operation. Chapters on Aeromarine Airways and the lighted airway round off an impressive contribution to the history of commerical aviation.

Airports

Arend, Geoffrey. *Air World's Great Airports: Newark, 1928–1952*. New York: Air Cargo News, 1978. Pp. 109. Illustr.

Cited herein as item 933.

Arend, Geoffrey. *Air World's Great Airports: La Guardia, 1939–1979*. New York: Air Cargo News, 1979. Pp. 152. Illustr.

Cited herein as item 934.

Arend, Geoffrey. *Great Airports: Kennedy International*. New York: Air Cargo News, 1981. Pp. 200. Illustr.

Cited herein as item 935.

Arend, Geoffrey. *Great Airports: Miami International*. New York: Air Cargo News, 1986. Pp. 320. Illustr.

Cited herein as item 936.

624. Duke, Donald G. *Airports and Airways, Cost Operation and Maintenance*. New York: Ronald, 1927. Pp. xii + 178. Index, Illustr.

One of the earliest serious attempts to state a procedure for the establishment and operation of airports and the promotion of airways, written by the chief of the Army Air Corps Airways Section.

625. Hanks, Stedman S. *International Airports*. New York: Ronald, 1929. Pp. x + 195. Illustr.

A fascinating contemporary (late 1920s) review of U.S. and European flying fields, well illustrated with appendixes that contain a selection of international conventions and regulations.

626. Horonjeff, Robert. *Planning and Design of Airports*. 2d ed. New York: McGraw–Hill, 1975. Pp. 460. Index, Bibliog., Illustr.

A recent text with much useful information that provides an interesting counterpoint to Duke's *Airports and Airways, Cost Operation and Maintenance* (cited herein as item 624). Discusses the principles that govern the airport design–planning process.

627. Stroud, John. *Airports of the World*. London: Putnam, 1980. Pp. xxiv + 605. Index, Illustr.

A most thoroughly researched, comprehensive reference book that covers 495 airports in 117 countries around the world. Includes information concerning the primary features of each airport such as operating authority, runway dimensions, elevation, lighting, navigation aids, and so on, with diagrams and photographs, plus a brief historical sketch of its development.

GENERAL AVIATION

One of the largest sectors of the aviation world, general aviation is often understood by the layman to be synonymous with recreational or "private" flying in light, low–horsepower aircraft. Although general aviation does indeed include recreational flying, the term also refers to a variety of other types of flying and to numerous aircraft. This section therefore includes books on aerial photography, gliding and soaring, hang gliding, homebuilt aircraft, human–powered flight, private and business flying, and ultralight aircraft.

The works in each subsection reflect a wide range of source material, from practical information to definitive scholarly works, and should answer the needs of a variety of researchers. Obviously, many additional titles could have been included. The reader who wishes further information should consult "Flying," Chapter 5 in Bernard Mergen's *Recreational Vehicles and Travel: A Resource Guide* (Westport, Conn.: Greenwood, 1985, pp. 143–174). Mergen's extensive and informative bibliographic essay cites more than 300 books and articles that are relevant not only to "the expressive dimensions of flying," as he terms it, but also to the entire sweep of the history of aviation.

Barbara J. Irwin
Russell E. Lee
Jay P. Spenser
Deborah G. Douglas
Dorothy S. Cochrane

Aerial Photography

628. Bagley, James W. *Aerophotography and Aerosurveying.* New York: McGraw–Hill, 1941. Pp. x + 324. Index, Bibliog., Illustr.

    An indispensable technical book for the student of the history of aerial photography and aerial surveying that provides a systematic study of the subject in the years before World War II. Bagley, the developer of the Bagley Tri–lens aerial camera, covers in detail the entire range of the subject.

629. Ives, Herbert Eugene. *Airplane Photography.* Philadelphia, Pa.: J.P. Lippincott, 1920. Pp. 422. Index, Illustr.

    An essential volume for early aerial photographic research as well as an excellent reference for the science of aerial photography. This well–illustrated book provides a complete education on early cameras, lenses, the interpretation of photographs, and most aspects of aerial photography. Certain sections are technical in nature.

631. Newhall, Beaumont. *Airborne Camera: The World from the Air and Outer Space.* New York: Hastings House, 1969. Pp. 144. Index, Bibliog., Illustr.

    A general history of aerial photography from balloons and kites to aircraft and spacecraft, written by the prominent historian of photography. Newhall examines both cameras and their modes of aerial transportation, along with mapping, reconnaissance, and meteorology. The book is well illustrated with a wide variety of interesting and beautiful photographs.

631. Smith, John T., and Abraham Anson, eds. *Manual of Color Aerial Photography.* Falls Church, Va.: American Society of Photogrammetry, 1968. Pp. xv + 550. Index, Bibliog., Illustr.

    A formidable study of color aerial photography authored by an impressive collection of experts in the field. The complex science is studied in a richly illustrated, technical volume that covers equipment, chemistry, and the interpretation of color photographs for a wide range of subjects. Includes many graphs, charts, and three appendixes.

Gliding and Soaring

632. Barringer, Lewin B. *Flight without Power: The Art of Gliding and Soaring*. New York: Pitman, 1940. Pp. ix + 251. Index, Bibliog., Illustr.

    The author, who held a world distance record for gliders and was quite active in soaring in the 1930s, provides a good overview of U.S. gliding and soaring during the period. Brief historical chapter at the beginning.

633. Bowers, Peter. *Modern Soaring Guide*. 2d ed. Blue Ridge Summit, Pa.: TAB, 1979. Pp. 256. Index, Illustr.

    Small but good summary that includes brief history of gliding/soaring, specific types, related equipment, soaring, techniques, and so on.

634. *Bungee Cord*. Lovettsville, Va.: Vintage Sailplane Association. Quarterly.

    Although too brief to include but a few photographs, this quarterly publication is now in 11 volumes and contains the most detailed English-language accounts of glider history available. Published by the Vintage Sailplane Association, a subsidiary of the Soaring Society of America, an organization devoted to documenting, preserving, and flying vintage sailplanes.

635. Devlin, Gerard M. *Silent Wings: The Saga of U.S. Army and Marine Combat Glider Pilots during World War II*. New York: St. Martin's, 1985. Pp. xxii + 410. Index, Bibliog., Illustr.

    Superb historical account of U.S. combat glider activities during World War II. Emphasizes battles, tactics, and operational use and includes British, Soviet, German, and Japanese glider operations. Entertaining and well written.

636. Dwiggins, Don. *On Silent Wings: Adventures in Motorless Flight*. New York: Grosset and Dunlap, 1970. Pp. 151. Illustr.

    Excellent history and summary of gliding/soaring. Many rare photographs.

637. Ellison, Norman H. *British Gliders and Sailplanes, 1922–1970*.
     New York: Barnes and Noble, 1971. Pp. 296. Index, Bibliog.,
     Illustr.

     Complete history of gliding in Great Britain. An adequate
     review of events and personalities is followed by a complete list
     of glider types from 1922 to 1970. Good three–view aircraft
     drawings.

638. Joss, John. *SoarAmerica*. Los Altos, Calif.: Soaring, 1976. Pp.
     xii + 216. Bibliog., Illustr.

     A compilation of articles from *Soaring* magazine that con-
     sists of memorable flights and special flying sites. Articles
     include photographs and drawings that teach gliding concepts.

639. Lincoln, Joseph Colville. *On Quiet Wings: A Soaring Anthology*.
     Flagstaff, Ariz.: Northland, 1972. Pp. xx + 397. Index, Illustr.

     Some of the best articles from *Soaring* magazine are com-
     bined with photographs and drawings in this quality hardback.
     The principles and techniques of gliding are introduced.

640. Mrazek, James E. *Fighting Gliders of World War II*. New York:
     St. Martin's, 1977. Pp. 207. Index, Illustr.

     Best work available on all known combat gliders of World War
     II. Mrazek emphasizes technological development and glider
     types. Well written and contains interesting photographs and
     drawings.

641. Piggot, Derek. *Understanding Gliding: The Principles of Soaring
     Flight*. New York: Barnes and Noble, 1977. Pp. 259. Illustr.,
     Index.

     Soaring techniques, sailplane structures, and the like.

642. Riedel, Peter. *Start in dem Wind* (*Takeoff into the wind*). Stutt-
     gart, Germany: Motorbuch Verlag, 1977. Pp. 281. Index,
     Illustr.

     Most accurate account of German gliding activities before
     World War II. Although the text is in German, the photographs

are worth the price of the book. This is the first of three volumes and covers the period from 1911 to 1926.

643. Riedel, Peter. *Vom Hangwind zur Thermik (From calm to thermal)*. Stuttgart, Germany: Motorbuch Verlag, 1984. Pp. 226. Illustr.

The second volume in Riedel's classic work on German glider activities covers the period 1927–1932. German text and hundreds of superb photographs.

644. Riedel, Peter. *Über sonnige Weiten (Over sunny expanses)*. Stuttgart, Germany: Motorbuch Verlag, 1985. Pp. 271. Index, Illustr.

Third and final volume (1933–1939) in series on history of German glider activities. German text and excellent illustrations.

645. *Soaring and Motorgliding*. Santa Monica, Calif.: Soaring Society of America. Monthly.

Contains the best and most exhaustive coverage of modern gliding (emphasis on the United States). Well illustrated with occasional articles about the history of gliding.

Hang Gliding

646. Carrier, Frederick "Rick" G. *Fly: The Complete Book of Sky Sailing*. New York: McGraw–Hill, 1974. Pp. 128. Bibliog., Illustr.

Thorough coverage of hang gliding history, aircraft types, and pilot training. Profusely illustrated.

647. Halacy, D.S., Jr. *The Complete Book of Hang Gliding*. New York: Hawthorn, 1975. Pp. 183., Index, Bibliog., Illustr.

Well–written and informative analysis of mid–70s hang gliding with sections on history and future of the sport.

648. Hunt, Martin. *Hang Gliding*. New York: Arco, 1977. Pp. 128. Illustr.

   Comprehensive view of world hang gliding. Brief history included.

649. Markowski, Michael A. *The Hang Glider's Bible*. Blue Ridge Summit, Pa.: TAB, 1977. Pp. 480. Index, Bibliog., Illustr.

   When it was published in 1977, *The Hang Glider's Bible* was the definitive work on the sport. The book is well written, well illustrated, and thorough. It begins with a history of hang gliding that includes Lilienthal, Chanute, and others.

650. Mrazek, James E. *Hang Gliding and Soaring*. Rev. ed. New York: St. Martin's, 1981. Pp. viii + 215. Illustr.

   Well illustrated and nicely written, with chapters on Paul MacCready's human–powered aircraft and powered ultralights, both of which are related to hang gliders.

651. Poynter, Dan. *Hang Gliding: The Basic Handbook of Skysurfing*. Santa Barbara, Calif.: Parachuting, 1979. Pp. viii + 181. Bibliog., Illustr.

   Exhaustive account of technical aspects of hang gliding, circa 1983. Includes historical chapter. Very well illustrated.

652. Wills, Maralys. *Manbirds: Hang Gliders and Hang Gliding*. Englewood Cliffs, N.J.: Prentice–Hall, 1981. Pp. 242. Index, Bibliog., Illustr.

   An excellent short history on hang gliding that includes a chapter on the fundamentals of flying and lists clubs, schools, and sites for hang gliding around the country.

Homebuilt Aircraft

   Bingelis, Antoni. *Firewall Forward: Engine Installation Methods*. Edited by David A. Rivers. Austin, Tex.: Tony Bingelis, 1983. Pp. 303. Illustr.

   Cited herein as item 349.

653. Bird, P.E. *Elements of Sport Airplane Design for the Home-builder*. Los Angeles, Calif.: Vogel Aviation, 1977. Pp. 95. Bibliog., Illustr.

Brief but good basic handbook for those who want to design a sport airplane.

654. Bowers, Peter M. *Guide to Homebuilts*. 8th ed. Modern Aviation Series. Blue Ridge Summit, Pa.: TAB, 1981. Pp. 208. Index, Illustr.

Easy-to-read book that concentrates on the history of home-builts. Covers modern, traditional designs but excludes more up-to-date composite material, the so-called plastic homebuilts.

655. Dwiggins, Don. *Build Your Own Sport Plane*. New York: Hawthorn, 1975. Pp. viii + 259. Index, Bibliog., Illustr.

Adequate general overview of homebuilt aircraft movement in the early 1970s.

656. Experimental Aircraft Association. *EAA Data Book for the Aircraft Homebuilder*. 4th ed. Hales Corners, Wisc., 1964. Pp. 54. Illustr.

Analyzes the Experimental Aircraft Association and home-built aircraft in the early 1960s. A number of good photographs highlight a lively text.

657. Forrest, Richard I., and Paul H. Poberezny. *EAA's Aircraft Builders Handbook*. Hales Corners, Wisc.: Experimental Aircraft Association, 1965. Pp. 62. Illustr.

Good historical reference that contains general technical information governing homebuilts in the United States and Canada.

658. Garrison, Peter. *Homebuilt Airplanes*. San Francisco, Calif.: Chronicle, 1979. Pp. 95. Illustr.

Describes specific homebuilt airplanes, from ultralights to helicopters, in well-written anecdotes. Excellent color illustrations highlight each chapter.

659. Lambie, Jack. *Composite Construction for Homebuilt Aircraft.*
     Sport Aviation Series Book no. 6. Hummelstown, Pa.: Ultra-
     light, 1984. Pp. 238. Illustr.

     An excellent text on the most recent technological revolution
     in the construction of homebuilt aircraft. Thorough and well-
     written.

660. Markowski, Michael A. *The Encyclopedia of Homebuilt Air-
     craft.* Model Aviation Series. Blue Ridge Summit, Pa.: TAB,
     1980. Pp. 576.

     Contains a listing of almost every homebuilt known. Speci-
     fications are included with each aircraft and there are 10
     appendixes of related information. The work is somewhat dated
     because it was published just before the revolutionary use of
     composite materials in homebuilts began.

661. Markowski, Michael A. *ARV: The Encyclopedia of Aircraft
     Recreational Vehicles.* Hummelstown, Pa.: Ultralight, 1984.
     Pp. 350, Illustr.

     Attempts to describe aircraft, primarily homebuilts, that fall
     within the newly defined category of aircraft recreation vehi-
     cles—between kite–like ultralights and traditional single-
     engine, all–metal airplanes. The book goes back to the earliest
     days of aviation to trace the evolution of this new aircraft
     category. Interesting to read, with useful appendixes and an
     adequate glossary.

662. Thomas, Kas, and Jack Lambie. *The Complete Guide to Home-
     built Rotorcraft.* Blue Ridge Summit, Pa.: TAB, 1982. Pp. viii
     + 120. Index, Illustr.

     Clearly explains small, personal helicopters built from plans
     or kits. Includes easy–to–read text and adequate illustrations.
     Contains a list of design and construction source material.

663. Thurston, David B. *Homebuilt Aircraft.* New York: McGraw-
     Hill, 1982. Pp. xiv + 210. Index, Bibliog., Illustr.

     An aeronautical engineer's overview of U.S. general aviation
     movement known as "homebuilding," with details of designs,
     construction materials, and techniques. This book gives

in–depth coverage on the technical requirements for building airplanes at home. Shop requirements, insurance and safety, and a thorough chapter on powerplants are included.

Human–Powered Flight

664. Grosser, Morton. *Gossamer Odyssey: The Triumph of Human Powered Flight.* Boston: Houghton Mifflin, 1981. Pp. xxi + 298. Index, Bibliog., Illustr.

    Documentary of Paul MacCready's two human–powered aircraft, the *Gossamer Condor* and *Gossamer Albatross*, and the background of the Kremer prizes. Contains brief historical introduction.

665. Reay, David A. *The History of Man–Powered Flight.* Oxford: Pergamon, 1977. Pp. x + 355. Index, Bibliog., Illustr.

    Excellent history of human–powered flight through 1977, just before Paul MacCready's successful *Gossamer Condor.* Text includes early material on flight mythology, Leonardo da Vinci, and 19th–century ornithopters.

666. Schulze, Hans G., and Willi Stiasny. *Flug durch Muskelkraft* (Flight through muscle power). Frankfurt: Verlag Fritz Knapp, 1936. Pp. 223. Index, Bibliog., Illustr.

    Superb history of human–powered flight through 1936. Included is valuable material on the Muskelflug–Institut (Muscle Flight Institute) that was quite active in Germany during the interwar years. Contains excellent illustrations and diagrams.

Private and Business Flying

667. Bilstein, Roger E. "Technology and Commerce: Aviation in the Context of American Business, 1918–1929." *Technology and Culture* 10 (July, 1969): 392–411.

    Examines the effect of aviation on business in the years following World War I. Includes the effect of airmail on banking, air cargo express, and early business and commercial passenger flying.

668. Bollinger, Lynn L., and Arthur J. Tully, Jr. *Personal Aircraft Business at Airports*. Elmsford, N.Y.: Maxwell Reprint, 1948. Pp. xi + 348. Index.

This extensive study of the commercial interests created by the growth of fixed–base operation was conducted by the Harvard Business School. Because the study was undertaken during the post–World War II years, the boom in general aviation growth figures significantly in the data presented. Also critically examines aviation as an industry and its financial implications.

669. Boughton, Terence. *The Story of the British Light Aeroplane*. London: John Murray, 1963. Pp. xiv + 321. Index, Bibliog., Illustr.

Chronicles the development of British light aviation from 1911 to 1939, with special emphasis on events from the 1920s and 1930s. Not only examines the staggering number of airplane designs that were developed during these years, but also includes data on the many air contests and record–breaking flights that resulted. Boughton is critically reviewed by Kenneth Razak in *Technology and Culture* 5 (Summer 1964), 457–459.

670. Crouch, Tom D. "General Aviation: The Search for a Market, 1910–1976." In *Two Hundred Years of Flight in America*, ed. Eugene Emme, 111–135. San Diego, Calif.: American Astronautical Society, 1977. Bibliog., Illustr.

Measures the impact of general aviation on the American economy from 1919 until the late 1960s. Emphasis is placed on the diversity of early general aviation, which had a hand in everything from crop dusting to surveying. The problems of civil aviation, especially that of high operational and maintenance costs, are examined, as well as the push to produce a "poor man's airplane." Includes information on homebuilts and soaring.

671. Ethell, Jeffrey L. *NASA and General Aviation*. NASA SP–485. Washington, D.C.: National Aeronautics and Space Administration, Scientific and Technical Information Branch, 1986. Pp. ix + 131. Illustr.

An excellent, tightly written account that reviews the

research efforts of the National Aeronautics and Space Administration in regard to improving general aviation. Topics of discussion include aerodynamic efficiency, internal combustion and turbine engines, commuter aviation, safety, and electronics and avionics.

672. *Flying* Magazine. *The Best of Flying.* New York: Van Nostrand Reinhold, 1977. Pp. 352. Index, Illustr.

A sampler of articles that have appeared in the magazine, published to celebrate *Flying*'s 50th birthday. Not only does it reflect changing thought during aviation's rapid development, but it is also an excellent source of information concerning events and personalities involved.

673. Francis, Devon. *Mr. Piper and His Cubs.* Ames: Iowa State University Press, 1973. Pp. xi + 256. Index, Bibliog., Illustr.

A corporate history of Piper Aircraft and founder William T. Piper. A good deal of attention is given to the Piper Cub, the company's most successful plane. The heightened production during World War II is also well documented. The word "Cubs" in the title does not refer to the airplane so much as to the family–run business that Piper Aircraft eventually became.

674. Juptner, Joseph P. *U.S. Civil Aircraft.* 9 vols. Los Angeles, Calif.: Aero, 1962–. Index. Bibliog., Illustr.

Juptner presents every civil aircraft to recieve an ATC (Approved Type Certificate) in chronological order, beginning with no. 1, the Buhl–Verville J4 Airster, in 1927 and ending with no. 817, the Fokker Friendship F–27, in 1957. Through extensive use of photographs, combined with detailed statistics and information, Juptner fills a void where precise data are needed. Volume 9 contains a section entitled "ATC Update" that corrects errors found in previous volumes; Volume 9 also provides ATC listings and the master index for the series.

675. Langewiesche, Wolfgang. *Stick and Rudder; An Explanation of the Art of Flying.* New York: McGraw–Hill, 1944. Pp. vi + 389. Index, Illustr.

The classic flying manual, this book covers the basics of private flying, including elementary maneuvers and controls, landings, simple aerodynamics, and problem solving.

676. McDaniel, William H. *The History of Beech: Four Decades of Aeronautical and Aerospace Achievement.* Wichita, Kans.: McCormick–Armstrong, 1976. Pp. xii + 480. Index, Illustr.

An extensive and complete corporate history of the Beech Aircraft, with emphasis on the success of the various Beech models during and following World War II. Beech is unique in that for half of its business life, it has been managed by Olive Ann Beech, widow of founder Walter Beech. Includes many photos.

677. Munson, Kenneth. *Private Aircraft: Business and General Purpose, since 1946.* New York: Macmillan, 1967. Pp. 173. Index, Illustr.

Focuses on both business and general postwar aircraft and has a worldwide scope. The 80 aircraft appear in three–view color drawings together with a brief descriptive paragraph.

678. Nicholson, Norman, ed. *Readings on Post War Personal Aircraft.* Fort Worth, Tex.: Globe Aircraft, 1944. Pp. 100.

A collection of short articles derived from prominent national publications and well–known authors of the aviation world that outline predictions for the future of general aviation following the war. The expected sales boom of the postwar years is a prominent theme, as is the idea of the availability of aviation to the average man.

679. R. Dixon Speas Associates. *The Magnitude and Economic Impact of General Aviation, 1968–1980.* Manhasset, N.Y.: Aero House, 1970. Pp. xi + 154. Bibliog.

Thoroughly examines general aviation from the industry itself to geographical distribution and composition of the general aviation fleet. Also provides information on passenger and cargo transport, and on many aspects of economic implications and impact. An extensive study that conveys much information through the use of graphs and tables.

680. Robertson, F.H. "Light and Executive Aircraft and Their Future Prospects in the United Kingdom." *Royal Aeronautical Society Journal* 67 (October 1963): 637–650.

The text of a lecture given on this subject. Centers on the complaint that the British aircraft industry had failed to include light aircraft manufacture as a profit–making venture. Explores the profitability and possible form for the basis of a strong light aircraft industry and discusses the history of light aircraft in Great Britain. Includes the text of the discussion that followed the lecture.

681. Smith, Frank Kingston. *Week–End Pilot.* New York: Random House, 1957. Pp. vii + 242. Illustr.

Although somewhat dated, *Week–End Pilot* provides practical piloting information through an amusing, anecdotal writing style most useful for the beginner pilot. Smith later authored *Weekend Wings*, which documented his further experiences.

682. Smith, Frank Kingston. "The Turbulent Decade." *Flying*, September 1977, 200–208. Illustr.

An interesting account of the post–World War II "boom and bust" in the private aircraft industry viewed from the mid-1970s, a prosperous time for general aviation. It is worthwhile to contrast this article with Thompson's "Hard Times in Hangar Town," also cited in this section.

683. Smith, Frank Kingston. *Weekend Wings.* New York: Random House, 1982. Pp. 193.

A highly entertaining tale of the experiences of a recreational pilot. Although the stories he relates are amusing, they also contain practical information that will be useful to the private pilot, or to those interested in learning more about recreational private flying. See also Smith's earlier volume *Week–End Pilot* (cited herein as item 681).

684. Spenser, Jay P. *Aeronca C–2: The Story of the Flying Bathtub.* Famous Aircraft of the National Air and Space Museum, vol. 2. Washington, D.C.: Smithsonian Institution Press, 1978. Pp. 72. Illustr.

Documentation of the research toward and development of the Aeronca C–2, the first practical general aviation airplane, including subsequent modifications. A large portion of this work centers on the National Air and Space Museum's restoration of the Aeronca C–2, serial no. 1, utilizing detailed photo documentation. Numerous photos throughout the volume enhance the succinct text.

685. Thomson, Steven L. "Hard Times in Hangar Town." *Air and Space* 1 (April–May 1986): 76–84. Illustr.

Chronicles the up–and–down nature of general aviation sales since 1946 and gives special consideration to the sales slump currently plaguing the general aviation industry. Also cites theories as to why sales continue to plummet, such as increased product liability, lack of interest by the public, and stifling tax laws.

686. Trimble, William F. *High Frontier: A History of Aeronautics in Pennsylvania*. Pittsburgh, Pa.: University of Pittsburgh Press, 1982. Pp. xiv + 344. Index, Bibliog., Illustr.

Valuable in a general aviation context primarily for its concise historical account of the Piper Aircraft Corporation. Although the treatment is necessarily shorter than Francis's *Mr. Piper and His Cubs* (cited herein as item 673), it is much more matter–of–fact. Mention of Piper is found throughout the book.

687. Warford, Jeremy J. *Public Policy toward General Aviation*. Washington, D.C.: Brookings Institution, 1971. Pp. xii + 193.

The outcome of a study sponsored by the Brookings Institution as a part of its Studies in the Regulation of Economic Activity series. Warford critically analyzes the method public authorities use to deal with the strains placed on the airport and airways system by the growth of general aviation. Practical solutions are suggested.

688. Zuck, Daniel R. *An Airplane in Every Garage*. New York: Vantage, 1958. Pp. 192. Illustr.

Largely the result of the post–World War II move to make personal aviation available to everyone. Zuck presents his idea of the "planemobile," a combination airplane and automobile, as a solution to this problem, as well as a method of rapid evacuation in the event of an atomic attack. Zuck actually constructed a prototype, which crashed during a test flight.

Ultralights

689. Adkins, Hal. *The Directory of Homebuilt Ultralight Aircraft.* La
      Moille, Ill.: Haljan, 1982. Pp. 106. Illustr.

      Contains a list of aircraft types, a chapter on published
      material about ultralights, and information on building mate-
      rials and supplies. Insurance and ultralight group organization
      types are illustrated.

690. Berger, Alain–Yves, and Norman Burr. *Berger–Burr's Ultralight
      and Microlight Aircraft of the World.* Newberry Park, Calif.:
      Haynes, 1983. Pp. 285. Index, Illustr.

      Describes more than 250 aircraft and 70 powerplants. Lists
      all known ultralight aircraft, including several types from the
      Soviet Union. Many good photographs and drawings supplement
      the detailed text.

      Brinks, Glenn. *Ultralight Propulsion: The Basic Handbook of
      Ultralight Engines, Drives and Propellers.* Ultralight Aviation
      Series, no. 4. Hummelstown, Pa.: Ultralight, 1982. Pp. 192.
      Illustr.

      Cited herein as item 350.

691. Carrier, Frederick "Rick" G. *Ultralights: The Complete Book of
      Flying, Training, and Safety.* Garden City, N.Y.: Doubleday,
      1985. Pp. 140. Illustr.

      One of the most clearly written and illustrated of the ultra-
      light flight manuals, this book also has some valuable passages
      about the psychology of the accident–prone pilot.

692. Drisdale, Tommy, and Steven Hanes. *The Ultralight Aviator's
      Handbook.* Manhattan Beach, Calif.: Sky Flight International,
      1982. Pp. 294. Illustr.

      A handbook of ultralight flight that includes a list of types,
      rules of flight, and a reprint of sections from the Federal
      Aviation Agency's *Airman's Information Manual.*

693. Markowski, Michael A. *Ultralight Aircraft: The Basic Handbook of Ultralight Aviation.* Hummelstown, Pa.: Ultralight Publications, 1983. Pp. 336. Bibliog., Illustr.

A complete manual of ultralight flying that includes descriptions of over 60 different aircraft types, and sections on powerplants, flight training, and navigation.

694. Mrazek, James E., Jr., and James E. Mrazek, Sr. *Ultralights: A Complete Introduction to the Revolutionary New Way to Fly.* New York: St. Martin's, 1982. Pp. ix + 195. Bibliog., Illustr.

Although somewhat dated, a good introduction to ultralights. Includes a section on international regulations as of 1982.

NAVIGATION, COMMUNICATION, AND METEOROLOGY

This section covers sources of detailed information for researchers interested in the function, construction, and operation of instruments (including radar) used to navigate aircraft and to maintain voice communication with aircraft, and in the science of weather and climate as it relates to aeronautics. The citations are listed under the following headings: General Instruments, Instrument Flying, Communications Systems, Radar, Air Navigation, and Meteorology.

The sources chosen to represent the subject of aerial navigation deal with specific techniques and instruments (e.g., sextants) whereas texts on general theory have been excluded. Every effort was made to find both historical and technical works; few of the former are available. Although the intent is to represent instruments of all periods, the majority of sources date to World War II and, to a lesser extent, the immediate prewar and postwar period.

Works of general theory have been omitted as they tend to be superficial and provide little useful information. Instrument makers' manuals and catalogs are also excluded but should not be overlooked in a literature search; they are readily available and contain a great amount of valuable information and detailed photographs. This type of material was not included here because it would take a large number of sources to properly represent the evolution and development of instruments and navigational aids. Foreign-language sources and works that contain highly technical material have also been excluded as they are beyond the scope of the average researcher.

Samuel B. Fishbein
Thomas J. Noon
Dominick A. Pisano

General Instruments

695. Bendix Corporation. Eclipse–Pioneer Division. *Pioneer Aircraft Instruments: Fundamentals of Operation and Principal Uses.* Teterboro, N.J., 1943. Pp. 76. Illustr.

Provides clear explanations of flight and engine instruments, sextant, drift meter, oxygen regulator, prop synchronizer, and other World War II military instrument equipment. Contains illustrations of Pioneer instruments with cutaway diagrams.

696. Bose, Keith W. *Aviation Electronics Handbook.* Indianapolis, Ind.: Howard W. Sams, 1962. Pp. 224. Illustr.

A practical handbook that benefits aircraft owners, pilots, technicians, engineers, and others requiring a knowledge of aviation electronics equipment (ca. 1962). Covers the design, maintenance, and operation of automatic direction finders, distance–measuring equipment, weather radar, instrument-landing systems, communications systems, and other such equipment. Also includes discussions of equipment standardization and installation, aviation organizations, and shop facilities.

697. Broadbent, Stephen R., ed. *Jane's Avionics, 1986–87.* 5th ed. London: Jane's, 1986. Pp. 540 Index, Illustr.

A comprehensive compilation of the world's avionics systems and equipment, together with descriptions of each product, names of companies (by country), and a foreword that describes developments in avionics.

698. Cochrane, Rexmond C., and James R. Newman. *Measures for Progress: A History of the National Bureau of Standards.* Washington D.C.: U.S. Department of Commerce, National Bureau of Standards, 1966. Pp. xxv + 703. Index, Bibliog., Illustr.

The need for a definitive history of the National Bureau of Standards developed primarily from the very rapid expansion of the role of government in the scientific and technological progress of the nation and the evolution of the bureau's role in this expansion. Although the subject matter of the book is exceptionally broad, a good bit of the early work in radio telegraphy and aeronautical instruments is recorded herein.

699. Coulthard, W.H. *Aircraft Instrument Design.* London: Sir Isaac Pitman and Sons, 1952. Pp. 309. Index, Illustr.

Reviews physical design principles of aircraft instruments. Excellent source on early jet–age aircraft instruments, their design, and operation. Section on sextants. Superb photographs and cutaway illustrations.

700. DeBaud, Gene C. *Pilots' and Mechanics' Aircraft Instrument Manual.* New York: Ronald, 1942. Pp. xx + 490. Illustr.

Discusses operation, maintenance, and usage of aircraft instruments of the 1930s and early 1940s. Photographs and descriptive data on specific manufacturers' types and models. Radar altimeter, radium dial painting, sextants, and so on. Best source for World War II instruments.

701. De Ferranti, Sebastian. "Instruments and Electronics in Aviation." *The Aeronautical Journal of the Royal Aeronautical Society* 74 (1970): 718–723.

In the 23d of a series of Louis Bleriot Memorial Lectures to the Royal Aeronautical Society, the author traces the history of instruments and electronics in aviation, and the reasons for their development.

702. Jordanoff, Assen. *Dials and Flight.* New York: Harper and Brothers, 1947. Pp. vi + 359. Illustr.

How modern (ca. 1947) aircraft instruments are built, how they function, and how they are serviced.

703. Kelly, Lloyd [as told to] Robert B. Parke. *The Pilot Maker.* Foreword by Alan B. Shepard, Jr. New York: Grosset and Dunlap, 1970. Pp. vii + 195. Index, Illustr.

Chronicles the development of flight simulators, from Edwin A. Link's pioneering "pilot maker" in 1929, to the sophisticated systems used for flight training in military and commercial aviation and the space program. An indispensable guide to flight simulation.

704. Pallett, E.H.J. *Aircraft Instruments: Principles and Applications*. London: Pitman, 1972. Pp. ix + 371. Index, Illustr.

Modern reference book on aircraft flight instrumentation that provides excellent historical background. Includes photographs and drawings.

705. Safford, Edward L. *Aviation Electronics Handbook*. Blue Ridge Summit, Pa: TAB, 1975. Pp. 404. Index, Illustr.

A general guide to the electronic equipment and systems used in aviation. Encompasses the simple and the complex, and includes systems used in private and commercial aircraft as well as key military equipment. Designed to give those readers who are more concerned with the actual flying and navigation of aircraft a greater understanding of the various instruments and systems than they would normally obtain from texts on flying.

706. Werner, Earl F. *Aircraft Instrument Maintenance*. New York: McGraw–Hill, 1948. Pp. viii + 466. Index, Illustr.

Discusses the initial installation, removal, replacement, and reinstallation of basic aircraft instruments. Excellent reference source.

Instrument Flying

707. The Daniel Guggenheim Fund for the Promotion of Aeronautics. *Solving the Problem of Fog Flying; A Record of the Activities of the Fund's Full Flight Laboratory to Date*. New York, 1929. Pp. 52.

A record of the activities of the fund's Full Flight Laboratory (up to publication date) with special emphasis on early efforts at "blind flying" (fog flying). A full report of the experiment conducted by Lt. James H. "Jimmy" Doolittle, who successfully demonstrated fog flying on September 24, 1929.

708. Doolittle, James H. "Early Experiments in Instrument Flying." *Annual Report of the Board of Regents of the Smithsonian Institution*, 1961. Pp. 337–355. Illustr.

Account of the first successful instrument flight from take-off to landing by the man who made it.

709. Ocker, William C., and Carl J. Crane. *Blind Flight in Theory and Practice*. San Antonio, Tex.: Naylor, 1932. Pp. 200. Index, Illustr.

Excellent book by pioneering army experimenters both famous for their work on first–generation instrument flight and procedures. Contains many fine photos of instruments.

710. Smith, Frederick H. *Flying by Instruments*. New York: National Aeronautics Council, 1942. Pp. 153. Illustr.

Detailed and well–illustrated manual on instrument techniques and procedures written by an airline pilot.

711. Weems, Philip V.H., Charles A. Zweng, and H.C. Stark. *Instrument Flying*. Annapolis, Md.: Weems System of Navigation, 1947. Pp. vi + 486. Index, Illustr.

Based on Howard Stark's 1934 work of the same name. Excellent schematic diagrams of all types of aircraft instruments, with step–by–step instruction of instrument usage in various flight situations. An informative work, especially for pilots, that gives historical insight to war–era methods of instrument flying.

Communications Systems

712. Braband, Ken C. *The First 50 Years: A History of Collins Radio Company and the Collins Divisions of Rockwell International*. Cedar Rapids, Iowa: Rockwell International, 1983. Pp. ix + 218. Bibliog., Illustr.

A chronological history of Collins Radio Company and its founder, Arthur Collins. The scope of the work is from the earliest days of shortwave transmitters to today's satellite navigation and flight management systems. From its inception, Collins has been involved in producing state–of–the–art equipment.

713. Hansford, R.F. *Radio Aids to Civil Aviation*. London: Heywood, 1960. Pp. 623. Bibliog., Illustr.

   One hundred and one items that cover the period from 1926 to 1958. Chapter headings include "Principles of Radio," "Aircraft Communication Systems," "En–route Aids," "Aids to Air Traffic Control," "Aids to Approach Landing and Surface Movement," "Weather Radar," and "Radar Links."

714. Holahan, Jim. *Aviation Radio for Pilots*. New York: Sports Car, 1964. Pp. 136. Illustr.

   A nontechnical book that gives the lightplane pilot a better understanding of the scope of aviation radio and workings of the "Navcom" equipment he uses. Explains the basic terms of aviation radio and basic electronic concepts, discusses every piece of equipment in use in 1964, gives tips on buying new and used equipment, and includes government flight regulations.

715. Johnson, Allen L. "Two Hundred Years of Airborne Communications." *Aerospace Historian*, September 1984. Pp. 185–193.

   Two hundred years ago the brothers Etienne and Joseph Montgolfier made a 25–minute flight across Paris. Their communications during this first airborne flight consisted of shouting warnings to the people below. The author traces 200 years of communications development from its inception to high–speed laser beams.

716. Roberts, Henry W. *Aviation Radio*. New York: William Morrow, 1945. Pp. xv + 637. Illustr.

   An authoritative treatise on aviation radio written by an acknowledged expert in his time. Having won the Harmon Trophy for "literary contributions to the science of aeronautics and radio communications," Roberts was especially qualified to write this book. From basic scientific principles to the technological achievements of the early 1940s, the text is prepared in a simple and easy–to–understand manner.

717. Sandretto, Peter C. *Principles of Aeronautical Radio Engineering*. New York: McGraw–Hill, 1942. Pp. viii + 414. Bibliog., Illustr.

As the title implies, the book adheres strictly to aircraft applications. The author assumes that the reader has some preliminary knowledge of radio and understands the terms used in describing the characteristics of the apparatus. The book is also sprinkled with a liberal treatment of the history and philosophy behind each development and brings to the reader an up–to–date (1942) review of the technology involved.

718. *Sparks Journal: Society of Wireless Pioneers, Radio Aviation Edition* (newspaper). Santa Rosa, Calif.: Society of Wireless Pioneers, 1983.

A historical and scientific record of the early days of "wireless" and its indispensable value to commercial flying on the 200th anniversary of manned flight (1783–1983). The primary purpose of the society is collecting, researching, and recording the history of communications. This edition is primarily devoted to the early "pioneers," whether they be aircraft, airway radio stations aviation organizations, or staffs of the Civil Aeronautics Administration and the Federal Aviation Administration.

Radar

719. Allison, David K. *New Eye for the Navy: The Origin of Radar at the Naval Research Laboratory.* Washington, D.C.: Naval Research Laboratory, 1981. Pp. xi + 228. Index, Bibliog., Illustr.

A revision of the author's doctoral dissertation that utilizes the Naval Research Laboratory's development of radar to characterize the institutional process involved in mission-oriented research and development. The work traces, in detail, the events from the development of the first practical radar device to the introduction of operational equipment into the fleet. The work also discusses projects that later evolved from the original radar program at the laboratory. A remarkably thorough historical work that should not be overlooked.

720. Clark, Ronald W. *Tizard.* Cambridge, Mass.: MIT Press, 1965. Pp. xvii + 458. Bibliog., Illustr.

A key figure in the development of England's system of national defense in the World War II era, especially the chain of radar stations that assured the RAF's victory in the Battle of

Britain. This biography predominantly documents Tizard's work in developing a science of defense.

721. Dunlap, Orrin E., Jr. *Radar; What Radar Is and How It Works.* New York: Harper and Brothers, 1946. Pp. 208. Bibliog., Illustr.

Traces the history of radar from the early reflected wave experiments of Hertz and Marconi through the application of the radio "echo" to push–button warfare. Dunlap then looks ahead to radar's promising future and peacetime applications. The bibliography serves as an excellent suggested reading list.

722. Fagen, M.D., ed. *A History of Engineering and Science in the Bell System: National Service in War and Peace, 1925–1975.* New York: Bell Telephone Laboratories, 1978. Pp. xv + 757. Index, Bibliog., Illustr.

The second in a four–volume series. Devotes a large part of the text to a nontechnical discussion of Bell Laboratories' involvement in the development of radar during World War II. Attempts to assess the long–range importance of the laboratory's many technical contributions.

723. Price, Alfred. *Instruments of Darkness: The History of Electronic Warfare.* London: Macdonald and Jane's, 1977. Pp. 284. Index, Illustr.

Regarded as the standard reference work on the World War II radar battle. The author has profited by the lapse of 30 years to put his story of World War II into perspective. At each stage of the evolution, he presents both the British and the German story, and he shows how closely developments on one side were matched on the other. A salutary reminder that the impressive performance of modern weapons depends ultimately on the survival, in war, of their guidance and control systems.

724. Stimson, George W. *Introduction to Airborne Radar.* El Segundo, Calif.: Hughes Aircraft, 1983. Pp. ix + 621. Index, Bibliog., Illustr.

A comprehensive treatise on radar that provides an overview and covers essential background information, basic design considerations, aspects of detection and ranging, doppler effects, the sources of technical problems, and high–resolution ground mapping. Also gives the reader a glimpse into the future (constrained only by proprietary and military security restrictions).

725. Sun, Jack K. and various authors. *AWACS Radar Program: "The Eyes of the Eagle."* Baltimore: Westinghouse, 1985. Pp. 23.

A need existed for detection and tracking of low–flying targets for surveillance, command, and control. Initiation of effort to attain that capability started in the mid to late 1950s. Describes the evolution of the Airborne Warning and Control System program from 1959 to 1970: the competition, design, development, test, and production. Details specifications for the various elements of the system.

726. Swords, Sean S. *Technical History of the Beginnings of Radar.* London: Peregrinus, 1986. Pp. xiv + 325. Index, Bibliog., Illustr.

As the title suggests, this work is of both technical and historical value to the reader. Maintaining a wide, international scope, it records the emergence of radar in those countries where independent development of radar occurred. The development of radar in the United Kingdom is then chosen for more detailed attention. Provides an annotated bibliography.

727. U.S. Air Force. *Electronics and Radar: Principles and Uses.* Air Force Manual 51–6. Washington, D.C., 1953. Pp. 136. Illustr.

Prepared to serve mainly as an introduction to the uses of radar and other electronic equipment in the U.S. Air Force. Excludes complete technical details and covers these topics in a general manner. Discusses basic electricity and radio theory along with current (1953) aircraft communications equipment, airborne and ground navigational aids, and fundamental principles of radar.

728. Wells, Robert, and C.R. Whiting. *Early Warning, Electronic Guardians of Our Country.* Englewood Cliffs, N.J.: Prentice-Hall, 1962. Pp. 120. Illustr.

A dramatically written, nontechnical account of the U.S. Early Warning System, its mode of operation, and its capability of meeting a potential alert. The book centers on America's capabilities that are concentrated in the Polar region ground-based systems.

Air Navigation

729. Kayton, Myron, and Walter R. Fried, eds. *Avionics Navigation Systems.* New York: John Wiley and Sons, 1969. Pp. xviv + 666. Bibliog., Illustr.

Presents a unified treatment of the principles and practices of modern aircraft navigation systems. Prepared for the navigation system engineer, it favors integrated design in an effort to reduce duplication of costly subsystems. This engineer-oriented text should serve a wide spectrum of readers, from the systems analyst to the operations personnel. The state of the art is discussed as well as the development for the five years after 1969.

730. Orman, Leonard M. *Electronic Navigation.* North Hollywood, Calif.: Pan American Navigation Service, 1950. Pp. xiii + 222. Bibliog., Illustr.

Restricted to the broad field of electronic radar navigation and designed to supply the need for a balanced text suitable for use in technical high schools and colleges. Stresses the user's viewpoint and avoids detailed technical descriptions. Although the title uses the term "navigation," the information contained therein speaks only of "radar navigation."

731. Pierce, John A., A.A. McKenzie, and R.H. Woodward, eds. *Loran: Long Range Navigation.* MIT Radiation Laboratories Series, vol. 4. New York: McGraw-Hill, 1948. Pp. xiv + 476. Bibliog., Illustr.

Contains 171 items covering the period from 1942 to 1946. Describes in full the long-range navigation system. Bibliography includes reports, magazine articles, instruction books, and internal memoranda.

732. Shields, Bert A. *Principles of Air Navigation.* New York: McGraw-Hill, 1943. Pp. vii + 451. Illustr.

Written for young students. Presents the subject matter according to the pilot's viewpoint. Discusses various types of aviation problems and explains in detail how each should be solved. One chapter is devoted to the use of computers and calculators and another deals with radio ranges and how they are used in airway flying (ca. 1943).

733. *United States Air Force, Summary Report of Electronic Aids to Air Navigation.* Wright Field, Ohio: Air Materiel Command, 1947. Pp. 96.

Intended to provide interested military, governmental, commercial, and industrial groups with a review of the USAF's past, present, and projected future research and development activities, objectives, and policies in the general and specific fields relating to navigation of aircraft by electronic means. Although directed basically at military aircraft, the report may also be applicable to the problems of commercial and civilian aviation.

734. U.S. Federal Aviation Administration Academy. Airways Facilities Branch. *Flight: The Story of Electronic Navigation.* Oklahoma City: U.S. Department of Transportation, 1974. Pp. 41. Illustr.

A brochure designed for use in facility familiarization courses conducted by the FAA. A flight is simulated and takes the student through all the planning phases to takeoff: provides en route and approach aids. Enables the reader to gain an appreciation of the skill required by a pilot, as well as the services provided by the FAA controllers and flight specialists and the electronic facilities.

735. Weems, Philip V.H. *Air Navigation.* New York: McGraw-Hill, 1938. Pp. xiv + 587. Index, Illustr.

Although the first edition was published in 1931, the second, printed in 1938, serves to illuminate air navigation methods in the years immediately before World War II. This comprehensive work encompasses every aspect of aerial navigation and the corresponding instrumentation. Discusses methods and techniques commonly employed and includes a brief treatment of meteorology.

736. Wright, Monte D. *Most Probable Position; A History of Aerial Navigation to 1941*. Lawrence: University Press of Kansas, 1972. Pp. xi + 280. Index, Bibliog., Illustr.

   A general explanation of aerial navigation and the solutions found to navigation problems in the pre–electronic era. Endows the reader with a knowledge of navigation methods. Deals with civil and military aspects on an international scale. A well-researched work, accompanied by an extensive bibliography.

Meteorology

737. Bates, Charles C., and John C. Fuller. *America's Weather Warriors, 1814–1985*. College Station: Texas A&M University Press, 1986. Pp. xiv + 360. Index, Bibliog., Illustr.

   The first full–fledged study of the military uses of meteorology, with much information on the connection between aviation and weather forecasting. Especially good on the influence of meteorology on World War II, in both the European and Pacific theaters, the Korean War, and the war in Vietnam. Contains a comprehensive bibliographic essay that covers books, bulletins, periodicals and articles, theses and dissertations, oral histories, and public documents.

738. Jonasson, Jonas A. "The AAF Weather Service." In *The Army Air Forces in World War II*, ed. Wesley F. Craven and James L. Cate. Vol. 7. Chicago: University of Chicago Press, 1958, 311–338. Index, Illustr.

   A tightly written, succinct account of the development of the Army Air Forces' Air Weather Service and its effect on World War II air operations in Europe, Africa, and the Far East.

739. Whitnah, Donald R. *A History of the United States Weather Bureau*. Urbana: University of Illinois Press, 1961. Pp. ix + 267. Index, Bibliog., Illustr.

   A pioneering work that contains a great deal of useful information concerning the relationship between aeronautics and meteorology, especially in the Army Signal Service/Corps. Of particular interest is Chapter 9, "Aviation Forecasts: A New Enterprise, 1913–41," which outlines the growth of meteorology as an aid to aviation.

FLIGHT EQUIPMENT

To better assist researchers who are trying to make their way through the variety of subject matter classified under flight equipment, I have organized this section around the following categories: armament, personal equipment (including uniforms), and awards and memorabilia. Because flight equipment encompasses such a wide range of material, each category includes many types of items. Researchers should keep in mind that the list is not all-inclusive and is intended to be only an introduction to the subject.

Although bibliographic sources on the topic are scarce, additional information may be obtained from several institutions that offer research material to the general public. Among these are the National Air and Space Museum, Smithsonian Institution, Washington, D.C.; National Museum of American History, Smithsonian Institution, Washington, D.C.; U.S. Air Force Museum, Wright-Patterson AFB, Ohio; Harry G. Armstrong Aerospace Medical Research Laboratory, Wright-Patterson AFB, Ohio; The National Archives and Records Service, Washington, D.C.; U.S. Army Center of Military History, Washington, D.C.; Royal Air Force Museum, London, United Kingdom; Imperial War Museum, London, United Kingdom; Deutsches Museum, Munich, Federal Republic of Germany; Musee de L'Air, Paris, France.

Karl S. Schneide

Armament

740. Barnes, G.M. *Weapons of World War II.* New York: Van Nostrand, 1947. Pp. 317. Index, Illustr.

Deals mainly with weapons, tanks, and other armament of the U.S Army ground forces, but also includes some information on the armament used by the Army Air Forces. A must for the military historian looking for facts about World War II ordnance. A well-organized reference tool.

741. Chinn, George M. *The Machine Gun: History, Evolution and Development of Manual, Automatic, and Airborne Repeating Weapons.* 4 vols. Washington, D.C.: U.S. Department of the Navy, Bureau of Ordnance, 1951–55. Various pagination. Index, Bibliog., Illustr.

Volume 1 of this standard reference work is most commonly used, but it contains numerous errors. Three other volumes, formerly classified, have now been privately reprinted. Because so little research has been done in this area, Chinn's work is a handy source of information.

742. Ezell, Edward C., Thomas M. Pegg, and Walter H.B. Smith. *Small Arms of the World: The Basic Manual of Small Arms.* 12th ed., rev. Harrisburg, Pa.: Stackpole, 1983. Pp. 894. Index, Bibliog., Illustr.

The first picture study of small arms of World War I through World War II. Includes recently reprinted field-stripping information. Revision of wartime *Small Arms of the World* by Walter H.B. Smith and Joseph E. Smith. Of limited value for aviation armament research.

743. Gervasi, Tom. *Arsenal of Democracy II: American Military Power in the 1980s and the Origins of the New Cold War, with a Survey of American Weapons and Arms Exports: The Export of American Weapons.* New York: Grove, 1981. Pp. 300. Index, Bibliog., Illustr.

A nontechnical, illustrated inventory of all types of modern U.S. arms, munitions, and equipment. A handy reference.

744. King, H.F. *Armament of British Aircraft, 1909–1939*. London: Putnam, 1971. Pp. xii + 457. Illustr.

A work with limited technical data but much general information on British aircraft armament during the period.

745. Lusar, Rudolf. *Die Deutschen Waffen und Geheimwaffen des 2. Welt Krieges und ihre weiterenwicklung* (German weapons and secret weapons of World War II and their subsequent development). Munich: J.F. Lehmann, 1964. Pp. 379. Illustr.

Studies the development of advanced German weapons and secret weapons in World War II. Includes information on aircraft and rockets.

746. Quick, John. *Dictionary of Weapons and Military Terms*. New York: McGraw–Hill, 1973. Pp. xii + 515. Bibliog., Illustr.

A concise, nondetailed reference on all types of armament. Very handy reference that is adequate to answer simple questions.

747. Rowland, Buford, and William B. Boyd. *U.S. Navy Bureau of Ordnance in World War II*. Washington, D.C.: Department of the Navy, Bureau of Ordnance, 1953. Pp. 539. Index, Illustr.

An excellent detailed study that includes aircraft weapons. No longer in print.

748. U.S. Department of the Navy. Bureau of Ordnance. *Navy Ordnance Activities: World War, 1917–1918*. Washington, D.C.: U.S. Government Printing Office, 1920. Pp. 323. Illustr.

A classic reference work that includes aircraft armament. Should be used in conjunction with *America's Munitions* by Benedict Crowell. The best work on the subject. No longer in print.

749. U.S. Department of War. *America's Munitions, 1917–1918*. Report of Benedict Crowell, Asst. Secretary of War, Director of Munitions. Washington, D.C.: U.S. Government Printing Office, 1919. Pp. 592. Index, Illustr.

Outstanding reference work, with details, photos, and illustrations of all types of U.S. Army weapons (including aircraft guns, bombs, sights, etc.), planes, engines, artillery, optics, tanks, vehicles, and personal equipment for soldiers. The basic reference on the war materiel of World War I. The best study ever made on the subject.

Personal Equipment (including uniforms)

750. Bender, Roger James. *Air Organizations of the Third Reich: The Luftwaffe.* Mountain View, Calif.: R. James Bender Publishing, 1972. Pp. 320.

Covers all World War II German Air Force uniforms and insignia, including flight clothing. Good illustrations and line drawings of articles mentioned. Also includes many contemporary wartime drawings. Excellent reference.

751. Greer, Louise, and Anthony Harold. *Flying Clothing: The Story of Its Development.* Shrewsbury, England: Airlife, 1979. Pp. 176. Index, Bibliog., Illustr.

Surveys the history of flight clothing of major nations since World War I from a British perspective. Best descriptive and historical coverage is on early developments. Overall, a good background study but could use more technical coverage on specific items of clothing.

752. Horan, Michael. *Index to Parachuting, 1900–1975: An Annotated Bibliography.* New York: Garland, 1977. Pp. xlii + 173. Illustr.

An excellent, well–organized guide to sources of information on all aspects of parachutes and parachuting. Includes sections on military parachuting, the aerospace medicine of parachuting, and a brief historical essay.

Mohler, Stanley, R., and Bobby H. Johnson. *Wiley Post, His Winnie Mae, and the World's First Pressure Suit.* Smithsonian Annals of Flight, no. 8. Washington, D.C.: Smithsonian Institution Press, 1971. Pp. vii + 127. Bibliog., Illustr.

Cited herein as item 864.

753. Mollo, Andrew. *Army Uniforms of World War I: European and United States Armies and Aviation Services*. New York: Arco, 1978. Pp. 219. Index, Illustr.

The best English–language reference on World War I uniforms. Limited space, however, does not allow for expansive or detailed coverage of field equipment such as helmets, backpacks, canteens, and the like, but type names are included. Another drawback is the lack of coverage on all global combatants, including Japan, China, and colonial troops.

754. *Parachutes, Aircraft Fabric, and Clothing*. TM–1–440. Washington, D.C.: U.S. War Department, 1945. Pp. 156. Illustr.

The most informative source on U.S. armed forces parachutes in World War II. Although historical information is lacking, it is the best reference on the subject from a technical standpoint. Should be reprinted.

755. Sweeting, C.G. *Combat Flying Clothing: Army Air Forces Clothing during World War II*. Washington, D.C.: Smithsonian Institution Press, 1984. Pp. ix + 229. Index, Bibliog., Illustr.

The finest and most comprehensive survey of U.S. military flying clothing and accessories from World War I through World War II based on official regulations. Good illustrations. A second volume, now in preparation, will complete coverage on oxygen systems, survival gear, and parachutes.

756. U.S. Army Air Forces. *Illustrated Catalog. Class 13, Clothing, Parachutes, Equipment and Supplies, September 30, 1943*. Reprint. Springfield, Va.: George A. Petersen, n.d. Pp. 108. Illustr.

Currently available reprint that lists and illustrates every item of personal equipment issued by the Army Air Forces. Includes parachutes, flight clothing, oxygen equipment, mechanics' clothing, emergency kits, life vests, and miscellaneous equipment.

757. Weld, Jim. *Flying Headgear of the World, 1934–45*. Huntington Beach, Calif.: J. Weld, 1980. Pp. 50. Illustr.

Includes coverage of flight helmets and goggles of the major

World War II belligerents—the United States, United Kingdom, Germany, Japan, France, Russia, and Italy. Each article is well illustrated with official designation noted wherever possible. Very good illustrations.

Awards and Memorabilia

758. Chalif, Don, and Roger J. Bender. *Military Pilot and Aircrew Badges of the World, 1870–Present.* [Volume I—Europe (Albania–Hungary)]. San Jose, Calif.: R. James Bender, 1982. Pp. 224. Index, Bibliog., Illustr.

Provides historical information and material on the traditions surrounding designs for badges, with each chapter surveying a particular nation. Collectively, a comprehensive list of aircrew badges with excellent, detailed illustrations and notes on dimensions and construction. Illustrates badge placement on uniforms. Outstanding reference. Second volume is awaiting publication and is equally outstanding.

759. Grosvenor, Gilbert, et al. *Insignia and Decorations of the U.S. Armed Forces.* Rev. ed. Washington, D.C.: National Geographic Society, 1944. Pp. 208. Illustr.

Covers thousands of insignia, badges, and medals, including those that pertain to aviation. Originally published in the June, October, and December 1943 issues of the *National Geographic*, and updated and republished as an offprint in December 1944. One of the best wartime references available. Used by the military. Does not, however, include unofficial insignia, which were plentiful during the period.

760. Huff, Russell J. *Wings of World War II: The Military Flight Qualification Badges of the Second World War.* Sarasota, Fla.: R.J. Huff and Associates, 1981. Pp. 250. Illustr.

Rather comprehensive collection of wing badges used in World War II. Illustrations vary greatly in quality and the layout of photographs and corresponding captions is confusing at times. Contains some detail on the manufacture of badges.

761. Mollo, Andrew. *The Armed Forces of World War II: Uniforms, Insignia and Organization.* New York: Crown, 1981. Pp. 312. Index, Illustr.

Standard reference work, very useful because it deals with military forces background first, then describes uniforms and organization. Lacks coverage on noncombatants and neutrals for completeness.

762. Rosignoli, Guido. *Air Force Badges and Insignia of World War 2.* New York: Arco, 1977. Pp. 200. Index, Illustr.

A generally accurate source that includes good sections on pre–World War II insignia. Color illustrations are excellent and depict insignia not generally available elsewhere. Coverage of unofficial insignia is also quite valuable, since it appears in few other places.

763. Williams, Dion. *Army and Navy Uniforms and Insignia; How to Know Rank, Corps and Service in the Military and Naval Forces of the United States and Foreign Countries.* Rev. ed. New York: Frederick A. Stokes, 1918. Pp. 333. Illustr.

A classic reference work on U.S. and foreign uniforms, insignia, and medals of World War I with coverage of airmen. Some minor errors on basic uniforms and insignia. No longer in print.

SAFETY

This section presents a wide range of publications that deal with safety in aviation. However, the list should be considered mainly an introduction to the subject and a starting point for the beginning researcher. Other publications—and there are many—have not been included primarily for lack of space. Pilot instruction manuals, which are available in abundance, were excluded as the intent was to select volumes on safety in the air rather than manuals on how to fly.

Passenger safety on commercial flights has long been a subject of controversy, and both defenders and detractors are represented here. The growth of air regulations and the recent deregulation of the industry have been discussed in many reports pertaining to the aircraft industry, the FAA, and other topics related to air safety. In fact, so many have been presented in congressional hearings alone, that only a few could be listed here. Accident investigation, a key to securing future air safety, is another area that has been examined by the private and public sectors.

Two excellent bibliographies that should be of great assistance to the researcher are Frank H. King and Viola W. King, *Aviation Safety Bibliography and Source Book* (Basin, Wyo.: Aviation Maintenance Publishers, 1980); and James J. Pelouch and Paul T. Hacker, *Bibliography on Aircraft Fire Hazards and Safety*, 2 vols. (Cleveland, Ohio: Aerospace Safety Research and Data Institute, 1974).

Although this section is devoted almost exclusively to books on aviation safety, many aviation periodicals such as *AOPA Pilot* and *Flying* frequently publish timely articles and editorials on the subject. In addition, the following organizations regularly publish materials related to aviation safety: American Institute of Aeronautics and Astronautics, New York, N.Y.; Aircraft Owners and Pilots Association, Air Safety Foundation, Frederick, Maryland; Airline Pilots Association, Herndon, Virginia; Federal Aviation Administration, Department of Transportation, Washington, D.C.; Flight Safety Foundation, Arlington, Virginia; International Air Transport Association, Montreal, Canada; International Civil Aviation Organization, Montreal, Canada; International Society of Air Safety Investigators, Washington National Airport, Washington, D.C.; National Aeronautics and Space Administration, Washington, D.C.; National Fire Protective Association, Aviation Fire Division, Quincy, Massachusetts.

Dorothy S. Cochrane

764. *Aeronautics Safety Code.* New York: Society of Automotive Engineers, 1925. Pp. 32.

The Aeronautics Safety Code was the first concerted effort by the United States to formulate national standards for the growing aviation community. Cosponsored by the U.S. Bureau of Standards and the Society of Automotive Engineers, the code was drawn up by a committee of representatives from the National Advisory Committee for Aeronautics, aircraft and insurance companies, and the military and encompassed everything from design to power plants and from pilot qualifications to airfields.

765. *Aviation Safety.* Riverside, Conn.: Belvoir, 1985. Bimonthly.

A bimonthly private general aviation publication that reviews recent accidents and provides aircraft safety ratings for selected aircraft. Also includes news items and safety tips. Worthwhile, especially for the aircraft safety ratings.

766. Bailey, F. Lee. *Cleared for the Approach: F. Lee Bailey in Defense of Flying.* Englewood Cliffs, N.J.: Prentice–Hall, 1977. Pp. vii + 211.

Reviews aviation in the United States and tries to allay the fear of flying. Although Bailey extols the joys of flying, he also criticizes the industry and the Federal Aviation Administration for reacting to crashes rather than improving faulty conditions.

767. Barclay, Stephen. *The Search for Air Safety: An International Documentary Report on the Investigation of Commercial Aviation Accidents.* New York: William Morrow, 1970. Pp. viii + 376. Index, Bibliog., Illustr.

A fascinating look at the investigation of commercial aviation accidents. Several international crashes are viewed through the eyes of investigators who reveal the detective skills necessary to piece together the reasons for the crash. Includes a three–page bibliography along with a section of photographs.

768. Bramson, Alan E. *Be a Better Pilot.* New York: Arco, 1980. Pp. 239. Index, Illustr.

An excellent guide for becoming and staying a good general aviation pilot. The author covers preflight preparation, instrument flying, takeoffs and landings, engines and engine failures, handling faults, and weather. Extensively illustrated.

769. Buck, Robert N. *Flying Know-How*. New York: Delacorte, 1975. Pp. 264. Index.

A practical guide to safe flying written by an airline pilot who flew DC-2s and 747s. Reviews important topics such as communications, checklists, and air temperature and its effects on the aircraft. Also includes a chapter on flight above 18,000 ft.

770. Buck, Robert N. *Weather Flying*. New York: Macmillan, 1978. Pp. xxi + 296. Index, Bibliog., Illustr.

A thorough and detailed account of natural (and man-made) atmospheric conditions and how to fly through them. Covers rules and regulations, theory, psychology, the airplane, and instruments. A very readable and succinct guide to the hazards of flying.

771. Collins, Richard L. *Flying Safely*. New York: Delacorte, 1977. Pp. x + 276. Index.

Safety advice for the general aviation pilot. Examines the most common hazards and mistakes and concludes that the pilot should exercise common sense and follow all rules and regulations.

772. *Contributions to Flying Safety; The Eighteen Year History of the Daniel and Florence Guggenheim Aviation Safety Center at Cornell University, 1950-1968*. New York: Cornell University, Daniel and Florence Guggenheim Aviation Safety Center, 1968. Pp. 24. Illustr.

Looks at the progress in aviation safety between 1950 and 1968 and at the center's many contributions to the field through its committees, publications, and projects. The center was dissolved with the establishment of the National Transportation Safety Board.

773. Dempster, Derek D. *The Tale of the Comet*. New York: David McKay, 1958. Pp. 218. Bibliog., Illustr.

A fascinating and often gripping account of the investigation into the cause of the de Havilland Comet I crashes by a team of engineers from the Royal Aircraft Establishment at Farnborough. Although the book is packed with information about how the structural failure of the Comet I was discovered, Dempster has managed to make it read like a mystery thriller. A pleasant departure from the run–of–the–mill aircraft safety book.

774. Flight Safety Foundation. *International Air Safety Seminar Proceedings*. Arlington, Va.: Flight Safety Foundation. Annual.

Reviews the proceedings of the yearly meeting of safety experts from around the world. Presents current topics in air safety and evaluates air crashes that occurred during the year.

775. *Flying* Magazine. *Pilot Error: Anatomies of Aircraft Accidents*. New York: Van Nostrand Reinhold, 1977. Pp. 160. Index.

A collection of 25 accident reports that originally appeared in *Flying* magazine's bimonthly column entitled "Pilot Error." The reports include actual conversations between aircraft and tower/control and an analysis of each predicament and crash.

776. Fowler, Ron. *Preflight Planning*. New York: Macmillan, 1983. Pp. ix + 257. Illustr.

A preflight advice book for general aviation pilots that is divided into three sections: pilot, airplane, and environment. Concentrates on knowing yourself, the aircraft, the conditions, and the Federal Aviation Regulations. Lists common mistakes and reviews pertinent information.

777. Hoekstra, Harold D., and Shung–Chai Huang. *Safety in General Aviation*. Arlington, Va.: Flight Safety Foundation, 1971. Pp. iv + 126. Index, Bibliog., Illustr.

Examines general aviation (through 1970) from the perspective of accidents and regulations. Statistics and charts assist and point to areas that need improvement. The authors find that the leading causes of accidents are the pilot, weather, and mechanical problems.

778. Hurst, Ronald, ed. *Pilot Error: A Professional Study of Contributory Factors.* London: Crosby Lockwood Staples, 1976. Pp. 282. Index, Bibliog., Illustr.

Examines human error in the cockpit and the factors that contribute to it. Chapters are authored by a pilot, a doctor, an aircraft designer, and an air traffic controller. Also explores relations between airline management and pilots and the legal complications of pilot error. An appendix reviews current research activities in pilot error.

779. Johnson, Daniel A. *Just in Case: A Passenger's Guide to Airplane Safety and Survival.* New York: Plenum, 1984. Pp. xvi + 268. Index.

An excellent air safety guide aimed at improving the chances of surviving an airline emergency. Covers inflight and ground emergencies, crash landings on land and water, and the use of safety equipment. Chapters are also devoted to human reaction to emergencies and to stress reactions following emergencies. Research studies and actual incidents are cited throughout the book. The lifesaving procedures are presented in a factual manner, many complete with illustrations and tables. References follow each chapter.

780. Jordanoff, Assen. *Safety in Flight.* New York: Funk and Wagnalls, 1941. Pp. ix + 371. Index, Illustr.

A classic guide to aviation safety with aircraft, engines, instruments, and navigation aids of the day. Amply illustrated with photos, charts, and cartoons. Includes an informative section on power plants and propellers.

781. Knauth, Percy. *Safety in the Skies.* Blue Ridge Summit, Pa.: TAB, 1982. Pp. vi + 154. Index, Illustr.

An excellent history of air safety and a look at today's problems. Covers the introduction of air traffic control and radio navigation aids and discusses positive control of air traffic and midair collisions. Also looks at advances in instruments and air navigation aids.

782. Lafferty, Perry F. *How to Lose Your Fear of Flying.* Los Angeles, Calif.: Price, Stern, Sloan, 1980. Pp. 95. Illustr.

A question–and–answer book of basic airline information designed to allay the fear of flying. Simple aerodynamics, air traffic control procedures, flight emergencies, and aircraft familiarity are the topics.

783. Lederer, Jerome. *Safety in the Operations of Air Transportation; A Lecture Delivered by Jerome Lederer, M.E., under the James Jackson Cabot Professorship of Air Traffic Regulation and Air Transportation of Norwich University, April 20, 1939.* Northfield, Vt.: Norwich University, 1939. Pp. v + 69. Illustr.

A report on the status of air safety in 1939 written by an expert in the field. The author follows the development of new instruments and procedures during the 1930s and touches on all of the important elements of air safety. This historic look at aviation and safety was expanded from a speech delivered at Norwich University in Vermont, April 20, 1939 (one of the James Jackson Cabot Professorship Lectures).

784. Lederer, Jerome. *Aviation Safety Perspectives: Hindsight, Insight, Foresight, Presented at the Wings Club on April 21, 1982, New York City.* New York: The Wings Club, 1982. Pp. 40. Illustr.

Lederer, in the 19th Wings Club "Sight" lecture delivered on April 21, 1982, discusses safety measures developed by the aviation industry (beginning with the first flight recorder installed by the Wright Brothers on the 1903 Flyer) and current issues such as terrorism, wind shear, and collision avoidance. A concise survey of airline safety today.

785. Lowell, Vernon W. *Airline Safety Is a Myth.* New York: Bartholomew House, 1967. Pp. 211. Illustr.

The TWA pilot of a Boeing 707 that crashed in Rome in 1964 recounts the tragedy and goes on to criticize air safety conditions. Hazards cited include noise–abatement procedures, fuel and fire, fatigue, and dangerous airports. Calls for less intervention by the Federal Aviation Administration and more flexible federal aviation regulations. An appendix contains all of the U.S. air carrier crashes between 1960 and 1965.

786. McClement, Fred. *It Doesn't Matter Where You Sit.* New York: Holt, Rinehart and Winston, 1969. Pp. xi + 238.

Looks at the alarming rate of midair collisions and questions the air traffic control system and the Federal Aviation Administration's commitment to safety. Also investigates clear air turbulence and lightning.

787. McFarland, Ross A. *Human Factors in Air Transportation*: *Occupational Health and Safety.* New York: McGraw–Hill, 1953. Pp. 830. Index, Bibliog., Illustr.

A textbook of aviation medicine and its relationship to airline personnel, passengers, and facilities. A major part of the book studies the human variables of flight and ground personnel. Also investigates sanitation, quarantine regulations, and the care and comfort of passengers and provides crash and survival information. Statistics and charts abound, and an extensive bibliography follows each chapter.

788. Mason, Sammy. *Stalls, Spins, and Safety.* New York: McGraw–Hill, 1982. Pp. xviii + 165. Index, Bibliog., Illustr.

An excellent book written by a veteran aerobatic and test pilot who believes in the importance of stall and spin training for all pilots. Mason covers aerodynamics, inducement, recovery, aerobatics, and the stall and spin characteristics of aircraft.

789. Newton, Dennis W. *Severe Weather Flying.* New York: McGraw–Hill, 1983. Pp. xix + 149. Index, Illustr.

Aimed at the general aviation pilot, Newton explores the fundamentals of flying, or not flying, through adverse weather conditions. Thunderstorms and icing comprise most of the book. The second book in a general aviation series sponsored by the Aircraft Owners and Pilot's Association and McGraw–Hill.

790. North Atlantic Treaty Organization. Advisory Group for Aeronautical Research and Development. Aeromedical Panel. *Medical Aspects of Flight Safety: The Unexplained Aircraft Accident.* London: Pergamon, 1959. Pp. ix + 308. Index, Bibliog., Illustr.

An international panel of medical experts authored this study of the human element in the operation of aircraft and as the cause of accidents. High-altitude flight is the major focus of the book, but it also includes chapters devoted to pathology and flight safety. Some chapters are written in French. References follow each report.

791. Powers-Waters, Brian. *Safety Last*. Rev. ed. New York: Pinnacle, 1975. Pp. 317. Index, Illustr.

A scathing attack on the Federal Aviation Administration by a former airline pilot who claims that aviation safety is all but ignored. Negligence of duty and the setting of minimum standards by the FAA combined with a lack of communication within the aviation community allow disasters to happen over and over again.

792. Ramsden, J.M. *The Safe Airline*. London: Macdonald and Jane's, 1976. Pp. 231. Index, Illustr.

A comprehensive study of airline safety principles that includes design, crew, navigation, airports, crime, economics, government regulation, and the law. Full of facts, statistics, and detailed explanations of aeronautical terms and procedures. A worthwhile source of information.

793. Rubinstein, Richard I., James J. Pinto, and Sanford Z. Meschkow. *Directory of Aerospace Safety Specialized Information Sources*. Vol. 2. Washington, D.C.: National Aeronautics and Space Administration, Lewis Research Center, 1976. Pp. xiii + 235.

A handbook of organizations and experts in specific areas of safety technology and engineering. Provides useful information on how to locate experts and sources of data in the field. Includes 159 organizations and approximately 580 names.

794. Roed, Aage. *Flight Safety Aerodynamics*. Rev. ed. Washington, D.C.: U.S. Government Printing Office, 1976. Pp. 158. Illustr.

A layman's explanation of airflow, performance, handling qualities, aircraft load, and operational problems and their effects on air safety. Well illustrated.

795. Ryther, Philip I., and Stephen M. Aug. *Who's Watching the Airways? The Dangerous Games of the FAA*. Garden City, N.Y.: Doubleday, 1972. Pp. x + 296.

An indictment of the Federal Aviation Administration, specifically top management, by a former employee. The charges include government inaction in aviation safety and poor attention to the regulations it imposes, and a too–close relationship with industry.

796. Serling, Robert J. *The Probable Cause: The Truth about Air Travel Today*. Garden City, N.Y.: Doubleday, 1960. Pp. 287.

A study of piston–powered passenger aircraft in the late 1940s and the 1950s that points out the progress that had been made in air safety. Specific crashes, individuals, and federal agencies all contribute to the story.

797. Serling, Robert J. *Loud and Clear: The Full Answer to Aviation's Vital Question: Are the Jets Really Safe?* Garden City, N.Y.: Doubleday, 1969. Pp. 327.

Examines the onset of the jet age in air transportation. Most of Serling's attention is directed toward 707s, Constellations, and 727s. Includes crash reports and the resultant improvements in aircraft and regulations.

798. Stewart, Oliver. *Danger in the Air*. New York: Philosophical Library, 1958. Pp. 194. Index, Illustr.

Looks at air safety from a British perspective. Investigates the airship R–101 and the de Havilland Comet and the causes of accidents, including fatigue, weather, and structural failure. Well–researched.

799. Thurston, David B. *Design for Safety*. New York: McGraw–Hill, 1980. Pp. x + 196. Index, Bibliog., Illustr.

Evaluates general aviation aircraft designs along with aircraft systems, equipment, facilities, and power plants. Concludes that safety and efficiency are the key qualities of good aircraft design.

800. Trammell, Archie. *Cause and Circumstance: Aircraft Accidents and How to Avoid Them.* New York: Ziff–Davis, 1980. Pp. x + 210. Illustr.

An updated and revised collection of monthly columns (1972–1978) written by the editor of *Business and Commercial Aviation.* Covers classic crashes, do's and don'ts of flying, and provides general advice for the professional, business, or general aviation pilot.

801. Traveler's Insurance Company. *Airplanes and Safety.* Hartford, Conn., 1921. Pp. x + 127. Illustr.

An insurance company takes a look at the airplane of 1921—its construction, operation, and maintenance—and at the business of insurance rates and contracts.

802. U.S. Civil Aeronautics Board. *Accident Investigation Report.* Washington, D.C.: U.S. Government Printing Office, 1934–1965.

Detailed studies of commercial aircraft accidents. Includes probable cause and all circumstances that surrounded the crash. Issued annually. Continued by U.S. National Transportation Safety Board, Bureau of Accident Investigation, *Aircraft Accident Report* (cited herein as item 813).

803. U.S. Congress. House. Committee on Interstate and Foreign Commerce. *Independent Office of Air Safety; Hearing before the Committee on Interstate and Foreign Commerce.* 80th Cong., 2d Sess., 20 and 21 April 1948. Washington, D.C.: U.S. Government Printing Office, 1948. Pp. iii + 114.

Testimony regarding the enactment of a bill (H.R. 6144) to provide for the coordination of aviation policy, improve the administration of the Civil Aeronautics Act of 1938, and to provide for an independent Office of Air Safety.

804. U.S. Congress. House. Committee on Interstate and Foreign Commerce. Special Subcommittee on Investigation. *Air Safety: Selected Review of FAA Performance.* Washington, D.C.: U.S. Government Printing Office, 1974. Pp. 263. Illustr.

Reviews the Federal Aviation Administration's handling of

the DC-10 cargo door problem, air transport of hazardous materials, the CF-6 engine-DC-10 problem, and ground proximity warning systems. Questions the FAA's commitment to leadership in safety and its willingness to allow industry to conduct self-regulation.

805. U.S. Congress. House. Committee on Public Works and Transportation. *Status of the Air Traffic Control System: Hearings before the Subcommittee on Investigations and Oversight of the Committee on Public Works and Transportation.* 98th Cong., 1st and 2d Sess., 4 May–27 June 1984. Washington, D.C.: U.S. Government Printing Office, 1984. Pp. iv + 1441. Bibliog., Illustr.

A year-long investigation of air traffic control that began 21 months after the controllers' walkout. During that year the air traffic control picture seemed to worsen with regard to safety and overwork.

806. U.S. Congress. Senate. Committee on Commerce. *Safety in Air: Hearings before a Subcommittee of the Committee on Commerce.* 74th Cong., 2d Sess. Washington, D.C.: U.S. Government Printing Office, 1936–1937.

The report of the politically motivated Copeland committee, which conducted hearings on the airliner crash in 1935 that killed Senator Bronson Cutting of New Mexico. A comprehensive, but often bitter investigation of air safety that contributed to the passage of the Civil Aeronautics Act of 1938.

807. U.S. Department of Commerce. Weather Bureau. *Design for a Modern National Aviation Weather System: A Plan for Modernizing the National Aviation Weather Service to Promote the Safety and Efficiency of Air Operations (through FY 1963).* Washington, D.C.: U.S. Government Printing Office, 1958. Pp. 53. Illustr.

A five-year plan to improve the existing weather service. Recommends installing current and new data collection instruments at more airports; upper air probing; information dissemination through radio, telephone, and pictorial displays; strengthened weather network using high-activity airports and geographically strategic weather stations; and research and development.

808. U.S. Department of Transportation. Federal Aviation Admin-
      istration. *FAA General Aviation News.* Washington, D.C.:
      U.S. Government Printing Office. Bimonthly. Illustr.

      A bimonthly publication that serves as the agency's aviation
      safety magazine for aircraft, helicopters, balloons, gliders, and
      the like. Contains the latest regulation problems in air safety
      and helps pilots review their flying skills.

809. U.S. Department of Transportation. Federal Aviation Admin-
      istration. *Guide to Federal Aviation Administration Publica-
      tions.* Washington, D.C.: U.S. Government Printing Office,
      1986. Pp. vi + 60.

      An indispensable guide to the publications of the FAA.
      Includes all regulatory (Federal Aviation Regulations, certi-
      fication) and nonregulatory (advisory circulars, flight safety
      materials, handbooks) items, which cover just about any subject
      on aviation within the United States.

810. U.S. Department of Transportation. *Annual Report on the
      Effect of the Airline Deregulation Act on the Level of Air
      Safety.* Washington, D.C.: U.S. Government Printing Office,
      1979. Pp. 50.

      This statistical study checks the adequacy of air safety
      regulations, reviews accidents, and records air safety violations.

811. U.S. National Transportation Safety Board. Bureau of Accident
      Investigation. *Annual Review of U.S. General Aviation Acci-
      dents.* Washington, D.C.: U.S. Government Printing Office,
      1947–.

      A yearly review of all general aviation accidents within the
      United States.

812. U.S. National Transportation Safety Board. Bureau of Accident
      Investigation. *Briefs of Accidents; U.S. Civil Aviation.* Wash-
      ington, D.C.: U.S. Government Printing Office, 1959–.

      A report of all accidents in U.S. civil aviation by year that
      cites the important facts of each accident in a brief format.
      Distributed by the National Technical Information Service,
      Springfield, Virginia.

813. U.S. National Transportation Safety Board. Bureau of Accident
      Investigation. *Aircraft Accident Report*. Washington, D.C.:
      U.S. Government Printing Office, 1966–.

      Detailed studies of commercial aircraft accidents by year.
      Includes probable cause and all circumstances that surrounded
      the crash. Distributed by the National Technical Information
      Service, Springfield, Virginia.

814. U.S. National Transportation Safety Board. Bureau of Accident
      Investigation. *Aircraft Accident Reports: Brief Format; U.S.
      Civil Aviation*. Washington, D.C.: U.S. Government Printing
      Office, 1968–.

      Reviews selected aircraft accidents in U.S. civil and foreign
      aviation; issued several times a year. Distributed by the Na-
      tional Technical Information Service, Springfield Virginia.

815. U.S. National Transportation Safety Board. Bureau of Accident
      Investigation. *Annual Review of U.S. Air Carrier Accidents*.
      Washington, D.C.: U.S. Government Printing Office, 1969–.

      A yearly review of accidents for all U.S. air carriers in
      passenger operations. Statistics and tables provide information
      on type of accident, characteristics, losses, and other pertinent
      factors.

816. U.S. Navy Department. Naval Aviation Safety Center. *Hand-
      book for Aircraft Accident Investigators*. Washington, D.C.:
      U.S. Government Printing Office, 1957. Pp. 70.

      A thorough technical guide to aircraft investigations by the
      Navy that has obvious application to the public sector. Covers
      how to organize and investigate a crash, from recovering and
      analyzing the wreckage to questioning witnesses.

817. Weston, Richard, and Ronald Hurst. *Zagreb One Four: Cleared
      to Collide*? London: Granada, 1982. Pp. 198. Illustr.

      Recounts the story of a midair collision of a British Airways
      Trident 3 and an Inex Adria DC–9 over Yugoslavia in 1976 and
      the resulting investigation that led to the imprisonment of an
      air traffic controller who was convicted of negligence. Co-
      authored by a lawyer who represented one of the British Air-

ways flight attendants killed in the crash. Weston eventually helped to clear the air traffic controller of the charges.

Whitnah, Donald R. *Safer Skyways: Federal Control of Aviation, 1926–1966.* Ames: Iowa State University, 1966. Pp. xii + 417. Index, Bibliog., Illustr.

Cited herein as item 557.

EVENTS

The works in this section are representative samples of the broad range of material available on aviation "events," for lack of a better descriptive term, and the persons associated with them. The category includes, but is not limited to, books on record–breaking first flights, transatlantic–transpacific flights, barnstorming, air racing, and air exploration, especially of the Arctic and Antarctic regions. Although the chronological span covered varies, the emphasis is on aviation's "golden age," the years between the two world wars.

The bibliography attempts to provide the reader with the best or most representative books on the subject. These are by and large good, easy–to–read works about the myriad events of the period, the development of the flying machines, and the breathtaking exploits of the participants.

Samuel B. Fishbein
Thomas J. Noon

818. Alcock, Sir John, and Sir Arthur Whitten Brown. *Our Trans-atlantic Flight*. London: William Kimber, 1969. Pp. 195. Illustr.

Chronicles the successful pioneering attempt to cross the Atlantic in June 1919. The first direct transatlantic flight of Sir John Alcock and Sir Arthur Whitten Brown was an example of courage and endurance, navigational skill, and the reliability attained by a relatively crude aircraft. Before it was included in this book, Sir John's account of his transatlantic flight was published in the September issue of *Badminton Magazine* of 1919.

819. Amundsen, Roald E.G. *My Polar Flight*. London: Hutchinson, 1925. Pp. 292. Illustr.

The trials and tribulations of Roald Amundsen during one of his polar expeditions, wherein both of his aircraft were disabled and he and five others were considered "lost." After 14 days, Amundsen and his party finally were rescued by the cutter *Sjoliv*. This expedition was the first attempt to use airplanes for exploration of the Arctic.

820. Andrée, S.A. *Andrée's Story: The Complete Record of His Polar Flight, 1897*. Translated by Edward Adams-Ray. New York: Viking, 1930. Pp. xiv + 389. Illustr.

The complete record of Andrée's ill-fated polar balloon flight in 1897. From the journals of S.A. Andrée, Nils Strindberg, and K. Froenkel, found on White Island in the summer of 1930 and edited by the Swedish Society for Anthropology and Geography.

821. Archbold, Richard, and A.L. Rand. *New Guinea Expedition: Fly River Area, 1936–1937*. New York: Robert M. McBride, 1940. Reprint. New York: AMS, 1979. Pp. xviii + 206. Index, Illustr.

Although this volume recounts the experiences of the author on his second biographical expedition, it was only made possible by the use of the airplane, parachute, the radio telephone, and other 20th-century devices. With these, Archbold has penetrated some of the secrets locked in the Pleistocene era. The lay reader will be fascinated by the struggles of the two men of science and their machine, against jungle, mountain, and prehistoric man.

822. Balchen, Bernt. *Come North with Me, an Autobiography.* New York: E.P. Dutton, 1958. Pp. 318. Illustr.

Starting with the year 1926, the author recounts in some detail the trials and tribulations experienced during his expedition to the North Pole. The story takes us through the expedition to Antarctica (1928–1930), the flight over the South Pole, and continues through 1957.

823. Barker, Ralph. *The Schneider Trophy Races.* London: Chatto and Windus, 1971. Pp. 272. Bibliog., Illustr.

The story of Jacques Schneider, a visionary who saw in the seaplane the brightest hope for spanning the oceans. Because of an accident while hydroplaning at Monte Carlo in 1910 that restricted his active life, Schneider turned to organizing aviation events and competitions. His concept of a special contest for seaplanes combined a vision of maritime aviation with a passion for speed. On December 5, 1912, he presented the trophy that bears his name. A story of the rivalry of men, machines, and countries during the early period of aviation history.

824. Bartlett, Donald L., and James B. Steele. *Empire: The Life, Legend, and Madness of Howard Hughes.* New York: W.W. Norton, 1979. Pp. 687. Index, Bibliog., Illustr.

A thorough biography of an epic figure who finally came to be ruled by his madness. Good coverage of Hughes's aviation career, especially the development of the Hughes Racer and "Spruce Goose," and the struggle over Trans World Airlines.

825. Bertram, Hans. *Flight to Hell.* Translated by Jan Noble. New York: Harper and Brothers, 1936. Pp. 236. Illustr.

The story of Hans Bertram, who, with his comrades Lagorio, Klausmann, and Thom, on February 29, 1932, took off for a flight from Germany to Australia in the Junkers seaplane *Atlantis* to demonstrate the excellence of German aircraft. A forced landing on the northwest coast of Australia brought on the terrible ordeal of 53 days in an inhospitable environment, but the company was eventually rescued. Told with many personal anecdotes.

826. Binney, George. *With Seaplane and Sledge in the Arctic*. New York: George H. Doran, 1926. Pp. 287. Illustr.

Chronicles three Oxford expeditions led by Binney between 1921 and 1924 to the polar regions. Although none of those setting out in 1921 had previous experience in the Arctic, they developed new methods and safeguards in exploration. The decision to experiment with the use of aircraft was partly due to the belief that certain regions would be inaccessible except from the air.

827. *The Bush Pilots*. Alexandria, Va.: Time–Life, 1983. Pp. 176. Index, Bibliog., Illustr.

A compendium of photos and stories of the early bush pilots, their aircraft, and exploits all over the world. A tough, independent lot, these pilots pioneered the use of airplanes to carry people and goods to places that had been accessible only on horseback, or by oxcart, dog sled, or canoe.

828. Byrd, Richard E. *Skyward; Man's Mastery of the Air as Shown by the Brilliant Flights of America's Leading Air Explorer*. Foreword by William Moffett. New York: Halcyon House, 1928. Pp. xiv + 359. Illustr.

Focuses on man's mastery of the air as it relates to the flights of the most famous air explorer of his time. The book recounts Byrd's life, his thrilling adventures, his North Pole and transatlantic flight, and his plans for conquering the Antarctic by air.

829. Casey, Louis S. *The First Nonstop Coast-to-Coast Flight and The Historic T-2 Airplane*. Smithsonian Annals of Flight, no. 1. Washington, D.C.: Smithsonian Institution Press, 1964. Pp. 90. Bibliog., Illustr.

Relates the history of the first successful nonstop coast-to-coast flight of the historic Fokker T-2 now in the collection of the Smithsonian Institution's National Air and Space Museum. Describes the two attempts that preceded the flight and provides a technical description of the T-2. Well illustrated with drawings and photographs, plus a complete genealogy of the aircraft.

A boyish–looking Charles A. Lindbergh stands in front of his aircraft, the Ryan NYP "Spirit of St. Louis," at Roosevelt Field, New York, before departing on his solo, nonstop transatlantic flight, May 20, 1927. (SI Photo A336)

830. Chamberlin, Clarence D. *Record Flights.* Philadelphia, Pa.: Dorrance, 1928. Pp. 286. Illustr.

Chronicles the trials and tribulations of the Chamberlin–Levine flight from New York to Europe. Also reviews a chapter from the early days of flying, including the politics, motivation, and financial strains concerned with the developing industry. Part 2 is devoted to Chamberlin's early days at school and his military service during World War I.

831. Christy, Joe. *Racing Planes and Pilots: Aircraft Competition, Past and Present.* Blue Ridge Summit, Pa.: TAB, 1982. Pp. xi + 198. Index, Illustr.

Traces the history of air racing over the years from the world's first, held in August 1909, near Rheims, France, to 1980. Lists events and aircraft, with commentary on each.

832. Cobham, Alan J. *A Time to Fly.* London: Shepheard–Walwyn, 1978. Pp. x + 214. Illustr.

The autobiography of a British pilot whose long–distance exploration flights expanded public awareness of the technical advancements that were making civil air transportation feasible and safe. The author discusses his flights in Africa, the Middle East, Southeast Asia, and Australia, and shows that, although difficult, flying in isolated regions was not only possible but commercially viable.

833. Cohen, Rose N. *The Men Who Gave Us Wings.* New York: Macmillan, 1944. Pp. vi + 210. Illustr.

Takes the reader from the time men dreamed of flying through the various periods of ballooning, gliders, and powered flight. Also contains a chronology of important dates in the history of aviation through 1937. Prepared as a text for school children with questions and "things to do" at the end of each chapter.

834. Crouch, Tom D., ed. *Charles A. Lindbergh, an American Life.* Washington, D.C.: Smithsonian Institution Press, 1977. Pp. xv + 119. Bibliog., Illustr.

A compendium of five lectures presented at the National Air

and Space Museum, Smithsonian Institution, on May 20, 1976, to commemorate the 50th anniversary of Lindbergh's flight. A contribution to a more complete understanding of the achievements of a great airman. Contains many photos.

835. Davis, Burke. *Amelia Earhart*. New York: G.P. Putnam's Sons, 1972. Pp. 189.

Recounts the life story of Amelia Earhart, the first woman to fly solo across the Atlantic on May 20, 1931. Earhart dared to defy the beliefs and customs of her day just as she braved the dangers of the sky and the oceans; the mystery concerning her life and disappearance remains. Concludes with a description of the search conducted after she disappeared in July 1937.

836. Dwiggins, Don. *They Flew the Bendix Race: The History of the Competition for the Bendix Trophy*. Philadelphia, Pa.: Lippincott, 1965. Pp. 198. Illustr.

From the start, the Bendix classic was a wide–open contest with a substantial cash incentive. Vincent Bendix, an industrialist, was convinced by Clifford Henderson, originator and promoter of the National Air Races, to sponsor an annual cross–country airplane race. The first annual race was flown in the fall of 1931, from Los Angeles to Cleveland. An interesting story of early pilots and their planes and their efforts to capture this prestigious trophy.

837. Dwiggins, Don. *The Air Devils: The Story of Balloonists, Barnstormers, and Stunt Pilots*. Philadelphia, Pa.: Lippincott, 1966. Pp. 226. Illustr.

Much of the book is based on the personal recollections of airmen the author had known or flown with in the previous 20 years. To get to stories prior to this time, Dwiggins's research extended over many published and unpublished materials. An excellent history of early flight in story form.

838. Dwiggins, Don. *The Barnstormers: Flying Daredevils of the Roaring Twenties*. New York: Grosset and Dunlap, 1968. Pp. 151. Bibliog., Illustr.

An important and colorful story of the early barnstormers, the madcap daredevils who once entertained and electrified audiences all over the United States with their death–defying feats. The story begins with the days before World War I, when pioneer aerial performers risked their necks in frail–looking wood and wire aircraft. The main part of the story is set against the "roaring twenties," a period that produced many legendary flying heroes.

839. Earhart, Amelia. *20 Hrs. 40 Min.; Our Flight in the Friendship.* New York: Grosset and Dunlap, 1928. Pp. 314. Illustr.

Through this revealing look at Amelia Earhart's life, the reader is able to understand the ambitions and motivations that led her to participate in a transatlantic flight in 1928. Two other books by Earhart that are worth reading are *The Fun of It; Random Records of My Own Flying and of Women in Aviation* (cited herein as item 959), published in 1932 and *Last Flight* (cited herein as item 840), a record of her transglobal flight attempt during which she was lost at sea.

840. Earhart, Amelia. *Last Flight.* Arranged by George Palmer Putnam. New York: Harcourt, Brace, 1937. Pp. xvi + 226. Illustr.

The author's own story of her nearly transglobal flight that ended in her tragic disappearance somewhere in the mid–Pacific. As she completed each stage of her journey, she sent back not only her dispatches and personal letters, but diaries, charts, and logs. The text was arranged by Earhart's husband, George Palmer Putnam, and is illustrated with maps and many photographs.

Earhart, Amelia. *The Fun of It; Random Records of My Own Flying and of Women in Aviation.* Reprint. Chicago: Academy, 1977. Pp. 218. Illustr.

Cited herein as item 959.

841. Ekins, Herbert R. *Around the World in Eighteen Days and How To Do It.* New York: Longmans, Green, 1936. Pp. xiii + 186. Illustr.

Ever since Jules Verne sent his fictitious Phileas Fogg "around the world in eighty days," hardly a year went by without new attempts to circumnavigate the globe and establish

speed records. Discusses the author's 1936, 25,794-mile trip in
18½ days as a passenger on established airlines.

842. Eustis, Hamilton Nelson. *The Greatest Air Race, England to
     Australia—1919.* Foreword by Air Marshal Sir Richard
     Williams. Adelaide: Rigby, 1969. Pp. 188. Illustr.

     Following World War I, the Commonwealth government
     offered a prize of 10,000 pounds to the first Australian to fly a
     British aircraft from England to Australia within a period of 30
     days. The author relates the story of the results of that offer
     and the primitive state of aviation in 1919—there were no
     instruments, radio communications between air and ground, or
     cabin pressurization.

843. Fleisher, Suri, and Arleen Keylin, eds. *Flight, as Reported by
     the N.Y. Times.* Introduction by Norbert Slepyan. New York:
     Arno, 1977. Pp. 279. Illustr.

     A compendium of newspaper headlines and articles pertaining
     to the growth of aviation that appeared in the *New York Times*
     from July 25, 1909, to July 21, 1976. The reader will note that
     the articles do not speak of the many disasters throughout this
     period, but only about the adventure associated with the history
     of aviation.

844. Foxworth, Thomas G. *The Speed Seekers.* New York: Doubleday,
     1976. Pp. xi + 560. Index, Illustr.

     Flawed but useful survey of international air racing in the
     1920s with emphasis on technological developments. One wishes
     Foxworth had carried the story on into the 1930s. Good
     appendixes.

845. Glines, C.V., ed. *Polar Aviation.* New York: Franklin Watts,
     1964. Pp. xii + 289. Illustr.

     An anthology that represents the history of flight in the polar
     regions. Although it does not contain all the stories (and moti-
     vations) that could be told, it does relate man's progress as he
     first tried flight in balloons, then dirigibles, and finally aircraft
     to bring the inaccessible polar areas of the world within easy
     reach. Flights into these areas of the world were first fool-
     hardy, then daring, then routine.

Gordon, Arthur. *The American Heritage History of Flight.* Edited by Alvin M. Josephy Jr. New York: American Heritage, 1962. Pp. 416. Index, Illustr.

Cited herein as item 64.

846. Grierson, John. *Challenge to the Poles: Highlights of Arctic and Antarctic Aviation.* Foreword by Charles A. Lindbergh. Hamden, Conn.: Archon Books, 1964. Pp. 695. Illustr.

John Grierson, a professional pilot with experience in the Arctic and Antarctic, takes his readers through "fantastic" experiences of early polar flying, the sighting of new lands and mountain ranges, the relief and tragedy of rescue missions, over blinding snowfields, and under spirit–blanketing fogs. Covers the period 1896–1954.

847. Hull, Robert. *September Champions: The Story of America's Air Racing Pioneers.* Harrisburg, Pa.: Stackpole, 1979. Pp. 223. Index, Bibliog., Illustr.

The author takes us back to the central arena of aviation derring–do in the 1930s, the Cleveland Air Races. The story of an individualistic era and its heroes in which the fastest airplanes in the world were strained to, and often beyond, their limits by pilots such as Jimmy Doolittle, Roscoe Turner, Steve Wittman, Louise Thaden, and Jacqueline Cochran.

848. Huttig, Jack. *1927: A Summer of Eagles.* Chicago: Nelson–Hall, 1980. Pp. xiv + 147. Index, Bibliog., Illustr.

A popular narrative of North Atlantic crossing attempts and other long–distance flights made between March and September 1927, including Lindbergh's successful solo flight in May. The author skillfully portrays the hoopla and excitement attendant upon these flights.

849. Jackson, Donald D. *The Explorers.* Alexandria, Va.: Time–Life, 1983. Pp. 176. Index, Bibliog., Illustr.

Traces in words and pictures the stories of the exploration of some of Earth's last frontiers by air. At the end of World War I there were numerous trained pilots looking for new challenges who could potentially reach places that were hitherto con–

sidered unexplorable. To the public, following their exploits from the sidelines, the fliers seemed to be living one of the great adventures of the age.

850. Joerg, Wolfgang L.G. *Brief History of Polar Exploration since the Introduction of Flying.* New York: American Geographical Society, 1930. Pp. 50. Bibliog., Illustr.

The text is accompanied by a physical map of the Arctic and a bathymetric map of the Antarctic. With the aid of these and a number of text maps, the author first reviews the history of polar exploration since the introduction of flying, briefly discusses the special methods of air navigation in the polar regions, takes up the present (ca. 1930) status of political sovereignty in the Arctic and Antarctic, and ends with a description of the two maps and the major physical features they display.

851. Kilgallen, Dorothy. *Girl around the World.* Philadelphia, Pa.: David McKay, 1936. Pp. 219. Illustr.

The author, a member of the New York *Evening Journal* and International News Service staff correspondent, entered a race to circle the globe (by any means). At age 23, she was the first woman to break the then–existing record of 72 days, 6 hours, and 11 minutes established by Nellie Bly in 1889. This is the exciting story of her 22,000–mile journey by air in which she girdled the globe in 24 days, 12 hours, and 51 minutes.

852. Kinert, Reed C., and Dustin W. Carter. *Racing Planes and Air Races.* 13 vols. Fallbrook, Calif.: Aero, 1967–. Illustr.

A complete history of racing events from 1909 to 1967 dedicated to the designers, builders, and pilots of racing aircraft and their contribution to the science of flight. From the beginning of air racing in 1909, the development of racing planes and engines contributed directly to the technology applied to aircraft built in assembly–line quantity, both military and commercial. Originally issued annually in serial form.

853. Larsen, Jim. *Air Racers: Directory of Unlimited Class Pylon Racers.* Kirkland, Wash.: American Air Museum, 1971. Pp. 161. Illustr.

A directory of unlimited class pylon air racers with three objectives: (1) to provide a quick reference to the racers that participated in sanctioned, unlimited class, closed–course racing events from 1964 through 1970; (2) to record in sufficient detail some of the colorful racer markings and physical specifications necessary for model builders to construct accurate aircraft miniatures; and (3) to provide a material legacy for the many individuals who have devoted time, and in some cases, their lives to the sport of air racing.

854. Lewis, Peter M.H. *British Racing and Recordbreaking Aircraft*. London: Putnam, 1971. Pp. 496. Illustr.

A comprehensive illustrated account of the competitive aspects of British flying. This succint narrative records in detail over 400 diverse airplane types, many of standard or modified form, others evolved specifically for extreme speed, high altitude, or ultimate range. The narrative also embraces gliders, balloons, and airships, together with extensive descriptions of more than 1,400 events and nearly 2,000 men and women who have achieved distinction by flying in them.

855. Light, Richard Upjohn. *Focus on Africa*. New York: American Geographical Society, 1941. Pp. xv + 229. Bibliog., Illustr.

With text and aerial photographs, the author presents a portrait of Africa in 1937–1938. Written during the era of the start of world conflict, the author's reflections on Africa are as true today as they were in 1941. An excellent work.

856. Lindbergh, Anne Morrow. *North to the Orient*. New York: Harcourt, Brace, 1935. Pp. 255. Illustr.

The memoirs of Anne Morrow Lindbergh's flight with her husband in their Lockheed Sirius around a great circle route from New York to Tokyo to Nanking. Eloquently portrays her experiences and thoughts during this tour of the cold northern reaches and the mysterious east. Mrs. Lindbergh served as navigator for this flight, in which the couple searched out future air routes for commercial aviation.

857. Lindbergh, Anne Morrow. *Listen! The Wind*. Foreword and Map Drawings by Charles A. Lindbergh. New York: Harcourt, Brace, 1938. Pp. xii + 275. Illustr.

Anne Morrow Lindbergh's memoirs of her flight with husband
Charles around the North Atlantic Ocean, from Africa to South
America, in search of new commercial air routes. The splendid
narrative combines aviation and adventure, transoceanic flight,
and accounts of the natives of the countries the Lindberghs
visited during the flight.

858. Lindbergh, Charles A. *"We."* New York: G.P. Putnam's Sons,
     1927. Pp. 318. Illustr.

     A quickly written autobiographical memoir in which Lind-
     bergh discusses his exploits as a barnstormer, his year as an
     Army flight training cadet, his work as an airmail pilot, and his
     epochal transatlantic flight from New York to Paris in 1927.

859. Lindbergh, Charles A. *The Spirit of St. Louis.* New York:
     Charles Scribner's Sons, 1953. Pp. xii + 562. Illustr.

     A more complete and thoughtful account of the New York to
     Paris flight of May 1927. Lindbergh spent nearly a decade and a
     half composing the book, working and reworking it, until he was
     satisfied. The results are readily apparent. Awarded the Pul-
     itzer Prize for biography in 1954.

860. Mendenhall, Charles A. *The National Air Racers in 3-views,
     1929-1949.* Rochester, N.Y.: Diane, 1971. Pp. 62. Bibliog.,
     Illustr.

     A collection of drawings of over 90 racing planes that il-
     lustrates all of the aircraft of the National Air Races (1929 to
     1949) era in pictorial form. Interestingly, in some cases, no
     formal plans of the racers ever existed and, in some others, the
     original drawings have long since been lost or destroyed.

861. Mendenhall, Charles A. *The Modern Air Racers in 3-views,
     1949-1975.* Rochester, N.Y.: Pylon, 1975. Pp. 62. Bibliog.,
     Illustr.

     As with the first volume, *The National Air Racers in 3-views,
     1929-1949*, this book was written with the idea of providing
     graphic three-view drawings of all the modern racing aircraft
     (to 1975) under one cover. Includes notes concerning construc-
     tion data, performance specifications, color schemes, pilots,
     and other related details.

862. Miller, Francis Trevelyan. *The Flight to Conquer the Ends of the Earth; Byrd's Great Adventure: With the Complete Story of All Polar Explorations for One Thousand Years.* Philadelphia, Pa.: John C. Winston, 1930. Pp. 383. Illustr.

A story of one of the world's great adventures, the flight from the ends of the earth. A drama that began three centuries before Christ and comes to a climax in the year 1930 with the triumphant return of Admiral Byrd. He was the first man to fly over both ends of the earth, and futhermore to fly the Atlantic Ocean from the Western Hemisphere to the Eastern Hemisphere.

863. Mills, Stephen E., and James W. Phillips. *Sourdough Sky, A Pictorial History of Flights and Flyers in the Bush Country.* Seattle, Wash.: Superior, 1969. Pp. 176. Illustr.

A pictorial history of flights and flyers in the bush country (interior Alaska). Although in many areas the airplane is considered a convenience, in Alaska it was a vital part of day-to-day life. Among "bush pilots," a knowledge of how to cope with the bush is as much a part of life as how to pilot an aircraft. Contains a partly annotated list of 100 pilots of the North.

864. Mohler, Stanley R., and Bobby H. Johnson. *Wiley Post, His Winnie Mae, and the World's First Pressure Suit.* Smithsonian Annals of Flight, no. 8. Washington, D.C.: Smithsonian Institution Press, 1971. Pp. vii + 127. Bibliog., Illustr.

A journey through the exciting life of Wiley Post. The narrative provides the story of the man, his beloved Lockheed Vega, the *Winnie Mae*, and the world's first practical pressure suit. The book also includes Post's studies of biological rhythms and their relation to flight (the world's first such studies), his discovery of the jet stream, and other experiments.

865. Mondey, David. *The Schneider Trophy: A History of the Contests for la Coupe d'Aviation Maritime Jacques Schneider.* London: Robert Hale, 1975. Pp. 303. Index, Illustr.

A history of the contests, men, and planes of the era, starting in 1913, with some diagrams and photos of the international Schneider competition. A detailed description of the amphibious machines and their development. The wish of Jacques Schneider to advance long-range maritime aviation was not realized directly, but the aviation industry of the world owes much to the little man who dared to dream. Schneider Trophy results appear in the appendix.

866. Nevin, David. *The Pathfinders*. Alexandria, Va.: Time–Life, 1980. Pp. 176. Index, Bibliog., Illustr.

Anthologizes in words and pictures the history–making flights that took place between 1909 and 1938. Special attention is given to Lindbergh's transatlantic flight to France on May 21, 1927.

867. Post, Wiley, and Harold Gatty. *Around the World in Eight Days: The Flight of the Winnie Mae*. Introduction by Will Rogers. New York: Rand, McNally, 1931. Pp. 304. Illustr.

Post and Gatty's account of their epochal flight around the world in 1931 in a modified Lockheed Vega, the *Winnie Mae*.

868. Potter, Jean Clark. *The Flying North*. New York: Macmillan, 1947. Pp. xvi + 261. Illustr.

Chronicles the bush pilots of Alaska and their role in the great saga of pioneer history. By 1939 the small airlines of the Territory were hauling 23 times as many passengers and 1,000 times as much freight, per capita, as the airlines of the continental United States.

869. Putnam, George P. *Andrée, the Record of a Tragic Adventure*. New York: Brewer and Warren, 1930. Pp. 239. Illustr.

The saga of Andrée and two associates in their unsuccessful quest to reach the North Pole by balloon in 1897. The flight ended after only a few days, when the balloon was forced down, perhaps less than 200 miles from its starting point. The bones of these three brave men were found some 33 years later at their last camp.

870. Rhode, Bill. *Baling Wire, Chewing Gum, and Guts; The Story of the Gates Flying Circus*. Port Washington, N.Y.: Kennikat, 1970. Pp. xi + 194. Index, Bibliog., Illustr.

An entertaining account of one of the most popular and

profitable stunt flying circuses of the 1920s. Founder Ivan D. Gates estimated that in a four-year period between 1922 and 1926, his flying circus had put on 1,836 exhibitions in 1,042 cities and towns and had traveled throughout 41 states.

871. Ronnie, Art. *Locklear: The Man Who Walked on Wings.* South Brunswick, N.J.: A.S. Barnes, 1973. Pp. 333. Bibliog., Illustr.

Details the life of Ormer Locklear, a popular stunt pilot whose brief career as a Hollywood aviator-actor ended in tragedy 16 months after his first film. Ronnie goes beyond the mere facts to portray the motivations behind Locklear's death-defying feats.

872. Roseberry, Cecil R. *The Challenging Skies: The Colorful Story of Aviation's Most Exciting Years, 1919-1939.* Garden City, N.Y.: Doubleday, 1966. Pp. 533. Index, Bibliog., Illustr.

A popular narrative treatment of aviation's most glamorous and romantic era, the period between the World Wars. Although Roseberry's focus is on events and personalities, the book is nonetheless intelligently written and comprehensive. Especially good on distance flying, aerial exploration, and air racing. A fine introduction to aviation in the 1920s and 1930s.

873. Schmid, Sylvester H., and Truman C. Weaver. *The Golden Age of Air Racing—Pre 1940.* Hales Corners, Wisc.: EAA Air Museum Foundation, 1963. Pp. 167. Illustr.

Captures the color and atmosphere of the golden age of air racing. The book is a tribute to the pilots, designers, and build-ers of the racing craft of that era and to the present-day (1963) EAA members. Specifies National Air Race results year by year and gives details of various winning aircraft.

864. Sinclair, James P. *Wings of Gold: How the Aeroplane Developed New Guinea.* Bathurst, Australia: Robert Brown, 1983. Pp. 326. Index, Bibliog., Illustr.

A thorough and well-written account of aerial exploration and its role in the development of New Guinea. Spanning the period from 1922 to 1942, the book provides an overview of how the airplane was used in exploring the country, and takes reader from the early anthropological expeditions of Matthew W.

Stirling to the gold prospectors and mining operations to the onslaught of Japanese forces in World War II. First published in 1978 by Pacific Publications.

875. Smith, Richard K. *First Across! The U.S. Navy's Transatlantic Flight of 1919.* Annapolis, Md.: Naval Institute, 1973. Pp. 279. Bibliog., Illustr.

The classic treatment of the Navy's pioneering 1919 transatlantic flight that used the Curtiss NC–series flying boats. Awarded the American Institute of Aeronautics and Astronautics prize for history in 1972.

876. Sutherland, Alice Gibson. *Canada's Aviation Pioneers: 50 Years of McKee Trophy Winners.* Foreword by Fred W. Hotson. Toronto: McGraw–Hill Ryerson, 1978. Pp. xiii + 304. Index, Illustr.

Provides a unique look at the people who built the aviation industry in Canada. The story is one of people, and, although the sphere of their efforts was wide and varied over 50 years, the common denominator was achievement. This story of the winners of the Trans–Canada Trophy, also known as the Mckee Trophy, was completed on the eve of the 50th anniversary of its award.

877. Swinson, Arthur. *The Great Air Race, England–Australia, 1934.* London: Cassell, 1968. Pp. xix + 236. Bibliog., Illustr.

The England–Australia Air Race of 1934 remains a unique event in aviation history. It halved the flying time from Europe to the Far East, paving the way for long–distance commercial aviation and making a powerful impact on strategic concepts. It spurred the development of revolutionary aircraft and brought to world notice the surging power and skill of American aeronautical engineering. It also brought together the great figures of the heroic, pioneer age of aviation.

878. Thomas, Lowell. *The First World Flight; Being the Personal Narratives of Lowell Smith, Erik Nelson, Leigh Wade, Leslie Arnold, Henry Ogden, John Harding.* New York: Houghton Mifflin, 1925. Pp. xxii + 328. Illustr.

The story of a pioneering round–the–world flight of the

Douglas World Cruisers, as related to Lowell Thomas by Lowell Smith, Erik Nelson, Leigh Wade, Leslie Arnold, Harry Ogden, and John Harding, all of whom were young officers in the U.S. Army Air Service. The flight was completed on September 28, 1924. Emphasizes the skill and courage exhibited by the participants and the fact that the aircraft used were the best that could be produced. Well written and entertaining.

879. Wilkins, George H. *Flying the Arctic*. New York: G.P. Putnam's Sons, 1928. Pp. xv + 336. Illustr.

Details some of Wilkins's experiences while studying universal meteorology and its association with world weather. Contends that from evidence collected over many years, meteorologists deduced the theory that data collected in polar regions and correlated with meteorological information from other latitudes would enable scientists to forecast the seasons with comparative accuracy.

880. Winter, Lumen, and Glenn Degner. *Minute Epics of Flight*. New York: Grosset and Dunlap, 1933. Pp. 160. Bibliog., Illustr.

Recaptures, in picture and word, the great moments connected with the story of flight. The authors have drawn upon a variety of sources to present a chronological history that begins with man's first urge to fly, as recorded in ancient legend and folklore, and ends with the year 1932.

881. Wood, Martha. *Heroes of the Air*. Rev. ed. New York: Thomas Y. Crowell, 1946. Pp. vi + 484. Illustr.

A detailed, flight–by–flight description of aeronautical exploits from the late 18th century to the end of World War II. Contains information on more than 100 separate flights and fliers and includes an annotated chronology that lists each flight from 1783 to 1946. Continues the work done in previous editions by Chelsea Fraser.

SOCIAL AND CULTURAL ASPECTS OF AVIATION

This section of the NASM bibliography encompasses a number of subjects that have to do with aviation's effect on culture and society. Broadly speaking, the works cited here should give the reader an idea of aviation's impact on society and the creative arts, its use as a tool of education and a symbol of progress, and the slow, often grudging assimilation of all members of society into its community. The entries are divided into 10 sections, which list overviews of aviation in culture and society; representative works on aviation in literature, education, film, the visual arts, architecture and design, music, and the comics; and sources on blacks and women in aviation.

Within the social and cultural context of aviation, an attempt has been made to select general studies that examine the discovery of the airplane and its proposed future uses. Because many literary works are also concerned with aviation's progress and society's reaction, a variety of anthologies of prose and verse, works of fiction, and analyses of the genre have been included. For those who seek additional bibliographic material in this area, Laurence Goldstein's *The Flying Machine and Modern Literature* (see item 907), contains source notes and a fine bibliography that covers anthologies, nonfiction prose, fiction, poetry, and drama. Aviation fiction is dealt with specifically in a useful article titled "Aviation Literature, A Changing Art," by Charles D. Bright (see item 901), which cites most of the classics. World War II spawned a number of educational programs in aviation, and the Civil Aeronautics Administration's Air Age Education series is particularly illuminating. Hollywood's long and stormy relationship with the airplane has given aviation a good deal of exposure to the public, even though most aviation films have been only modest box-office successes. General information on aviation themes in music and art is limited, but a number of sources have examined aviation's significant impact on the visual arts, design, and architecture, and many of these works are included here.

Blacks in aviation is, unfortunately, still a relatively unexplored topic. However, the recent interest in black history and the exhibition, Black Wings: The American Black in Aviation, at the National Air and Space Museum, have gone a long way toward identifying participants and locating collections for further research. Sources that deal with women in aviation constitute a sizable part of the section; these works include individual biographies and autobiographies, surveys, and military studies. One key item is Dorothy Niekamp's *Women and Flight, 1910–1978: An Annotated Bibliography* (see item 966), which cites many useful sources. Although secondary literature on women in aviation is, in general, quite limited, the works listed provide a sample of some of the most significant titles.

Dorothy S. Cochrane
Deborah G. Douglas
Dominick A. Pisano

Aviation in Culture and Society—General Overviews

882. Bernardo, James V. *Aviation in the Modern World; The Dra-
      matic Impact upon Our Lives of Aircraft, Missiles, and
      Space Vehicles.* New York: E.P. Dutton, 1960. Pp. 352.
      Index, Bibliog., Illustr.

      A general look at aviation and future space travel in 1960.
      Includes topics such as aviation's wide influence on the world,
      as it has broken geographic boundaries, affected how we eat
      and dress, and affected our military posture. Aimed primarily
      at young people, encouraging them to pursue aviation careers.
      Contains a large appendix of research materials.

883. Bilstein, Roger E. "The Public Attitude toward the Airplane in
      the United States, 1910–1925." Master's Thesis, The Ohio
      State University, 1960. Bibliog.

      A survey of early aeronautics and the public's response to
      aviation. The author finds that despite growing enthusiasm,
      the airplane in the period immediately before and after World
      War I was regarded as a stunt machine with few practical
      applications beside military use, and its acceptance as a means
      of transportation does not materialize until the mid–1920s.
      Good notes at the end of each chapter.

884. Bilstein, Roger E. "Symbolism and Imagery." In *Flight Pat-
      terns: Trends of Aeronautical Development in the United
      States, 1918–1927*, 147–163. Athens: University of Georgia
      Press, 1983. Bibliog., Illustr.

      Documents the emergence of aviation onto the social and
      cultural scene in the 1920s. The author cites examples of
      literature, film, music, and art, but also points to the tech-
      nological benefits and aesthetic qualities that broadened
      the appeal of aviation. Bilstein highlights the role of women
      in aviation because their participation prompted a wider
      acceptance of aviation.

885. Bilstein, Roger E. "'Folklore, Fantasy and Artifacts,' Aero-
      space Perspectives, 1975–1983." In *Flight in America, 1900–
      1983: From the Wrights to the Astronauts*, 307–318. Balti-
      more, Md.: The Johns Hopkins University Press, 1984. Index,
      Bibliog., Illustr.

In a short space, the author gives an excellent account of aviation and space literature (fiction and nonfiction) and films; also touches on television, music, and art. These media seem to reflect the impact of air and space upon society. Many of the books and films were produced for propaganda purposes, whereas others were for pure amusement, but they all reveal how flights into air and space began as spectacles and became integrated into everyday life.

886. Brooks, Courtney G. "American Aeronautics as Spectacle and Sport." Ph.D. diss., Tulane University, 1969. Pp. 241. Bibliog.

Studies aeronautics as recreation and public spectacle made popular by barnstormers and air circuses as well as Hollywood and the Civilian Pilot Training Program sponsored by the Civil Aeronautics Authority in 1939. The first half of the work is devoted to balloonists, and the second half to pioneers, racers, and explorers. Includes a section on the rise of private aviation.

887. Corn, Joseph J. *The Winged Gospel: America's Romance with Aviation, 1900–1950.* New York: Oxford University Press, 1983. Pp. x + 177. Index, Illustr.

Beside addressing the hero worship of aviators, the author comments on the aviation education of children by schools and popular culture, the positive impact of women in aviation, and the concept of an airplane in every garage. Also investigates the "religion" of aviation and the divine and evangelistic terms attributed to it by members of the aviation community and the general public.

888. Davy, M.J.B. *Air Power and Civilization.* London: George Allen and Unwin, 1941. Pp. vii + 202. Index, Illustr.

A thought–provoking book on the effects of aviation on society: Do the positive factors outweigh the negative? Condemns the development and uses of aircraft and even considers abolishing them (or at least their military uses).

889. Davis, Kenneth S. *The Hero: Charles A. Lindbergh and the American Dream.* Garden City, N.Y.: Doubleday, 1959. Pp. 527. Index, Bibliog.

An excellent biography of Charles A. Lindbergh and a fine study of the rise and fall of an American hero. Although sympathetic to Lindbergh, the author does an admirable job of exploring the controversial nature of the subject and, in addition, presents a good look at the public and press in the years between 1927 and 1941. Of great value is the extensive and comprehensive chapter–by–chapter bibliographical essay.

Hudson, Kenneth, and Julian Pettifer. *Diamonds in the Sky: A Social History of Air Travel.* London: Bodley Head, 1979. Pp. 240. Index, Bibliog., Illustr.

Cited herein as item 519.

890.   Jacobs, Anne M. *Knights of the Wing.* New York: Century, 1928. Pp. xii + 240. Illustr.

A popular book that investigates the progress of aviation in the 1920s. Interestingly, the book is written by a woman who frequented military aviation fields for 10 years. Orville Wright wrote the introductory note.

891.   Lardner, John. "The Lindbergh Legends." In *The Aspirin Age,* ed. Isabel Leighton, 190–213. New York: Simon and Shuster, 1949.

Studies the constant publicity surrounding Charles Lindbergh and argues that much of it was self–perpetuated. Challenges the notion that Lindbergh preferred privacy by detailing how he sought publicity through his upper–crust acquaintances and controversial philosophies. Also suggests that Lindbergh sought to influence American thought by using his aviation talents and position in society. A strikingly different look at the legend of the American hero.

892.   Lindbergh, Charles A. *Of Flight and Life.* New York: Charles Scribner's Sons, 1948. Pp. viii + 56.

Recounts Lindbergh's personal journey as he moves from being an idealistic young man, enraptured with aviation and scientific progress, to an apprehensive postwar man, fearful of the scientific materialism he feels has mankind in its grip in 1948. An insightful look at the future of a civilization living in the shadow of atomic weapons and airborne destruction.

893. Lindbergh, Charles A. *Autobiography of Values.* Edited by William Jovanovich and Judith Schiff. New York: Harcourt Brace Jovanovich, 1977. Pp. xxi + 423. Index, Bibliog., Illustr.

A remarkable autobiography in which Lindbergh examines his early interest in aviation, space, and medicine and then his changing philosophy toward nature, civilization, and life. Throughout the critical period of his rise and fall as an American hero, he intertwines his personal feelings and sacrifices with his ambition to serve and promote aviation. Contains good photographs and a bibliography of Lindbergh's own literary works.

894. Luckett, Perry D. *Charles A. Lindbergh: A Bio–Bibliography.* Westport, Conn.: Greenwood Press, 1986. Pp. xii + 147. Index, Bibliog., Illustr.

A clearly written, concise study of Lindbergh that includes a brief narrative biography, a sharply focused bibliographical essay, and an extensive and thoroughly researched selective bibliography. What sets this book apart from all the other studies of the subject, however, is Luckett's inclusion of an all–too–brief chapter on Lindbergh's effect on popular culture in America, an aspect of his life that represents a veritable goldmine of new insights on a much written about public figure.

895. Ogburn, William F. *The Social Effects of Aviation.* Boston: Houghton Mifflin, 1946. Pp. vi + 755. Index, Bibliog., Illustr.

A comprehensive study of how aviation will influence society: helicopter rescue and transport; general aviation costs and regulations; air transportation's effects on industry, government, and families; and international transportation and its relation to politics. Ogburn covers almost all nonmilitary topics, and many of his predictions are accurate.

896. Pisano, Dominick. "The Airplane as a Cultural and Aesthetic Symbol, 1909–1940." [Unpubl. paper, January 1981.] Pp. 54.

A significant study of the airplane's influence on society in the 1920s and 1930s, as manifested in architecture and design, with references to literature, painting, and popular culture. The author traces from their European sources various cultural and aesthetic movements that use the airplane as a symbol of modernity and progress and that culminate in the pervasive streamlined era in American popular culture and design.

897.   Ross, Walter S. *The Last Hero: Charles A. Lindbergh.* New York: Harper and Row, 1964. Pp. xv + 400. Index, Illustr.

Examines Lindbergh's life as an aviator and as an American hero. Ross believes that Lindbergh was the last living American hero, that is, one whose fame surrounded him as he lived. His influence on aviation (sometimes bold, sometimes controversial) and on Americans began 60 years ago and continues today.

898.   Turner, Charles C. *The Romance of Aeronautics: An Interesting Account of the Growth and Achievements of All Kinds of Aerial Craft.* London: Seeley, Service, 1913. Pp. 314. Index, Illustr.

Focuses on early aviation events and people. The work is well written and designed to introduce the general reader to the new world of aeronautics and aerial craft (including balloons).

899.   Ward, John W. "The Meaning of Lindbergh's Flight." In *Studies in American Culture: Dominant Ideas and Images,* ed. Joseph J. Kwiat and Mary C. Turpie, 27–40. Minneapolis: University of Minnesota Press, 1960.

The Lindbergh phenomenon is analyzed in terms of a twofold meaning: one, as a triumph of the solitary American pioneer and, two, as a celebration of the progress of machines and technology in society. The author explains that these two manifestations caused the phenomenon to last far longer than the actual flight warranted.

900.   Wecter, Dixon. "Gods from the Machine: Edison, Ford, Lindbergh." In *The Hero in America: A Chronicle of Hero-Worship,* 415–444. New York: Charles Scribner's Sons, 1972. Index, Bibliog., Illustr.

Deals with the heroes of the machine—Edison, Ford, and Lindbergh. Of these three, Wecter claims, Lindbergh was by far the most significant and enduring. Follows Lindbergh's evolution from a wildly popular "boy" to a controversial, articulate man. Despite the fact that the book was originally written in 1941, when Lindbergh's inflammatory statements had greatly reduced his popularity, Wecter treats Lindbergh sympathetically.

Aviation in Literature

901. Bright, Charles D. "Aviation Literature—A Changing Art." *Aerospace Historian* 31 (1984): 68–73.

An excellent article that reviews the classic aviation novels, almost all military, and examines trends in aviation fiction from pulps to comic strips to novels. The heroic status of the pilot passes through a number of stages as a result of wars, television, and the nuclear age.

902. Bryden, H.G., ed. *Wings: An Anthology of Flight.* London: Faber and Faber, 1942. Pp. 320.

A wonderful collection of flight verse and prose that extends from myths and legends through actual flights. Contains many pieces written by aviation figures like Otto Lilienthal, the Wrights, and Richard Byrd, and others by classic authors like Euripides, John Keats, Jules Verne, and H.G. Wells.

903. de la Bère, Rupert. *Icarus: An Anthology of the Poetry of Flight.* London: Macmillan, 1938. Pp. xxvii + 191. Illustr.

A compilation of flight verse written in extremely romantic and philosophical terms. Called a poetry of flight, not of the airplane. Includes material on gliding, kites, and aircraft, as well as flight in nature and myth.

904. de la Bère, Rupert. *The Unending Conquest: Being an Anthology of Flight.* London: J.M. Dent, 1938. Pp. 252. Illustr.

First-person prose accounts of flying by aviators with emphasis on World War I, the RAF, air races, and flying clubs.

Social and Cultural Aspects of Aviation

905.   Dillon, Richard Taylor. "The Sound of Wings: Aviation in
       Twentieth-Century Literature." Ph.D. diss., University of
       California, Berkeley, 1970. Pp. 337. Bibliog.

       Traces literary attitudes toward the airplane, pilots, and
       aviation throughout the 20th century, with special emphasis on
       the work of William Faulkner. A fine analysis of the use of
       aviation motifs in literature that investigates the work of
       writers who were not themselves involved in aviation.

906.   Gilbert, James, comp. *Skywriting: An Aviation Anthology.*
       London: M&J Hobbs, 1978. Pp. 269. Bibliog.

       A roughly chronological selection of aviation literature that
       includes the classic authors and personalities who wrote about
       almost every aspect of flying, as well as recent authors like
       Michael Collins, Scott Crossfield, and Richard Bach. A very
       satisfying volume.

907.   Goldstein, Laurence. *The Flying Machine and Modern Litera-
       ture.* Bloomington: Indiana University Press, 1986. Pp. xiv +
       253. Index, Bibliog., Illustr.

       Explores the age-old link between flying and imaginative
       literature, from Leonardo da Vinci's treatise *On the Flight of
       Birds* to Norman Mailer's *Of a Fire on the Moon.* Goldstein
       makes a compelling argument for the simultaneously positive
       and negative attitude writers have had toward flight, which,
       he says, ranges from ideas of self-transcendence to fear and
       loathing. A thoughtful and much-needed analysis of the air-
       plane and modern literature.

908.   Herzberg, Max J., Merrill P. Paine, and Austin M. Works.
       Happy Landings. Boston: Houghton Mifflin, 1942. Pp. v + 321.

       A collection of prose written by well-known aviators who
       describe the romance and adventure of flight as well as the
       rigors of combat flying. Includes John Magee, Ernest Gann,
       Anne Morrow Lindbergh, Alexander de Seversky, and Antoine
       de Saint-Exupéry.

909.   McCullough, David. "Aviation Authors: Saint-Exupéry's 'War-
       time Writings' Recalls a Remarkable Body of Work." *New
       York Times* Magazine, 12 October 1986, 50, 81-83, 85.

An excellent study of the best of the aviator authors—Charles and Anne Lindbergh, Saint-Exupéry, and Beryl Markham—that recalls their love of flight and their gift for writing. Quoting liberally from their work, McCullough explores his subjects' pioneering spirit, their almost spiritual love of flying, and their personal transformations through the years.

910. Markham, Beryl. *West with the Night*. Boston: Houghton Mifflin, 1942; San Francisco, Calif.: North Point, 1983. Pp. 293.

Markham's only written work is a remembrance of her life in Africa, which included raising horses, flying the mail, and running a business that involved spotting big game from the air. Markham provides a fascinating look at colonial Africa, but the beauty of the book lies in her poetic descriptions of the land and wildlife as she flies over the Serengeti or fog-shrouded mountain country. Markham was the first person to fly solo across the Atlantic from east to west.

911. Migeo, Marcel. *Saint-Exupéry; A Biography*. New York: McGraw-Hill, 1961. Pp. 335. Index, Bibliog., Illustr.

A remarkable biography written by an old flying companion of Saint-Exupéry who removes the myths surrounding the renowned writer, airmail pilot, corporate director, and reconnaissance pilot. Migeo's thorough research is evident throughout as he links passages from Saint-Exupéry's writings with detailed events of his rich life. A fascinating look at developing transcontinental airlines, World War II, and a unique individual. Excellent bibliography.

912. Murray, Stella Wolfe, comp. *The Poetry of Flight; An Anthology*. London: Heath Cranton, 1925. Pp. x + 144.

A poetry anthology divided into four sections: myth and legend, European, American, and verse written by women. Aims to show the poetry of flight and thereby avoid the history of flight or the unpleasant aspects of war.

913. Penrose, Harald. *Cloud Cuckooland*. Shrewsbury, England: Airlife, 1981. Pp. 155. Illustr.

The noted British aviation writer offers 18 personal glimpses of his love of flight, manned and winged, powered and unpowered. A beautifully written book, full of nostalia, but with an eye toward the future.

914.   Roberts, Joseph Baxley, and Paul L. Briand, eds. *The Sound of Wings; Readings for the Air Age.* New York: Henry Holt, 1957. Pp. xi + 303. Index.

A fine anthology of prose and poetry that includes a wider variety of material than is usually found in flight anthologies. The book is divided into five time periods and includes classic and 20th-century authors such as James Thurber, as well as aviator authors. Very satisfying reading.

915.   Rodman, Selden. *The Poetry of Flight.* New York: Duell, Sloan and Pearce, 1941. Pp. 190.

A large anthology of the prose and poetry of flight from antiquity to World War II. The wide variety of authors includes Goethe, da Vinci, Anne Morrow Lindbergh, and Saint-Exupéry. A thought-provoking and pleasurable book.

916.   Saint-Exupéry, Antoine de. *Airman's Odyssey.* New York: Regnal and Hitchcock, 1942. Pp. 437.

A trilogy comprising *Wind, Sand and Stars*, *Night Flight*, and *Flight to Arras*, three separate literary works of aviation adventure and exaggerated expression. Recognized as one of the most accomplished aviation writers, Saint-Exupéry mixes his adventures and thoughts generously with philosophy and the realities of the period just before World War II.

917.   Walker, Dale. "We Die in Glory: A Fond Reminiscence of the Air-War Pulps." *Aviation Quarterly* 3 (1977): 268–289.

A nostalgic look at the popular literary phenomenon of the post-World War I era, the aviation pulp novel. These dime novels, which glorified the men and aircraft of the Great War, are reviewed in terms of their literary, artistic, and popular value to a generation of avid readers. Pulp writer George Bruce and illustrator Rudolph Belarski receive well-deserved recognition.

918. Vale, Charles. *The Spirit of St. Louis—One Hundred Poems*. New York: George H. Doran, 1927. Pp. vii + 256.

One hundred poems devoted to Charles Lindbergh and his epic flight, drawn from over 4,000 poems entered in a "Spirit of St. Louis" competition in 1927. Selected on their literary merit, the poems reveal the impact of his flight in particular, aviation in general, and, most important, Charles Lindbergh as an American hero.

919. Verne, Jules. *Five Weeks in a Balloon, or Journeys and Discoveries in Africa by Three Englishmen*. London: George Routledge and Sons, n.d. Pp. 249. Illustr.

The classic of early stories about flying. Jules Verne's fictional account of a balloon flight through Africa presents the reader with a new mode of transportation as well as an introduction to the Dark Continent. The balloon *Victoria* provides ample excitement and reliable service until it is swept over a waterfall at the end of the book.

Aviation and Education

920. Air Age Education Series. New York: Macmillan, 1942.

The 20-volume Air Age Education series, sponsored by the Institute of the Aeronautical Sciences in cooperation with the Civil Aeronautics Administration, was produced to promote "air mindedness" among elementary and secondary students during World War II. Includes flight anthologies and aeronautical social and science studies along with pre-flight aeronautics and teachers' manuals, all designed to capture the interest of the young. Each book provides student activities, notes, film, and bibliographies.

Aviation in the Visual Arts

921. Ballantine, Ian, ed. *The Aviation Art of Keith Ferris*. New York: Peacock/Bantam, 1978. Pp. 91. Illustr.

The artist himself wrote a biographical sketch for the book's introduction that adds insight to his painting style and methodology. A personal observation or story by the artist accompanies each color plate and adds to the illustration's meaning.

922.   Berman, Greta. "Does 'Flight' Have a Future?" *Art in America*, September/October 1976, 97–99.

Studies James Brooks's mural *Flight* in the Marine Air Terminal at La Guardia Airport in detail both as a work of art and as a depiction of the history of flight. The article attempts to define the three major sections of the painting in terms of reality and fantasy, abstraction, and representation.

923.   Bowman, Ruth. *Murals without Walls: Arshile Gorky's Aviation Mural Rediscovered*. Newark, N.J.: Newark Museum, 1978. Pp. 96. Bibliog., Illustr.

Informative and well–researched articles that follow the commission, painting, and rediscovery of the aviation murals of Arshile Gorky at Newark Airport. Published on the 50th anniversary of the airport, this book reveals the rediscovered mural panels in all their boldness and intensity.

924.   Farmer, James H. *Celluloid Wings: The Impact of Movies on Aviation*. Blue Ridge Summit, Pa.: TAB, 1984. Pp. xiii + 369. Index, Bibliog., Illustr.

A well–researched, documented, and illustrated survey of aviation films from 1908 to 1950. The book also includes two appendixes: The first contains capsule reviews of 300 aviation films; the second, a list of screen appearances by type of aircraft. Overall, an excellent guide to aviation films.

925.   Flick, Al. "Flying in the Funnies." *Aviation Quarterly* 8 (1985): 4–47.

A nostalgic study of the aviation comics that were extremely popular in the 1920s through the 1940s, and that still survive today in Milton Caniff's "Steve Canyon." The air hero comic strips entertained America with romantic, daring adventures rooted in World War I aviation and the barnstormers. A look at an important segment of aviation popular culture.

926. Orriss, Bruce W. *When Hollywood Ruled the Skies*. Hawthorne, Calif.: Aero Associates, 1984. Pp. viii + 219. Index, Bibliog., Illustr.

Reviews selected aviation combat films from World War II through 1980 with an eye toward their content and the changes that have taken place in them over the years. Studies the subject matter of the film, be it a historic event or theme used for recruitment purposes, as well as the logistics of recreating the period with aircraft. A fascinating look at how Hollywood shaped aviation history.

927. Pendo, Stephen. *Aviation in the Cinema*. Metuchen, N.J.: Scarecrow, 1985. Pp. viii + 402. Index, Bibliog., Illustr.

A comprehensive guide to the aviation films produced by Hollywood. Includes aviation films whose themes encompass comedy, propaganda, combat, and disaster and provides a look at the logistical problems of aviation filmmaking. The author concludes that the main attraction of aviation films is their escapist entertainment and portrayal of human experiences. A first–rate source of information for the aviation film enthusiast.

928. Skogsberg, Bertil. *Wings on the Screen: A Pictorial History of Air Movies*. San Diego, Calif.: A.S. Barnes, 1981. Pp. 210. Index, Bibliog., Illustr.

A review of international and American aviation films beginning in 1927. The major attraction of the book is its coverage of films for Germany, Great Britain, Japan, and other European countries. Well illustrated.

929. Sochor, Eugene. "Aviation and Art Have Evolved Together in This Century." *ICAO* [International Civil Aviation Organization] *Bulletin* 37 (July–August 1982): 79–86.

Although this article claims to be a survey of aviation art over the past seven decades, it is actually concerned only with "serious" artists of the early part of this century, such as Ernst and Klee. Although the popular art of the last 30 years is given only cursory treatment, the article is still a valuable source of information on the role of art in aviation history.

930.   Valdivia, Mary Henderson. *At Home in the Sky: The Aviation Art of Frank Wootton.* Washington, D.C.: Smithsonian Institution Press, 1984. Pp. 76. Bibliog., Illustr.

A short biography of Frank Wootton, one of aviation's most prominent aritists. A member of the RAF during World War II, Wootton has been lauded for his treatment of the aircraft's environment as well as the aircraft itself. Includes an examination of Wootton's artistic style as well as many color plates.

931.   Wooldridge, E.T. *Focus on Flight: The Aviation Photography of Hans Groenhoff.* Washington, D.C.: Smithsonian Institution Press, 1985. Pp. 108. Illustr.

A showcase for the beautiful aviation photography of Hans Groenhoff, who captured flying in the romantic era of the 1930s through World War II on film. One hundred and twenty of his photographs (in color and black and white) appear here, culled from the collection he accumulated while a photographer for aviation journals, popular periodicals, and newspapers, as well as the airlines and the general aviation industry. A narrative text accompanies each chapter of the book.

932.   Wooldridge, E.T. *Images of Flight: The Aviation Photography of Rudy Arnold.* Washington, D.C.: Smithsonian Institution Press, 1986. Pp. 160. Illustr.

A selection of stunning photographs by aerial news photographer Rudy Arnold, who was the first official photographer for Floyd Bennett Field and also covered stories for the New York newspapers, the wire services, the newsreel companies, and the leading periodicals from the 1930s into the jet age. One hundred and twenty-four photographs (color, as well as black and white) are accompanied by a narrative text.

Aviation in Architecture and Design

933.   Arend, Geoffrey. *Air World's Great Airports: Newark, 1928–1952.* New York: Air Cargo News, 1978. Pp. 109. Illustr.

A picture history that celebrates Newark Airport's 50th year, especially its reign as the most modern airport of the 1930s. Arshile Gorky's abstract aviation murals, commissioned by the Federal Art Program of the Works Progress Administration, are of special interest here.

934. Arend, Geoffrey. *Air World's Great Airports: La Guardia, 1939-1979*. New York: Air Cargo News, 1979. Pp. 152. Illustr.

Celebrates La Guardia Airport's 40th anniversary in 1979 in picture-history fashion. Of special importance is the section on James Brooks's mural *Flight*, painted on the rotunda walls in the Marine Terminal between 1938 and 1942 as part of the Federal Art Program of the Works Progress Administration. Also contains a good general history of commercial aviation in the period.

935. Arend, Geoffrey. *Great Airports: Kennedy International*. New York: Air Cargo News, 1981. Pp. 200. Illustr.

The third in Arend's continuing series of pictorial histories of well-known airports. Less important than the previous works on LaGuardia and Newark in terms of airport architecture, but interesting for its illustrations of the "lost" murals of Eugene Chodorow and August Henkel at Floyd Bennett Field, funded, like those of Gorky and Brooks, by the WPA's Federal Art Program.

936. Arend, Geoffrey. *Great Airports: Miami International*. New York: Air Cargo News, 1986. Pp. 320. Illustr.

The fourth in Arend's continuing series of illustrated histories of well-known airports, but more comprehensive in scope. Contains useful information and photographs relating to Pan American Airways Dinner Key flying boat terminal, gateway to the Caribbean, Central and South America.

937. Bush, Donald J. *The Streamlined Decade*. New York: George Braziller, 1975. Pp. viii + 214. Index, Bibliog., Illustr.

Looks at the designers who promulgated the streamlining movement in the 1930s as well as their designs. Drawing its inspiration from nature, aeronautics, and hydraulics, the streamlined aesthetic became the focus of industrial design, architecture, and, later, fashion and popular design. The debt owed by the streamlining adherents to aviation is highlighted in a chapter entitled "Ideal Forms" and is acknowledged throughout the book.

938.   Jeanneret–Gris, Charles E. [Le Corbusier]. *Aircraft.* New York: Studio Publications, 1935. Pp. 123. Illustr.

Celebrates the future of aviation and architecture as envisioned by the author, one of the most prominent architects of the 20th century. In an attempt to break away from the old regimented styles, Le Corbusier envisions aircraft as the symbol of a new age that will incorporate modern technology into the planning and design of cities.

939.   Jeanneret–Gris, Charles E. [Le Corbusier]. *Towards a New Architecture.* Translated by Frederick Etchells. New York: Praeger, 1970. Pp. 269. Illustr.

The revolutionary designer known as Le Corbusier worked for a "modern movement" in architecture throughout his career, believing that architecture should be approached through the engineering, planning process that produced the age of machines and technology. One chapter is devoted to airplanes and how they influence not only design, but the thought process. Originally published in Paris in 1923 by Editions Crès under the title *Vers une architecture.*

940.   Lehigh Portland Cement Company. *American Airport Designs.* New York: Taylor Rogers and Bliss, 1930. Pp. 96. Illustr.

A pictorial volume devoted to airport design and planning. Reviews the top 28 designs of the Lehigh Airports Competition of 1929, the first attempt at regional planning of airports for the future. It is interesting to note that many of these designs were actually built.

941.   Plummer, Kathleen C. "The Streamlined Moderne." *Art in America* 62 (1974): 46–54.

This well–researched article links the beginnings of Streamlined Moderne design with the clean, orderly world of H.G. Wells's science fiction stories. It studies the relationship between science fiction, industrial designers, and machines of transportation, most important, the airplane, throughout the 1930s.

Aviation in Music

942.   Cameron, Peggy. "Aviation History Is Carefully Recorded in Tin Pan Alley." *Washington Post*, 24 February 1935, 3–4.

An excellent article that reviews the Bella C. Landauer exhibition of aeronautical sheet music at the Old Print Shop in New York City in 1935. The author notes that no serious composer has as yet found aviation a subject of lasting merit.

Blacks in Aviation

943.   Carisella, P.J., and James W. Ryan. *The Black Swallow of Death; the Incredible Story of Eugene Jacques Bullard, the World's First Black Combat Aviator.* Boston: Marlborough House, 1972. Pp. xii + 271. Bibliog., Illustr.

The biography of the first known black combat pilot, Eugene J. Bullard, who in early youth left the United States in search of racial equality. Bullard eventually joined the French Foreign Legion, fought at Verdun, was accepted into the French army air service, and became a pilot in the French escadrilles. He applied to join the U.S. Army Air Service, but was rejected and grounded soon thereafter by the French for assaulting a superior officer.

944.   Francis, Charles E. *The Tuskegee Airmen: The Story of the Negro in the U.S. Air Force.* Boston: Bruce Humphries, 1956. Pp. 225. Bibliog., Illustr.

A narrative history of the black pilots of World War II based on their personal experiences, a variety of publications, and official reports. The incidents related follow the training and actual aerial combat activities of the various all–black fighter squadrons.

945.   Gropman, Alan, L. *The Air Force Integrates, 1945–1964.* Washington, D.C.: Office of Air Force History, 1978. Pp. x + 384. Index, Bibliog., Illustr.

A comprehensive study that documents the long road toward integration in the U.S. Army Air Forces and U.S. Air Force from the post–World War II era to the mid-1960s. Pays par–

ticular attention to the effect of presidential administrations on integration in the military over the years. Almost one–third of the book is devoted to useful tables, appendixes, and notes.

946.   Hardesty, Von, and Dominick Pisano. *Black Wings: The American Black in Aviation.* Washington, D.C.: Smithsonian Institution Press, 1983. Pp. 80. Bibliog. Illustr.

The outgrowth of an exhibition presented at the National Air and Space Museum in 1982 that traces the history of black aviators in the United States. The book is a pictorial history that draws extensively from the private collections of the pilots themselves. The photographs are excellent in quality and are woven together with an informative text to present a valuable historical resource.

947.   Lee, Ulysses G. *The Employment of Negro Troops.* U.S. Army in World War II. Washington, D.C.: Department of the Army, Office of the Chief of Military History, 1966. Pp. xix + 740. Index, Bibliog., Illustr.

Studies the development and application of Army policies for the employment of blacks in the military in World War II, with emphasis on combat troops. Although not a full history of all blacks in the war, it is a comprehensive study of the mobilization, training, deployment, and experiences of ground and air troops, with minor references to service troops.

Northrup, Herbert R. *The Negro in the Aerospace Industry.* The Racial Policies of American Industry, Report no. 2. Philadelphia: University of Pennsylvania, Industrial Research Unit, Department of Industry, Wharton School of Finance and Commerce, 1968. Pp. ix + 90. Index, Bibliog., Illustr.

Cited herein as item 992.

Northrup, Herbert R., Armand J. Thieblot, Jr., and William H. Chernish. *The Negro in the Air Transport Industry.* The Racial Policies of American Industry, Report no. 23. Philadelphia: University of Pennsylvania, Industrial Research Unit, Department of Industry, Wharton School of Finance and Commerce, 1968. Pp. x + 146. Index.

Cited herein as item 993.

948.   Osur, Alan M. *Blacks in the Army Air Force during World War II: The Problem of Race Relations.* Washington, D.C.: Office of Air Force History, 1977. Pp. 227. Index, Bibliog., Illustr.

An exceptionally important study of racial policies and relations during World War II. Based on the premise that the Army Air Forces was pressured by the War Department to admit blacks, the book studies the alleged separate–but–equal policy, the attempt to utilize blacks efficiently, and the racial problems and accomplishments that resulted from official AAF policies during World War II. The appendixes contain informative tables on blacks in the AAF and their units.

949.   Patterson, Elois. *Memoirs of the Late Bessie Coleman.* N.p., 1969. Pp. 9. Illustr.

Although this is a very short and personal account of Bessie Coleman's life (written by her sister), her pioneering achievements in aviation in the face of racial discrimination are well recorded. Important for the study of blacks and women in aviation.

950.   Powell, William J. *Black Wings.* Los Angeles, Calif.: Ivan Deach, Jr., 1934. Pp. xiii + 218. Illustr.

Written by the man who organized the Los Angeles–based Bessie Coleman Aero Club in 1929 and the first all–black air show in 1931, *Black Wings* is a plea for black youth to become involved in aviation. Powell recounts his entry into the field of aviation and provides the names and events that shaped black involvement in flying, and all the while promotes air-mindedness within the black community.

Women in Aviation

951.   Adams, Jean Margaret Kimball. *Heroines of the Sky.* Garden City, N.Y.: Doubleday, Doran, 1942. Pp. xviii + 295. Illustr.

Profiles of 17 famous women flyers aimed at the secondary school reader during World War II. The warm accounts of aviators such as Amelia Earhart and Anne Lindbergh portray these women as pioneers and daredevils, and most important, as women with dreams and perseverance.

952.   Auriol, Jacqueline. *I Live to Fly*. New York: E.P. Dutton, 1970. Pp. 197. Index, Illustr.

The French test pilot who traded speed records with Jacqueline Cochran tells of her career, which included helicopter training in the United States and a devastating crash early in her career.

953.   Brooks–Pazmany, Kathleen. *United States Women in Aviation 1919–1929*. Smithsonian Studies in Air and Space, no. 5. Washington, D.C.: Smithsonian Institution Press, 1983. Pp. iii + 57. Bibliog., Illustr.

Follows barnstorming and record–setting women through the roaring twenties. Focuses on the National Women's Air Derby of 1929, the first women's cross–country race that began in Santa Monica, California, and ended at the National Air Races in Cleveland, Ohio. This grueling race gave women the recognition they deserved as well–qualified, talented pilots.

954.   Chapelle, Georgette. [Dickey Meyer, pseud.]. *Girls at Work in Aviation*. Garden City, N.Y.: Doubleday, Doran, 1943. Pp. xvii + 209. Illustr.

Surveys women's participation in aviation during World War II. Part of a national propaganda effort to encourage women to volunteer their labor in nontraditional vocations. Aviation is construed in its broadest sense, hence the book has chapters on aeronautical engineers, flight attendants, and factory workers, as well as pilots. Chapelle also wrote a companion volume entitled *Needed—Women in Aviation*.

955.   Cochran, Jacqueline. *Final Report on Women Pilot Program*. Washington, D.C.: U.S. Army Air Forces, n.d. Pp. 53.

A valuable source of information on the Women's Airforce Service Pilots program, which was highly successful in providing competent women pilots to the Army Air Forces for various flying duties, thus freeing male pilots for combat duty. Cochran compiled a short, but detailed account of the Women Pilot Program, complete with extensive comparisons of male and female training and flying records.

956. Cochran, Jacqueline. *The Stars at Noon*. Boston: Little, Brown, 1954. Pp. 274. Illustr.

Jacqueline Cochran's autobiography is an interesting though shallow account of a woman who pulled herself up by her bootstraps to become a successful aviator and businesswoman. With her aggressive personality, Cochran broke through some of the barriers that held women back and established herself as an accomplished racer and record holder. In World War II, she was the director of the Women's Auxiliary Service Pilots (WASPs), opening the door of opportunity to many women in aviation.

957. Cochran, Jacqueline, and Maryann Bucknum Brinley. *Jackie Cochran: An Autobiography*. New York: Bantam Books, 1987. Pp. 358. Index, Illustr.

Despite a somewhat misleading subtitle (the book was published seven years after Cochran's death), this book, although not a definitive, critical biography, does provide insight into the complex character and mystique of Jackie Cochran. Based on Brinley's oral history research and Cochran's own writings, supplemented by comments from her friends.

958. Curtis, Lettice. *The Forgotten Pilots: A Story of the Air Transport Auxiliary, 1939–45*. Henley-on-Thames, Oxfordshire: G.T. Foulis, 1971. Pp. xv + 337. Illustr.

A comprehensive history of the Air Transport Auxiliary and the ferry pilots who kept the RAF flying as well as an excellent account of women ferry pilots and their role as capable contributors to the war effort. The book also explores ATA's relations with its parent company, BOAC, and the British Air Ministry.

Davis, Burke. *Amelia Earhart*. New York: G.P. Putnam's Sons, 1972. Pp. 189.

Cited herein as item 835.

Earhart, Amelia. *20 Hrs. 40 Min.; Our Flight in the Friendship*. New York: Grosset and Dunlap, 1928. Pp. 314. Illustr.

Cited herein as item 839.

One of the most famous women flyers of her time, Amelia Earhart poses beside her Lockheed 5B Vega. On May 21, 1932, in this aircraft, Earhart became the first woman to complete a nonstop solo flight across the Atlantic. (SI Photo A45905C)

Earhart, Amelia. *Last Flight*. Arranged by George Palmer Putnam. New York: Harcourt, Brace, 1937. Pp. xvi + 226. Illustr.

Cited herein as item 840.

959. Earhart, Amelia. *The Fun of It; Random Records of My Own Flying and of Women in Aviation*. Reprint. Chicago: Academy, 1977. Pp. 218. Illustr.

Earhart's autobiography has historic value beyond her own story because she devotes chapters to women pilots of the day, women in aviation, and the establishment of the Ninety–Nines. Original edition published by Harcourt Brace in 1932.

960. Earhart, Amelia. *Letters from Amelia, 1901–1937*. Edited by Jean L. Backus. Boston: Beacon, 1982. Pp. 253. Bibliog., Illustr.

A well–researched collection of Earhart's correspondence that provides insights into her personality. Also serves as a detailed biographical work in the absence of a comprehensive life of Earhart.

961. Keil, Sally van Wagenen. *Those Wonderful Women in Their Flying Machines: The Unknown Heroines of World War II*. New York: Rawson Wade, 1979. Pp. x + 334. Index, Illustr.

An excellent account of the Women's Airforce Service Pilots program that necessarily includes a look at the Women's Auxiliary Ferrying Squadron and Air Transport Auxiliary pilots in Britain. Among the details of these programs are found the real stories of individual women who wanted to fly.

962. May, Charles P. *Women in Aeronautics*. New York: Thomas Nelson and Sons, 1962. Pp. 260. Index, Bibliog., Illustr.

Surveys the history of women in aviation. Text is organized thematically—lighter than air, parachuting, World War II, racing and so on. The material is accurate (if dated and lacking any serious conclusions) but geared to a secondary school audience.

963.   Moolman, Valerie. *Women Aloft*. The Epic of Flight. Alexan-
       dria, Va.: Time–Life, 1981. Pp. 176. Index, Bibliog., Illustr.

       Looks at women in aviation through World War II. The book
       dwells on the most well–known women aviators, especially
       Amelia Earhart, but it also gives an overview of women pilots
       around the world as barnstormers, racers, long–distance flyers,
       ferry pilots, and even Russian combat pilots.

964.   Myles, Bruce. *Night Witches: The Untold Story of Soviet
       Women in Combat*. Novato, Calif.: Presidio, 1981. Pp. viii +
       278. Illustr.

       Chronicles the Soviet air regiments, composed of women
       who flew bombers and fighters and fought alongside their male
       counterparts in combat missions throughout World War II. An
       interesting and rare look at women in combat that makes use
       of personal narratives and official Soviet histories.

965.   Nichols, Ruth. *Wings for Life*. Philadelphia, Pa.: Lippincott,
       1957. Pp. 317. Illustr.

       The autobiography of an aviation pioneer whose flying
       career began in the "golden age" of aviation and extended into
       the jet age. A woman noted for record setting and firsts in
       aviation, Nichols became deeply involved with airborne relief
       efforts around the world.

966.   Niekamp, Dorothy R. *Women and Flight, 1910–1978: An Anno-
       tated Bibliography*. Oklahoma City: The Ninety–Nines, 1980.
       Pp. 232. Index.

       The most important research source on women in aviation.
       Includes an exhaustive index of *New York Times* articles, a
       comprehensive index of periodicals, and a good section on
       books. A special section is devoted to Amelia Earhart. (Note:
       Researchers must obtain permission to use the bibliography
       from the Ninety–Nines or the author.)

967.   The Ninety–Nines. *History of the Ninety–Nines, Inc.* Oklahoma
       City, 1979. Pp. 552. Illustr.

       A glossy picture book that contains a wealth of information.
       Although not a scholarly history, the biographical paragraphs

and photographs of several hundred Ninety–Nines are valuable.

968. Oakes, Claudia M. *United States Women in Aviation through World War I.* Smithsonian Studies in Air and Space, no. 2. Washington, D.C.: Smithsonian Institution Press, 1978. Pp. iii + 44. Bibliog., Illustr.

A short survey of women aviation pioneers. Five women are featured and many others are mentioned in this study of women who got in on the ground floor of aviation.

969. Oakes, Claudia M. *United States Women in Aviation, 1930–1939.* Smithsonian Studies in Air and Space, no. 6. Washington, D.C.: Smithsonian Institution Press, 1985. Pp. iii + 70. Bibliog., Illustr.

The third book of the U.S. Women in Aviation series chronicles the entry of women into the business of aviation and air racing. These women became involved in a variety of businesses, careers, and promotions with the aviation industry and slowly gained some measure of acceptance. In air racing, women began the 1930s competing against themselves but soon joined the men on the circuit and, on occasion, even beat them.

970. Planck, Charles. *Women with Wings.* New York: Harper and Brothers, 1942. Pp. 333. Index, Illustr.

An excellent survey of pre–World War II women flyers complete with a chronology, a section on records, and a listing of the winners of national aviation events. The book is especially interesting because it includes short sketches of a wide variety of women as well as the famous flyers of the period.

971. Reitsch, Hanna. *Flying Is My Life.* New York: G.P. Putnam's Sons, 1954. Pp. 246. Index, Illustr.

The autobiography of the woman who flew as a test pilot in Hitler's Luftwaffe. Reitsch's fascinating story includes a long career as a glider pilot, complete with many records, and test pilot of the V-1 bomber. Her account of Hitler's last days is of great importance as well.

972.   Thaden, Louise. *High, Wide and Frightened.* New   York: Stackpole Sons, 1938. Pp. 263. Illustr.

The winner of the 1936 Bendix race recalls her life in aviation. Thaden's book is an important firsthand account of the Women's Air Derby of 1929, and of many endurance and speed races of the 1920s and 1930s.

973.   Treadwell, Mattie E. *The Women's Army Corps.* U.S. Army in World War II. Washington, D.C.: Office of the Chief of Military History, Department of the Army, 1954. Pp. xxvi + 841. Index, Bibliog., Illustr.

Within this comprehensive official account of The Women's Army Corps are found the stories of the Air–WACs and, to a lesser degree, the Women's Airforce Service Pilots. Points to the Army Air Forces as a progressive part of the military, and cites the contributions of and problems encountered by women who became clerks, radio operators, mechanics, Link trainer instructors, and pilots.

AVIATION INDUSTRY

The aircraft industry in the United States rose from humble beginnings to world prominence. In 1914, according to Census Bureau figures, 16 companies were listed as aircraft manufacturers. Together they produced 49 aircraft. During World War II, the industry built 300,000 aircraft and 800,000 engines, and from 1939 to 1944, it rose from 44th to 1st in terms of dollar value of output. The economics of the present–day industry has become increasingly complex, with sales volume in the billions of dollars. Because of its size, political power, and interdependence with the federal government, the industry plays an important role in our national life.

Phenomenal growth and influence have been accompanied by controversy over many issues: the alleged Aircraft Production Board "scandal" of World War I; the so–called Lindbergh Boom and manipulation of aviation stocks in the late 1920s; the Hugo Black Senate committee investigation in 1934; and post–World War II assaults on certain sectors of the industry as part of the military–industrial complex.

Historical literature on the aviation industry is mixed and uneven in quality. Some aspects of it have been studied in an objective way, other key themes have been ignored. Surprisingly few works have analyzed the industry in all of its complexity. Predominant are promotional corporate publications written by public relations staffs. More recently, exposés of the industry's darker side have appeared. Although the titles in this section often err on the side of "company history," a few works by professional historians have attempted to chronicle in a broad, scholarly way the industry's growth and development and its relationship to the U.S. economy. John B. Rae's *Climb to Greatness: The American Aircraft Industry, 1920–1960* (see item 997) comes to mind immediately. What is lacking is an analytical historical survey of the industry from its origins to the present; for now, researchers are left to seek out the thread of the story from the welter of confusing and often contradictory material that exists.

Those interested in the defense industry at large should see Jacques S. Gansler's *The Defense Industry* (see item 982), pp. 321–330, for a good selective bibliography, which includes economic analyses and congressional reports pertaining to the aircraft manufacturing sector. For material on more specific aspects of the air–

craft industry, the researcher should review other sections of the bibliography, in particular, Air Transportation, General Aviation, and Propulsion.

Dominick A. Pisano
Von D. Hardesty
Samuel B. Fishbein

974. Allen, Hugh. *Goodyear Aircraft: A Story of Man and Industry.* Cleveland, Ohio: Corday & Gross, 1947. Pp. 162. Index, Illustr.

Typifies how in scores of cities all over the country American industry and American men and women met an emergency and won a war. The story of Akron, Ohio, an industrial community transformed under pressure of war into a boomtown, having much of the aspect of a mining camp.

975. Bluestone, Barry, et al. *Aircraft Industry Dynamics: An Analysis of Competition, Capital and Labor.* Boston: Auburn House, 1981. Pp. xv + 208. Index, Bibliog.

A well–documented industrial history that focuses on the problems and distinctions that make the aircraft industry a unique component of the U.S. economy. As a result of the currency of this work, the section on future trends has a great deal to do with the rise of high technology in the aviation industry. A comprehensive, current economic evaluation of the industry also makes this work stand out.

976. Bright, Charles D. *The Jet Makers: The Aerospace Industry from 1945 to 1972.* Lawrence, Kans.: Regent's Press, 1978. Pp xvii + 228. Index, Bibliog., Illustr.

A survey history of the American aerospace industry since World War II. The first chapters summarize the major themes in the story. Each subsequent chapter delves into one of the previously identified themes. The book's material is ordered chronologically. Particularly strong is Bright's discussion of the Cold War period and the impact on the industry as a result of the political climate.

977. Coulam, Robert F. *Illusions of Choice: The F–111 and the Problem of Weapons Acquisition Reform.* Princeton, N.J.: Princeton University Press, 1977. Pp. xiii + 432. Index, Bibliog., Illustr.

A pivotal study of the controversial Tactical Fighter Experiment (TFX) program (later called the F–111), an early effort of the 1960s to produce a multipurpose fighter that would be used by both the Air Force and Navy. Beset by numerous development problems, the program was eventually abandoned by the Navy; the Air Force decided to continue, but the difficulties persisted. Coulam's title aptly points up the fact that as air-

craft development proceeds, a point of no return is reached, at
which choices become minimal. Given the complex and
ingrained nature of the weapons acquisitions process, prospects
for reform, Coulam says, are doubtful unless the institutions
involved in the process are changed.

978. Cunningham, Frank. *Sky Master: The Story of Donald Douglas.*
      Philadelphia, Pa.: Dorrance, 1943. Pp. xii + 321. Illustr.

      The standard biography of Donald Douglas, noted aircraft
      designer and manufacturer.

979. Cunningham, William G. *The Aircraft Industry: A Study of
      Industrial Location.* Foreword by Carl Hinshaw. Los Angeles,
      Calif: Lorin L. Morrison, 1951. Pp. xvi + 247. Index, Bibliog.,
      Illustr.

      Shows how economic and geographic factors influence indus-
      trial location in the aircraft industry. The author endeavors to
      demonstrate how aircraft manufacture evolved in the first
      half-century following the invention of the airplane in 1903.
      Broadly chronological in approach, the book focuses on the
      various stages of growth in the aircraft industry and provides
      insight into how aircraft companies decide on plant location.
      Supplementing the text are statistical tables and maps that
      illustrate the author's findings. An update of an earlier report,
      "The Location of the Aircraft Industry," prepared in 1940.

980. Fernandez, Ronald. *Excess Profits: The Rise of United Technol-
      ogies.* Reading, Mass.: Addison Wesley, 1983. Pp. xii + 320.
      Index, Bibliog., Illustr.

      Critical account of the corporate history of United Technol-
      ogies and its predecessors from the time of the Great Depres-
      sion to the 1980s.

981. Freudenthal, Elsbeth E. *The Aviation Business; From Kitty
      Hawk to Wall Street.* New York: Vanguard, 1940. Pp. xii +
      342. Index, Bibliog.

      The first book to be written in the United States that criti-
      cally analyzes aircraft manufacturing and air transportation
      companies from their beginnings to World War II. Rather than

taking the romanticized operational and technical approach that had characterized previous writings, Freudenthal focuses on the financial and economic side of the story and emphasizes the role of the government, contracts, regulation of the industry, and so on.

982. Gansler, Jacques. *The Defense Industry.* Cambridge, Mass., MIT Press, 1982. Pp. 346. Index, Bibliog., Illustr.

Essential for understanding the place of the aerospace industry within the larger context of the defense industry and the place of the defense industry within the American economy. Contains many references to both aviation and aerospace and summarizes the economics of the aircraft industry.

983. Gorham, James E. *The Economic Impact of Energy Shortages on Commercial Air Transportation and Aviation Manufacture, Volume II.* Washington, D.C.: Federal Energy Administration, 1975. Pp. xi + 271.

A highly technical, somewhat complicated study concerning the effects of the energy crises of the mid–1970s on all aspects of the aviation industry, including the airlines and general aviation manufacturing. Extensive, detailed tables and graphs contribute to the volume, an excellent source for precise factual material, as well as historical data on the aviation industry during those years.

984. Grumman Aircraft Engineering. *Grumman at War.* Bethpage, Long Island, N.Y., 1945. Pp. 46. Illustr.

Published as a tribute to Grumman on the occasion of the company's 15th anniversary. The story of Grumman's contribution to the war effort.

985. Harding, William Barclay. *The Aviation Industry.* New York: Charles D. Barney, 1937. Pp. x + 74. Illustr.

An early account of the aviation industry in the United States written during the first years of FDR's New Deal.

986. *A History of Eastern Aircraft Division, General Motors Corporation.* Linden, N.J.: Eastern Aircraft Division, 1944. Pp. 157. Illustr.

The story of Eastern Aircraft Division's vast and widely scattered production program and its employees as well as General Motors' switchover from making automobiles to building fighter planes for the Navy.

Holley, I.B., Jr. *Buying Aircraft: Materiel Procurement for the Army Air Forces.* Washington, D.C.: Office of the Chief of Military History, Department of the Army, 1964. Pp. xviii + 643. Index, Bibliog., Illustr.

Cited herein as item 477.

Holley, I.B., Jr. *Ideas and Weapons: Exploitation of the Aerial Weapon by the United States during World War I; A Study in the Relationship of Technological Advance, Military Doctrine and the Development of Weapons.* Washington, D.C.: Office of Air Force History. 1983. Pp. xii + 222. Index, Bibliog.

Cited herein as item 478.

Kelsey, Benjamin S. *The Dragon's Teeth? The Creation of United States Air Power for World War II.* Washington, D.C.: Smithsonian Institution Press, 1982. Pp. 148. Index, Illustr.

Cited herein as item 487.

Kuter, Laurence S. *The Great Gamble: The Boeing 747; The Boeing–Pan Am Project to Develop, Produce and Introduce the 747.* University, Ala.: University of Alabama Press, 1973. Pp. ix + 134.

Cited herein as item 539.

987. Lilley, Tom, et al. *Problems of Accelerating Aircraft Production during World War II.* Elmsford, N.Y.: Maxwell Reprint, 1970. Pp. viii + 112.

Valuable primarily for historical documentation, this study brings to light the private and public reasons behind the difficulties experienced by the aviation industry as it was forced into large–scale wartime production. The major blame is directed toward the government, the industry, and the public itself—for poor management and apathy, in addition to production shortages.

988. Litchfield, Paul W. *Industrial Voyage*. Garden City, N.Y.: Doubleday, 1954. Pp. 347. Index, Illustr.

A personal narrative by the author, who started work at the Goodyear Tire and Rubber Company in the early 1900s as a plant superintendent and later became head of the company. Litchfield discusses his early life in New England, his austere upbringing, how he brought his background to Akron, Ohio, and how that background pervaded his philosophy of the development of the corporation.

989. Maynard, Crosby, comp. and ed. *Flight Plan for Tomorrow. The Douglas Story: A Condensed History*. 2d ed. Santa Monica, Calif.: Douglas Aircraft, 1966. Pp. 92. Illustr.

A popular history of the Douglas Aircraft Company. Traces the growth of the company after its founding in 1920, gives detailed attention to events of major importance, and examines decisions that were critical to its expansion.

990. Mead, Cary Hoge. *Wings over the World: The Life of George Jackson Mead*. Wauwatosa, Wisc.: Swannet, 1971. Pp. x + 314. Bibliog., Illustr.

Biography of George Jackson Mead who, along with Frederick Rentscheler, became an important aviation industrialist in the 1920s.

991. Mingos, Howard. *The Birth of an Industry*. New York: Howard Mingos, 1930. Pp. 95. Illustr.

An early classic that documents the influential events and personalities that spurred rapid growth within the aviation industry, the founding and early history of the Manufacturer's Aircraft Association, and problems caused by its rapid expansion and World War I. Much information is also devoted to the affairs of the Aeronautical Chamber of Commerce of America. Although this volume is very short, its value as a legal history of the early aviation industry should not be underestimated.

Newhouse, John. *The Sporty Game: The High–Risk Competitive Business of Making and Selling Commercial Airliners*. New York: Knopf, 1983. Pp. 242. Index, Bibliog.

Cited herein as item 522.

992. Northrup, Herbert R. *The Negro in the Aerospace Industry.* The Racial Policies of American Industry, Report no. 2. Philadelphia: University of Pennsylvania, Industrial Research Unit, Department of Industry, Wharton School of Finance and Commerce, 1968. Pp. ix + 90. Index.

Follows the employment of blacks in a highly technological industry dependent on the federal government. Begins with the entry of blacks into the industry in World War II and ends with the early results of affirmative action in the mid–1960s. Tables break down the industry by occupations, selected states, and years.

993. Northrup, Herbert R., Armand J. Thieblot, Jr., and William H. Chernish. *The Negro in the Air Transport Industry.* The Racial Policies of American Industry, Report no. 23. Philadelphia: University of Pennsylvania, Industrial Research Unit, Department of Industry, Wharton School of Finance and Commerce, 1971. Pp. x + 146. Index.

This study of black employment in air transport analyzes 12 major air carriers (which employ 90 percent of all airline personnel). Investigates the fortunes of the industry as well as racial factors. Tables break down the industry by groups, occupations, and regions.

994. *Of Men and Stars: A History of Lockheed Aircraft Corporation, 1913–1957.* Burbank, Calif.: Lockheed Aircraft, 1957. Various pagination. Illustr.

A history of Lockheed that spans very nearly a half–century of aviation progress. Within the decade that followed the Wright brothers' 59–second flight in 1903, the first airplane bearing the Lockheed name took to the skies. Presented in a series of chapters, each prepared (or published) at a different time.

995. *Pedigree of Champions: Boeing since 1916.* 4th ed. Seattle, Wash.: Boeing, 1977. Pp. 78. Illustr.

A capsule history of Boeing's evolution from the stick–and–wire Model 1 (B&W) of 1916 to today's globe–girdling military and commercial jets, missiles, and space vehicles. The early fame of Boeing was earned by its position as the leading U.S. supplier of single–seat fighting planes. Boeing expanded rapidly into the transport field and developed larger aircraft for the passenger trade.

996. Phillips, Almarin. *Technology and Market Structure: A Study of the Aircraft Industry.* Lexington, Mass.: Heath Lexington, 1971. Pp. xviii + 235. Index.

Highly technical analysis of the aircraft industry and its role in the market structure. The author begins with a historical overview, then covers economic and technological themes in detail with statis ical analysis.

997. Rae, John B. *Climb to Greatness: The American Aircraft Industry, 1920–1960.* Cambridge, Mass.: MIT Press, 1968. Pp. 280.

Provides an overview of the American aircraft industry, a unique intertwining of business, politics, and technology, from 1920 to 1960. Describes the evolution of the industry from its inception to the jet age, giving ample coverage to commercial, political, and technological themes and how they interrelated to shape the industry.

998. Rentschler, Frederick B. *An Account of Pratt & Whitney Aircraft Company, 1925–1950.* East Hartford, Conn.: Pratt & Whitney, 1950. Pp. 51.

Rentschler, founder of Pratt & Whitney, gives a personal account of his career and of the development of the company into the post–World War II era.

999. Rice, Berkeley. *The C–5A Scandal; An Inside Story of the Military Industrial Complex.* Boston: Houghton Mifflin, 1971. Pp. xiv + 238. Index, Bibliog.

A critical analysis of U.S. Air Force procurement of the Lockheed C–5A jet transport. The author views the C–5A program as an example of a flawed procurement process of the Defense Department. Cost overruns, defective technology, sloppy accounting procedures, inefficiency, concealment, and mismanagement punctuate this melancholy story of the military–industrial complex. The book endeavors not merely to critique military contracting, but to show how it actually works in relationship to Congress and the private sector.

1000. Ross, Donald. *An Appraisal of Prospects for the Aircraft Manufacturing Industry*. New York: White, Weld, 1940. Pp. 82.

Presents an evaluation of every domestic firm that manu-factured aircraft and equipment during the report's time–span. Each citation provides a brief corporate history, models manufactured, assets, and much more pertinent information. Also has a short section dealing with future prospects for the industry as a whole. This volume is invaluable for statistics and research dealing with the aviation industry.

Shrader, Welman A. *Fifty Years of Flight: A Chronicle of the Aviation Industry in America, 1903–1953*. Cleveland, Ohio: Eaton, 1953. Pp. 178. Illustr.

Cited herein as item 26.

1001. Simonson, Gene R. *The History of the American Aircraft Industry: An Anthology*. Cambridge, Mass.: MIT Press, 1968. Pp. x + 276. Index, Bibliog.

A collection of articles that deal with economic, political, and military influences on the American aircraft industry from its beginnings to 1965. Strong emphasis on post–1940 military impact on the development of aircraft production in the United States.

1002. Stekler, Herman O. *The Structure and Performance of the Aerospace Industry*. Berkeley: University of California Press, 1965. Pp. xvi + 223. Index, Bibliog.

Published by the Institute of Business and Economic Research at the University of California, Berkeley. Focuses on industrial organization as it relates to the American aerospace industry. Gives attention to historical developments and the interaction of government and private sectors.

AIR AND SPACE HISTORY

AN ANNOTATED BIBLIOGRAPHY

SPACE

Cathleen S. Lewis, Editor

Model of the first artificial satellite of the Earth, Sputnik, on display in the Milestones of Flight Gallery at the National Air and Space Museum. Sputnik was launched on 4 October 1957 by the USSR. Instrumentation was designed by scientists of the Academy of Sciences of the USSR. This model is on loan to the Museum from the Soviet Academy of Sciences. (Dale Hrabak, Smithsonian Institution)

BIBLIOGRAPHIES

This section describes published bibliographies and several principal complete databases relating to the history of space science, technology, and exploration. The bulk of the published entries are concentrated in the period through 1968. Interest in preparing and publishing bibliographies after this date seems to have diminished considerably. This trend may be due to the increasing use of computer databases and to the subsequent decline in public interest in the space program.

The best introduction to relevant historical literature in the early period of the space program is Katherine Dickson's excellent *History of Aeronautics and Astronautics: A Preliminary Bibliography* (item 1008). This resource primarily identifies and annotates books, monographs, and reference works, with much lesser emphasis on journal literature. The entries reflect a preponderant concern for scientific and technical issues as well as the early development of a historical literature, mostly biographical and anecdotal. Many of the entries for bibliographies in Dickson's work are included throughout this volume.

A second important source, nicely complementing the coverage of Dickson's bibliography, is John J. Looney's *Bibliography of Space Books and Non-Aerospace Journals, 1957-1977* (item 1019). His purpose is to provide an introduction to secondary literature published outside of the space science and engineering field—primarily social, economic, political, legal—on NASA and, more generally, is intended to serve as an adjunct to the technical literature found in NASA's *Scientific and Technical Aerospace Reports* and in *International Aerospace Reports* (see respectively item 1026 and 1013), the two principal abstracting and indexing services for the subject. Looney's introduction is essential reading, for both its discussion of trends in the non-specialist literature and its elucidation of the bibliographic approach followed. The work is a model of systematic bibliographic scholarship that greatly enhances its value to the historian.

Although other bibliographies listed in this section tend to be less comprehensive and more highly specialized, considerable information is available on given topics. These bibliographies cover more that the history of space exploration. Their range includes scientific and technical articles and books on a variety of topics as well as more general reference works. Note, too, that many works cited in this book contain excellent bibliographies.

Martin J. Collins

1003. Beard, Robert. *Soviet Cosmonautics, 1957–69. A Bibliography of Articles Published in British Periodicals and of British and Foreign Books.* Swindon: R. Beard, 1970. Pp. 43.

Lists articles and monographs on the Soviet space program which were published in Great Britain between 1957 and 1969 in a privately published pamphlet. Provides no annotations.

1004. Benton, Mildred C. "Artificial Satellites: A Bibliography of Recent Literature." *Jet Propulsion* 28 (1958): 301–302, 352–361, and 399–401.

Arranges over 300 annotated references to technical articles alphabetically by author in two parts. Part 1 covers 1956; Part 2 covers 1957–1958. Includes many references to *Vanguard, Sputnik*, and *Explorer*.

1005. Benton, Mildred C. *Literature of Space Science and Exploration.* Washington, D.C.: U.S. Naval Research Laboratory, 1958. Pp. 264.

An annotated list of over 2,000 monographs, articles, and research reports covering the period 1903 through June 1958. References are listed chronologically. Includes author and subject indexes. Emphasizes the development and scientific uses of instruments on vehicles.

1006. Benton, Mildred C. *Use of High Altitude Rockets for Scientific Research: An Annotated Bibliography.* Washington, D.C.: U.S. Naval Research Laboratory, 1959. Pp. 123.

Chronological list of periodical articles, technical reports, and papers on high–altitude rocket research published between 1946 and June 1959. Entries arranged alphabetically within years. Author and subject indexes.

1007. *Bibliography on Space Sciences: United States.* Washington, D.C.: National Academy of Sciences, 1956 to date (Annual).

Appended to *United States Space Science Program: Report to the Committee on Space Research* (COSPAR) that NAS furnishes annually to COSPAR. Reports contain bibliographies of U.S. works from 1956.

1008. Dickson, Katherine M. *History of Aeronautics and Astro-
       nautics: A Preliminary Bibliography.* Washington, D.C.:
       National Aeronautics and Space Administration, 1968. Pp.
       420. Index.

       Provides an introduction to historical literature and other
       sources published mainly during 1945–1967. Despite the
       implication of the title, the work's primary emphasis is on
       the historical literature on space. Concise, analytical anno-
       tations are arranged according to broad subject categories.
       Coverage includes English and foreign language publications.
       Author, title, and subject indexes.

1009. Filipoulsky, Richard F., and L. Bickford, eds. *Space Com-
       munications: Theory and Applications, A Bibliography.* 4
       vols. Washington, D.C.: National Aeronautics and Space
       Administration, 1965.

       Contains annotated references to technical reprints,
       articles, and books published between 1958 and 1963.
       Arranged in seven main subject categories: modulation and
       channels (Vol. 1); coding and detection theory (Vol. 2);
       information processing (Vol. 3A); advanced techniques (Vol.
       3B); communications satellites (Vol. 4A); deep space appli-
       cations (Vol. 4B); manned spaceflight applications (Vol. 4C).

1010. Fry, Bernard M., and F. Mohrhart, eds. *Guide to Information
       Sources in Space Science and Technology.* New York: Inter-
       science, 1963. Pp. 579.

       Nearly 4,000 references arranged alphabetically under 19
       subject headings, which include Soviet astronautics, space
       law, the International Geophysical Year, U.S. space pro-
       grams, history, biographies, and space centers. Six appendixes
       include a summary of satellites and planetoids, a list of U.S.
       missions utilizing large boosters, and a list of journals pub-
       lished in the space and aeronautics fields. Detailed subject-
       author index.

1011. Hallion, Richard. *The Literature of Aeronautics, Astro-
       nautics and Air Power.* Washington, D.C.: U.S. Air Force
       Office of Air Force History, 1984. Pp. xi + 66. Index.

       Outlines available introductory literature on the history of
       aeronautics from prehistory to the present in the form of a

bibliographic essay. Briefly touches on the history of space exploration. Comments on the sparsity of space–related studies. Includes more extensive coverage of the history of rocketry.

1012. Hogan, John C. "A Guide to the Study of Space Law, including a Selective Bibliography of the Legal and Political Aspects of Space." *St. Louis University Law Journal* 5 (1958): 79–107.

Contains over 250 selected references from books, law reviews, political journals, and scientific and technical journals (American and foreign). Also issued as Rand Corporation Paper P–1290 (Santa Monica, Calif., 1958).

1013. *International Aerospace Abstracts*. New York: American Institute of Aeronautics and Astronautics, 1961–. Semi-monthly.

The IAA surveys an international range of technical periodicals, serials, books, proceedings, transactions, and translations on aeronautics, space science, and technology. Complements STAR (item 1026) which covers the world's technical report literature. Each issue is organized by broad subject fields. Contains subject, personal author, report number, and accession number indexes. Like STAR, IAA is also available on online computer database through NASA's RECON system and through commercial databases. Selectively useful to the historian for researching scientific and technical issues.

1014. Jacobs, Horace. *Numerical/Chronological/Author Index, 1954–1978, Advances in the Astronautical Sciences, Science and Technology Series, and Other AAS Publications*. San Diego, Calif.: Univelt, 1979. Pp. 446.

Cites all articles and papers published by, for, or in conjunction with the American Astronomical Society (AAS) for the period indicated as well as some reports from 1979. Includes a numerical index arranged by AAS technical paper number, a chronological index of the contents of the *Astronautical Sciences Review*, a chronological index of the Journal of the *Astronautical Sciences*, and a comprehensive author index. Appendixes list AAS meetings, Goddard Memorial Symposia, and AAS published books.

1015.   Kehrberger, H. Peter. *Legal and Political Implications of Space Research*. Hamburg: Verlag Weltarchiv, 1965. Pp. 365.

Subtitled "Space Law and Its Background: Political, Military, Economical Aspects and Techno–Scientific Problems of Astronautics, a Selective Bibliography of Eastern and Western Sources." Covers literature from 55 nations. Includes a comprehensive index to abbreviations, transliterations, periodicals, honorary collections, subjects, and authors.

1016.   Kendon, Anthony. "A Guide to the Study of the Soviet Space Program." *Spaceflight*, May 1975, 175–179.

Presents a comprehensive, unannotated listing of non-technical, English–language, and translated works on the Soviet space program. Particularly useful is the complete listing of U.S. congressional reports and Library of Congress research reports through 1975.

1017.   Kliss, Elmer. *Bibliography on Meteorological Satellites, 1952–1962*. Washington, D.C.: Weather Bureau, 1963. Pp. 380.

Nearly 1,000 annotated references to books, technical reports, conference papers, and articles arranged chronologically by year and alphabetically by author within each year. Includes author and serial indexes as well as subject and geographical outlines.

1018.   Krull, Alan R. "A History of the Artificial Satellite." *Jet Propulsion* 26 (May 1956): 369–383.

Contains approximately 350 annotated references to the significant publications on artificial, manned, and unmanned satellites of the earth. Arranged chronologically (1879–1955).

1019.   Looney, John J. *Bibliography of Space Books and Articles from Non–Aerospace Journals, 1957–1977*. Washington, D.C.: National Aeronautics and Space Administration, 1979. Pp. 243.

Attempts to "identify the non–specialized, secondary literature relating to NASA in particular and spaceflight more generally" (see his introduction) and to complement

Scientific and Technical Aerospace Reports and *International Aerospace Abstracts* coverage of the technical literature. The introduction defines the scope and methods of the work. Entries (no annotations) are arranged in 14 broad subject categories, with headings for scientific and technical aspects of spaceflight, as well as its legal, social, economic, and international implications. No index.

1020.   Luisis, Andy. *Astronomy and Astronautics.* New York: Facts on File, 1986. Pp. xvii + 292. Index.

Provides a broad spectrum of articles and monographs grouped under various topics covering technical as well as historical subject matter. Annotations indicate the level of readership and point out significant features. Makes few qualitative judgments.

1021.   Magnolia, L.R. "The Soviet Space Program: A Selected Bibliography." *TRW Space Log* 5, no. 1 (Spring 1965): 23–25.

An unannotated list of English–language and translated sources on the Soviet space program, 1957–1964. Includes many technical papers.

1022.   Magnolia, L.R. "Selective Bibliography on the Soviet Space Program: 1965–1968." *TRW Space Log* 8, no. 4 (Winter 1968/69): 24–29.

Selects a variety of articles and monographs on Soviet space activities during 1965–1968. No annotations.

1023.   Meshkov, V.M. and Z.P. Dzhinova., comp. *Kosmos dalekii i blizkii* (Space: near and far). Moscow: Kniga, 1987. Pp. 97. Index.

Commemorates the thirtieth anniversary of spaceflight with a bibliographic essay on the history of space travel. A project of the Lenin Library in Moscow, this bibliography reports on western scholarship in the history of space exploration, as well as Soviet works. [In Russian]

1024.   Ordway, Frederick I. *Annotated Bibliography of Space Science and Technology with an Astronautical Supplement. A*

*History of Astronautical Book Literature—1931 through
1961.* 3d ed. Washington, D.C.: Arfor, 1962. Pp. 77.

Lists over 500 English–language books on astronautics and
astronomy arranged chronologically. Author and title indexes.
Includes proceedings of international conferences.

1025.   RAND Corporation. *An Annotated Bibliography of RAND
Space Flight Publications.* Santa Monica, Calif. 1959. Pp.
53.

Abstracts over 200 classified and unclassified reports
issued from 1948 to 1959 that cover various aspects of space–
flight, including some of the earliest U.S. plans for a space
program.

1026.   *Scientific and Technical Aerospace Reports.* Washington,
D.C.: National Aeronautics and Space Administration,
1963–. Semi–monthly.

An abstracting service, commonly known as STAR, which
covers unclassified technical reports of research sponsored by
the United States and other national governments on the science and technology of space and astronautics. Classified
literature is abstracted in NASA's *Limited Scientific and
Technical Aerospace Reports.* STAR also includes some dissertations, translations, and patents. STAR's coverage is
complemented by International Aerospace Abstracts which
covers the journal literature (see item 1013). Each issue of
STAR contains an abstract section arranged by subject
categories and an indexes of subjects, corporate authors,
personal authors, reports numbers, and accession numbers.
STAR is primarily of value to the historian for selective
exploration of scientific and technical developments and
activity. STAR is now available as an online computer
database through NASA and through some of the commercial
database vendors.
    For further information on NASA's information services
see the pamphlet *The NASA Information System: And How to
Use It* available from the NASA Scientific and Technical
Information Facility, P.O. Box 8757, BWI Airport, Md. 21240.

1027.   United Nations. *International Space Bibliography.* New York,
1966. Pp. iv + 166.

Contains worldwide sources on space exploration written

for the nonspecialist. Unannotated. Compiled as part of an effort to help people throughout the world understand space.

1028. U.S. Congress. House. Committee on Science and Astronautics. *Publications of the Committee on Science and Astronautics, United States House of Representatives, from February 1959–May 1969.* Washington, D.C.: U.S. Government Printing Office, 1969. Pp. iv + 13.

Lists chronologically all published works including hearings, testimony, and selected readings generated by the House Committee for Science and Astronautics during the period February 1959 through May 1969. Includes the publication number of works. Omits works that were no longer available at the time. Does not indicate length or provide annotations.

1029. U.S. Congress. House. Committee on Science and Astronautics. *Publications of the Committee on Science and Astronautics, United States House of Representatives, from February 1959–August 1969.* Washington, D.C.: U.S. Government Printing Office, 1969. Pp. iv + 12.

Has the same format as the preceding citation. Contents cover the period February 1959 through August 1969.

1030. U.S. Congress. House. Committee on Science and Astronautics. *Publications of the Committee on Science and Astronautics, United States House of Representatives from February 1959–December 1970.* Washington, D.C.: U.S. Government Printing Office, 1970. Pp. ii + 15.

Has the same format as the preceding citations. Covers the period February 1959 through October 1970.

1031. U.S. Congress. House. Committee on Science and Astronautics. *Publications of the Committee on Science and Astronautics, United States House of Representatives, from February 1959–February 1972.* Washington, D.C.: U.S. Government Printing Office, 1972. Pp. ii + 17.

Has the same format as the three preceding citations. Covers the period February 1959 through February 1972.

1032.   U.S. Department of the Army. *Missiles, Rockets and Satel-
        lites.* 5 vols. Washington, D.C., June 1958. Irregular
        pagination.

        Covers rocket, missile, and space literature from 1957 to
        the end of March 1958. Presents annotations on scientific and
        popular literature. Covers the following topics: USSR, United
        States, Great Britain, France and other free countries of the
        world, technology (means and methods), and earth satellites
        and space exploration. At the time of publication, all cita-
        tions were available in the Army Library or the Library of
        Congress.

1033.   U.S. Library of Congress. Science and Technology Division.
        List of Selected References on NASA Programs. NASA
        SP-3. Washington, D.C.: U.S. National Aeronautics and
        Space Administration, 1962. Pp. 236.

        Contains a list of selected publications, speeches, and
        releases of NASA and congressional documents relating to
        NASA activities from October 1958 through 1961.

1034.   U.S. Library of Congress. Science and Technology Division.
        Space Science and Technology Books, 1957–1961. Washing-
        ton, D.C.: U.S. Government Printing Office, 1962. Pp. 133.

        Lists over 400 publications arranged chronologically by
        year and by country within each year. Includes subject and
        author indexes. Covers allied areas such as space law, inter-
        national cooperation in space exploration, reports and com-
        mittee publications of U.S. Congress, and commercial
        applications of space technology.

1035.   U.S. Library of Congress. Science and Technology Division.
        *United States IGY Bibliography, 1953–1960: An Annotated
        Bibliography of United States Contributions to the IGY and
        IGC (1957–1959).* Washington, D.C.: National Academy of
        Sciences/National Research Council, 1963. Pp. viii + 391.

        Section "Rocket and Satellites" (pp. 297–354), lists over
        500 references, arranged alphabetically by author. Pertinent
        material also listed under other discipline headings.

1036.   U.S. National Aeronautics and Space Administration. *Bibliog-*

raphies of Aerospace Science: A Continuing Bibliography. Springfield, Va.: Clearinghouse for Federal Scientific and Technical Information, 1962/1964–. Irregular pagination.

Published periodically. Contains annotated references to unclassified bibliographies in the NASA information system. All references are to bibliographies annotated either as reports in Scientific and Technical Aerospace Reports (STAR) or as articles of books in International Aerospace Abstracts (IAS). Provides a subject index but no author index.

1037. U.S. National Aeronautics and Space Administration. *Aerospace Medicine and Biology—A Continuing Bibliography.* Springfield, Va.: Clearinghouse for Federal and Scientific Technical Information, 1964 to date (quarterly). Irregular pagination.

Contains annotated references to unclassified reports and journal articles compiled by the American Institute of Aeronautics and Astronautics in cooperation with NASA and the Aerospace Medicine and Biology Bibliography Project of the Library of Congress. Topics include biological, physiological, psychological, and environmental effects on flight personnel during and following simulated or actual flight within or beyond the Earth's atmosphere. Provides subject, personal author, and corporate source indexes as well as annual cumulative indexes.

1038. U.S. National Aeronautics and Space Administration. Scientific and Technical Information Branch. *A Catalog of NASA Special Publications.* Washington, D.C., 1981. Pp. vii + 104.

Lists all NASA Special Publications issued from 1961 to the end of 1981. Includes NASA histories, data books, chronologies, and bibliographies. Useful NASA source materials relevant to historical research.

GENERAL SOURCES

This section presents a list of research tools (chronologies, collected biographies, dictionaries, and encyclopedias) basic to the field. The following are brief descriptions of the selection criteria used here.

The chronologies listed below are the exclusive product of the NASA History Office and NASA historians. The chronologies available concentrate on the manned spaceflight programs of NASA and provide lesser detail on NASA's unmanned and other non-NASA programs.

Collected biographies included here are useful reference tools containing statistical and biographical information on selected groups of aerospace personalities. Astronauts and cosmonauts, more than any other group, have attracted the efforts of compilers. For biographical and memoir information on specific individuals, the reader should refer to the sections most closely related to that individual's career.

The selected list of dictionaries includes those compiling technical terms, jargon, and acronyms of the space age, as well as foreign-language aerospace and rocketry dictionaries.

Encyclopedias are loosely defined here as that body of reference material that provides dates, capsules of information, and statistics on a wide range of spaceflight and rocketry interests. Most of the juvenile literature that dominates this genre have been omitted. Interestingly, the Soviet encyclopedias, most notably Glushko's most recent one (see item 1075), are the most thorough and provide information on national programs and hardware outside the Soviet Union.

Martin J. Collins
Derek W. Elliott
Deborah L. Hickle
Sophie Mayr

Chronologies

1039. Akens, David S. *Saturn: Illustrated Chronology Saturn's First Eleven Years, April 1957 through April 1968.* Huntsville, Ala.: National Aeronautics and Space Administration, 20 January 1971. Pp. 303. Index, Illustr.

Traces the development of the Saturn launch vehicle chronologically, from April 1957 to April 1968, with footnotes to major citations. Appendixes include Saturn vehicle configurations, launch summaries, Apollo mission profile, and glossary of abbreviations. Based on 528 cited sources which are numbered sequentially at the end of the book.

1040. Brooks, Courtney G., and I. Ertel. *The Apollo Spacecraft: A Chronology.* Vol. 3, *October 1, 1964–January 20, 1966.* NASA SP–4009. Washington, D.C.: National Aeronautics and Space Administration, 1976. Pp. xiv + 269. Index, Illustr.

Third in the series of four NASA chronologies of the development of the Apollo spacecraft and the manned lunar program. Concentrates on the advanced design, fabrication and testing of the craft.

1041. Emme, Eugene M. *Aeronautics and Astronautics: An American Chronology of Science and Technology in the Exploration of Space, 1915–1960.* Washington, D.C.: U.S. Government Printing Office, 1961. Pp. xi + 240. Index, Bibliog.

Provides an outline of major achievements in terrestrial and extraterrestrial flight, centering on the history of the National Advisory Committee on Aeronautics and the first years of the National Aeronautics and Space Administration. Appendixes.

1042. Ertel, Ivan D., and M. Morse. *The Apollo Spacecraft: A Chronology.* Vol. 1, *Through November 7, 1962.* NASA SP–4009. Washington, D.C.: National Aeronautics and Space Administration, 1969. Pp. xiv + 269. Index, Illustr.

First of a series of four volumes that chronicle the development of the Apollo spacecraft and the manned lunar exploration program. Divided into three sections: concepts, design decisions, and lunar orbit rendezvous mode.

1043. Ertel, Ivan D., and R. Newkirk, with C. Brooks. *The Apollo Spacecraft: A Chronology.* Vol. 4, *January 21, 1966–July 13, 1974.* NASA SP–4009. Washington, D.C.: National Aeronautics and Space Administration, 1978. Pp. xiv + 463. Index, Illustr.

Concluding volume of NASA chronology of the Apollo spacecraft and the manned lunar program. Divided into three sections: preparing for the first manned launch, recovery from the spacecraft fire, and unmanned lunar exploration.

1044. Grimwood, James M. *Project Mercury: A Chronology.* NASA SP–4001. Washington, D.C.: National Aeronautics and Space Administration, 1963. Pp. xiv + 238. Index, Illustr.

Briefly sums up major events in the development of Project Mercury. Divided into three sections: major events leading to Project Mercury, research and development phase, and the operational phase. One appendix presents a budget summary of the program.

1045. Grimwood, James M., and B. Hacker, with P. Vorzimmer. *Project Gemini Technology and Operations: A Chronology.* NASA SP–4002. Washington, D.C.: National Aeronautics and Space Administration, 1969. Pp. xvi + 308. Index, Illustr.

Part of the NASA History Series. Chronicles Project Gemini, NASA's second manned spacecraft program. Each mission is recounted in detail, along with other important issues relevant to Gemini, including some that predated Gemini. Divided into three sections: concept and design, development and qualification, and flight tests.

1046. Morse, Mary L., and J. Bays. *The Apollo Spacecraft: A Chronology.* Vol. 2, *November 8, 1962–September 30, 1964.* NASA SP–4009. Washington, D.C.: National Aeronautics and Space Administration, 1973. Pp. xiv + 277. Index, Illustr.

Second of four volumes that chronicle the development of

the Apollo spacecraft and the manned lunar exploration program. Divided into three sections: defining contractual relations, developing hardware distinctions, and developing software ground rules. Useful appendixes include abbreviations, a glossary, a flight summary, and organizational charts.

1047.   Newkirk, Roland W., and I. Ertel, with C. Brooks. *Skylab: A Chronology.* NASA SP–4011. Washington, D.C.: National Aeronautics and Space Administration, 1977. Pp. xvii + 458. Index, Illustr.

Chronicles the post–Apollo Skylab program through the conclusion of Skylab operations in 1974. Divided into three sections: early space station activities, the Apollo Applications Program, and Skylab development and operations.

Collected Biographies

1048.   Baker, Norman L., and L. Weiser, eds. *Who's Who in Space.* Washington, D.C.: Space, 1966–1967. Pp. 328.

Presents brief biographies of leaders in the American space community. Provides, in abbreviated form, full name, position, age, family history, education, career history, memberships, and affiliations. Serves as a concise reference guide for professionals and laymen.

1049.   Furniss, Tim. *Manned Spaceflight Log.* London: Jane's, 1983. Pp. 160. Index, Illustr.

Logs the first 103 manned spaceflights from Iurii Gagarin's April 12, 1961, flight on board *Vostok* through Shuttle flight STS–5 of November 11, 1982, including the U.S. Air Force's X–15 flights for which astronauts' wings were awarded. Numerous pictures of each astronaut or team. Appendixes include lists of training groups, a table of cumulative space experience, and a table of the scheduled Shuttle flights at that time.

1050.   Furniss, Tim. *Guinness Space: The Records.* London: Guinness Superlatives, 1985. Pp. 168. Illustr.

A collection of tables and information on all manned spaceflights through the date of publication. Brief biographies of all astronauts and cosmonauts are included. Tables include information on space records such as the spaceflight of the longest duration, extravehicular activity of the longest duration, and oldest and youngest astronauts to fly.

1051. National Air and Space Museum. *International Handbook of Aerospace Awards and Trophies.* Washington, D.C.: Smithsonian Institution Press, 1978. Pp. xi + ca. [200]. Index, Illustr.

Lists awards and trophies alphabetically by sponsoring organizations. Provides full title, date of establishment, frequency, brief description, and list of recipients. Handbook includes alphabetical index of awards and trophies, personal name index, and a list of illustrations.

1052. U.S. Library of Congress. Congressional Research Service. *Astronaut Information: American and Soviet.* 4th ed. rev. Washington, D.C., 1974. Pp. 82.

Provides a general biographical reference on American astronauts and Soviet cosmonauts. Contains six sections, covering astronauts of the NASA, X-15 program, Dyna-Soar (X-20) program, and Manned Orbiting Laboratory program; Soviet cosmonauts; and comparative data on American and Soviet spaceflight. Entries are brief and present position, age, education, career highlights, and marital status. Includes summary and comparative tables and charts.

Dictionaries

1053. Allen, William H., ed. *Dictionary of Technical Terms for Aerospace Use.* 1st ed. NASA SP-7. Washington, D.C.: National Aeronautics and Space Administration, Scientific and Technical Information Division, 1965. Pp. xi + 313. Bibliog.

Defines 6,000 technical terms of aerospace research unique to the many disciplines concerned with the space environment. Attempts to explain terms by their operational uses, but frequently relies on equations.

1054. Angelo, Joseph A. *Dictionary of Space Technology.* New York: Facts on File, 1982. Pp. 380. Illustr.

Presents abbreviated explanations with occasional illustrations for terms commonly used in the fields of aerospace, physics, chemistry, and astronomy. Provides synonyms and cross-references.

1055. *Aviation and Space Dictionary.* 6th ed. Los Angeles: Aero, 1940–1980. Pp. 272. Illustr.

Emphasizes complete, technically correct, concise definitions of aviation. Explains terminology and concepts, connected with spaceflight and related fields such as computer technology, nucleonics, and meteorology. Covers different usages of a single term. Includes cross-references, synonyms, acronyms, abbreviations, and symbols.

1056. Caidin, Martin. *Man–in–Space Dictionary.* 1st ed. New York: Dutton, 1963. Pp. 224. Illustr.

Defines briefly and illustrates, in a non-technical manner, terms relating to the manned exploration of space. Includes expressions referring to the mechanics of spaceflight, rocket engineering, medicine, physiology, and astronomy as they relate to manned spaceflight.

1057. *Dictionary of Guided Missiles and Space Flight.* Princeton, N.J.: Van Nostrand, 1959. Pp. 688. Illustr.

Fifth volume in the series *Principles of Guided Missile Design.* A large compendium of detailed explanations of the names and terms commonly used in reference to mechanical construction, components, and utilization of guided missiles and spacecraft. Includes related terms from aerodynamics, astrodynamics, electronics, astronomy, and physics. Includes list of synonyms and cross-references.

1058. Goursau, Henri. *Dictionnaire de L'Aéronautique et de L'Espace, Anglais–Francais* (English–French dictionary of aeronautics and space). 1st ed. Paris: Conseil International de la Lange Francais, 1984. Pp. 727.

Dictionary of aeronautics and space technology, from

English to French. Presents brief, concise French equivalents
for English technical terms. Provides five conversion tables
of metric equivalents for English measurements and physical
units.

1059.   Gunston, Bill. *Jane's Aerospace Dictionary*. London: Jane's
         1980. Pp. 493.

         Presents, in abbreviated form, precise definitions to tech-
         nical aerospace terms. Lists various usages of terms. Omits
         most proper names, abbreviations, and acronyms.

1060.   Hyman, Charles J. *German–English, English–German Astro-
         nautics Dictionary*. New York: Consultants Bureau, 1968.
         Pp. viii + 237.

         Lists German and English astronautics vocabulary and their
         translations. Written for use by translators.

1061.   International Academy of Astronautics. *Astronautical Multi-
         lingual Dictionary of the International Academy of Astro-
         nautics*. Prague: Academia, 1970. Pp. 936.

         Provides word or phrase equivalents in seven languages
         (English, Russian, German, French, Italian, Spanish, and
         Czech). Covers astronautical terms drawn from the vocabu-
         laries of astronomy, mechanics, fluid dynamics, rocketry,
         nuclear physics, chemistry, and biology. Includes index for
         each language.

1062.   Konarski, Col. Michael M., OBE. *Russian–English Space
         Technology Dictionary*. London: Pergamon, 1970. Pp. x +
         416. Index, Illustr.

         Contains over 10,000 Russian terms related to space
         science and exploration. Includes an index of American terms
         and brief glossary of Russian biomedical terms. The appendix
         contains a list of Russian spellings of the family names of
         many well-known scientists.

1063.   Kotik, Mikhail Grigor'yevich, comp. *Dictionary of Aerospace
         Engineering in Three Languages: Russian, English, German*.
         Amsterdam: Elsevier, 1986. Pp. 879. Index.

Arranged alphabetically in Russian. Lists Russian, English and German language expressions for aerospace terms, many of which have emerged in the last decade. English and German indexes provide cross references to numbered Russian terms. Provides some cross references in the text. The most comprehensive multi-lingual aerospace dictionary available, although awkward for use by the non-Russian speaker.

1064.   McLaughlin, Charles. *Space Age Dictionary.* 2d ed. Princeton, N.J.: Van Nostrand, 1963. Pp. 233. Illustr.

Presents simple graphic explanations and definitions of aerospace terminology with background information to provide the layman with a general understanding of outer space.

1065.   Marks, Robert W. *New Dictionary and Handbook of Aerospace.* New York: Praeger, 1969. Pp. 531.

Contains a special section on the Moon and Project Apollo. Introduces the layman to the subject structure and vocabulary of aerospace science, with particular emphasis on lunar flight and the topography of the Moon. Provides star charts, tables of astrophysical values and constants, and an index.

1066.   Moser, Reta C. *Space-Age Acronyms.* 2d ed. New York: IFI/Plenum, 1969. Pp. 534.

Presents concise definitions of acronyms and abbreviations commonly used in the aerospace vocabulary. Gives alternative definitions for acronyms. Includes separate appendixes for ships, aircraft, missiles, rockets, and communications.

1067.   Nayler, Joseph L. *Dictionary of Astronautics.* New York: Hart, 1964. Pp. 316. Illustr.

Presents brief, and sometimes illustrated, definitions of space terms. Provides detailed information on topics such as the launching, orbits, and instrumentation of satellites, conditions on planets, and navigation in space.

1068.   Newlon, Clarke. *Aerospace Age Dictionary.* New York: F. Watts, 1965. Pp. 282.

Compiles brief explanations of the terms, phrases, and expressions commonly used in the aerospace vocabulary. Indicates pronunciation of certain words. Appendixes include biographies, lists of NASA centers, military commands, and conversion factors.

1069.   Sneshko, Iu.I., A. Murashkevich, V. Borshch, V. Shchelkin, and Iu. Maslenov. *Frantsuzko–russkii aviatsionno–kosmicheskii slovar'* (French–Russian aviation space dictionary). Moscow: Voenizdat, 1982. Pp. 872.

Prepared by the Ministry of Defense of the Soviet Union. Contains over 60,000 French aviation and space terms and their Russian translations. Provides a brief list of Russian, French, and English acronyms common to the aerospace industry.

1070.   Turnill, Reginald. *Language of Space*. New York: John Day, 1971. Pp. 165.

Defines astronautical terms and phrases for the layman. Includes words and jargon new to the vocabulary of space and emphasizes related terms and concepts. References appear in bold face. Provides separate list of abbreviations and a chronology.

1071.   U.S. Library of Congress. Reference Department. *Russian–English Glossary of Guided Missile, Rocket and Satellites Terms*. Washington, D.C., 1958. Pp. vi + 352.

Lists the 4,000 most common Russian technical words and phrases drawn from Soviet rocketry and space publications during 1955–1958. Translations are based on English and American space publications.

1072.   U.S. National Aeronautics and Space Administration. Scientific and Technical Information Branch. *Space Transportation System and Associated Payloads: Glossary, Acronyms, and Abbreviations*. Washington, D.C.: U.S. Government Printing Office, 1981. Pp. 261.

Handy reference to the large "space vocabulary" adopted by NASA during the Shuttle program. Divided into two sections: a glossary with useful definitions and a list of acronyms and abbreviations.

1073. Wells, Helen T., S. Whiteley, and C. Karegeannes. *Origins of NASA Names.* NASA SP–4402. Washington, D.C.: U.S. Government Printing Office, 1976. Pp. 227. Index, Illustr.

Presents meanings, origins, and brief descriptions of names and acronyms of NASA projects, programs, spacecraft, and launch vehicles approved or flown through 1974. The names are alphabetically arranged in six categories: launch vehicles, satellites, space probes, manned spaceflight, sounding rockets, and NASA installations. Appendixes, notes.

Encyclopedias

1074. Berkner, Lloyd V., ed. *Manual on Rockets and Satellites.* London: Pergamon 1958. Pp. 508.

Includes three sections: International Geophysical Year Rocket Program, IGY Earth Satellite Program, and the Special Committee for the International Geophysical Year Conference Resolutions and Data Guide. Presents comprehensive articles well illustrated with photographs and diagrams. Contains a detailed table of contents, lists of illustrations and tables, references, and index.

1075. Glushko, V.P., ed. *Kosmonavtika: entsiklopediia* (Space encyclopedia). Moscow: Izdatel'stvo "sovetskaia entsiklopediia," 1985. Pp. 527. Index, Bibliog., Illustr.

A completely revised version of earlier Soviet space encyclopedias. Stresses Soviet achievements in space, but also covers non–Soviet space topics. Well illustrated with drawings and photographs. Index is by subject. Bibliography includes extensive list of Soviet and Western secondary literature.

1076. Government Data Publications. *Space Systems Volume and Directory.* Washington, D.C., 1963. Pp. 351. Illustr.

Presents extensive political and historical data on U.S. government and industry space projects in various stages of development. Detailed explanations include chronologies, technical specifications, and illustrations. Contains four sections: boosters, satellites, space vehicles, and others. Table of contents lists projects alphabetically within sections, indicating the contractor and government service affiliation.

1077.   Jacobs, Horace, and E. Whitney. *Missile and Space Projects Guide*. New York: Plenum, 1962. Pp. 235.

Presents concise basic reference material on all missile and space projects up to 1962, including pilot projects, concepts and studies, and foreign projects. Provides names, acronyms, numerical designations, and organizational affiliation of country. Includes cross-references.

1078.   *New Space Encyclopedia: A Guide to Astronomy and Space Exploration*. Rev. ed. Horsham, Sussex: Artemis, 1973. Pp. 326. Illustr.

Presents detailed explanations of special phenomena, emphasizing astronomy, cosmology, radio astronomy, artificial satellites, and rocketry. Illustrations include charts, diagrams, and photographs. Arranged alphabetically by subject.

1079.   Petrovich, G.V., ed. *The Soviet Encyclopedia of Space Flight*. Moscow: Mir, 1969. Pp. 620. Index, Bibliog. Illustr.

Concise encyclopedia of space science, technology, and exploration from early rocketry experiments to the present. Contains many entries on the U.S. space program. Appendixes include tables of space launches and features of the surface of the Moon. Bibliography cites Russian-language as well as English standard works, along with related foreign periodicals.

1080.   Rynin, Nikolai A. *Mezhplanetnie soobshcheniia* (Interplanetary communications). 3 vols. (9 parts). Leningrad: Kooperativnaia Artel "Pechatniia," etc., 1928–1932. Illustr.

Presents a comprehensive compendium of the history of interplanetary space travel. Covers a range of subjects including science fiction, rockets, theory of rocket propulsion, superaviation and superartillery, the life of K. E.

Tsiolkovskii, the theory of spaceflight, and astronavigation. Includes a bibliography of all articles written about rockets in any language up to 1931. Also provides a table of contents, subject indexes, drawings, diagrams, tables, charts, and photographs.

1081. U.S. Congress. Select Committee on Astronautics and Space Exploration. *Space Handbook: Astronautics and Its Applications.* Washington, D.C.: U.S. Government Printing Office, 1959. Pp. 252. Illustr.

Special congressional staff report written under contract by the RAND Corporation for Congress and the public. Presents in lay terms technical and scientific analyses of the state of spaceflight. Includes table of contents, detailed topical outline, and lists of tables and illustrations.

1082. Van Nimmen, Jane, and L.C. Bruno, with R.L. Rosholt. *NASA Historical Data Book, 1958-1968.* Vol. 1. *NASA Resources.* NASA SP-4012. Washington, D.C.: National Aeronautics and Space Administration, 1976.

The first in a planned series, this volume is intended primarily as a reference data book. Provides a statistical summary of NASA's first ten years, focusing on organization and management, manpower, budget resources, academic and industrial contractors, and the various field facilities. Contains appendixes, organization charts, and a brief bibliography of NASA historical publications.

1083. Willmore, A.P., and S. Willmore. *Aerospace Research Index.* Harlow, England: F. Hodgson, 1981; distributed by Gale Research Company. Pp. 597.

Provides a comprehensive list of worldwide government establishments, industrial laboratories, colleges, and universities involved in aerospace research and projects up to 1979. Covers research in astronomy, aeronautics, meteorology, and space science. Contains separate sections for each country and provides relevant full titles with acronym, plus English translation, address, affiliation, staff, budget, special facilities, customers, current activities, and publications for each organization. Includes a subject index and a title and keyword index.

PERIODICALS

There is no single, well–defined body of space history periodicals. The journals commonly consulted in researching space history represent a broad range of content and various levels of scholarship. With some guidance, all are useful. The following compilation is by no means comprehensive, but conveys the flavor of the available journal literature.

Although periodicals that address only space issues are ideal for gaining an overall appreciation of the history of space exploration, researchers should also consider the scientific, military, and trade journals as well as some of the periodicals aimed at the general public. However, such a broad range of journals cannot be expected to have a uniform level of scholarship. Even so, the wary researcher should be able to tell from their presentation and context whether the sources are credible.

The ideal source is a well–written historical essay with references to primary sources. But the relatively recent emergence of space exploration and the consequent sparsity of scholarly material on this subject make it necessary to evaluate other, undocumented sources. Historians of space exploration frequently refer to reports, newspapers, undocumented pieces in magazines, and technical reports, all of which have their intrinsic value. Popular journals, for example, often report on the social, political, and cultural impact of space-flight; military and trade journals discuss space systems, goals, and programs; and technical publications document research programs as well as raw scientific data.

To obtain an overview of space history, the lay reader is advised to start with the journals exclusively dedicated to space topics. Most of these are published by organizations promoting space activities and understanding. By far the most useful in this category are the publications of the British Interplanetary Society (BIS), which was established in 1933. *Spaceflight*, published 10 times a year since 1959, is chiefly a historical magazine that also features logs of current space activities. The BIS publishes *Spaceflight* to promote an understanding of space research and technology among the general public. The journal contains articles by well–respected space writers and often carries reports on special projects by the participating scientists and engineers. Of special note are the continuing features, which range from biographies of astronauts and cosmonauts and other space personalities, to logs of satellite launches.

The *Journal of the British Interplanetary Society (JBIS)*, published 10 times a year, provides more technical, yet still historical 'information on space exploration. The articles focus almost exclusively on space projects and are often written by engineers, although not necessarily by those who participated in the project. In contrast to the feature articles in *Spaceflight*, *JBIS* frequently indicates the primary sources for its articles. *JBIS* is also distinguished from the publications of other organizations by the international scope of its articles. Of special interest to the historian is the annual history issue.

In the United States, one finds *Aerospace America* (published as *Astronautics and Aeronautics* until January 1984), which is the official monthly journal of the American Institute of Aeronautics and Astronautics (AIAA), the largest aerospace organization in the country. *Aerospace America* occasionally publishes retrospectives that emphasize the development of weapons and space systems and aerospace weapons doctrines. Since 1972, the magazine has also featured the column, "Out of the Past—An Aerospace Chronology," which briefly commemorates aerospace events of 25, 50, and 75 years ago.

Space World is the monthly publication of the National Space Society (the merged outcome of the L-5 Society and the National Space Institute). The magazine is known for its short, lightly documented articles, mainly about the U.S. space program, especially the activities of NASA. In addition to its articles that address historical topics, *Space World* publishes announcements of events, conferences, and new publications. The most common criticism of the journal, however, is that the coverage of NASA activities is unwaveringly favorable.

One journal which offers an alternative perspective to that of *Space World*, is *Columbus Logbook*, a publication of the European Space Agency. *Columbus Logbook* is ESA's quarterly popular journal which covers European manned activities in space; including, but not limited to European experiments on board the Space Shuttle, and European development of their own indigenous piloted flight capability.

The only Soviet publication that regularly features historical pieces on spaceflight is the monthly journal of the Soviet Air Forces, *Aviatsiia i kosmonavtika (AiK)*. Beside publishing an annual log of all space launches in the April issue of each year, *AiK* features personal accounts of space flight by cosmonauts. The regular column, "In answer to our reader's question," features technical responses to inquiries about spaceflight and navigation, and are often written by scientists associated with the Soviet Academy of Sciences' Institute for the History of Natural Science and Technology. Unfortunately, these features suffer from a common Soviet problem—lack of documentation. *AiK* is noteworthy in that it publishes announcements of new historical works that inevitably make their way to libraries in the United States. Other articles include summaries and projections of current programs and official government statements and criticisms on a wide range of space activities. Articles from *Aviatsiia i kosmonavtika* frequently appear in translation in the Joint Publications Research Service's publication *USSR Space*.

Military history journals are concerned with a narrower range of space-related issues, but present no less a valuable body of literature. The *American Aviation Historical Journal* features histories of major missile weapons systems such as the Navaho. *The Proceedings of the United States' Naval Institute* is well-known for its historical essays, which include coverage of early Navy missile programs and analysis of naval communications and navigations systems. Researchers interested in military-related topics should peruse back-issues of the *Air University Review*, which, on occasion, published unclassified versions of restricted studies. The *Air Power Historian*, which is now published as *Aerospace Historian*, features similar articles.

Space historians frequently publish in journals dedicated to the history of science and technology. *ISIS* and *Technology and Culture*, the quarterly journals of the History of Science Society and the Society for the History of Technology, respectively, from time-to-time publish articles on the history of space exploration. However, a general search through these journals for space-related titles might not be fruitful. The tactic recommended here is to identify a specialist before going through back issues. One source of guidance in seeking these authors is the special interest group for Air and Space history of the Society for the History of Technology, the Albatrosses. A newsletter detailing the activities of the group, and its members, *The Albatross* is published quarterly. *The American Historical Review* and the *Southwestern Historical Review* often publish articles generated from universities with strong space history programs. Specific topics are usually covered in highly specialized journals, such as the *Annals of the History of Computing*, which prints many papers and notes on aerospace-related projects.

Although not purely historical in approach, social science journals often provide invaluable studies on the social and political effects of space exploration. The Society for the Social Studies of Science publishes a journal, *Technology Studies*. The British journal, *Space Policy*, features coverage of international space policy issues, written by key figures in various space agencies.

Probably the most widely consulted publications on space activities are the periodicals that report on current space events. Although not historical, they are useful in determining salient trends in space and space-related activities, development, and policy. For the most part, these periodicals deal with military topics. Perhaps the most encyclopedic of these is the new annual *Jane's Space Directory*. It lists aerospace contractors, space launch tables, manned and unmanned spaceflight programs, and military space activities. *Jane's* also provides analyses of space programs.

A regular appraisal of space-related activities can be found in the weekly *Aviation Week and Space Technology (AW&ST)*, a publication of the McGraw-Hill Company. *AW&ST* goes beyond weekly reports on space-related activities with supplemental space reports on areas that have not received close attention in the past. *Aviation Week's* unique situation as a commercial publication makes it an unrivaled reflection of the aerospace industry. It is the journal of record of the aerospace industry. Weekly calendars and bulletin board provide information on meetings and appointments in aerospace organizations. Despite frequent anonymous citations, *AW&ST* offers invaluable background sources for all space history research.

On a much smaller scale, but no less informative is the ESA quarterly periodical, *ESA Bulletin*. This publication offers periodic updates on the European Space Agency's current projects, as well as measured speculation on future activities and cooperation with other organization. Although *ESA Bulletin* is not purely historical, it does however, offer the reader a unique overview of ESA's programs and their participants.

In recent years, space bulletins have grown in size and number. They publish news shorts on their own specialized space areas. Of note are *Space Commerce Bulletin*, published weekly by Television Digest, Inc., which reports on space applications and commercial space ventures, and *Space Daily* from Santa Clara, California, which publishes wire service news bulletins and, on occasion, interviews with noted space experts. One such journal which has a very specific focus is *Soviet Aerospace*. The quarterly of the European Space Agency, *ESA Journal* presents scientific papers from ESA investigators. Many of the papers discuss the problems of project development, as well as the results of research in space.

News reports from magazines that do not exclusively cover space topics provide valuable current information. These include periodicals such as *Science News*, which provides good coverage of scientific events, especially in the articles by Jonathan Eberhardt. *Science* magazine regularly carries features and reports on scientific and policy issues. *Technology Review* frequently offers reports on aerospace-related technologies. Another useful periodical is *Air Force and Space Digest*, which covers space-related issues in a format similar to that of space bulletins. Interested researchers will go further and explore a variety of new trade journals such as *Datamation*, the weekly trade journal of the computer industry, which provides a useful guide to the activities of the computer divisions of the aerospace companies. For specific programs and technologies in countries outside of the United States, the readers should also consult *Science and Technology Perspectives*, a monthly publication of the Federal Broadcast Information Service and *USSR Technology Update*, a bi-weekly report from Delphic Associates in Falls Church,

Va. Additional scientific details on space science research can be found in regular scientific periodicals. Of note are the reports of the Space Science Board of the National Academy of Sciences, which are issued twice a year and report on the results of NAS–funded space science research projects.

Many popular journals report on events and significant issues pertaining to space activities. *Scientific American* frequently carries reports on contemporary problems of space science and planetary exploration. More popular accounts can be found in the *New Yorker*, in the thoughtful and analytical articles by Henry S.F. Cooper. Finally, the popular, though at times checkered, features of *Omni* should not be neglected.

Cathleen S. Lewis

RESEARCH SOURCES

There have been no comprehensive attempts to survey national and international holdings of primary papers and records relating to space history. As in other areas of post–World War II science and technology, concern over the preservation of personal papers and corporate and government records documenting the various national space programs has only recently emerged. In part, this reflects both the sheer magnitude of the task and the space program's youthful history. In the United States, the post–war alliance of government, industry, and universities to execute large–scale scientific and technical projects such as the space program has resulted in a commensurately large quantity of documentary material. This material is dispersed among individuals, numerous corporations and universities, professional organizations and societies, and several government agencies and departments. To the extent that such material survives, it demonstrates the complex relationships and associations among the above groups and the broad commitment of resources necessary to execute the space program.

In the government sphere, NASA and the Department of Defense (DOD) were, and continue to be, the principal focus of U.S. space activity. Both have a statutory responsibility to preserve records documenting their activity, and both have established a network of history offices to guide scholars and researchers in the use of these records. For addresses and telephone numbers of these offices, see *The Directory of Federal Historical Programs* (see item 1085).

The NASA History Office has recently published a revised edition of its very useful *History at NASA* (see item 1086). The guide provides a fine preliminary introduction to research in federal records, and, more specifically, outlines the character and organization of NASA agency records, as well as the historical document holdings of the various NASA history offices. Of equal interest is a description of the NASA history and publications program.

The DOD has not prepared a comprehensive guide to historical research for its holdings, in part due to the greater complexity of DOD organization as well as the problem of classified information. Individual services, however, have published guides to sources. The most useful and relevant of these is the Office of Air Force History's *Guide to Documentary Sources* (see item 1089). In addition to describing Air Force historical holdings, the guide covers the relevant holdings of the National Archives and other government agencies, university archives, and other private collections.

The Air Force and Navy have published catalogs to their extensive oral history holdings, some of which deal with space themes (see items 1092 and 1088, respectively). The Navy catalog, which is devoted to interviews on naval research and development, also includes listings from other depositories. Complementing these holdings is a recent catalog from the

National Air and Space Museum (see item 1084) describing its oral history program on the origins of space astronomy. Many of the interviews recount Navy, Air Force, and to a lesser extent, Army contributions to rocket and satellite technology and the services interaction with scientists who employed this new capability.

For additional information on conducting research in the historical collections or records of the various services, and research information on other government agencies that have contributed to the U.S. space programs, contact the appropriate history office as listed in item 1085.

The National Archives and Records Agency (NARA) now has some records pertaining to the space programs, most relating to the early period of space activity. Records of the National Space Council have been accessioned and are described in a finding aid (see item 1093). Records of other agencies that have had a role in the space program are also available, although these are not described in published finding aids (for example, records of OMB and the House Science and Technology Committee and its subcommittee, Space Science and Applications). Since the date ranges of materials available for research vary from agency to agency, the researcher should consult the appropriate division of NARA for further information.

The presidential libraries administered by NARA house a number of significant primary source documents and other historical materials relating to the space program dating from the Truman through the Carter administrations. Most have published general guides and catalogues to their collection; space-related materials can often be found in the various official presidential files and in the personal papers and oral history interviews of administration personnel. To facilitate research in this area some of the presidential libraries have prepared brief, descriptive outlines of relevant material. For information on space holdings contact the appropriate presidential libraries as listed in item 1085.

In addition to records of congressional committees at NARA, the personal papers of individual members of Congress are also useful sources for the political history of the space program. In celebration of the bicentennial of Congress in 1987, the history offices of the Senate and the House have been preparing guides on the availability and location of such papers. The Senate guide has already been published (see item 1087); for information on the House project, contact the history office (see item 1085).

No systematic survey has been done of the historical holdings of aerospace corporations. To determine the availability of such materials, contact the appropriate corporation directly.

Universities, too, have not systematically preserved the records of their participation in space programs or the participation of faculty and professional departments. Occasionally the papers of notable alumni who have contributed to the space program find a home at university archives. In seeking any of these records it is best to contact the individual university archives or search the National Union Catalog of Manuscripts for the location of the papers of specific individuals.

Several university archives, however, have programs aimed at preserving institutional and personal contributions to the space program beyond their own or their faculty's participation. Two will be mentioned here. Rice University's Woodson Research Center has joined in a cooperative venture with NASA's Johnson Space Center to make available to scholars research materials originally collected by Johnson History Office staff. The material, on indefinite loan to the Woodson research Center, falls into four series relating to major space programs (Mercury, Gemini, Skylab, Apollo–Soiuz Test Project) and one of miscellaneous general documents. A preliminary guide has been prepared for the collection; an online computer finding aid is planned.

Virginia Polytechnic Institute and State University Library has embarked on an ambitious program to collect the personal papers of prominent scientists, engineers, and managers in the space program. The Archives of Aerospace Exploration has recently been established to facilitate this effort and already has acquired a number of useful collections, the most notable of which is Christopher Kraft, Jr.'s. For more information on their holdings contact the University Libraries, Blacksburg, Virginia 24061.

Finally, a small number of the museums devoted to the collection of air and space artifacts also actively collect historical papers an records. Most notable of these is the Smithsonian Institution's National Air and Space Museum. Their oral history collection has already been mentioned above. An unpublished guide to their other extensive holdings can be obtained from the National Air and Space Archives, National Air and Space Museum, Washington, D.C. 20560.

Martin J. Collins
Deborah L. Hickle

1084.   DeVorkin, David H., and M.J. Collins. *Space Astronomy Oral History Project Catalogue.* Washington, D.C.: National Air and Space Museum. Smithsonian Institution, 1985. Pp. x + 227. Index.

Descriptive catalog of 54 oral history interviews with scientists, engineers, and administrators involved in the early use of rockets and satellites to do astronomy from above the Earth's atmosphere. Interview descriptions include abstracts and running tables of contents. Includes name, institution, and subject indexes. Includes appendixes.

1085.   *The Directory of Federal Historical Programs and Activities.* Washington, D.C.: Society for History in the Federal Government, 1984. Pp. xv + 86.

An invaluable guide to history programs in the federal government. Provides addresses, phone numbers, lists of personnel, and brief descriptions of the mission of the various history offices.

1086.   *History at NASA.* NASA HHR–50. Washington, D.C.: U.S. National Aeronautics and Space Administration, June 1986. Pp. ix + 61. Illustr.

Provides a thoughtful, well–rounded introduction to conducting research in NASA history. Focuses primarily on descriptions of historical document collections at NASA Headquarters and at the NASA centers. Also provides useful information on negotiating the federal records system, other Washington–area research facilities, and the programs and activities of the NASA History Office.

1087.   Jacob, Kathryn A., ed. *Guide to Research Collections of Former United States Senators, 1789–1982.* Washington, D.C.: Historical Office, United States Senate, 1983. Pp. viii + 362. Supplement. 1985. Pp. 23.

Comprehensive location guide to papers, oral histories, and other documentary materials relating to former U.S. senators. Arranged alphabetically by name. Includes appendixes of senators by state and repositories with senatorial collections by state.

1088. Nowicke, Carole E., D.K. Allison, and P.S. Buchanan. *Index of Oral Histories Relating to Naval Research and Development*. Bethesda, Md.: David W. Taylor Naval Ship Research and Development Center, 1985. Pp. xiv + 259.

Provides brief descriptive information on oral histories relating to naval research and development, with some pertaining to space topics. Primarily covers interviews conducted under Navy auspices, but also includes interviews conducted and held at other repositories. Includes name and subject indexes.

1089. Paszek, Lawrence J., comp. *United States Air Force History: A Guide to Documentary Sources*. Washington, D.C.: Office of Air Force History, 1973. Pp. v + 245.

Extensive but somewhat dated guide to historical collections relating to many aspects of Air Force activity. Repositories covered include the Albert F. Simpson Historical Research Center, the Air Force's primary facility for historical research and collections, other Air Force repositories, the record centers and presidential libraries in the National Archives system, university archives, and other private collections. Collections described encompass personal papers as well as records of various Air Force organizational units, with emphasis on aviation, but also including materials relating to space missiles and rockets. Includes repository and general subject indexes.

1090. Scott, Catherine D., guest editor. "Aeronautics and Space Flight Collections." *Special Collections*, vol. 3, no. 1/2 (Fall 1985, Winter 1985/86).

This volume is devoted to several essay reviews of noted aeronautics and spaceflight collections in the United States. In an introductory essay, Catherine Scott provides an overview of the state of the art and history of such collections. Also included is an essay on aerospace bibliographic control, emphasizing NACA and NASA contributions. Major collections or libraries covered are the Library of Congress, New York Public Library, U.S. Air Force Academy Library, U.S. Air Force Historical Collection of the Simpson Historical Research Center at Maxwell Air Force Base, GALCIT's Aero Library, History of Aviation Collection at University of Texas at Dallas, Ordway Aerospace Collection at the Alabama Space and Rocket Center, and the National Air and Space Museum Library.

1091. Smith, Richard K., comp. and ed. *The Hugh L. Dryden Papers, 1898–1965.* Baltimore, Md.: Johns Hopkins University Press, 1974. Pp. 166, Index.

Detailed inventory of the Dryden Papers located at Johns Hopkins University.

1092. *U.S. Air Force Oral History Catalog.* Maxwell AFB, Ala.: Albert F. Simpson Historical Research Center, Office of Air Force History, 1982. Pp. vi + 761.

Comprehensive catalog of Air Force oral history interviews, covering a wide range of service activity including space topics. Includes a combined name and subject index.

1093. Wolfinger, Jarritus, comp. *Preliminary Inventory of the Records of the National Aeronautics and Space Council.* Washington, D.C.: National Archives and Records Service, General Services Administration, 1977. Pp. vii + 12.

Provides a brief introductory history of the Space Council and short descriptions of the 13 series comprising the collection. Collection consists mainly of minutes, correspondence and memoranda.

GENERAL HISTORIES

To date, only a few histories summarize the themes and salient events of rocketry development and space exploration, and their quality is thin. Included below are examples of the best and the broadest histories. There is not a large body of work in this area because the field of space history is still at an early stage of development and few specialized studies have been undertaken by trained historians. The literature cited below will provide the reader with a general understanding of some of the historical issues and themes of space exploration.

Cathleen S. Lewis
Frank H. Winter

The V-2 guided missile, which was assembled from components of several rockets, on display in Space Hall in the National Air and Space Museum. Developed during World War II by German engineers at Peenemünde under the leadership of Wernher von Braun, the V-2 was the world's first long-range ballistic missile. In the last year of the war, more than three thousand of these rockets were launched against Allied targets. After the war, both American and Soviet engineers utilized captured V-2 components, engineers, and technicians to augment their own rocket programs. The first launch vehicles to send the artificial satellites into earth orbit were based on this technology. The paint design of the craft on display is the same at that of the first successfully launched V-2 from 3 October 1942. (Dale Hrabak, Smithsonian Institution)

1094. Anderson, Frank W., Jr. *Orders of Magnitude: A History of NACA and NASA, 1915–1980.* 2d ed. NASA SP–4403. Washington, D.C.: National Aeronautics and Space Administration, 1981. Pp. 99. Index, Bibliog. Illustr.

Reviews major events in the history of the National Advisory Committee for Aeronautics and the National Aeronautics and Space Administration, including the creation of research centers and laboratories, major test and development programs, and major manned and unmanned missions. Although it contains no footnotes or references, it provides a useful chronology of administrative and technical developments of the US space programs.

1095. Anoschenko, Nikolai D., ed. *A History of Aviation and Cosmonautics.* 5 vols. Washington, D.C.: National Aeronautics and Space Administration, 1967.

Translation of *Iz istorii aviatsii i kosmonavtiki* (Moscow: USSR Academy of Sciences, 1964). Miscellaneous collection of brief technical histories on a variety of aviation and space subjects. Includes articles on the development of rocket planes and ramjet engines, the development of U.S. rocket boosters, evaluation of Tsiolkovskii's contribution to rocket technology, and problems in the conquest of space. Articles tend to be straightforward narratives of technical progress.

1096. Blaine, James C.D. *The End of an Era in Space Exploration: From International Rivalry to International Cooperation.* American Astronautical Society Science and Technology Series, Vol. 42. San Diego, Calif.: Univelt, 1976. Pp. xvi + 199. Index, Bibliog., Illustr.

Draws on the history of rocketry and spaceflight to illustrate the convergent paths of U.S. and Soviet space exploration. Concludes that although the development of modern rocketry took place throughout the world with little interaction between researchers, the continuation of the current rate of space exploration necessitates cooperation between the superpowers.

1097. Cornelius, Michel. *De Spoutnik à Spacelab* (From Sputnik to Spacelab). Brussels: Editions du Perron, 1983. Pp. 218. Illustr.

Provides a journalistic account of space activities from the perspective of a Belgian space watcher. Begins with the first artificial satellite of the Earth and covers the next 25 years of spaceflight with emphasis on the U.S.–manned program and the Space Shuttle. Well illustrated by official program photographs and those from the author's personal collection.

Cox, Donald W. *The Space Race: From Sputnik to Apollo and Beyond.* Philadelphia: Chilton Books, 1962. Pp. 393.

Cited herein as item 1144.

Durant, Frederick C. III, ed. *Between Sputnik and the Shuttle. New Perspectives on American Astronautics,* vol. 3, American Astronautical Society History Series. San Diego, Calif.: Univelt, 1981. Pp. viii + 334. Index, Illustr.

Cited herein as item 1147.

1098. Emme, Eugene M. "The Historiography of Rocket Technology and Space Exploration." *Actes XIIIe Congrès internationale d'histoire* 12 (1971), 43–60.

Description of the state of space history in 1971 by the director of the NASA history program at the time. Discusses historical works completed and in progress, active questions, and issues and includes some discussion of technique.

Hanle, Paul A. and V. Chamberlain, eds. *Space Science Comes of Age: Perspectives in the History of the Space Sciences.* Washington, D.C.: Smithsonian Institution Press, 1982. Pp. xiii + 194. Index, Illustr.

Cited herein as item 1344.

1099. Hetine, R.D. *Space Age Fundamentals.* Santa Monica, Calif.: Douglas Aircraft, 1964. Pp. 107. Illustr.

Gives general information that provides a technical background on a broad range of space activities such as the solar system, space phenomena, and the effects of space travel on man.

1100. Lewis, Richard S. *From Vineland to Mars: A Thousand Years of Exploration.* New York: Quadrangle, 1976. Pp. 436. Index, Illustr.

Traces the history of the exploration of the Earth and stars, beginning in the year 985 with the Norse voyages to Greenland and Canada, and ending with the physical and technological discoveries that permit the continued exploration of our environment. Goal is to locate the roots of and motivation for the present–day space age. Illustrated with early charts of the Earth and recent astronomical photographs. Includes table of contents.

1101. Ley, Willy. *Rockets, Missiles, and Man in Space.* New York: Viking 1968. Pp. xvii + 557. Index, Bibliog., Illustr.

Popular historical narrative leading up to and including spaceflight, updating 1944 versions. Includes technical appendixes on rocket launchings and an addendum to early rocket history. There is a 16–page selected bibliography with annotations.

McDougall, Walter. *The Heavens and the Earth: A Political History of the Space Age.* New York: Basic Books, 1985. Pp. xviii + 555. Index, Illustr.

Cited herein as item 1171.

1102. Mack, Pamela E. "History of the Space Program." In *The Machine in the University: Sample Course Syllabi for the History of Technology and Technological Studies,* ed. Terry S. Reynolds, 107–112. Houghton, Mich. and Bethlehem, Penn.: Michigan Technological University and Lehigh University, 1987.

Presents a sample course syllabus for an undergraduate course on the history of space exploration. Includes a basic reading list. Outlines the salient issues in the field, providing a solid introduction to the subject matter.

1103. Mack, Pamela E. and D.H. DeVorkin. "Proseminar in Space History: The National Air and Space Museum, May 22, 1981." *Technology and Culture* 23 (1982): 202–206.

Reports on the proceedings of a conference held at the National Air and Space Museum on May 22, 1981. Brings forth current issues in the historiography of space exploration. Provides a clear, concise presentation of the concerns of historians who study space history.

1104. Mazlish, Bruce, ed. *The Railroad and the Space Program: An Exploration in Historical Analogy.* Cambridge, Mass.: MIT, 1965. Pp. xix + 223. Index.

Attempts to make the historical analogy between the space program and the development of the American railroad system through a collection of essays. Although the analogy is implicit throughout, the essays deal primarily with the issues of railroad development. Provides a useful perspective from which to approach the history of space exploration.

1105. Nicolson, Iain. *Sputnik to Space Shuttle.* New York: Dodd, Mead, 1985. Pp. 224. Index, Bibliog., Illustr.

Surveys the history of spaceflight. Provides little or no historical insight, but does present an accurate historical overview of the period 1957 through 1984.

1106. Odishaw, Hugh. *The Challenges of Space.* Chicago: University of Chicago Press, 1963. Pp. xviii + 379. Index.

Provides a collection of essays assessing the current level of development of many aspects of space technology and policy, written by leading figures in their field. Although emphasis is primarily on the U.S. space program, one paper discusses the national space programs of countries other than the United States. Each essay provides a list of selected readings.

1107. Peterson, Robert W. *Space: From Gemini to the Moon and Beyond.* New York: Facts on File, 1972. Pp. v + 323. Index.

Summarizes spaceflight events from 1965 through 1971. Contents are arranged topically with chronological discussions within sections. Information is presented in a handbook style for easy reference. A detailed index is included.

1108. Roland, Alex, ed. *A Spacefaring People: Perspectives on Early*

Spaceflight. NASA SP-4405. Washington, D.C.: National Aeronautics and Space Administration, 1985. Pp. viii + 156. Bibliog.

A collection of essays based on lectures at Yale University, held on February 6 and 7, 1981. Major themes include the management of science, applications development during NASA's first 20 years, international space activities, space policy, and the rationale for space exploration.

1109. Shelton, William. *American Space Exploration: The First Decade*. Boston: Little, Brown, 1967. Pp. xii + 367. Index, Illustr.

Presents a narrative account of the first 10 years of manned spaceflight, 1957–1967. Informs the layman of the background behind spaceflight and the individuals, discoveries, projects, and milestones important in this period. Includes index and table of contents.

U.S. Library of Congress. Congressional Research Service. *United States and Soviet Progress in Space through 1979 and a Forward Look*. Washington, D.C.: U.S. Government Printing Office, 1980. Pp. xiii + 91.

Cited herein as item 1674.

INSTITUTIONAL HISTORIES

Institutions of direct relevance to the history of space exploration include those government agencies that assumed responsibility for managing rocket and spacecraft development projects. Among these are agencies created specifically for that purpose, the laboratories and centers that have carried out or contracted for research and development, the funding and supervisory agencies of the Congress, industrial organizations, professional organizations of scientists and engineers, and other organized interest groups.

Of these, the various NASA centers and NASA itself have received the most attention, largely through NASA-sponsored histories. The most appropriate of these NASA—histories are cited here, along with the rarer independent histories. Several larger institutional histories (e.g., of the National Science Foundation and the House Committee on Science and Technology) are also included because these organizations have played an important role in supporting space activities. Specific "project histories" are cited, too, if they focus primarily on the administration and organization of the project, rather than on the technical and operational aspects. Additional histories which are applicable to institutional history, but which are more narrowly focused are included in the appropriate project or subject area throughout this bibliography.

Allan A. Needell

Ananoff, Alexandre. *Les Mémoirs d'un Astronaute, ou L'Astronautique Français*. Paris: Albert Blanchard, 1978. Pp. 197.

Cited herein as item 1735.

Anderson, Frank W., Jr. *Orders of Magnitude: A History of NACA and NASA, 1915–1980*. 2d ed. NASA SP–4403. Washington, D.C.: National Aeronautics and Space Administration, 1981. Pp. 99. Index, Bibliog. Illustr.

Cited herein as item 1094.

1110. Benson, Charles D., and G. Faherty. *Moonport: A History of Apollo Launch Facilities and Operations*. NASA SP–4204. Washington, D.C.: National Aeronautics and Space Administration, 1978. Pp. xx + 636. Index, Bibliog., Illustr.

Describes the origins, construction, and use of the Apollo launch facilities at Cape Canaveral, Florida, the complex that has become the NASA Kennedy Space Center. Concentrates on the development of the organization and procedures of "launch operations" as well as the establishment of launching structure, but also describes the effect of those activities on the neighboring landscape and population.

1111. Brown, Eunice H., J. Robertson, J. Kroehnke, et al. *White Sands History: Range Beginnings and Early Missile Testing*. White Sands, N.M.: White Sands, Public Affairs Office, 1959. Pp. v + 152.

Narrative history of White Sands Proving Grounds from 1945 through the mid–1950s. Reviews the facilities, founding fathers, and firings of Army ordnance.

1112. Chapman, Richard L. *Project Management in NASA: The System and the Men*. NASA SP–324. Washington, D.C.: National Aeronautics and Space Administration, 1973. Pp. x + 128. Bibliog.

Outlines uncritically the roles and structure of project management at NASA. Focuses primarily on the project management of the Office of Space Science and Applications. Based on interviews with NASA engineers and administrators and NASA documents. Contains notes. Useful source for research on NASA management.

Cleator, Philip E. *Rockets through Space: The Dawn of Interplanetary Travel*. New York: Simon and Schuster, 1936. Pp. 227. Index.

Cited herein as item 1193.

Corliss, William R. *NASA Sounding Rockets, 1958–1968: A Historical Summary*. NASA SP–4401. Washington, D.C.: National Aeronautics and Space Administration, 1971. Pp. vii + 155.

Cited herein as item 1456.

Corliss, William R. *The Interplanetary Pioneers*. NASA SP–279. 3 vols. Washington, D.C.: National Aeronautics and Space Administration, 1971–1973.

Cited herein as item 1379.

1113.   Corliss, William R. *A History of the Deep Space Network*. NASA CR–151915. Washington, D.C.: National Aeronautics and Space Administration, 1 May 1979. Pp. ix + 229. Bibliog.

Complements the author's history of NASA communications and Earth–orbital networks managed by the Goddard Space Flight Center. Summarizes both the technical and administrative history of the Deep Space Network, which is managed by the Jet Propulsion Laboratory (JPL) for NASA. Reviews early tracking and guidance experiments performed by JPL's precursor, the Guggenheim Aeronautical Laboratory, California Institute of Technology through the beginnings of the DSN during the Pioneer and Echo programs to the Mariner missions to Mars. Illustrations include organizational diagrams and layouts of facilities.

1114.   Dryden, Hugh L. "Future Exploration and Utilization of Outer Space." *Technology and Culture* 2 (Spring 1961): 112–126.

Written by the then current administrator of NASA. Presents the official version of the future of utilization of outer

space. Contains brief descriptions of programs in their developmental stages. Avoids speculation on the distant future
in the light of notorious erroneous predictions. Published
version of a paper presented at the Seminar on Astronautical
Propulsion, Instituto Lombardo, Italy, September 1960.

Emme, Eugene M. "The Historiography of Rocket Technology
and Space Exploration." *Actes XIIIe Congrès internationale d'histoire* 12 (1971): 43–60.

Cited herein as item 1098.

1115. Emme, Eugene M., ed. *Twenty-Five Years of the American
Astronautical Society: Historical Reflections and Projections, 1954–1979.* American Astronautical Society History
Series, vol. 2. San Diego, Calif.: Univelt, 1980. Pp. xi +
248. Illustr.

Publishes memoir papers from the American Astronautical
Society History Workshop held in conjunction with the
Seventeenth Goddard Memorial Symposium in March 1979.
Papers were presented by members of the society. Purpose is
to document the history of the AAS through the memoirs of
participants dating from the establishment of the Staten
Island Interplanetary Society in 1954 through 1979.

1116. England, J. Merton. *A Patron for Pure Science. The National
Science Foundation's Formative Years, 1945–1957.* Wash-
ington, D.C.: National Science Foundation, 1982. Pp. 423.
Index, Bibliog., Illustr.

Part of the history of the National Science Foundation.
Treats the institutional arrangements for the International
Geophysical Year and the associated earth satellite and other
high-altitude science programs in some detail. Appendixes,
notes.

European Space Research Organization. *Europe in Space.*
Paris: 1974. Pp. 168.

Cited herein as item 1741.

Fry, Bernard M., and F. Mohrhart, eds. *Guide to Information*

Sources in Space Science and Technology. New York: Inter-science, 1963. Pp. 579.

Cited herein as item 1010.

1117.   Green, Constance M., and M. Lomask. *Vanguard: A History.* NASA SP–4202. Washington, D.C.: National Aeronautics and Space Administration, 1970. Pp. xvi + 257. Index, Illustr.

Traces the American International Geophysical Year satellite program from its origins in Navy post–World War II planning through its approval and the conception, design, construction, and testing of the Vanguard launch vehicle. Also traces the development of the experimental payloads for the Vanguard satellite. Well documented and authoritative; uses primary, secondary, and interview sources, to recount the events leading up to the successful and unsuccessful Vanguard missions and to explain the external factors that influenced those events. Appendixes.

Griffith, Alison. *The National Aeronautics and Space Act: A Study of the Development of Public Policy.* Washington, D.C.: Public Affairs Press, 1962. Pp. vi + 119. Index, Bibliog.

Cited herein as item 1155.

Hall, R. Cargill. *Lunar Impact: A History of Project Ranger.* History Series. Washington, D.C.: National Aeronautics and Space Administration, 1977. Pp. 314. Index, Bibliog.

Cited herein as item 1385.

1118.   Hallion, Richard P. *On the Frontier: Flight Research at Dryden, 1946–1981.* History Series. Washington, D.C., National Aeronautics and Space Administration, 1984. Pp. 258. Index, Illustr.

Provides a comprehensive account of the establishment and activities of the NASA Hugh L. Dryden Flight Research Center at Muroc Dry Lake in the southwest corner of the Mojave Desert, California. Tracing its origins to the formal establishment by the National Advisory Committee for

Aeronautics of a High–Speed Flight Research Station at the
Muroc Air Force Base in November 1949, Hallion describes
the previous activities at the site and the various administrative and organizational changes that have taken place. He
also focuses on the major flight–test programs, including the
testing of supersonic aircraft, the "X" series of aircraft tests
associated with the Gemini and Apollo programs, the NASA
"lifting body" program, and the Space Shuttle test program.
Appendixes.

1119. Hartmann, Edwin P. *Adventures in Research: A History of
       Ames Research Center, 1940–1965.* NASA SP–4302. Wash-
       ington, D.C.: National Aeronautics and Space Administra-
       tion 1970. Pp. 511. Index, Illustr.

       Provides a chronological overview of the programs, people,
       and organization of the NASA (originally NACA) Ames
       Research Center, from the extended debate over its creation
       beginning in 1936 to its 25th anniversary in 1965. Rich in
       detail and containing considerable insight, the book is lightly
       documented and written from the insider's point of view. It
       addresses political, institutional, and technical developments.
       Appendixes.

       Hayes, E. Nelson. *Trackers of the Skies.* Cambridge, Mass.:
       Howard A. Doyle, 1968. Pp. xiii + 169.

       Cited herein as item 1345.

1120. Hechler, Ken. *Toward the Endless Frontier: History of the
       Committee on Science and Technology.* Washington, D.C.:
       U.S. Government Printing Office, 1980. Pp. xxxvi + 1073.
       Index, Bibliog., Illustr.

       Celebrates the 20–year history of one of the congressional
       committees responsible for the NASA budget, the House
       Committee on Science and Technology. Provides a rare
       perspective on space science programs from the view of the
       organization whose fiscal decisions ultimately have a great
       effect on space policy. Notes.

1121. Hetherington, Norriss S. "Winning the Initiative: NASA and
       the U.S. Space Science Program." *Prologue* 7 (1975): 99–
       107.

Describes the space science programs contemplated or already under way during the formative months of NASA. Contends that NASA emerged in control of the civilian space science program only through deliberate efforts to gain and maintain institutional control.

1122.   Hirsch, Richard, and J. Trento. *The National Aeronautics and Space Administration*. New York: Praeger, 1973. Pp. x + 245. Index, Bibliog.

Uncritical history of the National Aeronautics and Space Administration (NASA) from the founding of the National Advisory Committee for Aeronautics through discussions during the early 1970s about the future of the space program. Addresses the legislative as well as programmatic history of NASA. Concludes with discussions on the future of NASA.

1123.   Hunsaker, Jerome C., and R. Seamans, Jr. *Hugh Latimer Dryden, 1898–1965*. Washington, D.C.: National Academy of Sciences, 1969. Pp. 68. Bibliog., Illustr.

Memorializes the life of Dr. Hugh L. Dryden, first deputy administrator of NASA from 1958 to his death in 1965. Dryden was lauded for his efforts in promoting peaceful uses of outer space and international space cooperation. He was previously a leading aerodynamicist, known for his wind tunnel studies, and from 1947 to 1958 was the administrator of the National Advisory Council for Aeronautics.

1124.   Jones, Bessie Z. *Lighthouse of the Skies: The Smithsonian Astrophysical Observatory, Background and History*. Washington, D.C.: Smithsonian Institution Press, 1965. Pp. 293. Index, Illustr.

A glowing institutional history of the Smithsonian Astrophysical Observatory (SAO). Begins with the establishment of the Smithsonian Institution in 1846 and traces astronomical and related research through the creation of SAO in 1890 to the transfer of the Observatory to Cambridge, Massachusetts, in 1955. Combines biographical accounts with quotations from advocates and opponents of the Smithsonian's programs. Appendixes.

Kármán, Theodore von, and L. Edson. *Wind and Beyond:*

Theodore von Kármán, Pioneer in Aviation and Pathfinder in Space. Boston: Little, Brown, 1967. Pp. 376. Index, Illustr.

Cited herein as item 1241.

Kash, Don E. *The Politics of Space Cooperation.* Lafayette, Ind.: Purdue University Studies, 1967. Pp. xii + 137.

Cited herein as item 1660.

Kit, Boris V. *USSR Space Program.* College Park: University of Maryland, 1964. Pp: Vol. 1, 318; Vol. 2; 282.

Cited herein as item 1682.

1125. Kloman, Eramus H. *Space Project Management: Surveyor and Lunar Orbiter.* NASA SP–4901. Washington, D.C.: National Aeronautics and Space Administration, 1972. Pp. 41.

Provides case studies of the Surveyor and Lunar Orbiter projects from the perspective of a student of public administration and management. Management issues are discussed in terms of the institutional environments, the roles of individuals, teamwork, the definition of roles and missions, maintaining original objectives, organization, systems capability management, the role of headquarters, incentive contracting, cost performance, and science/engineering relations. Extensive use is made of interviews with managers. Valuable as an indication of concern with management issues associated with NASA's Apollo–era programs.

1126. Koppes, Clayton R. *JPL and the American Space Program.* New Haven, Conn.: Yale University Press, 1982. Pp. xiii + 299. Index, Illustr.

Summarizes the history of the Jet Propulsion Laboratory from the early days of the California Institute of Technology research, through the JPL's deep involvement in U.S. military research. Concludes with the success of the Mariner and Viking programs. Documents the history by government reports and inquiries, personal reminiscences, and secondary sources. Focuses closely on the conflicts between JPL,

NASA, and Caltech throughout the existence of the laboratory. Notes.

Lay, Bierne. *Earthbound Astronautics: The Builders of Apollo-Saturn.* Englewood Cliffs, N.J.: Prentice-Hall, 1971. Pp. 198. Illustr.

Cited herein as item 1302.

1127. Levine, Arnold S. *Managing NASA in the Apollo Era.* Washington, D.C.: National Aeronautics and Space Administration. Scientific and Technical Information Branch, 1982. Pp. xxi + 342. Index.

Documents NASA's organization and management during the Apollo program. Emphasizes issues related to the Apollo program. Observes that its current management style diverged from the traditional Department of Defense style. Argues that the management structure and style evolved as a direct consequence of the changing goals of the institution. Written as part of the NASA History Series. Notes.

Levy, Lillian. *Space, Its Impact on Man and Society.* New York: Norton, 1965. Pp. xv + 228.

Cited herein as item 1167.

Medaris, John B. *Countdown for Decision.* Princeton, N.J.: Van Nostrand, 1959. Pp. 303.

Cited herein as item 1490.

1128. Muenger, Elizabeth A. *Searching the Horizon: A History of Ames Research Center 1940-1976.* NASA SP-4304. Washington, D.C.: National Aeronautics and Space Administration, 1985. Pp. 284. Index, Bibliog.

Provides an institutional history of the Ames Research Center from its establishment in 1940 through 1980. Based on primary records and personal interviews, it is less technical and anecdotal than the earlier Hartmann history of Ames and extends that history through the Apollo and post-Apollo periods. Appendixes.

1129. Oates, Stephen B. "NASA's Manned Spacecraft Center of Houston, Texas." *Southwestern Quarterly Journal* 67, no. 3 (January 1964): 350–375.

Examines the choice of Houston as the location for the Manned Spacecraft Center in the light of the history of the early years of NASA. Describes the center, its personnel, and associated industries and institutions.

Ordway, Frederick I. III, and M. Sharpe. *The Rocket Team.* New York: Thomas Y. Crowell, 1979. Pp. xvii + 462. Index, Bibliog., Illustr.

Cited herein as item 1249.

Pellegrino, Charles R., and J. Stoff. *Chariots for Apollo: The Making of the Lunar Module.* New York: Atheneum, 1985. Pp. xvi + 238. Bibliog., Illustr.

Cited herein as item 1613.

Pitts, John A. *The Human Factor.* Washington, D.C.: National Aeronautics and Space Administration, 1985. Pp. xii + 389. Index, Bibliog., Illustr.

Cited herein as item 1553.

Pritchard, Wilbur L., and J. Harford. *China Space Report.* New York: American Institute of Aeronautics and Astronautics, 1980. Pp. 208. Index, Illustr.

Cited herein as item 1761.

1130. Rosenthal, Alfred. *Venture into Space: Early Years of the Goddard Space Flight Center.* NASA SP–4301. Washington, D.C.: National Aeronautics and Space Administration, 1968. Pp. 135. Index, Bibliog., Illustr.

A short, heroic insider's account of the establishment of the NASA Goddard Space Flight Center and the projects and programs undertaken there from 1959 to 1963. Contains several appendixes, including a chronology and listings of satellite and rocket projects and flights. Also reproduces several central documents and provides a useful bibliography. Appendixes.

1131.   Rosholt, Robert L. *An Administrative History of NASA, 1958–1963*. NASA SP–4101. Washington, D. C.: National Aeronautics and Space Administration, Scientific and Technical Information Division, 1966. Pp. xviii + 381. Index, Bibliog.

Draws on public documents and statements to tell the official history of the administration of the National Aeronautics and Space Administration (NASA). Traces the history from the reorganization of the National Advisory Committee for Aeronautics into NASA. Provides detailed information on fiscal allocations for the first six years of NASA in addition to charts describing the organizational structure. Distinguishes between the need for flexibility and continuity throughout the years of growth of the program.

1132.   Seamans, Robert C., Jr., and F. Ordway. "Apollo Tradition: An Object Lesson for the Management of Large–Scale Technological Endeavors." *Interdisciplinary Science Reviews* 2, no. 4 (1977): 270–304.

Review of the managerial processes and skills that were required to achieve the goal of landing a man on the Moon in less that a decade. Seamans served as a key manager at NASA headquarters during the 1960s; Ordway was with NASA at Huntsville. Article covers manpower, funding, planning, and the role played by industry. Special emphasis on managing a large–scale program that is continually changing and evolving.

1133.   Stehling, Kurt R. *Project Vanguard*. New York: Doubleday, 1961. Pp. 263. Index, Illustr.

First–person narrative account of the American International Geophysical Year satellite project by a senior engineer and head of the propulsion division at the Naval Research Laboratory. Contains several technical appendixes that provide details on the contractors and subcontractors as well as on the individual Vanguard launch attempts.

Swenson, Lloyd S., Jr. "The Fertile Crescent: The South's

Role in the National Space Program." *Southwestern Historical Quarterly* 71, no. 3 (January 1968): 377–392.

Cited herein as item 1184.

1134. U.S. Congress. House of Representatives. Committee on Government Operations. Subcommittee on Military Operations. 86th Congress. *Organization and Management of Missile Programs*. Washington, D.C.: U.S. Government Printing Office, 1960. Pp. iii + 228.

Contains the texts of hearings held on the organization and management of missile programs by the Department of Defense, as a whole, and the Air Defenses and the Air Force. The subcommittee made recommendations for the reorganization of these missile programs on the basis of these testimonies.

1135. U.S. Congress. Committee on Science and Technology. Subcommittee on Space Science and Applications. *United States Civilian Space Programs, 1958–1978*. Washington, D.C.: U.S. Government Printing Office, 1981. Pp. 1100. Illustr.

Massive reference volume compiled for congressional committees. Contains short historical essays on all suborbital, earth–orbiting, and lunar and planetary space programs conducted during the first 20 years of NASA. Summarizes major scientific and engineering results of each mission, describes spacecraft and launch vehicles, and includes pre-launch development. Although some discussion of issues is included, emphasis is on basic chronology and information. Appendixes.

U.S. Library of Congress. Congressional Research Service. *Soviet Space Programs: 1971–75*. Vol. 2, *Goals and Purposes, Organization, Research Allocations, Attitudes toward International Cooperation and Space Law*. Washington, D.C.: U.S. Government Printing Office, 1976. Pp. xii + 221.

Cited herein as item 1694.

U.S. Library of Congress. Congressional Research Service. *Soviet Space Programs, 1976–1980, Part 1, Supporting*

Vehicles and Launch Vehicles, Political Goals and Purposes, International Cooperation in Space, Administration, Resource Burden, Future Outlook. Washington, D.C.: U.S. Government Printing Office, December 1982. Pp. xvi + 445. Illustr.

Cited herein as item 1695.

U.S. Library of Congress. Congressional Research Service. *Soviet Space Programs: 1971–75.* Vol. 1, *Overview, Facilities and Hardware, Manned and Unmanned Flight Programs, Bioastronautics, Civil and Military Applications, Projections of Future Plans.* Washington, D.C.: U.S. Government Printing Office, 1976. Pp. xx + 668. Illustr.

Cited herein as item 1693.

The United States' Military Space Defense Market. New York: Frost and Sullivan, 1980. Pp. 200.

Cited herein as item 1502.

U.S. Presidential Commission on the Space Shuttle Challenger Accident. *Report on the Presidential Commission on the Space Shuttle Challenger Accident.* Vol. 1 Washington, D.C.: U.S. Government Printing Office, 6 June 1986. Pp. 256. Bibliog., Illustr.

Attributes the explosion of the Solid Rocket Booster (SRB) and subsequent loss of the Space Shuttle Challenger to flaws in the decisionmaking process within NASA. Reports testimony given before the commission. Details the history of the SRB O-ring seals, as well as other safety features of the Shuttle. Although the focus is primarily on the Challenger incident, this volume provides a basis for examining the NASA administration in the post-Apollo period. Appendixes provide primary documents connected with the investigation. Notes.

1137.   Webb, James E. *Space Age Management: The Large-Scale Approach.* New York: McGraw-Hill, 1969. Pp. 173.

Developed from a series of lectures at Columbia University delivered in 1968 by the then administrator of NASA on the eve of the manned missions to the moon. Webb carefully articulates his growing convictions about the management of large–scale, technological projects. Emphasizes the impor-tance of learning how to accomplish the urgent and complex tasks that require that management.

Wells, Helen T., S. Whiteley, and C. Karegeannes. *Origins of NASA Names*. NASA SP–4402. Washington, D.C.: U.S. Gov-ernment Printing Office, 1976. Pp. 227. Index, Illustr.

Cited herein as item 1073.

1138.   Winter, Frank H. "The American Rocket Society Story, 1930–1962." *Journal of the British Interplanetary Society* 33 (August 1980): 303–311.

Summarizes the history of the American Rocket Society (ARS), which later merged with the American Interplanetary Society to become the American Institute for Aeronautics and Astronautics. Emphasizes the early philosophical aims of the organization and the rocketry experiments that it sup-ported. Based on the personal papers of and interviews with some of the founding members of the ARS.

1139.   Winter, Frank H. *Prelude to the Space Age: The Rocket So-cieties: 1924–40*. Washington, D.C.: Smithsonian Institution Press, 1983. Pp. 207. Index, Bibliog. Illustr.

Identifies the groups and individuals involved in rocketry experimentation throughout the world during the interwar period. Traces the actions of key individuals within these groups. Bases this history on interview material, memoirs, and documents. Lists experiments performed and individuals involved. Appendixes.

POLITICAL AND ECONOMIC ISSUES

The political, economic, and policy issues arising out of the space program have been addressed in as many fashions as there are academic histories. An attempt has been made here to balance the wide range of political and economic issues with the available body of historical studies. The entries below represent the wide range of policy issues that have developed since the end of World War II; however, little secondary work has yet been done on the political and economic history of specific programs. Legal issues are presented only within their historical context. Works dealing with international cooperation in outer space can be found both here and in the section on international space activities. Studies that focus on the political and diplomatic issues surrounding international activities are listed here. Those that focus on international space programs are listed in the international section. In many instances, works have been cross-referenced to both sections.

For the most part, works that are profoundly economic or policy oriented in scope have been excluded. However, a few of these have been included in the cases where they are the only available work on that subject matter. Readers should refer to histories of specific programs and subjects for further information on political and economic histories. As is true throughout this volume, the policy studies of the Office of Technology Assessment and the Congressional Research Service are invaluable sources of technical and political information.

Cathleen S. Lewis

1140.   Anaejinou, Paul, N. Goldman, and P. Meeks, eds. *Space and Society—Challenges and Choices.* Vol. 1. American Astronautical Society, Science and Technology Series, vol. 59. San Diego, Calif.: Univelt, 1984. Pp. 442.

Proceedings of a conference held April 14–16, 1982, at the University of Texas at Austin. Papers discuss the political and policy issues that have arisen out of the first 25 years of spaceflight. Contributions are grouped around five major areas: U.S. government operations in space (including military activities), the political economy of space exploration, foreign space programs, space applications, and speculation on the future. Notes.

1141.   Armacost, Michael H. *The Politics of Weapons Innovation: The Thor–Jupiter Controversy.* New York: University Press, 1969. Pp. 293. Index.

Demonstrates the impact of interservice rivalry on the political dimensions surrounding weapons development, using the competition between the Air Force and Army over the design, production, and operation of an Intermediate Range Ballistic Missile (IRBM) system as a case study. The Thor-Jupiter competition is placed in the context of technical uncertainty, industrial rivalries, and domestic and international pressures. The study relies primarily on public records and congressional testimony given during the 1950s.

1142.   Bainbridge, William S. *The Spaceflight Revolution: A Sociological Study.* New York: Wiley, 1976. Pp. 249. Index, Bibliog.

A study of 19th–and early 20th–century communities of rocket pioneers and spaceflight promoters. Argues against the popular thesis that the military co–opted these groups, and instead suggests that pioneers, such as von Braun, maneuvered the government and military into providing the means for achieving spaceflight. Appendixes, notes.

1143.   Bauer, Raymond A. *Second-Order Consequences.* Cambridge, Mass.: MIT, 1969. Pp. xii + 240. Index.

Third in a series of books analyzing the space program by the American Academy of Arts and Sciences under a grant from NASA. Attempts to explore the social implications of the space program in terms of the problems of anticipating and measuring effects. Argues for greater understanding on the part of society in order to anticipate the consequences, and an improved mechanism to quickly detect unanticipated consequences. Appendixes.

Blaine, James C.D. *The End of an Era in Space Exploration: From International Rivalry to International Cooperation.* American Astronautical Society Science and Technology Series, vol. 42. San Diego, Calif.: Univelt, 1976. Pp. xvi + 199. Index, Bibliog., Illustr.

Cited herein as item 1096.

Caidin, Martin. *Red Star in Space.* New York: Crowell–Collier, 1963. Pp. 246. Illustr.

Cited herein as item 1679.

Chapman, Richard L. *A Case Study of the U.S. Weather Satellite Program: The Interaction of Science and Politics.* Ph.D. Diss., Syracuse University, 1967. Pp. 451. Bibliog.

Cited herein as item 1431.

Cleaver, A.V. "European Space Activities since World War II: A Personal View." *AIAA 11th Annual Meeting.* AIAA Paper 75–313, February 1975, 1–18.

Cited herein as item 1740.

1144.   Cox, Donald W. *The Space Race: From Sputnik to Apollo, and Beyond.* Philadelphia: Chilton Books, 1962. Pp. xvi + 371. Index.

Written as a sequel to the author's book *Spacepower.* Presents a narrative political history of the relative levels of U.S. and Soviet prestige as a function of Soviet secrecy versus early U.S. space failures. Attributes initial U.S. lag to post–World War II military policy. Appendixes.

Daniloff, Nicholas. *The Kremlin and the Cosmos.* New

York: Alfred A. Knopf, 1972. Pp. ix + 258. Bibliog., Illustr.

Cited herein as item 1680.

1145.   Diamond, Edwin. *The Rise and Fall of the Space Age.*
        Garden City, N.Y.: Doubleday, 1964. Pp. ix + 158. Index.

        Expresses disappointment with the outcome of the promise
        of space exploration, which the author attributes to the
        influence of politics, public relations, and the rush for prof-
        its. Concludes that the space program has become a public
        works project, with little indication of a coherent plan.

1146.   Dupas, Alain. *La lutte pour l'espace* (The battle for space).
        Paris: Seuil, 1977. Pp. 281. Illustr.

        Examines the space race in light of U.S.–Soviet relations
        on earth. Speculates on the future of space detente. Asserts
        that satellite reconnaissance has played an important role in
        diffusing international crises, not only on the tactical, but
        also the strategic level.

1147.   Durant, Frederick C. III, ed. *Between Sputnik and the
        Shuttle. New Perspectives on American Astronautics.*
        American Astronautical Society History Series, vol. 3. San
        Diego, Calif.: Univelt, Inc., 1981. Pp. viii + 334. Index,
        Illustr.

        Provides a collection of nine essays that address a wide
        range of various perspectives of the U.S. space program.
        Initial essays look at economic and political issues; remaining
        ones cover topics such as space transportation, liquid hydro-
        gen propulsion, and the arts and space.

1148.   Etzioni, Amitai. *The Moondoggle: Domestic and Interna-
        tional Implications of the Space Race.* Garden City, N.Y.:
        Doubleday, 1964. Pp. xv + 198.

        Argues that the moon race is an inappropriate response
        either to domestic problems (notably unemployment and
        economic stagnation) or to international concerns (in partic-
        ular, national security of the perceived loss of international
        prestige). Also argues that the moon race demonstrates the
        failure of existing U.S. policymaking institutions to establish

clear national priorities, particularly in the areas of man-power development and the allocation of funds. Written as an "expression of deep concern" rather than as an academic study.

Ezell, Edward C., and L. Ezell. *The Partnership: A History of the Apollo Soyuz Test Project*. Washington, D.C.: National Aeronautics and Space Administration, 1978. Pp. xx + 560. Index, Bibliog., Illustr.

Cited herein as item 1584.

1149.   Fortune Magazine. *The Space Industry: America's Newest Giant*. Englewood Cliffs, N.J.: Prentice-Hall, 1962. Pp. xii + 178.

Forms a basis from which to analyze the economic effect of the U.S. space program from a detailed description of the engineering, scientific, and institutional factors involved.

Frutkin, Arnold. *International Cooperation in Space*. Englewood Cliffs, N.J.: Prentice-Hall, 1965. Pp. iv + 186. Index.

Cited herein as item 1656.

1150.   Frye, William Emerson. *Impact of Space Exploration on Society*. Tarzana, Calif.: American Astronautical Society, 1966. Pp. xii + 370. Illustr.

Proceedings of American Astronautical Society meeting in San Francisco August 18–20, 1965. Examines the values of space exploration on the 20th anniversary of the founding of the United Nations. Papers examine the effects and benefits of space exploration to economic, geopolitical, cultural, scientific, and educational fields.

1151.   Galloway, Jonathan F. *The Politics and Technology of Satellite Communications*. Lexington, Mass.: Lexington Books, 1972. Pp. xiii + 247. Index, Bibliog.

Examines the role of satellite communications in both domestic and foreign policy decisionmaking. Describes the salient features that distinguish decisionmaking for satellite communications. Written primarily for policy analysts, but contains valuable information and source material for the historian. Appendixes, notes.

Gatland, Kenneth W. "Project Orion—America's Semi–Secret Project of the Fifties to Develop a Nuclear Pulse Rocket." *Spaceflight* 16 (December 1974): 454–455.

Cited herein as item 1286.

Giarini, Orio. *L'Europe et l'Espace.* Lausanne: Centre de Recherches Européenes, 1968. Pp. 255. Illustr.

Cited herein as item 1742.

1152. Gibney, Frank B., and G. Feldman. *The Reluctant Space–Farers.* New York: New American Library, 1965. Pp. xiv + 174.

Speculates on the political and economic consequences of what the authors refer to as space discovery. Focuses on the political process that has determined the direction of the U.S. space program. Criticizes what the authors view to be public and official apathy and indecision holding the space program back from its true potential.

1153. Ginzberg, Eli, J. Schnee, and B. Yavitz. "Transformation of a Science: NASA's Impact on Astronomy" In Economic *Impact of Large Public Programs: The NASA Experience.* 81–114. Salt Lake City: Olympus, 1976.

Results of a Columbia University study commissioned by NASA. Argues that NASA transformed astronomy from a small observation–oriented science into a "Big Science," experimentally oriented and with all of the attendant problems of manpower.

1154. Gray, Colin S. "The ABM and the Arms Race." *Aerospace Historian* 18 (December 1971): 26–32.

Attempts to define the arms race and the role antiballistic missiles (ABM) have played in it. Contends that the current missile race shares certain characteristics with arms races throughout the centuries.

1155.   Griffith, Alison. *The National Aeronautics and Space Act: A Study of the Development of Public Policy.* Washington, D.C.: Public Affairs Press, 1962. Pp. vi + 119. Index, Bibliog.

Reports on the legislative history of the National Aeronautics and Space Act of 1958. Pays close attention to the personalities and organizations involved in drafting the act and related documents. Sets out the major issues discussed by Congress during the hearings preceding the debates. Concludes with brief discussions of the House and Senate bills and the conference that followed.

1156.   Hall, R. Cargill. "Early U.S. Satellite Proposals." *Technology and Culture* 4 (Fall 1963): 410–434.

Reviews the studies and proposals made by the Army and Navy immediately following World War II through 1949 for satellite programs. Pays close attention to the conclusions of project RAND. Argues that the RAND conclusions were based on inappropriate assumptions about the post–Stalinist Soviet Union, and that these incorrect conclusions are at the root of U.S. concern with the political and psychological repercussions over spaceflight.

Harvey, Dodd L., and L. Ciocoritti. *U.S.–Soviet Cooperation in Space.* Miami: University of Miami, 1974. Pp. xxxiii + 279. Index, Bibliog.

Cited herein as item 1658.

Hechler, Ken. *Toward the Endless Frontier: History of the Committee on Science and Technology.* Washington, D.C.: U.S. Government Printing Office, 1980. Pp. xxxvi + 1073. Index, Bibliog., Illustr.

Cited herein as item 1120.

Hetherington, Norriss S. "Winning the Initiative: NASA and the U.S. Space Science Program." *Prologue* 7 (1975): 99–107.

Cited herein as item 1121.

1157. Holman, Mary A. *The Political Economy of the Space Program.* Palo Alto, Calif.: Pacific Books, 1974. Pp. xviii + 398. Index, Bibliog.

Analyzes both the fiscal aspect of NASA and second–order politico–economic effects of the space program. Makes brief comparisons with available Soviet data. Attempts to establish cost–benefit criteria for selecting programs by comparing the initial costs and anticipated and actual benefits.

1158. Holmes, Jay. *America on the Moon: The Enterprise of the Sixties.* Philadelphia: J.B. Lippincott, 1962. Pp. 272. Index.

Presents a broad picture of the U.S. space program in the form of a general history. Makes comparisons to the Soviet program on the basis of currently available data. Argues that the importance of the space program lies in proving superiority to the Soviets. Includes histories of the institutions of spaceflight and space science. Appendixes.

1159. Hoyt, Edwin P. *The Space Dealers: A Hard Look at the Role of American Business in Our Space Effort.* New York: John Day, 1971. Pp. ix + 243. Index.

Warns against what the author perceives as "the concentration of economic power in a small number of hands" and the resultant uncoordinated nature of the U.S. space effort.

James, Peter N. *Soviet Conquest from Space.* New Rochelle: Arlington House 1974. Pp. 206. Index, Bibliog.

Cited herein as item 1681.

1160. Jastrow, Robert, and H. Newell. "The Space Program and the National Interest." *Foreign Affairs* 50 (April 1972): 532–544.

Addresses the contemporary concern over the cost of the U.S. space program in the post–Apollo era by reviewing the policy decisions made 15 years earlier that established NASA. Points out the potential fiscal and financial budgets required to continue the space program at a high level. Special emphasis on the potential returns to meteorology, mineral reserves, and communications. Argues that the Space Shuttle would be the most economic carrier to put these programs into action. The authors were the director of NASA's Institute for Space Studies and associate administrator of NASA, respectively.

Johnson, Nicholas L. "Apollo and Zond—Race around the Moon." *Spaceflight* 20 (December 1978): 403–412.

Cited herein as item 1659.

Kash, Don E. *The Politics of Space Cooperation.* Lafayette, Ind.: Purdue University Studies, 1967. Pp. xii + 137.

Cited herein as item 1660.

Kehrberger, H. Peter. *Legal and Political Implications of Space Research.* Hamburg: Verlag Weltarchiv, 1965. Pp. 365.

Cited herein as item 1015.

1161.   Kennan, Erland A., and E.H. Harvey, Jr. *Mission to the Moon: A Critical Examination of NASA and the Space Program.* New York: Morrow, 1969. Pp. 396. Bibliog., Illustr.

Analyzes the causes of the fire in Apollo test mission 204 (Apollo 1), and the resulting deaths of astronauts Gus Grissom, Roger Chaffee, and Ed White. Argues that negligence on the part of NASA was the main cause of the tragedy and that the rapid growth of the aerospace industry has gone unchecked during the space program, and has taken over the direction of the program.

1162.   Killian, James R., Jr. *Sputnik, Scientists and Eisenhower: A Memoir of the First Special Assistant to the President for Science and Technology.* Cambridge, Mass.: MIT Press, 1977. Pp. 271. Index, Bibliog.

Written by the first special assistant to the president for science and technology, recounts the development of post-Sputnik science policy in the United States with emphasis on space and nuclear policies of the time. Justifies the cautious approach of Eisenhower's space exploration policy. Focuses on the relationship between scientists and politicians. Also reflects on the development of science policy since Eisenhower in the light of the early days of the President's Science Advisory Committee.

Kinsley, Michael E. *Outer Space and Inner Sanctums*. London: John Wiley and Sons, 1976. Pp. xiii + 280. Index.

Cited herein as item 1442.

1163.   Kistiakowsky, George. *A Scientist at the White House: The Private Diary of President Eisenhower's Special Assistant for Science and Technology*. Cambridge, Mass.: Harvard University Press, 1976. Pp. lxvii + 448. Index.

The unannotated entries of George Kistiakowsky's diary. Written during his tenure as Eisenhower's special assistant for science and technology (1959–1960), who advised Eisenhower on science policy as a whole and who was instrumental in shaping the president's space policy. The preface outlines the operations of the Presidential Science Advisory Committee and summarizes the author's feelings about the committee.

Koppes, Clayton R. *JPL and the American Space Program*. New Haven, Conn.: Yale University Press, 1982. Pp. xiii + 299. Index, Illustr.

Cited herein as item 1126.

Kovrizhkin, Sergei V. *Kosmicheskie issledovaniia v iaponiia: sotsial'no ekonomicheskie i politicheskie aspekty* (Space research in Japan: socioeconomic and political aspects). Moscow: Nauka, 1979. Pp. 153. Bibliog.

Cited herein as item 1768.

Kushin, Mikhail A. *Zapadnaia evropa: kosmicheskaia tekhnika i ekonomika* (Western europe: space technology and economics). Minsk: Izdatel'stvo Belorusskoi Gosudarstvennoi Universitety, 1975. Pp. 167. Bibliog.

Cited herein as item 1745.

1164.   Lapidus, Robert D. "Sputnik and Its Repercussions: A His-
        torical Catalyst." *Aerospace*, 17 (1970): 88–93.

        Analyzes the impact of the launch of Sputnik on society
        and politics. Argues that the launch awakened America to the
        danger of Soviet world dominance.

1165.   Laskin, Paul L. *Communicating by Satellite*. New York:
        Twentieth Century Fund, 1969. Pp. 79.

        Argues that institutions should be fashioned to maximize
        the rapid development of commercial communications sat-
        elite technology. Suggests fiscal and organizational modifi-
        cations to the then current International Telecommunications
        Satellite Consortium to allow more flexibility in responding
        to varying demands and to better distribute satellite tech-
        nology throughout the world. Briefly describes many of the
        alternative proposals for international communications
        satellite systems.

1166.   Levine, Arthur L. *The Future of the U.S. Space Program*.
        New York: Praeger, 1975. Pp. xi + 197. Index.

        Written before the flight of the Apollo–Soiuz Test Project.
        Attempts to decipher the historical ingredients of U.S. space
        policy in an effort to speculate on the future of the U.S.
        program. Relies on sources generated from NASA and other
        governmental agencies and personal interviews with NASA
        officials. Concludes with a summary of potential controver-
        sies in U.S. space policy during the 1980s. Appendixes, notes.

1167.   Levy, Lillian. *Space, Its Impact on Man and Society*. New
        York: Norton, 1965. Pp. xv + 228.

        A collection of essays by some of the leading figures in the
        American space program and related fields that examine the
        political, economic, social, religious, and philosophical issues
        of space exploration. Useful as a source for the thoughts of
        certain figures of the time. Provides no references.

1168.   Lewis, Richard S. *Appointment on the Moon*. New York:
        Viking Press, 1969. Pp. xiii + 538. Index.

        Traces the history of American space science from *Ex–*

plorer 1 to the moon landing. Presents a close examination of the Jet Propulsion Laboratory's lunar and planetary exploration programs. Discusses scientific as well as policy issues of the space program. Notes.

1169.   Logsdon, John M. *The Decision to Go to the Moon: Project Apollo and the National Interest.* Cambridge, Mass.: MIT, 1970. Pp. xiii + 187. Index, Bibliog.

Analyzes the development of the decision to plan a manned mission to the Moon in U.S. political institutions from the Eisenhower administration through the Kennedy administration. Argues that the Apollo program is symbolic of the motivations and characteristics of American civilization, and that the decision for the Moon program was purely political.

Logsdon, John M. "Selecting the Way to the Moon: The Choice of the Lunar Orbital Rendezvous Mode." *Aerospace Historian* 18 (June 1971): 63–70.

Cited herein as item 1602.

Lovell, Sir Bernard. "The Effects of Defense Science on the Advance of Astronomy." *Journal for the History of Astronomy* 8 (1977): 151–173.

Cited herein as item 1346.

1170.   Lovell, Sir Bernard. *The Origins and International Economics of Space Exploration.* Edinburgh: Edinburgh University Press, 1973. Pp. viii + 104. Index, Bibliog., Illustr.

Traces the history, since 1957, emphasizing political and economic issues that influenced the advancement of space programs in the United Kingdom, Europe, the United States, and the Soviet Union. Appendixes.

Low, George M. *The Apollo Program: A Midstream Appraisal.* Washington, D.C.: Smithsonian Institution Press, 1969. Pp. 22. Illustr.

Cited herein as item 1604.

1171.   McDougall, Walter A. *The Heavens and the Earth: A Political History of the Space Age.* New York: Basic Books, 1985. Pp. xviii + 555. Index, Illustr.

Presents the first detailed discussion on the effects the space age has had on the role of government. Attributes the development of post–World War II technocracy in the United States to competition with the Soviet Union during the Cold War. Argues that the development of this technocracy has made the Cold War total, placing the state in the forefront of the promotion of change. Discussion alternates between the American situation and that of the Soviets. The author was awarded the 1986 Pulitzer Prize for History for this work. Notes.

1172.   McDougall, Walter A. "Technology and Statecraft in the Space Age: Toward the History of a Saltation." *American Historical Review* 87 (1982): 1010–1040.

Asserts that the space race has caused irreversable transformations in our society, which the author summarizes as the "institutionalization of technological change for state purposes." Presents a more strongly stated version of the author's chief argument in his book *The Heavens and the Earth* (see item 1171).

McDougall, Walter A. "Space Age Europe: Gaullism, Euro–Gaullism, and the American Dilemma." *Technology and Culture* 26 (April 1985): 179–203.

Cited herein as item 1746.

Mack, Pamela E. *The Politics of Technological Change: A History of Landsat.* Ph.D diss., University of Pennsylvania, 1983. Pp. xii + 367. Bibliog.

Cited herein as item 1444.

Manno, Jack. *Arming the Heavens.* New York: Dodd, Mead, 1984. Pp. 197. Index, Bibliog.

Cited herein as item 1489.

1173. Michael, Donald N. *Implications of Peaceful Space Activities for Human Affairs.* Washington, D.C.: U.S. Government Printing Office, 1961. Pp. ix + 272.

Identifies areas in which the author foresees spaceflight having an impact on society. Written under contract for NASA. Based on research by the staff of Brookings Institution.

Mitroff, Ian. *The Subjective Side of Science: A Philosophical Inquiry into the Psychology of the Apollo Moon Scientists.* New York: American Elsevier, 1974. Pp. 329. Index, Bibliog., Illustr.

Cited herein as item 1390.

Molloy, James A., Jr. "The Dryden–Blagonravov Era of Space Cooperation, 1962–1965." *Aerospace Historian* 24 (1977): 40–46.

Cited herein as item 1664.

Murray, Bruce, and M. Davis. "Detente in Space." *Science* 192 (11 June 1978): 1067–1074.

Cited herein as item 1666.

1174. Musolf, Lloyd D., ed. *Communications Satellites in Political Orbit.* San Francisco: Chandler, 1968. Pp. xii + 189.

Provides a collection of public statements, reports, and papers related to the issues surrounding communications satellites. Presents a wide variety of approaches to and thoughts about commercial communications satellites. Useful in reviewing the discussion of communications satellites in historical context.

1175. Needell, Allan A. *The First Twenty–five Years in Space: A Symposium.* Washington, D.C.: Smithsonian Institution Press, 1983. Pp. 147. Index.

Collection of essays from the symposium: "The First Twenty–five Years in Space," sponsored by the National Air and Space Museum and the National Academy of Sciences. Includes comments made on the papers as well as the discussion afterward. Represents a wide range of opinions as to the motivations and economic and scientific issues of space-flight in this country as they have evolved over the past 25 years.

1176. Nieburg, H.P. *In the Name of Science.* Chicago: Quadrangle, 1966. Pp. ix + 384. Index, Bibliog.

Critical examination of the issue of science and exploration to justify space activities. Extensive discussion of the interaction between NASA, the military agencies, the political process, and the private aerospace industry.

Oberg, James E. *Red Star in Orbit.* New York: Random House, 1981. Pp. xiii + 272. Index, Illustr.

Cited herein as item 1684.

O'Leary, Brian. *Project Space Station—Plans for a Permanent Manned Space Center.* Harrisburg, Pa.: Stackpole Books, 1983. Pp. xv + 159. Index, Bibliog., Illustr.

Cited herein as item 1609.

1177. Ordway, Frederick I. III, C. Adams, and M. Sharpe. *Dividends from Space.* New York: Thomas Y. Crowell, 1971. Pp. xi + 309. Index, Bibliog.

Argues that the decline in popularity of the U.S. space program in the early 1970s could have been prevented if NASA had publicized space spin-offs better. Gives brief histories of products, systems, and research that were originally pioneered by NASA and that now have commercial and personal applications, such as home products, medicine, management and information systems, earth resources observation, satellite communications, and basic research in space. Bibliography lists sources of information on space technology and its applications.

1178. Pelton, Joseph N., and E. Burgess. *Global Communications Satellite Policy: Intelsat, Politics and Functionalism.* Mt. Airy, Md.: Lomond Books, 1974. Pp. xi + 183. Index, Bibliog., Illustr.

Analyzes the development of the International Telecommunications Satellite Consortium (INTELSAT) according to the functionalist theory of international relations. Reviews the history of communications systems as well as communications satellites. Begins analysis with the first INTELSAT launch, April 1965. Contains extensive footnotes, and makes many citations to primary INTELSAT and United Nations documents.

1179.   Pelton, Joseph N., and M. Snow, eds. *Economic and Policy Problems in Satellite Communications.* Praeger Special Studies in International Economics and Development. New York, 1977. Pp. x + 242. Index.

Collection of six papers on the economic and policy issues surrounding satellite communications. Papers are divided between economic and policy issues with introductions to each section by the editors. Part I introduced by Snow, inquires into the economic issues, including the International Telecommunications Satellite Consortium's pricing policy, the Federal Communication Commission's influence on domestic communications, and the FCC's regulation of the Communications Satellite Corporation (Comsat). Part II addresses the political issues of communications satellites, including the global political issues; the social, economic, and political role of communications satellites in both developing and developed countries; and the overall history of U.S. communications policy. Includes listings of the world's communication satellite systems and major cable systems. Appendixes.

Petrov, B.H., and V.C. Berreschetin, eds. *Orbity sotrudnichestva* (Orbits of cooperation). Moscow: Mashinostroenie, 1983. Pp. 177. Illustr.

Cited herein as item 1667.

Ploman, Edward. *Space, Earth and Communications.* London: Frances Pinter, 1984. Pp. ix + 237. Index, Bibliog.

Cited herein as item 1449.

1180.   Rabinowitch, Eugene, and R. Lewis, eds. *Man on the Moon. The Impact on Science, Technology and International Cooperation.* New York: Basic Books, 1969. Pp. xiv + 204.

Reprint of a series of articles that originally appeared in a special issue of *Bulletin of the Atomic Scientists*. Contains articles by Freeman Dyson, Mose L. Harvey, Sidney Hyman, John A. O'Keefe, William Leavitt, Franklin A. Long, Sir Bernard Lovell, Irving Michelson, Thornton Page, Eugene Rabinowitch, Charles S. Sheldon, Philip M. Smith, Sidney Sternberg, Ernst Stuhlinger, Harold Urey, and Wernher von Braun.

1181.   Rechtschaffen, Oscar H., ed. *Reflections on Space: Its Implications for Domestic and International Affairs*. Colorado Springs, Colo.: U.S. Air Force Academy, 1964. Pp. x + 344.

A collection of papers that discuss a wide range of issues connected with space exploration. Areas covered include the social, political, economic, and military aspects of space exploration as well as the Soviet perspective.

Ritchie, David. *Space War*. New York: Atheneum, 1982. Pp. 224. Illustr.

Cited herein as item 1493.

Roland, Alex, ed. *A Spacefaring People: Perspectives on Early Spaceflight*. NASA SP–4405. Washington, D.C.: National Aeronautics and Space Administration, 1985. Pp. viii + 156. Bibliog.

Cited herein as item 1108.

1182.   Rostow, Eugene V. *Satellite Communications and Educational Television in Less Developed Countries*. Washington, D.C.: National Bureau of Standards. Institute for Applied Technology, June 1969. Irregular pagination. Illustr.

Makes the argument for the existence of the International Telecommunications Satellite Consortium on the basis of economics and educational uses of satellite broadcasts. Proposes communication satellite system for use in Latin America. Uses the example of India and the country's use of the Applications Technology Satellite to illustrate the potential educational benefits of a communications satellite system. Now known as the Rostow Report, this is a comprehensive examination of the communications industry by the special communications task force of 1967, headed by Rostow.

Salkeld, Robert. *War and Space.* Garden City, N.Y.: Prentice–Hall, 1970. Pp. xxiv + 195.

Cited herein as item 1495.

Seamans, Robert C., Jr., and F. Ordway. "Apollo Tradition: An Object Lesson for the Management of Large–Scale Technological Endeavors." *Interdisciplinary Science Reviews* 2, no. 4 (1977): 270–304.

Cited herein as item 1132.

Schauer, William H. *The Politics of Space: A Comparison of the Soviet and American Space Programs.* New York: Holmes and Meier, 1976. Pp. vii + 317. Index, Bibliog.

Cited herein as item 1669.

Smith, Delbert D. *Communication via Satellite.* Leydon, England: A.W. Sijthoff, 1976. Pp. xviii + 335. Index, Bibliog.

Cited herein as item 1453.

1183. Snow, Marcellus S. *Marketplace for Telecommunications: Regulation and Deregulation in Industrialized Democracies.* New York: Longman, 1986. Pp. xvi + 304. Index.

Selects seven industrialized democracies and analyzes the decisionmaking processes surrounding satellite communications. Provides microeconomic analyses of the effects of regulation on communications systems. Although written by and for economists, this work touches on significant historical issues and provides source materials useful for all scholars.

1184. Swenson, Lloyd S., Jr. "The Fertile Crescent: The South's Role in the National Space Program." *Southwestern Historical Quarterly* 71, no. 3 (January 1968): 377–392.

Examines the economic impact of the Apollo program on

the American South. Briefly touches on the significance of the South to the history of aeronautics. Reviews the selection of southern sites for NASA space centers by Congress. Asserts that the locations of these centers has brought southerners to the forefront of the space program.

Tatarewicz, Joseph N. "Federal Funding and Planetary Astronomy, 1950–1975." *Social Studies of Science* 16, no. 1 (February 1986): 80–103.

Cited herein as item 1396.

1185.   Van Dyke, Vernon. *Pride and Power: The Rationale of the Space Program.* Urbana, Ill.: University of Illinois Press, 1964. Pp. xiii + 285.

Outlines the motivations and methods of the political decisions concerning the U.S. space program. Endeavors to explain the distinction between peaceful uses of space and the complete preclusion of military uses, as well as that between government–directed development of science and technology and enhancement of national prestige. Provides citations to news reports, statements by public officials, and congressional publications.

Vladimirov, Leonid. *The Russian Space Bluff.* London: Tom Stacey, 1971. Pp. 192. Index.

Cited herein as item 1700.

1186.   Webb, James E. "NASA and USAF: A Space Age Partnership." *The Airman*, August 1964, 6–11.

Written by the administrator of NASA, commemorates the traditional cooperation between NASA and the USAF, especially in the area of launch–vehicle development, ground support, and astronaut training.

SPECULATION ON SPACEFLIGHT

The concept behind this section on speculation on spaceflight is difficult to define. The section represents an attempt to compile a broad listing of the salient, historical works that speculated on the future of spaceflight and those that laid the groundwork for serious studies. As a result, this section includes both the classic writings by Konstantin Tsiolkovskii on the principles of spaceflight, and Wernher von Braun's in *Collier's* series on the future of man in space. Ideally, this section should contain works that relate speculative writings to the development of space exploration; the small number of such works presented here reflects the absence of such studies in the literature as a whole. In order to maintain the historical tone of this volume, current speculative volumes have been purposedly omitted.

Frank H. Winter

1187. Braun, Wernher von, and C. Ryan. "Baby Space Station." *Collier's* 131 (27 June 1953): 33–40.

   Introduces one of the earliest concepts of an artificial satellite and speculates on its scientific uses and the benefits of space exploration to mankind. Illustrations are by the leading space artist, Chesley Bonestell.

1188. Braun, Wernher von, W. Ley, F. Whipple, J. Kaplan, H. Haber, and O. Schachter. "Man Will Conquer Space Soon." *Collier's* 129 (March 1952): 22–36.

   An influential series of articles, illustrated by Chesley Bonestell, which played a major role in promoting the idea of spaceflight to both the general public and the scientific community. Articles include "Crossing the Last Frontier" by von Braun, "A Station in Space" by Ley, "The Heavens Open" by Whipple, "This Side of Infinity" by Kaplan, "Can We Survive in Space" by Haber, and "Who Owns the Universe" by Schachter.

1189. Carter, Paul A. "Rockets to the Moon: A Dialogue between Fiction and Reality." *American Studies* 15, no. 1 (1974): 31–46.

   Contends that rocketry pioneers Oberth, Tsiolkovskii, and Goddard, never distinguished between the reality of the practical problems of spaceflight and the fantasy of the concept. Carter shows how the most accurate descriptions of space travel, including descriptions of weightlessness and of the effects of the vacuum of space, were to be found not in the scientific press, where factual errors abounded, but rather in the science fiction literature.

1190. Clarke, Arthur C. "Space Travel in Fact and Fiction." *Journal of the British Interplanetary Society* 9 (September 1950): 213–230.

   Surveys the speculative literature of spaceflight from the ancient Greek Lucian of Samosota to the motion picture *Destination Moon*, released in 1950, with a perspective on the potential use of advanced versions of the V–2 rocket for realizing spaceflight. A noted spaceflight authority and science fiction author, Arthur C. Clarke contributed to the speculative literature and continued to be an influential advocate.

1191. Clarke, Arthur C. *The Exploration of Space*. New York: Harper, 1959. Pp. ix + 197. Index, Illustr.

First written in 1951 and updated in 1959, this book presents a scientific analysis of the problems inherent in space travel.

1192. Clarke, Arthur C. *Ascent to Orbit. A Scientific Autobiography*. New York: Wiley–Interscience 1984. Pp. 226. Illustr.

Presents a collection of technical writings along with the author's introductory autobiographical remarks on the evolution of his thinking. Of special note is the reprint of his pioneering articles on communications satellites, titled "Extra-Terrestrial Relays," which originally appeared in *Wireless World* in October 1945.

1193. Cleator, Philip E. *Rockets through Space: The Dawn of Interplanetary Travel*. New York: Simon and Schuster, 1936. Pp. 227. Index.

Speculates on the possibilities of spaceflight on the basis of the results of liquid–fuel rocket tests by the German and American rocket societies of the early 1930s. This work is Great Britain's earliest book on spaceflight, written by the founder and first president of the British Interplanetary Society (BIS) in 1933. Provides information on the first BIS attempts to initiate similar rocket programs, which were unsuccessful owing to the restrictive laws pertaining to non-private rocket experiments.

1194. Curtis, Hebert D. "Voyages to the Moon." *Publications of the Astronomical Society of the Pacific* 32 (1920): 145–150.

Brief review of early fanciful speculation on modes of travel in space and of the doctrine of plurality of worlds acts as a preamble to the objective positive assessment of Robert Goddard's rocket experiments.

1195. Deisch, Noel. "Navigation of Space in Early Speculation and in Modern Research." *Popular Astronomy* 38 (February 1930): 73–88.

Surveys the literature that speculates on the plurality of worlds and interplanetary flight, from the writing of the ancient Greeks to Miral–Viger's 1922 novel, *L'Anneau de Feu*. Concludes with a survey of reaction–propelled flying craft and astronautical research by N. Kibaltchich in 1882 to the work of R.H. Goddard in 1930. The article was the first chapter in a 172–page manuscript titled "Navigation of Space" that received an honorable mention for the 1928 REP–Hirsch international astronautical prize awarded by the Société Astronomique de France.

Dick, Stephen J. *Plurality of Worlds*. Cambridge: Cambridge University Press, 1982; paperback ed., 1984. Pp. x + 246. Index, Bibliog.

Cited herein as item 1342.

Durant, Frederick C. III, and G. James, eds. *First Steps toward Space*. Smithsonian Annals of Flight, no. 10. Washington, D.C.: Smithsonian Institution Press, 1974. Pp. 307. Index, Illustr.

Cited herein as item 1283.

1196. Emme, Eugene M., ed. *Science Fiction and Space Futures: Past and Present*. San Diego, Calif.: Univelt 1982. Pp. 270. Bibliog., Illustr.

Proceedings of the Third American Astronautical Society History Symposium on Science Fiction and Space Futures, held at Pentagon City, Virginia, March 27, 1981. Papers by Tom D. Crouch, Frederick I. Ordway III, Ron Miller, William Sims Bainbridge, and Jesco von Puttkamer survey interplanetary voyages in literature, space fiction in films, a history of space art, the impact of science fiction on attitudes toward technology, and philosophical perspectives on the role of space fiction. Includes transcripts of a panel discussion, a bibliography of space futures, and profiles of the contributors.

1197. Esnault–Pelterie, Robert. *Exploration par Fusées de la Très Haute Atmosphère et la Possibilité des Voyages Interplanétaires* (The exploration of the upper atmosphere by rockets and the possibility of interplanetary flight). Paris: Société Astronomique de France, 1928. Pp. 96. Illustr.

Expounds original hypotheses of spaceflight that the author began to formulate in 1908 independently of the rocketry and astronautical ideas of pioneers Konstantin E. Tsiolkovskii, R.H. Goddard, and Hermann Oberth. Calculates optimum rocket shapes, motion of a rocket in a vacuum, and safe acceleration speeds for manned flight. Presents the earliest known suggestions of atomic or nuclear rocket propulsion for planetary space missions, and considers the possibility of extraterrestrial life.

Goddard, Esther C., and G.E. Pendray, eds. *The Papers of Robert H. Goddard.* New York: McGraw–Hill, 1970. Pp. 1707. Index, Illustr.

Cited herein as item 1234.

1198. Hacker, Barton C. "The Idea of Rendezvous: From Space Station to Orbital Operations in Space Travel Thought, 1895–1951." *Technology and Culture* 15, no. 3 (July 1974): 373–388.

Traces the history of the concept of space rendezvous from Lasswitz and Tsiolkovskii through Oberth, Noondung and Goddard. Mentions the role of The British Interplanetary Society in the development of space travel ideas.

1199. Kondratiuk, Iurii. *Zavoevanie mezhplanetnykh prostranstv* (The conquest of interplanetary space). Moscow: Oborongiz, 1947. Pp. 81

Introduces original theories of rocket dynamics and rocket engineering that are independent of those of K.E. Tsiolkovskii. The author worked out his own equations for maximum–energy spaceflight trajectories, a theory of multistage rockets, intermediate interplanetary rocket–refueling bases (space stations or planetary satellite bases), landing of rockets with atmospheric drag, and suggestions for the use of metals and metalloids and their hydrogen compounds as future propellants for interplanetary rockets. [In Russian]

Kosmodemianskii, Arkadii A. *K. E. Tsiolkovskii.* Moscow: Voennoe Izdatel'stvo, 1960. Pp. 186. Illustr.

Cited herein as item 1243.

1200. Lasser, David. *The Conquest of Space*. New York: Penguin, 1931. Pp. 271. Illustr.

Discusses possibilities of spaceflight, barriers to spaceflight, and spaceships. The first English–language book on these topics, by one of the founders and the first president of the American Interplanetary Society (later the American Rocket Society). This work was influential in arousing early interest in spaceflight in the United States.

1201. Ley, Willy. *Die Fahrt ins Weltall* (Travel into the cosmos). Leipzig: Hachmeister und Thal, 1926. Pp. 68. Illustr.

Popularizes the earliest writings of Hermann Oberth, Walter Hohmann, and others concerning the possibilities of spaceflight. Is considered one of the first and most effective popularizations in spreading the concept of spaceflight.

1202. Ley, Willy. *Rockets, Missiles, and Men in Space*. New York: Viking, 1968. Pp. 557. Bibliog., Illustr.

Popularizes the history of rocketry and spaceflight from the earliest cosmological theories to Project Apollo and artificial satellites. Expands considerably the first edition of 1944, entitled *Rockets*. Contains an extensive, multilingual bibliography. Invaluable for personal recollections of the author's association with the early Verein für Raumschiffahrt (the German Rocket Society) of circa 1927–1933. Appendixes include performance characteristics of German World War II missiles, tables of U.S. V–2 and Viking launches.

1203. Ley, Willy, and W. von Braun. *The Exploration of Mars*. New York: Viking, 1956. Pp. 176. Bibliog., Illustr.

Presents one of the earliest serious proposals for a manned expedition to planet Mars, with engineering projections by the leading rocket pioneer Wernher von Braun. Beautifully illustrated by dean of space art, Chesley Bonestell. Includes hypothetical logistical tables for missions and an extensive bibliography of literature on Mars. Based on von Braun's *Das Marsprojekt* (The Mars project).

1204. Ley, Willy, H. Oberth, F. von Hoefft, W. Hohmann, K. Debus, G. von Pirquet, and F. Sander, eds., *Die Moglichkeit der*

Weltraumfahrt: Allgemeinverstandliche Beitrage zum Raum-schiffahrtsproblem (The possibility of spaceflight: universally understandable articles on the space travel problem). Leipzig: Hachmeister und Thal, 1928. Pp. 344. Illustr.

Contains chapters on spaceflight and rocket theories by the pioneers Hermann Oberth, Franz von Hoefft, Walter Hohmann, Karl Debus, Guido von Pirquet, Friedrich W. Sander, and the author. Broadened popular interest in spaceflight and rocketry in German–speaking countries and established the author as a popularizer of this genre.

1205. Nicolson, Marjorie H. *Voyages to the Moon*. Reprinted. 1960. New York: Macmillan, 1948. Pp. xiii + 297. Index, Bibliog.

Delightful compendium of 17th- and 18th-century literature and thought of supernatural voyages, spaceflight borne by birds, artificial wings, and flying chariots.

1206. Noordung, Hermann. *Das Problem der Befahrung des Welt-raums* (The problem of navigating in space). Berlin: R.C. Schmidt, 1929. Pp. 188. Illustr.

Presents earliest engineering projection of a manned geosynchronously orbiting space station. Presents separate "living wheel" (*wohnrad*), solar ray collector for power, and telescope observatory elements joined by electrical and umbilical cables. Expands the 1923 suggestion of space stations by Hermann Oberth in his *Die Rakete zu den Planetenräumen*. Starts with an elementary lecture on space and rocket physics.

Oberth, Hermann. *Die Rakete zu den Planetenraumen*. (Rockets into orbit) Nuremberg: Reproduktionsdruck von Uni-Verlag, 1960. Pp. 92. Illustr.

Cited herein as item 1309.

1207. Ordway, Frederick I. III. "The History, Evolution, and Benefits of the Space Station." *Proceedings of the USSR Academy of Sciences*, 17, no. 1 (1972): 90–111.

Traces history of space stations from fictional "Brick Moon" of Edward Everett Hale, 1869–1870, through Hermann Oberth's

1923 suggestion of a bona fide space station, to concepts of the 1970s.

1208.   Ordway, Frederick I. III. "Evolution of Space Fiction in Film." *Earth-Oriented Applications of Space Technology* 3 (March/April 1983): 249–253.

Traces history of the popularization of the concept of spaceflight in film, from Georges Melies' 1902 *Voyages dans la Lune* to the *Star Wars* series of the late 1970s. Emphasizes the film *2001: A Space Odyssey*, of 1968, for which the author was a technical consultant.

1209.   Parkinson, Bob and R. Smith. *High Road to the Moon from Imagination to Reality.* London: British Interplanetary Society, 1979. Pp. 120. Illustr.

Compiles 52 space paintings by R.A. Smith, executed between 1945 and 1955, depicting concepts of all phases of spaceflight, with lengthy articles describing the developments in reality. Includes photos and artwork that are contrasted with the earlier concepts of Smith, who was a long-time member of the British Interplanetary Society.

1210.   Perkins, Adrian. "The 1950's—A Pivotal Decade." *Spaceflight* 24 (July/August 1983): 321–325.

Analyzes public awareness of space science fiction and spaceflight speculation during the 1950s. Discusses, for example, the importance of the Hayden Planetarium spaceflight symposia from 1951 that led to the influential Collier's magazine series by Wernher von Braun and others, and the Walt Disney television series on spaceflight.

1211.   Pizor, Faith K. *The Man in the Moone and Other Lunar Fantasies.* New York: Praeger, 1971. Pp. 230. Illustr.

Excerpts from 17th- and 19th-century literary works on interplanetary flight, with emphasis on lunar voyages. Also includes selections from Richard Adams Locke's 1835 pamphlet on the celebrated "Moon Hoax," which reported the discovery of a civilization on the Moon by astronomer Sir John Herschel. Also discusses an 1841 concept of a reaction-propelled (steam) flying machine, which is actually a parody of absurd ideas proposed to enable men to fly.

1212. Ryan, C., W. von Braun, F.L. Whipple, and W. Ley, eds., *Conquest of the Moon.* New York: Viking, 1953. Pp. 126.

Expands the "Man on the Moon" symposium published in *Collier's* magazine, October 18, 1952. Contains chapters by Wernher von Braun, Willy Ley, and Fred L. Whipple on space stations, lunar expeditions, lunar exploration, and lunar bases. Illustrated by Chesley Bonestell, and others.

1213. Ryan, Cornelius, J. Kaplan, C. Bonestell, et al. *Across the Space Frontier.* New York: Viking, 1952. Pp. 147. Illustr.

Offers early popular discussion of spaceflight, artificial satellite, space station and space medicine projections by some of the leading authorities in these fields. Contributions by Wernher von Braun, Willy Ley, Fred L. Whipple, Heinz Haber, Joseph Kaplan, and Oscar Schachter, with color illustrations by Chesley Bonestell. Expands *Collier's* "Man Will Conquer Space Soon" Symposium held on March 22, 1952.

1214. Shternfeld, Arno A. *Interplanetary Travel.* Moscow: Foreign Languages, 1958. Pp. 126. Illustr.

Popularizes, from the Soviet point of view, the history of spaceflight concepts up to the realization of first Sputnik artificial satellites.

Simpson, Theodore R., M. Smith, et al., eds. *The Space Station: An Idea Whose Time Has Come.* New York: Institute of Electrical and Electronic Engineers, 1984. Pp. 295. Index, Illustr.

Cited herein as item 1620.

1215. Stapledon, Olaf. "Interplanetary Man." *Journal of the British Interplanetary Society* 7 (November 1948): 213–233.

Philosophy of man's role in and motivation for space flight, by a well-known British science fiction writer. This is one of the earliest articles on this topic and a milestone in the history of the British Interplanetary Society.

1216. Tsiolkovsky, Konstantin E. "Beyond the Atmosphere: A 1923 Essay." *Spaceflight* 9 (January 1967): 9–11.

Enumerates the advantages to mankind of establishing a space colony utilizing solar energy. Despite the title, the introductory remarks by Kenneth W. Gatland state that this essay was originally written in March 1932, and not 1923.

1217. Tsiolkovsky, Konstantin E., and K. Syers, trans. *Beyond the Planet Earth*. New York: Pergamon, 1960. Pp. 190. Illustr.

Translates the author's 1920 fictional account of a large internationally manned space station in which undiluted sunlight is harnessed to provide energy for the station's factory and for the growth of plants for its food supply.

1218. Tsiolkovsky, Konstantin E. *Call of the Cosmos*. Edited by V. Dutt. Moscow: Foreign Languages, 1960. Pp. 471. Illustr.

Collects the interplanetary science fiction of Russian astronautical pioneer Konstantin E. Tsiolkovskii, who attempted to popularize his theories of spaceflight. Includes an essay by B.N. Vorbyov on the science fiction in Tsiolkovskii's writings, two brief essays by Tsiolkovskii, and seven drawings of his spaceship concepts, reproduced photographically.

U.S. Congress. Office of Technology Assessment. *Civilian Space Stations and the U.S. Future in Space*. OTA–STI–241. Washington, D.C.: U.S. Government Printing Office, 1984. Pp. 234. Index, Illustr.

Cited herein as item 1624.

Walters, Helen B. *Hermann Oberth: Father of Space Travel*. New York: Macmillan, 1962. Pp. 169. Bibliog., Illustr.

Cited herein as item 1256.

1219. Winter, Frank H. "Observatories in Space, 1920's Style." *The Griffith Observer* 46 (June 1982): 2–8.

Narrates the history of the earliest space station concepts, including those of Hermann Oberth and Hermann Noondung.

Treats Noondung's 1928 proposal at length, with original illustrations from Noordung's *Das Problem der Befarhrung des Weltraums* (The problem of space travel).

1220. Winter, Frank H. "The Strange Case of Madame Guzman and the Mars Mystique." *The Griffith Observer* 48 (February 1984): 2–15.

Narrates the history of the world's earliest astronautical prize, the Guzman Award, founded in 1893. It was ultimately won by the *Apollo 11* astronauts. Includes some background material on the Mars canal controversy.

1221. Winterberg, F. "Hermann Ganswindt und seine Gendanken zur Weltraumfahrt im Jahre 1891" (Hermann Ganswindt and his thoughts on space travel in the year 1891). *Astronautik* 1 (1973): 127–140. Illustr.

Analyzes the reaction–propelled 1891 spacecraft concepts of German spaceflight pioneer Hermann Ganswindt. Includes biographical sketch of Ganswindt and coverage of his aircraft and other inventions. Contains some mathematical computations on the probable performance of Ganswindt's spacecraft.

1222. Wright, Hamilton, H. Wright, and S. Rappaport, eds. *To the Moon!* New York: Meredith, 1968. Pp. 300. Illustr.

An anthology of moon legends, moon poetry, fictional accounts of lunar voyages, popular scientific lunar observations, and modern essays on lunar exploration. The last section includes Iurii Gagarin's account of his Earth–orbiting flight in the *Vostok* spacecraft in 1961; the Jet Propulsion Lab's report on the flight of the Ranger VII unmanned lunar probe, a description of the first U.S. "soft" landing on the Moon by Surveyor 1, and articles on future lunar colonies and the motivations for manned lunar exploration.

A Proof Test Capsule of the Viking Lander on display on simulated Martian terrain in the Milestones of Flight Gallery at the National Air and Space Museum. This capsule was assembled from flight type hardware and was refurbished by Martin Marietta Corporation before donation to the National Air and Space Museum. Two indentical spacecraft, Viking 1 and Viking 2 were launched from the Kennedy Space Center on 20 August and 9 September 1975 and landed on Mars on 20 July and 3 September 1976. The Viking 1 lander is NASM's only space artifact on another planet. (Dale Hrabak, Smithsonian Institution)

ROCKETS, LAUNCH VEHICLES, AND MISSILES

Researching the history of the development of rocketry presents problems because much of the material is not readily available or is of poor quality. One general rule applied in selecting items for this section was that if a book or article was not available at the Library of Congress, NASA History Office or Library, or the National Air and Space Museum Library, it was not included. As a result, some of the favorite references have been omitted because they are too hard to find. For those interested in undertaking further and more detailed research, the following journals should also be consulted: the journals of the German Rocket Society, the American Rocket Society, and the earliest journal numbers of the British Interplanetary Society. The same applies to the many International Astronautical Federation (IAF) and other memoir papers, many of which have not been published as yet but may be available as preprints.

Another criterion for selection was that the work should stress the historical side of a given subject or, if technical, the work's historical importance should be unrivaled (for example, the reprints of Goddard's 1919 and 1936 papers, or Oberth's 1923 *Die Rakete* fall in this category.

The search here was much the same as for the other sections. First searched were the NASM Library, the Library of Congress, and NASA's Library. Bibliographies in works such as Willy Ley's *Rockets, Missiles, and Men into Space* and Ordway's *Annotated Bibliography of Space Science and Technology* were indispensable. The annual Air University bibliographies, too, were useful. The annual indexes of *Spaceflight* and the *Journal of the British Interplanetary Society* yielded valuable articles in the form of historical retrospectives on every phase of spaceflight. In particular, the "Personal Profiles," written by the pioneers, contain firsthand details and perspectives found nowhere else.

Good references were also difficult to find for the biographical section. There are few in-depth biographies of rocketry and spaceflight pioneers. Many biographies of astronauts and cosmonauts, particularly from the Soviet Union, are shamelessly propagandistic. On the other hand, the Soviets have surpassed the West in producing biographies of several of their "rocket technologists," such as Iangel and Isaev. Overall, the most worthy Western collected biography is

Shirley Thomas's *Men of Space. Who's Who in Space* and a *Who's Who in Aerospace* also provide information that is not available elsewhere, although the information is often very dated.

Frank H. Winter

Biographies and Memoir Materials

> Atashenkov, Petr T. *Akademik S.P. Korolev* (Academician S. P. Korolev). Moscow: Mashinostroenie, 1969. Pp. 208. Bibliog., Illustr.
>
> Cited herein as item 1677.

1223. Barth, Hans. *Hermann Oberth Leben–Werk–Wirkung* (Hermann Oberth life–work–impact). Feucht: Uni–Verlag, 1985. Pp. 415. Bibliog., Illustr.

> German–language narration of the life and works of Rumanian–born German spaceflight pioneer, Hermann Oberth. Chronological milestones in his life, honors, patents, biographies, and lengthy notes on the text are included.

1224. Barth, Hans, ed. *Hermann Oberth Briefwechsel* (Hermann Oberth's correspondence). Bucharest: Kriterion Verlag, 1979. Pp. 295. Index, Illustr.

> Compilation of selected letters of Hermann Oberth, recognized dean of astronautical pioneers. Letters are arranged chronologically from 1922 to 1954. Includes both subject and name indexes, notes on some of the letters, and translations of selected "foreign" letters (i.e. non–German).

1225. Beckman, Col. Henry J.H., W. Congreve, and J. Jocelyn. "The Connection of the Ordnance Department with National and Royal Tire–Works." *Journal of the Royal Artillery* 32 (February 1906): 481–503.

> A comprehensive biographical study of Sir William Congreve, 19th–century British rocket pioneer, with footnotes.

1226. Bergaust, Eric. *Wernher von Braun*. Washington, D.C.: National Space Institute, 1976. Pp. 589. Index, Illustr.

> Authorized biography of Wernher von Braun, the German rocket pioneer and long–time spaceflight advocate, by a close personal friend and well–known spaceflight journalist. Published one year before von Braun's death.

1227. Braun, Wernher von, "Dr. Wernher von Braun: An Historical Essay." *Spaceflight* 14 (November 1972): 409–412.

Reprints an article originally titled "Survey of Development of Liquid Rockets in Germany and Their Future Prospects," written by von Braun in June 1945. Summarizes the German Army's rocket program from 1932 to 1945, with speculations on uses of an improved V-2 (A9—A10 combination) as a precursor launch vehicle for orbiting a space station for Earth and astronautical observations, as well as weather control. Also suggests a space shuttle.

1228. Bush, G.F. "Princeton's Rocket Pioneer." *Princeton Engineer* 28 (December 1968): 9, 12–13, 22–23, 25; 29 (January 1969): 14, 18, 20, 22.

Relates the life of the American pioneer James H. Wyld and how he developed the regeneratively cooled rocket engine in 1938–1941, prompting him and three other members of the American Rocket Society to form Reaction Motors, Inc., a pioneering American rocket company. Refers to original source material.

1229. Clarke, Arthur C., W. Neat, A. Bond, et al. "Arthur Valentine Cleaver, OBE, an Appreciation." *Spaceflight* 20 (January 1978): 19–20.

Biography of A.V. Cleaver, Britain's most prominent rocket engineer, who was chief engineer for rocket propulsion of Aero Engine Division of Rolls Royce Ltd., which designed the Black Arrow and Blue Streak missiles, and Sprite jet–assisted takeoff unit. Cleaver is the most prolific, albeit unsuccessful, spokesman for England's role in space exploration.

1230. Codd, Lee A. "Pioneers in Rocketry, II (Col. Leslie A. Skinner)." *Ordnance* 43 (January/February 1959): 586–588.

Sketches the life of Col. Leslie A. Skinner, American rocket pioneer and developer of the Bazooka antitank rocket weapon of World War II.

1231. Essers, Ilse. *Max Valier—A Pioneer of Space Travel.* NASA TTF–664. Washington, D.C.: National Aeronautics and Space Administration, 1976. Pp. 263. Index, Illustr.

The life and accomplishments of Austrian rocketry and spaceflight pioneer Max Valier, who undertook solid- and liquid-propellant rocket experiments from the late 1920s until his death in 1930. Valier also lectured and wrote extensively on the possibilities of spaceflight.

1232. Essers, Ilse. *Hermann Ganswindt: Vorkämpfer d. Raumfahrt mit seiner Weltenfahrzeug seit 1881* (Hermann Ganswindt: Pioneer of spaceflight with his world vehicle from 1881). Düsseldorf: VDI-Verlag, 1977. Pp. 210. Index, Illustr.

Documents the life and accomplishments of German aviation and astronautics pioneer Hermann Ganswindt, designer and promoter of a reaction-propelled spacecraft in the 1890s.

1233. Gartmann, Heinz. *Men Behind the Space Rockets*. New York: D. McKay, 1956. Pp. 185. Index, Illustr.

Presents brief biographies of various individuals who played important roles in the development of the science and technology of rockets. Devotes one chapter to each of the following: Ganswindt, Tsiolkovskii, Goddard, Oberth, Valier, Sänger, Zborowski, and von Braun. Includes a table of contents, lists of illustrations, and a name index.

1234. Goddard, Esther C., and G.E. Pendray, eds. *The Papers of Robert H. Goddard*. New York: McGraw-Hill, 1970. Pp. 1707. Index, Illustr.

Selected diary entries, notes, letters, reports, and articles of American rocket pioneer Robert H. Goddard. Contains a reprint of Goddard's classic 1919 Smithsonian report, "A Method of Reaching Extreme Altitudes." Useful chronology of Goddard's important rocket tests, patents, and awards listed in the appendixes. In three volumes.

1235. Golovanov, Yareslav K. *Sergei Korolev: The Apprenticeship of a Space Pioneer*. Moscow: Mir, 1975. Pp. 295. Illustr.

Narrates the prewar phase of the career of Soviet rocket pioneer Sergei P. Korolev. Stresses Korolev's role as a leading member of the Group for the Study of Reactive Motion (Gruppa po izucheniiu reativnogo dvizheniia, GIRD) during the early 1930s. Based on interviews with GIRD members and

Korolev family members and friends. Korolev later became
the USSR's leading rocket scientist and administrator. He was
responsible for designing the first Sputnik launch vehicles.

1236. Gröttrup, Irmgard, and S. Hughes, trans. *Rocket Wife*. London:
A. Deutsche, 1959. Pp. 188. Illustr.

A rare view of postwar Soviet rocketry activities. The
author's husband was Helmut Gröttrup, the leading German
V–2 rocket scientist who joined the Soviets after Germany's
defeat. Gröttrup, along with other V–2 technicians, was sent
to the USSR to teach the Soviets about large–scale liquid–fuel
rocket technology.

Gubarev, V. *Konstruktor—neskol'ko stranits iz zhizni Mikhaila
Kuz'micha Iangelia* (Designer—a few pages from the life of
Mikhail Kuz'mich Iangel). Moscow: Izdatel'stvo politichesko
literaturi, 1977. Pp. 109. Illustr.

Cited herein as item 1733.

1237. Hartl, Hans. *Hermann Oberth Vorkämpfer der Weltraumfahrt*
(Hermann Oberth, pioneer of spaceflight). Hanover: Theodor
Oppermann Verlag, 1958. Pp. 239. Bibliog., Illustr.

The life of Hermann Oberth, one of the foremost pioneers of
spaceflight, whose books established some of the foundations
of modern spaceflight technology.

1238. Huzel, Deiter K. *From Peenemünde to Canaveral*. Englewood
Cliffs, N.J.: Prentice-Hall, 1962. Pp. 247. Illustr.

Memoirs of the author's career from a test engineer and
later manager of the V–2 rocket static firing and launch
complex at German rocket facility of Peenemünde during
World War II to development engineer of the Redstone missile
and its first launching at Cape Canaveral in 1953. It is essentially the story of Peenemünde and Operation Paperclip.
Appendixes include chronology of rocketry in Germany
1923–1945 and notes on the "A" series of German rockets and
Peenemünde test facilities.

1239. Ingenhaag, Karl–Heinz. "Walter Hohmann Leben und Werk des Raumfahrt—Theoretikers" (Walter Hohmann's life and work on flight theories). *Luftfarht International*, 7 (1980): 296– 299.

The life of German spaceflight pioneer, Walter Hohmann, known for his early theoretical study *Die Erreichbarkeit der Himmelskörper*, published in 1925, and for formulating the Hohmann ellipse flight path for interplanetary travel.

1240. Jacques, Robert. "From V–2 to Saturn V (The Story of Dr. Eberhard Rees)." *American Aviation Historical Society Journal* 1 (Spring 1984); 42–43.

Traces the career of Dr. Eberhard Rees from the head of manufacturing prototype V–2 rockets at Peenemünde Rocket Center during World War II to the director of the Marshall Space Flight Center. He was one of the original von Braun team.

1241. Kármán, Theodore von, and L. Edson. *Wind and Beyond: Theodore von Kármán, Pioneer in Aviation and Pathfinder in Space.* Boston: Little, Brown, 1967. Pp. 376. Index, Illustr.

Provides a candid portrait of the famous aerodynamicist, astronautical pioneer, and administrator. He is known for the vortex theory of drag, supersonic drag, and for directing the development of the Air Force's jet–assisted takeoff. He also assisted in the founding of the Jet Propulsion Lab and Aero– jet–General Corp. The bibliography of von Kármán's works is arranged chronologically, and includes a chronological list of his honorary degrees, titles, decorations, orders, and awards.

1242. Khramov, A.V. *Konstantin Ivanovich Konstantinov.* Moscow: Gosenergoizdat, 1951. Pp. 113. Bibliog., Illustr.

Details the life and career of 19th–century Russian rocket pioneer Konstantin Ivanovich Konstantinov, who attempted to create a science of rocket technology. He designed and con- structed an electric ballistic rocket pendulum in 1849, with which he arrived at fundamental equations of rocket dynamics. As head of the Russian war rocket establishment from 1849 to 1870, he designed some of the most advanced rockets in the 19th century and was a prolific writer on rocketry, artillery, and electricity.

1243. Kosmodemianskii, Arkadii A. *K.E. Tsiolkovsky.* Moscow: Voennoe Izdatel'stvo, 1960. Pp. 186. Illustr.

Narrates the life of Konstantin E. Tsiolkovskii, Russian astronautics pioneer, called "the father of cosmonautics," because of his fundamental theoretical studies of spaceflight undertaken from 1883 up to his death in 1935. It does not, however, analyze his true impact on the development of spaceflight, nor on the spaceflight movement in the West during the 1920s and 1930s. [In English]

1244. Lehman, Milton. *This High Man: The Life of Robert H. Goddard.* New York: Farrar, Straus, 1963. Pp. 430. Index, Illustr.

The authorized biography of American rocket pioneer Robert H. Goddard. Goddard's impact on contemporary and subsequent rocket technology is addressed, although overstated. Perpetuates the myth of Goddard as "father of modern rocketry," without full consideration of independent German and other developments. However, it is an invaluable and readable account of the life of Goddard. Primary documents and interviews are employed.

1245. Malina, Frank J. "Theodor von Kármán and the Development of Long Duration Composite Solid Propellant Rocket Engines." *Journal of the British Interplanetary Society* 35 (December 1982): 550–551.

A brief but important memoir on the author's and Theodor von Kármán's role in computing long–duration solid propellant rocket formulas. The author contends they were the origin of modern large–scale, solid–fuel rockets, such as the boosters used on the space shuttle.

1246. Nebel, Rudolf. *Die Narren von Tegel: ein Pionier der Raumfahrt Erzählt* (The fools of Tegel: The story of a space pioneer). Düsseldorf: Droste Verlag, 1972. Pp. 180. Index, Illustr.

Reminisces about the author's 1928–1929 collaboration with spaceflight pioneer Hermann Oberth and his subsequent role in the Verein für Raumschiffahrt (German Rocket Society) from 1930 to 1934. However, Nebel's perspective is that of an administrator, and not of a technologist.

1247. Neufeld, Jacob. "Col. George V. Holloman: Missile Pioneer." *Aerospace Historian* 27 (June 1980): 101–102.

A brief biography of Col. George V. Holloman, who directed several U.S. guided missile projects during and following World War II, including the Razon and Tarzon projects.

1248. Oberth, Hermann. "From My Life." *Astronautics* 4 (June 1959): 38–39, 100, 102–104, 106.

A brief autobiography by Oberth, with emphasis on childhood years when he first became interested in rocketry and space travel. He credits a reading of Verne's *From Earth to the Moon* as the spark that led him to become a space scientist.

1249. Ordway, Frederick I. III, and M. Sharpe. *The Rocket Team.* New York: Thomas Y. Crowell, 1979. Pp. xvii + 462. Index, Bibliog., Illustr.

Draws on personal reminiscences and letters to tell the story of German rocketry development from the very early years through the death of Wernher von Braun in 1977. A particularly useful starting point for the study of the history of rocketry. Although extensive quotations are provided, there are no direct citations made to the bibliography that is provided. Initially focuses closely on the Peenemünde years and the development of the A–4 (V–2); also reviews the fate of German rocket scientists who went to the United States and the Soviet Union. The bibliography provides an extensive list of relevant documents and interviews that were conducted by the authors.

1250. Päch, Susanne. "Rolf Engel—Fifty Years of Activity in Rocketry and Space Flight." *Spaceflight* 22 (June 1980): 231–236.

Recounts the accomplishments of German rocket pioneer Rolf Engel, who began his career of more than 50 years as a junior member of the German Rocket Society (Verein für Raumschiffahrt, VfR) in 1929 and as assistant to rocket pioneer Johannes Winkler. Engel subsequently directed some solid–propellant rocket developments for the German military during World War II. Following the war he contributed toward both solid and liquid fuel technology for the French Office

National d'Etudes et Recherches Aéronautique, the German Messerschmit–Boëlkow firm, and other organizations.

1251. Romanov, Aleksandr P. *Raketam pokoriaetsia prostranstvo* (Space succumbs to rockets). Moscow: Izdatel'stvo politicheskoi literatury, 1976. Pp. 111. Illustr.

The life of Valentin Glushko, one of the Soviet Union's leading rocket pioneers whose career spanned more than 50 years, from his first space writings in the late 1920s and experimentation in the 1930s, to launch vehicles up to his death in 1982. He was considered, after Sergei Korolev, his long–time coworker, to be the second most prominent Soviet rocketeer.

1252. Ruland, Bernd. "The Kurt Debus Story (3 parts)." *Bunte Illustrierte* (Offenburg), 5 May, 52–60, and 109–111; 26 May 1970, 56–64. Illustr.

Relates the life story of Kurt Debus, one of the leading rocket scientists at Peenemünde during World War II. Debus came with Wernher von Braun to the United States and from 1962 to 1974 he was director of the Kennedy Space Center, and he also directed the launch of America's first satellite, *Explorer 1* on January 31, 1958. Interview between Debus and von Braun is presented.

1253. Strandh, Sigvard. "Wilhelm Teodore Unge: A Swedish Pioneer in Rocketry." *Daedalus* (1984): 88–108.

Recounts the technical accomplishments of late 19th–century Swedish rocket pioneer Wilhelm Teodore Unge who may have developed the world's first ballistite (double–base) smokeless rocket propellant and use of finless, spin–stabilized rockets for life–saving and for military purposes.

1254. Subotowicz, M., and N. Orng, trans. "Kazimeriercz Siemieno-wicz, Polish Rocket Pioneer." *Spaceflight* 2 (April 1959): 15–17.

Sketches the life and contributions of Siemienowicz, variously cited as a Polish or Lithuanian rocket pioneer of the 17th century, who has been acclaimed for his detailed descriptions of the manufacture of rockets (1650), and for his then-advanced designs of finned (winged) and multiple–step rockets. Plates from his widely published and translated *Ars Artillerie Magnae* (Great art of artillery) are included.

1255. Tsander, F.A. *From a Scientific Heritage.* NASA TTF–541. Moscow: Nauka, 1967. Pp. 92. Bibliog., Illustr.

Compiles lecture transcripts, reports, work plans, manuscripts, and selected correspondence of Soviet rocket and spaceflight theorist Tsander, from 1923 to 1931. Includes bibliography of Tsander's printed works. Material compiled by Asta F. Tsander, his daughter.

Wachtel, C. "The Chief Designers of the Soviet Space Programme." *Journal of the British Interplanetary Society* 38 (1985): 561–563.

Cited herein as item 1701.

1256. Walters, Helen B. *Hermann Oberth: Father of Space Travel.* New York: Macmillan, 1962. Pp. 169. Bibliog., Illustr.

Popularizes the life of Hermann Oberth. Includes a glossary and synoptic calendar of milestones in Oberth's life. To date, it is the only English–language biography of Oberth.

1257. Winter, Frank H. "Sir William Congreve: A Bi–Centennial Memorial." *Spaceflight* 14 (September 1972): 333–334.

Commemorates the 200th anniversary of the birth of British 19th–century rocket pioneer, Sir William Congreve, who introduced the world's first rocket weapons system and who instituted several technological improvements, such as mass production of rockets.

1258. Winter, Frank H. "William Hale—A Forgotten British Rocket Pioneer." *Spaceflight* 15 (January 1973): 31–33.

Presents biographical details on British 19th–century rocket pioneer William Hale, who invented the first successful stickless, spin–stabilized gunpowder war rockets, which superseded the Congreve rocket and were extensively used by England up to the turn of the century. Hale's rockets were also used by several other nations. Summarizes the technological evolution of Hale's concepts.

1259. Winter, Frank H. "Nikolai Alexseyevich Rynin (1877–1942), Soviet Astronautical Pioneer: An American Appreciation." *Earth–Oriented Applications of Space Technology* 2 (1982): 69–80.

Details the life and accomplishments of Soviet aeronautical and astronautical pioneer Nikolai Alexseyevich Rynin, best known for producing the world's first spaceflight encyclopedia, *Mezhplanetnie soobshcheniia* (Interplanetary communications), 9 vols., 1928–1932. It also treats Rynin's aeronautical career, dating from 1910, when Rynin was a balloonist, prolific writer on worldwide aviation, and a professor of aeronautics. He was also an organizer of an early Soviet astronautics group in the 1930s.

Winterberg, F. "Hermann Ganswindt und seine Gendanken zur Weltraumfahrt im Jahre 1891 (Hermann Ganswindt and his thoughts on spaceflight in the year 1891)." *Astronautik* 1 (1973): 127–140.

Cited herein as item 1221.

1260. Witze, Claude. "Walter Dornberger—Space Pioneer and Visionary." *Air Force Magazine*, October 1965, 80–88.

Summarizes career of Walter R. Dornberger, commander of the German prewar and World War II Peenemünde rocket center and who afterwards came to the United States and became a vice–president for Bell Aerosystems Co. Dornberger was an outstanding spokesman for the early U.S. space program and had designed several shuttle–type vehicles.

Hardware and Program Development

1261. Aldrich, David E., and D. Sanchini. "F–1 Engine Development." *Astronautics* 6 (March 1961): 24–25, 46, 48.

Provides some historical background on the development of the U.S.'s most powerful single–chamber 1,500,000 lb.–thrust liquid–propellant rocket, the F–1, which powered the Saturn

V–Project Apollo launch vehicle. Authored by the manager and chief engineer and the assistant engineer of the F–1 program, respectively.

1262. Anonymous. "Rocketry at Ansty (1946–1967)." *Spaceflight* 9 (September 1967): 311–313.

Reviews rocketry developments at Ansty, near Coventry, England, from 1946 to 1967. Describes work on liquid–fuel rocket engines for primary propulsion and assisted takeoff for aircraft, guided missiles, reentry research vehicles, and small satellite launch vehicles. The engines include the Snarler, Sprite, Spectre series, Stentor, Blue Steel, and Black Arrow powerplants.

1263. Baker, David. *The Rocket: The History and Development of Rocket and Missile Technology.* London: New Cavendish Books, 1978. Pp. 276. Index, Bibliog., Illustr.

Traces the evolution of rocket technology, stressing mid–20th century launch vehicles and missile rocket engine developments. Research is based on secondary sources almost exclusively.

1264. Benecke, T., and A. Quick, eds. *History of German Guided Missiles Development.* Brunswick, Germany: Verlag E. Appelhaus, 1957. Pp. 420. Illustr.

Proceedings of the First Guided Missile Seminar held by the Advisory Group for Aerospace Research and Development in Munich, April 1956. Includes 26 separate papers covering most aspects of German missile activities during and immediately before World War II. Emphasizes powerplant and guidance systems and contains technical drawings and schematic diagrams.

1265. Bilstein, Roger E. "From the S–IV to the S–IVB: The Evolution of a Rocket Stage for Space Exploration." *Journal of the British Interplanetary Society* 32, no. 12 (December 1979): 452–458.

Details the development of the S–IV liquid–oxygen, liquid–hydrogen, high–energy upper stages of the Saturn launch vehicle. Includes both policy and engineering decisions. Men–

tions influence of RL–10 and J–2 rocket engines in S–IV design. This paper won the 1977 Robert H. Goddard Historical Essay Award in the annual competition sponsored by the National Space Club, Washington, D.C.

1266. Bilstein, Roger E. *Stages to Saturn: A Technological History of the Apollo/Saturn Launch Vehicles.* NASA SP–4206. Washington, D.C.: National Aeronautics and Space Administration, 1980. Pp. xx + 511. Index, Illustr.

Official NASA account of the history of the Project Apollo and Skylab launch vehicle, the Saturn rocket. Continues the NASA history series on the U.S.–manned space program, which began with Project Mercury. Extensive appendixes include schematic diagrams of Saturn V, development costs, launch sequences, tabulated Saturn flight history, Saturn V contractors, NASA Apollo–era organizational charts, manpower statistics, and extensive notes.

1267. Blagonravov, A.A. *Soviet Rocketry, Some Contributions to Its History.* NASA TTF–343. Jerusalem: Israeli Program for Scientific Translations, 1966. Pp. iii + 204. Bibliog., Illustr.

Nine essays on the history of Soviet rocketry from the second half of the 19th century to the 1930s, with emphasis on the achievements of the pioneers K.E. Tsiolkovskii, F.A. Tsander, and Iu.V. Kondratiuk. Includes memoir paper by the pioneer I.A. Merkulov, a useful bibliography of printed and manuscript works of Tsiolkovskii, and an explanatory list of Russian aerospace acronyms.

1268. Bramscher, Robert G. "A Survey of Launch Vehicle Failures." *Spaceflight* 22 (November/December 1980): 351–358.

Expendable launch vehicle failures of the United States, United Kingdom, the former European Launcher Development Organization, and Japan from 1957 to 1979 are surveyed with an analysis of trends. Tables of Early Launch Vehicle Failures (Vanguard, Juno, Thor–Able, Atlas Able, and Scout vehicles), 1957–1975; Thor Boosted Vehicles, 1960–1966; Atlas and Titan Boosted Vehicles, 1960–1974; and Third Power Launch Vehicles, 1968–1970, are surveyed.

1269. Braun, Wernher von, "The Redstone, Jupiter, and Juno." *Technology and Culture* 4, no. 4 (Fall 1963): 452–465.

Recounts the history of the Redstone missile and its variants, Jupiter and Juno. The author played the leading role in directing the development of these projects and the most significant application of the Jupiter–C rocket (also called Juno–1), as the launch vehicle for America's first satellite, *Explorer 1*. Includes useful list of Redstone milestones.

1270. Braun, Wernher von, and F. Ordway. *History of Rocketry and Space Travel*. New York: Thomas Y. Crowell, 1966. Pp. 244. Index, Bibliog., Illustr.

Treats the broad history of rocketry and spaceflight from the earliest Chinese rockets and first speculative history on spaceflight up to the initiation of Project Apollo. A useful source book.

1271. Braun, Wernher von, and F. Ordway. *The Rockets' Red Glare*. Garden City, N.Y.: Anchor, 1970. Pp. 212. Index, Illustr.

Treats the history of rocketry with emphasis on pre-Congreve pyrotechnics and Congreve–Hale era rockets up to World War II. Final chapter deals with space–age developments. Contains a useful chronology on earliest developments.

1272. Clark, John D. *Ignition! An Informal History of Liquid Rocket Propellants*. New Brunswick, N.J.: Rutgers University Press, 1972. Pp. 214. Index, Illustr.

Popularizes the history of liquid fuel rocket propellants by a technician associated with rocketry from 1949 to 1970. Contains anecdotes and technical descriptions, some with chemical formulas, explaining why certain propellants or propellant systems were chosen, and the difficulties involved.

1273. Clark, Philip S. "The Proton Launch Vehicle." *Spaceflight* 19 (September 1977): 330–333, 340.

Analyzes probable configurations and development of the Soviet Union's heavy Proton launch vehicle, used since 1965 to orbit Proton, Saliut, Luna, Zond, Mars, Raduga, Venera, and some Kosmos spacecraft. Uses literature open to the public

and formulas to arrive at performance, mass, and other estimates. Includes tables of characteristics and performances of
different Proton configurations.

1274. Clark, Philip S. "The Skean Programme." *Spaceflight* 20 (August 1978): 298–304.

Analyzes history and development of the Soviet Skean (SS–5)
intermediate–range launch vehicle, which orbited Kosmos,
Interkosmos, and some non–Soviet satellites, namely, India's
Aryabhata and France's *Signe* satellite. It is one of the most
used launch vehicles in the world. Five tables of Skean characteristics and payloads are included.

1275. Clark, Philip S. "The Sapwood Launch Vehicle." *Journal of the
British Interplanetary Society* 34 (1981): 437–443.

Analyzes the history and development of the Soviet Union's
Sapwood (SS–6) launch vehicle used to orbit *Sputnik 1* to *3*,
Luna 1 to *3*, *Vostok, Voskhod, Meteor, Soiuz, Venera, Molniia,
Prognoz,* and *Mars* spacecraft. Includes tables.

1276. Clark, Philip S. "The Sapwood Launch Vehicle—Revisited."
Journal of the British Interplanetary Society 35 (1982):
79–81.

Continues the review of Soviet Sapwood (SS–6) launch
vehicle from an earlier article, but presents new details based
upon later published Soviet sources. Includes a summary table
of Sapwood configurations and missions.

1277. Clark, Philip S. "Soviet Launch Vehicles: An Overview." *Journal of the British Interplanetary Society* 35, no. 2 (February
1982): 51–58.

Summarizes the history and development of five basic
Soviet launch vehicles, including the Sapwood (SS–6) family,
Sandal (SS–4), Skean (SS–5), Scarp (SS–9) family, and Proton
series, with less emphasis on the Sapwood. Includes five tables
of vehicle characteristics and reproductions of Soviet drawings
of some vehicles, including the rarely shown Sputnik 1
launcher.

Clark, Philip S. "The Chinese Space Programme." *Journal of the British Interplanetary Society* 37 (1984): 195–206.

Cited herein as item 1744.

1278. Cooksley, Peter G. *Flying Bomb: The Story of Hitler's V–Weapons of World War II.* New York: Charles Scribner's Sons, 1979. Pp. 208. Index, Bibliog., Illustr.

Narrates the tactical use against England of the German V–1 pulse–jet powered missile of World War II, with a brief account of the technical development of the weapon and its powerplant.

1279. Covault, Craig. "Chinese Rocket Test Center to Aid Large Engine Development." *Aviation Week and Space Technology,* 22 July 1985, 69–75.

Scrutinizes Chinese plans for the development of a Saturn 1 class launch vehicle at the rocket test center outside of Beijing. Comments on continued Chinese secrecy surrounding development and preflight testing.

Curtis, Hebert D. "Voyages to the Moon." *Publications of the Astronomical Society of the Pacific* 32 (1920): 145–150.

Cited herein as item 1194.

Curtis, S.A. "The Uses of the German V–2 in the U.S. for Upper Atmosphere Research." *Journal of the British Interplanetary Society* 32 (1979): 442–448.

Cited herein as item 1357.

1280. Dornberger, Walter R. *V–2.* New York: Viking, 1954. Pp. 281. Index, Illustr.

Reminiscences of the internal political–military history of V–2 rocket development and other German rocket projects from 1930 to 1945 by the commander of the German Army's Peenemünde rocket development center. A personal rather than technical account of the V–2, the world's first large–scale liquid–fuel rocket, with a useful appendix giving dimensions and performance of the rocket.

1281. Dornberger, Walter R., and G. Sutton. "European Rocketry after World War I." *Journal of the British Interplanetary Society* 13 (September 1954): 245–268.

Reviews German rocketry from 1927 to 1946, with emphasis on German Army developments at the rocket research centers of Kummersdorf and Peenemünde. Covers the V–2, JATOS, Wasserfall, X–4, Rheinbote, Me 163, Natter and other developments. Some production and development costs for the V–2 are provided, as well as some photos not published elsewhere.

1282. Duhem, Jules. *Histoire des origines du vol à réaction* (History of the origins of jet–powered flight). Paris: Novelles Editions Latines, 1959. Pp. 338. Index, Illustr.

French–language history of reactive flight, factual and fictional, from Greek legends to René Leduc's jet– and ramjet–powered aircraft of 1949. Offers extensive treatment of earliest concepts and experiments with rocket propulsion for manned flight as well as rocket–propelled watercraft. In some instances patents are employed as sources.

1283. Durant, Frederick C. III, and G. James, eds. *First Steps toward Space.* Smithsonian Annals of Flight, no. 10. Washington, D.C.: Smithsonian Institution Press, 1974. Pp. 307. Index, Illustr.

Twenty–seven papers presented at the First and Second History Symposia of the International Academy of Astronautics, Belgrade and New York, 1967 and 1968. Includes valuable memoirs by pioneers L. Crocco, L. Damblanc, D.J. Generales, Jr., S. Herrick, O. Lutz, F.J. Malina, H. Oberth, G.E. Pendray, A.I. Polyarny, H.E. Ross, I. Sänger–Bredt, R. Engel, E.A. Steinhoff, M.K. Tikhonravov, and R.C. Truax. Reprinted as American Astronautical Society History Series, vol. 6 (San Diego: Univelt, Inc., 1985).

1284. Emme, Eugene M., W. Bland, Jr., et al., eds. *The History of Rocket Technology: Essays on Research, Development and Utility.* Detroit: Wayne State University Press, 1964. Pp. 320. Index, Bibliog., Illustr.

Thirteen essays, some originally published in *Technology and Culture* 4 (Fall 1963), on the history of rocketry from the establishment of the American Rocket Society of the 1930s to

Project Mercury. Also contains histories of Jet Propulsion Laboratory, the first U.S. satellite proposals, launch vehicles and missiles, rocket airplanes, rocket belts, space telemetry, and early Soviet space developments. Extensive bibliographic notes are provided.

1285. Gantz, Kenneth F., ed. *Nuclear Flight: The United States Air Force Programs for Atomic Jets, Missiles, and Rockets.* New York: Duell, 1960. Pp. 216. Index, Illustr.

Twenty-two papers concerning the U.S. Air Force applications of nuclear energy for rocket and aircraft propulsion. Includes historical background.

1286. Gatland, Kenneth W. "Project Orion—America's Semi-Secret Project of the Fifties to Develop a Nuclear Pulse Rocket." *Spaceflight* 16 (December 1974): 454–455.

A brief history of the controversial American Project Orion nuclear pulse program from 1955 to 1963, with a useful Project Orion chronological summary digest.

1287. Glushko, Valentin P. *Rocket Engines GDL–OKB.* Moscow: Novosti Press, 1975. Pp. 75. Illustr.

Developmental history of rocket engines by the Soviet Union's Gas Dynamics Laboratory-Experimental Bureau (GDL–OKB) from 1929 to 1974, by the first head of GDL's section for the development of electric and liquid-propellant rocket engines. Includes useful chronology of GDL–OKB milestones, portraits of the organization's early leaders, and photos of GDL–OKB engines.

1288. Glushko, Valentin P. "Development of Rocketry and Space Technology in the USSR." *Space World* M–4–148 (April 1976): 4–32.

Summarizes the history of Soviet rocketry and spaceflight from the Russian Army and Navy's signal rocket-manufacturing plant of 1680 to the *Soiuz 11–Saliut 1* space station mission of 1971, and various satellites up to 1973. Highlights firsts, both in Soviet and non-Soviet space achievements. Includes brief coverage of international cooperative space ventures with the Soviet Union and names various Soviet space and rocketry museums.

1289. Goddard, Robert H. *Liquid–Propellant Rocket Development.* Washington, D.C.: Smithsonian Institution Press, 1936. Pp. 10. Illustr.

A report written late in 1935 to the Daniel and Florence Guggenheim Foundation by Robert H. Goddard concerning his liquid–fuel rocket experiments funded by the foundation and performed at Roswell, New Mexico, from July 1930 to July 1932 and September 1934 to September 1935. Published by another Goddard sponsor as Smithsonian Publication 3381. This first public mention of his successful March 16, 1926, liquid-fuel rocket flight was published on the 10th anniversary of that flight.

1290. Goddard, Robert H. *Rockets.* New York: American Rocket Society, 1946. Pp. 69 + 10. Illustr.

Exact facsimiles of Robert H. Goddard's two Smithsonian papers: "A Method of Reaching Extreme Altitudes" (1919, Smithsonian Publication 2540), and "Liquid–Propellant Rocket Development" (1936, Smithsonian Publication 3381). Contains a foreword by Goddard, dated May 1, 1945, an historical introductory note on liquid–propellant rocket development, and a biographic "Note and Appreciation" by G. Edward Pendray, written August 15, 1945, five days after Goddard's death.

1291. Goddard, Robert H. *Rocket Development: Liquid–Fuel Rocket Research, 1929–1941.* Edited by E. Goddard and G. Pendray. New York: Prentice–Hall, 1960. Pp. 222. Index, Illustr.

Condenses Robert H. Goddard's notes of his rocket experiments, from December 1929 to October 1941, sponsored largely by the Daniel and Florence Guggenheim Foundation. Includes a foreword by Harry F. Guggenheim, a reprint of a biographical article on Goddard by G. Edward Pendray, and an introduction by the editors.

Gray, Colin S. "The ABM and the Arms Race." *Aerospace Historian* 18 (December 1971): 26–32.

Cited herein as item 1154.

Green, Constance M., and M. Lomask. *Vanguard: A History* NASA SP–4202. Washington, D.C.: National Aeronautics and Space Administration, 1970. Pp. xvi + 257. Index, Illustr.

Cited herein as item 1117.

1292. Hagen, John P. "The Viking and the Vanguard." *Technology and Culture* 4 (Fall 1963): 435–451

Recounts the scientific and technological accomplishments of the Viking large–scale liquid–fuel sounding rocket and Project Vanguard, which used an upgraded Viking vehicle, authored by the director of Project Vanguard, the first U.S. scientific earth satellite program.

1293. Hall, R. Cargill, ed. *Essays on the History of Rocketry and Astronautics: Proceedings of the Third through Sixth History Symposium of the International Academy of Astronautics.* 2 vols. NASA CP–2014. Washington, D.C.: National Aeronautics and Space Administration, 1977. Pp. 238 + 474. Illustr.

Contains thirty–nine papers, arranged chronologically, covering the history of rocketry and spaceflight from the 16th century to 1958. Both volumes are in two parts: Volume 1 presents early solid–propellant rocketry, astronautical concepts, theories, and analyses after 1880; Volume 2 describes liquid– and solid–propellant rockets 1880–1945. Included are memoirs by rocket pioneers T.M. Mel'kumov, I. Sänger–Bredt, I.A. Merkulov, Iu.S. Shchetinkov, Iu.A. Pobedonostev, M.K. Tikhonravov, V.P. Zaytsev, and others.

1294. Holden, William G. *Saturn V: The Moon Rocket.* New York: Julian Messner, 1969. Pp. 190. Index, Illustr.

Popularizes the development of the Saturn V launch vehicle.

1295. Holmes, Jay. "Nuclear Rocketry: How are we doing?" *Missiles and Rockets* 6 (21 March 1960), 18–27.

Reports progress of U.S. nuclear rocket programs, (Rover, Orion, Kiwi), with brief background, and emphasis on financial and political problems.

1296. Irving, David. *The Mare's Nest*. London: William Kimber, 1964.
       Pp. 320. Index, Illustr.

       Describes the destruction of British and other cities by V–1
       and V–2 missiles of World War II, how British Intelligence
       learned details of these weapons, and the British efforts to
       counteract or destroy them.

1297. Kennedy, Gregory P. *Vengeance Weapon 2: The V–2 Guided
       Missile*. Washington, D.C.: Smithsonian Institution Press,
       1983. Pp. 87. Bibliog., Illustr.

       The technical history of the V–2 (A–4) rocket, the world's
       first large–scale, liquid–fuel rocket produced by the German
       Army prior to and during World War II. Includes production and
       missile statistical tables, as well as engineering drawings of
       V–2 components and support vehicles. Appendixes.

1298. Kharitonov, N. "The Legendary Katyusha." *Soviet Military
       Review* 4 (April 1975): 24–25.

       The history of the development and deployment of the
       Soviet Union's most famous rocket weapons of World War II,
       the solid–fuel barrage rocket, nicknamed by the Russians
       "Katiusha" (Little Kitty).

1299. Klee, Ernst, and O. Merk. *The Birth of the Missile: The Secrets
       of Peenemünde*. New York: Dutton, 1965. Pp. 126. Illustr.

       Reviews the technical development of the V–1, V–2, and
       other German missiles of World War II, mainly through illus-
       trations. Uses primary source material from the Deutsches
       Museum, Munich. The principal author was an archivist at that
       museum.

       Lapidus, Robert D. "Sputnik and its Repercussions: An His-
       torical Catalyst." *Aerospace* 17 (1970): 88–93.

       Cited herein as item 1164.

1300. Lasby, Clarence G. *Project Paperclip: German Scientists and
       the Cold War*. Reprint. New York: Atheneum, 1975. Pp. x +
       338.

Definitive review of the capture of German ordnance and material establishing German technical expertise at the end of World War II. Describes German rocketry and the transfer of rocketry efforts to the United States.

1301. Laukamann, Wolf. "Germany's V–1 and V–2." *Military Review* 48 (October 1968): 88–91.

Summarizes military history of the V–1 and V–2 weapons from 1942 to 1945, but offers no technical account of their development. Provides interesting information on the deployment of V–1s from He 111 bombers. Translated from an article appearing in *Soldat und Technik* in September 1964.

1302. Lay, Bierne. *Earthbound Astronautics: The Builders of Apollo–Saturn*. Englewood Cliffs, N.J.: Prentice–Hall, 1971. Pp. 198. Illustr.

Popularizes the complex history of the design, construction, and testing of the Saturn V launch vehicle with emphasis on the human side of this history. A tribute to administrators, engineers, aerodynamicists, machinists, electricians and other technicians involved in constructing the Saturn V. Includes list of NASA Distinguished Service Medal winners who contributed to the program.

Ley, Willy. *Rockets, Missiles, and Men in Space*. New York: Viking, 1968. Pp. xviii + 557. Index, Bibliog., Illustr.

Cited herein as item 1101.

1303. Lloyd, Christopher, and H. Craig, eds. "Congreve's Rockets, 1805–1806." In *The Naval Miscellany*. Vol. 4., 424–468 London: Navy Records Society, 1952. Index, Illustr.

Chronicles the earliest attempts by British rocket pioneer Congreve to promote the use of his rockets by the British Navy, culminating in their employment in the first Boulogne rocket attacks of 1805 and 1806. Uses original Congreve and Royal Navy correspondence arranged chronologically, with notes.

1304. McGovern, James. *Crossbow and Overcast*. New York: W. Morrow, 1964. Pp. 279. Index, Illustr.

> Narrates the stories of the World War II Operation Crossbow, from 1943 to 1945, as an allied offensive campaign against V-1 and V-2 installations, supply dumps, and factories; and Operation Overcast (later renamed Operation Paperclip), an intelligence-gathering operation during the final year of the war. Also relates the U.S. campaign from 1945 to 1949 to exploit former German rocket scientists who had worked on the V-2, to develop advanced U.S. rocket and missile technology during the postwar period.

1305. Michelson, Louis. "General Electric's X-405 Vanguard and Engine—Where It Is and How It Got There." *Missiles and Rockets* 3 (May 1958): 139-147.

> Details the development and construction of the General Electric X-405 rocket engine that provided the first-stage power for the Vanguard launch vehicle, designed for the first U.S. satellite program.

1306. Molton, P.M. "The Nuclear Rocket." *Spaceflight* 12 (October 1970: 390-394.

> Promotes application of nuclear-propelled rockets for the exploration of deep space and includes extensive historical background, with a useful chronological milestone table covering developments from 1955 to 1969.

1307. Morey, Loren. *The Powder Rockets*. New York: Military Affairs/Aerospace Historian, 1982. Pp. 197. Index, Illustr.

> History and development of U.S. double-base (nitrocellulose-nitroglycerine) solid-propellant rockets and rocketry from the experiments of Robert H. Goddard in 1915 to bazooka rockets of World War II. Primary sources are used extensively. The author was a rocket propellant chemist with the Hercules Powder Co. for 25 years.

1308. Moshkin, Evgenii K. *Razvitie otechestvennogo raketnogo dvigatelestroeniia* (Development of Russian rocket engine technology). Moscow: Mashinostroenie, 1973. Pp. 255. Bibliog., Illustr.

Details the development of the USSR's first liquid–fuel rocket engines, from the 1930s to immediate post–World War II. Numerous schematic drawings of the famous ORM and RD series. Some coverage on post–Sputnik engines. Includes rare organization chart of the Soviet Group for the Study of Reactive Motion (Gruppa po izucheniiu reativnogo dvizheniia, GIRD) rocket group of the 1930s.

1309. Oberth, Hermann. *Die Rakete zu den Planetenräumen* (The rocket into planetary space). Nuremberg: Reproduktonsdruck von Uni–Verlag, 1960. Pp. 92. Illustr.

Reproduces Hermann Oberth's famous 1923 work, which describes two hypothetical liquid–fuel (liquid–oxygen, liquid–alcohol) rockets for manned interplanetary flights and other aspects of spaceflight. This edition contains foreword by Wernher von Braun and a postscript announcing that the book was awarded the G. Edward Pendray Prize in 1956 by the American Rocket Society.

1310. Oberth, Hermann. *Ways to Spaceflight*. NASA TTF–622. Washington, D.C.: National Aeronautics and Space Administration, 1972. Pp. xiv + 597. Index, Illustr.

Translates Hermann Oberth's 1929 work *Wege zur Raumschiffahrt* with an added index and epilogue stating that the book won the 1930 REP–Hirsch international astronautical prize.

1311. Pendray, G. Edward. *The Coming Age of Rocket Power*. New York: Harper and Brothers, 1945. Pp. 244 Index, Illustr.

Outlines the long history of rocketry from the 12th century in China to the close of World War II, with emphasis on the American Rocket Society. The author was one of the founders and a leading member of the society.

Pirard, Theo. "Chinese Secrets' Orbiting the Earth." *Spaceflight* 19, no. 10 (October 1977): 355–361.

Cited herein as item 1760.

1312. Pockok, Rowland F. *German Guided Missiles*. Shepperton (Middlesex): Ian Allan, 1967. Pp. 120. Index, Bibliog., Illustr.

Surveys German guided missiles of World War II, particularly their guidance systems. Describes principles of these systems with accompanying simplified diagrams. Excludes unguided missiles and scientific research vehicles and is therefore not comprehensive. Appendixes include principal guided weapons' powerplants, code names of missile propellants, and German missile–carrying aircraft.

Pritchard, Wilbur L., and James J. Harford. *China Space Report*. New York: American Institute of Aeronautics and Astronautics, 1980. Pp. 208. Index, Illustr.

Cited herein as item 1761.

Rao, B. Radhakrishna. "China: New Space Power of Threat to Stability in Asia?" *Spaceworld* R–3–207 (March 1981): 19–20.

Cited herein as item 1762.

Raushenbakh, B.V. *Iz istorii sovetskoi kosmonavtiki* (From the history of Soviet cosmonautics). Moscow: Izdatel'stvo Nauka, 1983. Pp. 263. Illustr.

Cited herein as item 1687.

1313. Riedel, W.H.J. "A Chapter in Rocket History." *Journal of the British Interplanetary Society* 13 (July 1954): 208–212.

Narrates the little–known but important story of the first application of liquid–fuel rockets in Germany and their use in the rocket cars of Max Valier and Dr. Paul Heyland from 1929 to 1930. The author participated in these early experiments and later became a prominent rocket scientist at Peenemünde, helping to develop the V–2. Includes a rare photo of a 1931 alcohol/gaseous oxygen rocket motor, although it is not described in the text.

1314. Rosne, Milton W. *The Viking Rocket Story*. London: Faber and Faber, 1956. Pp. 248. Index, Illustr.

Examines the politics and technology leading up to the development of the first large–scale U.S. liquid–fuel rocket, the Viking, which was intended for use in exploring the upper atmosphere. The Viking was also the immediate forerunner of the Vanguard artificial satellite launch vehicle. The author helped create and direct the Viking project and was a leading early proponent of artificial satellites.

1315. Sampson, D.R., ed. *Development of the Blue Streak Satellite Launcher.* Oxford: Pergamon, 1963. Pp. 128. Bibliog., Illustr.

Six papers read at the Second Space Engineering Symposium, Hatfield College of Technology, England, February 22, 1963. The papers are concerned with the engineering development of the de Havilland Aircraft Company's Blue Streak liquid–propellant launch vehicle, which was to have been used by the European Launcher Development Organization (ELDO) as a satellite booster, but was cancelled in 1973. Provides 275 references.

1316. Sharpe, Mitchell E. *Development of the Lifesaving Rocket.* Huntsville, Ala.: National Aeronautics and Space Administration. George C. Marshall Space Flight Center, 1969. Pp. 72. Bibliog., Illustr.

Presents a detailed history of the solid–fuel (gunpowder) lifesaving rocket considered to be the most humane and prolific application of the rocket to emerge from 19th–century rocket technology. This book won the 1968 Robert H. Goddard Essay Award competition sponsored by the National Space Club.

Sheldon, Charles S. II. "The Soviet Space Program: A Growing Enterprise." *TRW Space Log,* Winter 1968–1969, 2–23.

Cited herein as item 1689.

1317. Sloop, John L. *Liquid Hydrogen as a Propulsion Fuel, 1945–1959.* NASA SP-4404. Washington, D.C.: National Aeronautics and Space Administration, 1978. Pp. 325. Index, Bibliog., Illustr.

Details the little–known, yet important history of the application of liquid hydrogen as a high–energy rocket, jet, and pulse–jet fuel from 1945 to 1959. Emphasis is on its use and significance in the Saturn launch vehicle. Also covers the earliest theoretical studies, before World War II, of hydrogen as a rocket fuel by K.E. Tsiolkovskii, R.H. Goddard, and H. Oberth. Includes useful appendixes on history of hydrogen technology, 19th century to 1945, and performance parameters of rocket engines using hydrogen.

1318.   Slukhai, Ivan A. *Russian Rocketry, a Historical Survey*. NASA TTF–426. Jerusalem: Israeli Program for Scientific Translations, 1968. Pp. 149. Bibliog., Illustr.

Discusses the history of military rocketry in the Soviet Union from the 17th century to Soviet ballistic rockets around 1969 in narrative, non–technical style. Contains extensive coverage of the history of the World War II Katiusha Soviet ground–to–ground barrage rocket. Includes an account of Soviet surface–to–air–missile (SAM-2, and the downing of the U.S. U–2 reconnaissance aircraft flown by Frances Gary Powers.

1319.   Sokolskii, Viktor N. and S. Kozlov, eds., H. Needler, trans. *Russian Solid–Fuel Rockets*. NASA TTF–415. Jerusalem: Israeli Program for Scientific Translations, 1967. Pp. 236. Index, Illustr.

History of gunpowder and other solid–propellant rockets in Russia from 1675 to 1913, based mainly on primary sources. Includes extensive treatment of 19th century war rocket manufacturing techniques by the pioneer K. Konstantinov and others. Contains appendixes of 16 selected 17th and early 20th century documents concerning rockets, such as experiment reports, calculations, and proposals. Also includes a list of abbreviations.

1320.   Spense, Roderick W. "Rover Nuclear Rocket Program." *Science* 160 (1968): 953–959. Illustr.

Traces the development and state of the art of nuclear rocket propulsion for spaceflight from early post–World War II U.S. and British studies through the Kiwi, Nerva, and Rover projects. The author was a division leader of N–Division at the Los Alamos Scientific Laboratory in New Mexico.

1321. Stuhlinger, Ernst, ed. *From Peenemünde to Outer Space: Commemorating the Fiftieth Birthday of Wernher von Braun, March 23, 1962.* Huntsville, Ala.: National Aeronautics and Space Administration, 1962. Pp. xiv + 853. Bibliog., Illustr.

Pays tribute to rocket and spaceflight pioneer Wernher von Braun on his 50th birthday, with a published collection of 38 papers on the history and development of space science and engineering by leading authorities in their respective fields. Main sections include: systems and operations, spacecraft design and engineering, propulsion, guidance and control, instrumentation and tracking, engineering components, and physics and biology. Prologue by James E. Webb, epilogue by Walter R. Dornberger.

1322. Sun, Fang–Toh. "Rockets and Rocket Propulsion Devices in Ancient China." *Journal of the Astronautical Sciences* 29 (July–September 1981): 289–305.

Traces the history of the earliest Chinese rockets and rocket–propelled devices, during the 10th through 17th centuries. Uses primary and secondary Chinese sources. Reproduces illustrations of Chinese rockets from these sources.

1323. Tokaty, G.A. "Soviet Rocket Technology." *Technology and Culture* 4, no. 4 (Fall 1963): 515–528.

Summarizes the history of Soviet rocket technology and Soviet rocket organizations from the mid–19th century to the launch of *Sputnik 1* in 1957. Emphasizes immediate postwar developments in which the author played a role as chief rocket scientist of the Soviet government in Germany, 1946–1947. Includes a brief list of references.

1324. Tokaty, G.A. "Foundations of Soviet Cosmonautics," *Spaceflight* 10 (October 1968): 335–346.

Surveys 19th–century Russian war rocket developments, late 19th–century Russian concepts of manned flight and spacecraft rockets, and Soviet liquid–fuel rocket developments from 1920 to 1950. The author was in charge of rounding up German rocket scientists for the Soviet Union after the conclusion of World War II.

1325. Tsander, Fridrikh A., and L. Korneev, eds. *Problems of Flight by Jet Propulsion—Interplanetary Flights.* NASA TTF–147. Jerusalem: Israeli Program for Scientific Translations, 1964. Pp. 390. Illustr.

Translates Soviet rocket pioneer Tsander's book *Problema poleta pri pomoshchi reativnykh apparatov* (1932), as well as his articles on spaceflight and previously unpublished steno-graphic and lecture notes. Includes a lengthy chapter by the editor on the life and work of Tsander.

1326. Tsiolkovsky, Konstantin. *Works on Rocket Technology.* Edited by M. Tikhonravov, et al. NASA TTF–243. Washington, D.C.: National Aeronautics and Space Administration, 1965. Pp. 434. Illustr.

Translates the essential writings of the Russian rocketry-astronomical theorist, Tsiolkovskii, who began his speculations in the 1880s and continued them until his death in 1935. It is arranged chronologically and edited with notes by a pioneer Soviet rocket scientist closely associated with Tsiolkovskii during his final years.

U.S. Congress. Committee on Science and Technology. Sub-committee on Space Science and Applications. *United States Civilian Space Programs, 1958–1978.* Washington, D.C.: U.S. Government Printing Office, 1981. Pp. 1100. Illustr.

Cited herein as item 1135.

U.S. Library of Congress. Congressional Research Service. *Soviet Space Programs, 1976–1980 Part I, Supporting Vehi-cles and Launch Vehicles, Political Goals and Purposes, In-ternational Cooperation in Space, Administration, Resource Burden, Future Outlook.* Washington, D.C.: U.S. Government Printing Office, December 1982. Pp xvi + 445. Illustr.

Cited herein as item 1695.

Van Allen, James A., ed. *Scientific Uses of Earth Satellites.* Ann Arbor: University of Michigan Press, 1956. Pp. 316. Illustr.

Cited herein as item 1370.

1327. Vick, Charles P. "The Soviet Super Boosters, Parts 1 and 2." *Spaceflight* 15 (December 1973): 457–460; 16 (March 1974): 94–104.

Analyzes the development of the Soviet Union's largest launch vehicles. Considered one of the most thorough private investigations of the design history of Soviet launch vehicles. Includes configuration drawings, a table of Proton launch history, and photos of models of vehicle types constructed by the author.

1328. Vick, Charles P. "The Soviet G–1–e Manned Lunar Landing Programme Booster." *Journal of the British Interplanetary Society*, 38 (January 1985): 11–18.

Analyzes the probable development of the Soviet G–1–e launch vehicle for contemplated manned lunar missions from the 1960s. Includes scale drawings by the author and tables of vehicle characteristics. References are provided.

1329. Wiggins, Joseph W. "Hermes—Milestone in U.S. Aerospace Progress." *Aerospace Historian* 21, no. 1 (Spring 1974): 34–40.

Tells the important technological story of the development of the first U.S. large–scale, solid–propellant rocket, the Hermes RV–A–10. Uses primary sources. Includes propellant configuration, schematic diagrams, and manufacturing and testing photos.

1330. Wilson, Andrew. "Agena—1959 to 1979." *Journal of the British Interplanetary Society* 34 (July 1981): 298–306.

Details the development of Agena rocket, NASA's most used and successful upper–stage liquid–propellant rocket, which served a variety of missions from 1959 to 1979, from orbiting reconnaissance satellites to interplantary probes. Agena also served as a rendezvous target and booster for Project Gemini.

1331. Wilson, Andrew. "Centaur Reaches Fifty." *Spaceflight* 20 (September/October 1978): 333–337.

Recounts the history of the liquid–oxygen, liquid–hydrogen upper–stage Centaur rocket on the occasion of its 59th suc–

cessful launch. Includes schematic diagrams of this important engine and Centaur launch list covering its flights from 1962 to 1978.

1332. Wilson, Andrew. "Scout—NASA's Small Satellite Launcher." *Spaceflight* 21 (November 1979): 446–459.

A comprehensive history of the Scout, NASA's only solid-propellant launch vehicle, includes several development charts and a launch list from 1960 to 1978, giving launch dates, configuration types, launch sites, and satellite payloads.

1333. Winter, Frank H. "The Rocket in India from Ancient Times to the 19th Century." *Journal of the British Interplanetary Society* 32 (December 1979): 467–471.

Uses the 17th– and 20th–century European sources to relate history of the rocket in India up to the 19th century. Maintains the Indian period led directly to the age of Congreve and development of modern rocketry in Europe.

1334. Winter, Frank H. "A New Look at Early Chinese Rocketry, 1200's to 1900." *Journal of the British Interplanetary Society* 35 (December 1982): 522–529.

Offers new interpretations of the possible origin and spread of the first rockets in China. Nineteenth–century Chinese rocket developments are discussed.

Yevsikov, Victor. *Re–Entry Technology and the Soviet Space Program* (Some Personal Observations). Falls Church, Va.: Delphic Associates, 1982. Pp. 112. Illustr.

Cited herein as item 1719.

Zaehringer, Alfred J. *Soviet Space Technology*. New York: Harper, 1961. Pp. xii + 179. Index, Bibliog., Illustr.

Cited herein as item 1734.

ROCKET SONDES, SPACE SCIENCE,
SCIENTIFIC SATELLITES, AND PROBES

This selection reflects the concentration of literature on the early period of space science prior to the NASA era. For the most part, the post–NASA period is covered in a number of NASA special publications (SP series) which include at least some historical treatment of their subjects. Many of these works were not fully documented, and not written by professional historians.

Few competent historical reviews of space science topics are available at present, although interest in this area is increasing rapidly among historians of modern science and technology. As a result, many of the citations provided here are not by historians but by scientists, engineers, and administrators who, as pioneer participants in their field, have taken an interest in its history and have labored to preserve it through personal reminiscences, technical reviews and summaries, and, in a few cases, large–scale technical histories.

As a result of the paucity of historical works and the self–imposed restrictions of the selection process (preference was given to works in English that will introduce the reader to useful literature on the history of space science topics, and to works that are well documented enough to lead the reader to primary literature and archival sources), the selection in this section is quite thin.

Although competent popular reviews have not been overlooked, considerable care has been taken to make sure that the authors whose works are cited are well versed and objective reviewers of their chosen fields; however, some works that lack adequate documentation are still included here if they are considered stepping stones to scholarly historical research for those just entering the field. While the field is yet thin it has provoked popular interest, and hence popular reviews without complete documentation are more common that scholarly reviews. Thus these works are included with a view to providing topical completeness as well as an idea of the present state of writing in the area.

David H. DeVorkin
Joseph N. Tatarewicz

General Histories

1335. Akasofu, Syun-Ichi, B. Fogle, and B. Haurwitz, eds. *Sydney Chapman, Eighty.* Boulder, Colo.: National Center for Atmospheric Research and University of Colorado, 1968. Pp. ix + 230. Bibliog., Illustr.

Volume honoring Sydney Chapman in recognition of his influence on the progress of geophysics, atmospheric physics, and planetary atmospheres. Includes biographical sketches, testimonials, anecdotes, personal reminiscences, and a review of his contributions to science by his friends and associates. Contains reprints of three of his autobiographical reminiscences.

1336. Alperin, Mortin, ed. *Vistas in Astronautics.* Vol. 2. New York: Pergamon, 1959. Pp. x + 318. Index, Bibliog., Illustr.

Symposium sponsored by the U.S. Air Force and others to consider potential directions for space exploration. Topics include scientific work to be done in space, and applications of science to civilian and military space programs. Contains presentations by many eminent astronomers and scientists. Appendixes, notes.

Bainbridge, William S. *The Spaceflight Revolution: A Sociological Study.* New York: Wiley, 1976. Pp. 249. Index, Bibliog.

Cited herein as item 1142.

1337. Bates, D.R., ed. *Space Research and Exploration.* London: Eyre and Spottiswoode, 1957. Pp. 224. Index, Bibilog.

Compendium of essays by Bates, Clarke, Massey, Ovendon, and others relating to aspects of space exploration on the eve of satellites. Covers rockets and propellants, orbit theory, studies of the atmosphere and near space, unmanned and manned satellites, space navigation, and meteor hazards. Appendixes.

1338. Beatty, J. Kelley. *The New Solar System.* Cambridge, Mass.: Sky, 1981. Pp. 224. Index, Bibliog., Ilustr.

Compendium of short chapters, each written by an active specialist, presenting knowledge gained from two decades of solar system exploration. Some chapters present mostly historical material. The introductory essays by Carl Sagan and Noel Hinners and the closing essay by John S. Lewis are explicitly historical. Appendixes, Notes.

Berkner, Lloyd V., ed. *Manual on Rockets and Satellites.* London: Pergamon 1958. Pp. 508.

Cited herein as item 1074.

1339. Berkner, Lloyd, and H. Odishaw, eds. *Science in Space.* New York: McGraw–Hill, 1961. Pp. x + 439. Index, Illustr.

A primer written by the members of the Space Science Board of the National Academy of Sciences to educate scientists to the possibilities for research in space. Each chapter treats a different discipline of space science and is "directed to research workers whose scientific activities may be influenced by the new opportunities for experiments offered by growing access to space" (Preface, p. v). Appendixes, Notes.

Brown, Eunice H., J. Robertson, J. Kroehnke, et al. *White Sands History: Range Beginnings and Early Missile Testing.* White Sands, N.M.: White Sands, Public Affairs Office, 1959. Pp. v + 152.

Cited herein as item 1111.

Bryant, C.R.J. "ESRO II: 20 Years Ago." *Journal of the British Interplanetary Society* 38 (1985): 553–560.

Cited herein as item 1737.

Carter, L.J. and P. Bainum, eds. *Space: A Developing Role for Europe.* American Astronautical Society Science and Technology Series, vol. 56. San Diego, Calif. Univelt, 1984. Pp. 278.

Cited herein as item 1739.

Clarke, Arthur C. *Ascent to Orbit*. A Scientific Autobiography. New York: Wiley–Interscience, 1984. Pp. 226. Illustr.

Cited herein as item 1192.

1340. Cleaver, A.V. "European Space Activities since World War II: A Personal View." *AIAA 11th Annual Meeting*. AIAA Paper 75–313, (February 1975), 1–18.

Heavily illustrated and detailed treatment of photography of planetary surfaces taken from space. Discusses optical and electronic systems, camera and support equipment design, and problems and potential of interpreting the observations.

1341. Corliss, William R. *Scientific Satellites*. NASA SP–133. Washington, D.C.: National Aeronautics and Space Administration, 1967. Pp. vii + 822. Index, Bibilog., Illustr.

Comprehensive review of the technical history of scientific satellites. Describes in detail major missions, spacecraft, launch systems, ground–based facilities, and the scientific instruments, by discipline—geophysics, solar physics, astronomy, and biology. There are extensive bibliographical citations and satellite descriptions. This work is noteworthy for its comparative analysis of instrument design.

1342. Dick, Stephen J. *Plurality of Worlds*. Cambridge: Cambridge University Press, 1982; paperback ed., 1984 Pp. x + 246. Index, Bibilog.

Broad review of the question of extraterrestrial life as raised by Democritus and philosophers up to the time of Kant. Examines the acceptance of the plurality doctrine as a symptom of the scientific revolution.

Durant, Frederick C. III, and G. James, eds. *First Steps toward Space*. Smithsonian Annals of Flight, no. 10. Washington, D.C.: Smithsonian Institution Press, 1974. Pp. 307. Index, Illustr.

Cited herein as item 1283.

Fishlock, David, ed. *A Guide to Earth Satellites.* New York: American Elsevier, 1971. Pp. 159. Index.

Cited herein as item 1434.

1343. Friedman, Herbert. *Reminiscences of Thirty Years of Space Research.* NRL Report 8113. Washington, D.C.: Naval Research Laboratory, 1976. Pp. 23. Illustr.

Well–illustrated popular review of major contributions to space research at the Naval Research Laboratory.

Gartmann, Heinz. *Men Behind the Space Rockets.* New York: D. McKay, 1956. Pp. 185. Index, Illustr.

Cited herein as item 1233.

1344. Hanle, Paul A., and V. Chamberlain, eds. *Space Science Comes of Age: Perspectives in the History of the Space Sciences.* Washington, D.C.: Smithsonian Institution Press, 1982. Pp. xiii + 194. Index, Illustr.

Collected essays on the various origins of space science, presented on March 23 and 24, 1981, at the National Air and Space Museum. Eleven space scientists and historians provided commentaries on solar physics, the development of American launch vehicles, lunar geology, the origin of the solar system, early studies of the ionosphere, cosmic rays and other topics. Notes.

1345. Hayes, E. Nelson. *Trackers of the Skies.* Cambridge, Mass.: Howard A. Doyle, 1968. Pp. xiii + 169.

Narrative of the Smithsonian Astrophysical Observatory's program to create an optical satellite tracking program in the mid–1950s.

Hetherington, Norriss S. "Winning the Initiative: NASA and the U.S. Space Science Program." *Prologue* 7 (1975): 99–107.

Cited herein as item 1121.

Kármán, Theodore von, and L. Edison. *Wind and Beyond: Theodore von Kármán, Pioneer in Aviation and Pathfinder in Space.* Boston: Little, Brown, 1967. Pp. 376. Index, Illustr.

Cited herein as item 1241.

Lasby, Clarence G. *Project Paperclip: German Scientists and the Cold War.* Reprint. New York: Atheneum, 1975. Pp. x + 338.

Cited herein as item 1300.

Lasser, David. *The Conquest of Space.* New York: Penguin, 1931. Pp. 271. Illustr.

Cited herein as item 1200.

Ley, Willy. *Rockets, Missiles, and Man in Space.* New York: Viking, 1968. Pp. xvii + 557. Index, Bibliog., Illustr.

Cited herein as item 1101.

Lovell, Sir Bernard. *The Origins and International Economics of Space Exploration.* Edinburgh: Edinburgh University Press, 1973. Pp. viii + 104. Index, Bibliog., Illustr.

Cited herein as item 1170.

1346. Lovell, Sir Bernard. "The Effects of Defense Science on the Advance of Astronomy." *Journal for the History of Astronomy* 8 (1977): 151–173.

Reviews funding priorities, policies, and conditions before and after World War II for astronomy, showing how wartime technology—specifically radar, rocketry, and scientific manpower—and expertise in electronics revolutionized the science.

Massey, Harrie, and M.O. Robins. *History of British Space Science.* Cambridge, Mass.: Cambridge University Press, 1986. Pp. xxi + 514. Index, Bibliog., Illustr.

Cited herein as item 1748.

1347. Mayo–Wells, Wilfred J. "The Origins of Space Telemetry." *Technology and Culture* 4 (Fall 1963): 499–514.

Reviews technical advances in telemetry systems during the 20th century. Looks in depth at the role of military needs in the development of long–distance communications. Describes different modes of multiple–channel telemetry developed during World War II at Princeton, standardization of telemetry by the JRDB, and the application to V–2 sounding rocket research and eventually to the first earth satellites.

1348. Newell, Homer E. *Beyond the Atmosphere: Early Years of Space Science.* Washington, D.C.: National Aeronautics and Space Administration, 1980. Pp. xviii + 497. Index, Bibliog., Illustr.

This major review analyzes the progress of space science from the V–2 era through the International Geophysical Year and Sputnik eras, and the NASA satellite era. The author was a central figure in the enterprise. Traces modes of decision-making within NASA and the federal government, discusses how space science developed, and relations between NASA, scientific centers and university investigators.

Nieburg, H.P. *In the Name of Science.* Chicago: Quadrangle, 1966. Pp. ix + 384. Index, Bibliog.

Cited herein as item 1176.

Petrov, B.H., V.C. Berreshchetin, eds. *Orbity sotrudnichestva* (Orbits of cooperation). Moscow: Mashinostroenie, 1983. Pp. 177. Illustr.

Cited herein as item 1667.

Popescu, Julian. *Russian Space Exploration.* Henley on Thames, England: Gothard House, 1979. Pp. viii + 150. Index, Bibliog.

Cited herein as item 1686.

1349. Porter, R.W. *The Versatile Satellite.* Oxford: Oxford University Press, 1977. Pp. vii + 173. Index.

Popular review of the many applications of satellites to science, global communications, navigation, weather forecasting, resource monitoring, and mapping. This is a well-illustrated review of major NASA missions. There is also a discussion of space for possible human habitation. The author was civilian head of "Project Hermes", the Army project to test captured German V–2 rockets, during and immediately after World War II and was a significant participant in the Committee on Space Research. Appendixes.

1350. Rabinowitch, Eugene, and R. Lewis, eds. *Man on the Moon. The Impact on Science, Technology and International Cooperation.* New York: Basic Books, 1969. Pp. xiv + 204.

Reprint of a series of articles that originally appeared in a special issue of the *Bulletin of the Atomic Scientists* dedicated to the effects of the Apollo program. Contains articles by Freeman Dyson, Mose L. Harvey, Sidney Hyman, John A. O'Keefe, William Leavitt, Franklin A. Long, Sir Bernard Lovell, Irving Michelson, Thornton Page, Eugene Rabinowitch, Charles S. Sheldon, Philip M. Smith, Sidney Sternberg, Ernest Stuhlinger, Harold Urey, and Wernher von Braun.

Roland, Alex, ed. *A Spacefaring People: Perspectives on Early Spaceflight.* NASA SP–4405. Washington, D.C.: National Aeronautics and Space Administration, 1985. Pp. viii + 156. Bibliog.

Cited herein as item 1108.

Sundra Rajan, Mahan. *India in Space.* New Delhi, India: Minister of Information and Broadcasting, 1976. Pp. 92. Illustr.

Cited herein as item 1764.

Tsiolkovsky, Konstantin L., and V. Dutt, ed. *Call of the Cosmos.* Moscow: Foreign Languages Publishing House, 1960. Pp. 471. Illustr.

Cited herein as item 1118.

U.S. Congress. Committee on Science and Technology. Subcommittee on Space Science and Applications. *United States*

Civilian Space Programs, 1958–1978. Washington, D.C.: U.S. Government Printing Office, 1981. Pp. 1100. Illustr.

Cited herein as item 1135.

1351. U.S. Congress. Office of Technology Assessment. *Space Science Research in the United States*. A Technical Memorandum. Washington, D.C.: U.S. Government Printing Office, September 1982. Pp. vii + 50. Illustr.

Public policy analysis of the development of space science through massive federal funding and the impact on the traditional scientific disciplines and their practitioners. Contains summary historical descriptions of scientific developments and tables and graphs of financial and demographic data.

U.S. Library of Congress. Congressional Research Service. *Soviet Space Programs, 1976–80. Part 3, Unmanned Space Activities*. Washington, D.C.: U.S. Government Printing Office, May 1985. Pp. xvii + 346. Illustr.

Cited herein as item 1696.

U.S. Library of Congress. Congressional Research Service. *Soviet Space Programs: 1966–70, Goals and Purposes, Organization, Resources, Facilities and Hardware, Manned and Unmanned Flight Programs, Bioastronautics, Civil and Military Applications, Projections for Future Plans, Attitudes Toward International Cooperation and Space Law*. Washington, D.C.: United States. Government Printing Office, 1971. Pp. xi + 670. Index.

Cited herein as item 1692.

U.S. Library of Congress. Science and Technology Section. Air Information Division. *Comprehensive Analysis of Soviet Space Program (Based on Soviet Open Literature, 1958–61)*. AID Report—72. Washington, D.C.: U.S. Library of Congress, May 22, 1961. Pp. 159. Illustr.

Cited herein as item 1699.

Webb, James E. "NASA and USAF: A Space Age Partnership."
The Airman, August 1964, 6–11.

Cited herein as item 1186.

Wukelic, George. *Handbook of Soviet Space Science Research*.
New York: Gordon and Breach, 1968. Pp. xx + 505. Illustr.

Cited herein as item 1724.

Earth and Atmospheric Studies

1352. Boyd, R.F.L., and M. Seaton. *Rocket Exploration of the Upper
Atmosphere*. New York: Wiley Interscience, 1954. Pp. 261.
Index, Bibliog., Illustr.

Forty–nine papers presented at a joint meeting of the
American Upper Atmosphere Rocket Research Panel and the
Gassiot Committee of the Royal Society of London, at Oxford
University, England, on August 24 and 26, 1953. Constitutes a
detailed review of sounding rocket techniques and the results
of studies of the high atmosphere, solar radiation, cosmic rays,
and related laboratory and theoretical research. Appendixes,
Notes.

1353. Briggs, Lyman J., et al. *The National Geographic Society—
U.S. Army Air Corps Stratosphere Flights of 1935 in the
Balloon "Explorer II"*. Stratospheric Series No. 2. Washing-
ton, D.C.: National Geographic Society, 1936. Pp. 278.
Index, Bibliog., Illustr.

Series of papers reviewing the successful manned balloon
ascent of *Explorer II*, and the scientific results obtained in the
areas of meteorology, aerial photography, and atmospheric
physics. An earlier volume (Stratospheric Series, no. 1) reviews
Explorer I and describes the instruments involved.

1354. Busse, Jon R., and M. Leffler. *A Compendium of Aerobee
Sounding Rocket Launchings from 1959 through 1963*. Washington, D.C.: National Aeronautics and Space Administration, 1966. Pp. viii + 170.

Includes detailed descriptions of the Aerobee 150, 150A,

300, 300A, and 100 sounding rockets, ancillary hardware, and an annotated general chronology of firings.

1355. Cook, A.H. "The Contribution of Observations of Satellites to the Determination of the Earth's Gravitational Potential." *Space Science Reviews* 2 (1963): 355–437.

Brief historical introduction to studies of the Earth's figure, beginning with Newton and Cassini. Reviews the technique for determining the Earth's gravitational potential.

1356. Corliss, William R. *NASA Sounding Rockets, 1958–1968: A Historical Summary*. NASA SP–4401. Washington, D.C.: National Aeronautics and Space Administration, 1971. Pp. vii + 155.

Provides useful introductory essays on pre–NASA rocketry (V–2 rockets, Aerobees), in addition to extensive tables identifying the firing dates, rocket performance, agency and experimenters, purpose and flight results of sounding rocket firings, and the history of sounding rocket development.

1357. Curtis, S.A. "The Uses of the German V–2 in the U.S. for Upper Atmosphere Research." *Journal of the British Interplanetary Society* 32 (1979): 442–448.

Reviews the characteristics of the V–2 rocket, and the execution of "Project Hermes" in the United States, an Army project conducted by General Electric to find, test, and evaluate captured German V–2 rockets. Identifies the ad hoc V–2 Upper Atmosphere Rocket Research Panel as a coordinating body whose purpose was to conduct scientific research with the V–2 rockets fired at White Sands between 1946 and 1951.

El–Baz, Farouk. *Astronaut Observations from the Apollo–Soyuz Mission*. Washington, D.C.: Smithsonian Institution Press, 1977. Pp. v + 210. Bibliog., Illustr.

Cited herein as item 1583.

Esnault–Pelterie, Robert. *Exploration par Fusées de la Très Haute Atmosphère et la possibilité des voyages interplanétaires* (The exploration of the upper atmosphere by rockets and the possibility of interplanatary flight). Paris: Société Astronomique de France, 1928. Pp. 96. Illustr.

Cited herein as item 1197.

1358. Fraser, Ronald. *Once around the Sun: The Story of the International Geophysical Year.* New York: Macmillan, 1957. Pp. 150. Illustr.

Published on the eve of the International Geophysical Year (July 1957–December 1958). Part I provides a contemporary review of the state of scientific knowledge of the earth, its atmosphere and oceans, and their interactions with the sun. Part II describes programs organized under the auspices of the IGY. Useful contemporary background for understanding the goals of the IGY, especially expectations for the planned satellite program.

1359. Goody, R.M. *The Physics of the Stratosphere.* Cambridge: Cambridge University Press, 1954. Pp. x + 187. Index, Bibliog.

Technical introduction to the physics of the high atmosphere, including reviews of the state of knowledge of its composition, temperature, ozone distribution, radiation, and turbulence. Incorporates historical remarks in narrative style, identifying advances from balloon and sounding rocket research.

Green, Constance M., and M. Lomask. *Vanguard: A History.* NASA SP–4202. Washington, D.C.: National Aeronautics and Space Administration, 1970. Pp. xvi + 257. Index, Illustr.

Cited herein as item 1117.

1360. Krause, Ernest H. "High Altitude Research with V–2 Rockets." *Proceedings of the American Philosophical Society* 91 (1947): 430–446.

Descriptive review of the various instruments and programs developed to conduct space science experiments with V–2 rockets at White Sands. The author was the head of the Rocket Sonde Research Section at Naval Research Laboratory during this early period. The work was reprinted in the Smithsonian Report for 1948, pp. 189–208. Contains extensive references.

1361. Massey, Harrie Stewart Wilson, and R.F.L. Boyd. *The Upper Atmosphere.* New York: Philosophical Library, 1959. Pp. xii + 333. Index, Bibliog., Illustr.

Textbook reviewing the state of knowledge of the Earth's atmosphere at the beginning of the satellite era. Reviews techniques of studying the atmosphere by ground–based radio, balloon–borne, and sounding rocket–borne experiments. Identifies basic types of atmospheric phenomena studied by these techniques and explains how artificial satellites might improve our understanding of these phenomena.

1362. Mitra, S.K. *The Upper Atmosphere.* Calcutta: The Royal Asiatic Society of Bengal, 1948. Pp. xix + 616. Index, Bibliog.

Exhaustive technical review of all aspects of atmospheric physics representing the state of knowledge gained from ground–based and balloon–borne studies. It was written on the eve of sounding rocket research.

1363. Nassau, J.J. "Conference on Astronomical Observations from above the Earth's Atmosphere." *The Astronomical Journal* 65 (June 1960): 239–290.

Papers presented at a one–day conference, held on December 30, 1959, at the Case Institute of Technology. Participants (N. Roman, H. Friedman, L. Spitzer, G.M. Clemence, L. Goldberg, A. Code, F. Whipple, and R.J. Davis) described plans for using satellites for research in all areas of astronomy. Includes descriptions of available vehicles and payloads, and plans for an orbiting space telescope.

1364. Newell, Homer E. *High Altitude Rocket Research.* New York: Academic Press, 1953. Pp. xiv + 298. Index, Bibliog., Illustr.

Early scientific review of the results of all types of rocket sonde experiments highlighting the work of the Naval Research Laboratory.

1365. Newell, Homer E., ed. *Sounding Rockets.* New York: McGraw–Hill, 1959. Pp. vii + 334. Index, Bibliog., Illustr.

Compendium of articles dealing with all aspects of sounding rocket research by such authors such as E. Pressly, S.F. Singer,

Newell, J.W. Townsend, Jr., and J. Van Allen. Describes all types of rockets used for solar and upper air research, including the Aerobee, Deacon, Cajun, ASP, Loki–WASP, Rockoons, Nike–Cajun, Nike–Deacon, Terrapin, Viking, Skylark, Veronique, Monica, Kappa, and Sigma. Coverage includes the United States, United Kingdom, France, and Japan.

1366. Pfotzer, G. "History of the Use of Balloons in Scientific Experiments." *Space Science Reviews* 13 (1974): 197–242.

Extensive review from 18th Century France to the 1960s. Traces advances in balloon technology, self–registering devices, and telemetry for both manned and unmanned scientific ballooning. Concentrates on German contributions and the work of Erich Regener. Numerous references.

1367. Sullivan, Walter. *Assault on the Unknown: The International Geophysical Year.* New York: McGraw–Hill, 1961. Pp. 418. Index, Illustr.

Provides an extremely readable, near contemporary account of the scientific research conducted under the auspices of the International Geophysical Year (IGY). The author, a respected science writer for the *New York Times*, was assigned full–time to cover the work of scientists associated with the IGY. Of special interest is the unique account of the secret Argus Project, in which the United States exploded small atomic bombs at high altitudes to determine the effect of such explosions on the radiation environment of near–earth space, including the formation of artificial radiation belts trapped by the earth's magnetic field.

1368. Vaeth, J. Gordon. *Two Hundred Miles Up.* New York: Ronald, 1955. Pp. 261. Index, Illustr.

Popular review of techniques and results of upper atmosphere research with sounding rockets. Describes work with captured V–2 rockets, and American–built Vikings, Aerobees, and satellites planned for the International Geophysical Year, including the controversial "Mouse", the Minimal Orbital Unmanned Satellite of the Earth, which was proposed be S. Fred Singer.

1369. Van Allen, James A. *Origins of Magnetospheric Physics.* Wash–

ington, D.C.: Smithsonian Institution Press, 1983. Pp. 144. Bibliog., Illustr.

Semi–autobiographical history centers on the discovery of the radiation belts of the earth from *Explorer I* and *III* data. Recounts earlier work with rocket sondes and balloons, and the results during that period that led to discoveries with satellites.

1370. Van Allen, James A., ed. *Scientific Uses of Earth Satellites*. Ann Arbor: University of Michigan Press, 1956. Pp. 316. Illustr.

Presents 33 papers given at the 10th anniversary meeting of the Upper Atmosphere Rocket Research Panel, Ann Arbor, June 26–27, 1956.

Lunar and Planetary Studies

Anonymous. "Russia's Project Far Side." *Astronautics* 4 (December 1959): 28–29.

Cited herein as item 1725.

1371. Brush, Stephen G. "Nickel for Your Thoughts: Urey and the Origin of the Moon." *Science* 217 (1982): 891–898.

Traces the early and continuing influence of Nobel Laureate chemist and geophysicist Harold Urey in providing the scientific rationale for going to the Moon. Follows the development of Urey's ideas and interaction with other scientists, especially John O'Keefe.

1372. Burgess, Eric. *To the Red Planet*. New York: Columbia University Press, 1978. Pp. 181. Index, Illustr.

Brief popular history of spacecraft exploration of the planet Mars. Concentrates on the U.S. Viking and Mariner missions from 1965 to 1976.

1373. Burgess, Eric. *By Jupiter*. New York: Columbia University Press, 1982. Pp. 155. Index, Bibliog., Illustr.

Short, popular history of the Pioneer 10 and 11 missions to Jupiter. Describes the spacecraft, scientific instruments, chief discoveries, and principal scientists and engineers involved.

1374. Byers, Bruce K. *Destination Moon: A History of the Lunar Orbiter Program.* NASA TM X–3487. Washington, D.C.: National Aeronautics and Space Administration, 1977. Pp. 412. Index, Bibliog., Illustr.

Chronology of a program that produced high–resolution photographic maps of the lunar surface in preparation for the Apollo landing missions. Appendixes.

Charon, Jean E. *Pourquoi la Lune?* (Why the Moon?). Paris: L´Encyclopédie Planète, 1968. Pp. 256. Bibliog., Illustr.

Cited herein as item 1576.

Clark, P.S. "The Soviet Venera Programme." *Journal of the British Interplanetary Society* 38 (1983): 74–93.

Cited herein as item 1726.

Cooper, Henry S.F. *Apollo on the Moon.* New York: Dial, 1969. Pp. 144.

Cited herein as item 1578.

1375. Cooper, Henry S.F. *Moon Rocks.* New York: Dial, 1970. Pp. 197.

Revised edition of Cooper's articles from the *New Yorker* chronicling the analysis of the first returned lunar samples.

1376. Cooper, Henry S.F. *Imaging Saturn.* New York: Holt, Reinhart, and Winston, 1980. Pp. 254.

Revised edition of Cooper's articles for the *New Yorker* chronicling the Pioneer and Voyager flybys of Saturn.

1377. Cooper, Henry S.F. *The Search for Life on Mars: Evolution of an Idea.* New York: Holt, Reinhart, and Wilson, 1980. Pp. 254. Index, Bibliog., Illustr.

Revised edition of Cooper's articles from the *New Yorker* chronicling the search for life on Mars. Concentrates on the Viking missions of 1976. Appendixes.

1378. Corliss, William R. *Space Probes and Planetary Exploration.* New York: Van Nostrand, 1965. Pp. ix + 542. Index, Bibliog., Illustr.

Provides highly detailed and technical descriptions explanations of the special characteristics of scientific spacecraft that operate beyond the Earth's orbit. One–third of the book is devoted to scientific instrumentation. Useful reference for the study of the history of these satellites. Appendixes, notes.

1379. Corliss, William R. *The Interplanetary Pioneers.* 3 vols. NASA SP–279. Washington, D.C.: National Aeronautics and Space Administration, 1971–1973. Illustr.

Detailed description and chronicle of the Ames Research Center series of Pioneer spacecraft launched into solar orbit during the 1960s, many of which are still operating. Each of the spacecraft and its scientific instruments are described in detail, as well as their mission operations and preliminary scientific results.

1380. Elliot, James L., and R. Kerr. *Rings: Discoveries from Galileo to Voyager.* Cambridge, Mass.: MIT Press, 1984. Pp. xi + 191. Index, Bibliog., Illustr.

Presents the contemporary state of knowledge of planetary rings in the Solar System. Includes accounts of the discoveries of the rings of Uranus and the rings of Jupiter. A personal and informative account of how planetary ring theory developed in response to new data from astronomical platforms of all kinds. Appendixes.

1381. Ezell, Edward C., and L. Ezell. *On Mars: Exploration of the Red Planet 1958–1978.* NASA SP–4212. Washington, D.C.: National Aeronautics and Space Administration, 1984. Pp. 423. Index, Bibliog., Illustr.

Provides a comprehensive and well–documented review of NASA's exploration of Mars, beginning with plans for Mariner's flyby missions and culminating with the landing on Mars by the two Viking craft and what they found. Identifies the interaction of NASA with the communities of scientists eager to study Mars, and describes technical problem areas, political pressures, and conflicting institutional styles. Appendixes, notes.

1382. Fimmel, Richard O., L. Colin, and E. Burgess. *Pioneer Venus.* NASA SP–461. Washington, D.C.: National Aeronautics and Space Administration, 1983. Pp. 253. Index, Illustr.

Detailed summary of the Pioneer Orbiter and Probe missions to Venus. Discusses the troubled history of mission proposal and approval, the development of the spacecraft and instruments, mission operations, and scientific results. Appendixes.

1383. Fimmel, Richard O., W. Swindell, and E. Burgess. *Pioneer Odyssey.* NASA SP–396. Washington, D.C.: National Aeronautics and Space Administration, 1977. Pp. 217. Index, Bibliog., Illustr.

Description of the Pioneer 10 and 11 missions to Jupiter. Treats the spacecraft, scientific instruments, mission development, and preliminary scientific results. Appendixes.

1384. Glasstone, Samuel. *The Book of Mars.* Washington, D.C.: National Aeronautics and Space Administration, 1968. Pp. vii + 315. Bibliog., Illustr.

Descriptive review of what was known about Mars before and after the first Mariner–Mars mission.

1385. Hall, R. Cargill. *Lunar Impact: A History of Project Ranger.* NASA SP–4210. Washington, D.C.: National Aeronautics and Space Administration, 1977. Pp. xvii + 450. Index, Bibliog., Illustr.

Provides a comprehensive and well–documented account of the first NASA program to design, construct, and launch an instrumented spacecraft on a trajectory to impact the lunar surface. Hall describes and analyzes organizational, political, personal, and technological factors within the project and develops themes of general interest in the history of large-scale science and technology projects. Notable themes are the tension between differing scientific and engineering motivations and procedures, the tension between academic and industrial communities, and the role of failure in technological progress. Appendixes.

Johnson, Nicholas L. "Apollo and Zond—Race around the Moon." *Spaceflight* 20 (December 1978), 403–412.

Cited herein as item 1659.

Johnson, Nicholas L. *Handbook of Soviet Lunar and Planetary Exploration.* American Astronautical Society Science and Technology Series, vol. 47. San Diego, Calif.: Univelt, 1979. Pp. xiv + 262. Index, Bibliog., Illustr.

Cited herein as item 1728.

1386. Kopal, Zdenek, and R. Carder. *Mapping of the Moon: Past and Present.* Dordrecht, Netherlands: Reidel, 1974. Pp. 237. Index, Bibliog., Illustr.

Heavily illustrated account of lunar mapping from the 18th century through the Apollo program. Emphasis is on the NASA years, but includes extensive coverage of mapping done by the U.S. Air Force, the U.S. Army, and the Soviet Union. Appendixes, notes.

1387. McCall, G.J.H. "The Lunar Controversy." *Journal of the British Interplanetary Society* 80 (1969): 19–29, 100–106, 190–199.

Reviews controversy over the origin of lunar features, noting progress in its resolution prior to and after Apollo 11.

1388. Masterson, Amanda R. *Index to the Proceedings of the Lunar and Planetary Science Conferences, Houston, Texas, 1970–1978.* New York: Pergamon, 1979. Pp. 261. Index, Bibliog., Illustr.

Provides keyword, missions, lunar sample numbers and author indices to the first nine issues of the *Proceedings*. Appendices, notes.

Masursky, Harold, G. Elton, and F. El–Baz, eds. *Apollo over the Moon: A View from Orbit*. NASA SP–362. Washington, D.C.: National Aeronautics and Space Administration, 1978. Pp. 255. Bibliog., Illustr.

Cited herein as item 1607.

1389. Mirabito, Michael M. *The Exploration of Outer Space with Cameras: A History of the NASA Unmanned Spacecraft Missions*. Jefferson, N.C.: McFarland, 1983. Pp. 170. Index, Bibliog., Illustr.

Account of the camera and imaging systems carried by the U.S. Mariner, Viking, Pioneer, and Voyager interplanetary spacecraft. Appendixes, notes.

1390. Mitroff, Ian. *The Subjective Side of Science: A Philosophical Inquiry into the Psychology of the Apollo Moon Scientists*. New York: American Elsevier, 1974. Pp. xv + 329. Index, Bibliog., Illustr.

Detailed and heavily documented sociological study of theories of the origin and development of the Moon as held by scientists involved in the Apollo program. Also reports how their opinions fared as confirming and contradictory evidence appeared. Relies on personal interviews with the scientists, but individual sources of quotations are not identified. Appendixes, notes.

1391. Morrison, David. *Voyages to Saturn*. NASA SP–451. Washington, D.C.: National Aeronautics and Space Administration, 1982. Pp. 227. Index, Bibliog., Illustr.

Sequel to *Voyage to Jupiter* covering the later encounters of *Voyager 1* and *2* with Saturn. Appendixes.

1392. Morrison, David, and J. Samz. *Voyage to Jupiter*. NASA SP–439. Washington, D.C.: National Aeronautics and Space Administration, 1980. Pp. 199. Index, Illustr.

Heavily illustrated narrative account of the *Voyager 1* and *2* missions to Jupiter. Discusses the prior Pioneer missions, the scientists involved, the spacecraft, scientific instruments, and the mission operations. Appendixes.

1393. Murray, Bruce C., and E. Burgess. *Flight to Mercury*. New York: Columbia University Press, 1977. Pp. xi + 162.

Heavily illustrated account of the Mariner 10 mission to Venus and Mercury.

Murray, B.C., and M. Davies. "A Comparison of U.S. and Soviet Exploration of Mars." *Science* 151, no. 3713 (February 25, 1966): 945–954.

Cited herein as item 1665.

1394. Newlan, Irl. *The Story of Mariner II*. New York: McGraw–Hill, 1963. Pp. 64.

Description for the lay reader of the *Mariner 2* mission to Venus, written by the staff of the Jet Propulsion Laboratory.

1395. Schorn, Ronald A. "The Spectroscopic Search for Water Vapor on Mars: A History." In *Planetary Atmospheres*. 223–236. Carl Sagan, et al., New York: Springer–Verlag, 1971.

Brief history of ground–based astronomical studies of Mars searching for traces of water vapor and the influence of the results of such studies upon the Mars–bound probe missions.

Shumilov, N. *Dva chuda kosmicheskoi tekhniki* (Two marvels of space technology). Moscow: Izvestiia, 1967. Pp. 191. Illustr.

Cited herein as item 1721.

1396. Tatarewicz, Joseph N. "Federal Funding and Planetary Astronomy, 1950–1975." *Social Studies of Science* 16 no. 1 (February 1986): 80–103.

Provides an historical and statistical demographic analysis of the impact of NASA on the planetary specialties within astronomy.

1397. Taylor, Stuart R. *Lunar Science: A Post–Apollo View*. New York: Pergamon, 1975. Pp. 372.

Detailed and highly technical assessment of knowledge of and theories about the Earth's moon in the aftermath of Apollo.

1398. Washburn, Mark. *Distant Encounters: The Exploration of Jupiter and Saturn.* New York: Harcourt Brace Jovanovich, 1983. Pp. xv + 272. Index, Illustr.

Chronicles the *Voyager 1* and *2* encounters with Jupiter and Saturn in the context of scientific, financial, and political issues of the day. The author describes both public and behind-the-scenes activities at the Jet Propulsion Laboratory during the encounters and at various scientific meetings where the results were presented. Includes first hand accounts of the community of planetary scientists confronting harsh budget realities immediately following highly successful and exciting missions.

Yefremov, Iu.I. *First Panoramic Views of the Lunar Surface.* Moscow: Nauka, 1966. Pp. 19. Illustr.

Cited herein as item 1730.

Solar Studies

1399. Bester, Alfred. *The Life and Death of a Satellite.* Boston: Little, Brown, 1966. Pp. xiv + 239. Index, Bibliog.

Popular and dramatic treatment of the history of the early phases of the NASA Orbiting Solar Observatory program through the first three flights. The author quotes extensively from meetings of experimenters and from written materials obtained through contact with NASA specialists and administrators, but provides no direct citations to sources. Numerous biographical and personality profiles of major participants are included but without explicit reference to source material.

1400. Dorman, L.I. *Cosmic Rays, Variations, and Space Exploration.* New York: American Elsevier, 1974. Pp. xv + 675. Index, Bibliog., Illustr.

Comprehensive review of the study of variations in cosmic ray flux. Includes a 12-page historical discussion that identifies periods in the history of the study. Appendixes.

1401. Eddy, John A. *A New Sun: The Solar Results from Skylab.* NASA SP–402. Washington, D.C.: National Aeronautical and Space Administration, 1979. Pp. xix + 198. Index, Illustr.

Lavishly illustrated review of the results from Skylab's Apollo Telescope Mount (ATM), a battery of eight major solar telescopes that monitored solar radiation and solar activity in the X–ray, ultraviolet, visible, and near–infrared regions of the spectrum during the 1973/1974 Skylab missions. Includes a historical introduction to the nature of solar studies, descriptions of the ATM instruments, and a detailed review of what was learned about the Sun.

1402. Ferraro, V.C.A. "The Solar–Terrestrial Environment: An Historical Survey." *Planetary and Space Sciences*, 17 (March 1969): 295–311.

Traces the progress since 1900 of understanding solar–terrestrial geomagnetic and magnetospheric relations.

1403. Friedman, Herbert. "Ultraviolet and X–rays from the Sun." *Annual Review of Astronomy and Astrophysics* 1 (1963): 59–96.

Description, by a pioneer in the field, of the history of rocket–borne instrumentation for the study of the high–energy portion of the solar spectrum.

1404. Goldberg, Leo. "Research with Solar Satellites." *Astrophysical Journal* 191 (July 1, 1974): 1–27.

Personal account by one of the pioneers in the field of space–based solar astronomy. Discusses scientific, bureaucratic, social, and personal aspects of space research in the early years of the space program.

1405. Liller, William, ed. *Space Astrophysics*. New York: McGraw-Hill, 1961. Pp. vii + 272.

Extensive series of essays covering practical instrumental problems and scientific goals of astronomy in space. Describes experimental techniques for observing the Sun from the Orbiting Solar Observatory (OSO) series and plans for astronom-

ical photometry and designing observing programs in space. Of
note are two chapters on attitude and pointing control problems. Useful for understanding the problems facing spacecraft
designers.

1406. Sekido, Y., and H. Elliot, eds. *Early History of Cosmic Ray
       Studies*. Dandrecht: D. Reidel, 1985. Pp. xvi + 444.

       Papers from a conference on cosmic rays held in Kyoto in
       August 1979. Extensive collection of personal accounts of the
       history of cosmic ray studies by numerous pioneer practi-
       tioners, describing balloon–borne experiments and early space
       physics.

1407. Singer, S.F. "The Mouse: A Minimum Orbital Unmanned Sat-
       ellite of the Earth for Astrophysical Research." *Journal of
       Astronautics* 2 (Fall 1955): 91–97.

       Proposes a small, artificial satellite for astrophysical stud-
       ies. This work is considered an important conceptual and
       planning milestone in the history of satellites.

1408. Tousey, R. "The Spectrum of the Sun in the Extreme Ultra-
       violet." *Quarterly Journal of the Royal Astronomical Soci-
       ety* 5 (1964): 123–144.

       Review observations of the nature of solar spectrum in the
       extreme ultraviolet and X–ray regions, since World War II.
       Identifies the continuum and emission spectra, spectrohelio-
       grams and line contour studies, noting refinements in the
       sounding rocket and early satellite eras. Concludes that the
       study of the high–energy solar spectrum is still in an observa-
       tional or discovery phase, with many features yet unidentified.

1409. Tousey, R. "Highlights of Twenty Years of Optical Space
       Research." *Applied Optics*, 6 (December 1967), 2044–2077.

       Reviews early discoveries about the Sun beginning in 1946,
       as gained from instruments sent into space aboard sounding
       rockets, earth–orbiting satellites (manned and unmanned),
       space probes, and lunar missions. Identifies basic optical
       systems employed to examine the solar spectrum, disk, and
       corona in the ultraviolet and X–ray regions. Advances in
       stellar and nebular studies from space observations are noted.
       The author is a pioneer in space solar physics.

1410. Tucker, Wallace H. *The Star Splitters: The High Energy Astronomy Observatories.* NASA SP-466. Washington, D.C.: National Aeronautics and Space Administration, 1984. Pp. 168. Index, Bibliog., Illustr.

General history of the High Energy Astronomy Observatories by a scientist who participated in the program.

1411. U.S. National Aeronautics and Space Administration. Goddard Space Flight Center. *Orbiting Solar Observatory Satellite: OSO I.* NASA SP-57. Washington, D.C.: U.S. Government Printing Office, 1965. Pp. vi + 306. Illustr.

Project summary of the construction, technical capabilities, and scientific work performed with the first orbiting solar observatory, which contained two biaxial-spin stabilized experiments and six single-axis stabilized scientific experiments. Launched in March 1962, it was the first in a series of seven such multi-experiment satellites.

1412. Widing, Kenneth G. "Solar Research from Rockets and Satellites." *Astronautics and Aeronautics* 7 (March 1969): 36–43.

Pictorial review of advancing of the ultraviolet and X-ray sun, as studied from rocket sondes and early Orbiting Solar Observatory satellites.

Astronomy from Space

1413. Berendzen, Richard. "On the Career Development and Education of Astronomers in the United States." Ph.D. diss., Harvard University, 1968. Index, Bibliog., Illustr.

Primarily a survey of the American astronomical community, presenting an extensive set of questions asked of all members of the American Astronautical Society concerning their attitudes toward NASA and space exploration. Appendixes, notes.

1414. Cornell, James, P., and P. Gorenstein, eds. *Astronomy from Space: Sputnik to Space Telescope.* Cambridge, Mass.: MIT Press, 1983. Pp. vii + 248. Index, Illustr.

Ten essays reviewing major aspects of planetary, solar, stellar, and galactic astronomy, with explicit discussions of the nature of ultraviolet (UV) and X-ray observations, planetary and lunar missions, and prospects for future research. Based on a lecture series held at Harvard University in 1982.

1415. Deutsch, Armin, and W. Klemperer. *Space Age Astronomy*. New York: Academic Press, 1962. Pp. xv + 526. Index, Bibliog., Illustr.

More than fifty papers presented at an international symposium sponsored by Douglas Aircraft Co. in conjunction with the Eleventh General Assembly of the International Astronomical Union. Includes contributions on a wide variety of space science topics, including engineering and science. Appendixes, notes.

1416. Friedman, Herbert. "Twenty-five Years of Rocket and Satellite Astronomy." *Nature* 234 (November 26, 1971): 181–183.

Traces highlights of the early history of developments in photometry, rocket technology, and earth satellites for the study of the Sun, background radiation, galaxies, and newly-discovered exotica in the ultraviolet and X-ray regions.

1417. Friedman, Herbert. "Rocket Astronomy." *New York Academy of Sciences* 198 (1972): 267–273.

Reviews 25 years of progress, identifying major events and advances in technical ability to observe astronomical objects from space. Recollects the author's contributions to ultraviolet and X-ray solar and stellar astronomy by the introduction and refinement of narrow-band Geiger counters flown on Aerobees and early satellites.

1418. Ginzberg, Eli, J. Schnee, and B. Yavitz. "Transformation of a Science: NASA's Impact on Astronomy." In *Economic Impact of Large Public Programs: The NASA Experience*, 81–114. Salt Lake City: Olympus, 1976.

This Columbia University study concludes that NASA altered the structure of astronomy as a discipline, raising new or formerly neglected specialties to roles of importance and influence. The authors claim that NASA helped move astronomy from little to big science through the large demands it placed on the discipline and the enormous resources it made available to the discipline to meet those needs.

1419. Henbest, Nigel. *Observing the Universe.* Oxford, United Kingdom: Basil Blackwell, 1984. Pp. 288. Index, Illustr.

Collection of articles by the author and others on current astronomy, which originally appeared in the *New Scientist.* Brief but informative selections on several space science missions include the International Ultraviolet Explorer, Infrared Astronomical Satellite, and other subjects.

1420. Hirsh, Richard F. *Glimpsing an Invisible Universe. The Emergence of X-Ray Astronomy.* New York: Cambridge University Press, 1983. Pp. viii + 186. Index, Bibliog., Illustr.

Examines the differing character of the major pioneer groups engaged in X-ray studies from sounding rockets and early satellites, including those at the Naval Research Laboratory and American Science and Engineering, Corp. from the 1950s through the launch of Uhuru (Solar Astronomical Satellite, SAS-A) in 1970. Reviews and critiques the growth of knowledge in various areas of solar and stellar astronomy resulting from the advent of X-ray astronomy. Appendixes, notes.

1421. Kopal, Zdenek. *Telescopes in Space.* New York: Hart, 1970. Pp. 140. Index, Illustr.

Describes the basic design principles used in astronomical telescopes; the means of putting telescopes into space; the nature of balloon, sounding rocket, and satellite astronomy; and the benefits of having a manned telescope in space. Discusses the Boeing Company, Aerospace Division plan for a Manned Orbiting Telescope.

1422. Lawton, A.T. *A Window in the Sky. Astronomy from Beyond the Earth's Atmosphere.* New York: Pergamon, 1979. Pp. 223. Index.

Brief descriptions of astronomical research performed on rockets and satellites. Concentrates on the advantages of doing astronomy beyond the atmosphere and on the potential for new and more advanced satellite platforms.

1423. Menzel, Donald H. "The Astronomer's Stake in Outer Space." *Atlantic Monthly*, November 1958, 95–99.

Essay, by a major astronomical figure, discusses the outer space environment and why astronomers want to place their telescopes there. Argues that "the Sputniks, in their way were probably the best thing that could have happened to America. They shocked us out of our complacency and revealed our vulnerability. Basic science began to live again" (p. 99).

1424. Newell, Homer E. *Astronomy in Space.* NASA SP–127. Washington, D.C.: National Aeronautics and Space Administration, 1967. Pp. 67. Index, Bibliog., Illustr.

Individual articles on the Orbiting Solar Observatory, Orbiting Astronomical Observatory, and other astronomy platforms. Includes descriptions of instruments and results, as well as the potential for larger and more complex observatories in the future.

1425. Pecker, Jean–Claude. *Space Observatories.* Dordrecht, the Netherlands: Reidel, 1970. Pp xvi + 120.

General review of reasons why astronomers have wanted to send astronomical instruments into space and an exposition of the types of astronomical information that can be acquired through space–borne research.

1426. Peterson, Lawrence E. "Instrumental Technique in X–Ray Astronomy." *Annual Reviews of Astronomy and Astrophysics* 13 (1975): 423–509.

Extensive review of detectors, collimating devices, and spacecraft housekeeping employed in high–energy observational astrophysics. Numerous citations.

1427. Spitzer, Lyman, Jr. "The Beginnings and Future of Space Astronomy." *American Scientist* 50 (1962): 473–484.

Identifies the limitations of ground–based astronomy and

early sounding rocket and satellite plans for observing celestial objects from space. It is useful in gauging a sense of the astronomical community's regard for observational astronomy from space. Written by a famous advocate of such observation.

1428. Spitzer, Lyman, Jr. *Searching between the Stars*. New Haven: Yale University Press, 1981. Pp. xv + 179. Index, Bibliog., Illustr.

Reviews recent knowledge of the interstellar medium gained with new technology. Text is based on the author's Yale Silliman lectures in 1978. Focuses on Princeton's Copernicus satellite, launched in 1972, which examined the ultraviolet (UV) high-dispersion spectra of material in the interstellar medium and in the atmospheres of hot stars. Discusses advances in understanding the evolution of stars, the cosmical abundances of the elements, and the dynamics of interstellar clouds resulting from experiments performed using Copernicus.

1429. Thompson, B.J., and R.R. Shannon, eds. *Space Optics*. Washington, D.C.: National Academy of Sciences, 1975. Pp. viii + 841.

Papers presented at the International Commission for Optics, October 9–13, 1972, held in Santa Monica. Reviews optical designs for satellite astronomy and is notable for the detailed description by Karl Henize of the Skylab Apollo Telescope Mount experiments.

APPLICATIONS SATELLITES AND
COMMERCIALIZATION OF SPACE

The application of spaceflight technology touches virtually everyone's life. Unfortunately, the literature on space applications has
been dominated by juvenile and engineering literature, and thus there
is little useful secondary material on applications satellites. Pertinent books were found at the Library of Congress and NASM and
NASA libraries, and the most simple and highly technical were elim-
inated immediately.

This section includes weather, communications, and some navigation satellites. All entries are satellite related (unmanned). For
information on manned spaceflight applications, the reader should
refer to the sections on aerospace medicine and manned spaceflight.

Janice L. Hill
Cathleen S. Lewis
Paul E. Ceruzzi

1430. Ashby, John H. *A Preliminary History of the Evolution of the Tiros Weather Satellite Program.* Greenbelt, Md.: National Aeronautics and Space Administration. Goddard Space Flight Center, 1964. Pp. 102. Bibliog., Illustr.

Discusses the evolution of the Tiros project. Details the events leading up to the launch of Tiros 1, including development of subsystems, testing of prototypes, and organization of participating agencies. Provides brief summary of the flights of Tiros 2 through 8.

Bainum, Peter M., ed. *Space in the 1980s and Beyond, 17th European Space Symposium.* Science and Technology Series of the American Astronautical Society, vol. 53. San Diego: Univelt, 1981. Pp. 302.

Cited herein as item 1736.

Carter, L.J., and P. Bainum, eds. *Space: A Developing Role for Europe.* American Astronautical Society Science and Technology Series, vol. 56. San Diego: Univelt, 1984. Pp. 278.

Cited herein as item 1739.

1431. Chapman, Richard L. *A Case Study of the U.S. Weather Satellite Program: The Interaction of Science and Politics.* Ph.D. Diss., Syracuse University, 1967. Pp. 451. Bibliog.

Ph.D. dissertation from Syracuse University examines early history of the U.S. weather satellites, particularly the development of the National Operational Meteorological Satellite System during the transition from the experimental to the operational system, with special emphasis on the interactions between NASA and the Weather Bureau.

Clarke, Arthur C. *Ascent to Orbit. A Scientific Autobiography.* New York: Wiley–Interscience, 1984. Pp. 226. Illustr.

Cited herein as item 1192.

1432. Covault, Craig. "Chinese Developing Satellites for Earth Resources Exploration." *Aviation Week and Space Technology*, 22 July 1985, 81–84.

Continues the series on the state of Chinese space technology. Describes Chinese plans for remote sensing technology—both domestic technology currently under development and images to be bought from the French company Spot-Image. Mentions specific Chinese uses for imaging, as well as technical obstacles that China will have to overcome in order to reach its goals.

1433. Cowen, Robert G. "Fulfilling the Promises." *Weatherwise* 37 (April 1984): 64–67.

Reviews the "promises," hopes, and official goals of the weather satellite program, and discusses how the goals were met and the promises fulfilled throughout the history of the program.

1434. Fishlock, David, ed. *A Guide to Earth Satellites*. New York: American Elsevier, 1971. Pp. 159. Index.

Explains how satellites work and describes existing systems used for communications, meteorology, earth resources, navigation, space research, and military purposes.

Galloway, Jonathan F. *The Politics and Technology of Satellite Communications*. Lexington, Mass.: Lexington Books, 1972. Pp. xiii + 247. Index, Bibliog.

Cited herein as item 1151.

Goddard Memorial Symposium. *Space, New Opportunities for International Ventures*. San Diego, Calif.: Univelt, 1980. Pp. x + 290. Illustr.

Cited herein as item 1657.

1435. Goldberg, E.A., and V.D. Landon. "Key Equipment for Tiros 1." *Astronautics* 5 (June 1960): 36–37, and 98–99.

Describes components of several Tiros 1 subsystems: TV camera, tracking and telemetry, position reference, power supply, and dynamics control. Discusses how these components interact during the operation of the spacecraft.

1436. Goldman, Nathan C. *Space Commerce: Free Enterprise on the High Frontier*. Cambridge, Mass.: Ballinger, 1985. Pp. xiii + 186. Index, Illustr.

Assesses the present state of national and international policy on commercial activities in space, and how it is formulated. Includes historical discussions of the evolution of attitudes towards commercial ventures and the evolution of the commercial ventures themselves, including transportation, telecommunications, and remote sensing. Warns against the military effects on space–related commercial ventures.

1437. Grey, Jerry, and C. Krop, ed. *Aerospace Technology and Marine Transport*. New York: American Institute of Aeronautics and Astronautics, 1977. Pp. 146. Illustr.

Discusses space technology spin–offs and direct space applications that have benefited the marine transport industry.

Hodgden, Louise. "Satellites at Sea: Space and Naval Warfare." In *National Interests and the Military Use in Space*, ed. William J. Durch, 113–133. Cambridge, Mass.: Ballinger, 1984.

Cited herein as item 1480.

1438. Hubert, Lester F., and P. Lehr. *Weather Satellites*. Waltham, Mass.: Blaisdell, 1967. Pp. 118. Index.

Discusses the development of U.S. weather satellites— Tiros, Nimbus, and Tiros Operational Satellites. Describes how they worked and how meteorologists used their data.

1439. Hughes, Patrick. "Weather Satellites Come of Age." *Weatherwise* 37 (April 1984): 68–75.

Discusses the current weather satellite systems of polar orbiting (NOAA) and geosynchronous (GOES) satellites. Covers several nonmeteorological applications of these satellites: detection of fire and smoke, use in the studies of vegetation and oceanography, and search and rescue. Also discusses international cooperation in sharing weather data.

1440. Jaffe, Leonard. *Communications in Space*. New York: Holt, Rinehart and Winston, 1966. Pp. 176. Index, Illustr.

Explains how the early communications satellites worked. Reviews the history of active and passive communications satellites. Explains how ground stations work. Devotes chapters to Comsat and future predictions.

1441. Kildow, Judith T. *Intelsat: Policy-Maker's Dilemma.* Lexington, Mass.: Lexington Books, 1973. Pp. xv + 118. Index, Bibliog.

Examines American policy toward Intelsat before, during, and after its formation. Discusses the effects of this policy and that of other nations involved in Intelsat.

1442. Kinsley, Michael E. *Outer Space and Inner Sanctums.* London: John Wiley and Sons, 1976. Pp. xiii + 280. Index, Notes.

Argues that the traditional cooperation between government and business in the area of commercial satellite communications has inhibited technological development. Compares the use of ground and transatlantic cables to communications satellites to argue for the deregulation of the Communications Satellite Corporation (Comsat). Notes.

Laskin, Paul L. *Communicating by Satellite.* New York: Twentieth Century Fund, 1969. Pp. 79.

Cited herein as item 1165.

1443. Leinwoll, Stanley. *Space Communications.* New York: John F. Rider, 1964. Pp. x + 166. Index, Bibliog., Illustr.

Explains the fundamental aspects of satellite communications technology. Reviews the history of active and passive communications technology, as well as the communications function of special purpose satellites, such as probes and manned spacecraft. Concludes with detailed discussions of Project OSCAR and other amateur radio operator projects. Although it was written primarily for the amateur radio operator, it can be understood by the general audience.

1444. Mack, Pamela E. *The Politics of Technological Change: A History of Landsat.* Ph.D diss., University of Pennsylvania, 1983. Pp. xii + 367. Bibliog.

Examines the history of the Landsat earth resources satellite program from the origins of the idea, through the first satellite launch in 1972 to 1975. Discusses the problems of putting the data returned by the satellite to effective and commercial use. Notes.

1445. Martin, James. *Communications Satellite Systems.* Englewood Cliffs, N.J.: Prentice–Hall, 1978. Pp. xv + 398. Index, Illustr.

Gives a clear and well–written overview of the basics of the technology of communications satellites, and how they fit into a total system of global voice, data, and television networks. Provides an in–depth treatment of the technical trade–offs in setting up typical systems. Contains charts, diagrams, photographs, and graphs.

Musolf, Lloyd D., ed. *Communications Satellites in Political Orbit.* San Francisco: Chandler, 1968. Pp. xii + 189.

Cited herein as item 1174.

1446. Ordway, Frederick I. III, C. Adams, and M. Sharpe. *Dividends from Space.* New York: Thomas Y. Crowell, 1971. Pp. xi + 309. Index, Bibliog., Illustr.

Discusses observation of Earth from orbit in order to study the oceans, the land, and the atmosphere. Includes chapters on communications via space and research in space. The first three chapters discuss earth–bound applications of space technology.

1447. Paul, Gunter, A. Lacy, and B. Lacy, trans. *The Satellite Spin-Off: The Achievements of Space Flight.* Washington, D.C.: Robert B. Luce, 1975. Pp. 272. Index, Illustr.

Reviews the history of several different satellite applications, including communications, earth resources, and meteorology. Discusses the political, scientific, and economic influences that affected the various programs.

Pelton, Joseph N. and E. Burgess. *Global Communications Satellite Policy: Intelsat, Politics and Functionalism.* Mt.

Airy, Md.: Lomond Books, 1974. Pp. xi + 183. Index, Bibliog., Illustr.

Cited herein as item 1178.

Pelton, Joseph N., and M. Snow, eds. *Economic and Policy Problems in Satellite Communications.* Praeger Special Studies in International Economics and Development. New York: Praeger, 1977. Pp. x + 242. Index.

Cited herein as item 1179.

1448. Pirard, Theo. "Twenty Years of Forecasting Progress: Weather from Space." *Aerospace International* 16, no. 4 (September/October 1980): 55–64.

Reviews thoroughly the history of weather satellites of all nations, from 1960 to 1980. Discusses instruments carried by the satellites and their capabilities.

1449. Ploman, Edward. *Space Earth and Communications.* London: Frances Printer, 1984. Pp. ix + 237. Index, Bibliog.

Examines the current context of space communications, including economic, military, and political aspects. Assesses the effects of satellite communications on education, development, and international affairs. Concludes that as the exchange of information via satellites has increased, so has the confusion over states' priorities for communications satellite development. Asserts that the potential for the use of space technology is not fully exploited as a result of international issues and the limits placed on the the flow of technology.

1450. Popham, Robert W. "A Personal Eye in Space." *Weatherwise* 37 (April 1984): 76–82.

Discusses direct interpretation of weather satellite data. Lists the various types of data available. Gives sources for information on direct readout, and more specifically, on how to build a station.

Porter, R.W. *The Versatile Satellite*. Oxford: Oxford University Press, 1977. Pp. vii + 173. Index.

Cited herein as item 1349.

1451. Ramo, Simon, ed. *Peacetime Uses of Outer Space*. New York: McGraw Hill, 1961. Pp. 279. Illustr.

Papers by leaders in various fields of research; each concerns a different use of space for peaceful purposes. Since this book was published early in the space age, much of the material predicts or proposes future uses of space.

Roland, Alex, ed. *A Spacefaring People: Perspectives on Early Spaceflight*. NASA SP-4405. Washington, D.C.: National Aeronautics and Space Administration, 1985. Pp. viii + 156. Bibliog.

Cited herein as item 1108.

Rostow, Eugene V. *Satellite Communications and Educational Television in Less Developed Countries*. Washington, D.C.: U.S. National Bureau of Standards. Institute for Applied Technology, June 1969. Irregular pagination. Illustr.

Cited herein as item 1182.

1452. Schnapf, A. "Global Weather Satellites—Two Decades of Accomplishment." *Space World* P-9-191 (November 1979): 10-23.

Summarizes the history of the U.S. weather satellite program from 1960 to 1979. Includes both the polar orbiting and the geostationary satellites. Provides several charts and drawings of the various programs and spacecraft. Describes capabilities of the craft.

1453. Smith, Delbert D. *Communication via Satellite*. Leydon, England: A.W. Sijthoff, 1976. Pp. xviii + 335. Index, Bibliog.

Proposes the Space Technology Integration model as a means of analyzing the development of communications satellites. Reviews the political and governmental history of commercial communications satellites. Presents the history as an interaction among scientific, government, and business forces.

1454. Smith, Michael L. "Selling the Moon: The U.S. Manned Space Program and the Triumph of Commodity Scientism," In R. W. Fox and T. J. Jackson Lears, eds. *The Culture of Consumption*. New York: Pantheon, 1983. Pp. 177–209.

Explores the forms of public display adopted by the planners of the U.S. manned space program, how they arose and were aided by the advertising industry, and argues that the display value of Apollo for national pride and prestige was a primary driver of the program. Places the stimulus for Apollo in the context of national recovery.

Snow, Marcellus S. *Marketplace for Telecommunications: Regulation and Deregulation in Industrialized Democracies.* New York: Longman, 1986. Pp. xvi + 304. Index.

Cited herein as item 1183.

Steinberg, Gerald M. *Satellite Reconnaissance.* New York: Praeger, 1983. Pp. 200. Bibliog.

Cited herein as item 1498.

1455. Sternberg, Sidney, and W. Strand. "TIROS 1—Meteorological Satellites." *Astronautics* 5 (June 1960): 32–34, 84–85.

Discusses the Tiros 1 system, launch, and orbit. Briefly touches on the success of Tiros 1 and its cloud pictures. Suggests additional readings.

Strasser, J.A. "New Details on Soviet Space Program: Report on Design of the Soviet Orbita–Molniya Comsat Network." *Aerospace Technology* 21 (22 April 1968): 16–21.

Cited herein as item 1722.

1456. Task Force on International Satellite Communications. *The Future of Satellite Communications.* New York: Twentieth Century Fund, 1970. Pp. 80.

Presents the recommendations of the task force for improved management of the radio spectrum resource and provides suggestions for better international cooperation in communications.

1457. United Nations Educational Scientific and Cultural Organization. *Communication in the Space Age.* Amsterdam, 1968. Pp. 200.

Discusses the potential for using satellites for various types of communications projects (radio and television, broadcasting to developing countries, and international cooperation programs). Compiles papers presented by various authors at the December 1965 meeting of the United Nations Educational, Scientific and Cultural Organization.

1458. U.S. Congress. House. Committee on Government Operations. Military Operations Subcommittee. *Satellite Communications (Military–Civil Roles and Relationships).* Washington, D.C.: U.S. Government Printing Office, October 1964. Pp. iv + 160.

Isolates the institutional and political character of satellite communications, while stressing the issues that divide civil and military uses of communications satellites. Touches on the international implications of satellite communications. Annexes include a brief history of communications satellite experiments, and a history of Project Advent.

1459. U.S. National Aeronautics and Space Administration, Goddard Space Flight Center. *Final Report on the Relay 1 Program.* NASA SP–76. Washington, D.C., 1965. Pp. 767. Illustr.

Gives the results of all aspects of the Relay 1 flight. Discusses design of the craft and ground communications stations.

1460. U.S. National Aeronautics and Space Administration, Goddard Space Flight Center. *Final Report on the Tiros 1 Meteorological Satellite System.* NASA TR–131. Washington, D.C., 1962. Pp. 355. Bibliog., Illustr.

Discusses the evolution of the Tiros program up to and including the flight of *Tiros 1*. Includes information on early attempts to observe the atmosphere from above. Gives detailed information on pre-launch tests and system design. The second half of the book presents papers of meteorologists discussing the use of *Tiros 1* photographs in the studies.

1461. U.S. National Aeronautics and Space Administration and Department of Commerce. *Proceedings of the International Meteorological Satellite Workshop, November 13–22, 1961*. Washington, D.C.: U.S. Government Printing Office, 1961. Pp. 226.

Begins with statements by members of NASA, the Weather Bureau, and other organizations. Papers cover a variety of subjects, including the Tiros spacecraft design, satellite picture gridding, and application of Tiros data to various areas of meteorological study. Includes a brief section on field trips to two NASA centers and the Weather Bureau. One appendix provides basic information on the first three Tiros satellites.

1462. U.S. National Aeronautics and Space Administration. Scientific and Technical Information Division. *Space Communications and Navigation, 1958–1964*. NASA SP–93. Washington, D.C., 1966. Pp. vii + 68. Bibliog., Illustr.

Briefly and clearly reviews the history of the National Aeronautics and Space Administration's development of telecommunications technology through the Application Technology Satellite (ATS) series. Written as part of a series of pamphlets describing NASA's achievements from 1958 to 1964 and contains a thorough, albeit unannotated, bibliography.

1463. U.S. National Aeronautics and Space Administration. Goddard Space Flight Center. *ATS–F Data Book*. Greenbelt, Md., 1974. Irregular pagination. Illustr.

Discusses all technical aspects of the ATS–F (ATS–6) mission, including the Titan III–C launch vehicle, orbit, spacecraft subsystems, ground operations, and scientific and technological experiments. Includes a section on the history of ATS–1 through 5.

1464. Wexler, Harry. "Observing the Weather from a Satellite Vehicle." *Journal of the British Interplanetary Society* 13 (September 1954): 269-276.

Proposes artificial satellite for forecasting weather. One of the earliest detailed concepts of weather satellites.

1465. Wexler, Harry, and J. Caskey, Jr., ed. *Proceedings of the First International Symposium on Rocket and Satellite Meteorology*. New York: John Wiley and Sons, 1963. Pp. 441. Index, Illustr.

Includes 40 papers, divided into the following categories: meteorological rockets (as used for both soundings and earth observation), meteorological satellites, including radiation studies, meteorological satellites, cloud studies, and meteorological satellites and special studies. Many of the papers discuss studies that made use of early Tiros data.

1466. White, Robert M. "Weather Satellite System." *The Military Engineer*, 58 (July/August 1966): 232-237.

Describes the Tiros Operational Satellite System, including the spacecraft, their orbits, and their capabilities. Discusses data transmission to the Command Data Acquisition stations and to the Automatic Picture Transmission stations. Covers many uses of satellite pictures, including the estimation of hurricane wind speeds. Concludes with a section on future development.

1467. Widger, William K., Jr., and J. Bernardo, eds. *Meteorological Satellites*. New York: Rinehart and Winston, 1966. Pp. 280. Index, Bibliog.

Reviews early history of weather satellites from the development of Tiros to Nimbus and Tiros Operational Satellite. Discusses various craft and orbits and how satellite data were used by meteorologists.

1468. Wohl, Richard. "Material Science: Soviets Lead the Way in Space Processing." *Defense Science* 3, no. 6 (December 1984): 52-55.

Cited herein as item 1724.

World Meteorological Organization. *Satellites in Meteorology, Oceanography, and Hydrology.* Geneva, 1982. Pp. 56. Bibliog., Illustr.

Summarizes the ways in which satellites are used in three areas of study, especially meteorology. Discusses the satellite systems launched by the United States and other nations, and summarizes the international programs of the World Meteorological Organization.

MILITARY USE OF SPACE

Despite the intertwined history of military projects and space exploration, serious unclassified historical studies of the military aspects
of spaceflight were not undertaken until very recently. As a result,
this section includes an eclectic sampling of monographs, studies,
articles, and histories of military space programs. Sources have been
gleaned not only from library databases, but also from Paul Stares's
bibliography (see item 1497).

A few studies of the Strategic Defense Initiative (SDI) are included, but only if SDI has been discussed in the historical perspective of Ballistic Missile Defense (BMD). A few congressional reports
on the military space programs of the United States have been added
for their historical perspective.

For additional sources, the reader should consult the institutional
and political sections of this bibliography, as well as the section on
the Soviet Union.

Cathleen S. Lewis

1469. Baker, David. *The Shape of Wars to Come*. New York: Stein and Day, 1982. Pp. 262. Index, Illustr.

Speculates on the role of space–based systems in future wars, based on the history of military use of space systems. Explains some of the fundamental techniques used on the satellites. Provides no scholarly citations.

Borrowman, Gerald L. "Kosmoljot–Soviet Wings into Space." *Journal of the British Interplanetary Society* 35 (1982): 75–79.

Cited herein as item 1704.

1470. Borrowman, Gerald L. "Soviet Military Activities in Space." *Journal of the British Interplanetary Society* 35 (1982): 86–92.

Examines the evidence of Soviet military activities in space with emphasis on manned activities on broad military Saliut stations, especially reconnaissance activities and laser experiments. Speculates on Soviet development of beam weapons. Refers to Chinese reconnaissance activities.

Braun, Wernher von. "Dr. Wernher von Braun: An Historical Essay." *Spaceflight* 14 (November 1972): 409–412.

Cited herein as item 1227.

1471. Burrows, William E. *Deep Black: Space Espionage and National Security*. New York: Random House, 1986. Pp. xvii + 401. Index, Bibliog., Illustr.

Traces the evolution of military reconnaissance and surveillance tactics and equipment. Presents the emergence of specific systems as the outcome of particular strategic approaches. Based entirely upon unclassified sources, reveals the preponderance of information available on what is often perceived to be highly secret. Touches on some issues surrounding national security and the author's method of researching this book. Includes discussion of Soviet space strategy and speculation on the future.

1472. Canan, James W. *The Superwarriors*. New York: Weybright and Talley, 1975. Pp. 361. Bibliog.

Discusses the role of research and development in weapons development, covering the controversy of funding private companies for research and development. Traces the history of laser technology through 1975 as an example, and speculates on its future use in strategic defense.

1473. Canan, James W. *War in Space*. New York: Harper and Row, 1982. Pp. 186.

Based on personal conversations with members of the defense community, describes the evolution of Defense Department strategic use of space. Touches on Soviet military satellite operations.

1474. Cassutt, Michael. "The Military Salyuts." *Space World*, April 1979, 18–25.

Reports on evidence that Soviet Saliut space stations are assigned either military or scientific activities that can be determined on the basis of orbital parameters, crew assignment, and the coding of communications. Concludes that even though it is primarily the military stations that participate in those activities, civilian stations may do so as well.

1475. Deudney, Daniel. *Space: The High Frontier in Perspective*. Washington, D.C.: Worldwatch Institute, 1982. Pp. 72. Illustr.

Argues that the presence of military instruments in space obscures the opening of the space frontier from the Earth. Briefly overviews these activities. Encourages cooperative ventures to hold the tide of militarization. Notes.

1476. Downs, Eldon W., ed. *The U.S. Air Force in Space*. New York: Praeger, 1966. Pp. 148. Index, Bibliog., Illustr.

Summary of U.S. Air Force involvement in space programs. Includes a discussion of scientific space research sponsored by the Air Force, as well as justification for the research. Appendixes.

Dupas, Alain. *La lutte pour l'espace.* Paris: Seuil, 1977. Pp. 281. Illustr.

Cited herein as item 1146

Fishlock, David, ed. *A Guide to Earth Satellites.* New York: American Elsevier, 1971. Pp. 159. Index.

Cited herein as item 1434.

Forbich, C. "The Soviet Space Shuttle Program." *Spaceworld,* January 1981, 4–8.

Cited herein as item 1706.

Gantz, Kenneth F., ed. *Man in Space: The United States Air Force Program for Developing the Spacecraft Crew.* New York: Duell, Sloan and Pearce, 1959. Pp. xv + 303. Index, Bibliog.

Cited herein as item 1588.

Gantz, Kenneth F., ed. *Nuclear Flight: The United States Air Force Programs for Atomic Jets, Missiles, and Rockets.* New York: Duell, 1960. Pp. 216. Index, Illustr.

Cited herein as item 1285.

1477. Graham, Daniel O. *A Defense That Defends.* Old Greenwich, Conn.: Devin–Adair, 1983. Pp. xiv + 158. Index, Bibliog., Illustr.

Proposes Strategic Defense as an alternative to Mutual Assured Destruction as a solution to the arms race. The author is considered the originator of the current concept of the Strategic Defense Initiative. Appendixes.

Gray, Colin S. "The ABM and the Arms Race." *Aerospace Historian* 18 (December 1971): 26–32.

Cited herein as item 1154.

1478. Grey, Colin S. *American Military Space Policy*. Cambridge, Mass: Abt Books, 1982. Pp. 106. Index.

Examines the current state of U.S. military space policy in the light of political, military, and scientific opportunities, problems, and necessities; mentions weapons, communications, and intelligence systems and frequently refers to Soviet policy. Considers the role of military space policy in arms control and the prospect for arms control negotiations over space weapons·systems. Annex analyzes Soviet Draft Space Treaty of 1981. Appendixes include texts of White House Fact Sheet on National Space Policy and the Soviet Draft Space Treaty of 1981. Provides extensive references to sources.

1479. Haggerty, James. "Military in Space." *Aerospace* 20, no. 2 (Spring 1982): 2–9.

Takes exception to the standard Department of Defense portrayal of the military balance in space. Outlines current military systems in use in the United States and speculates on systems currently under development. Well illustrated by painting and drawings of military satellites.

1480. Hodgden, Louise. "Satellites at Sea: Space and Naval Warfare." In *National Interests and the Military Use in Space*, ed. William J. Durch, 113–133. Cambridge, Mass.: Ballinger, 1984.

Asserts that the recent establishment of the Naval Space Command (October 1983) indicated a dramatic shift in naval thought toward the idea that space operations are peripheral to sea operations. Reviews the history of naval space operations.

James, Peter N. *Soviet Conquest from Space*. New Rochelle: Arlington House, 1974. Pp. 206. Index, Bibliog.

Cited herein as item 1681.

1481. Jasani, Bhupendra, ed. *Outer Space—A New Dimension of the Arms Race*. London: Taylor and Francis, 1982. Pp. xviii + 423. Illustr.

Divided in two parts. Part 1 surveys the history of space science and technology. Covers a wide range of topics such as orbital inclinations, vehicles, and propulsion, and touches briefly on the history of reconnaissance satellite techniques. States the inherent vulnerabilities and shortcomings of space-based strategic activities. Part 2 provides in–depth papers on selected areas related to the military use of space. Of particular interest to the historian are: "Reconnaissance Satellites" by Bruce G. Blair; "Banning All Weapons in Outer Space" by O.V. Bogdanov; "The Prospects for Beam Weapons." by A.M. Din;, "Recent Advances in the Use of Space for Military Purposes and on Second Generation Nuclear Weapons" by M. Felden; "What Additional Arms Control Measures Related to Outer Space Could Be Proposed" by D. Goedhuis; "Anti-Satellite Weapons: The Prospects for Arms Control." by D.L. Hafner; "Some Remarks on U.S. and Soviet Strategies Concerning Manned Activities in Outer Space" by H. Kautzleben; "Navigational Satellite Systems; Their Characteristics, Potential and Military Applications" by K.D. McDonald; "Orbital BMD and the Space Patrol" by P.J. Nahin; and "Use of Satellites in Crisis Monitoring" by K. Santhanam.

1482. Jiden, George F. "Space System Vulnerabilities and Countermeasures." In *National Interests and the Military Use of Space*, ed. William J. Durch, 89–112 Cambridge, Mass.: Ballinger, 1984.

Argues that the complex nature of satellite systems leaves them unavoidably vulnerable to attack. Concludes that despite elaborate countermeasures, satellite systems will always be vulnerable to offense.

Johnson, Nicholas L. "The Military and Civilian Salyut Space Programmes." *Spaceflight* 19 (August/September 1979): 364–370.

Cited herein as item 1709.

1483. Johnson, Nicholas L. *Soviet Military Strategy in Space*. London: Jane's, 1987. Pp. 287. Index.

Traces the history of the military activities of the Soviet Union in space, and what the author perceives to be the military, political, and economic unity of the Soviet space program. Based on unclassified reports of Soviet space activities and classic studies of military strategy. As the first book-length study of Soviet space policy, is indispensable for studying the history of the Soviet space program.

1484. Karas, Thomas. *The New High Ground.* New York: Touchstone, 1983. Pp. 224. Illustr.

Traces the organizational path of the command apparatus of U.S. military space policy from the initial design and budget debates through deployment. Uses the Space Shuttle as a primary example of U.S. space policy. Describes the history of current space weapons systems.

1485. Kendon, Anthony. "U.S. Reconnaissance Satellite Programmes." *Spaceflight* 20 (July 1978): 243-262.

Gathers published reports, dating from 1960, on U.S. reconnaissance satellites into a comprehensive record of reconnaissance activities. Lists U.S. reconnaissance and surveillance launches, including date of launch and information on launch vehicles and orbital parameters. Includes brief discussion of the evolution of U.S. strategy.

1486. Klass, Philip J. *Secret Sentries in Space.* New York: Random House, 1971. Pp. xvi + 236. Illustr.

Argues that reconnaissance satellites have helped to defuse the military strategic tension that has steadily increased since the end of World War II. Traces the history of strategic competition between the United States and the USSR. Describes the operations, uses, and retrieval of reconnaissance satellites. Although the coverage of the topic is comprehensive, no citations are provided.

Koppes, Clayton R. *JPL and the American Space Program.* New Haven, Conn.: Yale University Press, 1982. Pp. xiii + 299. Index, Illustr.

Cited herein as item 1126.

1487. Lang, Daniel. *From Hiroshima to the Moon.* New York: Simon and Schuster, 1959. Pp. xii + 496. Index.

Examines the scientific and military developments in the United States since the development of the atomic bomb, beginning with the Army's secret experiments during World War II. Based on interviews with individuals who took part in military research, including Wernher von Braun.

Levine, Arthur L. *The Future of the U.S. Space Program.* New York: Praeger, 1975. Pp. xi + 197. Index.

Cited herein as item 1166.

1488. Macvey, John W. *Space Weapons/Space War.* New York: Stein and Day, 1977. Pp. xvi + 245. Index, Bibliog., Illustr.

Claims not to support space war or its approach, but only to present the facts concerning a possibility of a space war. Presents popular discussions of potential space weapons.

1489. Manno, Jack. *Arming the Heavens.* New York: Dodd, Mead, 1984. Pp. 197. Index, Bibliog.

Asserts that the American space program is reactive to that of the Soviets and that the planners view the scientific merits of the program as secondary to the military aspects. Also discusses what the author believes to be the Nazi legacy of rocketry and space exploration. Includes list of organizations involved in the military uses of space.

1490. Medaris, John B. *Countdown for Decision.* Princeton, N.J.: Van Nostrand, 1959. Pp. 303.

The author's role is recounted in the then–crucial decision to proceed with the *Explorer 1* satellite crash program after the failures of the first Vanguard satellite vehicles. Maj. Gen. John B. Medaris, as commander of the Army Ballistic Missile Agency, proposed and directed the *Juno 1* (Jupiter C) vehicle program modified to launch the *Explorer 1*, the first U.S. satellite.

1491. Myer, Stephen M. "Space and Soviet Military Planning" In *National Interests and the Military Use of Space*, ed. William J. Durch, 61–68. Cambridge, Mass.: Ballinger, 1984. Bibliog.

Argues that the accelerated military–related space activities of the Soviet Union are directed specifically toward peacetime duties and crisis management, and although these activities might increase indirect Soviet involvement in war, they have no appreciable effect on Soviet activities on the ground.

O'Leary, Brian. *Project Space Station—Plans for a Permanent Manned Space Center.* Harrisburg, Pa.: Stackpole Books, 1983. Pp. xv + 159. Index, Bibliog., Illustr.

Cited herein as item 1609.

1492. Peebles, Curtis. *Battle for Space.* New York: Beaufort, 1983. Pp. 192. Illustr.

Reviews the history of military space systems and the issues surrounding them, including reconnaissance, surveillance, orbiting nuclear weapons in space, anti–satellite systems, the potential for the development of laser and particle weapons, and space law and arms control. Focuses almost exclusively on U.S. and Soviet programs, but gives some attention to Chinese reconnaissance activities. Proposes that the deployment of beam weapons may bring about a qualitative change in the arms race and supports their development. Includes a glossary of terms and extensive citations. Notes.

Pirard, Theo. "Chinese 'Secrets' Orbiting the Earth." *Spaceflight* 19, no. 10 (October 1977): 355–361.

Cited herein as item 1760.

Rao, B. Radhakrishna. "China: New Space Power of Threat to Stability in Asia?" *Spaceworld* R–3–207 (March 1981): 19–20.

Cited herein as item 1762.

1493. Ritchie, David. *Space War.* New York: Atheneum, 1982. Pp. 224. Illustr.

Asserts that the military legacy of the space programs of the United States and the USSR arose from mutual origins in German V–2 rockets. Traces the histories of both the Soviet and American military space programs.

1494. Russell, Malcolm. "Soviet Legal View of Military Space Activities." In *National Interests and the Military Use of Space,* ed. William J. Durch, 201–234. Cambridge, Mass.: Ballinger, 1984.

Assesses Soviet space policy by examining Soviet legal publications. Argues that the limited readership of these journals allows the authors to reveal more about Soviet policy on the use of space. Concludes that Soviet legal arguments closely parallel Soviet foreign policy statements, whose defensive character is manipulated to their offensive advantage.

1495. Salkeld, Robert. *War and Space*. Garden City, N.Y.: Prentice Hall, 1970. Pp. xxiv + 195. Bibliog.

Contrasts the immensity of space to the significance of wars. Narrates the history of the development of military space systems in the light of scientific discoveries and the political climate of the time.

Schauer, William H. *The Politics of Space: A Comparison of the Soviet and American Space Programs*. New York: Holmes and Meier, 1976. Pp. vii + 317. Index, Bibliog.

Cited herein as item 1669.

1496. Stares, Paul B. "Space and U.S. National Security." In: *National Interests and the Military Use of Space*, ed. William J. Durch, 35–59. Cambridge, Mass.: Ballinger, 1984. Bibliog.

Describes the evolution of U.S. military dependence on space systems. Attributes early international sanctions of military space activities to early U.S. aggressiveness in pursuing a policy to prevent Soviet military and political interference.

1497. Stares, Paul B. *The Militarization of Space: U.S. Policy, 1945–1984*. Ithaca, N.Y.: Cornell University Press, 1985. Pp. 334. Index, Bibliog.

Contends that as a result of the somewhat chaotic history of space doctrine, the U.S. government has returned to a strategic and rhetorical position similar to that of the late 1950s "space race." Traces the evolution of American military space systems from their early days, when they were plagued by interservice rivalries, through the formation of coherent programs and the maturation of technology. Focuses primarily on strategy of the U.S. military space effort. Refers to Soviet influences on U.S. policy and programs. Concludes that the consequences of developing further military space weapons cannot be predicted. Appendixes, notes.

1498. Steinberg, Gerald M. *Satellite Reconnaissance*. New York: Praeger, 1983. Pp. 200. Bibliog.

Begins with the U.S.–Soviet conflict over aerial reconnaissance. Discusses the policy changes in American and Soviet attitudes over this issue. Presents the policy issues involved in both the acceptance of reconnaissance satellites and that of anti–satellite operations and implications. Approaches the issues from the perspective of policy analysts.

1499. Stockholm International Peace Research Institute. *Outer Space—Battlefield of the Future?* London: Taylor and Francis, 1978. Pp. xvii + 202. Index, Illustr.

Sorts out the various military uses of satellites, including reconnaissance, communications, navigation, meteorology, geodesy, and interception/destruction. Provides the basic scientific concepts for the function of each type of satellite, followed by brief descriptions of national programs. Includes tables listing launch dates and parameters of satellites and a glossary of terms.

1500. Union of Concerned Scientists. *The Fallacy of Star Wars*. New York: Vintage, 1984. Pp. xiii + 293. Illustr.

Argues that President Ronald Reagan's proposed Strategic Defense Initiative (SDI) is based on the hope for improbable scientific and engineering breakthroughs and jeopardizes the Anti–Ballistic Missile (ABM) Treaty. Divided into three parts: Part 1 provides a historical background; Part 2 revises the Union of Concerned Scientists' (UCS) report, *Space–Based Missile Defense*; and Part 3 assesses the impact of SDI on the ABM treaty. Provides some technical information, but is primarily written for the lay reader. Notes.

U.S. Congress. House of Representatives. Committee on Government Operations. Subcommittee on Military Operations. 86th Congress. *Organization and Management of Missile Programs*. Washington, D.C.: U.S. Government Printing Office, 1960. Pp. iii + 228.

Cited herein as item 1134.

1501. U.S. Congress. House of Representatives. Committee on Science and Astronautics. 87th Congress. *Defense Space Interests*. Washington, D.C.: U.S. Government Printing Office, 1961. Pp. iii + 220.

Contains testimony from hearings before the House Committee on Science and Astronautics, which served as a basis for defining the Department of Defense's (DOD) space activities. Includes a chronology of DOD's Advanced Research Projects Agency activities.

U.S. Congress. House. Committee on Government Operations. Military Operations Subcommittee. *Satellite Communications (Military–Civil Roles and Relationships)*. Washington, D.C.: U.S. Government Printing Office, October 1964. Pp. iv + 160.

Cited herein as item 1458.

1502. *The United States' Military Space Defense Market*. New York: Frost and Sullivan, 1980. Pp. 200.

Reviews the role of space systems in the U.S. military in order to assess the importance of military space markets to business. Argues for further development to allow the United States to adequately defend these systems.

1503. Wilkening, Dean A. "Space–Based Weapons." In *National Interests and the Military Use of Space*, ed. William J. Durch, 135–167. Cambridge, Mass. Ballinger, 1984.

Asserts that in light of the history of previous proposals for technologies and missions of space–based weapons, as well as the history of the development of the technologies of the currently proposed system, any space–based weapons would make the strategic balance precarious.

Wohl, Richard. "Material Science: Soviets Lead the Way in Space Processing." *Defense Science* 3, no. 6 (December 1984): 52–55.

Cited herein as item 1723.

AEROSPACE MEDICINE

Original research in the history of aviation and aerospace medicine is exceedingly rare. However, this picture is changing for a number of reasons. For one thing, more historians of science, medicine, and technology are turning their attention to 20th century medicine and medical research, and aviation and aerospace medicine fall squarely within this area of interest. In addition, members of organizations such as the aerospace medical association continue to take an active interest in the history of their disciplines, and public agencies such as the Office of Air Force History have sponsored and conducted oral history interview programs for participants in contemporary work.

At this writing, the history of aviation and aerospace medicine remains a virtually unmined field of study. The following entries provide a rich introduction to the field and serve as a stepping stone to scholarly historical writing.

These entries were selected on the basis of several criteria: all are or lead to primary sources are readily available, and contain reliable historical documentation. In general, documents not found in collections at the National Library of Medicine, the Office of Air Force History, or the libraries of NASA or the Smithsonian Institution have been excluded because of obscurity. Popular reviews although not always historically accurate are included where possible, for they are useful as evidence of the widespread and consistently high level of interest in the field.

Second, the entries deal almost exclusively with American work. However, some references to international activities do exist, and although they are few in number, they are included wherever possible.

Third, the bibliography includes texts and classics that offer a historical perspective on the field or that are of historical signifi-cance in themselves.

The reader should be aware that the richest sources can be found in the period after World War II, which is the time when official his-tories of medical activities in the Army Air Forces and the Office of Scientific Research and Development first appeared. These reports were followed by NASA mission reports on the early manned space-flight era of the 1960s. Government laboratories, research centers, and schools provided official histories of varying quality. Many are

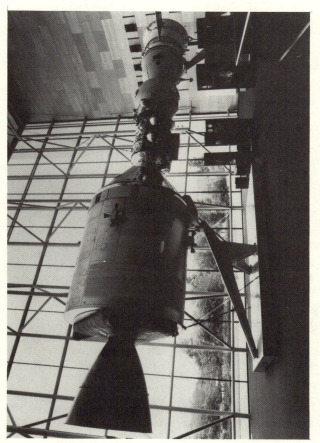

The Air and Space Museum's recreation of the Apollo–Soiuz Test Project, the first international piloted space mission during which an Apollo spacecraft docked with Soiuz 19 in space on 18 July 1975. This mock-up consists of an Apollo Command Service Module which had formerly been used for ground tests; an engineering model of the docking module, which was designed specifically for this mission, and a mock–up of a Soiuz spacecraft, which is on loan from the Soviet Academy of Sciences. A similar display is exhibited in Moscow in the Kosmos Pavilion of the Exhibition of Economic Achievements. (Dale Hrabak, Smithsonian Institution)

careful, balanced treatments of scholarly integrity, but others are of lesser value to the historian.

Finally, some topics are not covered here, notably, flight material, flight safety, and general space biology.

This bibliography may be supplemented with several useful bibliographies and chronologies. Part II of the Work Projects Administration *Bibliography of Aeronautics* includes international entries to its date of publication (1973). Ebbe C. Hoff and John F. Fulton prepared a comprehensive *Bibliography of Aviation Medicine* for the OSRD (Baltimore: C.C. Thomas) in 1942 and a supplement in 1944 (Yale University School of Medicine, Publication no. 9). Both include author and subject indexes. The National Library of Medicine publishes occasional bibliographies of space medicine; the most recent one appeared in 1986. NASA complies and publishes *Aerospace Medicine and Biology: A Continuing Bibliography* (1964 to date). John Bullard's *Chronology of the Aerospace Medical Division* (Air Force Systems Command, 1980) addresses that organization from 1960 to 1980. Several journals are helpful in the 1930s. *The Airline Pilot* for example, published intermittent articles on the health of the airman. Since its founding in 1929, the *Journal of Aviation, Space and Environmental Medicine* has included articles related to the history of the discipline and its practitioners. The entire May 1979 issue was devoted to the association's fiftieth anniversary. The January 1983 issue contains a list of selected classic aerospace medicine publications. Historical entries continue to appear regularly.

One important archival collection deserves special mention. The health sciences library of Wright State University holds the Ross A. McFarland archival collection. It is unrivaled as a single source of works on aviation medicine history.

Adrianne Noë

1504. Anderson, Henry G., M. Flack, and O.H. Gotch. *The Medical and Surgical Aspects of Aviation*. London: H. Frowde; Hodder and Stoughton, 1919. Pp. xvi + 255. Index, Illustr.

The earliest textbook on aviation medicine. Anderson analyzes the state of the field in Great Britain with a sensitivity to the medical problems inherent in aeronautics that is unusual in medical works of the period. Chapters of special interest are "Applied Physiology of Aviation" and "The Aero–Neuroses of War Pilots." Also includes an aeronautical glossary.

1505. Andrus, E.C., et al. *Advances in Military Medical Science in World War II* 2 vols. Boston: Little, Brown, 1948. Pp. 900. Index, Illustr.

Official history of the medical efforts of the Office of Scientific Research and Development. Includes extensive chapters on aviation medicine, crash injury analysis, acceleration, anoxia, and decompression. By way of introduction, Detlev W. Bronk, chair of the Division of Aviation Medicine for the Committee for Medical Research, gives a useful description of the state of the art in the field around 1945. Extremely useful appendix lists all OSRD medical contracts.

1506. Armstrong, Harry G., ed. *Aerospace Medicine*. Baltimore: Williams and Wilkins, 1961. Pp. 638. Index, Bibliog., Illustr.

A collection of scientific articles on early aerospace medicine, including several chapters by the editor, a founder in the field and formerly surgeon general, U.S. Air Force Includes an introductory essay on the history of aerospace medicine.

1507. Armstrong, Harry G. *Principles and Practice of Aviation Medicine*. Baltimore: Williams and Wilkins, 1939. Pp. xii + 496. Index, Bibliog., Illustr.

Presents an early text–book approach to aerospace medicine, written by an early pioneer in the field of aviation medicine. Although it was intended to be a text, it is a highly readable assessment of the state of the subject in 1939. By way of introduction, includes a good historical survey as well as 26 chapters on different topics of aviation medicine and related physiological and psychological research.

1508. Ashe, William F., et al. *Historical Survey of Inhabitable Artificial Atmospheres.* Columbus: Ohio State University Research Foundation, 1959. Pp. 154.

Published also as Wright Air Development Center Technical Report, WADC 58–154; PB Report 151277, Report AD–155 901. Provides abstracts of over 400 international articles and other 20th century publications on living organisms in artificial atmospheres.

1509. Bauer, Louis H. *Aviation Medicine.* Baltimore: Williams and Wilkins, 1926. Pp. xv + 241. Index, Bibliog., Illustr.

The first American text on aviation medicine. It has brought the subject to the attention of a wide medical and military audience. Contains historical introduction, and chapters on the essential tasks of the flight surgeon—pilot selection and classification, pilot care, and maintenance. Also includes technical supplements on the methods used to administer several medical tests widely used in World War I.

1510. Baxter, James P. III. *Scientists against Time.* Reprint. Cambridge, Mass.: MIT, 1968. Pp. xxi + 473.

This well–known official history of the Office of Scientific Research and Development includes several chapters on the advances in medicine under wartime pressures. Amid lengthy discussions of military medicine is a unit on aviation medicine, including a brief assessment of medical issues related to World War II. Traces official contributions to the military aviation medicine effort, such as work on oxygen delivery systems, decompression problems, and the visual problems of night flight. This is an excellent introduction to wartime aeromedical research.

1511. Benford, Robert J. *Doctors in the Sky—The Story of the Aero Medical Association.* Springfield, Ill.: Charles C. Thomas, 1955. Pp. xv + 326. Index, Bibliog., Illustr.

Chronicles the history of the Aero Medical Association from 1928 to 1955. Includes biographies of association presidents and other significant figures in the field, the establishment of aviation medicine as a specialty, information about the wives' wing, and a rich appendix that lists presidents of the association, its constitution and bylaws, awards, and a chronology of significant leaders in the discipline. A thorough history of the association.

1512. Benford, Robert J., comp. *The Heritage of Aviation Medicine: An Annotated Directory of Early Artifacts.* Washington, D.C.: Aerospace Medical Association, 1979. Pp. ix + 122. Index, Bibliog., Illustr.

A directory of aeromedical artifacts in public and private collections in the United States and abroad. Although not exhaustive, the entries span the period from early ballooning artifacts to those of the 1950s and form a highly usable guide to the rich history of the subject. Well–informed essays and intelligently chosen illustrations accompany the entries. A geographically organized index completes this indispensable work.

1513. Bert, Paul. *Barometric Pressure: Researches in Experimental Physiology.* Translated by Mary Alice Hitchcock and Fred A. Hitchcock. Columbus, Ohio: College Book, 1943. Pp. 1055. Index, Illustr.

A translation of Bert's 1877 work on the role of barometric pressure in physiology. In this three–part work, Bert offers a history of altitude physiology research, reports of his own experimentation, and his formidable conclusions. A classic work that for many years was a standard reference.

1514. Bond, Douglas D. *The Love and Fear of Flying.* Preface by Gen. James H. Doolittle, USAF. New York: International Universities Press, 1952. Pp. 190. Index.

The author, a professor of psychiatry and head of the medical school, Western Reserve University, gives a Freudian interpretation of such topics as the psychology of flight, fantasy and flight, the love of flight, its relation to aggression, and how flight relates to ego and reality. Also includes a section on diagnosis.

1515. Bushnell, David. *History of Research in Space Biology and Biodynamics.* Holloman Air Force Base, N.M.: U.S. Air Force, Missile Development Center, 1958. Pp. ix + 114. Illustr.

Carefully compiled official history of research activities. Includes numerous notes at the end of each chapter. Some material deals specifically with humans, other material is more general.

1516. Caidin, Martin, and G. Caidin. *Aviation and Space Medicine— Man Conquers the Vertical Frontier.* New York: E.P. Dutton 1962. Pp. 215. Illustr.

Presents a popular introduction to the history of early manned space travel, including aviation at high altitudes, the development of pressure and space suits, effects of gravitation forces, and escape and survival issues.

1517. Calloway, Doris Howes, ed. *Human Ecology in Space Flight.* New York: New York Academy of Sciences, Interdisciplinary Communications Program, 1966. Pp. 285. Bibliog., Illustr.

Proceedings of the First International Interdisciplinary Conference, 1963, Princeton. Authors discuss closed ecological systems—space cabin atmospheres.

1518. Calvin, Melvin, and O. Gazenko, eds. *Foundations of Space Biology and Medicine.* 3 vols. Washington, D.C.: U.S. National Aeronautics and Space Administration, 1975. Pp. 430 + 742 + 479. Index, Bibliog., Illustr.

A joint U.S./USSR publication. Volume 1, "Space as a Habitat," covers the physical properties of space and their biological significance, the planets and satellites of the solar system from physical and ecological points of view, and the problems of exobiology. Volume 2 (in 2 parts), "Ecological and Physiological Bases of Science Biology and Medicine," deals with the influence of an artificial gaseous atmosphere of spacecraft and space stations on the organism, the effect of radiant energy from space on the organism, the psycho-physiological problems of spaceflight, and the effects of spaceflight on man and animals. Volume 3, "Space Medicine and Biotechnology," looks at methods of providing life support, characteristics of life support systems protection, selection and training of astronauts, and future space biomedical research.

1519. Chase, John S., and N. Mumey. *Physical Requirements for Commercial Fliers*. Denver, Colo.: Clason, 1931. Pp. 31. Illustr.

Produced in an era of burgeoning civil aviation, this pilot's guide offers explanations of the effects of flight on the human body and explains physical examinations and testing equipment for flight examinations. Both authors were U.S. Department of Commerce medical examiners.

1520. Cosman, Bard C. "Birth of Aviation Medicine." *American Aviation Historical Society Journal* 29 (1984): 148–151.

Excellent concise treatment of the first years of organized aviation medicine in the United States.

1521. DeHart, Roy L., ed. *Fundamentals of Aerospace Medicine*. Philadelphia: Lea and Febiger, 1985. Pp. xviii + 985. Index, Bibliog., Illustr.

A professional technical text by respected experts in the field. Foreword, preface, and initial chapters address historical issues. Several of the essays contain useful historical overviews; sections include chapters on the physiology of flight, crew selection issues, flight operations, and overviews of particular topics. Includes a significant historical introduction and useful bibliography for historical work.

1522. Dempsey, Charles A. *Fifty Years of Research on Man in Flight*. Washington, D.C.: U.S. Air Force. Pp. 215. Illustr.

Celebrates the 50th anniversary of the organization now named the Air Force Aerospace Medical Research Laboratory. It is exceedingly useful for its photographs showing stages in the growth of the lab from a small unit in 1934 to the major research site it is today. Brief introductory remarks serve as a guide to the collection of illustrations and provides lists of participants, reports, and publications rather than as a useful synthesis of activities.

1523. Engle, Eloise. *Escape from the Air and from the Sea*. New York: John Day, 1963. Pp. 250. Index, Bibliog.

Offers a historical treatment of the development of aviation safety devices, such as the ejection seat and the parachute. Although not historically rigorous, the work is a useful introduction to certain developments in flight safety and provides a useful initial bibliography.

1524. Engle, Eloise, and A.S. Lott. *Man in Flight: Biomedical Achievements in Aerospace.* Annapolis, Md.: Leeward, 1979. Pp. xxvii + 396. Index, Bibliog., Illustr.

With an important seven–page foreword by Dr. Robert J. Benford, this broad historical treatment celebrates the first 50 years of the Aerospace Medical Association. Beginning with the first manned flights in balloons, the author traces the development of the field into the space program. Although concentrates on the later period, this usefully illustrated work is a basic introduction to the history of the topic.

1525. Fishbein, Morris, ed. *Doctors at War.* New York: E.P. Dutton, 1945. Pp. 398. Index, Illustr.

Fishbein was editor of the *Journal of the American Medical Association* and chairman of the Committee on Information, Division of Medical Sciences of the wartime National Research Council. Includes a chapter on the Mission of the Army Air Force by then Major David N.W. Grant. Traces issues of the evacuation of the wounded and gives a good historical perspective on the application of changes in the rules of flight surgeons, aviation psychologists and flight nurses. A good complement to Baxter's *Scientists against Time.*

1526. Fulton, John F. *Aviation Medicine in Its Preventive Aspects: An Historical Survey.* New York: Oxford University Press, 1948. Pp. viii + 174. Index, Bibliog., Illustr.

A concise work that gives a thoughtful broad history of prevention of altitude sickness, decompression sickness, pressure cabins, and acceleration. Concludes with a general chapter on safety in flight.

1527. Futrell, Robert F. *Development of Aeromedical Evacuation in the USAF, 1909–1960.* USAF Historical Studies, no. 23. Maxwell Air Force Base, Ala: Research Studies Institute, Air University, USAF Historical Division, 1960. Pp. approx. 900.

Thoroughly and carefully researched, extensively referenced and noted, this is one of the very few secondary documents on the topic of aeromedical evacuation of patients. Presents a chronology of developments organized by military action. Includes European developments.

1528. Gantz, Kenneth F., ed. *Man in Space: The United States Air Force Program for Developing the Spacecraft Crew.* New York: Duell, Sloan and Pearce, 1959. Pp. 303. Bibliog.

Collection of papers by premier life scientists participating in aerospace/aviation research. Contains extensive annotated references; particularly useful discussion of crew–selection.

1529. Gauer, Otto H., and G.D. Zuidema. *Gravitational Stress in Aerospace Medicine.* Boston: Little, Brown, 1961. Pp. 278. Bibliog.

First in a series of publications from the Guggenhein Center for Aviation Health Safety at the Harvard School of Public Health. Highly technical text includes a short history of gravitational aspects of aviation medicine. Most of the work treats issues in the physiology of acceleration in a careful technical, but readable, manner. Exceptionally well referenced.

1530. Gerathewohl, Siegfreid J. *Principles of Bioastronautics.* Englewood Cliffs, N.J.: Prentice–Hall, 1963. Pp. xvii + 557. Index, Illustr.

An important and relatively early handbook on the subject. Includes such topics as man's role in space, chapters on spacecraft, and space vehicle operations. Also includes extensive material on the environment, space and its biomedical effects, and physiology and life support in space. Includes both name and subject indices.

1531. Gibson, T.M. *Into Thin Air.* London: R. Hale, 1984. Pp. 279. Index, Bibliog., Illustr.

This is one of the few works to synthesize aviation medicine history. Subtitled "A History of Aviation Medicine in the RAF," this volume offers a rare historic perspective on European aviation medical issues. Bibliography is especially useful.

1532. Glasgow, Thurman A. "Father of Space Medicine: An Aero-space Profile." *Aerospace Historian* 17 (Spring 1970): 6–9. Illustr.

Profiles the career of Dr. Hubertus Strughold, considered the father of space medicine.

1533. Gillies, J.A., ed. *A Textbook on Aviation Physiology*. New York: Pergamon Press, 1965. Pp. viii + 1226. Index, Bibliog., Illustr.

A sophisticated classic text on the clinical medical aspects of aviation in medicine with a sharply focused historical introduction. Includes the following sections: "The Physical Environment of Flight," "The General Effects of Reduced Atmosphere Pressure," "Oxygen Depreciation at "Reduced Barometric Pressure (including the Principles of Pressure Suit Design)," "Thermal Stress and Survival," "Acceleration," "Noise and Vibration," "Visual Factors in Aviation Aircrew Performance," and "Aircraft Accidents."

1534. Haber, Heinz. *Man in Space*. Indianapolis, Ind.: Bobbs–Merrill, 1953. Pp. 219. Bibliog.

One of the earliest treatments of human issues in space-flight, along with those of McFarland. Predicts ways of han-dling the problems of space exploration anticipated in the early 1950s, such as weightlessness and cosmic radiation.

1535. Hanrahan, James S., and D. Bushnell. *Space Biology: The Human Factors in Space Flight*. New York: Science Editions, 1960. Pp. 285. Illustr., Bibliog.

Readable survey of human needs in the space environment —gravitation, radiation, closed systems as known and antic-ipated around 1960. Not a technical text, this is a review of research to date. Written at a level appropriate for high school and more advanced use. Extensive references.

1536. Hardy, James D., and R.J. Crosby. *Human Acceleration Studies for the Armed Forces—NRC Committee on Bio-Astronautics*. Washington, D.C.: National Academy of Sci-ences—National Research Council, 1961. Pp. 71. Bibliog.

Extensively referenced collection on flight acceleration and its effect on the human element. Includes a broad chronology of human acceleration events dating, from the middle ages to date of publication. Equally useful as a tool for names of researchers in the early spaceflight era.

1537. Henry, James P. *Biomedical Aspects of Space Flight.* New York: Holt, Rinehart and Winston, 1966. Pp. 184. Index, Bibliog., Illustr.

Written at the level of high school inquiry, this book provides well–illustrated explanations of the effects of high–altitude and gravitational forces, the nature of weightlessness, and related topics. Also includes chapters on space vehicles, radiation in space, human factors and the man–machine combination, and the selection and training of the astronaut around 1966.

1538. Holbrook, Heber A. *Civil Aviation Medicine in the Bureaucracy.* Bethesda, Md.: Banner, 1974. Pp. xviii + 347. Index, Illustr.

Written by a former executive officer of the Office of the Aviation Medicine, Federal Aviation Administration. Offers a useful institutional history of medical direction within the agency from 1926 to 1974. Particularly helpful for the Civil Aviation Administration period, 1938–1958.

1539. Hopson, J.A. "RAF Medicine—The First 50 Years." *British Medical Journal,* 4 (October 5, 1968), 48–50.

Brief institutional history of aviation medicine in the Royal Air Force from 1918 to 1968. Also includes comments on supplemental activities, such as casualty evacuation, nursing and specialist services, civilian research and rehabilitation.

1540. Johnston, Richard S., L.F. Dietlein, and C.A. Berry. *Biomedical Results of Apollo.* NASA SP–368. Washington, D.C.: U.S. National Aeronautics and Space Administration, Scientific and Technical Information Office, 1975. Pp. vii + 592. Illustr.

Official history of all Apollo medical projects. Topics include crew health, medical testing, and quantitative issues.

Experiments are described and results furnished. Mechanical systems for nutrition and waste management are evaluated. The chapter entitled "Perspectives on Apollo" provides a brief synopsis of matters of medical relevance from each mission.

1541. Johnston, Richard S., and L.F. Dietlein. *Biomedical Results from Skylab*. Washington, D.C.: U.S. National Aeronautics and Space Administration, Science and Technology Information Office, 1976. Pp. 491. Index, Illustr.

An official compilation of medical, life science, and human factors studies at the conclusion of NASA's Skylab Program. Chapters build on and give brief histories of earlier research in areas such as radiation, sleep patterns, and gravitation. This work addresses these and other issues in light of extended period flights which made it possible to collect in–depth data in flight. Includes an overview of all medical programs and extensive useful appendixes on life support and experimental hardware systems.

1542. Lam, Lt. Col. David M. "The Army Forward—Aeromedical EVAC Story." *U.S. Army Aviation Digest*, June 1981, 41–48; July 1981, 44–48; August 1981, 44–48; September 1981, 45–48.

Four carefully presented overviews on medical evacuation dealing with its origins to World War I, World War II, Korea, and Viet Nam. Useful as a starting point for in depth technological, military, or medicine history. Well illustrated.

1543. Link, Mae Mills. *Space Medicine in Project Mercury*. NASA SP–4003. Washington, D.C.: U.S. National Aeronautics and Space Administration, 1965. Pp. 198. Index, Bibliog., Illustr.

Includes examination of NASA and other private and government agency space medical studies to the end of project Mercury. Concentrates are on the development of closed-environment life support systems. Extensive bibliography.

1544. Link, Mae Mills, and H.A. Coleman. *Medical Support of the Army Air Forces in World War II*. Washington, D.C.: Office of the Surgeon General, U.S. Air Force, 1955. Pp. xxii + 1027. Index, Illustr.

An official history that offers in–depth treatment of the period as well as useful histories of the groups and institutions that played important roles in the World War II period. Includes numerous statistical tables and chapters on medical support worldwide.

1545. Livingston, R.B., A.A. Imshenstsky, and G.A. Derbyshire, eds. *Life Sciences and Space Research*. Amsterdam: North-Holland, 1963–. Illustr.

Sponsored by Committee on Space Research. Multivolume series. Recent volumes published by Pergamon Press.

1546. Lovelace, W.R., A.P. Gagge, and C.W. Bray. *Aviation Medicine and Psychology*. Dayton, Ohio: Air Material Command, May 1946. Pp. 137. Bibliog., Illustr.

Report prepared for the Air Army Forced Scientific Advisory Group, number 13 in a series. Outlines World War II American research efforts in both aviation medicine and aviation psychology. Well illustrated but superficial treatment. Includes excellent references that serve as a guide to other official technical reports on such topics as personal equipment.

1547. McFarland, Ross A. *Human Factors in Air Transport Design*. New York: McGraw–Hill Book Co., 1946. Pp. xix + 670. Index, Bibliog., Illustr.

Extensive work that traces the development of human factors to consider in aircraft. Includes numerous chapters on the nature of air transportation, pressurized cabins, comfort in travel, flight performance, and accident prevention. See also McFarland's later work, *Human Factors in Air Transportation: Occupational Health and Safety* (item 787.)

McFarland, Ross A. *Human Factors in Air Transportation: Occupational Health and Safety*. New York: McGraw–Hill, 1953. Pp. 830. Index, Bibliog., Illustr.

Cited herein as item 787.

1548. McFarland, Ross A. *The Psychological Effects of Oxygen Deprivation (Anoxemia) on Human Behavior*. New York: Archives of Psychology, 1932. Pp. 135. Bibliog., Illustr.

Reviews many of the ground–breaking studies of oxygen deprivation to 1932. Includes a clinical section that describes the physiological effects of oxygen deprivation and the relation of this phenomenon to drugs and climate.

Mandrovsky, Boris N., and E. Fortunow. *Soviet Bioastronautics*. Washington, D.C.: Library of Congress. Aerospace Technology Division, 1968. Pp. ii + 196. Illustr.

Cited herein as item 1712.

1549. Mason, J.K. *Aviation Accident Pathology—A Story of Fatalities*. London: Butterworth's, 1962. Pp. xvi + 358. Index, Bibliog., Illustr.

Written originally as an M.D. thesis, the work is one of the first major documents in the field of accident study, now recognized as a classic prepared by a modern founder of the field. Introduction contains a brief history of major disaster investigations, although most of the work is a text and guide for aircraft accident examiners. Highly technical, appropriately graphic.

1550. Medical Research Council, Privy Council. *The Medical Problems of Flying*. London: His Majesty's Stationary Office, 1920. Pp. 272.

British survey of aviation medical research immediately after World War I and incorporating wartime research. Includes the frequently cited first seven reports of the Air Medical Investigation Committee. Many remain standard references for two generations of aviation medical researchers and contain the now–classic papers of such scientists as Martin Flack.

1551. Mohler, Stanley R., and Bobby H. Johnson. *Wiley Post, His Winnie Mae, and the World's First Pressure Suit*. Washington, D.C.: Smithsonian Institution Press, 1971. Pp. vii + 127. Illustr.

See especially pp. 71–90 for information on the suit and a fine historical treatment of its development, including medical aspects.

National Research Council. Space Science Board. *Human Factors in Long–Duration Space Flight.* Washington, D.C.: National Academy of Sciences, 1972. Pp. xi + 272. Bibliog.

Cited herein as item 1608.

1552. Parin, V.V., ed. *Aviation and Space Medicine.* NASA TT–F–228. Washington, D.C: National Aeronautics and Space Administration, 1964. Pp. xv + 445.

Translation of 158 abstracts of papers published by Akademiia Meditsinskikh Nauk, SSSR, Moscow, 1963, as "Aviatsionnaia i kosmicheskaia meditsina." Articles cover a wide gamut of topics; particular attention is given to the effects of motion on human physiology.

1553. Pitts, John A.S. *The Human Factor: Biomedicine in the Manned Space Program to 1980.* NASA SP–4213. Washington, D.C.: National Aeronautics and Space Administration, 1985. Pp. xii + 389. Index, Bibliog., Illustr.

An in–depth history of medicine and the biological sciences in the manned space program. Sensitive to both the personalities and hardware involved, the author provides a concise treatment of the range of studies and policies at work. Includes a useful bibliographic essay as well as an extensive list of significant interviewees who contributed to the history.

1554. Randel, Hugh W., ed. *Aerospace Medicine.* Baltimore: Williams and Wilkins, 1971. Pp. xvi + 740. Index, Bibliog., Illustr.

A collection of highly significant articles, edited by the deputy director of space medicine, NASA. Includes Col. George Zimmerman's "Aerospace Medicine—Past, Present, and Future" (pp. 1–21), a good brief history of the field that concentrates on World War II issues and on professionalization within the medical field.

1555. Robinson, Douglas H. *The Dangerous Sky: A History of Aviation Medicine.* Seattle: University of Washington Press, 1973. Pp. xxiv + 292. Index, Bibliog., Illustr.

This basic introduction is a thorough chronological treatment of the history of aviation medicine through the jet age.

A good source on flight materiel and post–World War II physiological testing.

1556. Ruff, Siegfried, and Hubertus Strughold. *Compendium of Aviation Medicine.* Reproduced under a Licence Granted by the Alien Property Custodian, 1942. Pp. 129. Illustr.

Introduction by E. Hipphe, surgeon general chief of the Medical Staff of the German Aviation. The work deals mainly with the effects of altitude and acceleration, but also includes chapters on accident study and the psychophysiology of avia- tion. A short essay on the historical problems of aviation introduces the work.

1557. School of Aerospace Medicine. *Epitome of Space Medicine: Research Reports and Articles from Scientific Journals.* Randolph AFB, Texas: U.S. Air Force, School of Aerospace Medicine, 1957. Pp. various pagings. Bibliog.

Over three dozen noteworthy technical reports and pub- lished articles on space medicine from the conclusion of World War II to the beginnings of manned spaceflight. Includes Hubertus Strughold's significant historical essay chronicling the passage of aviation medicine to space medicine.

1558. Sells, Saul B., and C.A. Berry, eds. *Human Factors in Jet and Space Travel: A Medical and Psychological Analysis.* New York: Ronald, 1961. Pp. 386. Index, Illustr.

Concentrates on the human problems of high–performance flight. Includes 14 papers on both general and specific topics by founders in the field for example, and the flight environ- ment, group behavior problems in flight, reaction to jet travel, preventive medicine in jet and spaceflight, aircraft accidents, and a speculative chapter on space and human testing.

1559. Sergeyev, Aleksandr A. *Essays on the History of Aviation Medicine.* NASA TTF–176. Washington, D.C.: National Aero- nautics and Space Administration, 1965. Pp. 413. Bibliog.

Nine translated essays on the history of Soviet aviation medical researcher. An extensive bibliography of over 1,700 items makes this work doubly useful—as a reference docu- ment and as a statement of European research issues.

Swenson, Lloyd S., Jr., J. Grimwood, and C. Alexander. *This New Ocean: A History of Project Mercury*. NASA SP–4201. Washington, D.C.: National Aeronautics and Space Administration, 1966. Pp. xv + 681. Index, Bibliog., Illustr.

Cited herein as item 1621.

1560. U.S. Air Force Missile Development Center. *The Beginnings of Research in Space Biology of the Air Force Missile Development Center, Holloman AFB, New Mexico, 1946–1958*. Holloman AFB, N.M.: U.S. Air Force Historical Branch, Air Research and Development Command, 1958. Pp. iv + 28.

Includes a technical history of sub–gravity and zero gravity research through the late 1950s as well as collected papers on space biology and biodynamics. All chapters have bibliographical references, some extensive. (Note: Some of these essays have been published separately.)

1561. U.S. Air Force. School of Aerospace Medicine. *Fifty Years of Aerospace Medicine, 1918–1968: Its Evolution since the Founding of the United States School of Aerospace Medicine in January 1918*. AFSC Historical Publications Series no. 67–180. Brooks Air Force Base, Texas, 1968. Pp. iv + 284. Index, Bibliog., Illustr.

Traces the history of the school and its major participants through the late 1960s. Particularly useful for the World War II period.

1562. U.S. Congress. Senate. Committee on Aeronautical and Space Sciences. *Space Research in the Life Sciences: An Inventory of Related Programs, Resources and Facilities*. Washington, D.C.: U.S. Government Printing Office, 1960. Pp. vii + 269. Bibliog., Illustr.

A reference document on space medicine programs in the United States. Useful as a descriptive directory of space programs in NASA and the Department of Defense. Appendix material also includes several classic articles, such as H. Strughold's "From Aviation Medicine to Space Medicine," and Col. Paul A. Campbell's, "Man in Space—Where We Stand."

1563. U.S. Department of the Air Force. *German Aviation Medicine —World War II.* 2 vol. Pelham Manor, N.Y.: Scholium International, 1971. Pp. vii + 1302. Index, Bibliog., Illustr.

A reprint of an earlier work by 56 authors. Topics include a brief history of German aviation medicine, high–altitude research (including material on equipment,) and acceleration. Thoughtfully arranged with topics covered in considerable detail. Offers information unusual to the array of secondary literature.

U.S. Library of Congress. Congressional Research Service. *Soviet Space Programs: 1971–75. Vol. 1, Overview, Facilities and Hardware, Manned and Unmanned Flight Programs, Bio-astronautics, Civil and Military Applications, Projections of Future Plans.* Washington, D.C.: U.S. Government Printing Office, 1976. Pp. xx + 668. Illustr.

Cited herein as item 1693.

U.S. Library of Congress. Congressional Research Service. *Soviet Space Programs: 1976–80. Part 2, Manned Space Programs and Space Life Sciences.* Washington, D.C.: U.S. Government Printing Office, October 1984. Pp. xiv + 302. Illustr.

Cited herein as item 1718.

1564. U.S. National Aeronautics and Space Administration. Office of Manned Space Flight. *A Review of Medical Results of Gemini 7 and Related Flights.* Washington, D.C.: U.S. Government Printing Office, 1966. Pp. 287.

Presents the results of a conference held at the Management Center, John F. Kennedy Space Center, Florida, August 23, 1966.

1565. White, Clayton S., and Otis O. Benson, eds. *Physics and Medicine of the Upper Atmosphere: A Study of the Aeropause.* Albuquerque: University of New Mexico Press, 1952. Pp. xxiv + 611. Index, Bibliog., Illustr.

Edited by Clayton S. White, M.D., director of research, Lovelace Foundation for Medical Education and Research, and Brig. Gen. O.O. Benson, USAF (MC), commandant, USAF

School of Aviation Medicine. Presents the proceedings of a symposium on the physics and medicine and the upper atmosphere held at San Antonio, Texas, November 6–9, 1951. Includes articles on most aspects of aeropause (upper atmosphere) medicine. Particularly helpful is a section on research methodologies and a sophisticated treatment of the physics involved.

1566. White, William J. *A History of the Centrifuge in Aerospace Medicine.* Santa Monica, Calif.: Douglas Aircraft, 1964. N.p. Illustr.

Traces a well–illustrated international development of the centrifuge in aviation–related work from the late 18th century to the date of publication. Covers the World War II period particularly well. Although not a work of profound scholarship, this is one of a few attempts to trace a particular piece of aviation medical technology through the stages of both development and implementation.

PILOTED FLIGHT

No aspect of space exploration has captured the imagination of the world more than the idea of manned spaceflight. As a result, the volume of literature on this topic is unmatched by any other aspect of historical studies on space explorations. This body of literature is written to a broad spectrum of the community, but for the most part the literature included here represents the popular quality of the literature of piloted spaceflight. Therefore, in order to fully represent the broad range of subject matter within this field, much of the popular literature has been included here. Thus, many of the titles in this section are not included for their scholarly significance, but for their coverage of an otherwise unstudied area. As a rule, the most dependable, albeit often uncritical, studies available on manned spaceflight programs are those generated by the NASA History Office. The detailed bibliographies in the NASA History Series are invaluable for locating both published and unpublished sources.

For additional and detailed information on the scientific aspects of the manned spaceflight programs of NASA, the reader should consult the periodic NASA publications which present the scientific results of each mission. As in the case, of all NASA programs, reports from the Congressional Research Service and the Office of Technology Assessment often provide invaluable insights into the fiscal and policy issues which have shaped NASA's choices for missions.

Derek W. Elliott
Linda N. Ezell
Janice L. Hill
Lillian D. Kozloski
Cathleen S. Lewis

History of Manned Spaceflight Programs and Hardware

1567. Alexander, Thomas W. *Project Apollo: Man to the Moon.* New York: Harper and Row, 1964. Pp. v + 234. Index, Illustr.

Written during the height of the engineering and planning debates for the Apollo program. Explores the issues and anticipated problems of sending three men to the Moon and returning them to Earth. Discussion includes fiscal and policy issues as well as engineering problems. Drawings illustrate planned Apollo mission.

1568. Baker, David. *The History of Manned Spaceflight.* New York: Crown, 1981. Pp. 544. Illustr.

Thorough coverage of the American space program. All phases are researched and fully illustrated. Lacks scholarly notations.

1569. Belew, Leland F., ed. *Skylab: Our First Space Station.* NASA SP–400. Washington, D.C.: U.S. National Aeronautics and Space Administration, 1977. Pp. 164. Index, Illustr.

Heavily illustrated volume presenting the development of the Skylab program and events of the three manned visits to the station. The last chapter concerns scientific and medical benefits of the first U.S. orbiting laboratory.

1570. Belew, Leland F., and E. Stuhlinger. *Skylab: A Guidebook.* NASA EP–107. Washington, D.C.: National Aeronautics and Space Administration, 1973. Pp. x + 245. Bibliog., Illustr.

Well–illustrated guidebook by two major officials of the Skylab program at the Marshall Space Flight Center. Covers expectations and early history of the first U.S. orbiting laboratory with an excellent chapter on scientific equipment carried aboard Skylab. This work, prepared before the launch in 1973, is still useful as an introduction to this complex post–Apollo scientific program.

Benson, Charles and D.G. Faherty. *Moonport: A History of Apollo Launch Facilities and Operations.* NASA SP–4204.

Washington, D.C.: National Aeronautics and Space Administration, 1978. Pp. xx + 636. Index, Bibliog., Illustr.

Cited herein as item 1110.

Bilstein, Roger E. *Stages to Saturn: A Technological History of the Apollo/Saturn Launch Vehicles.* NASA SP–4206. Washington, D.C.: National Aeronautics and Space Administration, 1980. Pp. xx + 511. Index, Illustr.

Cited herein as item 1266.

1571. Bond, Aleck C., and M. Faget. *Technologies of Manned Space Systems.* New York: Gordon and Breach, 1965. Pp. x + 121. Index, Illustr.

Describes, in detail, the systems of Mercury, Gemini, and Apollo necessary for manned flight. Some explanations are presented in the form of chemical equations, but most of the information can be understood by the lay reader. This book is part of the Space Flight Technology Series edited by Enoch J. Durbin.

1572. Booker, Peter J., G. Freiver, and G. Pardoe. *Project Apollo: The Way to the Moon.* New York: American Elsevier, 1969. Pp. viii + 212. Index, Illustr.

History of the planning, design, and engineering associated with Project Apollo. Also discusses Surveyor and Ranger programs briefly. The design and operation of the Saturn launch vehicle and vehicle assembly are covered in depth. Illustrated with schematic drawings and photographs.

1573. Brooks, Courtney C., J. Grimwood, and L. Swenson, Jr. *Chariots for Apollo: A History of Manned Lunar Spacecraft.* NASA SP–4205. Washington, D.C.: National Aeronautics and Space Administration, 1979. Pp. xvii + 538. Bibliog., Illustr.

History of NASA's manned lunar exploration program—Apollo—from its conception through the first landing in July 1969. Extensive use is made of official NASA records and oral history interviews. This is the official program history.

Büdeler, Werner, and W. Goldman. *Spacelab: Europas Labor im Weltraum* (Spacelab: European work in space). Munich: Wilhelm Goldman, 1976. Pp. 287. Illustr.

Cited herein as item 1738.

1574. Caidin, Martin. *Man into Space.* New York: Pyramid, 1961. Pp. 192.

Describes the preparations for project Mercury through the *Freedom 7* flight of Alan Shepard, America's first man in space. Concludes with brief descriptions of Soviet space activities. Includes glossary of spaceflight terms.

1575. Caidin, Martin. *Rendezvous in Space.* New York: E.P. Dutton, Inc., 1962. Pp. xvi + 320. Index, Illustr.

Discusses Project Mercury through Scott Carpenter's *Mercury 7* mission. Presents an early analysis of the Gemini, Apollo, X–15, and X–20 programs, and the development of the Saturn launch vehicle, focusing on reaching the Moon and improving U.S. standing in space exploration.

1576. Charon, Jean E. *Pourquoi la Lune?* (Why the moon?). Paris: L'Encyclopedie Planete, 1968. Pp. 256. Bibliog., Illustr.

Recounts the history of the observations and the explorations of the Moon, with a view to explaining the lunar exploration activities of the United States and the Soviet Union. Although the book is dedicated to the three astronauts (White, Grissom, and Chaffee) and one cosmonaut (Komarov) who had lost their lives onboard *Apollo 1* and *Soiuz 1*, respectively, the book also discusses unmanned lunar activity. Glossary of space terms used is conveniently placed alongside the text.

1577. Compton, W. David, and C. Benson. *Living and Working in Space: A History of Skylab.* NASA SP–4208. Washington, D.C.: National Aeronautics and Space Administration, 1983. Pp. 449. Index, Bibliog., Illustr.

Part of the NASA History Series, it is probably the most comprehensive existing study ever made of the entire Skylab program. It includes a discussion of the station's last days in orbit. Presents a good discussion of funding problems and their effect on project planning

1578. Cooper, Henry S.F. *Apollo on the Moon.* New York: Dial, 1969. Pp. 144.

Describes what the astronauts actually did while on the Moon. Contains little reference to the spacecraft and equipment, but intimately describes the planning and execution of manned exploration on the Moon. Originally published as an article in the *New Yorker.*

1579. Cooper, Henry S.F. *Thirteen: The Flight That Failed.* New York: Dial, 1973. Pp. viii + 199.

Details the flight of Apollo 13, from the events before the oxygen tank explosion to splashdown. Specifically describes actions taken by Mission Control and the astronauts. Material originally appeared in the *New Yorker* in slightly different form.

1580. Cooper, Henry S.F. *A House in Space.* New York: Holt Rinehart and Winston, 1976. Pp. 184. Illustr.

Originally published as a series of articles in the *New Yorker*, describes the day–to–day life on board Skylab, with special focus on the third and last crew. Presents an intimate picture of the astronauts' lives. Illustrated with pictures taken on board the space station.

1581. Cortright, Edgar M., ed. *Apollo Expeditions to the Moon.* NASA SP–350. Washington, D.C.: National Aeronautics and Space Administration, 1975. Pp. 313. Index, Illustr.

Accounts of the Apollo program, mainly by astronauts and administrators. Numerous photographs highlight the book.

1582. Cromie, William J. *Skylab: The Story of Man's First Station in Space.* New York: David McKay, 1976. Pp. 146. Index, Illustr.

Skylab missions, starting with the launch of the space station, are recounted. Presents many details of the day–to–day life of the astronauts.

Eddy, John A. *A New Sun: The Solar Results for Skylab.* NASA

SP–402. Washington, D.C.: National Aeronautics and Space Administration, 1979. Pp. xix + 198. Index, Illustr.

Cited herein as item 1401.

1583. El–Baz, Farouk. *Astronaut Observations from the Apollo–Soyuz Mission.* Washington, D.C.: Smithsonian Institution Press, 1977. Pp. v + 210. Bibliog., Illustr.

History of the Apollo–Soiuz Earth Observations and Photography Experiment, including astronaut training, photographic results, and scientific observations based on the photographs. Comprehensive appendixes provide comments of the astronauts, as well as the training flight and the inflight manuals.

Emme, Eugene M. "The Historiography of Rocket Technology and Space Exploration." *Acts XIIIe Congrès international d'histoire* 12 (1971): 43–60.

Cited herein as item 1098.

1584. Ezell, Edward C., and L. Ezell. *The Partnership: A History of the Apollo Soyuz Test Project.* NASA SP–4209. Washington, D.C.: National Aeronautics and Space Administration, 1978. Pp. xx + 560. Index, Bibliog., Illustr.

Compares U.S.– and USSR–manned spaceflight programs from Mercury and Vostok through the joint Apollo–Soiuz Test Project (1975). Focuses on the years of negotiations, joint working sessions, and training leading up to the mission, more than on the actual flight. Authors were witnesses to many joint meetings and depended on primary sources and oral interviews. It is the official project history. Appendixes, notes.

1585. Faget, Maxime A. *Manned Space Flight.* New York: Holt Rinehart and Winston, 1965. Pp. 176. Index, Bibliog., Illustr.

Covers popular aspects of manned spaceflight in general with few references to specific flights. Describes the craft and on–board equipment and how they work. Satisfies popular interest in manned spaceflight during the Gemini and Apollo eras. Offers interesting insights into NASA attitudes toward space exploration. Written by the designer of the Mercury spacecraft who is a former Director of Development and Engineering as NASA.

1586. Farmer, G., and D. Hamblin. *First on the Moon.* Boston: Little, Brown, 1970. Pp. xiii + 434. Illustr.

Describes the lives of the Apollo 11 astronauts, their fam-ilies, and the people who worked with them during the earlier Apollo era through the first lunar landing.

1587. Froehlich, Walter. *Apollo–Soyuz.* NASA EP–109. Washington, D.C.: National Aeronautics and Space Administration, 1976. Pp. 131. Illustr.

A brief pictorial account produced by NASA on the first international manned spaceflight. Organized thematically, it describes the events preceding and including the 1975 Apollo-Soiuz mission.

1588. Gantz, Kenneth F., ed. *Man in Space: The United States Air Force Program for Developing the Spacecraft Crew.* New York: Duell, Sloan and Pearce, 1959. Pp. xv + 303. Index, Bibliog.

Written shortly before man went into space, it studies and predicts what may happen during a manned spaceflight.

1589. Gatland, Kenneth W. *Manned Spacecraft.* New York: Mac-millan, 1976. Pp. 304. Index, Illustr.

Narrates the history of the United States and Soviet space programs, stressing spacecraft design and the mechanics of the various flights. Includes schematic drawings of Apollo and Shuttle flight operations. Many tables of flights are presented, as well as a brief glossary of spaceflight terms.

1590. Grimwood, James M., and I. Ertel. "Project Gemini." *South-western Historical Quarterly* 71, no. 3 (January 1968): 393–418.

A brief history of the Gemini program, which includes a short discussion of pre–flight Gemini training, as well as a description of flight activities. Contains photographs taken by the Gemini astronauts while in flight. Both authors were historians at NASA's Manned Spacecraft Center.

1591. Gurney, Gene. *Walk in Space: The Story of Project Gemini.* New York: Random House, 1967. Pp. 186. Index, Illustr.

A popularized version of the 10 flights of Gemini, with brief biographies of each of the Gemini astronauts and a listing of American and Soviet manned spaceflights from 1961 through 1966.

Hacker, Barton C. "The Idea of Rendezvous: From Space Station to Orbital Operations in Space Travel Thought, 1895–1951." *Technology and Culture* 15, no. 3 (July 1974): 373–388.

Cited herein as item 1198.

1592. Hacker, Barton C., and J. Grimwood. *On the Shoulders of Titans: A History of Project Gemini.* NASA SP–4203. Washington, D.C.: National Aeronautics and Space Administration, 1977. Pp. xx + 625. Index, Illustr.

Official project history of NASA's second manned space-flight program during which many of the operations required for a lunar mission were tested. Authors had frequent access to program participants and documentation.

1593. Hallion, Richard P., T. Crouch, et al. *Apollo: Ten Years since Tranquility.* Washington, D.C.: Smithsonian Institution Press, 1979. Pp. xviii + 174. Bibliog., Illustr.

A collection of essays on the history, hardware, and results of Project Apollo. It was published in conjunction with a National Air and Space Museum symposium held on the 10th anniversary of the Apollo Moon landing.

Hechler, Ken. *Toward the Endless Frontier: History of the Committee on Science and Technology.* Washington, D.C.: U.S. Government Printing Office, 1980. Pp. xxxvi + 1073. Index, Bibliog., Illustr.

Cited herein as item 1120.

Holden, William G. *Saturn V: The Moon Rocket*. New York: Julian Messner, 1969. Pp. 190. Index, Illustr.

Cited herein as item 1294.

1594. Horowitz, Paul, ed. *Manned Space Reliability Symposium*. American Astronautical Society Science and Technology Series, vol. 1. New York: American Astronautical Society, 1964. Pp. 100.

Contains papers on investigations of problems associated with increased reliability requirements of manned spaceflight. Philosophical, scientific, engineering, and human factors are considered.

1595. Houbolt, John C. "Lunar Rendezvous." *International Science and Technology* 14 (February 1963): 62–65.

Outlines the author's development and promotion of a means for Apollo spacecraft to reach the Moon. Lunar rendezvous was ultimately chosen as the method for sending men to the Moon for the Apollo program.

Ivanov, V.A., T.F. Pazymova, and B.A. Sazhko. *Saliut 6–soiuz–progress*. Moscow: Mashinostroenie, 1983. Pp. 340. Illustr.

Cited herein as item 1708.

1596. Joëls, Kerry M., and G. Kennedy. *Space Shuttle Operator's Manual*. New York: Ballantine, 1982. Pp. 155. Illustr.

Describes in detail the Space Transportation System and what a prospective shuttle crew member can expect during flight. Included in the appendixes are technical details about the Shuttle's capabilities.

Johnson, Nicholas L. "Apollo and Zond—Race around the Moon." *Spaceflight* 20 (December 1978): 403–412.

Cited herein as item 1659.

Johnson, Nicholas L. "The Military and Civilian Saliut Space

Programmes." *Spaceflight* 19 (August/September 1979): 364–370.

Cited herein as item 1709.

Johnson, Nicholas L. *Handbook of Soviet Manned Spaceflight.* American Astronautical Society Science and Technology Series, vol. 48. San Diego, Calif.: Univelt, 1980. Pp. xii + 461. Index. Bibliog., Illustr.

Cited herein as item 1710.

1597. Johnston, Richard S., J. Correale, and M. Radnofsky. *Space Suit Development Status.* NASA TND–3291. Langley, Va.: National Aeronautics and Space Administration, February 1966. Pp. 26. Illustr.

Briefly reflects on the changing goals of each U.S. manned spaceflight mission and discusses the development of space suits through the Apollo program.

1598. Kent, Stan, ed. *Remember the Future: The Apollo Legacy.* San Diego, Calif.: Univelt, 1980. Pp. x + 207. Illustr.

A series of addresses commemorating the 10th anniversary of the flight of *Apollo 11*, covering a variety of subjects: prevention of nuclear conflict, a Solar Orbiting Mirror System, space colonies, advanced propulsion systems, the future in space, and space work environment. Presentations were made at the American Astronautical Society and American Institute for Aeronautics and Astronautics conference.

Lay, Bierne. *Earthbound Astronautics: The Builders of Apollo–Saturn.* Englewood Cliffs, N.J.: Prentice–Hall, 1971. Pp. 198. Illustr.

Cited herein as item 1302.

Lebedev, L.A. *Rendezvous in Space.* Moscow: Progress, 1979. Pp. 208. Illustr.

Cited herein as item 1662.

1599. Leondes, C.T., and R. Vance, eds. *Lunar Mission and Explora-*
tion. New York: John Wiley and Sons, 1964. Pp. 669. Index,
Illustr.

Presents reports from authorities in such fields as propulsion, facilities, trajectory analysis, mission analysis, life
support, and reentry through Earth's atmosphere, and others
which are required for a manned mission to the Moon. References appear at the end of each report.

Leonov, Alexei. "Cosmonaut Training." *Spaceflight* 20 (August
1978): 305–306.

Cited herein as item 1711.

Levine, Arnold S. *Managing NASA in the Apollo Era*. Washington, D.C.: National Aeronautics and Space Administration. Scientific and Technical Information Branch, 1982. Pp.
xxi + 342. Index.

Cited herein as item 1127.

1600. Lewis, Richard S. *Voyages of Columbia; The First True Space-*
ship. New York: Columbia University Press, 1984. Pp. 223.
Index, Illustr.

Details years of frustration, congressional criticism, and
mechanical breakdowns as NASA prepared the reusable Space
Transportation System. Provides journalistic account of how
indifference and doubt gave way to optimism that the shuttle
would open up new frontiers to commerce and industry.

Ley, Willy. *Rockets, Missiles, and Man in Space*. New York:
Viking Press, 1968. Pp. xvii + 557. Index, Bibliog., Illustr.

Cited herein as item 1101.

1601. Lloyd, Mallon. *Suiting up for Space*. New York: John Day,
1971. Pp. ix + 262. Illustr.

Documents the progress made in the United States and in
Europe on the early development of the space suit. Later chapters cover the evolution from partial pressure suits to full-
pressure garment used during Mercury, Gemini, and Apollo.

1602. Logsdon, John M. "Selecting the Way to the Moon: The Choice of the Lunar Orbital Rendezvous Mode." *Aerospace Historian* 18 (June 1971): 63–70.

Considers the choice of the lunar orbital rendezvous approach to accomplishing the manned lunar mission, which was the most significant factor contributing to the success of the Apollo program. Includes 50 references.

1603. Logsdon, John M. "Space Station: A Historical Perspective." In *Space Station: Policy Planning and Utilization*, ed. Mireille Gerard and P.W. Edwards, 14–22. New York: American Institute of Aeronautics and Astronautics, 1983.

Review the history of the planning for the space station. Relates the changing concepts of the station to the fiscal debates which shape them. Provides useful insights into the formation of space exploration policy.

1604. Low, George M. *The Apollo Program: A Midstream Appraisal.* Washington, D.C.: Smithsonian Institution Press, 1969. Pp. 22. Illustr.

This text of the Third Annual Edwin A. Link Lecture provides a brief overview of manned spaceflight from the perspective of the deputy administrator of NASA.

1605. Machell, R.M. *Summary of Gemini EVA.* NASA CR-1106. Langley, Va.: National Aeronautics and Space Administration, 1968. Pp. 274. Illustr.

Overview of Gemini extravehicular activities. Describes actual systems employed and how they were developed, testing and qualifications, preparation of astronauts, and operational and medical aspects, as well as significant mission results of the Gemini program.

Mandrovsky, Boris N., and E. Fortunow. *Soviet Bioastronautics.* Washington, D.C.: Library of Congress, Aerospace Technology Division. 1968. Pp. ii + 196. Illustr.

Cited herein as item 1712.

1606. Mark, Hans. *The Space Station: A Personal Journey.* Durham, N.C.: Duke University Press, 1987. Pp. vii + 264. Index.

Recalls the authors years and a physicist who worked on space science project in the U.S. Focuses most closely on his role in establishing policy for the development of the space station in the Carter and Reagan administrations. Provides insights in the space science community through anecdotes.

1607. Masursky, Harold, G. Elton, and F. El–Baz, eds. *Apollo over the Moon: A View from Orbit.* NASA SP–362. Washington, D.C.: National Aeronautics and Space Administration, 1978. Pp. 255. Bibliog., Illustr.

Describes how Apollo photographic equipment was chosen and used; how photos were selected to show broader lunar aspects; how the lunar surface is affected by cratering, tectonism, and volcanism, and other lunar features. Three appendixes cover photographic data, lunar probes, and data analysis for preparation of lunar maps. Also includes lunar geological glossary, selected references, and a bibliography.

1608. National Research Council. Space Science Board. *Human Factors in Long–Duration Space Flight.* Washington, D.C.: National Academy of Sciences, 1972. Pp. xi + 272. Bibliog.

Summarizes 10 years of results from biomedical experiments on board manned spaceflights in an effort to make recommendations for treatment, prophylaxis, and experiments on future long–duration flights. Discussions are presented topically with frequent historical references. Although many technical issues are discussed, the work is comprehensible to the lay reader. All citations are listed at the end.

Oates, Stephen B. "NASA's Manned Spacecraft Center of Houston, Texas." *Southwestern Quarterly Journal* 67, no. 3 (January 1964): 350–375.

Cited herein as item 1129.

Oberg, James E. *Red Star in Orbit.* New York: Random House, 1981. Pp. xiii + 272. Index, Illustr.

Cited herein as item 1684.

1609. O'Leary, Brian. *Project Space Station—Plans for a Permanent Manned Space Center.* Harrisburg, Pa.: Stackpole, 1983. Pp. xv + 159. Index, Bibliog., Illustr.

Written during the fiscal debates over the National Aeronautics and Space Administration's plans for building a space station. Vigorously argues for a U.S. space complex. Discusses the international and domestic imperatives for a space station. Surveys various preliminary designs for such a station. The author was a member of the astronaut corps until his resignation. Contains some mistakes, vis a vis Soviet space nomenclature.

1610. Peebles, Curtis. "The Manned Orbiting Laboratory, Part 1." *Spaceflight* 22 (April 1980): 155–160.

The first of a three–part series on the history of the ill–fated first attempt by the Department of Defense's (DOD) to establish a manned space station, the Manned Orbiting Laboratory (MOL). Chronicles the institutional, political, and fiscal history of the MOL program with mention of other DOD and NASA programs that undercut it. Includes some description of the proposed Gemini–Titan hardware.

1611. Peebles, Curtis. "The Manned Orbiting Laboratory, Part 2." *Spaceflight* 22 (June 1980): 248–253.

Continues the series on the Manned Orbiting Laboratory (MOL) based on engineering drawings and experiment descriptions released by the U.S. Air Force under the auspices of the Freedom of Information Act. All information provided is drawn from the Preliminary Technical Development Plan for the Manned Orbiting Laboratory from the Air Force Systems Command.

1612. Peebles, Curtis. "The Manned Orbiting Laboratory, Part 3." *Spaceflight* 24 (June 1982): 274–277.

Concludes the three–part series on the USAF's Manned Orbiting Laboratory with a discussion of various models made of the proposed spacecraft.

1613. Pellegrino, Charles R., and J. Stoff. *Chariots for Apollo: The Making of the Lunar Module.* New York: Atheneum, 1985. Pp. xvi + 238. Bibliog., Illustr.

Popular account of the development of the American space program, focusing closely on Grumman and the construction of the Lunar Module. Illustrated with photos of the developing module. Juxtaposes the accomplishments of the Soviet program with the state of mind of the engineers, scientists, and astronauts working on the programs. Lacks references. Contains a few historical inaccuracies. Appendix includes an update on what the primary participants in the Apollo program are doing now.

Pesavento, Peter. "Soviets to the Moon: the Untold Story." *Astronomy*, December 1984, 6–22.

Cited herein as item 1713.

Petrov, B.H., and V.C. Berreshchetin, eds. *Orbity sotrudnichestva* (Orbits of cooperation). Moscow: Mashinostroenie, 1983. Pp. 177. Illustr.

Cited herein as item 1667.

1614. Pierce, Roger J. "Mercury Capsule Communications." *Astronautics* 4 (December 1959): 24–27.

Describes the redundant communications systems of the Mercury spacecraft. Organized by functions: voice communications, command function, telemetry, orbital tracking, precise tracking, and rescue beacons. Written by one of the engineers of Collins Radio Company, which designed the systems.

Pitts, John A. *The Human Factor.* Washington, D.C.: National Aeronautics and Space Administration, 1985. Pp. xii + 389. Index, Bibliog., Illustr.

Cited herein as item 1553.

1615. Poole, Lynn, and G. Poole. *Scientists Who Work with Astronauts.* New York: Dodd, Mead, 1964. Pp. 172. Index, Illustr.

Sketches of eminent space scientists, administrators, physicians, and engineers. Included are Homer E. Newell, Nancy G. Roman, Eugene M. Shoemaker, Ernest Stuhlinger, Wernher von Braun, Robert R. Gilruth, Richard S. Johnston, Maxime A. Faget, Warren J. North, Charles A. Berry, Christopher C. Kraft, Jr., and Kenneth M. Nagler.

Popescu, Julian. *Russian Space Exploration.* Henley on Thames, England: Gothard House, 1979. Pp. viii + 150. Bibliog., Illustr.

Cited herein as item 1686.

1616. Powers, Robert M. *The World's First Spaceship: Shuttle.* Harrisburg, Pa.: Stackpole, 1981. Pp. 255. Index, Bibliog., Illustr.

A heavily illustrated account of the early years of the Shuttle program. Written in the excited tone of the early Shuttle period. A glossary of space terms is included.

Rabinowitch, Eugene, and R. Lewis, eds. *Man on the Moon. The Impact on Science, Technology and International Cooperation.* New York: Basic Books, 1969. Pp. xiv + 204.

Cited herein as item 1180.

Raushenbakh, B.V. *Iz istorii sovetskoi kosmonavtiki* (From the history of Soviet cosmonautics). Moscow: Izdatel'stvo Nauka, 1983. Pp. 263. Illustr.

Cited herein as item 1687.

Riabchikov, Evgenii Ivanovich. *Russians in Space.* Garden City, N.Y.: Doubleday, 1971. Pp. 300. Illustr.

Cited herein as item 1688.

1617. Roland, Alex. "The Shuttle Triumph or Turkey?" *Discover,* 6, November 1985, 29–49.

Contrasts the original promise of the space shuttle with the inevitable compromises which occurred during the budgeting and contracting processes from the original conception to the maiden voyage of *Columbia.* Describes the major technological short–comings of the Shuttle. Presents the divergent hopes of many individuals and agencies had had for the shuttle as the main reason for its short–comings. Concludes that the technological capabilities of the shuttle are improving, but the cost overruns on the project have made it a fiscal failure. Published three months prior to the *Challenger* explosion.

Seamans, Robert C., Jr., and F. Ordway. "Apollo Tradition: An Object Lesson for the Management of Large–Scale Technological Endeavors." *Interdisciplinary Science Reviews* 2, no. 4 (1977): 270–304.

Cited herein as item 1132.

1618. Shapland, David, and M. Rycroft. *Spacelab: Research in Earth Orbit.* Cambridge: Cambridge University Press, 1984. Pp. 192. Index, Illustr.

Heavily illustrated account of the European Space Agency's Spacelab program, written for the lay reader. There is coverage of Spacelab's construction, role, and shuttle operations, and a detailed account of *Spacelab 1*, flown on the Space Shuttle *Columbia* in November 1983. Appendixes list all experiments flown.

1619. Sharpe, Mitchell R. *Living in Space: The Astronaut and His Environment.* New York: Doubleday, 1969. Pp. 192. Index, Bibliog., Illustr.

Argues strongly for expansion of manned spaceflight programs. Discusses the hazards and advantages of spaceflight. Goes beyond the standard discussion of biomedical and psychological issues and predicts future accomplishments of manned spaceflight.

1620. Simpson, Theodore R., M. Smith, et al., eds. *The Space Station: An Idea Whose Time Has Come.* New York: Institute of Electrical and Electronic Engineers, 1984. Pp. 295. Index, Illustr.

Promotes the idea of space stations. Part 1 presents historical background and covers the Manned Orbiting Laboratory, Skylab, and Saliut programs. Part 2 covers policy decisions leading to presidential approval of the construction of a space station. Part 3 deals with space station concepts and uses; Part 4, with long-term potential. Part 5 consists of appendixes, which include transcripts of memos and speeches relating to NASA space station decisions and policies from 1961 to 1984. Included also are a list of acronyms and a glossary.

Smolders, Peter L., and Marian Powell, trans. *Soviets in Space.* London: Butterworth Press, 1973. Pp. 285. Index, Illustr.

Cited herein as item 1691.

Swenson, Lloyd S., Jr. "The Fertile Crescent: The South's Role in the National Space Program." *Southwestern Historical Quarterly*, 71, no. 3 (January 1968): 377–392.

Cited herein as item 1184.

1621. Swenson, Lloyd S., Jr., J. Grimwood, and C. Alexander. *This New Ocean: A History of Project Mercury.* NASA SP–4201. Washington, D.C.: National Aeronautics and Space Administration, 1966. Pp. 681. Index, Illustr.

Summarizes the history of the first U.S. manned spaceflight program—Mercury. Includes background material on pre-NASA research and looks at reentry body configurations. It is the official program history; it is noteworthy that the authors relied heavily on primary sources. Appendixes.

1622. Thomas, Davis, S. Bedini, W. von Braun, and F. Whipple, eds. *Moon: Man's Greatest Adventure.* New York: Harry N. Abrams, 1970. Pp. 267. Illustr.

Chronicles 4,000 years of man's fascination with the Moon, culminating in the successful mission of Apollo 11 in 1969. Text essays are written by historian of technology Silvio Bendini, rocketry pioneer Wernher von Braun, and astronomer Fred Whipple. Well-illustrated with photographs of related artifacts from ancient times through official NASA photographs of the Apollo 11 mission.

1623. Tomayko, James E. "NASA's Manned Spacecraft Computers." *Annals of the History of Computing* 7, no. 1 (January 1985): 7–18.

A study of the use of computers by NASA in its manned spacecraft, with an emphasis on the Apollo Guidance Computers and the Shuttle computer system. The author contends that NASA, in the interests of greater reliability, adopted a conservative approach in choosing hardware that was consistently behind the state of the art of then–current computer technology. In the areas of software verification and fault tolerance, however, NASA's approach was in the vanguard of computer technology.

U.S. Congress. Committee on Science and Technology. Subcommittee on Space Science and Applications. *United States Civilian Space Programs, 1958–1978*. Washington, D.C.: U.S. Government Printing Office, 1981. Pp. 1100. Illustr.

Cited herein as item 1135.

U.S. Congress. Office of Technology Assessment. *Saliut: Soviet Steps Toward Permanent Human Presence in Space —A Technical Memorandum*. OTA-TM STI-14. Washington, D.C.: U.S. Government Printing Office, December 1983. Pp. 113. Illustr.

Cited herein as item 1717.

1624. U.S. Congress. Office of Technology Assessment. *Civilian Space Stations and the U.S. Future in Space*. OTA–STI–241. Washington, D.C.: U.S. Government Printing Office, 1984. Pp. 234. Index, Illustr.

Critical review of the U.S. civilian space program, in particular NASA's plans for a space station. Considers long–term objectives, cost, private sector contributions, international activity, and the evolution of space station concepts.

1625. U.S. Congress. Senate. Committee on Aeronautics and Space Science. *Project Mercury: Man-in Space Program*. Washington, D.C.: U.S. Government Printing Office, 1 December 1959. Pp. vii + 97. Illustr.

Based on NASA briefings and other open literature, this congressional report was written during the testing phase of the Mercury program. Not only describes the testing program and mission profiles, but also reviews the fiscal, organizational, and political history of Mercury. Research preceding consideration of manned spaceflight done by the National Advisory Committee for Aeronautics is also discussed.

1626. U.S. Congress. Senate. Committee on Aeronautics and Space Administration. *Manned Space Flight Program of the National Aeronautics and Space Administration: Projects Mercury, Gemini, and Apollo.* Washington, D.C.: U.S. Government Printing Office, 4 September 1962. Pp. viii + 242. Illustr.

Expansion of the 1959 Congressional Report on Project Mercury. Describes the Mercury, Gemini, and Apollo programs to the extent of current nonclassified literature. Background on NASA's overall Manned Space Flight program is provided. The description of the Apollo program includes some of the early proposals for manned lunar flight. Appendixes include a description of the Department of Defense's X–20 program and a detailed chronology of manned spaceflight–related events.

U.S. Library of Congress. Congressional Research Service. *Soviet Space Programs: 1966–70, Goals and Purposes, Organization, Resources, Facilities and Hardware, Manned and Unmanned Flight Programs, Bioastronautics, Civil and Military Applications, Projections for Future Plans, Attitudes toward International Cooperation and Space Law.* Washington, D.C.: U.S. Government Printing Office, 1971. Pp. xi + 670. Index.

Cited herein as item 1692.

U.S. Library of Congress. Congressional Research Service. *Soviet Space Programs: 1971–75, Volume 1, Overview, Facilities and Hardware, Manned and Unmanned Flight Programs, Bioastronautics, Civil and Military Applications, Projections of Future Plans.* Washington, D.C.: U.S. Government Printing Office, 1976. Pp. xx + 668. Illustr.

Cited herein as item 1693.

U.S. Library of Congress. Congressional Research Service. *Soviet Space Programs: 1976–80. Part 2, Manned Space Programs and Space Life Sciences.* Washington, D.C.: U.S. Government Printing Office, October 1984. Pp. xiv + 302. Illustr.

Cited herein as item 1718.

1627. U.S. National Aeronautics and Space Administration. Office of Manned Space Flight. *NASA's Manned Space Flight Program.* Washington, D.C.: U.S. Government Printing Office, 29 April 1969. Pp. 139–262. Illustr.

Reprint of a portion of a NASA report to Congress as part of its testimony during the fiscal year 1970 budget authorization hearings. Although the emphasis is on the Apollo program, future plans for a space station and shuttle design are presented. Includes NASA budget projections.

1628. U.S. National Aeronautics and Space Administration. *What Made Apollo a Success?* NASA SP-287. Washington, D.C.: U.S. Government Printing Office, 1971. Pp. 75. Illustr.

Series of eight articles reprinted from March 1970 issues of *Astronautics and Aeronautics* by key Apollo program managers. Included are articles by George M. Low, Kenneth S. Kleinknecht, Eugene F. Kranz, and Howard W. Tindall, Jr. Topics include design principles, crew procedures, and flight control, mission planning.

U.S. Presidential Commission on the Space Shuttle Challenger Accident. *Report on the Presidential Commission on the Space Shuttle Challenger Accident, Vol. 1.* Washington, D.C.: U.S. Government Printing Office, 6 June 1986. Pp. 256. Bibliog., Illustr.

Cited herein as item 1136.

1629. Wilson, Keith T. "The Recovery of American Manned Spacecraft, 1961–1975." *Spaceflight* 24 (April 1982): 179–184.

Provides a brief overview of 24 years of American spacecraft recovery at sea. Focuses on the problems and adjustments made for these 31 splashdowns within programs as well as those occurring from program to program. Includes a table listing the recovery ship for each mission, as well as a brief bibliography.

Yevsikov, Victor. *Re-entry Technology and the Soviet Space Program* (Some Personal Observations). Falls Church, Va.: Delphic, 1982. Pp. 112. Illustr.

Cited herein as item 1719.

Personalities

1630. Aldrin, Col. Edwin E. "Buzz", Jr., and W. Warger. *Return to Earth*. New York: Random House, 1973. Pp. 338. Index, Illustr.

A personal account by the commander of the Apollo 11 Lunar Module of the first manned expedition to the Moon in 1969. Contains much useful detail on the personal thoughts and day–to–day activities of an astronaut preparing for such a mission.

1631. Bell, Joseph N. *Seven into Space; The Story of the Mercury Astronauts*. Chicago: Popular Mechanics, 1960. Pp. 197. Illustr.

Popular account of Project Mercury activities leading to the first suborbital flight.

1632. Caidin, Martin. *The Astronauts; The Story of Project Mercury, America's Man in Space Program*. New York: E.P. Dutton, Inc., 1961. Pp. 224. Index.

A well–illustrated history of the selection process, training, and preparation for the Mercury program. Includes photos and descriptions of pre–manned testing flights.

1633. Carpenter, M.S., G. Cooper, J. Glenn, V. Grissom, W. Shirra, A. Shepard, and D. Slayton. *We Seven, by the Astronauts Themselves*. New York: Simon and Schuster, 1962. Pp. 352. Illustr.

Presents a personal narrative of Project Mercury and related activities of the astronauts, with an introduction by John Dille of Life magazine. Chapters are compilations of separate articles written by each of the seven astronauts. A table of contents and an index are included.

1634. Cipriano, Anthony J. *America's Journeys into Space: The Astronauts of the United States*. New York: Julian Messner, 1979. Pp. xi + 212. Index, Illustr.

Briefly presents U.S.-manned missions through the Apollo–

Soiuz Test Project (ASTP) and biographies of all astronauts
who participated in them. Included are the rollout of Space
Shuttle Enterprise and glossary of space terms.

1635. Collins, Michael. *Carrying the Fire: An Astronaut's Journey*.
New York: Farrar, Straus and Giroux, 1974. Pp. 488.

The author piloted both the Gemini 10 and Apollo 11 missions. On *Gemini 10* he performed two spacewalks, including
one to an Agena spacecraft, to which his Gemini was docked.
On *Apollo 11* he orbited the Moon alone, while Neil Armstrong
and Edwin Aldrin made history on the surface below. This
autobiography presents one astronaut's story of the highs and
lows of involvement in the U.S. space program.

1636. Cooper, L. Gordon, et al. *The Astronauts, Pioneers in Space by
the Seven Astronauts of Project Mercury*. New York: Golden
Press, 1961. Pp. 95. Illustr.

This firsthand story describes experiences of the Mercury
astronauts from their training through Alan Shepard's flight.

1637. Cunningham, Walter, and M. Herskowitz. *The All-American
Boys*. New York: Macmillan, 1977. Pp. x + 321. Index, Illustr.

Autobiography of Walter Cunningham during his career as an
astronaut. Includes much information on other astronauts in
the program.

1638. Furniss, Tim. *Manned Spaceflight Log*. London: Jane's, 1983.
Pp. 160. Index, Illustr.

Logs the first 103 manned spaceflights from Iurii Gagarin's
April 12, 1961, flight on board *Vostok* through Shuttle flight
STS-5 of November 11, 1982, including the U.S. Air Force's
X-15 flights for which astronauts' wings were awarded. Il-
lustrated with numerous pictures of each astronaut or team.
Appendixes include lists of training groups, a table of cumula-
tive space experience, and one of the Shuttle scheduled flights
at that time.

1639. Grissom, Betty, and H. Still. *Starfall*. New York: Thomas Y.
Crowell, 1974. Pp. 276. Index, Bibliog., Illustr.

Presents an account by the wife of astronaut Virgil I. Grissom of the tragic Apollo 204 fire, in which her husband and
fellow astronauts Edward E. White and Roger B. Chaffee
perished on January 27, 1967.

1640. Grissom, Virgil I. *Gemini, A Personal Account of Man's Venture into Space.* New York: Macmillan, 1968. Pp. xi + 212.
Illustr.

Profiles the author's own experiences as one of the original
seven Project Mercury astronauts who made the second U.S.
suborbital flight, and who later flew in the *Gemini 3* mission
and joined Project Apollo. The book was published shortly
after Grissom's tragic death on January 27, 1967, when an
Apollo capsule caught fire during ground tests.

1641. Irwin, James B., and W. Amerson, Jr. *To Rule the Night, The
Discovery Voyage of Jim Irwin.* Philadelphia, Pa.: A.J. Holman, 1973. Pp. 251. Illustr.

Reveals religious and philosophical perspectives of astronaut
James B. Irwin, lunar module pilot on Apollo 15.

1642. O'Connor, Karen. *Sally Ride and the New Astronauts in Space.*
New York: F. Watts, 1983. Pp. 88. Illustr.

Describes experiences of the first American woman astronaut, Sally Ride, who flew aboard the Space Shuttle *Challenger* (STS–77) in 1983. It describes how shuttle astronauts are
selected and trained.

1643. Olney, Ross. *Americans in Space: Five Years of Manned Space
Travel.* Camden, N.J.: Thomas Nelson and Sons, 1966. Pp.
129. Index, Illustr.

Offers a personal account of the day–to–day and
moment–to–moment experiences of the first, second, and third
group of American astronauts. Focuses primarily on the first
six American Mercury flights, although some mention is made
of the Gemini and proposed Apollo programs. Reprints the
Short Glossary of Space Terms, NASA SP-1, as an appendix.
Provides a table of the first six years of manned spaceflight of
the the United States and the USSR.

1644. Pierce, Philip N. *John H. Glenn Astronaut.* New York: Franklin Watts, 1962. Pp. 207. Index, Illustr.

Popularizes the life of astronaut John Glenn, who made the first U.S. orbital flight aboard Mercury (MA-6) on February 20, 1962. It was written in the atmosphere of the time and before Glenn's subsequent career as a U.S. senator.

1645. Shaylor, David J. "John Young—One Man's Conquest of Space." *Spaceflight* 24 (May 1982): 221–224.

Reviews long-time space career of astronaut John W. Young, who joined NASA in 1962 and flew on *Gemini 3, Gemini 10, Apollo 10, Apollo 16,* and Space Shuttle *Columbia's* first mission.

1646. Sherrod, Robert. "Selling of the Astronauts." *Columbia International Review,* May/June 1973, 16–25.

Interesting account of how NASA managed press access to its astronaut corps during the 1960s.

1647. Silverberg, Robert. *First American into Space.* Derby, Conn.: Monarch, 1961. Pp. 142.

Popularly written biography of Alan Shepard.

1648. Smaus, Jewel S., and C. Spangler. *America's First Spaceman.* Garden City, N.Y.: Doubleday, 1962. Pp. 159. Illustr.

Popularizes the life and accomplishments of U.S. astronaut Alan B. Shepard, Jr., who made the first U.S.-manned sub-orbital spaceflight on May 5, 1961.

1649. Wolfe, Tom. *The Right Stuff.* New York: Farrar, Straus and Giroux, 1979. Pp. 436.

Narrates the development of the popular image of the early American astronauts, who, by definition, possess "the right stuff." Provides often critical insights into the flavor of the era.

INTERNATIONAL COOPERATION AND COMPETITION

By definition, the exploration of space transcends national borders. This is true literally, when one considers the concerns of the first space powers, the United States and the Soviet Union, over the ease with which cameras, radios and bombs could be placed over their territories once the space age began in 1957. The transcendence is less concrete but no less real when one considers the long list of nationalities which have contributed to the development of space science and technology. Today, the size of many space science projects has demanded international cooperative efforts.

The selections presented here describe the flavor of the issues surrounding international cooperation and competition in space. They range from the earliest comparative studies of the U.S. and Soviet space programs, through historical works which describe long-standing international relationships, to highly analytical pieces which attempt to enumerate the pros and cons of competition and cooperation.

For additional resources, the reader should proceed beyond this list of specialized works and examine the histories of national space programs, and the histories of space projects in which scientists throughout the world have shared their knowledge and expertise.

Cathleen S. Lewis

1650. Bainum, Peter M., and F. von Bun, eds. *Europe/United States Space Activities—With a Space Propulsion Supplement.* Science and Technology Series of the American Astronautical Society, vol. 61. San Diego, Calif.: Univelt, 1985. Pp. 442.

Based on the 23d Goddard Memorial Symposium/19th European Space Symposium held March 27, 1985, Greenbelt, Maryland.

1651. van den Berg, Anne. "The Intercosmos Programme." *Journal of the British Interplanetary Society* 35 (1982): 82–85.

Reviews the history of the East European Intersputnik and Intercosmos program. Includes a list of international manned spaceflights.

1652. Bryant, C.R.J. "ESRO II: 20 Years Ago." *Journal of the British Interplanetary Society* 38 (1985): 553–560.

Written by one of the British Aerospace engineers who designed European Space Research Organization II. Briefly describes the engineering and scientific planning of the first successful launch of an ESRO satellite on May 16, 1968, at Vandenberg, California. Explains the significant results of the IRIS satellite.

1653. Büdeler, Werner, and W. Goldman. *Spacelab: Europas Labor im Weltraum* (Spacelab: European labor in space). Munich: Wilhelm Goldman, 1976. Pp. 287. Illustr.

Describes the European participation in the Shuttle program through the development of Spacelab. Briefly reviews the history of the U.S. space program through the Shuttle. Explains the operations and engineering design of the Shuttle and Spacelab. Concludes with speculation on the construction of the space station.

1654. Carter, L.J., and P. Bainum, eds. *Space: A Developing Role for Europe.* American Astronautical Society Science and Technology Series, vol. 56. San Diego, Calif.: Univelt, 1984. Pp. 278.

Presents the proceedings of a conference sponsored by

European astronautical societies, June 6–9, 1983, in London, England, and hosted by the British Interplanetary Society. Papers report on European Space Agency programs currently under development, as well as propose future projects for ESA. Historical references throughout the papers. Citations are made to both technical and popular sources.

1655. Cleaver, A.V. "European Space Activities since World War II: A Personal View." *AIAA 11th Annual Meeting.* AIAA Paper 75–313 (February 1975): 1–18.

Reviews political and technical problems faced by European concerns during the period 1945–1960; emphasizes the achievements of European Launcher Development Organization and European Space Research Organization during the years 1960–1964 and subsequently to 1973. Examines parallel national programs in the United Kingdom, and bilateral efforts with the United States, Germany, and France. An excellent concise review of space policy in Europe.

Diamond, Edwin. *The Rise and Fall of the Space Age.* Garden City, N.Y.: Doubleday, 1964. Pp. ix + 158. Index.

Cited herein as item 1145.

Dupas, Alain. *La lutte pour l'espace* (The Battle for Space). Paris: Seuil, 1977. Pp. 281. Illustr.

Cited herein as item 1146.

European Space Research Organization. *Europe in Space.* Paris, 1974. Pp. 168.

Cited herein as item 1741.

Ezell, Edward C., and L. Ezell. *The Partnership: A History of the Apollo–Soyuz Test Project.* Washington, D.C.: National Aeronautics and Space Administration, 1978. Pp. xx + 560. Index, Bibliog., Illustr.

Cited herein as item 1584.

1656. Frutkin, Arnold. *International Cooperation in Space.* Englewood Cliffs, N.J.: Prentice-Hall, 1965. Pp. iv + 186. Index.

Examines the history of international cooperation in space as a balance between competition and cooperation. Speaks of cooperation on technical and editorial issues, as well as political cooperation. Takes the 19th-century acceptance of the internationality of science as the starting point for international cooperation in space. The author was NASA's assistant administrator for international programs.

Giarini, Orio. *L'Europe et l'Espace.* Lausanne: Centre de Rescherches Europeénes, 1968. Pp. 255. Illustr.

Cited herein as item 1742.

1657. Goddard Memorial Symposium. *Space, New Opportunities for International Ventures.* San Diego, Calif.: Univelt, 1980. Pp. x + 290. Illustr.

Papers from the 17th Goddard Memorial Symposium, held in 1980. Focuses on the international use of the Space Shuttle and Shuttle-related activities; some papers deal with applications. Incomplete and unrecorded papers are included.

1658. Harvey, Dodd L., and L. Ciocoritti. *U.S.-Soviet Cooperation in Space.* Miami: University of Miami, 1974. Pp. xxxiii + 279. Index, Bibliog.

Tells the story of U.S. and Soviet cooperation in space through relevant primary documents. Seeks to work out an understanding of Soviet behavior toward international space cooperation as a basis for understanding Soviet international behavior in general. All sources presented are available through the University of Miami's Center for Advanced International Studies' Documentary Collection on Science, Technology and International Affairs.

1659. Johnson, Nicholas L. "Apollo and Zond—Race around the Moon." *Spaceflight* 20 (December 1978): 403–412.

Comparison of American and Soviet manned spaceflight. Demonstrates calculations and risks both countries took to send a human being around the Moon, with the U.S. achieving its goal.

1660. Kash, Don E. *The Politics of Space Cooperation.* Lafayette, Ind.: Purdue University Studies, 1967. Pp. xii + 137.

Measures the history of international space cooperation against a spectrum ranging from conservative to innovative. Analyzes the actions relevant to NASA's international activities. Concludes that NASA's activities have been relatively conservative, but justifiably so, in the light of rapidly changing political climate.

1661. Kushin, Mikhail A. *Zapadnaia evropa: kosmicheskaia tekhnika i ekonomika* (Western Europe: space technology and economics). Minsk: Izdatel'stvo Belorusskoi Gosudarstvennoi Universitety, 1975. Pp. 167. Bibliog.

Analyzes the political–economic aspects of the national space programs of the United Kingdom, France, Italy, and other West European States. Evaluates the potential of the aerospace industry in Europe and the possibility for further European economic integration as a result of the development of space cooperation.

1662. Lebedev, L.A. *Rendezvous in Space.* Moscow: Progress, 1979. Pp. 208. Illustr.

Narrates the history of the Apollo–Soiuz Test Project through comments and interviews with Russian participants and observers. Provides the only Soviet version of the project. Includes very little in the way of analysis.

Lovell, Sir Bernard. *The Origins and International Economics of Space Exploration.* Edinburgh: Edinburgh University Press, 1973. Pp. viii + 104. Index, Bibliog., Illustr.

Cited herein as item 1170.

1663. Malyshev, Iurii V., M. Rebrov, and G. Strekalov. *SSSR–indiia na kosmicheskikh orbitakh* (USSR and India in space orbit). Moscow: Mashinostroenie, 1984. Pp. 128. Illustr.

Relates the history of USSR–Indian cooperation in space from the launch of the Indian satellite Aryabhata by the Soviet Union, through the mission to *Saliut 7* of the crew of *Soiuz T–11*, which included Indian cosmonaut Rakesh Sharma. Provides no references, but is very well illustrated.

1664. Molloy, James A., Jr. "The Dryden–Blagonravov Era of Space Cooperation, 1962–1965." *Aerospace Historian* 24 (1977): 40–46.

Narrates the history of the meetings between Hugh Latimer Dryden and Anatolii Arkadievich Blagonravov during the early 1960s. Asserts that the basis for U.S.–Soviet cooperation in space during the 1960s and 1970s rested on the personal relationship between these two men, but was disturbed by political realities as time progressed.

1665. Murray, Bruce C., and M. Davies. "A Comparison of U.S. and Soviet Exploration of Mars." *Science* 151, no. 3713 (February 25, 1966): 945–954.

Attempts to discern the goals, policies, and plans of Soviet and U.S. planetary exploration programs through a comparative analysis of the two countries' interplanetary missions flown to date, and insofar as possible, through analysis of the public plans.

1666. Murray, Bruce C., and M. Davies. "Detente in Space." *Science* 192 (June 11 1978): 1067–1074.

Takes the opportunity provided by the successful completion of the ASTP to compare the U.S. and Soviet space programs. Special emphasis on unmanned lunar and planetary probes. Argues that more meaningful cooperation than "a handshake in space" is needed. Believes that data exchange agreements would prove most profitable for both sides. Suggests that future collaborative efforts might include a Shuttle–Saliut rendezvous.

1667. Petrov, B.H., and V.C. Berreshchetin, eds. *Orbity sotrudnichestva* (Orbits of cooperation). Moscow: Mashinostroenie, 1983. Pp. 177. Illustr.

Chronicles the history of Soviet international space collaboration from *Intercosmos 1* solar experiments in 1969 to current Soviet international activities, including the guest cosmonaut program on Saliut space stations. Includes tables listing all Soviet collaborative efforts.

1668.   Rebrov, Mikhail F. *SSSR–frantsiia na kosmicheskikh orbitakh* (USSR–France in space orbit). Moscow: Mashinostroenie, 1982. Pp. 84. Illustr.

Illustrates the history of Soviet–French cooperation in space, but focuses primarily on the flight of *Soiuz T–6,* which carried the first Frenchman to fly in space, Jean Loup Chretien, to the Soviet space station *Saliut 7.* Provides a list of French experiments carried out on Soviet spacecraft.

1669.   Schauer, William H. *The Politics of Space: A Comparison of the Soviet and American Space Programs.* New York: Holmes and Meier, 1976. Pp. vii + 317. Index, Bibliog.

Compares the institutional, fiscal, and political organization of the U.S. and Soviet space programs. Focuses on those traits associated with the competition between the nations. Contrasts the impact space exploration has had on domestic issues and societies. Provides extensive references.

Shapland, David, and M. Rycroft. *Spacelab: Research in Earth Orbit.* Cambridge: Cambridge University Press, 1984. Pp. 192. Index, Illustr.

Cited herein as item 1618.

1670.   Sheldon, Charles S. II. *Review of the Soviet Space Program, with Comparative United States Data.* New York: McGraw–Hill, 1968. Pp. viii + 152. Index, Illustr.

Commercially published version of a report written for Congress analyzing Soviet space activities. Presents available unclassified information on Soviet programs in an attempt to provide sufficient information with which to make an informed judgment on relative U.S. and Soviet positions in space. Written by the then–acting chief of the Science Policy Research Division of the Legislative Research Service of the Library of Congress, who directed research on all such reports.

1671. United Nations. *The World in Space: A Survey of Space Activities and Issues Prepared for UNISPACE '82*. Englewoods Cliffs, N.J.: Prentice–Hall, 1982. Pp. xiv + 689. Index, Bibliog., Illustr.

Written in preparation for the Second United Nations Conference on the Exploration and Peaceful Uses of Outer Space '82 (UNISPACE '82). Surveys the state of space science and applications and current economic and technological issues in space research. Describes international cooperative programs in these areas and participating agencies.

1672. U.S. Congress. Office of Technology Assessment. *U.S.–Soviet Cooperation in Space*. OTA–TM–STI–27. Washington, D.C.: U.S. Government Printing Office, July 1985. Pp. x + 113. Illustr.

Examines the history of U.S.–Soviet cooperation in space, in order to evaluate the potential for further cooperative ventures. Treats both the scientific and political issues involved in such cooperation. Touches on Soviet cooperative projects with other nations. Appendixes include a list of U.S. cooperative programs in space science and applications. Makes many references to other OTA publications. Notes.

1673. U.S. Library of Congress. Congressional Research Service. *World–Wide Space Activities*. Washington, D.C.: U.S. Government Printing Office, 1977. Pp. xxix + 607. Illustr.

Presents a comprehensive documentation of the space activities of launching nations other than the United States and the Soviet Union. Lists the space activities and organizations of each nation. Summarizes international space activities of the world, including organizations and programs.

1674. U.S. Library of Congress. Congressional Research Service. *United States and Soviet Progress in Space through 1979 and a Forward Look*. Washington, D.C.: U.S. Government Printing Office, 1980. Pp. xiii + 91.

Compares the facilities and activities of the two space programs with the objective of providing information that can be used to make qualitative judgments by which to evaluate the two countries.

1675. U.S. Library of Congress. Congressional Research Service. *Space Activities of the United States, Soviet Union and Other Launching Countries, 1957–82.* Washington, D.C.: U.S. Government Printing Office, 1982. Pp. 133.

Updates two previous reports by the Library of Congress's Congressional Research Service: *U.S. and Soviet Progress in Space: Summary Data through 1979* and *World Wide Space Activities, 1977.*

1676. U.S. Library of Congress. Legislative Reference Service. Foreign Affairs Division. *International Cooperation and Organization for Outer Space.* Washington, D.C.: U.S. Government Printing Office, August 12, 1965. Pp. ix + 580. Index, Illustr.

Congressional report written to identify the character and organizations of international space cooperation. Reviews the history of NASA international activities, as well as the overall history of U.S. and Soviet space activities. Well illustrated by charts and tables.

THE SPACE PROGRAMS OF THE USSR

Since 1957 the space programs of the Soviet Union has been held as a measure of United States activities in space. The Soviet Union launched the first artificial satellite, the first man, and the first woman into space. Now the USSR is on the verge of establishing a permanent human presence in space. This was a goal once shared by early space visionaries in both the US and the USSR. As a result of this close identification with the US space program, a significant body of literature comparing the American and Soviet programs has emerged from the west over the last thirty years. Much of this literature has sought to assess the leadership in space. From the Soviet Union has come heroic accounts of the personalities and execution of their own space activities. The vast majority of literature on the history of the Soviet space program makes little or no attempt to conceal the strong political leanings of the authors. As a result, the selections which follow present a wide range of opinion of the goals, motivations, and origins of the Soviet space program. Also included are serious scientific accounts of Soviet activities, and the few scholarly accounts of the subject. The reader should bear in mind that the selections provided here are the most representative of the first generation of historiography of the Soviet space program, and will provide the groundwork for a more sophisticated next generation of historical analysis of Soviet activities in space.

Out of necessity, this section contains numerous Russian–language citations which are either not yet available in translation or for which the available translations are extremely poor. For the ease of identification and location, appropriate English titles have been provided. The first place to look for adequate translations would be the National Aeronautics and Space Administration's Technical Translations, which are available through the Joint Publications Research Service in Arlington, Virginia. As throughout the book, all Russian transliterations have been carried out according to a simplified version of the Library of Congress system, often presenting seemingly idiosyncratic spellings (eg., Soiuz, and not Soyuz), except in the case of published works).

Cathleen S. Lewis

General Histories

1677. Atashenkov, P.T. *Akademik S. P. Korolev* (Academician S. P. Korolev). Moscow: Mashinostroenie, 1969. Pp. 208. Bibliog., ·Illustr.

Chronicles the life of Soviet rocket pioneer Sergei Pavlovich Korolev, who became the USSR's "Chief Spacecraft Designer." He was responsible for the design bureau that constructed launch vehicles for the first Sputnik satellites. He also directed the development of many ballistic missiles, geophysical rockets, the Vostok and Voskhod spacecraft, until his death in 1966. Includes a chronology of milestones in Korolev's life and bibliography of 25 references.

1678. Baker, Norman L. *Soviet Space Log, 1957–1967*. Washington, D.C.: Space 1967. Pp. 59. Illustr.

Compiles the launch and orbital information on all known Soviet launch attempts for the period 1957–1967.

van den Berg, Anne. "The Intercosmos Programme." *Journal of the British Interplanetary Society* 35 (1982): 82–85.

Cited herein as item 1651.

Borrowman, Gerald L. "Soviet Military Activities in Space." *Journal of the British Interplanetary Society* 35 (1982): 86–92.

Cited herein as item 1470.

1679. Caidin, Martin. *Red Star in Space*. New York: Crowell–Collier, 1963. Pp. 246. Illustr.

Examines the beginning of Soviet scientific activities in space including discussion of the evolution of Soviet launch vehicles and cosmonaut biomedical training. Concludes with a discussion of the international political implications of space-flight. Appendixes.

1680. Daniloff, Nicholas. *The Kremlin and the Cosmos*. New York: Alfred A. Knopf, 1972. Pp. ix + 258. Bibliog., Illustr.

Speculates on the nature of the Soviet space program in the light of unofficial sources and the author's in–depth knowledge of the Soviet system. Suggests that Sergei Korolev's identity was widely known by those who had contacts with Soviet scientists and that Khrushchev's view of the space program was not as erratic as suggested by other authors. Includes interview with former Soviet rocket scientist G.A. Tokaty-Tokaev.

Frutkin, Arnold. *International Cooperation in Space*. Englewood Cliffs, N.J.: Prentice–Hall, 1965. Pp. iv + 186. Index.

Cited herein as item 1656.

Golovanov, Yareslav K. *Sergei Korolev: The Apprenticeship of a Space Pioneer*. Moscow: Mir, 1975. Pp. 295. Illustr.

Cited herein as item 1235.

Harvey, Dodd L., and L. Ciocoritti. *U.S.–Soviet Cooperation in Space*. Miami: University of Miami, 1974. Pp. xxxiii + 279. Index, Bibliog.

Cited herein as item 1658.

1681. James, Peter N. *Soviet Conquest from Space*. New Rochelle: Arlington House 1974. Pp. 206. Index, Bibliog.

Asserts that the Soviet Union is winning the real space race against the United States. Cites frequent U.S. breaches of security as an indication that the Soviets are achieving strategic domination from space.

1682. Kit, Boris V. *USSR. Space Program*. College Park: University of Maryland, 1964. Pp.: vol. 1, 318; vol. 2, 282.

Presents a scrupulous examination of the available information on all aspects of the Soviet space research in 1964. Includes professional and personal biographies of Soviet space scientists.

1683. Magnolia, L.R. "The Soviet Space Program." *TRW Space Log*, 1965, 2–22.

Reviews the first eight years of the Soviet space by program and project. Makes occasional comparisons to U.S. programs. Illustrated with drawings of spacecraft.

Malyshev, Iurii V., M. Rebrov, and G. Strekalov. *SSSR–indiia na kosmicheskikh orbitakh* (USSR and India in space orbit). Moscow: Mashinostroenie, 1984. Pp. 128. Illustr.

Cited herein as item 1663.

Molloy, James A., Jr. "The Dryden–Blagonravov Era of Space Cooperation, 1962–1965." *Aerospace Historian* 24 (1977): 40–46.

Cited herein as item 1664.

Murray, Bruce, and M. Davies. "Detente in Space." *Science* 192 (June 11 1978): 1067–1074.

Cited herein as item 1666.

1684.   Oberg, James E. *Red Star in Orbit*. New York: Random House, 1981. Pp. xiii + 272. Index, Illustr.

Popularizes the history of Soviet–manned spaceflight, beginning with background on Soviet space science and the launch of Sputnik and concluding with a discussion of the Saliut space station program. Includes an annotated bibliography and brief biographies of cosmonauts.

Petrov, B.H., and V.C. Berreshchetin, eds. *Orbity sotrudnichestva* (Orbits of cooperation). Moscow: Mashinostroenie, 1983. Pp. 177. Illustr.

Cited herein as item 1667.

1685.   Petrov, G.I. *Conquest of Outer Space in the USSR, 1967–1970*. New Delhi: National Aeronautics and Space Administration/ National Science Foundation (Amerind), 1973. Pp. xv + 444. Illustr.

Excerpts reports of Soviet space activities from the Soviet press, chronologically arranged by subject.

1686. Popescu, Julian. *Russian Space Exploration.* Henley on Thames, England: Gothard House, 1979. Pp. viii + 150. Index, Bibliog.

Describes the state of Soviet space science and launch activity from 1957 through 1976. Contains detailed sections on unmanned planetary, communications and navigation satellite development. Chronologies are included.

1687. Raushenbakh, B.V. *Iz istorii sovetskoi kosmonavtiki* (From the history of soviet cosmonautics). Moscow: Izdatel'stvo Nauka, 1983. Pp. 263. Illustrations, Notes.

Collection of papers presented at the symposia commemorating the 70th and 75th anniversaries of Sergei Pavlovich Korolev. All papers are written by prominent scientists who have participated in the Soviet space program and describe the role played by Korolev in the program. Notes.

Rebrov, Mikhail F. *SSSR–frantsiia na kosmicheskikh orbitakh* (USSR–France in space orbit). Moscow: Mashinostroenie, 1982. Pp. 84. Illustr.

Cited herein as item 1668.

1688. Riabchikov, Evgenii Ivanovich. *Russians in Space.* Garden City, N.Y.: Doubleday, 1971. Pp. 300. Illustr.

Provides the official Soviet history of their space program as prepared by the Novosti Press Agency. Heavily weighted to manned spaceflights. Consists of intimate descriptions of the lives of the early cosmonauts.

Schauer, William H. *The Politics of Space: A Comparison of the Soviet and American Space Programs.* New York: Holmes and Meier, 1976. Pp. vii + 317. Index, Bibliog.

Cited herein as item 1669.

Sheldon, Charles S. II. *Review of the Soviet Space Program, with Comparative United States Data.* New York: McGraw–Hill, 1968. Pp. viii + 152. Index Illustr.

Cited herein as item 1670.

1689. Sheldon, Charles S. II. "The Soviet Space Program: A Growing Enterprise." *TRW Space Log,* Winter 1968–69, 2–23.

Classifies Soviet launch vehicles according to the author's widely accepted alpha–numeric system. Gives examples of missions for each classification of vehicle. Includes a brief list of suggested readings. Illustrated by line drawings of launch vehicles.

1690. Shelton, William R. *Soviet Space Exploration: The First Decade.* London: Arthur Baker, 1969. Pp. 283. Index, Bibliog., Illustr.

Theorizes that the first 10 years of Soviet space exploration is a continuation of Russian and Soviet rocket research and the overall scientific endeavors of the past century. Draws heavily on interviews with Soviet space scientists. Makes early assertion that the Soviets did intend to make manned moonflights. Draws numerous analogies to U.S. space program. Introduction by Gherman Titov, the second man in space and the first man to spend a day in space.

Shternfeld, Arno A. *Interplanetary Travel.* Moscow: Foreign Languages, 1958. Pp. 126. Illustr.

Cited herein as item 1214.

1691. Smolders, Peter L., and Marian Powell, trans. *Soviets in Space.* London: Butterworth, 1973. Pp. 285. Index, Illustr.

Written immediately after the deaths of cosmonauts Georgii T. Dobrovol'skii, Vladislav N. Volkov, and Victor I. Patsaev on board Soiuz 11. Reviews the history of Soviet manned and unmanned space programs. Argues that the Soviet program has followed a more logical course than the U.S. space program. Heavily illustrated with photos and diagrams of Soviet spacecraft. No citations are provided.

U.S. Congress. Office of Technology Assessment. *U.S.–Soviet Cooperation in Space.* OTA–TM–STI–27. Washington, D.C., July 1985. Pp. x + 113. Illustr.

Cited herein as item 1672.

1692. U.S. Library of Congress. Congressional Research Service. *Soviet Space Programs: 1966–70, Goals and Purposes, Organization, Resources, Facilities and Hardware, Manned and Unmanned Flight Programs, Bioastronautics, Civil and Military Applications, Projections for Future Plans, Attitudes toward International Cooperation and Space Law.* Washington, D.C.: U.S. Government Printing Office, 1971. Pp. xi + 670. Index.

The third report to Congress on the Soviet Space program, covering the years 1966 through 1970. Based on unclassified materials and previous reports. Refers to years preceding those specifically covered by the report. Organized along the lines of previous reports. Relies on Soviet publications and statements more than previous reports. Contains some mild mistakes in translation and transliteration. Special emphasis is on Soviet military programs and the impact of these programs on American plans.

1693. U.S. Library of Congress. Congressional Research Service. *Soviet Space Programs: 1971–75,* Vol. 1, *Overview, Facilities and Hardware, Manned and Unmanned Flight Programs, Bioastronautics, Civil and Military Applications, Projections of Future Plans.* Washington, D.C.: U.S. Government Printing Office, 1976. Pp. xx + 668. Illustr.

The first volume of the fourth five–year report to Congress on the Soviet space program, covering the years 1971 through 1975. Updates previous reports in the light of interceding events. Provides much more detail on the Soviet program than previous reports as a result of public information received during the planning for the Apollo–Soiuz Test Project. Includes discussion and illustrations of Soviet sea–tracking vehicles and the Kaliningrad Space Control Center. Some inaccuracies are present vis-à-vis Soviet history. Contains many tables and charts. Detailed table of contents serves as index. Appendixes, notes.

1694. U.S. Library of Congress. Congressional Research Service.

Soviet Space Programs: 1971–75. Vol. 2, *Goals and Purposes, Organization, Research Allocations, Attitudes Toward International Cooperation and Space Law.* Washington, D.C.: U.S. Government Printing Office, 1976. Pp. xii + 221.

Volume 2 of the fourth five–year report to Congress on the Soviet space program. Examines the motivations, goals, and organization of the Soviet program and its potential impact on the U.S. program. Makes many new conclusions in the light of the successful completion of the Apollo–Soiuz Test Project. Appendixes, notes.

U.S. Library of Congress. Congressional Research Service. *United States and Soviet Progress in Space Through 1979 and a Forward Look.* Washington, D.C.: U.S. Government Printing Office, 1980. Pp. xiii + 91.

Cited herein as item 1674.

1695. U.S. Library of Congress. Congressional Research Service. *Soviet Space Programs, 1976–1980. Part 1, Supporting Vehicles and Launch Vehicles, Political Goals and Purposes, International Cooperation in Space, Administration, Resource Burden, Future Outlook.* Washington, D.C.: U.S. Government Printing Office, December 1982. Pp. xvi + 445. Illustr.

Part 1 of the fifth five–year report to Congress on the Soviet space program. Dissects every aspect of the administration and support of Soviet launching capabilities from ground–and ocean–station tracking to the recovery of satellites. Includes discussion of Soviet attitudes toward international cooperation in space, and future economic and fiscal constraints to the program. Appendixes, notes.

1696. U.S. Library of Congress. Congressional Research Service. *Soviet Space Programs, 1976–80, Part 3, Unmanned Space Activities.* Washington, D.C.: U.S. Government Printing Office, May 1985. Pp. xvii + 346. Illustr.

Part three of the fifth five–year report to Congress on the Soviet space program. Reviews Soviet unmanned activities in space as part of a report to Congress, published every five years on Soviet space activities. Special emphasis on Soviet military activities. Includes technical discussions of Soviet planetary exploration and space sciences.

1697. U.S. Library of Congress. Legislative Reference Service. *Soviet Space Programs: Organization, Plans, Goals and International Implications*. Washington, D.C.: U.S. Government Printing Office, 1962. Pp. xi + 399. Index, Illustr.

The first congressional report on the Soviet space program, prepared by the Legislative Reference Staff of the Library of Congress. Covers the period 1957 through 1962. Attempts to assess Soviet motivations and capabilities in space on the basis of published sources as well as widely accepted assessments from other fields. Concentrates on political, economic, and international political aspects of space exploration with little direct reference to scientific operations. Implicitly concerned with the effect on U.S. policy and operations. Appendixes notes.

1698. U.S. Library of Congress. Legislative Reference Service. *Soviet Space Programs, 1961–65: Goals and Purposes, Achievements, Plans, and International Implications*. Washington, D.C.: U.S. Government Printing Office, 1966. Pp. xii + 920. Index.

The second comprehensive report to Congress on the Soviet space program. Covers the years 1962 through 1965. Updates the previous report in the light of interim events. Continues the discussion of Soviet organization, motivations, and goals with special emphasis on the political implications of Soviet space achievements and their relevance to the U.S. space programs. Contains some discussion of science technology of the Soviet program of that period. Makes many comparisons to U.S. program. Contains first the official U.S. report identifying Sergei Korolev as chief designer of the Soviet program, based on G.A. Tokaty's statements. Appendixes, notes.

1699. U.S. Library of Congress. Science and Technology Section. Air Information Division. *Comprehensive Analysis of Soviet Space Program (Based on Soviet Open Literature, 1958–61)*. AID Report—72. Washington, D.C., May 22, 1961. Pp. 159. Illustr.

Reviews the Soviet space program for the years 1958–1961, on the basis of open Soviet literature from that period.

Attempts to define the configuration of the Soviet launch vehicle from published illustrations and written descriptions. Describes guidance and navigational systems from published reports. Sources range from popular to highly technical works. Appendixes, notes.

1700. Vladimirov, Leonid. *The Russian Space Bluff.* London: Tom Stacey, 1971. Pp. 192. Index.

Reveals the political and scientific uses of secrecy by Soviet officials in their space program. Also reveals heretofore unreported episodes of Soviet space exploration in intimate detail. Best available political history of the Soviet space program.

1701. Wachtel, C. "The Chief Designers of the Soviet Space Programme." *Journal of the British Interplanetary Society* 38 (1985): 561–563.

Condenses previously available information on the Soviet spacecraft designers. Overlooks some Soviet information on the topic.

1702. Wallisfurth, Rainer M. *Russlands Weg zum Mond.* (Russia's way to the Moon) Düsseldorf: Econ–Verlag, 1964. Pp. 434. Index, Bibliog., Illustr.

Detailed East German account of the early Soviet space program from *Sputnik 1* to *Vostok 6* and *Mars 1* spacecraft. Includes discussions of policy decisions and political ramifications. Addresses the *Vostok 6* flight of Valentina Tereshkova and the related scientific results. Provides a useful Russian and mainly German bibliography.

Piloted Flight

1703. Anonymous. *Soviet Man in Space.* Moscow: Foreign Languages, 1961. Pp. 93. Illustr.

Popularizes the life of Iurii Gagarin, the Soviet cosmonaut and first man in space, who made an orbital flight aboard the *Vostok* spacecraft, April 12, 1961.

1704. Borrowman, Gerald L. "Kosmoljot–Soviet Wings into Space." *Journal of the British Interplanetary Society* 35 (1982): 75–79.

Consolidates early reports of Soviet development of a multiuse winged vehicle (space shuttle).

1705. Burchett, W., and C.A. Purdy. *Cosmonaut Yuri Gagarin, First Man in Space*. London: Hamilton, 1961. Pp. 187. Index, Illustr.

Provides the first published evaluation of Soviet spaceflight in the west. Based on the authors' interviews and conversations with Soviet officials involved in their space program. Attempts to portray the behind–the–scenes atmosphere of the Soviet program. Topics discussed include manned spaceflight and planetary probes. Predicts the future of Soviet programs.

Cassutt, Michael. "The Military Salyuts." *Space World*, April 1979, 18–25.

Cited herein as item 1673.

Ezell, Edward C., and L. Ezell. *The Partnership: A History of the Apollo–Soyuz Test Project*. Washington, D.C.: National Aeronautics and Space Administration, 1978. Pp. xx + 560. Index, Bibliog., Illustr.

Cited herein as item 1584.

1706. Forbich, C. "The Soviet Space Shuttle Program." *Spaceworld*, January 1981, 4–8.

Based on unclassified and classified reports of the Soviet development of a space shuttle (Albatross). Predicts that the Soviets will attempt a shuttle launch before the United States. Abbreviated version of a classified report.

1707. Gagarin, Valentin A. *My Brother Yuri: Pages from the Life of the First Cosmonaut*. Moscow: Progress 1971. Pp. 218.

Recollects the life of Iurii Gagarin, who became the first man in space on April 12, 1961. Relates the tragic death of Iurii in an aircraft training accident on March 27, 1968.

1708. Ivanov, V.A., T.F. Pazymova, and B.A. Sazhko. *Saliut 6–soiuz–progress*. Moscow: Mashinostroenie, 1983. Pp. 340. Illustr.

Records the history of the Soviet Union's recently completed space station program, *Saliut 6*. Describes training and experiments for the program. Contains chronology of flights to *Saliut 6* and is illustrated by high–quality colorplates.

1709. Johnson, Nicholas L. "The Military and Civilian Saliut Space Programmes." *Spaceflight* 19 (August/September 1979): 364–370.

Analyzes the evidence of two separate Soviet Saliut space station programs—one military, one civilian. Describes the operations of both.

1710. Johnson, Nicholas L. *Handbook of Soviet Manned Spaceflight*. American Astronautical Society Science and Technology Series, vol. 48. San Diego, Calif.: Univelt, 1980. Pp. xii + 461. Index, Bibliog., Illustr.

Diagrams the engineering development of the Soviet manned space program. Features proposals for future manned spacecraft development. Notes.

Lebedev, L.A. *Rendezvous in Space*. Moscow: Progress, 1979. Pp. 208. Illustr.

Cited herein as item 1663.

1711. Leonov, Alexei. "Cosmonaut Training." *Spaceflight* 20 (August 1978): 305–306.

Briefly describes the goals and methods of cosmonaut training for long–term stays aboard Saliut space station. Written by Gen. Maj. Alexei Leonov, deputy director of the Gagarin Training Center.

1712. Mandrovsky, Boris N., and E. Fortunow. *Soviet Bioastronautics*. Washington, D.C.: Library of Congress, Aerospace Technology Division, 1968. Pp. ii + 196. Illustr.

Abstracts the Soviet open source literature from July 1967

through January 1968. Topics include: weightlessness and acceleration, noise and vibration, closed cabins and altered gas environment, hypodynamia and hypokinesia, hypothermia, effects of combined factors (except radiation), biorhythms, exobiology, and spacecraft sterilization.

1713. Pesavento, Peter. "Soviets to the Moon: the Untold Story." *Astronomy*, December 1984, 6–22.

Claims that the Soviets actually did plan a manned lunar program, but that engineering shortcomings forced the Soviet Union to forego landing a man on the Moon.

1714. Pesavento, Peter. "Space Shuttles—CCCP Style." *Griffith Observer* 48, no. 12 (December 1984): 2–11.

Assesses the potential uses for a Soviet Space Shuttle and the current debate on the stage of development the Soviets have achieved on their work on the Shuttle. Makes a strong argument for the existence of small shuttle for use as a space tug to the Soviet space station.

1715. Sharpe, Mitchell R. *It Is I, Seagull*. New York: Thomas Y. Crowell, 1975. Pp. 214. Index, Bibliog., Illustr.

A popular western biography of the first woman in space, Soviet cosmonaut Valentina Tereshkova, who flew on board *Vostok 6* June 16–19, 1963.

1716. Titov, Gherman, and M. Caidin. *I Am Eagle*. Indianapolis, Ind.: Bobbs–Merrill, 1962. Pp. 212. Illustr.

Recounts the impressions of cosmonaut Gherman S. Titov during his flight aboard Vostok 2, during August 6–7, 1961, the second manned orbital flight. Contains some biographical material. Based on interviews with Wilfred Burchett and Anthony Purdy, who traveled to the USSR. Appendixes include parameters of Vostok 2 and a Western analysis of the mission by coauthor Caidin.

1717. U.S. Congress. Office of Technology Assessment. *Salyut: Soviet Steps toward Permanent Human Presence in Space—A*

Technical Memorandum. OTA–TM STI–14. Washington, D.C., December 1983. Pp. 113. Illustr.

Examines the technical sophistication of the Soviet Union's Saliut space station program. Asserts that the Soviets adapt current technology to their needs and thus conserve time and expense in research and development.

1718. U.S. Library of Congress. Congressional Research Service. *Soviet Space Programs: 1976–80. Part 2, Manned Space Programs and Space Life Sciences.* Washington, D.C.: U.S. Government Printing Office, October 1984. Pp. xiv + 302. Illustr.

Part two of the fifth five–year report to Congress on the Soviet space program. Reviews Soviet manned spaceflight. Contains section on biomedical and space medicine; special emphasis is put on Soviet space station activities.

1719. Yevsikov, Victor. *Re–Entry Technology and the Soviet Space Program (Some Personal Observations).* Falls Church, Va.: Delphic, 1982. Pp. 112. Illustr.

Written as part of Delphic Associates' Soviet Emigre Series. Describes the organization, method, technology, and importance of various laboratories throughout the Soviet Union that worked on heat shield and insulation technology for the Soviet space program. Provides first hand insights into the most active period of this research for manned spacecraft (through 1969). Illustrated with diagrams on the use and application of insulation and heat shields on manned and unmanned space-craft, as well as fuel tanks and rocket engines.

Space Science and Applications

Johnson, Nicholas L. *Soviet Military Strategy in Space.* London: Jane's, 1987. Pp. 287. Index.

Cited herein as item 1483.

1720. Kreiger, F.J. *Behind the Sputniks: A Survey of Soviet Space Science.* Washington, D.C.: Public Affairs Press (RAND), 1958. Pp. 380. Index, Illustr.

Presents the state of Soviet space science from the open literature of the time. Contains translations of early writings of Soviet space scientists.

Meyer, Stephen M. "Space and Soviet Military Planning." In *National Interests and the Military Use of Space*, ed. William J. Durch, 61–68. Cambridge, Mass.: Ballinger 1984. Bibliog.

Cited herein as item 1491.

1721. Shumilov, N. *Dva chuda kosmicheskoi tekhniki* (Two marvels of space technology). Moscow: Izvestiia, 1967. Pp. 191. Illustr.

Recounts two early achievements in Soviet space science in October 1967: the success of *Venera 4*, the first spacecraft to land on Venus; and the first automatic docking in space by satellites *Kosmos 186* and *Kosmos 188*.

1722. Strasser, J.A. "New Details on Soviet Space Program: Report on Design of the Soviet Orbita–Molniya Comsat Network." *Aerospace Technology* 21 (22 April 1968): 16–21.

Describes the Soviet communications satellite system using the *Molniia 1* satellite and Orbita ground stations. Lists the ground stations and their relative power. Briefly discusses the meteorological and surveillance uses of the Molniia satellite.

1723. Wohl, Richard. "Material Science: Soviets Lead the Way in Space Processing." *Defense Science* 3, no. 6, December 1984, 52–55.

Briefly reviews the history of Soviet materials processing in space, especially those experiments performed on board Saliut 6. Argues that U.S. materials processing, under the auspices of Department of Defense Advanced Research Projects Administration has fallen behind that of the Soviet Union. Concludes with examples of how material processed in space by the Soviets might be put to military use.

1724. Wukelic, George. *Handbook of Soviet Space Science Research.* New York: Gordon and Breach, 1968. Pp. xx + 505. Illustr.

Summarizes the first 10 years of Soviet space science research. Classifies the most significant activities according to program. Lists major scientists conducting experiments and the period of their work, while noting absence of scientific literature preceding the initiation of specific programs.

Lunar and Planetary Exploration

1725. Anonymous. "Russia's Project Far Side." *Astronautics* 4 (December 1959): 28–29.

Briefly reports on Luna 3's successful flight around the far side of the Moon.

1726. Clark, P.S. "The Soviet Venera Programme." *Journal of the British Interplanetary Society* 38 (1983): 74–93.

Describes the evolution of the Soviet Venera (Venus) program. Includes detailed descriptions of spacecraft design, orbit and launch information, and scientific data collected on these missions.

1727. Johnson, Nicholas L. "Apollo and Zond—Race around the Moon." *Spaceflight* 20 (December 1978): 403–412.

Comparison of American– and Soviet–manned spaceflight. Demonstrates calculations and risks both countries took to send a human being around the Moon, with the U.S. achieving its goal.

1728. Johnson, Nicholas L. *Handbook of Soviet Lunar and Planetary Exploration.* American Astronautical Society Science and Technology Series, vol. 47. San Diego, Calif.: Univelt, 1979. Pp. xiv + 262. Index, Bibliog., Illustr.

Describes the detailed engineering history of Soviet lunar and planetary spacecraft from 1958 through 1978. Organized by objective (Moon, Mars, and Venus) and by generation and designation of probe. Traces the evolution of Soviet planetary and lunar objectives. Well illustrated with photographs and drawings. Includes programmic chronologies. Notes.

Kopal, Zdenek, and R. Carder. *Mapping of the Moon: Past and Present*. Dordrecht, Netherlands: Reidel, 1974. Pp. 237. Index, Bibliog., Illustr.

Cited herein as item 1386.

Murray, B.C., and M. Davies. "A Comparison of U.S. and Soviet Exploration of Mars." *Science* 151, no. 3713 (February 25, 1966): 945–954.

Cited herein as item 1665.

1729. U.S. Library of Congress. Aerospace Technology Division. *Spacecraft Sterilization Procedures in the USSR*. Washington, D.C., 1966. Pp. 11.

Answers inquiries about Soviet procedures to rid Venera and Mars spacecraft of earthbound organisms before launch.

1730. Yefremov, Iu.I. *First Panoramic Views of the Lunar Surface*. Moscow: Nauka, 1966. Pp. 19. Illustr.

Presents scientific analyses of photos broadcast to Earth from Luna 13.

Hardware Development

1731. Agranovsky, Anatoli. "A Lasting Trace." *Sputnik*, April 1973, 33–42.

Chronicles the story of Aleksei Isaev, one of the Soviet Union's leading rocket engine designers who died in 1971 and who specialized in creating engines for Soviet planetary probe launch vehicles.

Bramscher, Robert G. "A Survey of Launch Vehicle Failures." *Spaceflight* 22 (November/December 1980): 351–358.

Cited herein as item 1268.

Clark, Phillip S. "The Proton Launch Vehicle." *Spaceflight* 19 (September 1977): 330–333, 340.

Cited herein as item 1273.

Clark, Phillip S. "The Skean Programme." *Spaceflight* 20 (August 1978): 298–304.

Cited herein as item 1274.

Clark, Phillip S. "The Sapwood Launch Vehicle." *Journal of the British Interplanetary Society* 34 (1981): 437–443.

Cited herein as item 1275.

Clark, Phillip S. "The Sapwood Launch Vehicle—Revisited." *Journal of the British Interplanetary Society* 35 (1982): 79–81.

Cited herein as item 1276.

Clark, Phillip S. "Soviet Launch Vehicles: An Overview." *Journal of the British Interplanetary Society* 35, no. 2 (February 1982): 51–58.

Cited herein as item 1277.

1732. Geisler, Wladyslaw, and M. Subotowicz. *Ary Szternfeld Pioneer Kosmonautyki.* Warsaw: Ludowa Spoldzielnia Wydawnicza, 1981. Pp. 252. Illustr.

Relates the life and accomplishments of Ari Shternfeld, Polish–Soviet astronautical pioneer, winner of the 1934 REP-Hirsch Astronautical Prize; one of the most prolific spaceflight popularizers of Eastern Europe, who also contributed to Soviet rocket and spaceflight mathematical dynamics.

Glushko, Valentin P. *Rocket Engines GDL–OKB.* Moscow: Novosti, 1975. Pp. 75. Illustr.

Cited herein as item 1287.

Glushko, Valentin P. "Development of Rocketry and Space Technology in the USSR." *Space World* M–4–148 (April 1976): 4–32.

Cited herein as item 1288.

1733. Gubarev, V. *Konstruktor—neskol'ko stranits iz zhizni Mikhaila Kuz'micha Iangelia* (Designer—a few pages from the life of Mikhail Kuz'mich Iangel). Moscow: Izdatel'stvo politichesko literaturi, 1977. Pp. 109. Illustr.

Sketches the life of Soviet rocket pioneer Mikhail K. Iangel, who headed the USSR's space program after the death of Sergei P. Korolev in 1966 until his own death in 1971. Early in his career Iangel had been an aircraft and rocket engine designer.

Kosmodemianskii, Arkadii A. *K.E. Tsiolkovskii.* Moscow: Voennoe Izdatel'stvo, 1960. Pp. 186. Illustr.

Cited herein as item 1243.

Moshkin, Evgenii K. *Razvitie otechestvennogo raketnogo dvigatelestroeniia* (Development of Russian rocket engine technology). Moscow: Mashinostroenie, 1973. Pp. 255. Bibliog., Illustr.

Cited herein as item 1308.

Slukhai, Ivan A. *Russian Rocketry, a Historical Survey.* NASA TTF–426. Jerusalem: Israeli Program for Scientific Translations, 1968. Pp. 149. Bibliog., Illustr.

Cited herein as item 1318.

Tokaty, G.A. "Soviet Rocket Technology." *Technology and Culture* 4, no. 4 (Fall 1963): 515–528.

Cited herein as item 1323.

Tsander, F.A. *From a Scientific Heritage.* NASA TTF–541. Moscow: Nauka, 1967. Pp. 92. Bibliog., Illustr.

Cited herein as item 1255.

Tsander, Fridrikh A., and L. Korneev, ed. *Problems of Flight by Jet Propulsion—Interplanetary Flights.* NASA TTF–147. Jerusalem: Israeli Program for Scientific Translations, 1964. Pp. 390. Illustr.

Cited herein as item 1324.

Tsiolkovskii, Konstantin. *Works on Rocket Technology.* Edited by M. Tikhonravov. NASA TTF–243. Washington, D.C.: National Aeronautics and Space Administration, 1965. Pp. 434. Illustr.

Cited herein as item 1326.

Vick, Charles P. "The Soviet Super Boosters, Parts 1 and 2." *Spaceflight,* 15 (December 1973), 457–460; (March 1974), 94–104.

Cited herein as item 1327.

Vick, Charles P. "The Soviet G–1–e Manned Lunar Landing Programme Booster." *Journal of the British Interplanetary Society* (January 1985): 11–18.

Cited herein as item 1328.

Winter, Frank H. "Nikolai Alexseyevich Rynin (1877–1942), Soviet Astronautical Pioneer: An American Appreciation." *Earth–Oriented Applications of Space Technology* 2 (1982), 69–80.

Cited herein as item 1259.

1734. Zaehringer, Alfred J. *Soviet Space Technology.* New York: Harper, 1961. Pp. xii + 179. Index, Bibliog., Illustr.

Places the history of Soviet rocket technology in the historical context of Russian and early Soviet rocketry experiments. Uses a nomenclature for Soviet launch vehicles that is not commonly used today. Provides references to some of the earliest secondary writings on the Soviet space program.

THE SPACE PROGRAMS OF WESTERN EUROPE

In contrast to the space programs of the United States and the Soviet Union, the history space activities within Western Europe is one of efforts to overcome the tendencies for international competition, and to succeed at international cooperation. By virtue of this distinguishing feature, the history of the space programs of western Europe merits a separate discussion.

European participation in space research dates back to the end of World War II. The earliest activities took the form of cooperative efforts with the United States in sounding rocket research. In the last two decades, Europe has risen to the status of one of the three space powers in the arenas of communications, earth resources, and launch capability. Unfortunately, a complete history of the growth of European independence in space has yet to be written. The foundations for such histories can be found in Robert Massey's book on the history of British space science (item 1748) and in Walter McDougall's article (item 1746) on the early years of the French space program. The selections provided here are a sampling of the most descriptive and readily available works on the subject. The reader should confer with the technical publications of ESA and its predecessors, ELDO and ESRO for a more complete picture of European space research of the last three decades. Also of interest are NASA's annual reports on that agency's international programs.

Cathleen S. Lewis

1735. Ananoff, Alexandre. Les Mémoirs d'un Astronaut, ou L'Astronautique Français (The memoirs of an astronaut, or the French astronaut). Paris: Albert Blanchard, 1978. Pp. 197.

Relates the author's experiences as one of France's leading advocates and popularizers of spaceflight, from the 1930s to the present. Describes his role in the founding of France's first astronautical society and subsequently in the establishment of the first International Astronautical Federation Congress in 1950.

1736. Bainum, Peter M., and F. von Bun, eds. *Europe/United States Space Activities—With a Space Propulsion Supplement.* Science and Technology Series of the American Astronautical Society, vol. 61. San Diego, Calif.: Univelt, 1985. Pp. 442.

Based on the 23d Goddard Memorial Symposium/19th European Space Symposium held March 27, 1985, Greenbelt, Maryland.

1737. Bryant, C.R.J. "ESRO II: 20 Years Ago." *Journal of the British Interplanetary Society* 38 (1985): 553–560.

Written by one of the British Aerospace engineers who designed European Space Research Organization II. Briefly describes the engineering and scientific planning of the first successful launch of an ESRO satellite on May 16, 1968, at Vandenberg, California. Explains the significant results of the IRIS satellite.

1738. Büdeler, Werner, and W. Goldman. *Spacelab: Europas Labor im Weltraum* (Spacelab: European labor in space). Munich: Wilhelm Goldman, 1976. Pp. 287. Illustr.

Describes the European participation in the Shuttle program through the development of Spacelab. Briefly reviews the history of the U.S. space program through the Shuttle. Explains the operations and engineering design of the Shuttle and Spacelab. Concludes with speculation on the construction of the space station.

1739. Carter, L.J., and P. Bainum, eds. *Space: A Developing Role for*

Europe. American Astronautical Society Science and Technology Series, vol. 56. San Diego, Calif.: Univelt, 1984. Pp. 278.

Presents the proceedings of a conference sponsored by European astronautical societies, June 6–9, 1983, in London, England, and hosted by the British Interplanetary Society. Papers report on European Space Agency programs currently under development, as well as propose future projects for ESA. Historical references throughout the papers. Citations are made to both technical and popular sources.

1740.   Cleaver, A.V. "European Space Activities since World War II: A Personal View." *AIAA 11th Annual Meeting*. AIAA Paper 75–313 (February 1975): 1–18.

Reviews political and technical problems faced by European concerns during the period 1945–1960; emphasizes the achievements of European Launcher Development Organization and European Space Research Organization during the years 1960–1964 and subsequently to 1973. Examines parallel national programs in the United Kingdom, and bilateral efforts with the United States, Germany, and France. An excellent concise review of space policy in Europe.

1741.   European Space Research Organization. *Europe in Space*. Paris, 1974. Pp. 168.

Introduces the operations and participants of the European Space Research Organization and the European Space Agency. Includes descriptions of national programs and organizations of each member state.

Frutkin, Arnold. *International Cooperation in Space*. Englewood Cliffs, N.J.: Prentice–Hall, 1965. Pp. iv + 186. Index.

Cited herein as item 1656.

1742.   Giarini, Orio. *L'Europe et l'Espace* (Europe and space). Lausanne: Centre de Recherches Europeenes, 1968. Pp. 255. Illustr.

Attempts to inform a broad range of the European public about the issues and expectations of space exploration.

Contends that these technical issues must be thoroughly understood before the political and economic problems of rapid technological change can be addressed. Useful for understanding one sector of the pre–European Space Agency perspective on NASA.

1743. Gire, B. and J. Schibler, "The French National Space Program, 1950–1975." *Journal of the British Interplanetary Society* 40 (1987): 51–66.

Presents a well–illustrated technical overview of French national launch vehicles. Includes some discussion of the institutional history of French rocketry and of early French experiments with German V–2 rockets during the 1950s.

1744. Goddard Memorial Symposium. *Space, New Opportunities for International Ventures.* San Diego, Calif.: Univelt, 1980. Pp. x + 290. Illustr.

Papers from the 17th Goddard Memorial Symposium, held in 1980. Focuses on the international use of the Space Shuttle and Shuttle–related activities; some papers deal with applications. Incomplete and unrecorded papers are included.

1745. Kushin, Mikhail A. *Zapadnaia evropa: kosmicheskaia tekhnika i ekonomika* (Western Europe: space technology and economics). Minsk: Izdatel'stvo Belorusskoi Gosudarstvennoi Universitety, 1975. Pp. 167. Bibliog.

Analyzes the political–economic aspects of the national space programs of the United Kingdom, France, Italy, and other West European States. Evaluates the potential of the aerospace industry in Europe and the possibility for further European economic integration as a result of the development of space cooperation.

1746. McDougall, Walter A. "Space–Age Europe: Gaullism, Euro-Gaullism, and the American Dilemma," *Technology and Culture* 26 (1985): 179–203.

Approaches the history of the early French rocketry and

space program is the most sophisticated manner to date. Argues that the French (European) approach to space development presents an alternative to those of the United States and the Soviet Union. Makes a significant contribution to the understanding of the space programs of the European community.

1747. Marten, Neil. *Britain into Space*. London: Conservative Political Centre, 1968. Pp. 14. Illustr.

Encourages British participation in aerospace research. Briefly reviews the origins of the European Launcher Development Organization. Favorably portrays the role of the Conservative government in British aerospace research.

1748. Massey, Harrie, and M.O. Robins. *History of British Space Science*. Cambridge: Cambridge University Press, 1986. Pp. xxi + 514. Index, Bibliog., Illustr.

Tells how British sounding rocket studies of the ionosphere and atmosphere during the International Geophysical Year developed into major programs for satellite–borne research in the 1960s and 1970s. Analyzes the Commonwealth cooperative program in space research, continuing sounding rocket programs, and the structure of international cooperation in space research. The authors, both of whom are central players in this history, also provide extensive commentary on the history of the European Space Agency.

Rebrov, Mikhail F. *SSSR–frantsiia na kosmicheskikh orbitakh* (U.S.S.R.–France in space orbit). Moscow: Mashinostroenie, 1982. Pp. 84. Illustr.

Cited herein as item 1668.

1749. Ropelewski, Robert. "French Pursue Own Space Programs." *Aviation Week and Space Technology* 108 (12 June 1978): 21–22.

Reports on early Centre National d'Etude Spacial plans for exclusively French space program, outside the framework of the European Space Agency.

Shapland, David, and M. Rycroft. *Spacelab: Research in Earth Orbit.* Cambridge: Cambridge University Press, 1984. Pp. 192. Index, Illustr.

Cited herein as item 1618.

United Nations. *The World in Space: A Survey of Space Activities and Issues Prepared for UNISPACE '82.* Englewood Cliffs, N.J.: Prentice-Hall, 1982. Pp. xiv + 689. Index, Bibliog., Illustr.

Cited herein as item 1671.

U.S. Library of Congress. Congressional Research Service. *World-Wide Space Activities.* Washington, D.C.: U.S. Government Printing Office, 1977. Pp. xxix + 607. Illustr.

Cited herein as item 1673.

U.S. Library of Congress. Congressional Research Service. *Space Activities of the United States, Soviet Union and Other Launching Countries, 1957–82.* Washington, D.C.: U.S. Government Printing Office, 1982. Pp. 133.

Cited herein as item 1675.

THE OTHER SPACEFARING NATIONS

The decision to isolate the following nations in one section was not based on a technological judgment of these space programs, but on a judgment of the available literature. To date, there are few histories of the space programs of Canada, China, India, and Japan. This fact can be attributed to the relative youth of these space programs, and the commensurate sparsity of relevant primary sources. The lack of acceptable sources has also caused the omission of the emerging spacefaring nations; such as Brazil, Argentina, and the regional consortia of space applications users (e.g. Arabsat). For an overview of world-wide space activities, the reader should consult the Congressional Research Service's publication *World-Wide Space Activities* (item 1673)

The reader will note that longstanding cooperation with the European Space Agency notwithstanding, Canada space programs have largely been separate from that of ESA.

Cathleen S. Lewis

Canada

1750. Canada. Science Council of Canada. *A Space Program for Canada*. Report no. 1. Ottawa, July 1967. Pp. v + 31.

Reviews Canada's space activities and upper atmosphere research. Makes recommendations for specific experimental instrumentation and the future direction of Canadian space activities in the future.

1751. Canada. Department of Communications. *Alouette*. Ottawa, 1971. Pp. i + 20. Illustr.

Tells the story of Canada's first artificial satellite *Alouette*, which was launched on September 28, 1962, by the United States. Briefly describes the satellite's development, operations, and experiments.

1752. Canada. Department of Communications. *The Canadian Space Program: Five Year Plan (80/81–84/85)*. Serial no. DOC–6–79DP. Ottawa, Canada, January 1980. Pp. 67, 71. Illustr.

Proposes plans for the continued development of the Canadian space program. Begins with a historical account of the founding of the Interdepartmental Committee on Space and follows events through the development of the Canadian-designed Space Shuttle Remote Manipulator System. Includes tables of proposed expenditures and projects for the future. [In French and English]

China

1753. Clark, P.S. "The Chinese Space Programme." *Journal of the British Interplanetary Society* 37 (1984): 195–206.

Reviews the post–World War II history of Chinese rocketry development. Compares launch vehicle and military development. Presents overviews of civilian and military satellite programs.

1754. Clark, P.S. "The Chinese Space Year of 1984." *Journal of the British Interplanetary Society* 39 (1986): 29–34.

Comments on the surge in Chinese space activities during 1984, the most active year to date. Speculates on the missions of Chinese launches and on the possibility of misdesignation of these launches. Briefly presents the individual components of Chinese launching facilities. Mentions a rocket test accident in 1978. Provides references.

1755. Covault, Craig. "Austere Chinese Space Program Keyed toward Future Buildup." *Aviation Week and Space Technology*, 8 July 1985, 16–21.

Reports on Chinese current activities and plans for future space activities. Describes technical difficulties the Chinese have had in the past and the areas of their interests in obtaining Western (mostly U.S.) assistance and technology. First in a series based on the author's observations while on tour as part of a 16–member American space team to China.

1756. Covault, Craig. "Chinese Developing Satellites for Earth Resources Exploration." *Aviation Week and Space Technology* 22 July 1985, 81–84.

Continues the series on the state of space technology in the People's Republic of China. Describes Chinese plans for remote sensing technology, both domestic technology currently under development and images to be bought from the French company Spot–Image. Mentions specific China uses for imaging, as well as technical obstacles that will have to be overcome in order to accomplish its goals.

1757. Covault, Craig. "Chinese Modify CZ–2/3 Rocket Boosters, Focus on Commercial Launch Market." *Aviation Week and Space Technology* 22 July 1985, 77–79.

Outlines Chinese aspirations to enter the commercial launch–vehicle market. Provides some data on the capacities of Chinese launch vehicles.

Covault, Craig. "Chinese Rocket Test Center To Aid Large Engine Development." *Aviation Week and Space Technology* 22 July 1985, 69–75.

Cited herein as item 1279.

1758. Covault, Craig. "Contrasts across China." *Aviation Week and Space Technology*, 8 July 1985, 11.

Summarizes the author's impression of Chinese space technology, based on his observations during a trip to that country.

1759. Covault, Craig. "Test Centers near Beijing Expanding Space Design, Checkout Capabilities." *Aviation Week and Space Technology*, 15 July 1985, 71–76.

Evaluates spacecraft testing facilities of the Chinese Academy of Sciences in Beijing. Identifies computer hardware used in testing spacecraft.

1760. Pirard, Theo. "Chinese 'Secrets' Orbiting the Earth." *Spaceflight* 19, no. 10 (October 1977): 355–361.

Uses currently available data to speculate on the state of Chinese rocketry and satellite technology. Describes launch vehicles and satellites on the basis of orbital parameters. Attempts to discern the structure of China's space research institutions.

1761. Pritchard, Wilbur L., and J. Harford. *China Space Report*. New York: American Institute of Aeronautics and Astronautics, 1980. Pp. 208. Index, Illustr.

Narrates the American Institute of Aeronautics and Astronautics delegation's tour of Chinese space research facilities. Includes descriptions of facilities and personnel of academic institutions, government agencies, scientific laboratories, and space–related industries.

1762. Rao, B. Radhakrishna. "China: New Space Power of Threat to Stability in Asia?" *Spaceworld* R–3–207 (March 1981): 19–20.

Reviews China's rocketry, missile, and launch–vehicle activities. Concludes that China's space–launch capability has serious military and strategic consequences in Asia.

1763. Zhaoqian, Jing. "China's National Space Program." *Signal* June 1984, 40.

Highlights the significant activities of China's space program. Written by one of the leading figures in Chinese space
research.

India

1764. Sundra Rajan, Mahan. *India in Space*. New Delhi: Minister of
Information and Broadcasting, 1976. Pp. 92. Illustr.

One of two published histories on the Indian space program.
Contains history of launch facilities at Thumba and the Rohini
sounding rockets. Refers to ancient Indian astronomy and
potential benefits of the space program in India.

Malyshev, Iurii V., M. Rebrov, and G. Strekalov. *SSSR–indiia na
kosmicheskikh orbitakh* (USSR and India in space orbit).
Moscow: Mashinostroenie, 1984. Pp. 128. Illustr.

Cited herein as item 1663.

Japan

1765. Japan. Kagaku Gijutsucho. *Space in Japan*. Tokyo: Science and
Technology Agency, 1972. Pp. 20.

Provides background information of the previous year's
space activities, including resource allocation. Published
biennially.

1766. Japan. National Space Development Agency. *NASDA '83–'84*.
Tokyo, 1985. Pp. 48. Illustr.

Briefly reviews the history of Japan's National Space Development Agency as a basis for projecting the future of Japan's
space activities.

1767. Japan. Space Activities Commission. *Space Development
Program*. Tokyo: 13 March 1974. Pp. 45.

Reviews the space development program of Japan, which
encompasses the encouragement of research and the devel-

opment of satellite and communications technology, as well as
launch capability and participation in NASA's international
programs.

1768. Kovrizhkin, Sergei V. *Kosmicheskie issledovaniia v iaponiia:
sotsial'no ekonomicheskie i politicheskie aspekty* (Space
research in Japan: socioeconomic and political aspects).
Moscow: Nauka, 1979. Pp. 153. Bibliog.

Presents a political, socioeconomic analysis of Japan's space
program, especially the structure of the scientific, financial,
and industrial base. Asserts that the space program risks
falling prey to the military interests of the country as a result
of U.S. involvement. Applauds Japan's cooperation with the
European Space Agency.

AUTHOR INDEX

The author index is keyed to the item number of each individual bibliographic entry. Both personal and corporate authors are listed.

Ley, W., 1101, 1188, 1201, 1202, 1203, 1204, 1212
Lieberg, Owen S., 90
Light, Richard Upjohn, 855
Lilienthal, Otto, 91
Liller, William, 1405
Lilley, Tom, 987
Lincoln, Joseph Colville, 639
Lindbergh, Anne Morrow, 856, 857
Lindbergh, Charles A., 858, 859, 892, 893
Lindorm, Bo., 575
Link, Mae Mills, 1543, 1544
Linsley, H. L., 312
Lippisch, Alexander, 441
Lissitzyn, Oliver James, 520
Litchfield, Paul W., 988
Livingston, R. B., 1545
Lloyd, Christopher, 1303
Lloyd, Ian, 338
Lloyd, Mallon, 1601
Logsdon, John M., 1169, 1602, 1603
Loh, W. H. T., 330
Looney, John J., 1019
Lopez, Donald S., 255, 333
Lord, Clifford L., 510
Lott, A. S., 1524
Lovelace, 1546
Lovell, Sir Bernard, 1170, 1346
Low, George M., 1604
Lowell, Vernon W., 785
Lucke, Charles E., 296
Luckett, Perry D., 894
Luisis, Andy, 1020
Lusar, Rudolf, 745
Lybye, Knud, 576

M
McCall, G.J.H., 1387
McCary, Charles, 116
McClement, Fred, 786
McCready, Lauren S., 339
McCullough, David, 909
McDaniel, William H., 676
MacDonald, Hugh, 577
McDonald, John J., 270

McDougall, Walter A., 1171, 1172, 1746
McFarland, Marvin W., 92
McFarland, Ross A., 787, 1547, 1548
McGovern, James, 1304
Machell, R. M., 1605
McIntosh, R. H., 578
MacIsaac, David, 491
Mack, Pamela E., 1102, 1103, 1444
McKenzie, A.A., 731
McLaughlin, Charles, 1064
McPhee, John A., 150
McRuer, Duane T., 444
Macvey, John W., 1488
Magnolia, L.R. 1021, 1022, 1683
Maitland, Edward M., 151
Malina, Frank J., 1245
Malyshev, Iurii, 1663
Mancini, Luigi, 35
Mandrovsky, Boris N., 1712
Manly, Charles M., 383
Manno, Jack, 1489
Manoury, Paul, 52
Mark, Hans, 1606
Markey, Richard, 313
Markham, Beryl, 910
Markowski, Michael A., 649, 660, 661, 693
Marks, Robert W., 1065
Marten, Neil, 1747
Martin, James, 1445
Masefield, Peter G., 152
Maslenov, Iu., 1069
Mason, Francis K., 45, 214
Mason, J.K., 1549
Mason, Monck, 117
Mason, R.A., 492
Mason, Sammy, 788
Massey, Harrie Stewart Wilson, 1361, 1748
Masterson, Amanda R., 1388
Masursky, Harold, 1607
Mauer, Mauer, 492
May, Charles P., 962
May, Garry, 580
Maynard, Crosby, 989